"MY NAME IS JACK JOHNSON BUT I'M NOT THE SINGER."

Written by Jill Johnson

Copyright © 2018 by Jill Johnson.
Cover images by Jack Johnson.
Cover and Interior design copyright © 2018 by Two Peas Publishing.

All rights reserved. No part of this book may be used or reproduced in print, electronically, or otherwise without express written permission from the copyright holder. You may reproduce brief quotations in articles and reviews.

First Printing, 2018

ISBN: 978-1-938271-43-4

Two Peas Publishing
PO Box 1193
Franklin, TN 37065

www.twopeaspublishing.com

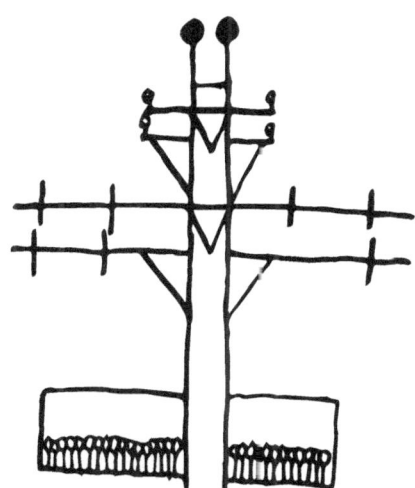

Dedicated to all families that find themselves
in a battle against a disability or disease.
May God give you the strength, the fortitude, the patience,
and the love to conquer the battle ahead.

Dedicated to my hero, my son, my motivation,
my light, my warrior, Jack. You touched so many
with your quirkiness, your quick wit,
your view of the world,
and your fearlessness that let you speak aloud
what the rest of us are afraid to say.
You will forever be missed and loved by all of us left
behind.

CHAPTER 1

We all have a story. Ours begins with the first meeting between Ben and me. A friend and I were at a dance club and, much to my surprise, she walked over to him once I picked him out as someone with whom I would like to dance. What stood out most was his plaid jacket, something that I didn't know at the time but learned later, was a window into his personality. Ben is a plaid jacket kind of guy: lots of wisecracks, a wicked sense of humor, and an ability to see the world in vivid detail which helps him in his chosen profession—an architectural renderer.

After dating for seventeen months, we were married in a small ceremony at my family's house. Our future was so bright and wonderful. I moved to his condo, and we started our married lives together. We enjoyed our quiet times on the lake. We had romantic evenings in front of the fire, dreaming of the future. Life was good.

After the first year, we started to think about starting a family. After trying unsuccessfully for six months, we sought the expertise of a fertility specialist. After an initial exploratory surgery and countless IUI's (Inter Uterine Insemination—collecting sperm which was injected directly into my uterus.) we still had not achieved a pregnancy. One day I went in to start yet another cycle and complained to the doctor I wasn't feeling well. She said since they had to take blood anyway, they would check to see if my blood counts were normal. I waited alone in the room by myself, the only time Ben had not gone with me in all my previous visits. I heard the nurse tell the doctor something and heard her say, "Do you want to tell her?" The door opened, the doctor walked in wearing a strange look on her face and said, "You're pregnant!" I had gotten pregnant without the help of drugs or tests or exams; I had gotten pregnant naturally. We were thrilled and relieved. The next week we were back at the infertility clinic having more blood tests and our first ultrasound. There it was on the screen, the very tiny flicker of a beating heart. We were mesmerized and in love. Seven weeks and several ultrasounds later, I started to spot. Nothing significant, but any blood is scary at any time during a pregnancy. We went in for another ultrasound, and the sight of that flickering heartbeat was a happy relief. Two days later, the spotting became worse, and another ultrasound was performed. The tiny flicker was gone. A dilation and curettage procedure at a local surgery center was performed. Most pregnancies last nine months and end with the joyous arrival of a new bundle of life. Mine was ending in a cold surgical room. That child today, if it had lived, would be twenty-six years old. One day I will get to meet him or her when this journey here is over for me.

I started to ask the question, "Why God?" Why would you make women unable to conceive a child when that is what their bodies are made for? Why do some women have it so easy and some so difficult? Do you love them more than me? Are we being punished for some horrible sin we committed, that for the life of me I can't remember? Being raised in the South, Ben and I grew up in a believing environment and attended church on a regular basis. Like most twenty-somethings, we had not attended a church regularly for quite some time, attending only on an occasional holy holiday or for weddings and funerals. Did our absence from a weekly religious service warrant this kind of pain? Why would a loving God give us this horrible existence? Why would He let us get pregnant after what we had been through and let us lose it? Nothing made sense, not in our heads or our hearts.

CHAPTER 2

Life continued with its highs and lows. Our lives reached another low with the unexpected death of my mother, a mere three months later. Mother, a petite lady, who in her later years, took better care of herself than she did when we were growing up. One night while lying in bed with Dad talking about their day and saying their goodnights, she turned out the light on the nightstand, said goodnight, and an aneurysm ruptured in her brain. There was no warning and no cure. She lived twenty-four hours in a semi-comatose state until her brain stopped all bodily functions. Mother was only sixty-five years old. As she lay slowly dying, somewhere nearby, a radio was on and the song "A Whole New World" was playing. Mother quietly passed into a whole new world. There were no goodbyes and hugs. There were no I love yous. There was no closure to a life that meant so much to our family. We were slapped in the face by the harsh reality of life. Sometimes we don't get to say goodbye, or get that final I love you. Life is ripped from our grasp like a toy ripped from the hands of a child. We are left with more questions than answers and with hearts broken in grief.

After her death, I was more determined than ever to get pregnant. Since the IUI's had not produced a pregnancy and there seemed to be nothing in any way affecting my ability to get pregnant, the infertility doctor suggested we do further testing not on me, but on Ben. To our surprise, Ben did indeed have lazy sperm that could not penetrate the exterior of my eggs without help. Our new plan changed to in vitro fertilization or better known as IVF. Since the infertility drugs were injected into the hip muscles, I could not inject myself with the drugs. The critical job of drug injector became Ben's. At first, he was a little squeamish, but the nurses gave him a good lesson on hip injections. Ben became the drug injecting king. Our first IVF attempt was unsuccessful from the start because the fertility drugs given did not produce enough eggs. We tried a second time with stronger drugs, and I produced nine eggs, three of which were not healthy. The remaining six eggs were placed

MY NAME IS JACK JOHNSON...

in lab dishes and mixed with Ben's sperm. After the implantation of three zygotes, I was so scared I would do something wrong or move the wrong way, I laid in the back seat of our SUV all the way home and stayed in bed the rest of the day. Days later after a blood test was taken, the phone rang, and on the other end, my fertility doctor congratulated me—I was pregnant!

Since we had become pregnant under the care of the infertility doctors, we continued to see them on a regular basis. On a routine check-up and ultrasound visit, Ben and I arrived at the doctor's office, signed in, and waited in the lobby to be called back. As we were waiting, I felt the urge to go to the restroom. I told Ben where I was going, started to walk down the hall and felt the strange sensation of moisture in my underwear. I walked in the bathroom, found an empty stall, pulled down my pants, and to my horror, found my underwear wet with blood. The world just stopped. My mind went blank, the world around me started to blur. I washed my hands and started the long trip back up the hall, my mind and eyes focused solely on the door of the doctor's office. I walked into the waiting area, past Ben and through the doors to the interior hallway of the office. Ben, not knowing what the heck was going on, followed me as I flagged down the first nurse I could find. The tears started falling as I tried to explain my situation. Our doctor came out of a patient's room and immediately told the nurses to get me to the ultrasound room. On the ultrasound table with the nurse and doctor both in the room, there on the screen was the familiar flicker of a heartbeat. So far, the baby was still alive, the heartbeat still strong. A blood test was ordered and it revealed low progesterone. Progesterone, a hormone made in the first 3 months of a pregnancy by the mother, is needed to keep the lining of the uterus receptive to the fertilized egg. Once the fertilized egg implants into the uterus, a woman keeps producing progesterone until the umbilical cord grows large enough to produce progesterone for the growing fetus. My body was not producing progesterone; therefore, the lining of the uterus was shedding in an attempt to have a menstrual period. Without the needed progesterone, my uterus would shed the pregnancy as well. I was immediately given an injection of progesterone to stop the process, and given a prescription for continued progesterone injections that I would need for the first few months of this pregnancy. Again, Ben would have to use his "Master Injector" skills for the next three months. Not only were the injections hard, but I never quit bleeding. I was put on full bed rest, not able to get out of bed for any reason other than trips to the bathroom, showering, and doctor visits. I was not allowed to cook, clean, nor go out to eat. Ben tried to work, moving his office to our house and tried to

... BUT I'M NOT THE SINGER

cook and clean, but it was too much for him. I became so tired of being in the bed but every time I got up and the bleeding started again, I panicked. Fear of losing another pregnancy ruled our lives. Some days seemed to last forever. I played cards. I watched TV. I read books. Finally, with my mind tired and bored, I decided to start journaling, sharing every day with my unborn child. He or she would get a glimpse of what life was like for us before, during and after their birth. Every day I tried to write something, giving a view of how Ben and I had gotten to this point.

At twelve weeks in the pregnancy, we said a tearful goodbye to the staff at the infertility center and were released into the care of Dr. S., our new obstetrician who specialized in high-risk pregnancies. Problems seemed to follow us. The bleeding continued for some unknown reason, baffling even Dr. S. At one of my routine ultrasounds, the technician took still picture after still picture of something on the screen. Dr. S. was called into the room, looked at the ultrasound screen, and explained to us that the source of the bleeding was a placenta previa. A placenta previa is a condition in which the umbilical cord that supplies all the needed blood, oxygen and nutrients to a growing fetus partially or fully covers the cervix. It causes bleeding in a pregnancy, and in some rare cases, can cause further severe complications and even death of the fetus. Luckily by the twentieth week of pregnancy, the placenta had moved away from the cervix, and all bleeding finally stopped. We found out during a routine ultrasound the baby was a boy. When the ultrasound technician told us, I looked at Ben, and he gave me the thumbs up sign.

At 6 months on a routine check-up, the doctor discovered I was in the first stages of premature labor. I was put on complete bed rest yet again. This time I didn't feel so alone since I now had the constant companionship of the active and ever-present baby I carried. He had become very animated and had the hiccups on a regular basis. I wrote about him in my journal every day, letting him know more about our past and keeping up to date on his progress. I wrote in my journal on August 9th, 1994:

"I'm twenty-eight weeks… This baby pushes his body parts into my skin, and we can almost make out which body parts. Most of the time his head pushes up but once I have seen an elbow or foot. It distorts my whole abdomen's shape."

Yet again, we were faced with another family member's death. Ben's father, John Paul, had previously been diagnosed with leukemia. He had fought

MY NAME IS JACK JOHNSON...

it for months and was holding onto hope that one day he would be cured. Our pregnancy had brightened his attitude, giving him something to fight harder for. Unfortunately, he never got a chance to meet his new grandson. He passed a mere three months before the baby was born. Sometimes life's timing can be very cruel.

At my thirty-eighth week appointment, my blood pressure had skyrocketed. I was diagnosed with pre-eclampsia, and the baby needed to be delivered. We were sent to the hospital, and I was admitted. After the labor-inducing drugs were administered, labor began and continued through the night and into the next day. On October 28 at 6:30pm, I was ready to begin pushing. After two long hours of pushing, a nurse laid something on my chest. I opened my eyes to the strangest thing I had ever seen: a squirming body, its skin a strange color of gray, with a head full of black hair. The little bundle was whisked away to a warming bed where he was measured and weighed. Mister Benjamin Paul Johnson Jr. (Benny for short) weighed in at 8 pounds, 13 ounces and was 21 inches long. A few of those ounces were the weight of his thick, dark hair.

How does anyone describe being a parent? It is a strange but wonderful feeling. As soon as you find out you are going to have a bundle of joy, your view of life takes a turn. Life is not only about you, your spouse, and your plans and goals for your life. It now includes another being. Once that human being is born into your world, magical things start to happen. Our focus changes from "us" to "him or her." An internal switch is turned on, a switch that never turns off. That switch opens our minds and hearts to a new dimension—unconditional love. Our hearts expand even though we never physically feel it. A road opens before us representing the future of that child. We never dream of them becoming destitute or old and frail in their later years. We dream of bright futures, scholar students, All American athletes, dainty ballerinas, classical musicians, and getting to enjoy seeing our genetic lineage continue life for years to come. I have personally never heard a parent ever say they wish their child would strive to be an average Joe. How many of us have told our offspring, "You can be anyone you want to be? You can be the President of the United States!" Our dreams for that child are laid out like the "yellow brick road," and they will follow it along to their lofty dream's end. There is a change in our soul, deep within us, that changes our core being. We become parents!

Benny was not the ideal Gerber baby. He cried and cried for hours, leaving us confused and exhausted. His pediatrician told us to put him in his crib so he could cry himself to sleep. After two hours of crying, we accepted what we could not change. It was a stress filled time for two inexperienced parents and one very unhappy baby.

"Right now, you are laying in your travel playpen on your back with your sleeper open down to your diaper. You look like Elvis trying to impress the girls with your good-looking chest. The real reason is that I opened it earlier hoping it would soothe your colic fit. The fit lasted an hour. I will try anything to keep you quiet and happy, but nothing seems to work. Today was better than yesterday when your first fit lasted two hours and the second lasted an hour. We had plans for lunch with your daddy's great aunts, but after you cried for an hour and a half, I called your daddy crying myself and asked him to call his great aunts to cancel our lunch date. After you quit crying, I sat down and had a beer before lunch. I haven't had a beer before lunch in years. Ben and I wish we knew what makes you so unhappy—we would gladly fix it!"

But life with Benny wasn't all bad. He was a handsome little boy with dark eyes and his famous head of hair. He brought joy to us that we had only dreamed of. Those first few months between the crying spells, he reached all his major milestones in development. His two top front teeth emerged at four months of age which could have been one of the reasons for the crying. One day I was thinking about how wonderful motherhood was, how too soon he would be blowing out birthday candles and I wrote in my journal:

"…Benny blowing out candles on a birthday cake. I know it will happen one day and like having Benny in our lives feels like a dream, so will Benny blowing out candles on his birthday cake. Our time together will go by so fast, it's scary. I wish I could see you through your life to adulthood and then magically go back to the delivery room and do it all again. Maybe that's what heaven will be—reliving great times over and over!"

CHAPTER 3

We adapted to living life as new parents with our new son. Some days were the best, and some days were a struggle. Life as we had known it was now completely different. Our focus, like any new parent, was Benny. The other things we thought were so important were often left undone or overlooked. As time went on, we fell into a rhythm of life. Ben worked from home or went into the office. Benny and I stayed home and bonded. Ben and I dreamed when Benny was older and in school, I could start back to work outside the home. We could eventually buy a bigger house one day. We had been told that we only had a six percent chance of ever conceiving again, so we envisioned life with just the three of us.

Sometimes God has other plans for us that we never see coming. Being so busy with Benny and our lives, I had forgotten entirely about my period. I couldn't remember when I was supposed to have it or when my last one was. I finally took the time, did a little detective work, and found that my period was indeed late. In true infertility mindset, I figured that I had skipped one because I was so busy with Benny or my schedule was messed up from the previous infertility treatments. Two more days passed and curiosity got the best of me. Once I told Ben, we decided to buy a pregnancy test just to satisfy our curiosity. I remember being in the bathroom, wetting the test, and waiting for the results. There are those times in life when you feel that life throws you a curve ball and for some strange reason, you put out your hands, and you catch the ball. The pregnancy test was positive! Ben and I were shocked, dumbfounded. Ben made another drug store visit for another pregnancy test. The next morning the second test was positive too. Later, so was the third one.

Still in total disbelief, I gave Dr. S.'s office a call. When the receptionist asked what I needed to see Dr. S. for, I told her I thought I was pregnant. She laughed, asked if I had taken a home pregnancy test and I had to fess up that all three tests were positive. She laughed again. At our appointment on August 29th, Dr. S., surprised to see us, confirmed I was indeed pregnant. He

...BUT I'M NOT THE SINGER

wanted us to see our infertility doctor first so she could make sure it was a viable pregnancy. Soon we were at the infertility office yet again, seeing the flicker of another heartbeat, our six percent chance of ever seeing this again. Our infertility doctor was thrilled for us and said everything looked normal, but Ben and I were both concerned about my progesterone level. Would it be any different with this baby than it was with Benny since I had gotten pregnant on my own? Dr. W. mentioned if we wanted to check my progesterone levels, we could easily do it. We left the office very worried. We decided that having the progesterone test was well worth the money when you factored in how much our peace of mind was worth. As soon as we got home, we called the doctor back and scheduled the test. As was our fear, the analysis revealed that indeed my progesterone levels were deficient. If we had not started the progesterone injections when we did, we might have lost this baby the same way we lost our first pregnancy before Benny was born. While embracing the good news about our new baby, the injections began.

On August 29, I wrote to Benny: "We just found out officially today that you are going to have a baby brother or sister. You're so small right now you can't understand this and won't understand when we bring the baby home in April. This is something Daddy and I thought would never happen. I am about six weeks into this pregnancy. You will be less than 18 months old when this new baby is born. Two kids in diapers, two baby beds, and two kids in a room together. Lots of twos. It's going to be hard, but I'm still happy about it all. Your dad is really excited. He loves you a lot and wants to give you everything in life. That includes a sibling. One day after we are both gone, you will have someone to share your life with who will know you and love you in that special way only brothers/sisters know. I know when my mother died, my sisters were the only other people on earth who knew how each other felt. It was a relief to know we weren't alone. Now you will be a big brother. What a special job!"

At 20 weeks, we found out the sex of baby number two: a boy. Two boys would make a fantastic family!

Before we knew it, we were closing in on another delivery due date. This baby was in a breech position and after a failed attempt to turn the baby, we knew I would need a Cesarean Section. In the wee hours on the morning April 10th, I was taken to the operating room for a C-section. With Ben dressed in surgical wear and me on the table, Dr. S gave a play by play of his

MY NAME IS JACK JOHNSON...

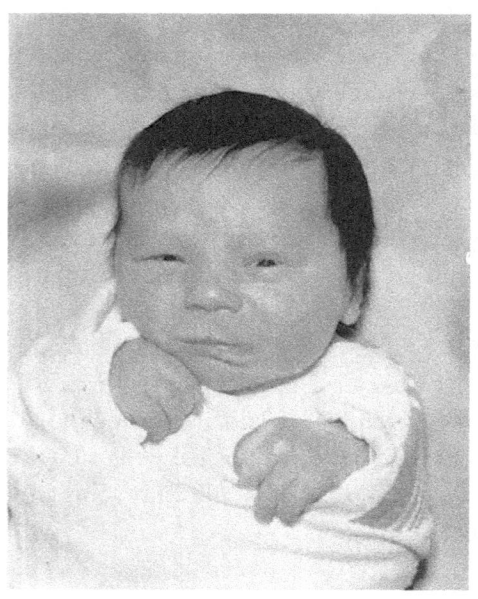

April 10, 1996 Jack's birth

actions. Once the baby was removed, Dr. S. said, "We have a boy. More like a linebacker!" The small baby screamed his unhappiness. Our new son weighed in at 8 pounds, 10 ounces, was 21 inches long, and like his older brother had a head full of hair. Jack Tolbert Johnson, named after his grandfather and great, great grandfather, was wrapped in a blanket and presented to me. The only thing I could do was give him a small kiss on his cheek.

Benny, once we all got back home and life restarted again, became a holy terror. He didn't like having a brother, someone who was taking Mom and Dad away from him. In his little toddler mind, Jack was the enemy taking time and attention from him. Ben and I learned to make special time with Benny and special time with Benny and Jack together. In no time, Benny was starting to enjoy his little brother and his new job as big brother.

A local church offered a Mother's Day Out Program. Ben and I decided it would be a wonderful thing for Benny, having both girl and boy playmates and time away from us. To enter the program, you had to be a year old, and since Benny was now over a year old, we signed him up. What we thought would be a wonderful experience for Benny became yet another problem: Benny's new Mother's Day Out Program quickly became a Mother's Day In program for me. Benny hated it. He didn't like being there. He didn't like me leaving him. He cried and cried until the program director would call me. I would pack Baby Jack up, and the two of us would check on Benny. If Jack and I stayed, Benny would play with the other children. If we left, he would realize I was gone and start crying again. I tried sneaking out; didn't work, I tried telling Benny goodbye with a big hug and kiss; didn't work. I tried telling him goodbye and letting him know I would be back soon to get him; didn't work either. The teachers tried to help by keeping Benny busy and happy with the other children, but when he discovered

... BUT I'M NOT THE SINGER

his mommy was gone, he cried and cried. Finally, one day, the call didn't come. I was worried and afraid something awful had happened. The opposite happened: Benny had decided that staying and playing with his newfound friends was more fun than being at home with his mommy and baby brother. It was a happy day!

Life with two little ones was hard, much harder than when we only had one. I was continuously changing diapers, feeding someone, putting them down for naps, playing with one or the other, or cleaning up after them.

DECEMBER 12, 1996—We are watching Bill Nye the Science Guy while I write this. It's a quiet moment in a very busy week. Benny has been sick with an ear infection and the croup, and Jack has picked this week to cut the 2 upper front teeth we have been waiting for. It has been a cry-a-thon around here this week. If Benny hasn't been crying and whining, then Jack has. Sometimes it was a crying chorus. It has not been fun. These are times I will not look back on fondly.

Somehow all the diaper changing, napping, cleaning and playing got easier and easier the further away from the land of babies we got. Thirteen months after Jack was born, he was scheduled for a minor surgery to correct a slight problem with the tear ducts in each of his eyes. Once the surgery was performed and Jack healed, we started living life again looking forward. Our next biggest hurdle with Jack seemed to be getting him to walk and to eat solid foods. For some strange reason, he rejected some solid table foods. He ate Cheerios, Fish Crackers, American cheese, but when we tried to sneak in some meat or veggies from the table, he refused to eat them and would only eat jarred baby foods. On his first birthday, he ate lots of cake and icing, getting it all over his face and hands just like Benny and every other kid in America does on their first birthday. Unfortunately, he cried through his first family attended birthday party. When Ben took him outside, Jack was fine but once inside in the living room packed with family and friends, he fell apart crying inconsolably. It seemed like it was just too much for him—the crowd, the attention, the unwrapping of presents. It left us feeling oddly disturbed.

He had not yet learned to walk, having trouble it seemed negotiating the ups and downs of traveling around furniture—a baby's first step on their way to walking independence. His ability to crawl was remarkable; he could fly. He could crawl as fast as Benny could walk across the floor. His arms and

MY NAME IS JACK JOHNSON...

legs seemed to travel at the speed of sound as he went from place to place on all fours. Once while having his tongue stuck out between his lips and crawling at warp speed, his fast-moving arms tangled up, and he fell on his chin, forcing his teeth into his tongue with such force that his tongue was almost cut through.

Jack started saying "mama," "da-da," and "bye." He loved his bed, was always eager to sleep, and was usually very happy. Benny and Jack interacted as brothers typically do with big physical hugs and lots of belly blowing. Benny found out at an early age how fun it was to make Jack laugh, so he took advantage of each opportunity. With both boys sitting in their car seats in the back seat, Benny discovered how Jack loved to watch him shake his head. Benny would shake his head from side to side, and Jack would cackle loudly. This would go on for miles. One day, Benny was not in a very good mood and shook his head at his seatmate only once. Jack would not be denied and shook his own head and bent over his car seat with laughter.

We started to experience more and more frequent crying episodes with Jack. One second, he would be fine, and from out of nowhere, he would burst into tears. I would check his clothes for pins or stray plastic accidentally left from a clothing item's price tag. I would check him for rashes, bug bites or pinch marks in case Benny had taken his frustrations out on Jack. I even took him several times to the pediatrician to see if there was a hidden ailment that was bothering him. But Jack was always given a clean bill of health.

We decided to put him in the Mother's Day Out Program Benny attended. We knew everyone, and they certainly knew us by now. One day the phone rang and yet again I was asked to come and pick one of the boys up. This time it was Jack. By what the teachers said, Jack was happily playing when something happened, they didn't know what, and he just fell apart and would not be consoled. I picked him up, his face red from crying, took him home, and immediately the exhausted child fell asleep. From that day forward, the fits of unexplained crying became a regular occurrence. At least once a week, the teachers would say Jack would cry out for no reason and would eventually cry himself to sleep. Once, while I was grocery shopping, one of the teachers called and left a message on our answering machine that Jack was totally inconsolable and that I needed to come and take him home. This was before the age of cell phones in our lives, so I didn't get the message until I arrived home. After quickly putting away the grocery perishables, I drove as fast as I could to the facility only to find Jack fast asleep. One of the teachers explained that the crying episode had been exceptional-

... BUT I'M NOT THE SINGER

ly difficult with Jack throwing himself on the ground.

Just like most new parents, Ben and I had trouble finding time to go grocery shopping We finally got in the habit of going at night after work and taking both boys with us. Ben and I pushed two grocery carts, one with one boy and one in the other. Even these trips soon became terror time for Jack for no reason at all. I accused Ben of mashing Jack's little fingers or pinching a tiny bit of Jack's skin while his hands were pushing the cart. But he cried when I pushed him and I know I never mashed his fingers or pinched his skin. Over time, his crying became so loud and obnoxious, one of us would have to take him to the car and wait with him until the other one and Benny completed the shopping. I had no idea what was causing the crying.

Time passed, and finally, at 16 months old, Jack started to walk We were thrilled. Before we knew it, he was running—something that thrilled his big brother. From that day forward, the two of them never went anywhere without running. They would run to their bedroom, to the kitchen, and through the family room. When they would run, they would look at each other, their faces lit with smiles, and they would laugh at each other and at themselves. The sound of their tiny, flat, little feet slapping against the floor was the percussion to the laughter. We began playing "naked boy time," the time right before their baths when I would let the boys run around the house without clothes or diapers. They loved it. I can still see their tiny little bare bottoms running away from me, the laughter coming from them as their feet slapped the linoleum floors and their arms reaching out to each other. They would race to the baby gate at the kitchen door, give each other a big goofy grin and turn toward me, running as fast as they could, squealing with each step, naked as the day they were born and in a complete place of true happiness.

One day when the weather was great, I took the boys to a nearby park that had a fantastic playground. We had taken them there before, and they always loved it. The playground had swings, slides of all shapes and sizes, sand pits, and lots of walkways, bridges, and hidey-holes for little ones to explore and enjoy. One of the slides was a spiral slide, corkscrewing from one of the walkways to the ground. Benny had come down the slide so many times on our previous trips that I thought Jack would enjoy it too. He and I climbed up through the maze of the playground equipment until we got to the spiral slide. I got Benny to stand at the bottom and put Jack at the top of the slide. But Jack would not go down. The slide was too much for him to do all by himself. I picked him up, sat down at the top of the slide, and sat him back down in my lap. I had seen so many parents coming down

MY NAME IS JACK JOHNSON...

the slide in this way, their children happy in their laps, that I didn't think anything about it. As we were coming down the slide, I noticed his little left foot tennis shoe caught on the shiny aluminum looking material the slide was made of, and his foot ended up underneath his leg at a funny angle when we came to a stop at the bottom of the slide. I picked him up from my lap and stood him on the ground, and he immediately started to touch his leg. He sat down and with his little chubby toddler hand started to flip his fingers back and forth at a certain spot on his leg while he whined. He never cried or screamed but refused to stand. I immediately picked him up, got him and Benny both in the car, and came home. Fortunately, Ben was working from home that day when we arrived home, and I explained to him what had happened. Jack still refused to stand up and continued to touch his leg and whine. We called the pediatrician and were told to bring Jack in. It was late in the day when we arrived at the pediatrician's office, but we were taken back, and an X-ray was made of Jack's leg. There on the X-ray was the tiniest fracture in his leg. I was heartbroken and washed with guilt. An appointment was made the next morning to get Jack's leg set in a cast. I didn't know I could feel so much guilt and pain. I was plagued by the "if only's." If only I had not put him in my lap. If only I had not taken them to the playground. If only I had put my hands on his legs and kept them together while we came down the slide. If only...

The next morning, we were at the orthopedic office to have Jack's leg set in a cast. Jack and I went back to an examining room where a nurse asked us the usual questions of what, where, when, and how. I told her the whole story about the playground and the spiral slide, but for some reason, I was getting a strange feeling from her about the whole situation. She left the room and went to get the doctor. I held Jack in my lap while listening to the conversation outside the examining room between the nurse and the doctor. The doctor asked what the story was and the nurse said, "The mom says he broke his leg coming down a slide" in her most sarcastic voice. I was shocked when I heard she was insinuating that I had done something to break Jack's leg. Her tone of voice and innuendo made my blood boil. When the doctor and nurse walked back into the room, he asked me to tell him the story of what happened, me knowing full well what had just been said in the hallway between the two of them. The doctor didn't stay long only to confirm the fracture in Jack's leg and to give him a quick once-over. Before the doctor left the room, he told me the nurse was going to put a cast on Jack's leg that would have to stay on for a few weeks. We would then

... BUT I'M NOT THE SINGER

bring Jack in and have the cast removed, and the leg would be healed. The nurse started getting together all the ingredients to make the cast for Jack's leg. I explained to her that Jack had always been a very strong child and that it might take more than just the two of us to hold him while she put the cast on. She smugly looked at me and said that she had put casts on lots of children, strong ones included, and that she and Jack would be alright. As soon as I laid Jack on the table, he started to cry, squirm and sit up. Soon, he was screaming and kicking his legs in all directions. After 30 minutes of cast making with Jack, the nurse was a little less smug, and Jack's big, new, purple cast was bent at the knee!

We had wanted Jack to walk for so long, and now he was back on the floor on all fours, except this time he would drag one leg covered in a dark purple cast. Jack never missed a beat playing with toys, chasing cats, and messing around with his big brother. He even went Trick or Treating that Halloween, purple cast and all, dressed in a homemade Dalmatian dog costume while riding in the boy's little red wagon around the neighborhood. Eventually, he did learn how to walk on the cast, even though it was bent at the knee. Weeks later, we returned to the orthopedist office and had it removed. Jack's leg was healed.

CHAPTER 4

With Jack's leg healed, we started getting back to a normal life. There were still questionable issues with his behavior and progression. Jack was walking again, but most of the time he ran. When I say ran, I mean an uncontrolled, no purpose run that would leave Ben and I bewildered and drained after trying to catch him all the time. He had no fear and acted like he didn't hear us calling his name as we ran after him. I was so afraid he would run out in our neighborhood street when a car was coming and I would not be able to stop him. I realized one day that I had not heard Jack call out for "daddy" or "mommy," some of his first words. He was still not eating whole foods, preferring only pureed baby foods. I would try to sneak solid foods into his baby foods but he would either vomit or he would work the solid piece of food out of his mouth and swallow the baby food. His screaming had escalated into full-blown tantrums. He would drop to the floor, his arms and legs flying, while rolling around on the floor inconsolable. I watched one day as Jack pulled a circular drink coaster off the coffee table and repeatedly threw it across the room making it spin like a top.... over and over again. I had read an article in a *Reader's Digest* a few years back about a mother discovering her son had a condition called autism. I remembered bits and pieces of the article and somewhere in my brain, I let the thought cross my mind, "Could Jack have autism?" I mentioned my autism fear to Ben, but he told me I had been cooped up with two boys for so long that I had lost my mind and that he needed to make sure I got out more.

In November, Jack had his 18-month well-baby visit with his pediatrician. Ben kept Benny at home and I took Jack to see the doctor. Jack was happy and busy playing like any other 18-month-old boy in the waiting room, but when the nurse came to get us, he started screaming. By the time we got to an examining room, he was screaming at the top of his lungs. I held him. I sang to him. I cuddled him, but nothing worked. The pediatrician came in and tried his best to comfort Jack, but nothing he did worked either. The doctor checked out my screaming son and everything was normal, including his lungs. The doctor asked about eating and talking, two of Jack's weaknesses. I explained Jack's refusal of solid foods, how some words had disappeared, and the full-blown tantrums. Finally, over the cries of Jack, the pediatrician asked if I had ever heard about the condition called autism. My heart sank in my chest. I told him I had and shared the coaster spinning I had witnessed one day. Dr. M. explained he could not diagnose autism or any other learning disability, but that he could get in touch with the right people who could. As much as my heart was aching, my brain was telling me that this is what Jack and we needed. We needed answers. Answers that a pediatrician could not provide. I cried all the way home.

The next week, a person from the Vanderbilt Behavior Clinic called and scheduled an appointment. Ben and I were to go without Jack to the clinic for a parent interview. The interviewer asked many questions about Jack. We shared the behaviors we had witnessed. As she wrote down all our answers, somewhere in the back of my mind I knew where this was going. Call it motherly instinct or a crazed mother, but I just knew. I just knew in my heart there was something different about Jack. He had been such a good baby—always smiling and cooing. His little round face would light up when

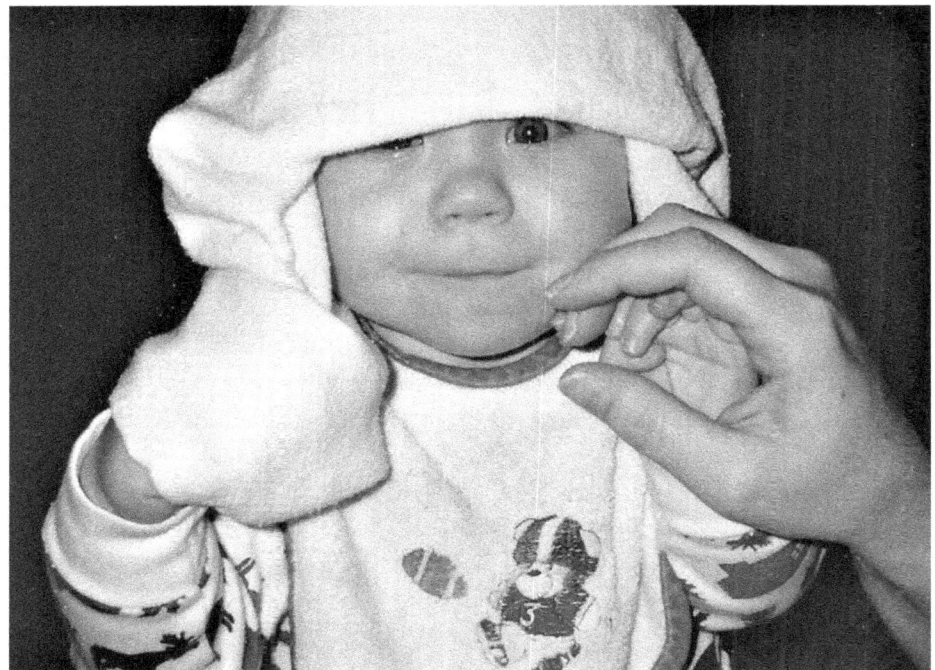

1996 Baby Jack after a bath and before autism diagnosis

MY NAME IS JACK JOHNSON...

he grinned that cute baby smile. He babbled and learned to say "mommy" and "daddy". He had a personality. He played with toys. He loved to watch TV and play with his never-stopping, big brother. But something was happening—or maybe I should say not happening—with his development. It seemed to me Jack got to a certain point in his development and it just stopped. I know you are not supposed to compare your children, but when they are young, near the same age and size, and are learning and changing so much each day, you find yourself comparing. Benny didn't have trouble eating. He was late to walk at 13 months, but not as late as Jack was at 16 months. Benny started to talk and thereafter every day brought new words and gestures. Benny did cry a lot, but his crying did not involve flaying arms or legs, no jerking of his body or being physically self-injurious. I had become troubled about the escalating intensity of Jack's tantrums. Ben and I both had already suffered busted lips and banged up noses while holding Jack when he jerked his head and banged it into ours. What if he did that to Benny? I was getting scared because I just didn't know what to do with Jack, especially during his frantic tantrums.

I left the Vanderbilt Behavior Clinic that day knowing in my heart that Jack had a significant condition, and Ben left in denial la-la land. I got in the car, started to cry and couldn't stop. Ben just kept saying that no diagnosis had been made and until then, he would not believe the worst. The interviewer had told us that she was going to schedule an appointment for Jack with the Child Development Center at Vanderbilt. Mr. Common, my nickname for common sense, told me that if there was the slightest chance that Jack's development was normal, then why the upcoming appointment? Ben and I decided to stop for lunch to discuss the interview without children around. Since we had a babysitter with the boys, we chose a restaurant that was not near our house nor was one we frequented. We sat down, started to order our lunch, and the background music in the restaurant took my breath away. I had to run to the bathroom where I couldn't control the sobs. The song playing was "A Whole New World." The same song that played as my mother passed away. And again, those words brought more tears. I didn't need a diagnosis. I just knew.

After that initial clinic visit, things started to happen. We were contacted by the state's Early Intervention Program and an appointment with Jack's caseworker was scheduled. Still, Ben lived in the land of denial, refusing to even talk about it. Me? I was ready. I was prepared to find some help, some guidance, some sense of comfort in the fact that Jack would get what he needed. Mostly, I was scared of the unpredictable future.

...BUT I'M NOT THE SINGER

DECEMBER 9, 1997—I hope and pray nothing will be wrong but maybe someone will have some kind of answer for us about the tantrums. I don't know what Ben and I will do if they continue with Jack getting stronger and bigger. Sometimes now if you don't get away from him while he's having a fit, he can hurt you. Of course, he doesn't mean to. I'm looking forward to getting some answers. I feel so guilty about the fact he won't eat whole foods and he doesn't talk as much as he should. I feel being his mother, I am not doing something right. I hope someone can help.

Jack was scheduled for a hearing test, but as we suspected, it came back normal. The audiologist said she agreed with Dr. M. that there was a suspicion of autism.

JANUARY 12, 1998—Yesterday I caught Jack beating his head against the couch cushion, just bouncing his head up and jerking it down so it would bounce back up again. I just sat there and watched. It's such a horrible feeling to see him do something like that. What pleasure is banging and bouncing your head on the couch? At least it was the couch cushion where it wasn't hurting him. Ben said that shows him that Jack at least is smart enough to not bang his head on the floor or wall. I wish he could talk better and let me know anything—I'm always guessing. When he cries I start asking—Are you hungry? Are you thirsty? Do you want to go night-night? Usually, he just cries without any change, no speaking, no reaching out, no pointing. It is so hard. I have cried a river thinking about our changing future and what could be in store for all of us. How hard is life going to be from now on? I hate being left out, on hold, waiting for other people. I am afraid of all this uncertainty.

The Child Development Center called and Jack's upcoming appointment was scheduled for February 18th. We were told the appointment would start at 9:15am and would last until 1pm. He was scheduled to see a medical doctor, a psychologist, a speech therapist, an occupational therapist, and a physical therapist. I was so tired of waiting for answers.

As we waited for the upcoming appointment, life with Jack continued to be difficult.

FEBRUARY 4, 1998—No one wants to keep Jack. Everyone fears Jack They're afraid he might have a tantrum and they won't know what to do. Well,

MY NAME IS JACK JOHNSON...

JUMP ON BOARD! We don't know what to do either. Just having Mommy and Daddy doesn't make him happy. He is not like other kids—they see Mommy and Daddy and instantly stop crying. Most of the time, Jack doesn't pay any attention to anything around him when he has a fit. Again, he had a fit at preschool Wednesday and they called me to come and get him. Of course. like so many times before, I was at the grocery store and didn't know until I got home that they had called. I went to get him as soon as I heard their message and by the time I got the message and got to preschool, he had cried himself to sleep. The teachers said they had never seen anything like it—the kicking, screaming and banging his head. One of the teachers called later that night to make sure Jack was OK. Previously we had ventured out for dinner and Jack started to get upset over something. Ben started to panic thinking a fit was coming. I followed Jack's eyes and he was looking straight at a drinking straw. Once I gave him the straw, he was fine. You must keep guessing what he is trying to say with his screams. Yesterday, Ben and I were getting the boys ready to walk out the door for school but Jack didn't want to go. Jack always wants to go—go bye-bye, go outside, go upstairs, go anywhere. He hardly ever fights when it's time to put on his coat, but he was not going to put his coat on or go anywhere. He started to cry and Ben picked him up to put his coat on the hard way (as we call it.) With one sniff Ben knew why Jack didn't want to go—his diaper was dirty! Jack was refusing to leave with a nasty bottom. Once Ben changed him, Jack was ready for his coat and ready to go. He never said poopy, he didn't gesture, he didn't say NO, he didn't say anything. He just cried. That's Jack's way of letting us know his wants, his dislikes, his needs, his would-likes, his have not's, and his can't-gets. This is like a puzzle—always trying to piece together the next dilemma. I hate this—I really, really hate this. I don't hate my child, I hate what is happening. Sometimes he likes this, other times he likes that. Sometimes he says this word, other days he doesn't speak. Some days he is so hard to be with, other days he is a pure joy. He can be the happiest child and then there is that other side. He can get so angry he kicks and hits at anything within his reach. Last week we had a lesson on OW! He kicked me and I said "OW!" I hit him back ever so lightly and I said "OW!" He kicked me again and I said "OW" again. I ever so lightly hit him and said "OW." Finally, he started to say "OW" when he kicked me or when I play hit him. I can only hope he understood some of it.

FEBRUARY 21, 1998—The day we had been waiting for has come and as suspected, Jack has autism. I was not surprised—actually relieved to finally know. The different doctors and therapists asked lots of questions and played with Jack. Each of them was looking for problems in their area of expertise. They all agreed Jack has autism, somewhere between mild and moderate autism. His inability to withstand textures was his biggest area of weakness throwing him more toward moderate autism. He has no problems with his physical abilities. He can solve small toddler problems like stacking blocks, putting pegs in shaped holes, and puzzle pieces in different shaped holes. The therapist called it fine and gross motor skills. Gross motor skills are running, jumping, sitting, and climbing. Fine motor skills are hand to hand, hand to mouth, picking up small objects, etc. Jack was normal in all these categories. His speech is definitely delayed. His intolerance to textures is a huge problem. He cannot stand whole foods or anything on his hands like food, finger paint, even soap. All the therapists agreed on several things: Jack needs to stay in preschool where he can interact with his normal peers, he needs to start going to a playgroup like Waves in Franklin, the early intervention program for kids Jack's age, and he will also need speech and occupational therapies.

With the diagnosis of autism, I was busier than ever. I stayed on the phone talking with our caseworker at the Early Intervention System in our state. The System was responsible for Jack's interventions until he reached the age of 3 and at that time, children with special needs started going to school through the local school system. I talked to the director of both preschools, letting them know the when, the how, and the why. The director of the Mother's Day Out program that Benny and Jack had been attending told us that the preschool was not a preschool for children with autism. She said Jack could continue to come to preschool as long as he didn't hurt himself or any other children. I found the number for our local chapter of the Autism Society of America and talked to the representative, a mother of a son with autism herself, for hours.

I started to take notes on the different behaviors I witnessed with Jack.
"Last week, he picked up a perfumed magazine insert and violently gagged. The gag seemed to make him sickly for several minutes afterward. Eventually, he drank some juice and wanted to be held. Soon he went back to playing but gagged violently again. I smelled his hands and the perfume smell was there too. After we washed his hands, he did not gag again. The smell of the perfume on his hands was not that strong to me. Jack likes

MY NAME IS JACK JOHNSON...

to eat chocolate yogurt but only if I am eating it and only if he is fed the yogurt out of my portion from my yogurt container. I tried to give him his own bowl and spoon but all he did was stir it disgustingly. He never tried to eat any from the bowl even when I tried to feed it to him. The next night I gave him a cup just like mine of yogurt and an identical spoon and he tried to feed himself. It was awkward but a good attempt."

MARCH 4, 1998—Now I'm in the process of learning everything I can about this condition—what is available in treating it, support groups for parents, money problems, and different therapists. Our world is changing daily. Jack can still be a great joy amid his problems. He finds pleasure in the cutest ways, even though they are different ways. Benny has started to understand with our help that Jack is different.

MARCH 9, 1998—Jack had his first day at Waves and he loved it! He didn't want to leave. I had to chase him down to put his coat on him.

CHAPTER 5

Autism. Just the word sends chills up the spine of most parents. Autism, or autism spectrum disorder, refers to a range of conditions characterized by challenges with social skills, repetitive behaviors, speech and nonverbal communication, as well as by unique strengths and differences. (www.autismspeaks.org/what-autism) The diagnosis does not mean people with autism are not capable of learning or are developmentally challenged. It means they learn differently than others. To put it in simple terms for understanding, think of your brain like a computer. The keys on the keyboard are your connection to what comes up on the screen in front of you. What would happen if the keys were scrambled? Your "s" key was your "y" key. The "delete" key was the "5" key? You couldn't just take the computer keyboard apart and fix it. You would do the only thing you could do: you would learn how to use the keys the way they are. That is like autism. The connections in the brain are just different from the ones typical people have in their brains. For the people who work with and love a person with autism, we must understand and learn their "new keyboard."

Our life became all about the boys. We wanted to grow healthy, happy, self-reliant children into adults responsible for themselves and not a burden on each other or our government. We were thinking into the future to a time when both boys were left to their own devices and didn't have us to help them. We were planning for the time after our own deaths. It sounds so morbid. Unemployment rates in the special needs community are very, very high. Housing and transportation are both huge problems. The future dreams of most special needs parents look nothing like the dreams of typical parents with typical children. (Note. In the special needs world we don't say "normal" but use the term "typical" instead. Being disabled in life is a normal state for all of us at some time in our lives, unable to do the things we typically had done before. The word normal implies that being disabled is not a normal state for humans. The term typical is used in its place.)

MY NAME IS JACK JOHNSON...

We started watching the life we thought we had slowly begin to disappear and found ourselves watching others enjoy the things we had planned for and dreamed about for so long. We watched as our friends, family, and neighbors prospered, vacationed, enjoyed evenings alone, had nights on the town, bought new cars, went to church, the park, the movies, the lake, had parties, went swimming, and all the other typical activities a family does in their everyday lives. We were held hostage, not from anything of our own doing, but by a circumstance of life. If we dared to go out for any reason, we never knew when the autism bomb would explode, causing public chaos. We couldn't spend money because we were living off one and only one paycheck, and any therapy or specialized doctor visits might or might not be covered by our health insurance. At that time, so little was known about autism that most insurance companies grouped autism treatments under mental health issues which had limited coverage. Since there was not a proven treatment for autism, a life-long disability, any therapy was classified as unnecessary, and insurance would not cover.

Life, in general, is hard. Life with autism is harder. Life with autism, a three-year-old, and a ticking time bomb disguised as a toddler is harder still. Daily we had to not only learn to handle Jack's autistic behaviors, but we had to adjust our way of doing things that for years had become second nature. Just pulling out of the driveway would sometimes produce a full-blown tantrum while Jack was strapped into a car seat in the backseat of our car. Getting a drink of water could yield a drop to the floor, head-banging, spit inspiring reaction. Ben and I lived each day confused by what caused these unexplained and unexpected reactions. What were we doing wrong? Our guilt at not knowing what to do with our own child and the burden of having such an explosive child was so heavy.

Not only was Jack going to a regular preschool and a developmental preschool, but he also started speech and occupational therapy. The whole family began seeing a social worker for issues with behavior. My days consisted of getting Benny and Jack ready for school, getting Jack ready for therapy, getting them fed, getting them bathed, and getting them to bed. Life was a blur. In between all this going and coming, and coming and going, I had to wash clothes, clean house, and cook meals. I also started attending a parent support group for parents of children with autism. I was the mother of the youngest child in the group and the mother of the most recently diagnosed child. I soaked up every word spoken and tried to remember so many words of advice. The one piece of advice that changed my life was about housework. I had asked the ladies in attendance how they did it all: the therapies, the wifely duties, the other childrearing, the cooking of meals and keeping a house clean. One lady spoke up as soon as I finished and said, "Forget the house cleaning. Who cares if your house is dirty? That should be the least of your worries. Your energy should be used to help your children, not make sure your house looks good." With those few words, my thinking changed and so did my constant chasing of my tail trying to be "Super Mommy."

MARCH 27, 1998—"Benny told me today that while I was in the shower, he had been killing dust bunnies. Must be time to clean the house."

To make matters worse, I received a call from the director of the preschool/Mother's Day Out Program that both the boys were attending. Again, she explained that their program was not set up to handle a child with special needs like Jack. The director said that if Jack decided to open a door and run away, something very common for kids with autism, the program was not set up to handle a situation like that. For Jack's welfare and the welfare of the program, the director and I decided to take Jack out of the typical preschool.

Since Jack did not have communication skills and he didn't talk as much as he should, we started teaching him through a communication system called the Picture Exchange System (PECS). We had received the initial beginnings of the system from a visit to the office of the Autism Society of Middle Tennessee. The system consisted of small, easy to read cards with black drawings on a white background. Each picture on the card depicts a word or action with that word or action written in black letters at the bottom of the card. The person using the cards can make his wants and needs known to others by looking for the appropriate word or action and giving the card to someone who can help him get what he needs or wants. The cards are laminated, and Velcro is attached to the back. I copied the cards, bought a laminator and Velcro, and began the arduous task of trying to get Jack to understand the concept. It didn't go well. The first few times we tried, he threw a fit. I would have to show him the picture and the actual item that went with the picture. For example, I would show him the PEC card for juice which showed a cup with fluid in it, and then show him his own sippy cup with his juice in it. We did the same for milk, cookies, fish crackers, Cheerios, and any other snack he liked, for toys and other fun things he enjoyed. The cards were put on a bigger strip of laminated and Velcro-ed construction paper, cut the right dimensions for small hands to easily maneuver. When Jack would sit to eat in his high

MY NAME IS JACK JOHNSON...

chair, I would attach two cards—the juice card and the milk card—on the strip, and while showing him the pictures, ask him if he wanted juice or milk. At first, he hated it, having to learn to choose between the two cards and not being able to drink whatever drink was put in front of him. To make things worse at the beginning of the process, I had to use my hand over his to show him how to choose the drink he would get by touching the picture of that drink. He didn't like my hand on his during this part of the lesson. Over and over we tried and tried. Finally, one day it happened; he touched the picture of the drink he wanted and said the word. I knew then there was still a little boy inside that body that was just waiting to come out and learn so much about the world around him.

MARCH 13, 1998—"We are only beginning this journey. Ben and I have started the PECS cards, and Jack is beginning to see how they work. If he hands me the card, he gets what's on the card. When he doesn't want it, he usually throws the card at me. At least it's a start."

We also began using some sign language. "More" was signed by bringing all your fingers and thumbs together on each hand and then touching both hands together. "Wait" was signed by turning your hand upward and wiggling your fingers back and forth. Jack's speech therapist used these and others during his therapy sessions, and I continued to use them at home. I made one of my own by first pointing to my chest, then crossing my arms across my chest, and lastly pointing my finger back to Jack, while saying "I love you" every night before he fell asleep.

    I also started taking Jack to a group speech therapy session twice a week in Nashville at the Bill Wilkerson Center. I will never forget our initial visit with the director at the time. She had an immense presence through her voice and her demeanor. I am not saying she wasn't kind, or that she was heartless. Let's just say she could be an acquired taste. We liked her because you knew from the beginning she was not one to hold back or beat around the bush. On Jack's first visit, she sat Ben and me in a neighboring classroom behind a one-way glass. We could see her and Jack, but they couldn't see us. In the next room, she sat Jack down at a child-size table in a small regular chair, started talking and showing him different toys. As soon as Jack sat in the chair, he was immediately up and walking about. Sitting was not his thing; moving constantly was. The center director grabbed another chair, this one different from the first chair. This chair we would find out later is called a Rifkin Chair. A Rifkin Chair is a chair with a higher solid back, solid sides with armrests, and a removable piece of wood in the seat of the chair. This piece of wood fit into a slot in the seat and sat between the legs of the child once in the chair. Along with a strap that fit across the lap of the child in the chair, the solid wood piece in the seat slot kept the child in the chair. The director put Jack in the chair and he so innocently watched as she strapped him in, placing the wood between his legs. For a few seconds, it didn't register with him what exactly had happened. As soon as he started to move, he realized he was strapped. He squirmed, lurched, and became a full-fledged bucking bronco. Jack bucked with so much force he moved the whole chair around the room. At first, he made unhappy noises that quickly escalated into screams. The director began explaining to us through the one-way glass that children with autism cannot learn if they do not first learn to sit in a chair. Since this was Jack's first time to be forced to sit and participate, his behavior was a very common reaction for children with autism. I understood what she was saying, but the tears flowed down my cheeks nevertheless. Watching my child crying and bucking while strapped to a wooden chair was not something I ever thought I would have to witness. Every instinct in me wanted to jump up and release my child from this torture. But somewhere deep inside of me, it made sense. Jack would have to learn everything. The things we learn by just living life every day surrounded by other humans showing us the things they already knew, Jack would have to be taught.

Jack was placed in a group speech class with several recently diagnosed children with autism. The other children came from different parts of our area, from different backgrounds, had different deficits such as sensory problems, speech problems, and fine motor skill problems. One child could not stand the feeling of his clothing, and as soon as he arrived, he would disrobe himself down to his diaper. The mothers sat together in a small room between two classrooms, each wall of the small room a one-way mirror where we could watch the therapy session. At first, Jack continued to sit in the Rifkin Chair, but he wasn't alone. Several other classmates were also learning how to sit and participate. Toys became part of the therapy with each child given a choice of which toy they wanted to play with. As the children played, the therapist coaxed them to use language at the appropriate times teaching them patience and language at the same time. PECS cards were used, and choices were made of toys, activities, and snacks. I was beginning to understand the concept of speech therapy especially for children like Jack. Not only were they teaching the child to say the word, but they were also putting a mental picture together with that word.

MY NAME IS JACK JOHNSON...

Looking at how the therapy room was labeled with PECS cards for each piece of furniture and each individual activity center, I decided to make our house look the same as the therapy room. I copied some of the PECS cards I had been given, attaching and labeling each piece of furniture and every appliance in our house. When Jack would cry, I would give him a choice of drink or dirty diaper PECS card letting him choose either one. Sometimes it worked, other times it didn't. On the few occasions that it worked, he would point to the picture card that told me, for example, that he was thirsty. I would say to Jack, "Let's go to the refrigerator," which was plainly marked with its own picture card, opened the door, and held up one of Jack's cups that had juice or milk in it, asking him if he wanted juice or milk. Sometimes he pointed, sometimes he said either juice or milk. It was a start, and it opened the door of communication between us.

Unfortunately, even with the progress, there were still lots of tantrums and "come aparts" as we called them. Even with Jack's newly discovered words, there were still lots of times where language did not happen, and communication was lacking. We would guess what Jack wanted, but more times than not, we were wrong which always made Jack's tantrums worse. He just couldn't understand that if he wanted something, we were supposed to know what he wanted just because he wanted it. It was so hard, the guessing games, the "come aparts," the frustration we all felt. No parent likes to feel helpless when their children need them but without a communication system and not being able to communicate wants and needs, Jack was still completely miserable, and in differing ways, we were too. Poor Benny was so confused by the things going on around him. The mommy and daddy he knew would do anything he asked. His brother was not as lucky. From the eyes of a three-year-old, it must have been a terrible situation. There were always surprise tears and arms and legs in the air that Benny had to run away from when the tantrums started. Mommy and daddy were always trying to make things better. I know some days were worse than others and it seemed that when Jack had a bad day, Benny had a bad day too. I can't imagine what his little, immature and inexperienced brain was thinking.

We began family therapy, something that was offered to us through the Early Intervention System. We started to see a social worker, a sweet lady who taught us how to be better parents and how to deal with the life we now found ourselves living. Miss Jane would talk to us while watching the boys play with the toys she had in her office. When a situation arose, she would help us with discipline and how to solve conflicts between the boys, be-

... BUT I'M NOT THE SINGER

tween the boys and us, and between Ben and me. As I have said before, life with a special needs child is hard, quite a bit harder than a life with a typical child who had typical, every day, common problems. Every day brought new and more difficult problems, like how to deal with the outside world during a very public come apart to financial problems to problems with outside family members. Miss Jane was a huge help by showing us how to discipline a child who didn't quite understand the world around him much less what he had done to deserve a timeout. She taught me how important I was to both of my boys even though Jack took up most of my time, but how time with only Benny was important to his self-confidence and self-worth. She talked to Ben and me about how important we both were to our family and that we had to make time for each other as hard as it was to find it. We talked about how to deal with the public, our extended families, and the heartbreak and inadequacy we both felt from living in the world of autism.

MARCH 29, 1998—Later in the week we went to see Miss Jane. She will teach us how to discipline Jack with ways that he can understand. Hopefully, we can find useful information to help with Benny's bad behavior too. Last week we thought we had put the boys to bed—said goodnight, kissed, tucked them in and then lights out. An hour later, Jack's still wiggling and crying out. I walked back to their room to check on him and "surprise"! There stands Benny in Jack's bed! Poor Jack was crying out because he was trying to sleep and couldn't because big brother was sneaking into and playing in his crib. This happened three times in one week! Finally, for punishment, we took away Benny's trip to his grandmother's house and all his treats. So far it has worked. So, yes, we can use Miss Jane's help for both boys.

Jack also began having individual therapy sessions with another speech therapist and an occupational therapist. During his first session with Miss Patti, the occupational therapist, she received an accidental black eye from Jack. Great way to start off with a new therapist! Patti worked with Jack's immature vestibular system, his sensory integration issues, his tactile defensiveness, and his fine motor skills. The vestibular system is the sensory system that provides information about movement and sense of balance. The brain uses this information from the vestibular system and from the proprioception (sensory receptors that receive stimuli from within the body, especially those that respond to position and movement) throughout the body to understand the body's position and acceleration from one moment

MY NAME IS JACK JOHNSON...

to the next. To put it in a very simple way, a person's ability to know where their body is in space at any given minute. Sensory integration is the process of integrating the information our body receives from our senses: sight, sound, smell, taste, touch, and the perception of movement and position. As a natural part of typical development, children process, interpret, and respond to sensory information. In autism, the sensory information children receive is not processed and interpreted effectively which creates a negative response from a child with autism. Tactile defensiveness is the hypersensitivity in some children to touch and the input that touch sends to the brain. Our new speech therapist worked one on one with Jack helping him to form and verbalize his needs and wants through speech.

APRIL 27, 1998—The boys are napping. The clothes are drying, and I will need to fold them up later. This afternoon after naps, we have our appointment with Miss Jane. Jack went to Waves today. We haven't had any problems with him there. He seems so happy and well adjusted, and he is learning so much. He ate a French fry this weekend. Of course, it was a small, thin fry but it was a new texture. He is learning his numbers and counts all the time now. Whenever he sees numbers, he has to count them aloud. He watches clocks, the numbers changing on the microwave timer, numbers he sees in stores......anywhere there are numbers. He only counts them to ten. He is also starting to recognize letters and says them aloud as well. He can sing all the little kid songs they sing at school and Waves. Of course, the only way we can tell what he is saying is by watching his body movements or by listening closely to each word he sings. Some words will sound close to what the word sounds like but most sound like a lot of mumbling. Hopefully, speech therapy will help with this.

APRIL 28, 1998—Speech therapy has been going well except for one day. Linda, the speech therapist, had given Jack some colored markers to color with. Quickly, things got out of hand. Jack cared less about coloring with them, he just wanted to line them up end to end. Linda tried to put the ones he was laying down back in their holder, but Jack wanted to play with all of them. I forgot to mention—the tops were off all the markers. Jack tried to pick up as many as he could so Linda couldn't put them back. She was trying to put them back before he could get a grip on them. He started repeating "No-no-no-no-no-no...." and Linda said, "Jill, help me!" By the time we got the markers away from Jack, my hands were colored with a few marks and Jack's hands, face and arms were covered with all the colors of the markers. Linda said she would not let him have markers again. Good idea!

CHAPTER 6

Our lives were in constant motion, running to therapies, doctor appointments, back and forth to preschool. Unfortunately, in the beginning, our families were in denial. Ben and I had tried to explain autism to our parents, but since autism was rare at the time and almost unheard of when they were growing up, they just could not accept this new, strange ailment that their grandson had been diagnosed with. For my family, the denial bubble burst on an otherwise quiet Sunday afternoon while having the Southern tradition of Sunday dinner. I do not remember what started the whole thing, but I remember the horror of it. My whole immediate family was gathered around the dining room table, the homemade foods lovingly prepared and ready to eat when Jack went into a full fledge, screaming, spitting, flailing, head banging, two-hour long tantrum. When words cannot describe, witnessing a tantrum can make a believer out of you. Ben and I took Jack into my dad's bedroom and shut the door while the others ate their meal. Jack was on the floor, in full tantrum mode, banging his head on the carpet. It was ugly. Occasionally a brave family member would venture in to help only to throw up their hands when nothing they did helped. From that day forward, there was no denying that there was something different about Jack.

When the denial became a reality, fear became the problem. No one wanted to spend time with Jack. We didn't have the every-weekend-call for free babysitting by grandparents that most parents enjoy. We had the occasional visit at our house or theirs. There was no joy at the idea of babysitting our boys together. Ben and I felt truly alone.

Determined to not become hermits in our own world, we started to venture out into the world around us. We attempted to go out to eat, an occasional treat and an opportunity to feel a sense of normalcy. I plainly remember an outing, one that is difficult to forget. We decided to meet some friends for dinner at a local Mexican restaurant. Our friends had a little girl about the age of Benny, and they enjoyed spending time together. We fed Jack his baby

. . . BUT I'M NOT THE SINGER

food before we left for the restaurant so he would be at least well fed. We were seated at a table for eight that sat on a platform higher than some of the other tables in the restaurant. We had brought some of Jack's favorite toys that were small and easily movable. He always loved small toys that he could carry in his small hands. The entertainment toys that night were small figurines of Barney, the purple dinosaur, and his friends BJ and Baby Bop: all three Jack's favorite TV show characters. We had finished eating and were sitting, talking while the little ones visited each other and while Jack was still in a good mood. Jack discovered how fun it was to drop his figurine buddies, one by one, on the floor below his chair and make his daddy pick them up. He dropped one, Ben picked it up placing it back on the table in front of Jack, and the next figurine was dropped, repeating the scenario over and over. Out of the blue, a newly received figurine placed back on the table was unexpectedly thrown backward by a sweeping motion across the table top by Jack. The sound of glass breaking was all we heard. With that one whip of his hand, Jack had thrown Barney across the room and straight into the margarita glass of a lady in the party sitting behind us, shattering the glass onto the table and into her plate. We were stunned. The lady started rubbing her eyes, saying she was afraid the shattered glass had gotten into her eyes. We apologized profusely and offered to pay for their dinner even though we really didn't have the extra money. We did buy her another drink, and thankfully she decided her eyes were fine. The people sitting around us were giving us that look even though we tried so hard to defuse the situation. It was so embarrassing for us and caused us yet another heartache.

We also, in our quest to live through the chaos, decided we needed a church home. Ben and I had attended and had joined a church right after Benny was born. But after a paid, unhappy nursery worker complained about Jack after complaining about Benny and his crying for years, we stopped going to that church. Our quest for another began.

There is a certain amount of grief that comes with a diagnosis of a lifelong disability for anyone, and we were no exception. We grieved the child we thought we had. All the dreams a parent has for their child comes crashing down around them when diagnosed with autism or any other intellectual or physical disability. It is not just the lack of fulfillment of dreams but also a realization of a completely unknown future. None of the doctors could give us an accurate picture of what our future looked like. Would Jack ever learn in a typical school, graduate from high school, drive a car, have a job, live by himself on his own, or have friends? Would Benny have to be Jack's caregiver for the rest of his life after Ben and I died? Each day there was a new unanswered question that no one had an answer to.

We humans take our futures for granted. We think if we believe it, it will happen. Nothing bad will ever happen to us, that only happens to other people. We try to protect ourselves and our children from the bad things in life because we want them to have the best of everything: the best home life, the best education, material things, be on the best winning teams, be the prettiest, the most popular, the most perfect child there ever could be. Such a wonderful fairy tale if this wasn't real life.

For us, we had to grieve the fairy tale we had written in our heads for them. We had to grieve the way of life we had previously known. We had to grieve our future for our family. We had to learn to live each day in the land of uncertainty. There was no roadmap, no GPS we could follow. I cried a lot, always questioning myself, my decisions. Ben worked a lot because it gave him a feeling of being in control of something. Anything. Because our world was anything but controllable. It was hard to do all the things we both needed to do while carrying the weight of uncertainty on our backs and still living each day with the magnitude of an unclear picture of what we were even living each day for. Where were we going? What would our lives look like in 10, 20, 30 plus years? It was scary.

MAY 20, 1998—We are in Gulf Shores, Alabama at the beach. We got here late yesterday and then went to the grocery last night. Today is our first day at the beach. Jack hates the sand. He has cried most of the time. With the sound of the waves crashing onto the shore, his cries don't carry very far. We are in a strange place with lots of sand and unfamiliar sounds. He even must sleep in a twin bed something he doesn't do at home yet, and he doesn't like it either.

Jack has finally gotten used to the sand and the ocean. He has even walked to the water by himself. We got him in the pool too.

MAY 29, 1998—On our trip, we only had one bad episode of rude people while we were there. At a family restaurant, an older couple was seated next to our table. As usual, we had fed Jack before we left the condo, planning ahead just in case we had to wait a long time. When Jack is hungry, he is not very happy. I thought the boys were good at the restaurant, just being kids, wiggling and noisy. There were other kids in the restaurant too who were crying and talking loudly. It took forever for our food to get ready and everyone was getting restless. After we ate, we left as soon as possible, knowing

... BUT I'M NOT THE SINGER

we had a limited time before the boys became rowdy. We paid for our meal, packed up our diaper/toy bag, and left. On our way out, I turned around to check to make sure we didn't leave anything, one of my many habits. I turned around just in time to see the woman at the next table making the hand-across-her-brow motion and mouthing her excitement that we had left. It made me so mad. I thought we had done so well—the boys didn't cry or scream or break anything. We were at a family restaurant being a family, kids and all, doing the best we could do when this person doesn't hide the fact that she is happy to see us go. I have made up my mind to get some cards from the Autism Society to give to people like her. The cards read something like "Pardon my son's behavior, but he has autism, a brain disorder..." I will use them on the assuming public to enlighten them on their misguided judgments of us while sharing with them why our family is different. I would hate to think there are this many heartless people in the world today.

On the trip to the beach, I got a new view of Jack and his abilities. Jack's car seat is behind the passenger seat of our car. When I am not driving, I can turn around and easily see him, or I can hear what he is doing. On the trip to the beach, we passed a house with an ADT security company sign in their front yard. I heard Jack read the letters on the sign, "ADT." I thought nothing about it, just that I had heard him read the letters. On the trip home, around the same area, I heard Jack saying, "ADT, ADT" over and over. It dawned on me when I looked out the window, we were near where he had seen the ADT sign on the way to the beach. I kept an eye on him as he looked out the window looking for that sign. When it came into view, he was so happy and repeated "ADT" for a while afterward. There is a mind in that seemingly hard head of his. It just is so different from ours!

    Jack has been clingy all week since we got home from the beach. Benny has been a poor example of a good boy. He was even grounded last night for biting poor Jack, a problem we have had before. One of the teachers at Waves commented to me that a mark on Jack's face looked like a bite mark. I told her it was just a rash, thinking she was talking about a rash he got on his right cheek while we were at the beach. After I picked him up, I noticed on the other cheek a mark that did indeed look like a bite mark. I wondered if someone at Waves had bitten him and then remembered the comment from the teacher at Waves earlier that day. Then I remember a skirmish the boys had that morning while I was getting dressed. I wasn't in the room with them when it happened but walked in and broke it up. I remembered they were both crying

MY NAME IS JACK JOHNSON...

on the couch together. I separated them and put the toys they were fighting over in time out. Having thought about all the things I had remembered from earlier that day, I asked Benny if he had bitten his brother. He grinned and said, "Yes." I asked him where and he told me, "On his cheek." He gave himself away like it was nothing. After dinner, Ben and Jack went outside to play while Benny stayed inside with me—grounded.

MAY 31, 1998—I worry too much about Jack, but I can't help it. He is doing better; he has voluntarily said "more." He has patted himself and said, "me." He mooed when I asked him what a cow says. And he said "wee, wee, wee" for the piggy that goes all the way home. That all happened just this weekend. But I still worry.

The other day at therapy, the poor child vomited. Patti, the OT, had him playing in the dried bean box and it made him sick. He gagged a few times and then just vomited. This was a first for therapy. He has vomited at home and in restaurants but not at therapy.

At Miss Jane's office Friday, Jack rammed his head into my face. Miss Jane saw it, and before I could think, she grabbed him and put him in a time-out chair. She faced him away from us and put his chair in front of hers. She held him in that chair with all her might until he finally stopped crying and bucking. He was shocked! I thought it was great in a strange way. I bet he will think a little harder about doing that again at her office.

JUNE 26, 1998—Jack has started going to summer group speech at Bill Wilkerson, and Benny started his summer session of preschool. I will be busy taking them to all their separate activities and working to make time with both boys.

JULY 11, 1998—We finally got a computer and are in the process of learning how to use it. I bought the boys some programs, and we have played some of them. Jack is doing better in some areas. He talks more and sings all the time. The therapist at BW has had to ask him to stop singing several times because it was inappropriate at the time. He loves to sing. He still has a hard time with using words for what he wants. He can say "help me"—not plain but understandable—but only when you ask, not when he needs to use it on his own. His sensory issues are still bad, and he has now vomited at all therapies. On a happier note, Jack made me laugh one day recently. He was riding his spring horsey, going back and forth, I was reading the newspaper, and Benny was

... BUT I'M NOT THE SINGER

at school. (We had a large horsy that sat on metal legs attached to the base by metal springs). Carmie, the cat and Benny's little sister as he calls her, was wild, jumping, running and sliding across the family room floor. Jack stopped riding and started laughing, something he doesn't do much of on his own. I stopped reading and watched. Carmie was enjoying herself sliding and running, Jack was enjoying Carmie, and I was enjoying Jack. The old cat finally tuckered out—she is 12 years old—and laid down on the floor between Jack and me. Jack looked down at Carmie from his horse and so eloquently said, "Kitty, ready, set, go!" I laughed and laughed thinking about Jack's request was his way of asking the kitty to do it all again. The old cat continued her rest, and Jack went back to riding his horse. I thought it was a funny request.

OCTOBER 8, 1998—A few things I have seen Jack do or heard him say......
He told me he had a dirty diaper by not wanting to sit down in his high chair. He said "Siper," his word for diaper.
He came to me the other day when the bath water was running and said "Ttthirt" so I would help him take off his shirt. He also touched his diaper several times and did the hand to his mouth "OOOOOO" for open so he could take off his diaper and get in the tub.

OCTOBER 9, 1998—Jack went to the refrigerator and said, "I want juice." It was a first. Later he handed me his juice glass, walked to the frig, and said, "Juice." On Saturday, he told me, "I want juice" and was not in the kitchen.

OCTOBER 21, 1998—Jack is now scarred on his face which will hopefully one day fade away. He was running too fast down a handicap ramp at Waves on the playground of the adjoining church. At the bottom, he couldn't stop himself and fell head first into a bench. I was home when they called from Waves. The preschool helper asked me if I wanted to come get him or have them call 911. That scared me. By the time I got to the car, Ben pulled up and once I told him what happened, we were on our way. Jack had about an inch gash on his forehead right above his eyebrow. He was in pain and upset. I had called the boy's pediatrician before we left home, so they were watching for us. Ben drove, Benny was in the backseat, and I had Jack in my lap in the front passenger seat. Jack was crying loudly, trying to rub his forehead while I was trying to keep his hands away from the gash as I held a rag over it. Ben drove very, very fast all the way to the doctor's office. Once there, they took us back and Jack had to have four stitches. What a stressful day for all of us!

MY NAME IS JACK JOHNSON...

Just this morning, Jack broke the rocking horse. When Ben and I ran from the kitchen toward the noise, Jack was on the floor still holding on to the horse's handles. Never a dull moment here!

Jack is making progress, sometimes very fast. He is using the Picture Exchange System some but he uses his language a lot. Now we can ask him "What do you want?" and 80% of the time he tells us with words, actions, or PEC cards. It has gotten easier but it seems life will always be hard for us.

JANUARY 29, 1999—I can't believe we lived through another Christmas. Benny really liked the Christmas tree; Jack didn't understand. Ben and I took the boys to see Santa. Benny was fine; Jack wasn't impressed. Our Santa picture looked like this: Santa smiling, Benny smiling, and Jack sitting beside them in his stroller not smiling.

For Christmas, Jack got Tinky Winky, a Teletubby, his new best friend. A Teletubby is a character on a kid's TV show. There are four of them: Tinky Winky, Dipsy, Laalaa, and Po. It is Jack's favorite TV show. Jack has carried Tinky Winky everywhere. Ben and I laughed when we noticed Tinky Winky had the dirtiest face which was almost black with dirt. When Jack got Tinky Winky, Benny wanted one too. So instead of them fighting over two of them, we bought all four of them (so they could fight over them all!). Each Teletubby says several phrases when you push their tummy's. Today, Ben tried to put the boys down for a nap and on his third trip to tell them to go to sleep, Teletubby Po burst into a big "Uh oh!"

APRIL 24, 1999—We have made it through the holidays, birthdays, and Easter. It's getting warmer outside and the boys are going outside to play more and more. We have a bumble bee that lives by the boy's playhouse in our backyard. Benny tries to kill it by pretending to be a Power Ranger. Jack thinks it's a butterfly. Benny can swing himself on a regular swing now. Jack cannot but has learned to swing by himself on the seesaw swing on the swing set. Benny is still at preschool: Jack started two weeks ago at Franklin Elementary in the autism preschool class. He is in class with 5 other little boys with autism. He gets speech and occupational therapy at school, too.

JUNE 19, 1999—Back in February of this year, it rained and rained and flooded the neighborhood. The water got in one neighbor's basement and a couple of other's garages. It didn't get inside any of the houses. The flood water blocked the road and brought all the neighbors out. It is amazing how fast it comes up when it starts but more amazing how fast it leaves. And it leaves such a mess. It didn't get in our house or even in our yard. The officials say it was the second biggest flood since the 100 years flood of 1975. Benny thought it was cool, all the water and excitement. Jack didn't even notice.

Jack is loving school. His strengths and weaknesses are growing further apart. Last week, I sat him down at the computer, and after making the lettering on the screen large enough to get his attention, I typed the letter "A" and asked Jack what letter came next. He proceeded to type each letter of the alphabet unassisted. He didn't want to stop. He typed capital letters and lower-case letters. He watched me backspace to erase an extra letter and he now types extra letters so he can backspace and erase them. Both boys have started swim lessons. Benny is in a group and Jack has private lessons from one of the recreational therapists at the nearby Rec center. We want them to both learn how to swim. Both boys are also working on handwriting. Benny is getting the hang of it but has a way to go. Jack is learning to hold a pencil the right way. I would say both have a long way to success.

Once in a conversation with an acquaintance, the lack of qualified preschools became the topic. In my naivety, I shared that Waves, Jack's developmental preschool was looking for preschool children to be peer models for children like Jack. I went on to say the teacher/student ratio would be small and there would be lots of learning opportunities for the peers. I even shared my enthusiasm for the program, teachers, and staff. My story of this wonderful preschool was met with a less than ecstatic facial expression and the words that cut me deeply, "Oh, no. None of my friends would want to put their children there!" I wasn't sure if that statement was meant to be so hurtful but no one said anything to the contrary. Did people shun children with special needs? Can people be this cruel?

One night while tucking the boys in the bed, I kissed Benny and said, "I love you" which was met with an "I love you, too." I kissed Jack, told him "I love you" while still doing the gestures for those heartfelt words, and was met with a surprise reply. He gestured "I love you" back, his first reply to those special words. I cried quiet tears of joy.

CHAPTER 7

Living day to day with autism brings a whole new set of problems into the life of a family living with this disability. Things that are easy for the average family are very problematic for a family living with autism.

Both of my boys were born with long, dark hair. In fact, both were born with such long hair, their first haircuts were both at six weeks old! After that initial haircut, Benny and Jack had several more during their baby days. Once they became toddlers, haircuts were easy. Until autism. It was like flipping a switch. Jack went from a passive baby getting a haircut to a mad animal. I was totally shocked and completely unprepared the first time it happened. Benny sat in the chair, being his charming self, happily talking to anyone who would listen. When Jack's turn came, I put him up in the stylist's chair, he stiffened into a board, and slid out. I picked him up and asked the stylist if I could just hold him. She said yes. I picked Jack up, sat down with him, got him into position, and once the cutting started, all hell broke loose. Jack jerked and thrashed. The tears started and then came the screams. He cried so much his nose ran down his face, mixing with his flowing tears. Once the cut hair landed on us, we were covered in a mixture of hair, snot, and spit from head to toe. He was such a strong kid. It took everything in me to hold him. I could not figure out what had happened. What made him go from a calm child to a wild child? Was he afraid? What changed to make him afraid? I had always been with the boys at haircut time so I knew neither one had been cut or snipped during a haircut. The poor stylist was a basket case. She was a smoker and I am sure she couldn't wait to have a cigarette after dealing with Jack. It was horrible. From that day forward, every haircut became a battle for Jack. Autism had reared its ugly head again.

AUGUST 6, 1999—We are at Gulf Shores, AL at the beach. Jack is taking a beach nap, I am writing, and Ben and Benny have gone to find some fresh shrimp for dinner. Today is our first full day and I must say it has been enjoyable. The boys have been great. They both like the sand, surf, and sun. Jack is not afraid of the ocean waves at all. He was a little at first but once he felt the waves, he was hooked. He would go out by himself if we let him. Benny hasn't given Ben a break always wanting to be in the waves. Ben and I have been pleasantly surprised by their behavior.

The next day, Jack has had an autistic day as Ben and I call it. He wanted to wander all day along the beach. He walked through several people's beach camps, walking across their towels and blankets. The folks look so funny when this little boy comes walking into their personal space not saying a word. Some were downright ugly about it and voiced their displeasure. He never even looks at them! It's like he doesn't see them. Ben and I have been apologizing all day long and chasing Jack. Then when he gets ready to come back to the condo, he just walks off toward the building. If you aren't watching him, he could be gone. We couldn't enjoy our day because we were trying to keep up with Jack.

We are back from the beach. I had had enough of two little boys, one husband, and a two-room condo. Ben was so glad to be back home. The boys wore him out. He is not accustomed to them all day for 5 days straight. He got a taste of my life and tired of it quickly. I love my children with everything in me but they fight, scream, hit, push and run causing me to dream of getting in the car and leaving. No wonder we feel like we didn't get a vacation.

Since we had left our previous church because of the rude comments from a nursery helper, we were lost without a church home. We started going to the church my dad and sister, and Ben's mother and grandmother attended. We found out the church had a children's church service downstairs while the worship service was being held upstairs. Since both boys were close in age, they were in the same class together. We informed the class helpers about Jack's autism and they responded positively. They seemed unafraid and confident so we felt comfortable leaving him there. Each week the boys went downstairs and we got to go to worship together with our families. One Sunday, the worship service concluded early and we were dismissed. Ben walked downstairs to get the boys where he found Benny sitting in a chair participating with the group of children. He found Jack sitting in a corner, alone, playing in some dirt. Not what we expected. We talked to the class helpers about it and they said Jack would sometimes sit with the others and sometimes would not. I went to the church's children's program minister and told her the story. She suggested we try to meet with the head minister of the church.

MY NAME IS JACK JOHNSON...

OCTOBER 20, 1999—I have been in contact with the minister at the church we have been attending about having a program for special needs children during church service. We have talked and are in the planning stages of meeting with all concerned parties. At least he seemed open to the idea. Maybe soon we will have a church to go to that welcomes all of us. Benny has gone with Katie and Susan (our nieces) to their church twice and comes home singing songs and showing off his Sunday School work. He really wants to go to church but I can't justify not taking Jack. What message would that send to Jack? What message would that send to other people? And lastly, what message would that send to Benny? Hopefully, this problem will be solved soon and both boys will come home singing Sunday School songs!

We asked the minister if we could get the church to agree to start a program for children with special needs where each child with needs would be paired with a friend, a person that could redirect them and keep them with the class. He went to the elders of the church and asked but was turned down. I was disappointed. Why were children like Jack not welcomed with open arms into the church, of all places? Isn't that a part of the whole story of Jesus? Love your neighbor; blessed are the children, do unto others as you would have them do to you? Are families like mine just supposed to stay home because they are too much trouble? We agonized over this. Even though we felt like outcasts, we continued to try to attend. Knowing Jack was not watched by

2000   Ben, Jill, Benny and an unhappy Jack
a few years after autism diagnosis

... BUT I'M NOT THE SINGER

anyone there made us uncomfortable. What were we to do?

Going out in public was still hard. Jack didn't like crowds, the noise, different smells, and he had no patience for waiting. If we went to a restaurant and had to wait to be seated, by the time we were seated, Jack was already unhappy and we were tired from trying to keep him busy and happy. Having a child with autism is a trial and error predicament. You don't know how the autism will affect a child in a certain situation until they are put into that position. If they have a bad experience, you first must figure out the reason why—was it the lights or the noise of the crowd, was the child hungry or tired at the time—then decide if it is a situation you want to put them in again. People don't realize children with autism must learn how to behave in public. Parents must teach them how to deal with those noises, crowds, smells, and textures. We cannot teach them how to behave in public if we don't take them out in public. I understand how obnoxious it is to be in a public place with someone's screaming child, but the only way a child with autism can learn about a certain experience is to be put into that experience.

Just getting ready to go somewhere was difficult at our house. Benny was easy; put his clothes out and he could do the rest. Jack was not so easy. First you had to catch him which wasn't easy especially if it was somewhere he didn't want to go or he was busy doing something else. Children with autism do not transition well, meaning they cannot go from one activity to another. If Jack was riding the boy's rocking horse, we couldn't grab him and expect him to go willingly with us. If he was busy watching TV, you couldn't pick him up and take him to the bathroom to brush his teeth. Trying to dress a child who is in the throes of a tantrum was a lot harder than dressing a calm child. Of course, we didn't really understand this at the time, being so new to the world of autism. We would pick him up no matter what he was doing at the time and he would fall apart. Not only did Jack need to learn about the world around him, but Ben and I also needed to learn how this disorder affected our son.

Jack, now three years old, was still in pull-ups and eating baby food. If we went anywhere, we still had to take plenty of each. If Jack was hungry, you were in luck. He would sit in any chair in any environment at any time to eat. But if he was not hungry, he would not sit in a high chair while the rest of us ate our meal. I quickly learned to keep some of his toys only for those times when I needed a distraction. That even became one of my mottos for Jack: D is for distraction. If we needed to get him into a high chair, we could break out a distraction that he could only have if he got in the chair. Once he

MY NAME IS JACK JOHNSON...

understood the concept, he would hold his arms up so he could sit and play with whatever the distraction was at the time. Our D for distraction could derail a come-apart, but usually only fifty percent of the time. We were happy we could stop some of them.

Then there were the times when we tried to introduce new foods to him. I never understood his aversion to food. Was it the smell, the look of it, or the whole texture dislike? I could understand if the food had reached his mouth and he didn't like the taste or the texture but he could go into the gag and vomit stage by just seeing a new food. None of this made sense to me.

Bathing was also a problem. It didn't occur to us for a while but every time we put the boys in the tub together, Benny had no problem, Jack would scream and cry. He would calm down after a while but he hated getting in the water. I used a floating toy boat thermometer to let me know the temperature of the bath water always making sure it wasn't too hot. I asked Benny if the water was too hot and he always said no. For Jack, the water must have been too hot for his over-sensitive system. It took us a while to figure this out but when we did, we made the temperature cooler and just carefully added hot water after both boys were in the tub. At first, Jack hated bubble baths. He again screamed and cried and, of course, we thought it was again the temperature of the water. We finally figured out it was the bubbles. By the time we figured it out, Jack had started to tolerate and even got to the point of loving bubble baths. Again, this all took a while to put all the pieces together. There were many unhappy episodes at bath time before it made sense.

One of the hardest challenges to figure out was the issue of riding in the car. We would get ready to leave and for some strange reason, Jack would go into full-blown tantrum stage once in the car. It was so frustrating for us and for Benny who had to sit in the seat next to Jack. After we traded our SUV for a van, we put Jack and his car seat in the back seat of the van so Benny wouldn't have to be so close to the screaming. Once Jack learned to walk, he would always go to the same car door to get in the car. If we were carrying him and tried to put him in the car from another door, he would resist. If he was with a relative and they tried to put him or his car seat in a different place than the spot it was in our car, he would fall apart. We could pull out of our driveway only by turning left. If we turned right, the screaming would immediately start. There were still other tantrum causing situations in the car that we had not figured out at the time. We only knew we would sometimes, for no apparent reason at all, have a bucking, flailing, screaming child in the back seat of our car. He kicked and flailed so much he tore the material on the back of the middle van seat to shreds.

After a particularly stress-filled day for me at home with both boys, Benny made us laugh. He had patiently waited and watched out the window for Ben to come home from work. When Ben pulled into the driveway, Benny ran to the door to meet him. When Ben opened the door, Benny told his dad, "Dad, let's get out of here! Mommy's dangerous!"

In the fall of 1999, Jack started preschool full time in a regular education setting. He had been going since his April birthday that year to another school on a part time basis. With the opening of a new school that was on what they called a balanced calendar year (a term used for a school calendar of three nine-week school sessions divided by two three-week breaks and one six-week break for summer. This type of calendar in a school is sometimes called year-round school.) Jack began his full-time education at Poplar Grove School, the only school in our district on the balanced calendar system. All the autistic preschool classrooms in our district were moved to this central location because of the balanced calendar. The nine weeks on and the breaks between gave the children with autism a much-needed break from the struggles of learning and gave the hard-working teachers a well-deserved break too. I thought it would be the ideal place for both my children. Benny was only four at the time and wasn't ready for Kindergarten until the next year, so Jack started school before Benny.

The first step in educating a child with special needs is to develop a yearly IEP, an Individual Education Plan, for that child. An IEP is a legal document between the parents of the child and the school system when goals are set for each individual child for their present grade and the school systems should meet those goals. For example, a goal for a young child in preschool might be learning to hold a pencil correctly. If a child isn't taught how to hold a pencil properly, handwriting will always be a problem. This goal would be written on the IEP for that individual child. Goals to work on and hopefully meet are decided by the ability of the individual child, their present level of understanding, their strengths and weaknesses, and the goals of each grade level set by that particular state's education system. An IEP meeting usually consists of the child's parents, the child's regular and/or special education teachers, the school principal, and any therapist that works with that child. Others can and will attend the IEP when their opinions are needed for the services the child may or may not need.

MY NAME IS JACK JOHNSON...

AUGUST 20, 1999—Jack had his IEP this week. Jack starts school next week. Going two days with a limited class and one day with all the children together. He will have a new teacher, Miss Kim.

SEPTEMBER 30, 1999—Jack is now in school every day and loves it. His speech has improved in quality and quantity. Miss Kim is a sweetheart. I volunteer to help her out with easy work and have already worked a couple of days. The workroom is next to her room divided by a wall containing a one-way mirror. I can see how Jack is doing while I volunteer. I can also watch for what is working with Jack and what is not so I can continue some of what I see at home. Jack is now talking in 4 to 5-word sentences. He is still eating baby food though. He has yet to go to the bathroom. He knows what to do—Miss Kim gave us PEC cards to use—but just will not sit down and try it. He is still taking swim lessons once a week and has gotten better at swimming too.

OCTOBER 20, 1999—Jack peed in the potty for the first time. It was a shotgun pee as I called it, meaning I made him do it. He had gotten up from his nap dry so I sat him on the potty. You could tell when the urge to pee started because he started to squirm and scream at me. I made him stay. He would only pee until he could hold it again. After 15 minutes of peeing and holding, we put a pull-up on him but he was so mad he cried and screamed for another 20 minutes. I don't think he understands the concept yet. We will wait until he does.

NOVEMBER 7, 1999—Jack has peed in the potty 2 times now. There was a lot of waiting involved—to be exact...4 hours—and a lot of stickers, books, games, and patience! We have only succeeded twice. We survived Halloween. Benny was a pirate; Jack was a football player. I have noticed Jack will not wear a mask of any kind so any costume he wears cannot have anything to go on his face. He doesn't have the capacity to tell us what he wants to be for Halloween, so I just put a costume together for him. I had an old football outfit that Benny got once for a gift, so it worked out for Jack. We are working on teaching him to say, "Trick or Treat" but it might be up to Benny to say it at the neighbor's door. Why would Jack want candy? He won't eat it!

NOVEMBER 14, 1999—Jack's language has gotten better. He said the other night, "glasses picking up" because he wanted me to pick up Mr. Potato Head's glasses which had fallen to the floor. Not just "glasses" but what he wanted me to do with the glasses. I was impressed!

... BUT I'M NOT THE SINGER

December 14, 1999—We just had our first Christmas celebration with distant relatives. Benny loves Christmas this year; Jack could care less. He seems to dislike the sound of paper ripping as you unwrap gifts. He makes that yucky face he does. He has been grouchy for days. Friday after a trip to the mall, he cried until 5 pm. He had another fit Sunday, one Monday night, and the latest one was this morning. He gets upset over the slightest change in routine. With all the goings and comings of Christmas, it is not easy to keep a routine. His speech has gotten so much better but he still gets agitated so easily. This week alone I have heard several new sentences or words. First, he screamed, "Benny, let's go jump on the bed!" Of course, they promptly did. Then the other night I hollered his name and he answered, "What?" A first! Last week he said, "Benny, let's brush our teeth so we can go to school." Quite amazing. But when he has a fit, I can't understand a word he says. His words are garbled and I can't make out what he is saying or whether he is talking words at all. He hits at me and kicks at me and spits on himself. It's ugly. It makes me feel awful when he tantrums. I feel so inadequate, blaming myself and my lack of parenting skills. Parenting him is such a challenge. I cry a lot about it. I also worry about how all of this is affecting Benny. At the Mother's support group yesterday, they said they had never mentioned the word "autism" to their typical children. I told Benny the first week after Jack's diagnosis! I wanted him to understand that Jack's behavior was not normal and was not something to copy or make fun of. The boys interact so much now but not the way I would like. It's more rough-housing, screaming, jumping and running which others tell me is just the boy in them. I would like to see them play something together—a sport, a game, or just pretend.

DECEMBER 27, 1999—Well, I missed Christmas. I was sick and had to stay in bed. Ben has tried to keep things together but I caught him drinking Old Charter last night. He confessed he drank some the night before. As he put it, he isn't a good mother. I guess that is a compliment to me—the boys in two days have made their dad drink. I'll remember this the next time he doesn't understand why I'm in a bad mood!

Benny enjoyed this Christmas more than any before. I guess he is at that age where his understanding of the magic of Santa, the birth of Jesus, and the lesson of giving and receiving has really kicked in. Jack got a small portable game computer that has this face on it and the mouth is the computer screen. The mouth moves with each word or question it asks. Jack loves it. I got up

MY NAME IS JACK JOHNSON...

yesterday morning and Ben was puzzled because Jack kept saying, "I want mouth." Ben was wiping and wiping the child's face and checking his mouth for a piece of paper, a hair, or something else. It finally dawned on me to ask the child if he wanted "mouth computer." He excitedly said "mouth comfuter." From now on, the toy will be forever known as "Mouth."

I forgot to describe Jack's school Christmas party. It went well until he had to put peanut butter on a pine cone and roll it in birdseed. Jack thought the birds would like a little vomit on theirs! Yes, he vomited at his Christmas party.

FEBRUARY 28, 2000—Jack is now eating peanut butter on crackers and bread. It has taken a few months but now it has become a Jack favorite. Last night he ate a french fry—one whole fry! His bites were tiny and it took him 30 minutes but he finally ate it. We are working on pieces of apple this week and so far, he is tasting them. Tasting, with Jack, is putting the food to his mouth or touching it to his tongue. A bite is taking a piece into his mouth no matter how small the piece of food is. He is "tasting" apples. Of course, he is still eating baby food vegetables.

APRIL 28, 2000—Jack is now eating whole bananas, peanut butter sandwiches, chips, and chocolate pudding for lunch just like the other typical kids at school. He is now 4 years old!

Jack's first year of school had come to an end. He was eating more food varieties, his language had grown, and he was maturing each day.

CHAPTER 8

JUNE 10, 2000—We are at the beach. The boys are enjoying the pool. Benny is swimming with water wings and Jack is a water monkey—no fear at all. Scares me to death because he doesn't grasp the danger of water. He has a floatation device that fits with lots of elastic and Velcro. It gives him freedom in his arms and legs. Benny wants to swim so badly and does a great job if he would only drop the water wings.

Our last beach day has been a fun day with Jack. He has rediscovered the ocean and loves it. Once his dad took him further out in the water, he has been going in ever since. If no one will go with him, he will wander in by himself. He doesn't mind the salt water, in fact, he licks it off his skin. He loves the pool too. He can swim around the pool alone with his swim device on. Benny has gotten better at swimming too. He still is wearing those dang water wings though. I have let most of the air out of them unbeknownst to him. They barely have any air in them at this point but he thinks he still needs them.

On our way home. Not too long ago, Jack was dancing in his car seat to a snappy jazz song on the radio. A non-prompted first for him.

I have been thinking about the boys and our different relationships. I don't think Benny would ever cry for me if he spent the night with someone. Maybe when he was younger he might have but not now. Jack, on the other hand, would be different. He misses me if I have been gone for one day! I have a strange bond with Jack which I think is connected to his lack of language and my understanding of this lack of communication. Sometimes I can feel what he is thinking or wanting and can make him ask or say whatever it is. Ben cannot do this. I think this is where their relationship has trouble. Ben can play rough and tough with Jack but has a difficult time communicating with him. It troubles me a lot, their lack of communication.

JULY 21, 2000—The boys have started school. This year is Benny's first year in real school and he is a kindergartener. I haven't met his teacher yet

MY NAME IS JACK JOHNSON...

but hope he likes her. Jack will have Miss Kim again this year. Next year, he will be included in a regular kindergarten class. Hopefully this year he will be potty trained. His eating has gotten better with him trying more and more new foods. Of course, it is with Miss Kim and his OT, not with Ben and me at home. Jack did try a green bean and a cucumber at Pawpaw's last Sunday. He likes all the clapping he receives there when he takes a bite of something new.

SEPTEMBER 2, 2000—Benny has discovered the joy of riding a bike. Since Benny started riding a bike without training wheels, Jack is riding Benny's old bike with training wheels. Jack even gets to join the other neighborhood kids when they ride in our driveway. He still doesn't understand danger like cars on the road or turning the bicycle wheel too sharp but we are glad he graduated to a bike from a tricycle.

Jack is now writing his name—not well, but the pencil control is better. The "J" is very legible but the rest of the letters need more work. It's a start. He is also reading books. Miss Kim has these very easy first reader books and Jack brings one home every night. He is learning to read "the," "my," "A," and is doing well with them. He has had a lot of trouble with potty training. Of course, he does fine with Miss Kim but for us, he just wants to hold it and he can hold it forever. Lately, he comes home from school, finds a pull-up, takes off his pants and underwear, puts the pull-up on, and proceeds to pee or poop in the pull-up. The only problem Miss Kim tells me she has with him at school besides not pooping in the potty is that he must have the bathroom door open when he goes. Here at home we never shut the bathroom door when one of the boys go to the bathroom because they might need us and can holler if they do. At school that is not acceptable behavior. She is teaching Jack to go with the door closed by closing the bathroom door a little more each day when he goes. At first, he hated it but now he is getting better with the door closed some.

SEPTEMBER 29, 2000—We are back at the beach.... this time for a friend's wedding. It is nice here....no crowds. Since we have 3 weeks off, we get the benefit of still warm water and nice weather but no crowds. It is so much better with the boys. They can get on the beach and run and scream their heads off and no one cares. Last night we ate at a restaurant, no wait for a table, no crowds. We thought Jack was going to lose it, but he didn't. He was upset over the ABC's on the kid's menu. Oh, autism... we love you so!

Jack has come so far, and so have Ben and I as parents. We are realizing some things will change, some won't and some will change at a snail's pace.

...BUT I'M NOT THE SINGER

Jack has finally started to pee in the potty for us. He peed in the potty for the babysitter while Ben and I were out and has continued to do it ever since. He is even peeing in different bathrooms, something he would not do at first. The urge to pee won out over the autism. As for pooping, we have tried and he is not ready. When he needs to poop at home while wearing big boy underwear, he will find a pull-up, go to his favorite quiet place, and poop in the pull-up. Then he comes and finds me innocently says, "I'm poopy." Life with him will never be dull.

A new year started, but still without pooping in the potty. Benny was six years old and turning seven in October. Jack was four but would be five in April. They were both growing and getting further away from being babies.

JANUARY 1, 2001—The new year is here, and so is the snow! We have about 2 inches on the ground. The four of us went out in it and we had a first.... Jack liked the snow! He has never liked the snow. Today, he ran, jumped, and fell into it. He didn't want to come back in the house. A nice way to start the new year.

JANUARY 2, 2001—Jack pooped in the potty today. Yahoo!
    How did we finally do it? Miss Kim is a miracle worker. Since Jack was coming home and finding his old pull-ups, then taking off his big boy underwear and putting on the pull-up so he could poop in it, Miss Kim suggested we not buy any more pull-ups. With the few we had left, she suggested I talk to Jack and explain that we only had 15 (a made-up number since I cannot remember how many we had) pull-ups left and couldn't buy any more. Each day when Jack came home to do the poopy pull-up switch-a-roo, I would reiterate that we only had so many more pull-ups left. We counted each pull-up until we were down to a few. I explained again to Jack that we only had so many left and then he would have to use the potty like big boys do when they need to poop. When there were only two left in the pull-up package, I told Jack he needed to try going to the potty first before putting on a pull-up since there were only two left. And he did. Amazing how Miss Kim's thinking outside the box helped with Jack being potty trained.

APRIL 5, 2001—One morning this week, Jack surprised Miss Kim. She has been meeting him at the front door of the school since that is the door he will enter next year in kindergarten. They are practicing it until the end of the

MY NAME IS JACK JOHNSON...

school year. As they were walking down the hall toward the classroom, Miss Kim asked Jack how he was doing that day. He replied, "I am so happy to be here." She was shocked. It was a wholly appropriate response with Jack describing his emotions of being happy!

Even though his speech has gotten better, his behavior has not. One day on break, he bit Benny. Luckily Benny had on long sleeves that kept Jack from biting a spot out of Benny's arm. Benny professed to be totally innocent in the whole biting episode. His first explanation was he was playing by himself and Jack just grabbed his arm and bit it. Then the story changed to them fighting and Jack just grabbed Benny's arm and bit it. The more I asked, the more I learned. The last and final story from Benny was that they were fighting, Benny pushed Jack, Benny's arm got too close to Jack's mouth, and Jack bit it. I hate all this boy fighting. Everyone says it is just the boy in them but I don't necessarily believe that. I guess I'm stupid but I think boys should not fight and rough-house ALL the time!

APRIL 10, 2001—Happy birthday to Jack! Today he is 5 years old.

APRIL 12, 2001—Jack had a good birthday. He seemed to finally understand it was his day. He opened presents, read the cards, and seemed to really enjoy his birthday. We had an open house birthday where family and friends could drop by at their leisure, assuring Jack was not overwhelmed by too many people at once. Jack got two Exit signs for his birthday which he loved. His big thing now is Exit signs in buildings. He loves looking at them. He loves spelling the word Exit. He loves looking for and finding them in buildings. He is a strange creature.

APRIL 22, 2001—The other night I was thinking about the boys and how much they have grown. Benny is getting so tall and thin and has that dark, soft hair and beautiful, dark brown eyes. He is so handsome and looks older than six years old. He has now gotten a few freckles across his nose. He is so big; I can't pick him up anymore. Jack is so completely different from Benny. His face is round and still baby-like. His green eyes are so deep; you feel you could almost see inside his head when you look deep into them. Jack's hair is so coarse and thick; you cannot see his scalp. He has tiny teeth that have perfect spacing between them. My boys are perfect in my eyes. They are true blessings. I thank God for them every day!

...BUT I'M NOT THE SINGER

APRIL 24, 2001—I am waiting for Jack to come home on the bus. He is riding the bus home every day.... a life skill he needs to learn.

JUNE 25, 2001—We are at the beach. Benny loves the ocean and loves the pool. Since he never met a stranger, he has already made friends with other boys his age staying at this condo complex. Jack could care less about making friends. When we are on the beach, he is either writing words in the sand or playing with a sand bucket of water. When we are at the pool, he becomes active, jumping, screaming, swimming and splashing in the water. I guess the ocean has way too many sensory inputs coming at Jack. The sounds of waves, the feel of the sand, the heat of the sun, the constant breeze off the water must be too much for his senses. He is very docile at the beach but comes alive at the pool.

JULY 23, 2001—Benny's first day as a first grader and Jack's first day as a kindergartener. Jack got the same teacher as Benny had last year, so we were familiar with her. I won't forget looking back at him when I was walking out of the classroom to leave and seeing him sitting at the table with five other children he did not know. Benny also had a first good day as a first grader. He was looking forward to riding the bus home, something he had wanted to do last year but I wouldn't let him, thinking he was just too young to ride as a kindergartener. He had a hard time understanding why Jack could ride the bus home—a special needs bus—and he couldn't ride one home (a K-8th grade bus). So, this year, I let him ride the bus home. He was so excited about being a first grader and getting to ride the bus. He found his bus, got on it, and on the way home, it broke down. The kids on the bus had to wait in the 90-degree heat for another bus to get them. The driver, not familiar with our neighborhood, dropped Benny off at the first house where another girl gets off—address #102—ours is #126. Benny had to walk home after sitting in a broken-down bus on his first day of first grade... in the 90 plus degree heat. The bus would normally drop him off around 3 (he got on the bus at 2 45). On this first day of first grade, it was a little after 4 when Ben and I, who had been waiting to take pictures of Benny's first school bus trip home, saw him walking around the curve of the street dragging his wheeled backpack. The first words out of his red and sweat covered face were "First grade is great!" His second words were "Bus riding is fun," and lastly, he said, "The bus broke down." I have yet to figure out which of those made his day!

MY NAME IS JACK JOHNSON...

Miss Kim was still a participant in Jack's education. She helped the regular education teacher understand the unique behaviors of a child with autism and helped the teacher with issues and modifications Jack might need to be able to learn. We all learned that successful inclusion of a special education student into a regular education classroom is a group effort. (Inclusion is the term for including a child with special needs into a classroom with a regular education curriculum, with or without an assistant for education support.)

A couple of the children in Jack's Kindergarten class became his friends. Both friends were girls and both were named Megan. I called it the Megan sandwich: two Megan's with a Jack in the middle. These girls were fantastic with him. They made sure he was doing what he was supposed to do. They helped him out with his assignments and told him what to do next. They were Jack's first real friends. They had no clue how happy this made me. Jack had never really had friends like the other children his age. His social skills were not age-appropriate so communication with typical children his age had been difficult. These two precious girls did not care if Jack didn't have appropriate social skills. They could get him to do almost anything and he always listened.

AUGUST 6, 2001—Jack and I are at Saddle Up! Saddle Up is a therapeutic horseback riding program for children with special needs. They will only take children after they turn five years old and then we were on a waiting list. We have been coming for a little while. The first few times Jack would not get near his pony. Slowly he started to touch it, brush it, and feed it. Finally, he sat in the saddle but would not let the pony move. Today he is riding his pony like the other children and is loving it.

Jack has been in a horrible mood lately. At school today, he was bad too. It is so sad for me to see him do things he has not done in years. Hitting himself, falling in the floor, walking like some computer cat he has seen on his computer, spinning in a circle, opening and closing cabinet doors, turning lights on and off... repeatedly. I hate this!

SEPTEMBER 7, 2001—Summer is now gone. The boys are doing well in the new school year. The Exit sign thing which had become a compulsion has gotten better but now he is into ceiling fans. Really into ceiling fans.

When Jack's compulsion with ceiling fans began, he liked to look at them, then he liked to draw them and talk about them, and soon he started to mem-

... BUT I'M NOT THE SINGER

orize them, which fans were in which restaurants. He could describe them when you mentioned a certain restaurant: "that restaurant has a white fan with five blades, a light kit, and a long string." He started to refuse to eat at a restaurant that did not have ceiling fans. He would have a come-apart forcing us to surrender. I remember once coming home from a trip to the lake. We had stopped at a restaurant that had food we thought everyone would enjoy, especially Jack, but it didn't have ceiling fans and he refused to go inside to eat. We had to get take-out and being that we were miles from home, our food was cold and soggy by the time we got home. Ceiling fans became a hardship and a blessing all at the same time.

The boys had their school pictures made. Benny was so photogenic and always took great pictures. Jack, on the other hand, had become more difficult to deal with when it came to taking his picture. It was not in his nature to pose or wait for the right moment. He had done well on the school's picture taking day until his Kindergarten picture. It seems the photographer got behind on his schedule and was not ready to take Jack's kindergarten class picture at their scheduled time. So, the class had to wait. Jack hated to wait. And from what I was told, they had to wait a long time. By the time it was his Kindergarten class's turn, Jack was not a happy boy. In the class picture, all the children are smiling, happy, and looking at the camera. When I saw the picture, I can imagine hearing the photographer tell them to "say cheese," and I can hear twenty-plus sweet, youthful voices saying "cheese" as the photograph was taken. All except my son. Oh no, there he is in the class picture surrounded by all the smiling faces of his happy classmates, looking off to his left, making this horrible I-smell-something-stinky-and-I-am-mad face. My son was that kid, the one who messes up the whole class picture. Ben cannot keep himself under control whenever he looks at the picture.

OCTOBER 30, 2001—Benny is now 7 years old. We just had his party and it was fun. He enjoyed it. He is growing up so fast. Jack is still Jack who right now is angry and very unhappy about something.

DECEMBER 4, 2001—Jack has been grouchy lately.... crying, whining, screaming....it has been a zoo. It shouldn't be this way. It could be the upcoming Christmas season with all the lights, sounds, and comings and goings.

Jack ate 3 pieces of pizza last Friday night at a restaurant. We had to pay for his meal... something we didn't have to do because we were always bringing his meal from home. I was shocked watching him cram piece after piece in his mouth. On his pizza, he also ate Canadian bacon and pepperoni too. Amazing.

You can ask poor Jack what he wants Santa to bring him for Christmas and he will say a candy cane. That's what the Santa at school gives children after they sit in his lap. So, in Jack's world, he thinks Santa only gives candy canes. Thank you, autism, for making Christmas way harder than it should be even making Santa no fun.

CHAPTER 9

The other day, Jack wanted something from his dad. He said to Ben, "Dad, you know when I was little, I hated you. But now that I am bigger, I really love you. Do you think you could take me for a car ride?" Ben couldn't keep from laughing at Jack's request. Unfortunately, the weather was too cold for a convertible ride but Ben promised Jack a car ride as soon as the weather was warmer. Jack is such a charmer!

MARCH 7, 2002—The boys are great. Benny is outgrowing all his clothes at a very fast rate. Jack's language has shot out of the roof. If he is not in the mood to talk, he will tell you, "Don't ask me no questions now!" Not the best response but, at least, he is speaking his mind.

MAY 7, 2002—Last night Jack ate a piece of chicken, a piece of pineapple and a piece of pasta. I think he must be getting bored with his current menu and wants to venture out He has asked for these foods.
   Jack and I are at Saddle Up! He is riding his buddy pony again. He loves coming here and riding his Saddle Up! pony.

MAY 7, 2002—We had Jack's IEP last week. His first-grade teacher will be Mrs. G. She has never taught a child with autism before but looks forward to the challenge. I look forward to working with her.

MAY 21, 2002—At Saddle Up! again. Last week Jack had a huge temper tantrum over who knows what and didn't get to ride. This week he was ready to ride. Only one more day to ride before this session is over.

JULY 1, 2002—We are in Naples, Florida staying at a condo owned by our previous neighbors who moved here a few years back. They invested in several rental properties and are letting us stay in one of them. We drove Saturday

MY NAME IS JACK JOHNSON...

to Gainesville and spent the night there. Since we had a double room with double beds, I slept with Jack and Ben slept with Benny. Jack is like sleeping with a worm in hot ashes. He moves and jerks all night long. With all his moving and jerking, I didn't sleep much that night. At breakfast Sunday morning, Jack had a huge come apart in the Waffle House because it didn't have ceiling fans. When I say a huge come apart, I mean a scream, cry and shake come apart. Ben and I had to remove Jack and play breakfast tag: I ate while Ben took Jack outside and after I ate, I relieved Ben who came inside and ate his breakfast while I held a still crying but tired out Jack. Poor Benny....it must be upsetting to him too. I would venture to say we will not be welcomed back at this Waffle House again. The boys are loving the ocean. Jack wasn't afraid of the water and waves at all, walking into the ocean until it was around his neck so he could bob along with the waves. Benny has been Jacques Cousteau spending time looking at every fish, shell, and rock he can find. Jack has been wearing Benny's old shark goggles—water goggles with shark skin-colored face and fin. He looks very silly in them but he doesn't care. Several people have passed remarking about the boy with the shark fin in the ocean. If they only knew....

JULY 2, 2002—After a quick trip today to the zoo, we walked to the pool at our condo complex. The boys were like fish. Benny sort of dives into the water; Jack jumps. We noticed both stay close to the ladder in the 7-foot water. Swimming lessons are finally paying off. Later, after a trip to downtown Naples, a little dinner at a nice restaurant, and a long walk on a fishing pier, we are bushed!

JULY 3, 2002—Another ocean day to a different beach. This beach had a walkway with a free golf cart ride over a growth of mangroves to the actual sandy beach. We have more sand stuff than most, so we looked like the Beverly Hillbillies with all our gear and toys. Once there, Jack borrowed Benny's surfboard while Ben and Benny walked to a nearby sandbar. Jack is having a blast by his laughter as he rides the waves. Everyone is having a good time. I should add that on our golf cart trip back to our car, we had a mishap with a dropped water noodle and the driver had to reverse to retrieve it. No harm, no foul, just embarrassment for the Beverly Hillbillies!

JULY 5, 2002—Our last day here. Yesterday the boys splashed and played at the pool most of the day. Last night we met our neighbors for dinner on the

... BUT I'M NOT THE SINGER

beach, watched the sunset, and fireworks for the 4th of July. It was beautiful, the colors of the fireworks reflecting off the ocean waters. I have never seen anything like it before. We were joined by 50,000 other folks all there to see the fireworks. It was a great last night in Naples!

JULY 15, 2002—The boys start back to school at the end of this week so we are at the pool trying to do as much as we can while we can. Jack is wearing Benny's shark goggles again. This time they are slightly to one side of his head making him look just a little goofier. I have asked him 2 times if I could straighten them but Nnnnnnoooooo! So yes, I am that mother.... the one who lets her child wear goofy looking shark goggles that aren't straight. Yes, I am that mom!

JULY 18, 2002—School registration day. The moms get to fill out the mounds of registration forms while the kids get to play with friends in their classrooms. Tomorrow, the boys have their first full day of school.

AUGUST 29, 2002—The boys are in school and mommy is running around again. Benny's teacher this year is one of those teachers no one likes. Some children in his class have been moved out to another class by their parents. I think this teacher is just older and is a no-nonsense educator. I think a lot of parents do not like that. Benny and I talked about him staying in her class, me sharing that in life we don't all get to choose who will be our future teachers, our professors in college, nor our future bosses or coworkers. I explained to him that I thought it would be best for him to learn to deal with people—all kinds of people at an early age. Sometimes we don't always get what we want and must deal with what we have been given. Benny told me he would try and give the teacher a chance. I told him if the situation warranted a change, I would take care of it.

Jack has had good days and bad days. There has been no obvious reason for the bad days... just Jack! I have talked to his class about Jack and autism. One of Jack's classmates stopped me in the hall at school one day and asked me why Jack did something he did. I thought that was compassionate for a 1st grader. We talked and I explained as best I could. Jack's school work has gotten harder and the homework has grown in amount. He doesn't enjoy this. Not that the work is that hard, he just doesn't want to do homework. Once he starts it, he finishes it quickly. For homework one night, he had to write in his classroom journal. He could write about anything he wanted. I suggested he write about riding his bike. He said no. I then suggested he write about our cats who he loves but no again from him. He finally wrote on his own, "A fan can keep me cool. I like one with five blades." Not exactly what I had in mind but it was what was on his mind. The school tested him to see his skill range. The teacher administering the test asked Jack to write the word "school." He wrote it correctly. She then said to him, "I bet you can also spell "dog" and "cat." Jack wrote for her "Dog and Cat." You must be specific with him.

The boys are both going to start Cub Scouts. This should be interesting because Ben will have to attend with Jack like all the other dads of 1st graders. Can't wait to see what happens with Scouts.

SEPTEMBER 7, 2002—A late Saturday night sitting in the bed writing while Jack is asleep in his bedroom next door. Ben and Benny are in Knoxville at Benny's first University of Tennessee football game. They spent the night in Knoxville because it was a night game. Ben called from Neyland Stadium and I got to talk to Benny who was having a great time. Benny and Jack talked to each other as well, a first for the two of them talking on the phone. I don't know what Benny said on his end but I know Jack's face lit up when he heard Benny's voice. Wish I could freeze those moments!

OCTOBER 1, 2002—While the boys are on fall break from their year-round school, we headed to Fort Morgan, Alabama for a few days. Last night we had dinner with friends who live here. The boys are growing fins they have been in the water so much this trip. Jack is so unaware of the dangers of the waters and I am hyper-aware of them.

Jack was very excited about this trip to the beach. I don't know why. I guess time away from school and home has become exciting. We had talked about coming here and what we were going to do and see. Before we left, Jack went to his room and gathered up some of his toys he wanted to take with him. He came to me and told me he had packed up some of his toys already for the trip. I told him, "Jack, that's great. Now you are ahead in packing than the rest of us." He stood there for a minute and said, "Mom, I am not just a head. I am a whole body." Oops! He had heard the word "ahead" and thought I said, "a head" as in a body part. Just because he can now talk doesn't mean he understands all the things the rest of us say.

OCTOBER 10, 2002—We are home and we hit the ground running once we returned. The boys are still on fall break. It seems they have been home for

... BUT I'M NOT THE SINGER

so long... maybe too long. We are at the dentist office. The boys are in the back getting their teeth cleaned. I am in the lobby writing while I wait for the sounds of screams and cries once Jack's cleaning starts. He does such a poor job at brushing his teeth that his teeth are yellow. I have tried to brush them but he throws a huge fit. I think his over sensitive mouth gags once his toothbrush hits one of those hyper-sensitive spots, and his weak fingers and hands just can't maneuver a toothbrush like they should. I really wish I could find a dentist who understands the challenges associated with children with autism. Strange I haven't heard any screams from the dentist chair yet! But wait, there are the screams and cries. Autism and teeth cleaning are not compatible!

Jack is getting older and more aware of the world around him. He doesn't always understand why he cannot do things others can do. One day, his teacher called to let me know Jack had a bad day. It had started in P.E. class and had gotten worse as the day went on. In P.E., Jack had not been able to do the P.E. exercise all the other students in his class were doing. They were bouncing a ball, volleying it into the wall, and catching it as it came back to them. The PE teacher said Jack attempted the maneuver during the whole class. She checked on him once and she said big old tears were rolling down his cheeks but he was still trying. He became so disappointed he had a come apart. On another day, he had a wonderful day at school and received a reward for his good day—a Three Musketeer candy bar—Jack's one and only favorite candy bar. He was so proud of himself when he got home sharing with me how he had been so good that day and that he was ready to eat his candy. I bragged on him while I opened his reward. It was a melted mess! He cried and cried and cried. He wanted to go back to school to get one that wasn't melted. I felt so sorry for him. I guessed he had clutched the candy bar all the way home on the hot bus in the heat. Needless to say, I will keep Three Musketeer bars around the house for reward time from now on! Recently, Ben found a map Jack had drawn of I-65 south exiting off to Highway 59 turning onto Highway 180. It was the exact road numbers where we had recently traveled on our last trip to Gulf Shores. How does he remember that?

NOVEMBER 3, 2002—We survived Benny's birthday and our Police Officer and Ninja Warrior Halloween. Candy wasn't a big hit with Benny now wearing braces on his teeth and Jack not eating candy much at all.

Jack has been a holy terror. We hate going out in public with him because his compulsiveness had gotten so bad. We are regulated to only restaurants with ceiling fans. And the restaurant's ceiling fans must be on. If not, he

MY NAME IS JACK JOHNSON...

throws a big fit. Ben took the boys trick or treating and instead of saying "trick or treat" when the neighbors answered the doorbell, Jack would ask to see their ceiling fans. Ben had to stop him several times since he would just start to walk in the neighbor's open door looking for their ceiling fans. Now he can identify each fan by make and model. We are constantly hearing things like, "My favorite fan is a Hunter Quik Connect fan with five blades" over and over. When he tells this to others, we must explain his strange behavior and language. He is even talking about asking Santa Claus for a ceiling fan. I need to call his autism doctor, Dr. McGrew, and make an appointment quickly.

DECEMBER 4, 2002—We made it through another Thanksgiving. The large crowds of family are so hard on Jack. Then there are the other children to deal with who have as many behavior problems as Jack but are not disabled. One young relative kicked Jack in the head while being ugly. It set off a temper tantrum with Jack that lasted about 45 minutes. The same relative threw another boy's toy across the yard, laughing the whole time. It is so hard for Jack to handle the whole social situation that Thanksgiving is for everyone which in turn means it is hard for us as well. I wish relatives would pay more attention to their own children and at least stop their children from creating more pain and suffering for Jack and for all of us. Jack did lose a front tooth—his first—over Thanksgiving. He was eating a Thanksgiving favorite—cheese balls—when it just fell out.

Ben and I took him to his autism doctor yesterday. Dr. McGrew told us definitely NO ceiling fan ("white with no light and four blades and a long string") and NO bucket lights (an outside light with a shade that looks like a bucket) from Santa Claus. She is afraid it would be playing into Jack's compulsive behaviors possibly making them worse. We are afraid Jack will be disappointed on Christmas morning.

DECEMBER 27, 2002—We survived Christmas! We had so many places to be but everything went well. Of course, we are still carrying Jack's meals because he still doesn't eat the foods offered and take some of his favorite toys just in case he needs something to play with that is familiar. Maybe one day I will stop carrying a "diaper bag without diapers." Jack did not get his perfect gift of a ceiling fan, but the toys he received kept him busy.

MARCH 28, 2003—It's the last day of the boy's spring break. Benny has played a lot with the neighborhood kids and he has enjoyed that. Jack has been

...BUT I'M NOT THE SINGER

Jack. He has watched TV, played outside, rode his bike, walked around the block, and played games on the computer almost every day. He has also cried and tantrum-ed several times as well. When he doesn't get "his way" he throws a fit. "His way" and the typical way are completely different. With Benny, if he doesn't get to do something he wants to do or buy a certain new toy he wants he might cry to get "his way." I think that is typical of most kids. With Jack, "his way" is about things we have no control over like ceiling fans in public places. And of course, those are the most fun tantrums of all... those performed in public places. The staring eyes of the judgmental onlookers, the blank, unemotional looks and my personal favorite and the most popular tantrum witnessing public eye reaction: the shaking of their heads. If I was standing close, they are probably saying "tsk, tsk, tsk!" at the behavior of my disabled child. They don't really care about Jack and us; we are just interrupting their beautiful, wonderful lives. Little do they understand our lives have been interrupted by autism for years. It has stolen my child and made him its slave. Makes me sad!

APRIL 16, 2003—It's almost Easter. Jack's birthday was last week. He is a big seven years old something I noticed the other night at bath time. He is starting to get rounder—not chubby or fat—just rounder. Benny is still tall, thin, muscular from his level of activity. Jack is soft, from his level activity as well. He is probably all wiener meat and chocolate pudding. What's a mother to do when the menu of choice is pudding and wieners? He did have a good birthday. For school, I sent mini Three Musketeer bars for a class birthday treat instead of cookies or cupcakes. Hey, the birthday boy should get what he desires! He asked me for brownies for his birthday open house here at home. His gift wish was for a Gameboy after Benny got his for his birthday in October. Jack and his Gameboy have been inseparable. The first night he got it, he slept with it. The boys have finally started to share... they swap Gameboys instead of Gameboy games. It works for them—today. Right this second as I am writing this, the boys are all playing touch football, even Jack. He does have a Powerpuff Girls Bubbles doll, some Powerpuff Girls stickers and a Powerpuff Girls birthday card lined up on the front porch so they can watch him play. I guess they are his personal cheering squad. What does that child think? Does he think since the characters are on the stickers and card that they are personally there as well?

MAY 20, 2003—We are at Saddle Up! Jack has started riding horses again and loves it. He doesn't ride a pony anymore; he rides a bigger horse and

MY NAME IS JACK JOHNSON...

still loves it. He loves coming here to ride because there are lots of electric poles—a Jack favorite. Today on the way here, he told me that he wants to spend the night with his favorite pole. Good grief! Can't you see him now, standing under an electric pole, in the bright light of the pole's attached street light, just standing there with darkness all around him where the light cannot reach? Poor Jack has yet to quite grasp the concept that all his "friends" are not human but are objects. Lord, give me strength to help him understand this thing called life.

CHAPTER 10

In our quest to find a church to call our home, we had spent lots and lots of time visiting and attending several just to find out in the long run that they were not going to be a perfect fit for us. Some of these churches greeted us with open arms only to find out down the road that Jack was just not going to fit into the box they had created for his age group. Benny was happy anywhere if there were other children his age to hang around with. Ben and I talked a lot about what we should do as Jack's parents. Do we find a church that will accept all of us with open arms or do we find a church that Benny really likes so at least he could grow up in a church? That would mean that one of us would go to church with Benny and one of us would stay home with Jack since he seemed to be the puzzle piece we could not fit into a church environment. And then the question became: what would Benny think about Jack not going to church? Would he think Jack wasn't worthy to go? Would he grow up believing Jack was not equal to him or other children just because he didn't do the things other children could do? And what about Jack? Would he realize one day that he wasn't invited to church because he was different? And what about Ben and me? Answering for myself, I know I could use a little more knowledge about God, grace, patience, and understanding in this crazy world my family lives in daily. The questions just continued to add up for Ben and me and there were no easy answers.

We had been told about a local church who had a specific program just for children with special needs. The program at this church paired a willing adult volunteer with a special needs child. The adult was called a "special friend" to the child with special needs. This adult would sit with the special needs child during the Sunday School class period and make sure the child was safe and participating as much as the child could despite his/her needs. It sounded too good to be true.

MY NAME IS JACK JOHNSON...

JULY 29, 2003—We have started going to a new-to-us church. The Franklin First Methodist Church is the same church my grandparents attended for years. So far, it has been great for us. The Sunday School is the same time as a church service so until we get acclimated, Ben and I go to a service while the boys go to Sunday School. Benny loves it since he knows other children who attend here. Jack has mixed feelings but is getting adjusted. The church provides a volunteer "special needs friend" who helps with Jack in his class. The church has been so wonderful and we find ourselves not dreading going to church.

Miss Kim, Jack's previous preschool teacher who also became our mentor and friend, knew a member of this church. She had discussed Jack and our situation with her. Kim's friend agreed to help us out. "Misses Luna" became Jack's special friend during his Sunday School time so Ben and I could attend service and, in the future, possibly join an adult Sunday School class of our own. Jack was excited to have his own friend and having time away from us. We were delighted to have time in church with others and relieved knowing that both of our children were safe in their own Sunday School classes.

AUGUST 11, 2003—Church went well this last Sunday. Jack's Sunday School theme class this week was drama class. The church had a rotating class schedule for children Jack's age. Each class had a Biblical basis but had a different activity. Some of the classes I can recall are: a movie theater with a popcorn machine and a small screen for watching Biblical themed short movies; an arts and crafts class where the children made a Biblically themed item that went along with their lesson; a drama class where the children dressed up as Bible characters in line with their lesson; and a computer class where children could play Bible-based games on the computers. When I picked Jack up from drama class, he had on angel wings. Jack with, of all things, angel wings!

After Ben and I saw things were working well for the boys in their Sunday School classes, we decided to find one for us. Once we did, we knew we had to start taking the boys in the sanctuary for the church service. Since we had been taking the boys on and off to different churches for most of their childhoods, they had some experience in sitting in a sanctuary environment. Of course, for a child with special needs, each week can be a new experience with their ever-changing mood swings, environmental factors like the lighting in a new place or the sound system and acoustics of certain rooms, the general

... BUT I'M NOT THE SINGER

health of the child that particular day, the smell of people sitting near them, loud noises like babies crying or squeaky, creaking wooden pews. This list goes on and on for each special need's child and their personal tolerance level. For Jack, it was all the above plus what side of the bed he woke up on and if he previously had a tantrum that morning. Then there were always the new developments that seemed to change and evolve in his world each day, those unseen, unplanned for complications that sent Jack into a huge, nasty come apart and sent us into a state of shock, not knowing or understanding where or what just happened to cause this latest tantrum. There were those Sundays that after a Saturday night dinner of pizza, Jack would release a bodily odor so bad that Ben and Benny could not hold in their laughter. Their laughter only escalated when Jack would respond to my stern, knowing-who-the-culprit-was look with the loud proclamation, "I'm gassy!" I knew it would be a challenge to teach Jack how to sit through a whole church service quietly.

We started to attend the Methodist church's service together as a family. The church had outgrown its historic, small sanctuary and had service in a nearby gymnasium of a building they owned across the street from the historic sanctuary. On our first few visits, we attended the historic sanctuary, but since Jack had trouble with learning to be still for long periods of time, the old wooden pews squeaked so badly we knew it had to be a distraction for other surrounding members who were trying to listen. We felt the gymnasium environment with its folding chairs divided into sections of pews would be easier for Jack. In case we had an emergency tantrum, we sat in the back row of the gym in the seats nearest to the back door. Ben and I decided that if we did have to take Jack out of the service for behavior issues, it would take both of us and it would be ugly with Jack screaming, kicking, and who knows what else. It would be easier for us and less troubling for others to witness if we stayed as close to the door as possible. Nothing like causing a big scene for the unsuspecting public in a church than to have a visiting family physically remove a bucking, screaming, wild child out of a religious function from the front pew of the church, walking down the aisle and across the sanctuary to the nearest exit. This scenario haunted mine and Ben's dreams every Saturday night before Sunday church.

Luckily for us, the change to the gym sanctuary worked. If Jack was wiggly and disruptive, he only bothered the few rows in front of us. Since no one sat behind us, there was no one to disrupt. I took a bag of toys for Jack to play with and things to keep him busy. I had to make sure the toys did not have sound because Jack would want them to do the things he had enjoyed previous-

MY NAME IS JACK JOHNSON...

ly, which meant if he remembered the toy had sound, he wanted it with sound. This became a problem and caused some outburst from Jack, so I left the toys with sound at home and replaced those toys with quieter ones. In his bag was a supply of Cheerios and a drink in a spill free sippy cup. I learned early on to make sure I held the container of Cheerios so they would not spill all over the floor. I am not saying these were foolproof, calming, nor quiet solutions. These were the first attempts at working to teach Jack how to sit still and be quiet in a large assembly. Some days were better than others. But it was a start.

MARCH 26, 2004—Church has been hard again for us. Last week, the back row was taken and Jack really didn't like it at all. So, we—me and Jack—rounded up some extra folding chairs and made our own back row. It didn't make any difference to him…. he was still bad. I will figure out a suitable punishment just for misbehaving in church…. something he won't like and will make him think about his behavior during the church service. Ben has been praying, "Hey, God! We're trying! Please give us a break!" If there are any two parents in need of religious guidance from God, it is us!

In my limited downtime, I think a lot about God, the Bible, and special needs people like Jack. I am not a Biblical scholar by any means but really want to learn what I can about what the Bible says about people with disabilities. I had recently read a book by Kathie Snow titled Disability Is Natural. In it, she describes a Greek and Roman society where human perfection was pleasing to the gods in that day. Therefore, babies with disabilities were left outside to die from exposure, thrown over cliffs, starved, or smothered because they were not perfect. In the time of Jesus, He healed the disabled so His followers and the non-believers of this time would know that through His miracles, Jesus was truly the son of God. Since we don't live in either one of these societies mentioned above, how did God see Jack? What is Jack's purpose in life? What is the purpose of any person with disabilities? Why did Jesus heal some people with disabilities in Biblical times but not all of them? What happened to those people? What exactly was the meaning of Jack's autism in the world? Why, God, why?

CHAPTER II

Ben and I have a lovely boat in our backyard. We have owned it for years. We used it in past summers, enjoying time in the sun, listening to music while leisurely floating around the water on floats, the gentle waves rocking our floats almost putting us to sleep. Benny had fun with us on the boat when he was a baby. That was before two children. Now it sits, covered, in our backyard. Lately, Ben has talked about trying to start it and trying to take the boys to the lake. It would be fun.

MAY 20, 2003—Ben has gotten serious about getting the boat up and running. He is planning on getting it in the repair shop and talks about us being in the water by July. I think he is kidding himself. He hasn't even taken the cover off yet! It will be an adventure to see how we all fit into the boat we have. I want a pontoon boat, but I think Ben wants to keep the ski boat we have so he can ski behind it again. And he wants to give the boys skiing lessons as well. I don't know how comfortable we will be in the boat. There is not a lot of room. With coolers, floats, skis, life jackets and then all of us, where will we ever sit? Maybe we will be OK and love the closeness. Maybe I have forgotten how much room it had and will be surprised. All of us can pack up and go every weekend we feel like going especially if we have the boat in a slip at a dock. Maybe Ben and I can go out on the lake by ourselves again during the week. Maybe sometime soon we will have lake time with the boys. Lots of maybes involved. I can see me now, all greasy with sunscreen, lying on a float bobbing with the waves, sunglasses on with a cold drink in my hand, the radio in the boat playing some lake floating music…. Yeah, right! Haha! More like…" Mommy, do this. Mommy, do that! Mommy, Mommy, Mommy, I want this!" I need to be a little more realistic! School will be out soon, and the boys are registered for camp. Jack will be going to a summer special needs camp, and Benny will be going to his typical camp. They are excited. Last night Ben and

MY NAME IS JACK JOHNSON...

the boys went to Cub Scouts Crossover, where the boys "crossover" to the next level of scouting. Benny went from Wolf to a Bear, and Jack went from Tiger Cub to Wolf. Ben came home exhausted and disappointed with Jack and his behavior. I told Ben he needed to stop thinking that Jack can be like the other boys when it comes to waiting and sitting for long periods of time. Jack cannot be like everyone else. Again, another fun activity between a father and his sons is made more difficult by autism.

Seems first grade flew by. Jack has done well in school. His teacher has not left school screaming. All parties concerned have worked together well. Some goals have been met while some have not and will be an on-going goal. Academically, Jack has learned quite a lot. His speech is so much better, but his handwriting is about the same. We have met his new teacher for 2nd grade, and Jack seems to like her. I love the eagerness of elementary teachers. I wonder every day what tomorrow and another school year will bring.

I found some of Jack's artwork from school. It is so special to see his drawings because one day not too long ago, we didn't know for sure if Jack would learn to hold a pencil. One drawing is of children at desks, each child with a ceiling fan above them. The ceiling fans all have four blades I noticed, Jack's favorite number of blades a fan should have. The caption on the drawing is "I am good at coloring," with coloring being spelled "Colering." At the bottom of the drawing, he wrote, "I'm a nice boy." I don't know why he wrote that, but I am glad he feels he is a nice boy.

JUNE 3, 2003—Back at Saddle Up! This is the last week of school. Tomorrow is party day and the next day is 2 hours of school. I am sure the teachers will be glad to get rid of them. Benny's teacher has probably aged several years this year having Benny in her class. Last week she sent home a note about Benny and another boy talking about their "wieners," which had upset her. Ben and I punished Benny, but I am afraid that will not be the last time he talks about his "wiener." I have never let the boys call "it" a wiener preferring they call it by its medical term. So, I figured Benny got that term from another boy in class. Goodness... how age appropriate for boys!

JUNE 17, 2003—The boys are enjoying camp. Jack has been swimming twice, and Benny goes Friday to the pool, and soon he will go to Nashville Shores with his camp buddies. Jack just gets to go swimming at the rec pool, but he thinks it is as cool as going to Nashville Shores.

...BUT I'M NOT THE SINGER

July 29, 2003—Recently the boys had a dentist appointment to have their teeth cleaned. Jack refused to sit in the dentist chair, refused to stand up from the floor where he collapsed during his I-will-not-get-in-the-dentist-chair fit. It was so fun. The dentist and assistants picked him up from the floor and physically put him in the chair and held him down while his teeth were cleaned. It wasn't the way I wanted it to be—having to restrain him physically—but what are you supposed to do? They could easily get to his teeth because his mouth was wide open from the screams and cries coming from him. He was mad at everyone about that trip for a while. School has started with everything going smoothly....so far. Each day I wait for the bomb to drop. Now, I am not sure from which child. Benny has gotten in trouble every day since school started. Not anything bad, just talking and not listening to the teacher's instructions. Jack loves his new teacher. What's not to love? She is young, sweet, cute, smiles all the time, is mild-mannered, and has a soft voice. I hope Jack doesn't burst her bubble. She tells me that, so far, Jack has been a dream child. No fits, no bad days. I talked to the class today about Jack and his autism. The children seemed to soak it in.

I received a booklet Jack wrote and drew pictures in from school. It is titled, "All About Me." There were pages and pages of questions so the teacher, Miss W., could learn more about her students. Some of the questions were like "list some things you will miss from 1st grade" or "there are some things I did over summer." Jack didn't answer very many of the questions, but he spent his time on the booklet drawing pictures of Exit signs and a classroom. Of course, the actual drawings are very primitive with lots of crooked lines and scribble marks. But if you really look at the drawing, he has a map drawn of part of the school building with the location of the Exit signs and fire alarms placed where they go at a certain place in the building. In a scene of a classroom, the student tables are color coded red, blue and yellow just like they are in the classroom. There are also several drawings from what I can decipher must be table lamps the teacher has around her room. Also included are chairs, computers, doors, and something that looks like an animal. The artwork is messy, but the amount of detail he put in the picture blows my mind.

AUGUST 19, 2003—Jack and I are at Saddle Up! I love watching him ride when he rides without a lead person. He looks so big sitting up there by himself, making the horse go where he wants him to go. But Jack has so little patience when he must wait for the instructor and easily becomes a holy terror. Only a couple of weeks more of riding, then we will take a break. Time for a

MY NAME IS JACK JOHNSON...

change in activities and special needs bowling starts in September. No more horseback riding for a while.

SEPTEMBER 5, 2003—Today has been a hard day for me. Miss W., Jack's 2nd-grade teacher, informed us that she planned on giving Jack and two other classmates a Pride Time Award. A Pride Time Award is an award given to students during a school-wide assembly for doing something good or out of the ordinary. Students can receive teacher given Pride Time Awards for excellent grades, behavior, or being an extraordinary friend. Miss W. thought Jack would be OK getting the award. She wanted it to be a surprise. Ben and I went to school without telling Jack about the award. We tried to sit where he couldn't see us so we could keep it a surprise as well. Miss W. got up in front of the whole school and announced the Pride Time Award to Jack and his buddies, Megan and Megan, who have always been Jack's biggest friends. Jack heard his name and just collapsed. He would not go up to the podium to get his award. Megan and Megan walked up, received theirs and got Jack's for him while he sat angrily in his seat. One father wanted to take a picture of the award winners together, but Jack flat refused. These two girls love Jack, always thinking of him before themselves and helping him out in all situations. They are the sweetest two girls I know. One Megan told her father she didn't want to have her picture made until Jack was ready to have his made with them. I was so angry…angry at autism for robbing my son of this happy moment. I was angry at autism for putting a damper on a meaningful moment for these selfless little girls. I was angry at autism for stealing a prideful mommy moment from me. Autism has robbed us of so much, and now I can add one more thing to the growing list. I hate it! I wish Jack could enjoy all the things other kids get to enjoy. He should be proud of himself but nnnnnoooooo. Instead, he folds into a heap of emotions when his good traits are acknowledged. How do I show him it is OK to be proud of himself when he does something good? How do you teach pride to someone with autism? Should we have warned him about the award? Should we have prepared him for what he should do? Would it have made any difference? So many questions and really no answers now.

Our local Recreation Department of our town has started a special needs bowling day once a week during the fall season. I have been taking Jack. We usually arrive after the older students with special needs have started bowling so if there are no other children around Jack's age, he bowls by himself, or I bowl with him. He seems to like to bowl but gets easily

... BUT I'M NOT THE SINGER

frustrated when he doesn't bowl as well as he thinks he should. He likes to watch the older students bowl but doesn't interact with them. We will see how this new adventure progresses.

OCTOBER 3, 2003—It has been a while since I have written. The boys are on fall break, and we have headed south to Orange Beach, AL. I am poolside while I write because all the boys are swimming in the pool. My biggest boy, Ben, is right there with them. I hope he wears them out. The boys received their report cards before we left. Jack's was as good as it can be despite his autism. Benny's was a mixed bag of needing improvement on spelling and grammar and A's and B's on the other subjects. Last night we had dinner with our Gulf Shores, AL friends at a local marina. Jack loved it because the restaurant had 12 ceiling fans, with one fan not having any blades attached at all. How exciting was that for him! He has had a hard trip which means it has been hard for us as well. He wants what he wants when he wants and to heck with the rest of us. Like right now, he is in timeout for fighting with Benny in the pool and for running away from me which meant I had to remove him from the pool physically. Once out of the pool, he then spits at me and screams at me. I just kept adding timeout time until he had a whole 15 minutes in timeout or should I say, "pool out!" Mean ole Mommy!

OCTOBER 11, 2003—We made it back from the beach in one piece and with Jack. We didn't leave him there, but we were tempted—haha. The day we left we had to travel to Gulf Shores for breakfast because the restaurant across the street from our condo didn't have ceiling fans. Jack flat refused to go, and we didn't want the fight... again.

NOVEMBER 11, 2003—October is always such a busy month for us, and I didn't get a chance to write. We had Benny a birthday wienie roast in the backyard for his friends. He is now nine years old! The next week was Halloween. Benny was a scary, white-faced creature I think came off a movie, and Jack was a fireman. I must say... Jack's costumes are so easy. "Easy"— not a word I usually associate with Jack.

On the 30th, Ben and I had gone out to eat lunch. When we got home, there was a message from Miss W. Jack had a bad day and had been "physical" with her and Miss Linda, her class assistant. I jumped in the car and took off for school. This is what happened: Jack's class was starting to take a test—a timed test—and were getting directions from Miss W. Jack started

MY NAME IS JACK JOHNSON...

his before she told her students to begin. Jack was asked three times to stop, and when he didn't, they took his test away. He exploded! From their description, Jack's explosion was like his younger year's tantrums. He was out of control with arms and legs flying around and that horrible spitting. The teacher and assistant thought it would be best to remove Jack from the classroom physically. With no training and no knowledge of Jack's strength, the two women both small in height and weight tried to pick him up. They got him to the door, and Miss Linda and Jack got tangled up, and Miss Linda fell with Jack falling on top of her. A janitor was nearby and was asked to help. They did remove Jack out of the classroom doorway and into a special education classroom. When Jack fell on top of Miss Linda, she sprained her wrist. The students who witnessed this were scared, and the teachers were exhausted. Jack was still upset as well. He had no clue what had just happened. I was a basket case myself. I was worried about Jack, the teacher, the assistant, the other students, and frankly, didn't know what to do. I have tried so hard to help Jack by talking about autism with the students and teachers, but with one come apart, he had possibly erased everything I had tried to accomplish. One of my greatest fears is that Jack will become an outcast in life. He has no concept that one outburst of bad behavior can make that happen. I was depressed and cried for days afterward. Since that day, we are in the process of making some better decisions about behavior issues at school. We also added on his IEP a modification.... Jack will not receive a timed test until the timer has started!

When our church's Sunday School classes dismiss the children, the hallway becomes very crowded with parents retrieving their children and stopping to talk to friends and neighbors. When Jack gets out of his class, he is ready to get to the car and is usually very vocal about his impatience with others gathering in the hallway. I must stay near him or hold his hand so I can keep up with him and make sure he is not pushing or shoving his way through the crowd. This particular Sunday, he was making his way through the crowd when a parent accidentally bumped into Jack. Jack loudly says, "Watch where you are going, you fool!" I was flabbergasted. I profusely apologized to the parent and ran after Jack. When we got to the car, in my most angry voice, I asked Jack where did you hear that ugly remark. He told me on the cartoon, "Courage, the Cowardly Dog," there was a character that always says that when someone bumps into them. Good grief, now I have to fight the words of characters on cartoons. Will life ever get easier?

... BUT I'M NOT THE SINGER

JANUARY 4, 2004—Another new year. We survived another Thanksgiving and Christmas. Oh halleluiah!

Before the boys were out of school for the holidays, I had a progress meeting with Miss W. Miss W. shared a story that happened in class recently. Setting up the story, she explains she is teaching the class carry-over subtraction. She is letting the students teach the class by choosing a student to go to the chalkboard and explain a carry-over problem to the other students. Miss W. takes the seat of the chosen student who has become the "teacher" of the subtraction problem that is written on the board. That student then chooses another student to be the teacher, and they explain the next subtraction problem to the class and on and on. Since Miss W. has "become" a student, she acts like a student sitting at a desk, raising her hand, and saying "Pick me!" so the student "teacher" can call on her as well. One of the students picked Jack to be the "teacher." He got up in front of the class and proceeded to mimic every word, every gesture, every change in voice that Miss W. has used to teach a problem in math. She shared that she never knew if Jack was really listening and understanding what she was teaching because he doesn't look at her like the other students in the class. She is now in awe of his memory and understands now that he has indeed been listening to everything she has said and done in class. She shares that during this math exercise, she gets teary-eyed thinking about Jack and his hidden abilities. As the tears fill her eyes, a female student sitting beside her saw the tears and gently touched Miss W's hand. The little girl said, "It's OK Miss W. Someone will call on you soon." Such a sweet story that I am so glad she shared with me

FEBRUARY 18, 2004—A long overdue update. Benny is doing better in school. He made the A-B honor roll the last nine weeks of school. Jack is doing OK with his academics. His behaviors are better, just different. His friend, Megan, sent him a hand-made Valentine. She had drawn a picture of the two of them with the caption, "Me and You." She also wrote "BFF"—best friends forever on the card. I almost cried. I wish all people could love Jack the same way.

MARCH 26, 2004—After selling the ski boat we had, we are now the proud owner of a pontoon boat that is docked at Sligo Marina on Center Hill Lake. The boys like the new to us boat but just want to get into the water. Way too

MY NAME IS JACK JOHNSON...

early for that! The weekend we moved the boat, Jack threw a big old fit about wearing a life jacket. Too bad for him... I won that fight. No life jacket, no boat riding. Plain and simple. He will soon be eight years old, and Benny turns 10 in October. Benny will be a 4th grader, and Jack will be a 3rd grader next year.

On April 4, the boys participated in the Pinewood Derby car race with their Cub Scout troop. The Scouts are instructed to buy a small Pinewood Derby model car kit, which was a small block of wood, and four plastic wheels, from a local hobby store. The Scouts design their Derby car and have someone cut their design from the block of wood that came with the kit. After their Derby car is cut, nails are threaded through a hole in each wheel and inserted into previously cut slots on the underside of the block of wood. After the wheels are attached, the boys are then free to paint and decorate their Derby car the way they want. Benny really got into decorating his car, painting it red with blue highlights and attaching cool stickers to it. Jack's car was painted mostly blue with a little red, and once the paint dried, he picked out stickers to attach to his. With help from his dad, Jack's chosen stickers were slowly and precisely placed on his Derby car, finishing with a carefully placed "Eat Dirt" sticker on the back.

On race day, the boy's cars had to be a certain weight to be "legal." Small weights were glued to the cars to achieve the weight limit. Both boy's Derby cars needed more weight, and since Ben didn't buy any extra weight, he found enough spare quarters and pennies to get the right amount of weight. The spare change was attached with Scotch Tape to the Pinewood cars alongside the proper Derby weights. The track itself was a wooden track with three slots where Derby cars were placed to keep them racing in a straight line. The beginning of the track was elevated so the cars would race downward toward the finish line at the bottom of the track.

Since Cub Scouts was a father/son activity, I let them have this time together and stayed home. Ben told me that some of the Derby cars were carefully cut into the shape of an actual race car and looked like they had been painted and decorated by the moms and dads instead of the boys themselves. He shared that some of the cars came wrapped in terrycloth and packaged in boxes to protect the alignment of the wheels and their custom paint jobs. Our sons carried theirs in their bare, probably sweaty and dirty hands. Ben also said that Jack's car was one of the least decorated cars in the race. With the added and unsightly taped quarters and pennies, I am sure Jack's Derby car

... BUT I'M NOT THE SINGER

looked pitiful sitting on the track next to the miniature NASCAR racers the other children entered in the race.

Ben said Jack eagerly gave the Scout Master his car when it was his car's turn to race while the other boys whose cars were to race with Jack's, proudly handed over their masterpieces to be placed on the track. The boys were instructed to sit near the finish line so they could retrieve their cars once the race was over. Once three Derby cars were placed in the three slots on the track, the track Scoutmaster pulled the trigger that dropped the pegs and released the cars to begin their downward trek. Within seconds the race was over. Much to Ben's surprise, Jack's car won! And it just kept winning. Jack understood his car had won but didn't quite understand that winning could take him and his quartered and penny-ed Pinewood Derby racer to the Regional Pinewood Derby Car Race.

The Regional Race was held a few weeks later at our local mall. We all happily walked through the parking lot and into the mall in search of the race. Somewhere along the way, Jack lost his grip on his racer, it hit the floor, and bent one of the wheels. The mall was very crowded, noisy, and the sounds echoed off the walls. It was not a good place for Jack to be. Then he was asked to stand in line for his turn in the race... an activity Jack was not able to do. Benny became Jack's waiting line stand-in while Jack was miserable, surrounded by mobs of children of all ages, parents, grandparents, and mall shoppers either talking, crying, or scurrying about. Jack took his stand in line when it was time for his car to race, but his car lost in the first race. He wasn't upset, just very happy to leave. For Jack, it was a win just to be going home.

APRIL 16, 2004—Jack is now an eight-year-old! We celebrated at three different places and at home. We gave him a stuffed Nemo which I guess was his favorite gift. Now he wants a Dory to match. Saturday night he told Benny he loved him. Benny told Ben about it. Ben asked Benny what he said back to Jack, and he said nothing. Boys! The next day I was praising Jack for being kind and telling Benny he loved him. Without missing a beat, Jack asked if that made the Easter Bunny come to his house. Jack had a motive for his "I love you" statement. The boys have been on spring break for two weeks, and things have been better than ever before. They have fought but not as bad as they have before. I took them to the dentist last Monday. The last time there, Jack had a complete come apart and had to be restrained while the dentist cleaned his teeth. This visit he did great. The difference? I went back with him, held his hand during the cleaning, and explained everything they said to

MY NAME IS JACK JOHNSON...

him. It was great. The dentist and assistants were pleasantly surprised. I think Jack surprised himself.

A recent episode at church turned out better than expected. First, let me add that I carry business cards with me that read, "Please excuse my son's behavior. He has autism, a brain disorder......." and describes how autism might affect someone diagnosed with it, and ends with, "For more information on autism, please call... (the telephone number of an autism society)" I carry these because I became sick of the stares and frowns of people in public places. There is nothing worse than having your child with autism have a very public tantrum only to look up while you are trying to calm your falling apart child to see you and your child have drawn a crowd of onlookers, stretching their necks, pushing each other, just to see the commotion. Instead of getting mad every time this happens to us, I have this card I can easily share with them so they will understand and hopefully move on with their lives. It gives me a sense of power in a powerless situation. One day at church, Jack was having a hard day. He was loud, combative, and down-right rude. A lady was sitting in front of us and was hearing the whole ugly scene. I had seen her before at church, and I thought she understood some days were not good for us. On this one day, she had had enough and let us know. She would turn around in her seat and give us the look... that look of disgust and anger mixed with a lot of impatience. When Jack would get loud, she would flinch in her chair. When she couldn't stand it anymore, she would again turn around and give us the look. I was doing all I could to keep Jack quiet, but it was not enough for her. We were disturbing her church service. I remember sweat popped out on my forehead and ran down my back from the nervousness I felt just trying to keep Jack happy and quiet. After the service was over, I stood and handed this lady one of my "Excuse my son's behavior" cards and walked away. I didn't say a word, just handed her the card. I felt so liberated. I had given her a reason why my son could not act the way SHE felt he should in her church.... a church that welcomed all. The very next week after church, this same lady stopped me and apologized for her behavior. She shared with me that she should have known what was happening since she had previously worked with special needs children. She was very sorry and sincere, and I believe we will now become friends. The card had worked its magic. God does work in mysterious ways.

MAY 5, 2004—Jack went to see his autism doctor yesterday. He has grown 2 inches and has gained 15 pounds in a year. As for his compulsions with

...BUT I'M NOT THE SINGER

ceiling fans, Dr. McGrew said we must get tougher with him about going into restaurants that do not have ceiling fans. She said to give him a choice—go into a restaurant without ceiling fans or go home. It is going to take some tantrums and come-aparts, but we need to stop his snowballing compulsions before they become worse. Once he understands that restaurants without ceiling fans have just as good food as ones with them, we hope he will be OK. This won't be easy and could get ugly.

MEMORIAL DAY, MAY 30, 2004—We are on the lake. We bought a tube for the boys to ride as we pull them with the boat. They have had fun tubing and swimming. Too bad the tube exploded just a few minutes ago. Maybe we can fix it.

MAY 31, 2004—We returned from the lake after having a great time. The boys were worn out.

This week I have Jack's first IEP for next year. The school still doesn't have a regular education teacher or a special education teacher for him. This should be an interesting meeting. Benny received a Pride Time Award last Friday. So proud of him.

Last week I read an article about kids with autism and cursive writing. The article said not to try to teach children with autism to print but to teach them cursive instead. With cursive writing, the pencil flows from letter-to-letter while with printing a student must constantly pick up and place down a pencil for each letter. I shared it with his teacher and asked her to try it with Jack. Oh. My. Goodness. What a difference! Jack wrote his name in cursive, and it looked like I had written it. I asked Jack to write his name in cursive for his dad and Ben was speechless. Ben and I were both amazed. Jack's printed handwriting is so bad and always has been. We have had it as a goal on his IEP for years because not only are his letters poorly written, but the spacing between the words is not there. His words look like one long word because there are no spaces between the words. It has been very hard to read. Maybe this can be the answer to this problem.

The boys got out of school. Another year behind us. Miss W. wrote on the back of Jack's report card, "What a wonderful year! I feel so blessed because Jack has been a part of my life this school year. I love him and will miss him!" I feel so blessed that Jack had such a wonderful and caring teacher!

Jack got a much loved but trouble-making game for his GameBoy for his birthday. He got a game called "Elf Bowling." Niece Katie gave it to him and

MY NAME IS JACK JOHNSON...

told me afterward that I might not be too happy with it. Oh, my goodness, how that child loves this game, but it is not appropriate for him. I didn't understand how inappropriate it was until I actually saw it while he was playing it. In the game, Santa's elves line up on a bowling alley in the shape that the bowling pins line up in a regular bowling alley. Santa takes a bowling ball, rolls the ball toward the elves, and knocks the elves away. Some of the elves are knocked down; some are not. Between the bowls, the elves say things to Santa like "Who's your daddy?" and "Is that all you've got, Santa?" There is also an occasional appearance by a reindeer who walks into the game, and if Santa bowls just the right way, his ball will hit the reindeer in the head, and it falls, making a "UH" sound as it hits the ground. AND then sometimes the elves will turn around, drop their elf pants, and pop themselves on their bare, little elf bottoms. So inappropriate for Jack. But he is obsessed with this game. I made him a deal: I will let him play the game as long as I do not hear any of the language from it, see him try to hit a cat with a ball in the head or do anything he sees the elves do on the game. If I do, the game will go in timeout. Stupid me, what do I really think he will say. Of course, he agrees to my rules. He happily plays the game, his laughter so loud and so hard it makes all of us laugh at how much he enjoys playing this silly game. That is until...Ben takes the boys to a Cub Scouts meeting one night. Ben has yet to understand how to control and help Jack get the most out of Cub Scouts. Each meeting has been a struggle for them. Benny has been complaining about going too because the meetings are becoming boring for him. On this particular night, Ben has lost sight of Jack. Frantically, he searches the Scouts meeting room, all its nooks, crannies, and dark places. Leaving the meeting room, Ben goes in search of Jack further and further into the other parts of the church where the meetings are held. Finally, he finds Jack, in a thankfully far-away-from-the-meeting hallway, bent over, his pants around his ankles, slapping his own bare bottom, saying "Who's your daddy, Santa?" Needless to say, the boys will not be going back to Cub Scouts.

CHAPTER 12

JUNE 27, 2004—We are spending time at the lake. Two weeks ago, we were here and were riding on the water when a storm blew up scaring us with deafening, hair-raising lightning. After we left the lake, we went in search of food. We stopped in Lebanon, but the restaurants with ceiling fans had huge waits for a table. The only restaurant we could find without a wait was Applebee's. It didn't have ceiling fans. But since Jack's autism doctor told us to be more forceful and not give in to Jack's ceiling fan compulsion, we explained the situation to him until he gave in. By this time, he was crying but not bad. I sat across the table from him so I could talk to him and reassure him everything would be alright and that the food was going to be just as good as a restaurant with ceiling fans. He was talking loudly, but the whole restaurant was noisy, so it wasn't too bad. Or so I thought. Unknown to us, an older couple sitting behind us was not happy with us sitting close to them with Jack. We were trying to calm him down and were gaining ground but it wasn't enough for them. I overheard the woman in the couple say, "And we thought things couldn't get worse!" but I had no idea she was referring to us. The man in the couple very loudly called for a waitress, announcing to everyone in the restaurant that they wanted to be moved "anywhere away from that kid!" while tipping his head in the direction of Jack. He didn't stop with saying it once but had to repeat it again. He was so loud people around the restaurant were staring and as he walked past our table, Ben and I at the same time said, "He is special needs!" referring to Jack. The man loudly replies, "WELL HE DOESN'T NEED TO BE HERE!" as the waitress took them to another table far away from us. Shocked and humiliated, Ben and I just looked at each other not knowing what to do or say. Our waitress came back, we ordered our food, and sat in silence. By this time, Jack was better and I had made the cutest little ceiling fan for him to hold out of pipe cleaners I kept in my purse for emergencies like this. Ben was still very quiet and Benny hadn't said anything either. A woman from another table with a large group walked up

MY NAME IS JACK JOHNSON...

to our table and squatted down. She told us she wanted to apologize for the couple's behavior and for the ugly remark the man had shouted even though she did not know them. She went on to explain she worked with children with special needs and asked if Jack had autism. We told her he did and she said she thought so. She shared with us how shocked her group had been and said she even cried as she witnessed the couple's behavior. She told us not to be ashamed because our son had every right to be there just like everyone else. It made us feel better but it was our first taste of public discrimination.

Once in the car, I cried all the way home. First, I was angry that people would act that way. I was shocked and confused because I had been in public places before when other children had acted so much worse than Jack had been that night. I really couldn't believe it had happened, that someone had caused such an outburst over how little Jack was crying. If he had been having a huge come apart, I would have understood. But he was barely crying and wasn't as loud as he could have been. Did this couple think that an Applebee's was a restaurant for adults? I thought it was a family restaurant because we had previously eaten there before. I had to hold myself back from marching across the restaurant and giving Mr. and Mrs. Ugly a piece of my mind. The person I felt sorry for the most was poor Benny. How do you explain that scene to him? How do you explain the behavior of rude, nasty people? I did talk to Benny about it later. I explained that some people were insensitive and selfish. Thankfully, since the other kind lady had come and talked to us, I used her as an example of how we should all act and how inappropriate the couple's attitude was toward people with special needs and just the public at large. It was an altercation none of us will ever forget.

AUGUST 7, 2004—The boys started back to school on July 20th. Benny's teacher is Ms. W., and Jack's is Mrs. H. Both boys like their teachers. This week is their 3rd full week of school and the start of true learning and the beginning of homework. Benny has already had some, but I think it will become more frequent. Jack has been finishing his homework at school before he comes home. His new teacher has experience with children with autism, so she has both Jack and JT in her class. JT has been with Jack on and off since WAVES days years ago. The special education teacher the school hired has already turned in her notice. Fine by me... she didn't seem to be very caring nor wanting to be involved with the students. I found out even though she has 20 years of experience with special education as a resource teacher, she had no experience with children with autism. Her first week was bad... just learn-

...BUT I'M NOT THE SINGER

ing the ropes, taking advice from others, and the day to day challenges with children with autism. Jack had a come apart that first week too, so it was just too much for her. She is going back to the school she came from. I suspected from day one that she wasn't up for the job. She didn't show for Jack's IEP at all; then she didn't want to discuss Jack and his needs. She didn't want to schedule another IEP but said, "I have his notes from last year that should be enough!" So, when Jack had his come apart, it was a strange poetic justice. If you don't want to take the time and energy to learn as much as you can about Jack, then don't complain to me when he falls apart. Good riddance for me! I hope they find a replacement soon.

SEPTEMBER 9, 2004—Jack and I are back at Saddle UP! We took a year off from horseback riding, and now Jack is back loving it again. I am so glad! Jack has been better at school and at home too. Over the weekend, Ben and I both noticed Jack did not have a come apart. Two weeks ago, we were talking about how the weight of the world was heavily pushing on our shoulders, and now things are so much better. Thank you, God!

SEPTEMBER 16, 2004—At Saddle Up! again. Jack did so well last week .. it was fun to watch and listen to him. I have been standing outside when they ride outside so I can hear and watch the riders in action. Other children ride in the same time slot as Jack. Listening to their comments is more fun than just watching them. Every week one horse needs to relieve itself one way or the other, and when it happens, all the boys and Jack too freak out over the horse's call of nature. Their comments are so funny.

Special needs bowling has started again. Jack has bowled a few times already. One day, he threw a little fit because he wasn't bowling well. His fit got the attention of some of the older students. A few of the older girls came over to me and asked me if Jack was OK. They would look at him as he cried and their faces would have so much sympathy for him. I thought one girl would cry herself. I reassured her Jack was fine; he was just mad he wasn't bowling like he wanted. Since he couldn't control the bowling ball the way he wanted, he started bowling with bumpers. I had never seen anyone use the bumpers to their advantage like he does. He understands he doesn't have the strength to roll the bowling ball the proper way—fingers and thumb in the holes on the ball, the ball heaved backward only to leave the hand and arm when released by the fingers and thumb. Instead, he holds the ball with both hands to his side, releases the ball from a standing position which releases the ball slower

MY NAME IS JACK JOHNSON...

than should be, making the ball slowly roll down the bowling lane. Once he saw all the gutter balls he was getting and that it took his ball forever to get to the pins, Jack got mad and demanded to use the bumpers to help him. He started aiming his ball toward the bumper where with each bumper tap the ball would ricochet to the opposite bumper giving the bowling ball a little more momentum with each bumper tap. Jack finally could achieve the score he wanted and even got several strikes this way. It was unbelievable to watch.

OCTOBER 14, 2004—Jack and I are at Saddle Up! and he is spreading his joy all around today. I do not know where this bad mood came from. I think it is time for fall break to be over. Jack does so much better with the schedule he gets at school. I cannot schedule his day at home like it is at school. Benny has been spending time with friends, and Jack has been watching quite a lot of the Weather Channel on TV. He loves the Weather Channel. He shares some of the facts and figures they talk about in different parts of the world. Benny's birthday is soon. He will be ten years old. Time does fly!

OCTOBER 21, 2004—I just got out of a school meeting where I finally met Jack's new special education teacher. I took brownies to share so everyone would be happy and fed with a little sugar and caffeine. (And because last year an assistant principal fell asleep in one of Jack's IEP meetings. So, from now on, I will bring chocolate to every IEP.)

OCTOBER 28, 2004—Benny's 10th birthday today. I am at Saddle Up! again as I write this. It's getting harder and harder to get Jack motivated to come here again. He is getting tired of horseback riding...again. Hopefully, the last session is coming up soon, and we can have some Saddle Up! time off. We are taking Benny out for dinner for his birthday tonight. We always let the boys choose where and what they want to eat on their special day since most of the time, their actual special day is during the week, not on weekend party time. Once his birthday celebrating is over, then it's on to Halloween.

NOVEMBER 4, 2004—At Saddle Up! for the last session. We gave Benny a new PlayStation game for his birthday that is rated Teen. Little did we know it had bad language that now Jack has heard and is using. Won't church be fun now! Here at Saddle Up!, the boys received blue ribbons for their great participation and for learning new riding skills during this session. The boys were so proud of them, touching them whenever they could. Jack was thrilled

... BUT I'M NOT THE SINGER

and very proud of his blue ribbon. After we got home, we went out to eat. Jack wanted to wear his blue ribbon to the restaurant. We loaded up in the van, but Benny remembered he had forgotten his Gameboy, so Ben took Benny back inside the house to find it. While they were gone, Jack and I were talking about the van being out of gas and eating out. I told him we were headed to the gas station and then we would go to eat. Jack replies to me, "Mom, let's go eat first and then get gas." I said, "Great idea Jack. I didn't think of that!" He said to me so calmly and seriously, "Mom, that's why I have this blue ribbon!" I love this child so much! Halloween is behind us. Benny wore a giant soccer ball head mask with a black cape, and Jack was a doctor. Benny took off with his neighborhood buddies and Ben took Jack around the neighborhood trick or treating. I stayed home and gave out candy.

NOVEMBER 14, 2004—I am sitting outside while Ben and Benny are playing soccer in the front yard with one of the neighborhood kids. Jack is inside playing with money, one of his new favorite things to do. As I was leaving the house to come outside, I told Jack where I would be. He told me, "OK. Look out for bears!" I have no clue where that one came from. He has been coming home telling us jokes he has heard at school from the other students. Some have been funny, some have been just downright silly, and some had been inappropriate. I explained to him that if he doesn't understand what a word means, he needs to come home and ask me before he repeats it. I think this will be a long and hard thing for him to learn. He also doesn't always know what is funny and what is not. Sometimes he will tell us a joke and ask us if it was funny. He wants to be funny but has no clue if some things are or not. I don't think it's very funny to have to teach my child what is funny and what is not.

He has been so good the last few days even eating out two times and not fretting over the absence of ceiling fans.

He was also reassessed for occupational services. Reevaluations can and usually are difficult for Jack. This one was not an exception. His therapist noted, "It is felt Jack's responses may or may not have consistently or accurately reflected his true abilities, and that should be taken into consideration with its interpretation. There were frequent times that Jack was distracted and required frequent redirecting to the task at hand." At one point during the assessment, he said, "This is hard. I want to be done." But of course, they must plow forward. He commented on the buzzing of the fluorescent lights during one part of the evaluation. He said, "I hear noises. I hate noises."

MY NAME IS JACK JOHNSON...

NOVEMBER 28, 2004—So much has happened lately. I am behind on writing. I will start with the passing of my sister's mother-in-law. Amy, my oldest sister, has been married several years and has always been close to her mother-in-law, Frances. Since Frances's other sons live out of town and she had no other family nearby, she had spent Thanksgiving and Christmas with our family at Amy's house. We always enjoyed her company, her prim and proper attitude, and her ability to withstand the noise and confusion that comes with being around a large family. After a short illness, she peacefully passed away wearing freshly applied makeup, always wanting to look her best. We didn't have a babysitter for Frances' visitation, so Amy suggested we bring the boys. Jack had never seen anyone in a funeral home and had lots of questions before and after we arrived. Once inside, Amy walked hand in hand with Jack up to the open casket so Jack could see Frances. Amy said to Jack, "Doesn't she look pretty?" Jack replied, "No." He asked Amy if the funeral home was Frances' home. Amy told him no. Then he asked if it was Jesus' home. I had previously explained to Jack that when we die, we go to see Jesus and since Frances was dead, he naturally thought she was with Jesus, and since he was seeing her at this place, it must be where Jesus lives. Amy turned to speak with some friends who had walked up to her, turning her back to Jack. Jack blurted out, "How old was that dead woman?" Embarrassed, I pulled Jack away and let Amy visit with her friends. I asked Jack if he had any more questions and he asked me, "Mom, under her eyes, are there X's?" It took a while for me to understand this question. I had to get Jack to explain what "X's" he was talking about. When I finally understood he was referring to X marks over someone's eyes, it dawned on me my child had watched too many cartoons. When a cartoon character dies, their eyes become "X" to insinuate that the character has passed away. The next day Ben had to go to Nashville and asked Jack if he wanted to go with him for the ride. Jack asked Ben, "Are we going back to see that dead woman?" Death is hard enough for us to understand much less someone with autism.

DECEMBER 30, 2004—The year is almost over. I am so behind on writing. I will start today with Jack and his new-found love of money. He loves it! He asks people for it, he plays with it and gives it back when he is finished. He has learned all the names of the pictured men on each bill. He doesn't want to spend it, he only plays with it, looks at it, recites each president's name, and it goes back to whoever gave it to him. At Thanksgiving at Amy's, he asked others for money, received one hundred and seventy-six dollars, played with

... BUT I'M NOT THE SINGER

it most of the time we were there and gave it all back when we got ready to leave. I received some Christmas money so one Sunday at church, I let him play with a hundred-dollar bill I had hidden in my billfold. Jack was so good all the way through church. Even the preacher said something about Jack's good behavior as we walked out of the sanctuary. He has learned so much about the presidents while he has been playing with money. One day he got off the bus crying. He had just been told that all the presidents on the money bills were dead. He had asked me before about the White House and how the presidents had all lived there. I didn't clarify they all lived at the White House but not at the same time! His literal mind thought ALL presidents still were alive and living at the White House! Jack was so, so sad about the presidents.

Before Christmas break, we joined some family members for a Christmas gathering at their house. Our hosts have a son of their own who is a few years younger than my boys, and other family members brought their son who is around the same age as our host's son. All four of the boys headed to our host's son room to play with his toys while all the adults sat and visited with each other. We had a wonderful meal, and when finished, all the boys ran back to play in the boy's bedroom. Ben and I were checking on the boys, making sure our two were playing nice, and everything was cohesive. We were sitting on the couch together when the host's son comes into the family room holding a stuffed Spiderman toy and crying. He walked straight to his mother who asked him what was wrong. The little boy said he was playing with his favorite toy, his stuffed Spiderman, when Jack grabbed it from his hands and ripped the arm of Spiderman in the process. This little guy was so heartbroken, sitting in his mother's lap, crying while holding onto his ripped and torn Spiderman. I began apologizing profusely and left the room to find my toy terrorizing son. I found Jack on the top bunk of the bedroom's bunk beds. I asked him to get down and told him what Spiderman's owner has said. Jack said nothing when I asked him why. I told him that he was in time-out and needed to sit with his father and me on the couch for the next few minutes.... after he apologized to everyone involved in the Spiderman incident. I was so mad at Jack. I could not believe he tried to take Spiderman away from anyone or that he had pulled so hard on it that it ripped. Finally, Ben and I decided to go home; we said our goodbyes with more apologies, got in our van and headed home. Again, I was still upset and mad over Jack's unexpected behavior. So, I asked Jack about it again. Before he could answer, Benny said, "Mom, I can't blame Jack for trying to take Spiderman away. The other boys were hitting Jack with their toys, and

MY NAME IS JACK JOHNSON...

when Jack got tired of it, he grabbed the toy that hit him next, and it ripped when he did." I almost fell out of my seat. I asked Benny to describe the whole scene again before Spiderman got ripped. Benny told us Jack was sitting on the bunk bed, playing by himself with a toy when the other two boys started hitting Jack with the toys they had been playing with. Jack told them to stop hitting him several times and just got tired of them hitting at him. So, when Spiderman hit Jack that last time, Jack grabbed at it and pulled it to get it away from the boy who was using it to hit him. When Jack pulled on Spiderman, his arm ripped. The owner of Spiderman started crying, left the room, and came to tell his mother what had happened. Unfortunately, the boy had left out the part about how he was hitting Jack with his beloved stuffed Spiderman. I asked Jack if that was what had happened and he shyly, with his head down said, "Yes." I then asked Benny why he didn't speak up and say something when we punished Jack for what we had been told had happened. Benny said, "I didn't want to get into an argument about what had happened with the other kid since we were at their house. And I didn't want to make the other kids mad at me either for taking up for Jack." What a mess! Jack didn't know to take up for himself, and Benny didn't feel comfortable at our host's house telling on the other children there. Before I talked to either one of them about this episode, I had to take a few minutes to decide what I wanted to say. So, the rest of the trip home, I cried. I felt so bad having put Jack in timeout for something that wasn't his fault. His only sin was pulling on the arm of Spiderman instead of coming to let us know what was happening. I felt so bad for Benny and the situation he had been put in and not feeling as if he could tell everyone there the real story. I just cried. After we got home and Ben and I discussed the whole scenario, we talked to Benny and told him that it was OK to let us know the whole story when he witnessed things were not right, not just for his brother but for anyone in his world. Right is right and wrong is wrong in any situation. If Benny witnessed a wrong of any kind, he needed to let us know. We reassured him we were not mad, but he needs to let us know when he sees some wrong being done to his brother or anyone else. As for Jack, we talked to him about coming to us when others are not treating him nicely so we can step in and deal with it. We reiterated how important it is for him to let an adult know with his words than to take matters into his own hands. This one day was a learning experience for all of us. Benny needed to learn to stand up for himself, his brother and anyone who is being wronged by another person. Jack learned he needed to tell others when he was being

...BUT I'M NOT THE SINGER

treated unfairly. Ben and I learned that we desperately need to investigate any situation that involves Jack and another person especially when we are only given one side of a two-sided ordeal. Each day is another day to learn for all of us.

FEBRUARY 4, 2005—For a few years, our church has been publishing a Lenten Devotional Book so members of our church could share a personal story with a Bible verse that goes with their story. The stories can be about certain occasions or a special time where you felt the presence of God in your world. The stories are as varied as the people who wrote and shared them. This year's "Seeds of Faith" had a very personal story in it about Jack written by his special friend, Misses Luna.

Scripture: Do not neglect to show hospitality to strangers, for by doing that some have entertained angels without knowing it. Hebrews 13:2.

He sits on the very back row of the 8:15 service every Sunday morning with his family. He always has a stuffed animal named "Dory" and sometimes his parents are troubled because his behavior is not ideal for an eight-year-old, but he is my "special friend," and God sends me a message through him each week. His name is Jack, and he has autism. I have learned to look at our church through Jack's eyes which means studying every exit sign and every ceiling fan in the building because taking a walk and looking at the same exit signs and ceiling fans is Jack's reward of choice for doing his work in Sunday School each week. If you ask Jack, he can tell you what exit signs have burned out lights and how many blades each ceiling fan has in the different classrooms. He has a wonderful sense of humor, and he is very smart. But if God had not sent Jack and his family into my life by way of a special teacher and friend, I would only see a little boy on the back row who talks out loud to a stuffed animal during church. I would probably roll my eyes when he acted inappropriately and never guess what an incredible compass this eight-year-old possesses. One day I went to the supply room to get him a piece of paper to draw exit signs on, and he stopped me and said, "No, Misses Luna, these are God's materials, and we shouldn't bother them." It was a comment that made me grin at the time, but I have often thought about it when I start to thoughtlessly borrow something from a classroom or the desk of a church secretary. Jack's autism affects his socialization skills, and he probably won't ever have a leading role in a children's pageant as an angel but make no mistake about it when you pass a noisy little boy on the back row at 8:15. He is a messenger from God for all who will "entertain strangers."

MY NAME IS JACK JOHNSON...

Prayer: Dear God, please don't let me judge others when I don't know them or understand their challenges. Help me to be open to the message you send to me through people who look at the world in a different way than I do. Thank you for the gift of "special friends" in this church. Amen.

CHAPTER 13

APRIL 4, 2005—Easter went by without a hitch. Jack's birthday is in six days, but we have already given him his gift: a trampoline. He needed the exercise so badly and something to do over spring break that we decided to give him an early gift. He jumps on it every day! Yay! —a useful gift!

JUNE 23, 2005—Ben and I finally did it! Something we have dreamed of since we have known each other! We finally bought a houseboat. We are thrilled! It is small and old, but it is still a houseboat. The houseboat has a queen-sized bed in the master bedroom, two bunk beds in the hallway across from a full bath with a shower, a small but usable kitchen with an eating area, and a living room space large enough for the four of us. We have the pontoon boat up for sale and Ben is selling his old, beloved Cadillac convertible to help pay for it. No more driving home in the dark, tired and worn out, from a day of sun and fun in the water. It is docked in Smithville, TN, about an hour and a half from home, the same dock the pontoon was docked in. We are so excited about getting away from the stress of life even hoping it will calm Jack too. We look forward to many happy times in our new boat. Benny chose the name of our new floating digs—"Our Happy Place."

JULY 3, 2005—We are celebrating the Fourth of July at the lake. It has just been the four of us. It is so nice to be surrounded by our stuff......sheets, towels, for the boys—toys. It is almost like home. The boys constantly fight over the GameCube when we are docked in the slip. They play well together when we are out on the water. We don't have electricity when we are away from the dock since the generator on the houseboat doesn't work so we head back to the dock when the sun starts to set. We did a lot of fishing yesterday. We found a quiet cove, anchored the boat, the boys got in the water, and we stayed anchored all day.

MY NAME IS JACK JOHNSON...

We celebrated our first Fourth of July on the lake in our new-to-us houseboat. The marina where the boat is docked puts on a Fourth of July firework show on the water. A barge carrying the fireworks is driven out into a large wide-open space in the lake between several hills, individual coves, and steep cliffs. People from neighboring towns find any open spot along the surrounding hills to watch the fireworks above the marina. Boats from many other marinas on the lake come to watch as well. The atmosphere is festive with boats of all kinds from massive houseboats to one-person kayaks. Once the sky becomes black, it starts—the sky seems to explode in color as each firework twists and turns its way skyward leaving a long trail of light like the tail of a comet. Once high in the sky, the fireworks burst, sending light across the sky. Each firework's shape and color is mirrored below in the black inky waters of the lake. The blasts of each firework as it explodes above our heads expels a mighty rumble that vibrates your organs and reverberates through the neighboring hills and valleys. It is a plethora of lights, sounds, and smells from the alternating colors of the sky and water, the sound of blast echoes moving further away, the smell of gunpowder from the overhead detonation, the sway of the boat on the water.... each adding to the ultimate firework extravaganza. Never will we be excited about land fireworks again.

We spent the whole summer enjoying the boat. We painted stripes on the outside and had the name, "Our Happy Place," put on as well. The boys loved going to the lake, staying in the water for hours at a time. I always took a supply of books to read while I was there so I could sit on the top of the boat for hours myself, listening to the boys play in the water or the birds chirping in the trees. I have always felt the spirit of God whenever I am near a body of water, and I felt it on those moments when the birds were chirping, and the boys were quiet. I justified our absence from Sunday morning church as getting to experience the gifts God gave us to enjoy. It was exciting to watch the boys interact and learn to enjoy each other's company in a different environment. They had this water game they played called "Train." Ben was usually the engine in the front, one boy would be next, and the last one was the caboose. As the engine, Ben would stretch out on his stomach in the water and the next boy would hold on to Ben's feet with his hands and stretch his legs out behind him. The caboose would then hold on to the second boy's feet and stretch his legs out behind him, making a long train of boys in life jackets, floating and swimming around the boat. It always brought a smile to my face to see them floating along, enjoying their time together.

... BUT I'M NOT THE SINGER

AUGUST 12, 2005—School has started, and the boys have been going for about three weeks. Benny won a Pride Time Award already for being a good math student and for helping others. This year in 5th grade he changes classes, but it doesn't seem to bother him a bit. He just goes with the flow. He likes all his teachers and is now having to take band. In fifth grade, the students get a choice between band or choir, and he chose band. He is playing the saxophone that is almost as big as he is even though Benny is a tall boy for his age.

On weekends when we stayed at the lake on the houseboat, at least one morning we woke up and instead of cooking breakfast, we took advantage of the marina restaurant. With the wide range of different breakfast foods, it was easier and less costly for us to eat at the restaurant than try to satisfy everyone's different wants on the houseboat. One restaurant breakfast morning, Jack ventured out from his regular breakfast diet and ordered pancakes. Jack had never eaten pancakes, but he wanted to try. He ordered scrambled eggs, bacon, and pancakes, but instead of eating pancakes smeared with butter and drowned in syrup, Jack ate his with ketchup. Yes, ketchup. It was the most disgusting thing for me to watch as he took a piece of pancake that had previously been cut into four equal pieces, and slowly and precisely pulled the pancake piece through his puddle of ketchup on his plate. I didn't have to eat them, thank goodness. Once he ate pancakes and ketchup, he looked forward to eating at the marina restaurant every time we stayed overnight on the houseboat.

Jack also started another houseboat routine. He would walk the docks to see all the ceiling fans on the other docked houseboats. After walking all the docks in the marina, memorizing every ceiling fan, he would come back to our houseboat and sit for hours drawing each fan he saw on his walk. This became a lake trip routine just in case someone put up another fan in the place of one he had drawn before or a new houseboat with a ceiling fan had recently docked at the marina. Since our boat did not have a ceiling fan and we needed to have some electrical work done, we also had electricity put on the front deck's ceiling of our houseboat so we could have a ceiling fan. Jack got to shop for it and helped pick out the one we put up. He was thrilled!

Jack told someone the other day, "I'm not even in your fan club!" I didn't know where it came from until Benny told me the line came from the "Cars" movie. We will have to make sure Jack only watches G rated movies since now he is repeating lines from movies. I cannot imagine what would come out of his mouth if he watched an R rated movie!

MY NAME IS JACK JOHNSON...

SEPTEMBER 19, 2005—Jack and I are at Saddle Up! He has decided to ride horses again. And this gives me a chance to write each week we are here. Ben has been away on a rare out of town job. It was just the boys and me for a few days. They were pretty good while Ben was gone. Last Sunday Jack had a real nasty come-apart at Sunday School. He even bit me! This past Sunday without Ben, I was a nervous wreck dreading another come-apart from Jack. I talked to him before church, and he shared with me that he would be OK if he had Sunday School class in the Computer Room. I don't have control over which class his age group attends, so we are at the mercy of the rotation system. I prayed God would intervene on my behalf and let Jack have Computer Class that Sunday. And behold! Jack had Computer Class, and all was right in Jack's world. Thanks, God. After church, we went to our every-two-week restaurant for lunch and behold again! —they had installed a new ceiling fan! Jack was in heaven on this particular day. Before church, Jack and I had made a deal.... if he was good for me at church and behaved, we would go to Home Depot after lunch to look at ceiling fans. Sunday was a Jack kind of day! Benny was like a little protective man in Ben's absence. He helped me out with Jack, did everything I asked him to do without complaint, and had an air of maturity about him. I let him sit up front in the passenger seat beside me in the van. I would watch him walk to the van passenger door, stop himself and run to the front seat door. For me, it was fun to have him up front with me. Last night, he asked if we could walk around the block... just the two of us. We walked for a mile and a half. At one time, he asked if we could hold hands. It was a special moment for me because I know one day he will not want to hold my hand anymore. It was something I will never forget.

Jack and I are bowling again with the special needs bowling crew. Last week, our bowling adventure took an unexpected turn. Usually, Jack bowls, not paying any attention to anyone there except the bowling alley's computerized scorecards. Between each player's bowl, the computer has some silly character that does a dance or goofy activity after a good score. When a bowler gets three consecutive strikes, the computer has three animated turkeys who run quickly around on the score screen. Jack loves to watch the turkeys running so he has been more aware of the other bowlers around him, watching for those bowlers who score strikes. This new-found awareness made Jack also aware of other things as well. I had noticed there was a young lady with special needs bowling in the lane next to Jack's that had an unusual way to bowl. This young lady also had a facial disability that

...BUT I'M NOT THE SINGER

affected her mouth. Even though she had a full set of teeth, her mouth was shaped as if she had lost her teeth. Her face was lovely even though different. Jack had never said anything to me about the way she or any other special needs student there looked. If you carefully watch anyone bowl, special needs or not, each bowler has their unique style when they bowl. On this particular day, Jack was more attentive than usual to his surroundings. Jack got up to bowl, picked up his ball, found his position on the lane, spread his legs wide, and with both hands, rolled his ball down the middle of his lane, something I had not seen him do before. He got a good score, and I didn't think anything else about it. The next time he bowled, he did it again. For Jack's next turn, he parted his legs again and rolled the ball down the middle of the lane, but instead of turning around, he threw his hands up into the air, something he hadn't done before. Still, I didn't think much about his unusual behavior. The next time he got up to bowl, I noticed he was standing in his lane but watching the person in the lane next to him. The young lady walked to the middle of her lane, parted her legs, rolled her bowling ball down the middle of her lane, and held her arms above her head before she turned around to walk back to her seat. I thought to myself surely Jack isn't imitating her. As I sat there pondering this scenario, I watched my son walk to the middle of his lane, open his legs, roll his bowling ball between them, and immediately throw his arms straight into the air.... just like the young lady had bowled in the lane next to him. And to make it worse, when he turned around to face me, he had his mouth drawn in, making his face look as close to her face as he could. I was horrified. I jumped up and asked him what he was doing. He looked at me so innocently and said, "Nothing." I asked him, "What are you doing with your mouth?" His reply caught me completely off guard when he said to me, "Well, she's doing it!" talking about the young lady bowling next to us. Jack had no clue that the young lady's mouth was part of her disability. He thought she was holding her mouth that way on purpose and if she could do it, then he could too. We had a long talk about the whole situation on the way home, but not after I talked to some of the recreation center personnel on whether anyone else had witnessed Jack's imitation skills. It was an embarrassing moment for me.

OCTOBER 10, 2005—At Saddle Up! again. I didn't think we would make it here. Jack cannot wear any of his pants from last year. We had to put on four pairs of pants before we found one to fit. The ones he has on are a little big, but they should be comfortable for riding horses.

MY NAME IS JACK JOHNSON...

At church Sunday, we were too late to get the back seats in the sanctuary. Our pastor was not there that day because when he is there, he makes sure we have extra chairs to make a back seat if needed. We had to sit three rows up from the back seat. Jack was not happy, started to blurt out his displeasure while getting louder and louder. I tried very hard to convince him it would be OK to sit where we were but he wasn't listening to me. Finally, he just picked up his chair, took it to the back of the church and made a new back row for himself. In moments like these, I have learned to assess the situation. First, I try to change his mind like I had done before he moved his chair. I tried to redirect him by distracting him with a toy or something else. While I am doing this, I am also thinking of a "plan B" just in case what I am doing is not working. I am also clicking off in my head the "should I" or "should I not" let him do or continue to do something. While these thoughts are moving around my brain, I am also pondering the "where" we are at that time. So, after my mind assesses the whole situation on this given day, I let him move his chair to the back row. I even moved my chair too. Don't think that is what I wanted to do—it was what I had to do in that situation. In the perfect world, I would convince him to stay in the row we had previously been sitting in because he should not be so rigid in his compulsive behaviors. Since we do not live in that perfect world, I did what I had to do... I moved my chair too. I decided to fight that battle away from the eyes of the members of our church and in a different environment where I might have a better chance of reasoning with Jack. You must choose your battles but also know your limitations. The whole congregation heard and witnessed the whole altercation and chair movement. Ben and Benny stayed in the seats three rows up from us in the "row seats picked" while Jack and I sat three rows back in the "row made" seats. To make matters worse, Jack started to put his ever-present stuffed Nemo and Dory on my head, in my face, and on my chest. I whispered to God to please give me a little extra strength and patience. When the sermon started, Jack talked and laughed through the whole thing. A late arrival came in, one of the ushers pulled up another chair and sat her beside Jack and me. Since Jack was still being a chatterbox, I had to keep reminding him to be quiet. Then he loudly asks, "Where's Jesus?" I whispered (trying to be an example of how he should talk to me in church) to him that Jesus was in heaven with God. The lady who had been seated next to us leaned toward me and said, "You are such a good mother. I'm visiting from New Orleans. You do a great job with him." After I said, "thank you," I felt so vindicated by her words since that day at church had been an unusually difficult one with Jack. It was nice to be

... BUT I'M NOT THE SINGER

noticed since most people noticed Jack and very loud and, in your face, bad behavior. It's a lot harder to see and recognize a mother's hard work when she is teaching a child of any age and ability how to act appropriately in a church environment. On this difficult day, this visitor was an angel of God to me. I wanted to thank her again for her sweet words, but as soon as the service was over, she disappeared. I looked and looked for her but did not see her in the moving crowd. I will never forget her words of encouragement to me that day.

We now have another special friend adult at church to help with Jack during Sunday School. Her name is Miss Stephanie, and she has a daughter in the same age group as Jack. She is a class assistant in her daughter's Sunday School class and has started to volunteer to help with Jack. It is great for Misses Luna and for us. Misses Luna always feels so bad when she is out of town knowing that if she is not there to help Jack, we usually don't attend Sunday School. With Miss Stephanie on board, Misses Luna can be out, and we can still attend Sunday School. Miss Stephanie and her daughter sit near us in the church service as well and will be there for us if needed during worship.

DECEMBER 27, 2005—For Benny's birthday we left Jack with babysitters and took Benny to a soccer tournament in Bowling Green, KY. That's what Benny wanted to do. Halloween was uneventful with Benny dressed as a hippie with peace signs and a big afro and Jack dressed as a referee with a yellow flag and whistle. I think by next year they will be too big for dressing up at Halloween. Our Thanksgiving was quiet with just the four of us staying home on Thanksgiving Day enjoying the food we like served in our own dining room on my unused Christmas bird china. It was nice to be by ourselves as a family.

Something wonderful happened a few Sundays ago. There is this sweet couple at church that have befriended us. They don't have children of their own but have always been so nice to both our boys. They understand Jack has autism, but it doesn't seem to bother them. This couple volunteers quite a lot at church as ushers and greeters. Mrs. H one Sunday asked Jack if he would like to help her as a greeter handing out the church bulletin at the door as members walk into the sanctuary. Much to my surprise, Jack said yes, helped, and loved it. This most recent Sunday, Mrs. H asked Jack if he would like to help her take up the offering during the service. I was skeptical, but he said he would like to do it. When time to take up the offering came, Mrs. H came and got Jack. She walked with him explaining what he was to do, which aisle to move the collection plate to, and where to wait. I stood up so I could see

MY NAME IS JACK JOHNSON...

them better since they were on the opposite side of the church than where we were sitting. Standing in the back of the church watching this child, who has given us so much grief, while he takes up the collection at church was a gift to my heart. I couldn't believe my eyes as Jack moved down the aisle handing the collection plate to the members seated in the rows. Tears flowed down my face as I watched. It was a great Christmas present for me. Once as the collection plate was moving along a row of members, Jack had to check on a nearby Exit sign while he was near it. The pastor said something to him after the service about how well he had done. Lots of other people told him "good job, Jack." I found Mrs. H after the service, hugged her, and told her how she had just given me the greatest Christmas present ever.

CHAPTER 14

What a way to start a new year! I got a phone call from Jack's special education teacher, Ms. P., formerly known as Miss D. She got married and just changing her name has been different for Jack. I had to explain why women change their names once they get married. But that wasn't why I got the phone call. Jack got on the school bus later than usual in the afternoon, and there wasn't an empty seat for him to sit. He walked through the bus looking for a seat with one person in it, so he explained to me. When he found a seat with one student in it, he asked if he could sit down and the student said "No!" So, Jack spit on him! He cannot act this way if he wants to continue to ride a regular education bus, not the special needs bus. Ben and I want him to ride the regular bus in case in the future he should use public transportation to get to and from a job, the grocery, or any other place an adult Jack would need transportation to and from. But he can't spit on people. The bus driver had to write up a "Bus Conduct Report" and report the behavior to the school's Central Office. Jack doesn't understand this type of social situation and we, as the adults in charge of him and his well-being, must step in for Jack's safety and welfare. Ms. P and I think it is necessary for Jack to have an assigned seat on the bus just in case another student will not let him sit with them. Was it right for Jack to spit on a student? No, but it also wasn't right for another student to deny an open seat for Jack, in my honest opinion. Ms. P is going to discuss the whole matter with Central Office, the bus driver, and Jack to make complete sure everyone knows and agrees to this arrangement. What a way to start the new year, I repeat!

MAY 20, 2006—It's the new year, and I haven't had time to write at all until now. We bought a new boat, a runabout as they call them. It is a small boat that we can use with the houseboat. The boys can tube behind it, Ben can ski behind it, and we can fish from it. Jack likes it because it goes fast

MY NAME IS JACK JOHNSON...

Ben's grandmother passed away in March, and my grandfather passed away in April. We called Ben's grandmother, Mimi. Jack once studied Mimi's face, placed his hand on her face, and told her, "Mimi, you sure have lots of wrinkles." With her true Southern Charm and manners, Mimi said to Jack, "Yes, I do." In Jack's true autistic say-anything mouth, he said, "I think you are old. I bet you die soon." Thank goodness, Mimi snickered as I corrected Jack and made him apologize. We called my grandfather "Pops" for as long as I can remember. He was living with my Dad at the time of his death under the care of hospice. Pops had a small viewing for just close family members and then a graveside service. Most of the family couldn't attend the private family viewing since it was during the week, but most of them came to the graveside service. My uncle Johnny said a few words and a prayer at the grave. Before the casket was lowered, my Dad, knowing so many in the family didn't get to say goodbye to Pops at the private viewing, asked if anyone wanted to see and say goodbye to Pops one final time. There was dead silence. A small, close-to-me voice said, "I want to see Pops, Pawpaw." It came from Jack. The funeral home worker opened the casket for the family who wanted to say their goodbyes. While he was doing this, Jack got up, took his ever-present stuffed Nemo and Dory, placed them on a nearby tombstone facing Pops' grave and walked over to the now open casket, standing with his Pawpaw. I will never forget Jack and his grandfather, Jack, standing there, side by side looking at Pops together. Then everyone who had not had the chance to say goodbye walked to the casket. There were lots of tears shed as each cousin said their goodbye to our grandfather that day. I was so proud of Jack for speaking up and unknowingly giving my extended family one last chance to say goodbye to our grandfather.

Again, we spent our Fourth of July watching the fireworks exploding over the water, but this year we watched from the runabout. We could lay down and watch from that view as the fireworks exploded above our heads. This year the overhead fireworks dropped small pieces of ash on us after each blast. We laughed and had so much fun.

One Sunday, while anchored in a cove, the boys swam in the water most of the day. Benny took a break from the water while Jack, in the water alone, asked Ben to come in the water with him. Ben, after drinking a bottled water, got in and threw the now empty bottle to Jack. Jack loved to play in the water and gladly grabbed the empty water bottle his dad had thrown to him. Jack filled the empty bottle with lake water. Out of the blue, he asked his dad to come to him. Then he poured the water over his dad's head. Then he shocked

...BUT I'M NOT THE SINGER

us both by telling his dad, "I now 'bab-tize' you in the name of the Father, Son, and Holy Ghost." Then he repeated the whole Lord's prayer, a prayer our church repeated each Sunday as long as we had been members. The same Lord's prayer I had asked Jack to read and repeat just like every other person in our church. The same Lord's prayer I believed my son did not know since he always refused to read or repeat each time I asked him to. As I sat on the top of our houseboat, tears filled my eyes as I heard and watched Jack pretend to "bab-tize" his dad while repeating the whole Lord's prayer, much to our delight and surprise.

We found another slight problem dealing with Jack or shall I say the problem found us.... through our noses. Jack had become a smelly cat. Body odor had started to reveal itself. When the weather was hot, and he had been in the water for a while, there was an imaginary green cloud of funky smells above his head. Ben and I talked to Jack about starting to wear deodorant much to his displeasure. He doesn't want to wear deodorant but must start wearing it because he smells. Ben tells Jack he smells like onions which makes Jack very mad. In reply, Jack will yell, "ONIONS ARE VEGETABLES AND I AM NOT A VEGETABLE!" This change for Jack is going to be another fun adventure.

SEPTEMBER 6, 2006—The boys are in full swing back to school. They are now 5th and 6th graders.

Both boys are in band this year. Benny is playing the saxophone again, and Jack is playing the xylophone or as they are now called, "the orchestra bells," the "bells" for short. It took some persuasion to get the band director to take on a band member with autism, but Jack has done well with it. He needs to have an assistant with him during band class and at his band concerts but hopefully, that won't always be the case. He follows the music well and likes to play. I hope this turns out to be a wonderful opportunity for him.

SEPTEMBER 19, 2006—Jack had his first band concert. It was called the "Premier Concert" and was the first time all the 5th grade classes had played together in one place. This concert was a trial run for upcoming concerts. His assistant came to sit with Jack to keep him focused. I was a nervous wreck, my mind a jumbled mess of "what if" scenarios. Putting it mildly, Jack's behavior was bad. I made a list of behaviors I thought were not appropriate for him; like talking out loud, pretending to shoot parents with his xylophone sticks, making faces at me and Ben and other parents, hitting his sticks

MY NAME IS JACK JOHNSON...

together, playing while the band teacher was talking to the audience, and not sitting up in his chair. Since this was a trial run for band concerts of the future, we now have behaviors that will have to be addressed in a social story to give him insight to what is expected of him during a concert.

Another strange learning experience for everyone at school with Jack and autism... Jack was in Science class sitting at the table with several other students. The class was playing a game of question ball—for lack of a better term—where the teacher throws a little, soft ball around the room for the students to catch after she has asked a question. The student that she throws the ball to has to answer the question. The student then throws the ball back to the teacher, and the whole process starts again with another new question. The teacher threw the ball to Jack, and the student nearest to him caught it instead. Jack did not like this and loudly said, "I do not like dark skinned people" because he was mad and the student who caught the ball was African American. Jack was pulled from the classroom by the teacher, and once in the hallway, she tells Jack how ugly his statement was and how we should be kind to all students of different colors, abilities, and ethnic backgrounds. All Jack heard was how bad he had been to another student even though the student had caught his question ball. The teacher gave Jack a punishment card which made Jack even madder. He went to Mrs. D.'s classroom. I received a phone call from the teacher about the situation, and we decided to meet briefly the next morning. At the meeting, I explained to everyone in attendance that Jack did not mean he didn't like African Americans; he was just mad, and the only thing he could come up with that wasn't out of line was that he didn't like "dark-skinned people." I asked the teachers if Jack was a prejudiced student didn't they think he would use a more inappropriate name than saying "dark-skinned people?" I also shared with them that if the student who caught the ball had been red-headed with freckles, Jack would have said, "I do not like red-heads with freckles." Jack knows no color when it comes to people. He has an understanding that some of us are different in how we look or act but he does not discriminate. He doesn't have the capacity to judge others by their skin color. He does judge others by the way they treat other people but not their outward appearance. We are not a prejudice family seeing everyone as equal. Funny too, that Jack's best friend is his African American friend who has autism too. After I explained all of this to the teachers, they were fine again. I did talk to Jack about what he had said, what the teacher thought he meant, and how the situation was misunderstood by all.

...BUT I'M NOT THE SINGER

Jack came home with a new saying. I had asked him to take the dishes out of the dishwasher. He responded that he could not take the dishes out because "I am weak and worthless and have tiny muscles and man boobs." I will never know where these things come from!

DECEMBER 5, 2006—Another band concert—this one better than the first Hopefully, one day soon, we can watch Jack play without an assistant and without any behaviors that are not appropriate for a band member.

DECEMBER 19, 2006—I am sitting in a local coffee shop drinking coffee, writing, and waiting for a 9:30 meeting at school. I have a meeting to meet Jack's teachers and his new classroom assistant. It has been a long, hard year for Jack in school. I believe he has had the wrong assistant. When I say the wrong assistant, I am not saying his assistant was bad. I am saying she was not a good match for Jack. Jack is a head-strong kiddo, needing structure and clear boundaries applied daily by a person who can be strong and firm themselves when Jack needs it. His assistant being such a wonderful person did not have the capacity to provide Jack with the consistent, never changing firmness he needs to understand his boundaries. She was a delightful free spirit who would give Jack anything he wanted, but this was not necessarily what he needed. Some days, he would be late for class or getting on the bus which would set him off into a come apart. She didn't understand the reality that if you let Jack do something once, he believes he should and will do it again. All the warning signs were there, but I think we—myself and Jack's teachers—thought with a little more direction, things would get better. It all came crashing down about two weeks ago. Jack had had a come apart on Friday at school that lasted two hours. Mrs. D had called me for helpful suggestions/ideas. Jack's assistant had done something that had set off the come apart. He did calm down but was not the same for the rest of that day or for the whole weekend that followed. On Monday, he seemed better. On my way to a luncheon, Ben called saying the school principal had called home and wanted to see us as soon as possible. Once at school, Ben and I were whisked away to a conference room where we were met with the long faces of Mrs. D and the principal. We were told Jack had had another bad morning. His assistant had given Jack 2 behavior warnings, and on the 3rd warning, he was asked to leave the classroom. His assistant and the classroom teacher forcefully and physically got Jack out in the hallway where he proceeded to explode in anger. He hit the teacher in the chest with his fist and kicked his assistant in the shin.

MY NAME IS JACK JOHNSON...

The assistant was fine, but the teacher had just returned to school from having open heart surgery weeks prior. Jack had hit the teacher in the chest right in the surgical scar that was still tender. The teacher had to leave school to see his doctor to make sure everything was alright. Ben and I were shocked! Jack had never been this violent before. If he had been a typical student, he would be expelled from school because this was classified as a criminal assault on a teacher. Because Jack had autism and was a special needs student, the school had to deal with this. The four of us in the meeting decided to send Jack home for the remainder of the day as punishment—something he did not want to do. He had no clue the magnitude of what he had done. As we went home with Jack in tow, my mind was racing with thoughts. Was the teacher still OK? Would Jack's school record be flagged with this incident for the rest of his life? I was feeling sick to my stomach. Then I thought about Jack. He was upset because he had to leave school early not because he had done a terrible thing. He had no understanding of the seriousness of his actions. I told Ben we needed to use this situation as a learning opportunity for Jack to help him understand how his actions have consequences. I asked Ben to call the city police department to see if anyone would be willing to talk to an autistic boy who had just crossed a line by hitting a teacher at school. Ben talked to a warden at the local juvenile detention center who said, "Bring him on in." We explained to Jack on the way there where we were going, what could have happened if he didn't have autism, and what he was going to see. He was afraid we were going to leave him and asked as we walked in if he could hold our hands. The warden gave us a tour of the facility with a view of some juveniles who were incarcerated there. We showed Jack the locked cells, explained the things you don't get to have there, and what his life would be like. Jack went into an empty jail cell and once inside, the warden shut and locked the cell door. There was a small vertical window in the door where we could see Jack, and he could see us. The look on his face told us we had indeed made our point. From that day forward, Jack has talked about "junior jail" or just "Jubie" for short. He hasn't hit or kicked anyone since.

JANUARY 2, 2007—Jack gave me the ultimate Christmas present this year. As I have written, Jack is playing the xylophone or bells in the 5th-grade band. On Christmas Day at Ben's sister's house, the adults were sitting around talking while the children were upstairs playing. I heard their piano start playing but thought that one of their children was sharing their musical talents with us. Ben, with a strange look on his face, said, "That piano music is the

...BUT I'M NOT THE SINGER

same music from Jack's Christmas band concert." We followed the music and there sitting at the piano playing the same songs from the band concert sat Jack. We were floored. How did he know how to take the music from the bells and play it on the piano, an instrument he has never played before? Of course, I cried. It was the perfect Christmas present. I see piano lessons in someone's future now.

CHAPTER 15

JANUARY 19, 2007—Both boys have recently received Pride Time awards at school. Benny received one for being an all-around good person at school. We were so proud of him.

Jack won a Pride Time award for having courage. His homeroom teacher, Mrs. G., called me the night before the award was presented. She told me the story of how Jack had received this award. The whole 5th grade at school had been learning and discussing courage, who were people they thought had courage and what made that person courageous. After they discussed courage, each 5th grade class took a vote to see who they thought was the most courageous boy or girl in each class. Jack was nominated as the most courageous boy in Mrs. G.'s class. Then the whole 5th grade took each classroom's most courageous person and took another vote of just those names to see who the entire 5th grade thought was the most courageous student in their 5th grade classes. Jack won by a landslide. Jack had previously won Pride Time awards in the past but had never walked to the stage to accept them himself. After his teacher called me to tell me about the award to be presented the next morning, I told Jack about how the whole 5th grade thought he had the most courage of any student in the 5th grade. He told me he didn't think he could walk up to the stage and get the award. I explained to him if all the students in 5th grade thought he was courageous, he had to show them how courageous he really was by walking to the stage and getting his award himself. Put in those terms, Jack agreed. The next morning, Ben and I got ready and took the boys to school. I was already an emotional wreck just thinking about other students thinking Jack had lots of courage even though he had autism. Ben and I found seats on the front row of the parent's section in the auditorium and watched Jack walk in and sit with his class in the bleachers. Some of Jack's previous teachers and even the principal walked over to me and Ben to tell us how proud they were of Jack and his award. By this time, my tears are flowing.

...BUT I'M NOT THE SINGER

The assembly started with awards given to the lower grade students first. When the 5th grade awards started, I still wasn't completely sure Jack would walk up to get his award. The principal read the award, announced the winner, Jack Johnson, and Jack and his assistance walked down the aisle to the podium. When Jack stood up to walk the aisle so did every 5th grade student, giving him a standing ovation! I was a crying mess by this time. I saw other teachers crying as well. Even Ben had tears in his eyes. Jack got his award, had his picture made, and walked back to the bleachers. The 5th graders on the front row of the bleachers gave Jack high fives as he walked back to the stairs. He did it! He showed his courage to everyone there! I was awestruck by the courage of the 5th grade students to give an award to a student with autism. There was no selfishness, no peer pressure to give the award to the most popular, no animosity. I saw a group of beyond-their-years wise students who had witnessed the struggles of a peer and recognized that student for his continued strength in the face of his many challenges. I saw the maturity of character in a group of young people who had seen and acknowledged the strife a peer faces daily from an obscure adversary. It takes a lot of insight to see this in others. I shared this story with the director of the school district who wrote a letter and a Certificate of Recognition that states:

"The Franklin Special School District presents this certificate to the 2006-2007 5th Grade Class.

"Your support and encouragement of a fellow student has been a shining example of compassion and kindness to others. You have provided the entire school with an extraordinary moment of greatness simply by living the character traits you have learned."

I also wrote the 5th graders a letter of appreciation and placed a library book in the school's library in honor of the entire 5th-grade class. What a wonderful moment it was for all of us especially Jack.

Jack's special education teacher started a new reward system for Jack to be used with his behavior plan. Mrs. D. has a classroom pet—a guinea pig named Pepper. Pepper is gray, lives in a large cage in Mrs. D.'s room, makes lots of noise and squeals, eats lots of vegetables and hay, and Jack has become smitten. He will do just about anything to spend time with Pepper. Jack had to be taught how to hold and treat Pepper the appropriate way and how to feed and give her fresh water. His love for Pepper became a great bargaining tool for good behavior from Jack. If he acted appropriately, did what was asked of him, used his time wisely, and was kind and respectful of his teachers, assistant, and other students, he could earn time with Pepper.

MY NAME IS JACK JOHNSON...

2007 Jack spending time with Pepper, the special education classroom pet

He has come home sharing with us stories about his new friend. I have found several pictures he has drawn of Pepper. He is calling her Pepper Ann now. What a great way to motivate him and teach him how to treat small animals.

Jack ended his fifth grade making all A and B averages in each subject on his final report card. He received a Certificate of Achievement recognizing all his hard work. Too bad the teachers didn't receive awards for all their patience and tolerance of Jack and his autistic habits, conduct, and actions. Before school ended, the whole 5th grade had a field trip to, of all places, the Juvenile Justice Center, better known to us as "Jubie Jail." We went to church, and during the pastor's sermon, the word "hell" was mentioned. Jack asked on the way home from church if the pastor was talking about that place we had taken him to after he hit a teacher. We laughed when we figured out Jack had mistaken the word "jail" for "hell." I guess for some criminals, jail can be hell!

Since summer for us is only 6 weeks, before we can turn around, it's back to school time for the boys. Benny is a 7th grader in middle school, and Jack is in the 6th grade. The school hired another special education teacher this year for Jack's grade. Luckily for us, she had been an assistant at the school, so Jack was familiar with her.

Jack had his yearly check-up with his autism doctor who monitors his progress physically, mentally, and socially, prescribes medicine for Jack's sensitivities and obsessions, and gives me information on programs that could be beneficial for Jack and his future. At his appointment, we are called back so Jack can be weighed, his height measured, and his vital signs

... BUT I'M NOT THE SINGER

recorded. Once his vitals are taken, and he is weighed, the nurse gets him to take off his shoes so she can get an accurate height. She takes Jack to a wall where a height measuring apparatus is attached. The nurse tells Jack to stand up against the wall, feet together, so she can get his height. Jack backs up to the measuring stick and puts his feet together, but with his feet touching together, his heels automatically rise, so Jack is standing on his toes. The nurse tells Jack to put his heels flat and put his feet together, but with his heels flat on the floor, Jack cannot put his feet together. When his feet are together, he can only stand on his toes. Since Jack had been toe-walking for so long, he can no longer physically put his feet together with his feet flat. He can flatten his feet, but the space between his feet is about eight inches apart. Jack's doctor recommends he see the school physical therapist for a full evaluation. She also tells us there is a chance Jack will have to wear leg braces to help stretch the tightened heel cords in his legs, a determination she leaves to the physical therapist.

On September 14, 2007, Jack had a full physical therapy evaluation. His teacher and I had prepared Jack for this evaluation in advance explaining what the physical therapist was going to ask him to do. Not only is Jack toe-walking, but his gait is also slower than it should be and his balance is being affected. His heel cords are so tight, they do not allow his feet to move correctly. The P.E. teacher stated to the physical therapist that Jack has difficulty running, jumping, and keeping up with his peers. She also stated that he has a hard time participating in her P.E. class because of the delay in gross motor skills. With the overall lack of strength, the tightness of his heel cords, and the difficulty of participating in physical activities, Jack will now start physical therapy at school once a week. We were also given stretching activities we will do at home with Jack daily.

I have so many questions about this. Why did I not see this problem before it got to this point? Jack has walked on his toes for years. Why didn't anyone say anything about it becoming such a problem to me before now? If he was having such a hard time in P.E. at school, why didn't someone say something to me? We knew he had a hard time participating in P.E. but we didn't understand it was something physical that was hampering him. Mommy guilt comes for a prolonged visit. My mind is full of why's and my heart is broken because I could have stopped this earlier if I had understood what to look for. Parenting is so dang hard especially when your child has special needs and doesn't communicate like a typical child. Surely, a typical child would complain to his parents that he was not able to do the same things in

MY NAME IS JACK JOHNSON...

P.E. as the other children. Jack never said a word except that he hated P.E. He has only complained to his P.E. teacher that he couldn't do an exercise once that I know of because she shared the story with me. But Jack does not share these things with me. When I think about it, Jack doesn't share much about his day with me at all. Unless he has had a bad day, I do not hear or know what has happened in his day if his teachers or assistant do not share it with me. I ask Jack every day how his day was and every day he says "fine" or "OK." So how do I get information from Jack? How do I ask him about his day in a more detailed manner? Since I am not physically at school and do not know exactly what went on each minute of his day, what question should I ask? I am perplexed, feeling so guilty, and wracking my brain trying to figure out what questions I need to ask Jack just to find out how his day truly was.

We expect Jack to become sore with all the physical therapy and heel cord stretching exercises we are doing at home and at school. He doesn't complain if he is in pain. Once the physical therapist began working with Jack on a weekly basis, she decided to bring in an orthotist, a person who equips people needing specialized devices to support or supplement their impaired limbs or joints, to evaluate whether there is a need for leg braces. Once the orthotist evaluated Jack's heel cords, he recommended leg braces that will force Jack's legs and feet into the proper position to correct his toe-walking and tight heel cords.

The orthotist came to school to begin the process of making leg braces for Jack. The leg braces are called AFO's, short for Ankle, Foot Orthotics. Once Jack and I met the orthotist in the physical therapy room, he began the process of making a mold of Jack's legs and feet. Jack never complained and watched as the orthotist covered his legs and feet with the different materials.

A few weeks later, the orthotist brought the braces to school where Jack and I met him again. Jack's feet and legs fit perfectly in the braces. The AFO's themselves are made of a hard plastic material. The upper part of the brace starts a few inches below the back of Jack's knee and attaches to the foot part of the brace. The leg braces only hold the back of Jack's leg stable. The braces are open in the front where Velcro straps hold the sides of the brace together. The foot brace holds Jack's foot in a flat position. It is shaped in the form of Jack's feet and has Velcro straps that hold Jack's feet in place in the brace. Jack has no problem with getting his feet in the braces comfortably. He is also given night braces to wear as he sleeps.

... BUT I'M NOT THE SINGER

OCTOBER 25, 2007—Jack and I are at Saddle Up! again. He trotted last week for the first time in a while. He liked it; his horse did not. On the way home, Jack told me he could feel the horse's sides go in and out when it breathed. I'm sure Jack is a load for a horse. On the way out here, I was talking to Jack, and for some reason, he told me to "speak freely." Where did that one come from?

NOVEMBER 28, 2007—Thanksgiving was peaceful. All Thanksgiving dinners were uneventful, a change from some of the previous years. The boys didn't dress up for Halloween this year—a first. I am having a hard time with Christmas this year since the boys have gotten older. The boys have no idea what they want for Christmas—they have so much already. Benny has gotten old enough to babysit his brother and has money to buy what he wants. Benny doesn't believe in Santa anymore, but Jack still does. I don't like this extra stress at Christmas.

Jack also still believes in the Tooth Fairy. He lost a tooth the other night without telling us, put the tooth under his pillow, and was highly disappointed the next morning when there was no money from the Tooth Fairy. He came downstairs and said, "I don't know what happened to the Tooth Fairy." I asked him, "What do you mean?" He said, "I lost a tooth yesterday, put it under my pillow, but the Tooth Fairy didn't come." Well, what do you say? I acted like I was thinking about his dilemma when I was thinking about mine and Ben's and how we hadn't left any money. I told Jack that maybe the money had fallen out from underneath his pillow since he tosses and turns all night long. I sent Ben upstairs to pick out Jack's clothes for the day and while he was up there, he "found" the Tooth Fairy's money under Jack's bed. Tooth Fairy—0; Mom and Dad—1!

DECEMBER 6, 2007—At Saddle Up! The next to the last session. Last week Jack and his horse trotted without a side walker which means Jack made the horse trot without any assistance. I think he even surprised himself. We found out today that Jack was voted by his classmates the most persevering student in the 6th grade. They will give him an award at the regular Friday school assembly tomorrow. Last year his class awarded him the most courageous student and now, this year, the most persevering. This class of students amazes me with their ability to see the goodness of others. I couldn't have asked for better classmates for him. These students are old souls, wise before their time. Jack has no clue. He would not and could not have gotten this far in school

MY NAME IS JACK JOHNSON...

without the support and love of these peers. There are no bullies in the group that I know of. We feel so blessed by God that Jack is part of such a caring group of students and faculty.

DECEMBER 13, 2007—Tonight is Benny's Christmas band concert at school. Last week at Jack's concert, he had about a 5-note solo which, of course, made me cry. He did well through the whole concert. At the award assembly, he did fine too, but his assistant had to walk with him to get the award. He just could not walk up there alone. I think he will in time.

JANUARY 17, 2008—Happy New Year! Christmas was fast and furious. There was a slight altercation between Jack and a cousin over a bean bag chair, but again some of that is my fault for not watching him more closely.

FEBRUARY 23, 2008—Jack is now wearing leg braces 24 hours a day. It took a while to build up time in the day braces, time for his feet and legs to get adjusted to them. We also had to have them adjusted several times where the braces rubbed red spots on his legs and feet. But now he wears them all day and even puts on his night braces by himself before bed. He is such a trooper. He hardly ever complains about having to wear them. We are so proud of him!

APRIL 10, 2008—Happy birthday to Jack! He is 12 years old today. Wow! After Jack's surprise piano playing at Christmas a few years ago, I have finally found him a piano teacher. He has a new assistant at school, a young lady who majored in music in college. She is very open to teaching Jack how to play piano giving the lessons here at home. Benny tells us he will not play a musical instrument in the future so maybe Jack will be our musician.

MAY 14, 2008—Last night Benny had his end-of-season lacrosse party, and Jack had his Spring band concert. Ben went with Benny, and I took Jack. Benny got a trophy and Ben got to play in a parent versus team pick-up game. Jack did well at the concert. His assistant, Miss S., who is also his piano teacher, sat in the audience and not beside Jack during the concert. This was a first—he has always had an assistant sit next to him at all the previous concerts since he started band. I guess this year has been the most significant year of personal growth for him. He is becoming a teenager and is maturing a lot before our eyes. Jack has been in his own way flirting with girls at school.

... BUT I'M NOT THE SINGER

He got into trouble for walking behind girls wearing flip-flops and stepping on the flip-flops. This is not only dangerous if someone falls but also a way of getting attention. Now watch, Jack will turn out to be a highly charged hormonal teenager and Benny will be the I-don't-care type.

We are now at a soccer game. This could be Benny's last outdoor soccer game since he has lost interest in soccer as his love for lacrosse and football has grown. Jack is sitting here drawing his favorite thing—florescent lights. He draws them over and over at school and at church. He memorizes which fluorescent bulbs are burned out and then draws a fluorescent light map of whichever room he is drawing. He uses blue, purple, and black for the different hues the bulbs give off and whether the bulb is out. What an amazing mind.

We had a new first for Jack recently: his first Special Olympics. The Special Ed department at PGS participates in the local, yearly Special Olympics and this year Jack was invited to participate. The event was held at the football stadium at the high school Jack will attend when he starts high school in a few years. Ben, Ben's mom, and I attended. Once the games started, the Olympians were separated into different sporting events. There was a ball throw, bocce balls tournament, and lots of running races. Jack ran in the 100-yard dash. We watched with apprehension when he lined up on

2008 Jack receiving his first Special Olympics award

MY NAME IS JACK JOHNSON...

the starting line. Ben and I had walked down closer to the track so I could get pictures and Ben could coach Jack. It was a warm day, and Jack had to run the race in his leg braces. We couldn't believe he did as well as he did, running in front of a crowd with leg braces, but he surprised us. He came in third in his race! Not having very much arm strength he threw the ball, but it didn't go very far. He was a little disappointed in his throw, but he still did an awesome job participating in a new-to-him activity.

At the Special Olympics, a local Sonic restaurant donates and serves lunch for all the participants in the games. All the PGS participants gathered together on the football field for lunch. Each one went through the lunch line and retrieved their hamburger, chips, cookie, and drink. Ben and I walked Jack over to the lunch tent to pick up his lunch. Jack chose a burger, some chips, a cookie, and water. We took his burger over to the condiment table, and when Jack opened his burger to add his ketchup, there was no cheese on his burger. He told us he wanted cheese on his burger. Ben asked the ladies manning the lunch tent if they had cheese to add to the burgers, but they did not. Jack complained he would not eat a hamburger if he didn't have cheese. Ben and I kept walking back to the group with Jack while explaining to him that it was OK to eat a hamburger without cheese. But Jack was adamant he was not going to eat a burger without cheese and was visibly becoming upset. When we got back to the group who were all eating their hamburgers, Jack fell apart. He started screaming and flailing on the ground. Between sobs, he was telling everyone on the football field that he was not going to eat a hamburger without cheese. All his fellow Olympians were shocked and a little frightened by his outburst. We kept explaining to him that it was fine to eat a burger without cheese but he refused to eat anything. He continued to scream, he rolled on the ground, he spat on the ground, he cried, he had a complete come apart for all the other Special Olympians to see. Finally, after several minutes of fit throwing, Ben decided to walk across the street from the school to the local Sonic and get Jack a hamburger with cheese. Only then did the come apart stop. By the time it ended, Jack was worn out and so were both of us. Later, I shared with Ben that Jack had never in his whole life had a hamburger without cheese. Every burger the child had ever had was a cheeseburger! Another day, another lesson learned!

Once the boys were out of school for the short summer, we were given a wonderful opportunity. A program based out of Dallas, Texas came to a town near us. The program, Challenge Air, is a free, not-for-profit organization that "offers inspiration and self-esteem building to children and youth with physical

... BUT I'M NOT THE SINGER

challenges through aviation by providing a day to focus on their abilities." Not only did this program offer their services to the physically challenged kids, but they also offered it to kids like Jack with intellectual challenges as well. Since he had never flown in a plane before, I told him about it, and we decided to sign him up. I shared with Jack how I had never flown in a plane before either, so it could be an exciting day for all of us. Benny was offered the opportunity to ride in the plane with Jack, but since he had flown before with Ben to a marine biology school in the Florida Keys, he gave me the chance to fly for the first time. We arrived at the airport, signed papers, were weighed, name tagged, and sent out to the airport's runways. After a few minutes of waiting and watching planes with children of all abilities come and go, we were introduced to our pilot. He didn't look much older than Benny, but he was very handsome. Mister Handsome, our pilot, Jack, myself, and two volunteers walked to our aircraft. I squeezed myself into the back seat of the cramped, four-seated plane. Jack climbed into his front seat with a huge smile on his face. Mister Handsome got in last and started explaining what was going to happen the next few minutes. Jack and I were given headphones so we could hear what the airport tower was saying and what our Mister Handsome had to say.

The plane started, we waved goodbye to Ben and Benny and started down the runaway. Mister Handsome had not closed the plane completely to let cool air in the cockpit, so the plane shook and clanked all the way down the runway. At a curve in the runway, we stopped and had to wait for takeoff while another small plane landed. Soon we shook and clanked to the main runway. I am sure if someone saw my face they would think I looked like a deer in the headlights. Mister Handsome turned around and gave me a brown paper bag just in case I felt sick. I must have looked worse than a deer in the headlights. I thought to myself as I looked down at the vomit bag, there was NO way I would do something as disgusting as vomit in front of or in the general area of a young man as handsome as this pilot.

Having made my mind entirely up on that issue, I turned my attention back to Jack. He was sitting in front of me so controlled, mature, and happy, answering all the questions Mister Handsome asked him and taking in every detail of the plane and his surroundings. I almost felt ashamed of myself for being so weak and afraid when I watched him from my back seat.

Once on the main runway, we were given the Ok to proceed. Mister Handsome reached up and quickly jerked the plane's top in place, secured it with its lock, and we started down the runway. Before I knew it, the runway started to change as the plane pulled away and started to fly. I couldn't take

MY NAME IS JACK JOHNSON...

my eyes away from the slowly widening view of the airport, the horizon, and the ground below. I checked on Jack who was wholly engrossed in his view out his side window. Mister Handsome was talking to us explaining our altitude and some of the points of interest in our new view of the world. Suddenly the plane dropped, but Mister Handsome didn't seem worried. Again, the plane lurched and dropped. That vomit bag was starting to call my name. I asked Mister Handsome what was wrong and he explained it was a normal thing for an ascending plane to go through pockets of atmosphere where the wind was blowing downward. Oh, that made me feel better as my hand got closer to the nearby vomit bag. Mister Handsome then added that the downward wind would stop as soon as we ascended further up. Even Jack shook his head to that one.

The view was incredible. We could see a nearby lake with boats on the water and the houses below in all shapes and sizes. I pointed out things I knew Jack liked. We had a bird's eye view of electric poles and radio antenna towers. I pointed out streets and interstates I knew we had traveled. As I was scanning the horizon for something else to point out to him, Mister Handsome's voice came over my headphones, "Look, Mom. Jack is flying the plane!" Much to my surprise, Mister Handsome with his hands held high in the air, had given the reins over to Jack and Jack was in control of the plane. I placed the vomit bag in my lap.

Before we knew it, we were facing the view of a long, black line—the runway back at the airport. We flew low over more houses, more of the lake, and to Jack's delight, more electric poles. As the ground grew closer and closer, I started to thank God for this opportunity to share with my son, for getting us safely back to the ground, for the technology that makes flying possible, and for sending us Mister Handsome, my personal motivation for not losing my lunch!

After we landed and removed ourselves from our tiny tin can with a propeller, Mister Handsome gave Jack a flying certificate and a pair of wings pin. Jack loves sharing the story of the day he flew a plane! It was indeed a great day for all of us.

JUNE 9, 2008—The boys are now out of school. We are at the dentist office. I sent both the boys back with the dental hygienists without me—a first for Jack. I had gone back with him but decided he could go back by himself this trip. I didn't tell him in advance; I just let the hygienist take him. This is the second trip to this dentist. The last dentist made me mad so the boys did

...BUT I'M NOT THE SINGER

not go back. I had written before about being at the previous dentist office and going back with Jack, holding his hand through his cleaning, and telling him exactly each step the hygienist was doing. That little extra bit of information for Jack made a complete difference for him and made getting his teeth cleaned so much easier. Then, at the last appointment, the hygienist and the dentist were both so rude and impatient when I went back with Jack and tried to explain the procedures like I did on the previous visit. Jack was in a bad mood, didn't want to cooperate with anyone, and add that to the impatience and rudeness of the staff, it was the trip from hell. Jack became obstinate and the staff decided they would just hold Jack in place while they cleaned his teeth It was ugly. The dentist acted so uncaring and unsympathetic that my child was so upset while being held down by several hygienists like an animal. No way could I ever take the boys back to her again. So far on this trip, I am still in the lobby and haven't been called back. Could we have reached yet another milestone? We do take baby steps but maybe, just maybe we will get there.

Speaking of milestones......Jack had a haircut recently. We still see the same barber as the boys had since they were young. Our barber, R., asked Jack while she was cutting his hair if he remembered how upset he had gotten years ago when she tried to cut his hair. He sadly told her yes, he remembered. On our way home, I asked him what he remembered about those first haircuts. He told me he didn't like to remember them because they were so upsetting for him. I asked why he got so upset when R. tried to cut his hair and he said it was because she held his hair up when she cut it and he was afraid she was going to pull it out. I had never thought about this point of view. Since we were talking about the past, I asked him about his dislike of grocery stores when he was a little boy. He told me he remembered getting sad because we didn't walk through each numbered aisle. I had no clue as a mother of a newly diagnosed child with autism that he needed to follow the number sequence in the grocery store.

JULY 7, 2008—We attended our church's Fourth of July picnic and watched our town's fireworks from the church property. At the church picnic, Jack was wild. The church had set up a few different blow-up bouncy houses, some for jumping and one for sliding. Jack loved the sliding bouncy house. We spent most of the time there at the slide. He surprised me twice by introducing himself to two different adults who were helping the sliders. Then he ate cotton candy! He had never eaten cotton candy before. You could tell

MY NAME IS JACK JOHNSON...

when he took a bite he didn't really enjoy it, but he ate it, and that's what counts. Later, we were sitting together resting after all his sliding when he leaned over to me and said, "Mom, did you see how good I did at the slide?" I said, "Yes, I did, Jack." He goes on, "You know what? I bet some of those people at the slide will come ask me for my autograph!" He is so funny at times you can't help but laugh.

JULY 14, 2008—Today we took Jack to his annual Dr. McGrew appointment, his autism doctor he sees once a year for follow-ups on his progress and medications. Per the doctor, Jack is doing great. He weighs 147 pounds and is 5 feet 2 and a half inches tall. Jack had a good trip to Nashville and was incredibly full of himself the whole trip. He loves getting on elevators and overseeing pushing the floor buttons for everyone on the elevator. He likes to interact with Dr. McGrew as she checks his vital signs. He told us while we were waiting for the doctor in the exam room that Dr. McGrew "was messing with his mojo" because she wasn't on time. Another where-did-he-get-that moment came when he started holding his breath trying to see if his face would turn blue if he held it too long. I think someone has been watching too many cartoons again. It was a good doctor visit and trip.... until next year.

AUGUST 7, 2008—Promotion Sunday is this Sunday at church where all the children in Sunday School get promoted to the next grade. This year Jack will get promoted to the Youth Floor and we still don't know what we are going to do with him. The Youth Floor is set up for typical teenagers with a pool table, a foosball table, a café for drinks and snacks, café tables with chairs, couches and comfy chairs for socializing, a large room with chairs facing a platform that contains the class leader's podium with a backdrop of musical instruments for the teen band who plays every Sunday. This teen hangout is on the third floor of our church and since the café/classroom is large with high ceilings, the acoustics are not good. When the band plays or when the room is full of socializing teens, the noise is deafening for Jack. It's a wonderful place for a typical teenager like Benny but not so for a teen with autism. This is not a good fit for Jack

Jack came home the other day and told me he had had a problem at school. It always scares me when he says this because he doesn't always understand our world and how it works. I never know what he is going to say or do so having a "problem" at school puts me on high alert. Jack tells me he had to

...BUT I'M NOT THE SINGER

poop at school the other day and when he finished, he saw there was no toilet paper in his stall to clean up with. He paused in his story and I asked him what he did.... dreading the answer I was about to hear. He said, "Oh, I found some scraps of toilet paper in the floor and used it. I asked if he got himself clean and he said he did. I then told him if that happened again he needed to check the other stalls for toilet paper before he needed the paper. With a strange look on his face, he asked me, "You mean you want me to walk around the bathroom looking in other stalls naked with my pants around my ankles?" Oops, had to correct that one by explaining to Jack to look for toilet paper in the stalls before he even starts to do his business. As I said, I never know what he will say or do next!

AUGUST 23, 2008—We are all at Benny's football game. Jack just ate a barbeque chip for the first time. His response to the chip—"That's delicious!"

SEPTEMBER 29, 2008—It has been a while since I had time to write. The boys are on fall break for three weeks. This Tuesday, September 30, we leave home for Florida and a visit to Disney. No one in my little family has ever been before with me being the exception. Ben's mom is going with us, and we are all staying with one of her cousins she hasn't seen in years. This cousin also works for Disney and can get us in and out of all the parks for a discount I don't like the idea of staying in someone's house, but I could not talk Ben out of staying at this relative's house.

After lots of preparation, we finally got on the road for our trip to Disney. We rented a van so we would all be comfortable and for hauling all our luggage. We planned to drive as far as we could, spend the night where ever we tire out, and finish the drive on the next day. On the second driving day, after having mechanical trouble with the rented van and having to wait for a replacement van, we arrived at our destination, Haines City, at 9pm, tired, hungry, and later than we had anticipated.

The next morning, we were up and headed to the Magic Kingdom. I had brought with me a letter from Jack's autism doctor stating that he has autism and could not be expected to stand in large lines for an extended period of time. We were given a "fast pass" which could get us in a faster waiting line for all the rides at the park. In all cases, we still had to wait, but our wait was less than the average park attendee. We rode lots of rides that first day with Ben and Benny enjoying Space Mountain by themselves. Jack really enjoyed

MY NAME IS JACK JOHNSON...

the Monorail that runs between the different parks and themed hotels, even getting to ride in the Monorail's cockpit which excited him.

Jack had a tough time distinguishing real from pretend at the Disney parks. A considerable part of the Disney magic is the make-believe aspect. Once we rode a ride and show at Epcot that told the story of recycling to the riders while it depicts the beginning, middle and ending to being "green." The ride part of the show started out in a large theater with theater seats. After watching a short movie, the theater seats separated into two seats together in a long train of seats. The train of seats then moved into a large area of pretend, moving dinosaurs animated with sound. Jack completely freaked out and grabbed my hand. Once we discussed real and pretend further, he relaxed and enjoyed trying to tell the difference himself.

Since we visited the Epcot Park the day before, Animal Kingdom was our next park to visit. There were many real animals in different settings all around the park. We went on a Safari ride through a pretend Africa and saw animals who inhabit that continent. We saw the Tree of Life where we caught a Bug's Life show. The theater was inside the massive Tree of Life. The Bug's Life characters in the movie were on the movie screen and flew at you in 3D. Not only did they fly at you, they also blew things at you and pretended to sting you. When the characters stung you, a pretend stinger popped up in your seat at the appropriate time in the movie and "stung" you. At one time in the movie, the main bug, "Flick" introduces his friend, an acid-spitting bug. I cannot remember the spitting bug's name because my mind was comprehending the idea of getting "acid" spit on us at some time in the future. Even Jack said, "Oh no, not an acid-spitting bug!" While the acid spitting bug is talking with Flick, it gets the urge to sneeze, which he stifles each time.... until the last time. When he sneezes at you, water comes out of the back of the seat in front of you simulating the fluid of a wet sneeze. It was funny. I don't think Jack liked it too much because he thought it was acid until I explained to him it was just water and it was just for fun. I was a little shocked that he actually thought the spray of fluid from the sneeze was acid. But he is a literal thinker and when a person says you are getting acid in your face, he believes he is getting acid in his face.

Next, we visited Hollywood Studios in Disney World, the park being mostly movie oriented. We rode a movie theater ride that had different movie scenes. Each scene had actors playing their parts in the movie while we watched from our ride seats. One of these scenes was a scene where the mob had a huge shoot-em-up. Jack thought the guns were real with real bullets. Another talk about real and pretend happened.

... BUT I'M NOT THE SINGER

Our last park at Disney was a water park, Typhoon Lagoon, a massive park with water activities of all kinds: a calm pool, a wave pool, water slides of all kinds, a snorkeling pool, and other pools we didn't have time to visit. Jack liked the water slide area. He wasn't afraid of the height of the slides or whether the slides tubes were open or closed. He would jump in the tube and away he would go. I rode one slide once but forgot to hold my breath and landed in the bottom pool taking in a mouth full of water. I spurted, spit, and gasped for air for about 30 minutes. I was asked by one of the slides personnel if I was alright. Yep, that's me.... the old lady who almost drowns at the water slide.

Our hosts on this trip had a very large dog that lived in a pen in their yard. This dog barked at us every time we left or came back. He also had a distinct, deep bark, sounding more like a low growl bark. Jack thought his bark was funny and started to imitate it. He amazes me with his incredible imitating skills. So, I wasn't surprised by his ability to imitate the dog's bark but was surprised at how well he did it. And shockingly, he did the imitation without opening his mouth.

At Typhoon Lagoon, Ben and boys decided to scuba dive at the scuba diving pool. While waiting in line for their turn in the pool, Jack started to do his imitation bark. Ben and Benny were snickering at Jack's new-found skill, when they overheard another person in line with an Australian accent say, "Someone has brought a dog to the park." This made Ben and Benny laugh even harder. On the way home, we stopped at a Waffle House to eat breakfast. The boys had never eaten at a bar on barstools before and wanted to sit there while they ate their breakfast. The three of us were nearby so we could watch them. Another man came in and sat beside Jack. He didn't seem to mind but kept us all in stitches when he started "barking" from his barstool, making the gentleman beside him confused by where the dog's barking was coming from. That child is too funny!

We had a wonderful time at Disney World. We made memories, took loads of pictures, enjoyed time with relatives, and will never forget our time there.

CHAPTER 16

Jack recently had an assignment in his Language Arts class. The assignment was to write a paper about something you are passionate about, and Jack is very passionate about his hatred for homework. He worked very hard on this paper and needed minimum help from me. His paper was titled,

"No More Homework."

"I hate homework in the seventh grade," or strongly dislike it. Students work hard enough at school. Too much free time is taken up due to homework. We should have longer school days or be given time to do the work at school. Less homework will eliminate heavy backpacks.

All students work hard enough at school each day. We must listen to the teacher when they are teaching us the lesson. We have to do the work in class. They also tell us to sit up and be quiet. We must work hard every day.

Homework takes up free time at home. There are other things I want to do besides homework. I would rather be watching T.V. Playing video games is something I would like to do. But I have to do homework instead! There are some things that can be done besides homework.

Maybe we could find time during the school day to do homework. Having the first fifteen minutes of class to do homework would be great. The teachers could stop their lesson early to do homework the last fifteen minutes of class. The teachers could change classes, while the student stayed at the same desk all day. No more wasting time getting books out of lockers.

We could make the school day longer. One hour could be enough time to get homework done. I would stay one hour longer to get homework finished. The teacher would be there to help with homework questions.

...BUT I'M NOT THE SINGER

Just think no more heavy backpacks. If there were no homework, we would keep our books at school. Without books at home, we would not have to wear or pack our backpacks. Even our buses would be lighter and less crowded without all those backpacks.

Life without homework would be excellent. I would have more free time and would not have to carry a heavy backpack. We could find extra time to do homework during the school day. I work hard enough at school, so let's get rid of homework.

You have got to love a guy who speaks his mind!

DECEMBER 30, 2008—Christmas has come and gone. I can't believe it is almost a new year. I cut back on gifts for everyone, and Ben and I didn't give each other anything. Money at our house is just too tight. We hope the New Year brings new work because Ben's business is slow...real slow. He has a few jobs in-house, but once they are done, he has nothing on the books. I keep reading about people in other parts of the country losing everything they have because they have no work or have been laid off from their jobs. Ben says he will get a part-time job if he must but I don't know where that will be because companies are not hiring either. I am scared.

Jack gave me a gift but he doesn't realize it. He had his first piano recital on December 19. It was so much more worth anything that money could buy! His school assistant has been teaching Jack piano for quite a while now. Miss S. put together the recital at school so more of his teachers and peers could attend. I invited several members of our family as well and Benny was excused from his class so he could be there too. At the recital, there were 15–20 people in attendance. Jack was very nervous about playing in front of so many people. A nervous Jack and Miss S. came in and he sat down at the keyboard that had been borrowed from the music department. Once Jack sat down in front of the keyboard, he cracked his knuckles and rubbed his hand through his hair. He then looked at Miss S. and she gave him the OK to start. His first song was *Silent Night*, then came *Angels We Have Heard on High, Amazing Grace, Old McDonald* and lastly, *Jingle Bells*. During *Angels We Have Heard on High*, a very soft, sweet, high voice sang during the chorus. To our surprise, it was JT, Jack's friend with autism who has limited communication skills. Even with JT's limited communication skills, Jack and JT have this special bond where they communicate with each other without talking. When Jack heard JT singing he laughed while he played. Before he

MY NAME IS JACK JOHNSON...

played *Old McDonald*, Jack turned and told the audience that no one should sing except for JT. While Jack played *Old McDonald*, JT stood in front of the audience and sang along. At first, he sang quietly but as the song went on, he got loud and swayed with the music. JT was so happy, and so was Jack. After *Old McDonald* was over, JT sat down but continued to quietly sing to each song. Of course, I cried through the whole recital, but I wasn't alone. I heard lots of sniffles and Ben even shed a few tears. Later at the after-recital reception, one of Jack's regular education teachers walked up to me and with tears in her eyes said that was the most touching thing she had seen the whole Christmas season. I hope she will always remember two special friends who have a wonderful, unique friendship that knows no bounds.

JANUARY 23, 2009—It's the new year, and the economy sucks! No one is building anything, so Ben's business has almost stopped. We are living off the savings account and cutting back on everything we can.

Jack's special education teacher shared with me how the other day Jack was singing in her classroom, and she had to ask him to stop. His song of choice: "I Like Big Butts, and I Cannot Lie." I blamed it on his dad.

FEBRUARY 16, 2009—The boys are both going through Confirmation at church. They attend Confirmation class the same time we would have been in worship on Sunday mornings. I go each Sunday with Jack to Confirmation. I am learning quite a lot; not sure whether Jack is learning much at all. During Confirmation class I take notes while the teachers talk. I show Jack my notes so he can see and hear the information two times.

APRIL 16, 2009—Happy 13th birthday to Jack! He didn't know what he wanted for his birthday at first, then told me he wanted his own Wii! I had to tell him no because we just don't have enough money for two Wii's. There were storms predicted for that day as well which upset Jack. The whole day upset Jack with him declaring it was the worst birthday ever. His trip through puberty has been rough but not totally unbearable. He has developed a sassy, grouchy mouth that drives me nuts. Since he doesn't have a brain filter that tells him what is appropriate to say and what is not, he blurts out whatever he wants at any time. When he acts this way around the unsuspecting masses, I must apologize for him and his behavior. I call it my "apology tour." After he behaves this way once he has been warned, I must think of appropriate punishments. One day I asked him what favorite item he didn't want to go in time

...BUT I'M NOT THE SINGER

out, and unfortunately for him, he told me. Guess what immediately went into time out? Bet he won't answer that question again!

Jack's special education teacher, his assistant, and the students in his special education class had a party for Jack's birthday. They had blue balloons, Jack's favorite color, Oreo cookies, and pepperoni pizza. They did not sing to him because he hates the Happy Birthday song. For years, Ben's side of the family has sung, "My Country Tis of Thee" instead of the Happy Birthday song. The things we do to keep Jack happy!

APRIL 23, 2009—Benny is now 6'2" tall! I cannot believe he is this tall!

MAY 16, 2009—We made it through Confirmation at church. It is one of those life steps we now have made it through. One Sunday during Confirmation, we had an art day. Each Confirmation class makes a banner to commemorate that particular class. The boy's class read John 15 for inspiration. This verse is about Jesus explaining—"I am the vine; you are the branches." (John 15:5) The art for their banner was vines, branches, and fruit. I didn't know how Jack could participate in the artwork so I improvised. I had recently seen some drawings of Jack's that he had memorized and drawn from a video game he had been playing. One of the pictures he had drawn was of two hands coming from opposite sides of the piece of paper, reaching out to each other. While we talked, I told Jack that John 15 was about being a part of a whole, Jesus being the main vine and us being the branches of the vine. This picture Jesus was describing with His words was how He is constantly reaching out to each of us. As I went on, I shared with Jack that the picture he had drawn of the reaching hands was what Jesus was doing to us......reaching out to us. After our talk, Jack drew another picture of Jesus' hand reaching out to us and the Confirmation teachers were impressed and used it in the banner. The final banner was pretty.... the hands reaching out to each other surrounded by the green vines and purple grapes. The ceremony started with the baptizing of ten of the members with two of them being my boys. I sat with the Confirmation class so I could sit with Jack to keep him in his chair and keep him quiet. Jack was VERY concerned about having water put on his head when it was time to baptize him because putting water on someone's head in church was not acceptable behavior in Jack's book. I had emailed the pastor and asked if he could use the smallest amount of water necessary to get the baptizing accomplished. Before I knew it, my boy's turn was up. Jack jumped up and was on the stage before I even got out of my chair. Benny took his place beside Jack and Ben

MY NAME IS JACK JOHNSON...

joined all of us from his seat in the audience. The pastor barely put water on his hand and touched Jack's head. Benny was next and both boys did so well. The sight of them kneeling during their baptism is something I will remember forever. After the baptisms were over, all the class had to be confirmed. Jack had to sit for an extended period of time and was getting very antsy to leave. Each class member was confirmed, and we celebrated the day with dinner out instead of the usual post Confirmation reception. It was a special day for us!

We also made it through another Special Olympics. Ben and I met the PGS Olympians bringing with us the highly cherished piece of cheese that was the instigator of the infamous there-is-no-cheese-on-my-burger come apart at last year's Special Olympics. We watched as Jack came in third in the softball throw event. Next was his run which turned out to be more than a 100-yard dash. It was a long run for someone like Jack, but he held on to third place and ran with all his might. It was the longest stretch we had ever seen Jack run. He proudly stood on the 3rd place podium during the race's ribbon ceremony. His face, even though still red from running, was filled with pride and we were filled with pride as well.

The school year is behind us. We celebrated Benny's graduation from PGS and celebrated Jack's end of the school year. Both boys received certificates of achievements in different ceremonies.

On June 13th, we again had the pleasure to participate in the Challenge Air "Fly Day" at a nearby airport. Again, we all attended with one change; this year Ben would be riding in the airplane with Jack. After we arrived at our scheduled time, we were introduced to the pilot who would be flying with Jack and Ben. It wasn't Mister Handsome we had last year, but he was still a nice looking, very young man. Before we knew it, Ben and Jack were strapped in their airplane seats and ready for take-off. Benny and I waited nearby so we could watch them take off and be there when they landed. Back on the ground, Ben and Jack emerged from their plane and started walking toward the family tent where we were waiting. Jack had a big smile when he saw us. Ben didn't look well at all. Jack had another great flight and even flew the plane again. Ben said his stomach was queasy from the bumpy ride, but he said he had not been sick. Jack again received a flying certificate and a set of wings pin. Ben got a day-long upset stomach.

JULY 3, 2009—At the lake for the first time this year. Ben has been out of work, and we have been out of money, so we just haven't had the money to even come to the boat. Jack goes back to school in two weeks, so the summer

...BUT I'M NOT THE SINGER

is almost over. Benny graduated from PGS in May, and soon he will start high school. Things are always changing for us!

AUGUST 22, 2009—Good grief! Summer is over already. Jack started 8th grade July 17th, and Benny started 9th grade August 13. I have been busy with school stuff—forms to fill out, meetings, homework, writing checks every few days.

AUGUST 31, 2009—Jack now has glasses. He had been telling me for months that he couldn't see the chalkboards at school. Of course, he told me this when he was supposed to be taking class notes from said chalkboards so his teachers, his assistant, and myself were not sure he was having trouble seeing the boards or if he was trying to get out of taking notes. I took him to get his eyes checked, and he did, in fact, need them. It's been a little over a month, and he hasn't broken or lost them yet.

Recently, Jack was delighted by a special treat. Our city's maintenance men had to change an electric pole light bulb. I saw them pull up outside, watched them set up their bucket truck, and immediately told Jack. He and I went outside and watched the men from the ground. He was fascinated! He watched every step as they changed the bulb. He even told one of the men, "Excuse me, sir, do you know the light is out on the pole at so and so address?" The guy told Jack he did know about the light bulb being out at that certain location while his face showed his shock at Jack's memory of electric pole lights needing to be replaced. Jack also told me, "Mom, I could do that job! I could be a 'bulb-er' one day."

Pepper, the guinea pig, passed away. It was hard on Jack. His special education teacher called to let me know and asked if Ben would dig a hole for her burial in the side garden outside her classroom. Ben agreed and on the day of the burial even though the ground was hard, Ben dug a final resting place for Pepper. Jack had told his teacher that Pepper needed a funeral, so Ben and I stayed for the funeral. Mrs. D., Jack, Ben, and I stood around Pepper's grave and from someplace I had never seen, my son says, "We are gathered here today to say goodbye to our friend, Pepper Ann. She was a good guinea pig, and she loved my vegetables...." Ben and I looked at each other with that "where did that come from" look and held back our snickers. Jack talked on with his guinea pig eulogy praising Pepper for being a good friend and pet. Then he says, "Shall we pray." Ben and I bow our heads only down enough where we can see each other, again looking at each other with the "where did

MY NAME IS JACK JOHNSON...

that come from" look, while Jack starts, "Dear God, thank you for Pepper Ann........." and finishes with "Amen." We all praised Jack for his leadership during Pepper's funeral while trying to stifle our snickers caused by what we had just witnessed. I am sure Pepper Ann's eulogy words and prayer could be found from a cartoon Jack had seen and memorized. At least it was appropriate, and Jack gave his friend, Pepper, a proper goodbye.

Jack came downstairs the other day laughing about how he had heard a song that was now "his" song. He had his computer downstairs and played the song for me. This "Jack" song is by Bruno Mars titled "The Lazy Song." It does remind me of Jack. The lyrics describe a person lying on their back looking up at their ceiling fan. That's Jack! Bruno sings about watching TV and doing a dance with his hands. That's Jack! The song talks about being in a Snuggie—that's Jack! And the first line states how today I don't feel like doing anything—definitely Jack! I agreed with Jack; this song is about him!

NOVEMBER 12, 2009—Lately, Jack has been acting like such a teenager, telling me what he wants to do and what he doesn't want to do. Too bad he hasn't figured out that is a battle he will not win. In the past few months, he has said he wished I would go to h#%&, called some football referees "Jack-us-es"—cussing but not using the correct pronunciation—and pretended to be sick to get out of school; a ploy that worked the first time but not the next after he told me he saw it on TV. Not too sure about these teenage years!

DECEMBER 7, 2009—Jack had his second piano recital. We had this one at our home. We moved furniture out of our dining room, lined up chairs in rows, and faced the chairs toward the piano in my office next to the dining room. Several family members and friends came. Right before he started to play, someone's phone rang. It was a family member who quickly tried to find and shut off his phone. But Jack, having seen a teacher at school do it, took the family member's phone in the kitchen, stating, "You can have it back after the recital." We all had a good laugh.

CHAPTER 17

JANUARY 2, 2010—Woo Hoo! It's 2010! For some reason, I am very optimistic about this even number year. Not that it makes a difference, just hoping the even number year will change our luck. We made it through another Christmas even though we didn't have money for Christmas. Ben's mom gave the boys an Xbox 360, so they never realized their parents didn't have much for them for Christmas.

JANUARY 6, 2010—The boys are back in school from Christmas break. Benny is sports free right now except for working out every afternoon at the school's gym. His body is already changing from a colt with long, skinny legs to a young man with muscles. My greatest joy is getting to watch these boys grow up! Jack is changing too. He has started to thin out and grow upward. He stepped in cat pee (one of the cats had an accident on the floor!) with his socked feet, and I had to wash his foot. I was surprised by the size of it! And the hair growing on the top of his foot... it wasn't a boy's foot but the foot of a man. He is having trouble with acne but will not keep his hands away from his face. Now he has some acne on his back as well. Two acne-faced, growing, facial haired teenagers live in my house now!

FEBRUARY 7, 2010—My new year optimism is gone. Ben had some work at the beginning of the year, but once he finished it, there was nothing. He is looking for another job. We have cut back on bills again, we have refinanced our house and lowered our house note, and we have had to borrow money from relatives. We are talking about selling both the boats but don't know in this economic climate if anyone would buy them.

February 23, 2010—Waiting to pick up Benny from school. Recently, I took Jack to the pediatrician because he has been complaining about his stomach hurting. The pediatrician said he thought Jack might have digestive issues and gave us some medicine to take. We have been giving him the meds, but he still is complaining. He also has had a few bouts of vomiting. Hope the meds kick in soon.

MARCH 18, 2010—Waiting for Benny at CHS. I had to leave Jack at home by himself to come pick up Benny. Jack came home again today sick to his stomach. He has been having stomach issues for a while, and we cannot figure out why. He was fine when I dropped him off this morning but vomited two times after he got to school. I picked him up about 9:30. I called Jack's pediatrician and told the nurse that the medicine they had given Jack a few weeks back for his stomach wasn't working. I also told her I thought he was getting worse.

MARCH 19, 2010—I did keep Jack home from school today. He has not eaten a good meal for two days. He ate a pretty good lunch, but it was still not his regular size meal. He is eating a fourth of his regular meals. He is tolerating the new medicine, but he is still not himself.

March 29, 2010—What a difference a day makes! Jack's stomach has been bothering him on and off for about six months now. I remember the first time he called from school and said he had a stomach ache. I went to school and got him even though he had no fever, no diarrhea, and no vomiting. Once he got home, he started acting like nothing was wrong. He was laughing and jumping around, not like a sick kid with a horrible stomach ache. So, I asked him about his stomach—how it felt and he told me it was well. No more hurting. I explained to him that you can't pretend you are sick to get out of school. His response was that he had seen someone on a TV show get to go home by saying they had a stomach ache like he had just done. We talked about how that was the wrong thing to do and that he would be in trouble if he did it again. I shared this with all his teachers for future reference. About a month later, he called again with a stomach ache and I reminded him of his previous stomach ache story. I also said if he did come home he was grounded from his favorite things and could only lay on the sofa where I could keep an eye on him. His response was "WHAT!" He decided to stay at school and tough it out. After then the stomach ache became more and more frequent. The school nurse asked for Tums to be brought to school for his aches. He would take the Tums and sometimes feel better and sometimes not. The last week of school before break he was home more than at school. Today is the 3rd straight day of vomiting. The vomiting happens in the morning but the stomach aches have come any time of the day. There is not a pattern. I

... BUT I'M NOT THE SINGER

took him to the doctor that last week of school and his pediatrician said it was gastritis, an infection of the stomach lining. He prescribed an over the counter dissolvable pill since Jack cannot swallow pills but this pill didn't dissolve well and made Jack vomit. The boy's pediatrician wanted to run some tests on Jack's blood and urine. Of course, Jack couldn't pee right then in the cup but we took it home and he eventually went. Jack had never had blood drawn before and told me he wasn't going to have any drawn then. He hollered and screamed about it but I kept him calm and between me, Ben, and the nurse, we got him to lay on the table and watch how she was going to take his blood. I stood beside the table and held his hand with one hand while I held his head up so he could watch with the other hand. The nurse explained how she would wrap his arm with the rubber band to make his vein stand up. And once it stood up, she would poke it with a pin like thing and his blood would come out. This must have fascinated him enough that he let her do it, watched, and counted the seconds the needle was in his arm. It took 58 seconds per his counting. The nurse took 3 vials of blood and Jack did not jerk, cry, or scream. Ben was holding Jack's hand—the one the blood was coming out of—and he wasn't doing well. He couldn't watch and was having to lean against the table. I thought he might pass out but he didn't. Jack did so well and I, surprised and shocked, told him how proud I was of him. So did the nurse. So now we are waiting... waiting for the lab tests to come back while Jack continues to vomit!

APRIL 7, 2010—Jack got sick again this morning. He has stopped eating breakfast, and he was sipping on some Gatorade when "BLAAAK" It came up all over the floor in the family room. He ran to the bathroom and vomited two more times. He did not drink that much to have vomited that much. It doesn't make sense. Where did all that fluid come from that he vomited up? He had just gotten out of bed and had nothing to drink before the Gatorade. But he just puked three times, way too much vomit for a few sips of drink. Maybe this is a clue to what is going on. This whole situation has been hard for Jack, but the guilt and helplessness I feel is making me a nervous wreck.

APRIL 13, 2010—We are at Vanderbilt waiting to see Jack's autism doctor. He got sick again Sunday, this time at church. No warning, he had had no breakfast. He said he vomited up his supper from the night before.... at 10 am Sunday morning! Why had that not digested? For two days, he has had only one small container of Jell-O for supper. Something is just not right!

MY NAME IS JACK JOHNSON...

After an hour with Dr. McGrew, we don't know much more than we did before. She looked in his eyes for swelling of the brain. Happily, there is no swelling. She is setting us up an appointment with a gastrointestinal doctor to whom she has sent other kids with autism. We wait again.

APRIL 14, 2010—I dropped off Jack at school, and before I could get anything done at home, I was called back to school to pick Jack up because he had vomited. Once a student vomits at school, he or she must be picked up and taken home. Jack said he was eating lunch and had to go to the bathroom. When he got there, he vomited three times and what he had eaten for lunch came back up. That was all he had eaten all day! Dr. McGrew said the blood tests showed no pancreatitis. She also said no signs of appendicitis. She thinks this is a gastro problem. She said to expect more blood work and an endoscope. She said she would try to pull some strings and see if she could get an appointment for next week. Again, we wait.

APRIL 18, 2010—Jack has now seen a gastrointestinal doctor. The doctor is planning on an endoscope and a colonoscopy to be done at the same time on Jack so they will have to put him to sleep for both procedures at the same time. We haven't told Jack any of this yet until we have a definitive date and time. There is no sense in worrying him about it until the time is closer. The gastro doctor did say he didn't think what Jack had was life-threatening but it could be a life-long condition where he might have to take medicine for years. I hope and pray they find a curable infection or treatable bacteria so Jack can get back to his old self.

APRIL 21, 2010—As of today, we have been a whole seven days without Jack vomiting. He has been taking his stomach pill each day, and it seems to help. He has on a pair of jeans that are literally falling off him. He took off his belt, and his jeans were falling off, so he had to tuck his shirt in his jeans to keep them from dropping to his ankles. We have an appointment to go to the hospital's preoperative department to tour the facilities and talk about anesthesia.

APRIL 23, 2010—Tomorrow is our town's Main Street Festival. Ben will have a tent and try to sell some of his prints. The weather is not going to be good, and lots of vendors have canceled their booths. Who could blame them, especially if the weather is going to be as bad as they are predicting?

... BUT I'M NOT THE SINGER

As predicted, the weather was so soggy on Saturday of the Main Street Festival; they closed it down. Sunday was pretty with lots of sunshine, and lots of people came, but it wasn't the same.

The weather had been a mixture of rain and sunshine for a few weeks, following the pattern of our springs in Middle Tennessee. On Friday, April 30th, the weather service had predicted a weather pattern of heavy rain for the weekend. In preparation for a long weekend indoors, I had cooked a large lasagna that Thursday night, something we could have again over the next few days.

Friday was a warm, windy, sunny day. That night, Benny, Ben and I watched the movie We Are Marshall, about the airplane crash that took the lives of the Marshall football team years ago. The rain started late Friday night, and we woke to heavy rain on Saturday morning. Since we had already had rain off and on for a while, the local Harpeth River was already higher than usual. It was still confined inside its banks but was not at its normal springtime water level. That Saturday morning with all the rain we were having, and with the prediction of more, some of our neighbors were expecting the river waters to rise out of its banks. In advance of this rise, one of our neighbors called early Saturday morning and asked for Ben and Benny's help to move furniture from their garage basement, a basement known to flood when the river overflowed its banks.

Ben came back after moving things for our neighbor and was alarmed by the rate of the rainfall that was now coming down in torrents and pooling in places around our neighborhood. Unlike other rains, this rain did not let up and continued to come down in buckets, hour after hour. Before we knew it, the river had come out of its banks and was quickly rising. During the afternoon, Ben walked outside in the heavy rain so he could watch the river water rise with the hard rainfall. I could tell he was getting concerned with each passing hour of constant rain and with the continuation of the rising river water.

By afternoon, I started to become concerned. The river was still rising, inching closer and closer to our neighbor's houses, the rain was still coming down in torrents, and the weather predictors were still saying more rain was on the way. Ben and I talked during the afternoon about the chances of us having to leave our house for higher ground if the rain continued and the river continued to rise. More of our neighbors left their homes, afraid if they stayed and the river continued its rise they would become trapped by the rising water. Their departures did not calm our concerns but just made

MY NAME IS JACK JOHNSON...

them worse. Ben and I were concerned about Jack as well, wondering if something was to happen to him because he had vomited so many times and we couldn't get out of our neighborhood because of the rising waters of the river, what would we do?

The river water slowly made its way into our neighborhood inching its way closer and closer to homes. Once the water covered our neighborhood street, we decided the boys and I would leave. I packed a bag for me and one for Jack while Benny packed one for himself. Ben called his step-mother who lived close by and asked if the boys and I could spend the night with her. Ben decided to stay behind just in case he was needed to help our other neighbors, and so he could be there with our pets: four cats and one guinea pig.

Ben helped us get to our car (we left the van with Ben in case he needed to haul things) through the torrential rain and told us goodbye. By this time, our neighborhood street was already covered at one end, so I drove the other way from our house. To our surprise, the road was covered this way too, but we made it through the rising water even though we couldn't see the road.

With the three of us safe at a relative's home, Ben started to devise a plan. Even though our neighborhood had in previous years dealt with the Harpeth River flooding, our house had never had water in it before. Some of the other homes closer to the river and those houses that sat lower to the ground had water enter them in previous floods. Since our house sat on a higher foundation, water had never been a problem. The confidence Ben had that our house was out of danger was slowly dissolving as he watched the water now visible out of our windows making its way up the street.

Years ago, before we purchased our house, the previous owners had converted a single garage to a mudroom and kitchen. Once we bought it, we had converted the kitchen back to its original spot and had made the converted kitchen into a separate office away from the rest of the house for Ben. The office was the same level as the rest of the house, but the mudroom sat on the concrete pad of the original garage. To get to Ben's office, you had to walk down three stairs into the mudroom, walk across the room, and go up three stairs. This arrangement made it harder for little boys to bother their dad while he worked and kept the noise factor for Ben at a minimum. Because of this difference in height in the floors, Ben surmised the rising waters would come in our house via the lowest point meaning it would first come onto the concrete pad of the ground level garage. For this reason, Ben started removing essential items from his office since the only entrance from the house to his office was through the ground level mud room.

... BUT I'M NOT THE SINGER

Ben removed important papers, equipment, and artwork from his office, stepped down three stairs into the mudroom, back up three stairs into the central part of the house, and up a flight of steps to our second floor where he would store the removed items. He repeated this over and over until he had removed what he deemed were the most critical items. Then he started on the appliances in the mudroom, stacking the washer and a chest freezer up on blocks. The dryer already was elevated two feet on a platform. Ben noticed the water from outside coming in under the mudroom door that opened to the outside. Within minutes, the trickle of water had become an inch and was rising quickly.

Ben and I started talking back and forth on our cell phones. He would call, and I would describe where in the house he could find our important papers. Once safely upstairs, he would call again, and we talked about where he would find our family photos. Again, once upstairs, he would call, and I would tell him the location of the things we wanted to save from the possible flood. Ben hauled our belongings to the second story out of the reach of the water should it find its way inside the main house. It had already found its way into the mudroom, now filled with two feet of water. Ben told me things were starting to float in the mudroom. Ben still had a few items left in his office he wanted to take upstairs and decided if he was going to wade into the mud room's two feet of standing water, he might as well change into his swimsuit. He noticed while making trips through the mudroom, the water was still rising higher and closer to the top stair into the main house.

Ben made another call letting me know what he was about to do. He had to turn off the electricity to the house since the water was still rising. Once he turned the electricity off, he would be working in the dark. He could be in danger of electrocution. He described to me what he had to do and told me he loved the boys and me. I told him to call me back as soon as possible because he was scaring me. We hung up. Ben had to wade into the two feet plus water, climb up on the dryer, try to dry off the best he could, open the fuse box above the dryer, and turn off the main electrical fuse to the house. He was afraid he would be electrocuted since he was soaking wet. He called me shortly after and told me he had prayed to God, before he threw the main switch, that if he was going to die, he hoped and prayed it would be easy and pain-free. I am glad God answers prayers!

All night Ben took trip after trip up our staircase hauling our belongings to the second floor. He called me to say the water now was nearing the first

MY NAME IS JACK JOHNSON...

step of our front porch inching its way toward our front door, a door that stood three feet off the ground. Shortly after, he called and told me water was coming into our house, not by way of the front door or the mudroom but was pushing its way up through the floor air vents under our house. And the water continued to make its way into our home, twisting and turning corners, following the low spots we didn't know we had. Soon it was an inch deep covering rugs and beginning to walk its way up the legs of our furniture. Ben called to tell me the water was quickly rising. We talked about other belongings to try to save. He also took the time to get the guinea pig and its cage upstairs, take the cat's food and litter box upstairs, and some food and drinks for himself in case he was upstairs for a while. His last call was at 2 am. His voice cracked as he told me he was sorry for his role in buying our house since it was so close to the nearby river, the same river now two feet inside our house. He apologized for telling me the house never flooded. He said he was exhausted and could do no more. He told me our furniture was now floating downstairs, bobbing along in the brown, smelly water that was now in our home.

Upstairs in the dark with the cats and the guinea pig, the only sounds Ben heard were water sloshing inside our house and the constant beeping of an abandoned car someone had tried to drive through the floodwaters. Once the water got inside the car's alarm system, the beeping began. The outside now was a vast wasteland of water. It had come into our house, the first floor three feet off the ground. Add to that there was now around two feet of water inside our house collectively making the water outside our home a whopping five-plus foot deep! Looking out the window, Ben said you could see the abandoned car's headlights shining through the water flashing along with the alarm beeping. It stopped somewhere Ben said in the early morning going from the constant beep, getting slower, and slower until it slowed to a "bbbeeeppp" and finally stopped.

As for the rest of us, we were safe and dry. Jack fell asleep alone in one bedroom at Ben's step-mother's house while Benny and I laid awake in the bed of another bedroom. Benny was worried about his dad, and I couldn't let him know I was as well. We talked about the cats, the guinea pig, the things we might have lost. I jokingly told Benny I had always wanted new hardwood floors and this could be the chance to get them. We snickered at that, but neither of us was in a laughing mood. Benny finally went to sleep, but I stayed up first checking on Jack, and then standing by a window, watching the rain continue to come down while the rain from my eyes rolled down my cheeks.

... BUT I'M NOT THE SINGER

I was up as soon as the sun was up. It was Sunday, May 2nd, but time had no meaning. I turned on a TV to see what was going on in the surrounding world. As soon as the picture popped up on the TV screen, the reporter was sharing story after story of water rescues in the area. She went on the say that a neighborhood in Franklin was evacuated during the night by boat. Several people were evacuated and taken by boat to higher ground. It was my neighborhood! I ran downstairs, found my mother-in-law in the kitchen, and told her what I had heard. I called Ben and asked, "Where are you?" In his morning voice, he answered, "I'm upstairs at the house. Why? Where did you think I would go?" I told him about the water rescues that had gone on during the night in our neighborhood. He said no one had been to our house during the night because he didn't hear anything. After we talked, my mother-in-law called 911 and asked about the night water rescues in our neighborhood. She shared with the 911 operator that Ben was still there in the upper floor of our home and needed to be rescued. The operator was going to send someone to pick up Ben.

Ben soon heard the knock on the front door. He waded through the water downstairs, opened the front door, and found two men in a boat pulled up to what had once been our front porch. Ben ran back upstairs, fed the cats several bowls of food to keep them fed for a few days, grabbed his packed bag and the guinea pig cage with the very unhappy guinea pig inside, and waded through the water of our downstairs to the waiting boat. I had left the boys with my mother-in-law, BR, and made my way through the short distance to my neighborhood through the deserted streets of our town. To my surprise, the closest I could get to my neighborhood was a few feet into the main entrance road. The floodwaters were blocking the entrance.

There was water everywhere. Walking to the entrance of my neighborhood, I found a small crowd of onlookers and rescue workers waiting for the boat making its way toward us, a boat carrying Ben. Tired from lack of sleep, full of emotional distress, and a bundle of nerves, as I waited, watching for the rescue boat, I fell apart.... tears overflowing after being held back from the day and the night before. Soon a boat came into view. It was a yellow rubber raft carrying three men and a giant guinea pig cage. The three men wore bright life jackets. The boat landed on what once was the road into our neighborhood, and Ben got out on dry land. He turned around and retrieved the guinea pig and cage. I was so happy to see him. He saw me and smiled.

We reunited at BR's house. The boys were excited to see Ben and the guinea pig. They were still worried about the cats. We reassured them the

MY NAME IS JACK JOHNSON...

cats were safe and dry upstairs with plenty of food and clean water for several days. Ben said the rescue personnel said they had knocked on our door during the night but Ben had not heard their knocks. He is a very hard sleeper. Rain had stopped briefly but started falling again. And again, it came in buckets at a very fast pace. We turned on the TV and watched the constant reports of flooding in the Middle Tennessee area. We had officially been the victims of a 500-year flood. The rainfall estimates were around 15 inches and counting. Roads were washed away. Communities were completely underwater. Rescues were happening all around; some from flooded homes and some from submerged cars. People were missing and unaccounted for. Some homes were utterly underwater with only their roofs exposed to the above hovering helicopters. The Red Cross was setting up shelters for those without a place to stay. Cars were stranded on flooded interstates. People couldn't get home because the water was blocking roads. There were mudslides that blocked roads as well. Parts of downtown Nashville were standing in water. Opryland Hotel and Opry Mills Mall were under siege by the nearby flooded river.

For me, life as I knew it was never going to be the same. There was a part of me that was in disbelief. I couldn't comprehend what was happening. What were we going to do? What were we going to find when we got back to our house? Could we live in our house again? I saw the pictures on the news of houses almost covered with floodwaters, and I wondered about my own home. Were our cats alright? Would they go downstairs and try to swim their way out looking for us? What about Jack and his health? We still did not know what was causing the vomiting. Family and friends called and checked on us. We were homeless. Our world was in total limbo. We waited for the floodwaters to recede.

Because of our proximity to the river, we did have flood insurance but only on our house, not on our belongings. And since our new temporary home was a mere mile away, Ben and I spent hours walking back and forth between our old home and our new home watching and measuring the rise and fall of the flood waters. There were a few homes in our neighborhood that did not flood. The owners had stayed and now found themselves stranded in a small area of the neighborhood that was not affected by the river's water. We found a yard in an adjacent neighborhood that backed up to one of the unaffected houses where we could walk through one yard and land in the yard of one of our neighbor's homes. Dry from the floodwaters but surrounded, these neighbors were willing to help us in any way they could.

... BUT I'M NOT THE SINGER

One of them found a canoe and another neighbor made some makeshift oars out of bits and pieces of things they had in their garage. Ben and another one of our homeless neighbors set off in the canoe to paddle their way to our houses to retrieve some things left behind and to check on our cats. While our neighbor went in her house, Ben kept the canoe near her front door and she did the same for Ben. He found our cats to be perfectly happy and dry in our upstairs.

On one of our many walks between homes, Ben and I witnessed parental craziness at its finest. While walking, an SUV drove through the police barricade and parked on the side of the road. A father got out of the driver's seat and walked to the back of the SUV. He pulled a camcorder from the back while two small children wearing swimsuits jumped out of the back seat. The father then said, "Get in the water while I film you and I will send this to Grandma and Grandpa." Ben and I were completely blown away. Did this father not know what was in that water? Floodwaters are full of sewage, gasoline, and oil from garages and submerged automobiles and lawn equipment, not to mention household chemicals of all kinds. Did he not understand the dangers of the floodwater current? One small slip into the current and the children could be swept away before that dad could put his camcorder down. Had he completely lost his mind? We walked away to the sounds of water splashing and laughing children. We wondered if the children would eventually become sick from the exposure to the floodwaters.

Monday morning, May 3rd, brought sunshine and some reduction of the water. By the afternoon, the floodwaters had receded enough for Ben and Benny to get to our house. They fed the cats, surveyed the damage, and brought home our basketball goal that had floated away to a neighbor's house from the high water and the current. It broke my heart to hear it had floated away since for months it had been the home of a toad. Each time we had mowed our grass, Ben had moved the basketball goal onto the driveway, and since the toad called underneath the goal his home, Ben also moved the toad away from the lawn mower's blade. Once the grass around the goal was mowed, he would put the goal back in its spot and shoo the toad back underneath where it was safe. I wondered since the goal had washed away, what had happened to the toad.

Tuesday morning, Ben took me to our house. We entered it gingerly not knowing what we would find. Everything in our home was covered with a layer of brown mud. The water line in the house was not up to the two-foot mark we had previously thought but the mark measured thirteen inches of

MY NAME IS JACK JOHNSON...

water; water that had stood inside our house for two days. All our furniture was wet, soaked from the flooding. Our kitchen cabinets and laminated floors had already started to buckle and bend from the moisture. With the thirteen inches marked on the walls by the water, it was apparent the water had gotten into our electrical system via the electric plugs located twelve inches from our floors. The cats who had been upstairs for the last few days had come downstairs by the sight of tiny paw prints in the mud on the floor. I walked through our house looking at the things that were ruined. I kept my shoes under our bed in a wheeled wire container. My shoes were soaked. All my shoes. Some of my clothes were in the bottom of my closet because our closets were so small. They were all soaked. Our long winter coats though hanging high in our closet had gotten wet by barely hanging near the water. And the list went on and on.

There was so much to do, so much to try and save. So much mud to clean. Where do you start? What do you do? My already overloaded brain was wracked with worry about Jack and his health and now had to deal with more worry and strife. What were we going to do?

Since our world had virtually come to a standstill, I had not noticed how the world around us had stopped too. The communities in and around Nashville stopped as well. Some commerce was going on, but many people took off from work, and some companies shut down for the rest of the week. The upcoming weekend had been deemed "Volunteer Weekend," a time for all people who wanted to help the flood victims to come together in an organized way to help. With the number of houses affected by the flood, thousands of volunteers would be needed. And thousands volunteered.

The first thing that had to be done was to take pictures of the damage. Ben and I walked through our house and our lives, taking pictures of each piece of furniture, each soggy and wet article of clothing, household appliances, our waterlogged bed and mattresses, the buckling floors, the warped kitchen cabinets, lawn equipment, our van. We had taken our van to higher ground to a neighbor's yard, but unfortunately, the water had also gotten in their house and inside our van. The actual damage was crushing. We had two visitors that day that would leave us with helpful ideas. A few of our pastors from church came by. Our lead pastor told us to be careful, that there would be people who wanted to help us and people who would be there to make themselves feel better and not us. Ben and I hoped we would know the difference. The other visitor would be our town's mayor. He and some other city officials walked our neighborhood telling us how sorry they were for our losses and how they would do anything to help us. The mayor said the city's trash department would pick up trash until we had no more. Ben and I shook their hands and felt confident we had their support.

A FEMA (Federal Emergency Management Agency) representative arrived. Flood insurance is not sold in a typical insurance agency but is only sold to homeowners through the federal government and only to those whose homes lie in the federally mandated flood areas of the United States. These areas are classified as flood areas by their proximity to waterways and by past flooding issues. With the amount of new growth in cities across the U.S., some homeowners might find themselves victims of floods where the new construction has changed the landscape. Homeowners like us live in areas close to waterways and understand there is a slight risk of a potential flood. No one expected this massive flooding. The FEMA representative told us an insurance adjuster would be by in the next few days to talk to us about our flood insurance and what the protocol would be for filing a claim. He also told us we would have to rebuild our first floor; we could not just clean it up and move back in.

Before we could start to rebuild, we needed to remove all belongings and furniture from the flooded house. Wednesday morning after leaving Benny at my mother-in-law's house to watch Jack, I went to our house to start packing. Not knowing what was causing Jack's vomiting, Ben and I decided we did not want him anywhere near the flooded areas since the flood water and the left-behind, ever-present mud had been so contaminated. I needed to pack the things we would need to live the next few months in someone else's home. I packed our financial materials, our essential records, clothes to last us for a while, and the boys' school materials that they would need to finish out the school year. The boy's clothes had been upstairs during the flood, so their clothing was clean and dry. Ben's and mine were not. I had always wondered what I would take when someone would say you had "X" amount of time to take some of your belongings and you had to start now. I never dreamed I would find myself in that situation. I took the things I thought I would need and planned to pack questionable things in boxes that could be easily accessed once they were packed.

The next morning, I left to head home to spend the day packing up our belongings that would go in storage. These belongings included things like towels, linens, dishes, pictures from the walls, office materials, books, small appliances that were out of the flood, lamps, electronics, bathroom items, and any other article we had stashed away in closets, cabinets, drawers, and

MY NAME IS JACK JOHNSON...

furniture. Much to my surprise, I was not alone. It seemed to me hundreds of people were there planning on where and how to pack boxes, bringing water to drink, and stepping up to do whatever was needed. Ben returned from a client's office and, much to his surprise, our neighborhood was inundated with the automobiles of friends, family, and complete strangers all wanting to help.

Unfortunately, I was in a state of shock. I had been so worried about Jack who continued to be sick while trying to get the boys back to some semblance of a routine in our changing world, and being completely overwhelmed by the sight of our house and our belongings, I quickly shut down. I was incapable of doing much. With the house full of people, I walked aimlessly about so paralyzed by the sheer amount of pandemonium our lives had become. Life had changed in what seemed like an instant and life would never be the same. I felt helpless in my own house while watching what felt like a movie in my view: people removing parts of my life from cabinets and drawers, wrapping them in paper, placing them in boxes, and sealing my world away in taped and marked boxes. They asked me questions I would try to answer but don't remember if I ever did. "Where do you want this?" "Do you know where this is?" "Do you want to keep this out before we pack it?" "Where does this go?" "What do you want to do with this?" Every room I walked into there were questions. I felt myself outside of my body. My head was spinning in a thousand ways. The visual of so many people in my house, the noise of their chatting and the questions, the overloaded emotional burden was too much. I walked outside and sat in silence. I wanted to leave, to walk away and hide, but knew I had to stay.

When I thought things couldn't get worse, Benny would call and say Jack had been sick. I would ask him if he thought Jack was better or if he thought I should come home—not our home but the home we found ourselves living in. My heart broke again.

Once the boxes were packed, the furniture had to be removed. It was divided into two groups: the keepers and the trash-ers. Our wood furniture had weathered the flood waters. With some special cleaning, it would be like new. Any upholstery furniture had to be trashed. The pile of trash in front of our house near the street grew by the minute. We salvaged some furniture not knowing whether it could be saved or not. Our next predicament was where to store the boxes packed full of our lives and history, and the furniture that was salvageable. Ben's sister had a rental house that was not being rented at the time that we could store our furniture and boxes

...BUT I'M NOT THE SINGER

until we could move back in ours. We were so grateful to have that house as a storage house and as a place to accommodate Ben's home office. Again, people were stepping up and out to help us.

Our two refrigerators and a freezer had to be emptied and removed as well. I found the lasagna I had cooked Thursday night, a mere seven days prior, hardened and ruined from being inside a refrigerator that had not worked in those seven days. Finding it was a reminder of what life was like before our world changed.

Our FEMA insurance adjuster came by and looked through our house. He took his pictures. He told us the first floor of the house would have to be dismantled, all wood joist and wall studs wholly dried out, sub-floors removed, all tile removed, all bathroom fixtures removed, and the drywall five feet from the floor removed. He walked through the house, surveyed the damage, and took notes in preparation for making his estimate on rebuilding cost. When the final figure was given, he would write us a check for that amount to rebuild our home.

By Friday night, our house was emptied of furniture and belongings. Our lives were now scattered in places, sent home with other people who would clean them and store them for us. Things were sent home with us; things we would need to live for however long it would take to rebuild. Other things were put upstairs in case we needed them quickly. Things were sent to storage. Things were hauled to the ever-growing pile of garbage that almost blocked our view of the house across the street.

Saturday morning brought in "Volunteer Weekend." Armies of volunteers waited to be sent to the homes of flood victims. When I arrived after getting the boys up and fed, I had a hard time getting into my neighborhood. People were everywhere. A police officer was stationed at the entrance of our neighborhood directing volunteers to the center across the street in a nearby park. Those volunteers could walk the short distance to our street. I had to stop and tell the officer I was a homeowner and was allowed through. Our street was almost inaccessible from the number of cars parked on either side of the road. My yard was a parking lot of trucks, cars and work vehicles. People were everywhere. The windows were open in our house and drywall, wood flooring, and other debris were being thrown out of the open windows to awaiting hands that wheel-barrowed the discarded materials to the trash pile. Trash trucks were circling the neighborhood, stopping to use their claws to pick up and release the trash into their truck-beds. Some of the trucks were from as far away as Knoxville. Helicopters flew overhead taking pictures of the thou-

MY NAME IS JACK JOHNSON...

sands of volunteers working together for the common good. It was a scene out of a movie happening before my eyes.

My house was being torn apart. Toilets, tubs, and sinks used for years by us were removed and littered our front lawn. Our kitchen cabinets and wood flooring joined the trash heap in our front yard. There were strangers, family and friends in every room of our house taking it apart piece by piece.

It was just too much for me, and I would make up reasons to leave the house and chaos. One day I left because I had to pay a bill. I left the chaos to pay the bill adorned in my muddy clothes, rubber boots, and mud-streaked face. I cried the whole way to the business, stood in line inside while others stared, got back in the car, and cried all the way back to the house.

With all the pandemonium at the house, it didn't end there for us; we still had a sick Jack. I would not let him go anywhere near the mud and muck with him being, at the time, so sick and not knowing what was wrong. The stress of not knowing why he was so sick was tearing me apart. I had researched every disorder and disease I could find on the internet that had vomiting as a symptom. My mother instinct was screaming to me that something was wrong. We went out to eat one night, and I noticed Jack's color was off. He had the skin pallor of cancer patients I had seen before. I finally broke down and said something to Ben fully expecting him to tell me "I think you have lost your mind." But to my surprise, Ben agreed with me, said he had also noticed Jack's color but didn't want to say anything to me for fear I would freak out. During each workday, whether on weekends or weekdays, we had to find someone to watch Jack. On other days, we were going to doctor's appointments or picking Jack up from school because he had vomited there yet again.

I remember a day when I was ultimately at my wit's end with the overload of life. At our flooded house, the helping masses had been there all day. In the quiet left behind, I took a load of trash from inside our house to the mountain of junk piled high by the road when something shiny caught my eye. Before the flood, I had a large glass container on the back porch that had clear, round glass beads in the bottom. Looking down, there was what was left of the glass container with all the glass beads scattered in the trash pile. For some reason, I sat down and started sobbing, all the while picking up each glass bead and putting them in a pocket I had made in the front of my t-shirt. You can buy a bag of those beads at Hobby Lobby every day for a few dollars, but there I was, sitting in my front yard for all the world to see, scrounging around a giant mountain of trash, crying my eyes out, while

... BUT I'M NOT THE SINGER

picking up clear glass beads. It had nothing to do with my love for those beads. Picking up those stupid beads was my only controllable moment in my out of control life. (I still have those glass beads; a reminder to me that only God has control, not us.)

CHAPTER 18

With the house empty, the drywall was removed. Instead of taking the time to cut all the drywall in half, we just decided to remove it all. Next, the subfloors were removed exposing the crawl space under our house. Plywood was placed on the joist while large, industrial fans began the drying process.

While the wood joist and wall studs dried out, we waited. This drying process would take time. A police officer was still guarding access to and from our neighborhood to make sure visitors were not allowed since our houses were opened and exposed while drying. We had the upstairs heating and cooling unit quickly repaired so the cats still living in our upstairs could have cool air. I know they were lonely and confused. So were we.

MAY 10, 2010—We are in the waiting area of Vanderbilt waiting for Jack to get called back for his prep for his endoscopy, colonoscopy, and biopsy. Even though we are displaced, we still are desperately trying to figure out what is going on with Jack's health. He has still been sick with random bouts of vomiting and stomach aches that do not have a set pattern. We pray these tests will give us answers.

We are now on our way home. The doctor said everything looked great—no ulcers, no bleeding, no Crohn's Disease and no Celiac Disease. We are relieved but still disappointed since we are now back to square one.

We celebrated Jack's graduation from Poplar Grove. He looked so mature and tall walking up to get his diploma. He was so happy and proud of himself. His smile was so big. He sat with his class during the ceremony, and as the speakers spoke, he glanced over at us and waved. He was the center of attention for this day, and he ate it up. We took lots of pictures of him with his teachers and with his friends. Miss D. had a little reception after the graduation for Jack and JT who also graduated. Those two, who had been together since they were two years old, would now be going to different high schools. That was the only dark cloud that hung over the joyful day.

...BUT I'M NOT THE SINGER

June 15, 2010—We are at Vanderbilt Children's Hospital with Jack in the emergency room. He has started vomiting more frequently, this time for three consecutive days. He doesn't have any of the extra weight he had in the beginning of this mess to have consecutive days of more vomiting. He looks awful—his color is so pale. Sometimes he feels good, other times he feels weak and tired. Some mornings he doesn't want to get up, like today. He stayed in bed until noon Friday. He stays in there and plays with his stuffed animals and his DS. He told me that when he lays down it keeps his stomach from hurting so I let him stay in bed. So, after three days of vomiting and feeling bad, we are here waiting to be seen by a doctor. Jack has had an endoscopy, a colonoscopy, biopsies, and an abdominal ultrasound. They have been negative: no bacteria, no ulcers, no nothing. We went to see Dr. McGrew last week for an autism check-up. She was shocked that he had lost 14 pounds since April 29th when he was last weighed. She even weighed him herself to make sure what she was seeing was indeed correct. Jack weighs 136 pounds. Ben and I were shocked to see he had lost another 5 pounds in 2 weeks since we had weighed him last. At Christmas, Jack had weighed somewhere around 168 pounds. That is a weight loss of 32 pounds in 6 months! And no one can tell us why. Dr. McGrew asked Jack lots of questions about being sad and depressed about having to leave our house and our stuff because of the flood. She wondered if he was having some mental issues that was causing any of this. But he told her he was OK with all of it and was happy in his temporary living arrangements. She asked

2010 Jack's graduation ceremony from PGS a few weeks before his cancer diagnosis

him if his stomach hurt all the time or just sometimes. He said sometimes. She asked him if his stomach ever kept him up at night and he said yes, it did. I had never asked him that question before so I did not know his stomach bothered him so bad it woke him up. I felt so bad for not asking that question. Dr. McGrew said she wanted to schedule a head CT scan for Jack as quickly as she could. It was scheduled for the next Monday but since he was so sick, we decided to bring him into the emergency room. Dr. McGrew had told us if Jack's condition seemed worse to take him to the emergency room so here we are. The emergency doctor just came in to let us know they are going to take Jack back for a CT scan. We wait. We are so tired of Jack being sick and not knowing why, not living in our own house, and the headache of rebuilding the house. I miss our old life.

The emergency doctor was a young, female doctor. Ben and I explained what had been going on with Jack, how much weight he had lost, what Dr. McGrew had said to us, and how we had a CT scan already scheduled for next Monday, but we felt Jack needed to be seen by a doctor now. The emergency doctor was cool toward us. There was no warm welcome, no attempt to talk to Jack or make him comfortable. She had a smug, know-it-all attitude I didn't like. I couldn't tell whether she didn't believe anything we had said or was just a cold person. Ben agreed with me. I wasn't sure she was going to agree to move up the scan. Ben and I had already talked between ourselves and were devising a plan B in case the doctor refused. But she agreed to do it. Reluctantly.

While we waited in the emergency room after Jack's scan, several nurses came in our room. I watched one as she started typing something on the room's computer. Then another nurse came in and whispered something in the first nurse's ear. A feeling of dread came over me. Soon the emergency doctor came in. She had a complete change in her demeanor, and her physical appearance had changed from her previous look of confidence to a look of having seen a ghost. She told us the CT scan showed a "crowding" and a "shadowing." When we asked for an explanation, she only said the scan showed them that further testing would be needed. She had already talked to the scheduling department, and Jack was already scheduled for an MRI the next day. We could leave but needed to be back the next morning. My acting career started that day as I told Jack that he would have to have another test the next day keeping my demeanor light and carefree when inside my heart was breaking, my stomach was in knots, and my palms were sweating.

... BUT I'M NOT THE SINGER

JUNE 16, 2010—At Vanderbilt again waiting for Jack—this time he is having an MRI of his brain. The CT scan we had yesterday showed a "crowding," a "shadowing," and a slight lack of fluid in the back of his brain. So today they worked us in for this MRI. They said it would take about 45 minutes to an hour, but it has already been an hour and 20 minutes. We could be called back anytime.

The next day we arrived for Jack's sedated MRI. We had prepared him the best we could. He was scared but was also so brave when they took him from us. After waiting for what seemed like forever to us, we were called back to the sedation recovery room. Jack was still asleep looking so peaceful laying on his back. His recovery nurse, J., was male, had a calming voice, and took loving care of his new patient. I asked J. if he knew the results of the MRI. He looked at me and Ben and said, "Jack has a mass in his brain. He is going to be admitted as soon as he wakes up and we can find him a room. He will be going to the Critical Care Unit so they can keep an eye on him until the doctors decide what to do." Tears fell down my face. My brain exploded with questions and worry. A crack formed in my heart. J. got me a chair. I looked at Ben and his expression said what words could not. We left the world we had known and entered another one. My son, my baby, my buddy, one of the loves of my life has a brain mass!

JUNE 17, 2010—4:15 am—In Pediatric Critical Care Unit at Vanderbilt Children's Hospital with Jack. They finally found what was causing his vomiting—a brain tumor! I am in shock. What do you do or say? I spent the night here with Jack and can't sleep right now. I need to get so much out right now... fear, sadness, helplessness, guilt, and I need a good, hard cry. I have been with Jack since the MRI and can't cry for fear it will upset him. And things are rough enough for him as it is without me falling apart in front of him.

This is what we know: there is a mass in the back of Jack's brain about the size of a walnut. The head neurologist is coming in early this morning to talk about where we go from here. Biopsy? Surgery? Benign? Malignant? We don't know. I am in a surreal world right now. Is this really happening? This child has been through so much and now this! In a strange, sick way there is relief that at least we know what has been causing all the vomiting. Jack has been so miserable hurting, feeling sick to his stomach, getting sick to his stomach or just thinking about getting sick to his stomach. Poor guy! I know how hard it has been for Ben, me and Benny and we had the easy parts. I hated to tell others what we found out. You want people to know but then you don't want

MY NAME IS JACK JOHNSON...

to upset them or make them sad. Then on the other hand, sharing this news is a way to reach out to others for comfort, a physical giving some of this hurt and pain we feel to someone else. Here, you take some of this burden because I cannot carry it all. Shifting this burden is kind of a selfish thing but if you held it all, you would collapse from the weight of it. Most people who go through this have a home—that sweet refuge from the rest of the world. Jack loves his room, his special space where he can be Jack without prying eyes and judgmental ears. But I can't give him that now. It's changed into a chaotic mess. We are gypsies riding around in our gypsy cars, living out of suitcases, eating other people's food... whatever they give us. I hate this!

We talked to Jack to let him know what was going on in his brain. We had to explain that he had something in his brain that wasn't supposed to be there and it would have to come out. I told Jack that we would call this thing a "wooly booger" since that is probably what it looks like. We explained that he would have to have surgery and that the doctor would take the wooly booger out. We told him he would be asleep for the whole thing and would not know what was going on. He asked a few questions about the wooly booger but seemed to accept what we had told him. I am so glad God gave me the words to explain this to Jack, and he received it well. No tears, no being afraid, no stress. Boy, I love this child so much!

We did talk to Jack's new doctor today. He is Dr. P from pediatric neurosurgery. He explained things to us...he explained how MRI's take pictures of sections of the brain from the top down to the bottom and from the left side to the right side of the brain. Jack's tumor (per Dr. P.—a tumor is a thing that takes up space) is the size of a quarter and sits low in the brain. The wooly booger as I call it to Jack is in between ventricles in the brain. Ventricles are open spaces in the brain where the brain is divided into sections and where spinal fluid is made. The tumor is in a ventricle between the cerebellum and the brain stem. The tumor is VERY close to the brain stem where lots of things are controlled like movement, breathing, and eye movement, to name a few. If Jack's wooly booger has grown veins into his brain stem, we could have some issues like a droopy face, strange eye movements or worse. Dr. P. said it didn't look like there were veins in the brain stem but he wouldn't know for sure until he got inside Jack's brain. After the tumor is removed, not only is there the issues with damaging the brain stem, there is the problem of malignancy. If the tumor is malignant, we have a long road ahead. If it's benign, Dr. P. said this would be a situation that will have to be closely monitored for the rest of Jack's life. We are not out of the woods by any means.

...BUT I'M NOT THE SINGER

JUNE 19, 2010—Sitting here by Jack's bed still in the PCCU waiting for a move to a private room. We have been told we are going to get one, but the last count was 30 other kids were waiting ahead of us. Jack felt good yesterday after he was given some anti-nausea medicine. He ate lunch and dinner.

Ben had a bad day yesterday. I think the pressure of it all was getting to him. He was clumsy and discombobulated more than usual. He tripped over Jack's potty chair. He teased Jack when he shouldn't have and made Jack mad. Ben and I gave Jack a bath in bed and had to get Jack to stand up to get his unmentionable parts washed properly. I took the used washcloth to the dirty linen box and while my back was turned, Ben walked away from Jack who without the extra support fell to the floor. I guess I took it for granted Ben would hold on to Jack but rattled Ben wasn't thinking. Jack wasn't hurt, just shook up. Last night the insurance adjuster called Ben and he had lost our information we had given him on the name and phone number of the regional director of the National Flood Insurance people so he could finish our estimate. Ben stopped by the house to get the mail that is still coming and ran over the neighbor's dog. It wasn't hurt badly. All these things together along with the stress of the flood aftermath, Jack's health situation and upcoming surgery, an uncertain future, and the pressure of life sent Ben into a sullen, depressed mood. I could tell he was bottling all of this inside and when those little things happen, he's not able to handle them. Whenever we talk, I am usually crying (I cry when I am not around Jack) and I can see Ben has tears in his eyes too but he won't cry. I can feel that old lump in my throat and know it's time to cry and relieve the pressure. I cry and feel better. I don't think Ben is doing anything, cry or otherwise, to relieve the pressure we feel right now. He really needs to let it all out somehow. Benny has been very neutral about the whole thing. I'm not getting a chance to talk one on one with him, but he seems so nonchalant about all of this. I hope he is OK too.

I still cannot comprehend that Jack has a brain tumor! It is still like a bad dream—that foggy, cloudy feeling in the brain that says this cannot be right. I look at him, and besides his color and weight loss, he is our same old Jack. But will he always be? What will this surgery do to him? Will he be the same Jack afterward? Will he have to take treatments for this? Can he make it through those treatments? Will my child make it to the other side of this and still be my child?

JUNE 21, 2010—Waiting again! That's all we seem to do now is wait. We are waiting for Jack to get to recovery after his second MRI. This MRI is to take

MY NAME IS JACK JOHNSON...

pictures of his brain and skull in preparation for his surgery tomorrow. His head is covered with these small, round markers that are attached to his head with sticky stuff. They are put in place, and the MRI is taken so the surgeon will have a map of Jack's head and brain.

We were finally moved into a private room. Jack was thrilled, and so was I. I can take a shower in the private bathroom and so can Jack. Once they put the stickers on his head, he cannot shower again. He has been in a great mood. To look at him, one could never tell how sick he truly is. The boy's pediatrician came to see us, and fortunately, Jack was asleep which gave me and Dr. M. a little time to talk about cancer, autism, and Jack. It was nice to see him. Lots of family and friends have come by to see Jack, and he has been delighted to see them. He has been laughing and joking, amusing me and Ben and all his nurses. He laughed so hard that one nurse stopped by to see why Jack was laughing. He was watching a video someone had put together of characters off Sesame Street paired together with popular music from today. The characters were dancing or walking to the beat of the music; music Jack listens to all the time. He was laughing so hard he was crying. All the laughter was a nice break from worrying about the next morning's surgery.

Jack and I were awake at the crack of dawn getting up and ready for surgery. Ben and Benny arrived soon after we got up. Jack's surgery was at 7am and could take all day. We just don't know until Dr. P. gets inside Jack's brain and sees what he is working with. We were taken downstairs to the surgical floor. Jack was not worried or upset, surprisingly very calm. They started another IV but it went well with not too much screaming. We were put in a large area separated by curtains. Jack was placed in a curtained unit that is across from the surgical chalkboard. Near the top of the list of names on the board is my son's name and the name of his surgeon. Reality took a bite out of me. Surgical nurses and the anesthesiologist drop in, say hello to Jack, ask me and Ben lots of questions. Some answers we know; some we don't. Dr. P. comes by and talks to us. I am in awe of someone who will see parts of my son I have never seen before, someone who I must give my child to, someone who holds my child's life in his hands. I choke back a huge lump in my throat.

The nurses came to get Jack. We told him goodbye. As soon as he was out of sight, I released the avalanche of tears I had been holding back: tears of fear, angst, denial, and disbelief. How could this be happening?

Ben and I walk to the surgical waiting room. Benny was waiting, and there was a large group of people waiting for us too. Our Sunday School Class had brought us food for the day. My dad, sister, Ben's mom, Rivers, Misses

... BUT I'M NOT THE SINGER

Luna and Miss Kim, Ben's sister and cousin are there waiting for us. One of our pastors from church was there. The waiting room was a large L shaped room. Our group took up a whole section of the L. We are gathered in a section that has windows and a separate kitchen area where we can eat when we get hungry. No food or drink is allowed in the waiting room. The surgical nurses had explained that they would call us during the surgery to let us know how Jack is doing and how the surgery is going. We have a phone in our area we can pick up when we get the call. Now we wait.

Just as expected, we get a call from the surgical nurse who tells us they have started the surgery. My mind cannot stop thinking about how a surgeon is opening the back of my baby's head, cutting out a tumor that is surrounded by the material in the body that controls every bodily function that happens to us each day. Our family and friends try hard to take our minds off what is happening to Jack a few walls away. Even though we talk and seem to be normal, we are anything but typical. We are living a real-life nightmare.

Other friends and family come and go, visiting during their lunch break or if they were near the area. We are hugged, touched, prayed for, prayed with, fed, hydrated, and loved. The surgical nurses call at intervals to let us know everything is well; Jack is doing great. The day drags by for us even with all the love and company we are blessed with that day.

We get the call at 1-ish that the surgery is almost finished and that Dr. P. will be out soon to talk to us. I pace the floor, my stomach in knots. Dr. P. walks in, and Ben, Benny, and I walk toward him. My sister joins us so she can listen and take notes as the doctor talks. We sit in chairs away from others, and Dr. P. sits in front of us. He tells us Jack is fine, he did well during the surgery, and there were no complications. Dr. P. tells us Jack has a brain tumor called Medulloblastoma, a stage four, malignant brain cancer. Since I had researched pediatric brain tumors online, I heard Dr. P. say the letter "M" and knew we were in trouble. I lowered my head to my chest while tears streamed down my face. Dr. P. dropped from his chair, leans on his knees, puts his hand under my chin, and raised my head to face him. He tells us that this cancer is not the death sentence it once was, that there are treatments today for it that are having good results, and that the researchers are coming out with new treatments all the time. He tells us Jack is in recovery and will be for a while, and he will then be moved up to PCCU where we can see him. Dr. P. tells us he will be back later to check on Jack and talk more to us.

Our world just shattered around us. Ben, Benny, and myself walked to the kitchen area where we cried and hugged each other. My sister had the task of letting the others waiting know the bad news. There were lots of tears and long faces. Some hugged us, some had no words. I sat in the children's play area of the waiting room, playing with toys, while I tried to absorb what had just happened. I didn't feel my body anymore. The waiting room disappears around me. The life we had known before is not the life we have now. I could not see, hear, or feel the world around me. I was not whole anymore. Tears rolled down my face uncontrolled. I didn't feel like I was crying but my eyes were shedding tears. I was numb, a void, yet living and breathing, the world had faded from around me. I was in total shock. Family and friends touched me to say goodbye. Something deep within me took over and said goodbye. It wasn't me but it was me. I heard their words but their words didn't penetrate my brain. I faked a smile at their "I'm sorry" and don't know if I replied. I hugged them but felt nothing. I was there but not there.

A nurse came to tell us Jack had been taken upstairs and we could see him now.

In PCCU, Jack was sitting upright in his bed, still hooked to tubes and machines. He looked good, his color was good, but he was sound asleep. There was a patch of hair missing from the back of his head. That was all I could see since his head was against an "O" shaped pillow which cradled his head without touching his incision. The PCCU nurse told us that Jack had not woken up yet but had stirred. Since he had been under anesthesia for such a long time, he would sleep for a while. Our family that remained at the hospital came to see him and left. Benny rode home with relatives after seeing his brother. Ben, and I left Jack in the hands of the PCCU nurse while we walked up the street for something to eat and to get out of the hospital for a while. We talked about what we know and what we don't know. We wondered what will happen to us in the days to come. We wondered what will happen to our son. How are we going to go through cancer treatments with Jack, a kiddo with autism, while not even living in our own house? How will we get by financially? How can Ben work if he must help me with Jack during these unknown treatments? What are we going to do?

After we got back, the nurse told us Jack had stirred more. When Jack heard our voices, he stirred again. We talked to him, he responded by shaking his head but didn't open his eyes. At least he knew us and was responding to us. Ben left for home, and I stayed with Jack. It had been a long day for all of us, and we were exhausted. Jack seemed to be resting so I laid down on the three-inch covered foam mattress in the PCCU room that substituted for a bed. I closed my eyes, but my brain was fretting, stressing; trying to come to

... BUT I'M NOT THE SINGER

terms with the events of the day. I found myself unable to stop the constant parade of noise in my brain. I sat up and stared aimlessly out the window into the darkness of night.

Jack's PCCU nurse came and went, periodically checking on his vitals and stats. In the quiet of the room, I heard a tiny "Mommy." Jack was asking for me. I rushed to his side and let him know I was there. We held hands and he shook his head lightly to my questions. He told me he doesn't feel well and felt sick. Our talking had gotten the attention of his nurse who came in and talked to Jack too. She grabbed a nearby container when he told her he felt bad, he opened his mouth, and a black, smelly vomit rolled out of his mouth into the container. I was shocked, afraid what I was seeing was blood. The nurse took the container, emptied it, washed it out, but before she could get back to Jack's bed, he needed it again. I finally asked what Jack's vomit was and the nurse told me it was the anesthesia from his surgery. I had never been the "vomit person" in our house. I could do anything else but vomit. Because of this, I was almost useless to Jack and the nurse. I just stood there in horror and disgust watching the vile smelling, thick black vomit roll out of my son. He didn't heave or gag; it just came out of his open mouth like water comes out of a hose. After a few minutes of being sick, Jack settled and fell asleep. The nurse left and I returned to my window of the world. Within a few minutes, Jack cried for me again and again he was sick. This went on most of the night. Not only was Jack patched together with stitches down the back of his head, on steroids to keep his brain from swelling, zoned out on residual anesthesia and strong pain medicine, he was also very sick from the huge quantities of anesthesia it took to keep him asleep during his seven-hour surgery. I had expected a long night but not in this way.

With the rise of the sun, Jack finally opened his eyes. His stomach settled once the anesthesia left his body. He was alert but only in intervals. He slept for a while and was coherent for a while. He could move his extremities and could hold up his head. He told us when he was hungry and when he wanted to watch TV. Dr. P. came by to let us know Jack was doing great and would be able to go home tomorrow if everything progressed as it seemed to be now. I was apprehensive about bringing Jack home so soon after major brain surgery, but the doctor was confident Jack was going to be able to convalesce at home better than being in the hospital. We would be sent home with precise instructions on how to take care of Jack.

A day later, we were back in our temporary home. Jack was still weak and not his old self but well enough to come home. Since we were living in the

MY NAME IS JACK JOHNSON...

upstairs of River's house, it was hard to get Jack up the stairs, but we did it. He was afraid of the stairs and falling since his balance was off. He was still on steroids for brain swelling and took his pain pills dissolved in his drinks. At first, he would wait until he was hurting before he would say something and it would take the pill longer to take effect. He didn't want to talk, just sat and stared at the TV, no laughter, no emotions. It worried me, but maybe it will just take him a little longer to get back to his old self. The surgeon shared with us after surgery that there was no brain stem involvement with Jack's tumor and Jack did not seem to have any after effects from the surgery itself. Some children after brain tumor surgery will have Posterior Fossa Syndrome, a condition that manifests after brain surgery leaving the patient with mutism (the inability to speak), decreased motor movement, cranial nerve paralysis, or temporary changes in emotions. No one knows why Posterior Fossa Syndrome happens in some children and doesn't in others. Jack did not seem to have any of these symptoms. He had a six-inch scar running from the top of his head to the bottom of his head just above his neck. We called it the "zipper." Although he was quiet and solemn, he could still talk, walk, and blessed us with an occasional smile.

Our church set up meals for us once we got back to our temporary home. It was so hard living in someone else's home. At least, they too were getting the benefit of the wonderful home-cooked meals we were receiving. It was our pleasure to share in our outpouring of support.

Our church has a Mission Team that every year travels to some needy area to help rebuild structures that are needing repair or to build new structures that are needed in neighboring churches or areas. They had previously gone to Mississippi to help in rebuilding churches after Katrina. This year they had helped in the aftermath of the flood including our house. Since Jack had been diagnosed with brain cancer, the Mission Team called Ben and offered to take over the task of rebuilding our house while Ben and I stayed with Jack during his upcoming treatments. Ben gladly told them yes. We had not known what we were going to do; trying to get Jack back and forth to the hospital, what Ben was going to do to keep a roof over our heads and trying to keep up with the everyday decisions and work it takes to rebuild a house. Their generous offer was a blessing. God was working through the people around us.

Each day Jack continued to improve. He ate more, was awake more, and moved around easier. On a day when Jack was feeling a little better, I had to talk to him about his wooly booger and the future. I told Jack that the wooly booger was wooly on the outside. Some of this wool could shed off while it

... BUT I'M NOT THE SINGER

was in his brain. This wool from the wooly booger was so small that no one could see it. And since no one could see it, the doctors wanted Jack to have treatments that would kill the wool the wooly booger might have left behind. I told him he would have to see lots of new doctors at different offices in the Children's Hospital. I tried to tell him just enough for him to grasp at one time. I decided that I would share things with him as those things were about to happen. I also had never mentioned the word "cancer" for fear of his reaction. We were going to take this one day at a time.

CHAPTER 19

Each day, family and friends called wanting to know how Jack was doing since every day he seemed different. All these calls were taking me away from my most important job: taking care of Jack. A friend suggested I start a CaringBridge site to keep everyone up to date on how Jack was doing. CaringBridge is a free online site that offers a place where patients or their loved ones can write in a journal format to let others know how the patient is on any given day. The journal readers can then leave well-wishers or words of encouragement for the patient or the family. On July 5th, I posted my first entry.

JULY 5, 2010—We—Rivers (also known as BR), Benny, Jack and I—just got back from an afternoon car ride. Jack wanted to go for a milkshake and a car ride, and we were excited he felt like going out. He told me which directions to go. We went all over our county once we stopped and bought the milkshakes. This ride was one that Ben has taken Jack on many times because Jack knew where to turn at every street we turned on. I am so glad he felt like getting out and that he remembered all the rides he had taken with his dad!! No surgery effects in Jack's brain today!

Jack felt so good a few days back—like his old self—happy, smiling and joking around the only way Jack can joke, but he hasn't felt well since. He told me last night he is itchy—he is covered in an acne-like rash caused by the steroids that keep his brain from swelling. He has been the biggest, bravest trooper I have seen. He has not cried—not once—through all of this. Through all the surgery stuff, the awful all night throwing up after the surgery, all the needles and medicines and smells (something that drives his autism crazy!) he has not shed one tear! To me that is amazing. What a wonderful person the good Lord gave us.

Thanks, God, for this strong, unique, quirky, loveable boy named Jack!

... BUT I'M NOT THE SINGER

JULY 8, 2010—Since we decided to put hardwood floors upstairs instead of carpet, today was carpet tear-out day. Benny is a workhorse when it comes to tearing up carpet even though he scared me to death with the razor-sharp blade he was using, but thankfully, he didn't cut himself. He got mad at me for saying "careful, careful" every time he had the razor in his hand. Mommy needs to chill. While Benny and I were pulling up carpet, Jack spent time at Ben's mother's house watching TV and playing poker—that always makes me laugh to say my Jack played poker. Winning several times made him happy. She said there were times he smiled and acted like the old Jack, but he is still quiet, subdued and not very energetic. She thinks he is still getting over major brain surgery and not to worry—it will just take time. I'll take her advice for today. Vanderbilt called to confirm our next week's appointments. Nurse J. at Dr. K.'s (Jack's oncologist) office called to let us know the when's and where's. We must be at the Children's Hospital (VCH) at 9 am Tuesday for Jack's next MRI at 10 am. They will be looking for any signs of cancer spreading into the spinal column. While they have him sedated, they will also do a spinal tap and take blood. On Wednesday, we have an appointment with the radiation oncologist at the Cancer Center at Vanderbilt. Thursday Jack has a hearing test at noon followed by a follow-up appointment with Dr. K. to discuss the results from Tuesday. The hearing test is to get a baseline of Jack's hearing before he starts radiation treatments. Hearing loss is one of the side effects of receiving radiation to the brain area.

JULY 9, 2010—Today at the house was hardwood floor day. My dad, one of my sisters, Ben and Benny put down hardwood floors in Jack's bedroom. It looks so much better than carpet. Jack told me today he is ready to be back in his bedroom. I asked him what he missed the most and he said his bed and his TV. He has been so good today—almost like his old self. He and I talked about home, the cats and the hospital. He said he didn't like hospital beds. Me neither. I took him to his grandmother's house today so I could help some at the house and she and Jack went to Ben and Jerry's for ice cream. He told me he didn't go inside, he sat in the car. He shared that he is afraid someone will make fun of his scar. I told him I would take care of anyone who made fun of his scar. I didn't tell him this but someone might have to post my bail on that one. He has played his DS a lot today and Benny said Jack got on the computer to watch his favorite YouTube videos. Sounds like the old Jack! Later we even talked him into going to Pancho's for Mexican food. We talked Jack into going to see his almost finished hardwood floors and, of course, he got to see

MY NAME IS JACK JOHNSON...

the cats. He really liked the floors and laughed at the cats meowing at him. It was a gift to see him up, out and smiling again.

Thanks, God, for the rain, for the good day, and for smiles.

JULY 13, 2010—What a long day. We started at VCH at 8:30 am in the hematology department. The nurse there took blood and put in the IV. Jack hates the IV part but likes to watch when they put IV's in and of course, scream a little too. He did great after the IV was secured. I walked beside his bed to the MRI room and held his hand while he was put to sleep. What was supposed to be 2 hours turned into 3 1/2 hours. Jack was a grizzly bear when he finally woke. He wanted the IV and monitors off. He didn't want to drink anything. He was too tired. He was too hungry. He went from a bear to a true Goldilocks. He wanted Arby's, one of his favorites. He ate two roast beef sandwiches, cheese sticks, peanut butter and an apple. I forgot to say that he has gained 4 pounds since the surgery. He probably gained four more just from lunch.

The oncology department did have a gift for me today. It's a 3-ring notebook divided into sections with bold letters on the front, "Childhood Cancer." It has everything a parent could want regarding information on cancer. My head feels like it could explode from information overload.

Thank you, blessed Father, for technology, for the kindness and patience of others, for voices that scream and give comfort, for good times and bad times that make us who we are, and for Your Son, Your love, and Your grace. Amen.

JULY 14, 2010—We visited with the radiation oncologist today. He did have good news—the MRI and spinal fluid from Tuesday were clear. Dr. T said radiation will start in 2 weeks and will occur five days each week for six weeks. Jack will have to be put to sleep every day because he MUST stay completely still for an hour while lying face down into a head brace with a helmet thing on his head with his head pointed upward while laying that way for an hour. Everyone raise your hand if you think you could do that. I don't see any hands. The radiation itself takes 5 minutes, the preparation and lining up the machines takes an hour. Then there are the side effects, so many that I couldn't write them all here. So, let's pick out the positives, shall we? The MRI was clear; the spinal fluid had no cancer cells, the doctor was friendly and very informative, Jack was yet again a trooper.

Thanks, God, for a beautiful day, the dinners provided by angels, the green passed tag on the heating and cooling system, Jack's ability to walk

...BUT I'M NOT THE SINGER

through today and not get upset, a roof over our heads and a bed on which to sleep. In His name, Amen.

JULY 15, 2010—Today Jack said, "I HATE VANDY!! Not the football team but the hospital." He is already so sick of going and we haven't even started the treatments. Jack's hearing is fine and the audiologist was cute...so said Ben. (She was. I will watch Ben for symptoms of hearing loss!) The oncologist moved Jack's CT scan for the radiation up to tomorrow. He will also have a Port-A-Cath inserted during another small operation on Monday. With all this accomplished, Jack will start radiation next week. Every day seems to be another procedure. I'm getting like Jack—I'm getting tired of Vandy. Not the football team The radiation will be for 6 weeks, then there is a month off, and then the chemo will start. Jack will get chemo once a month for the rest of the 9-10 months. Some months he will have to be hospitalized for the chemo but not all. The hospital stays will be 3 days. Jack did not want to stay again in the hospital—his reasons being they don't have Game Show Network and he doesn't like hospital food. With all this going on, the framing of our house passed inspection and we picked out kitchen cabinets.
   God, thank you for good news, good friends, good children, good health, good hearing and Your Son. Amen.

JULY 16, 2010—It's quiet tonight at our home away from home because Jack is spending the night at his Aunt Amy's house. She invited both the boys but Benny decided to stay with us. I called to tell Jack goodnight, and he was wrapped up in Amy's pink Snuggie drawing pictures of electric poles. He asked his dad before he went to Amy's to take him on a car ride and he got to see lots of electric poles. If you have never heard about Jack's drawings of electric poles, I will fill you in. Jack has a fascination with electric poles and how different each of them. Bet you didn't know all electric poles are different!! (Don't feel bad if you didn't, we had no clue until Jack showed us.) Some poles have street lights. Some have transformers. Some have several layers of wires. Some have only a few. The next time you are out on the roads, look at the poles, and you will see how different they indeed are. Jack likes to car ride, looks at the poles on his ride, memorizes the electric poles and draws them from memory. He will sit for hours and use reams of paper to draw all the poles he has seen on car rides. It is an amazing treat to see how the things we take for granted he is so tuned into. And it is unbelievable how his memory can work to remember each pole's difference. That's our Jack.

MY NAME IS JACK JOHNSON...

Today he had a CT scan of his brain and spine for the radiation technicians to map out a plan for the treatments. Dr. T. said the planning and mapping of the exact track the radiation must take is very intricate, complicated, and the most important part of the treatment. They are radiating two critical body parts—the brain and the spine—two places where the slightest mistakes could cause permanent damage. I can't imagine the pressure that would come with that job!

Thank you, God, for radiation techs, for blood sisters and friend sisters, for Snuggies, and for weekends. In Your Son's name, Amen.

JULY 18, 2010—We have almost finished Jack's bedroom. It's all painted, new floors, soon-to-be new mattress, new bedding, maybe a new TV. It looks nice and clean and happy and ready for him to be there. Hopefully, he will feel OK enough to go with us while we work on Benny's room and he can sit on his bed, watch his TV, play his Game Cube, draw at his desk and do all the things he loves to do in his room. I wish I had a magic wand and could have my house fixed today so we could get back in there.

Tomorrow is port surgery. The surgeon will cut a place in Jack's chest and insert a permanent IV port that will cut down on all the IV's, blood draws, and shots. Jack partly understands some of it—he likes the no more IV part. While he was at Aunt Amy's, he drew pictures of electric poles. Ben and I were thrilled he drew them. He hasn't drawn anything since before the surgery until he went to Amy's house, where pole drawing kicked in again.

God, thanks today for happy family times, feeling good, pictures drawn by little hands, friends and family who love and keep up with Jack, and Your love and grace. Amen.

JULY 19, 2010—Another long day. We got to VCH at 7:30am. We had to fill out paperwork, get our lovely paper bracelets, and Jack had to get his IV. This time the little nurse sprayed too much freezy spray and froze the vein and couldn't get it in. Someone else came in and put the IV in the other hand and got it on the first time. After talking to 4 other people answering the same questions over and over, they took Jack to surgery. Our Child Life specialist came and showed us what the port looks like and how it works. Jack has an incision for the port, and an incision where the tube was put in a neck artery. He is starting to look like a pincushion. He has marks and stickers all over his body, the two new incisions and they also covered his upper body with orange antiseptic. He is not happy he is orange. He said he wished he was blue! —his

... BUT I'M NOT THE SINGER

favorite color. They took him back at 9:15 and came for us at 10:30. He was waking up and already grouchy when we got to him. He didn't want to wake up, sit up, or drink water. He hurt but he didn't want to take any medicine. He let his presence be known to all who could hear. We finally left at 12:30. He has complained about his neck hurting so he has had another pain pill. He is now, after his pain pill, planning his next car ride tomorrow with his dad. His mouth has been running constantly the last hour or so. I'm not complaining—it just surprises me that he is so energized after taking a pain pill.

I must say whoever (Misses Luna) put together the Exit sign book from church (Misses Luna) was brilliant. He has already looked at it several times. He has talked about it to whoever will listen. He has told me stories about the pictures. He even slept with it during his nap this afternoon. Thank you, Misses Luna, for the great idea and the beautiful pictures. Thanks to all who posed for the pictures and held the signs. All of you made his day. I haven't seen him that excited in a very long time. He told me that one day maybe he could work for the church to make sure all the signs were always lit, maybe becoming a janitor so he could oversee changing all the lights on the Exit signs. He ended with saying he would have to get a Swiffer Sweeper. Can you tell he watches lots of TV?

Thank you, Lord, for Exit signs, pain pills, afternoon naps, pictures of friends, and things that bring us happiness—whatever it is for each of us. Amen.

JULY 21, 2010—Today was our practice run for Jack's upcoming radiation treatments at the Cancer Center. They must make sure they have all measurements for the treatments correct before the radiation begins tomorrow. The nurse, after getting us a room, had to access Jack's newly inserted port. Accessing, I have learned, is putting a needle with attached tubing in the port giving access to one of Jack's veins. Unfortunately, we must first take the sticky clear plastic covering off the newly inserted port. Next came the second bang of the day. Jack screamed and screamed while the plastic bandage was slowly peeled away from the port sight. I am sure the port site was still very sore from the implanting surgery and the little stitches it took to close the skin. Slowly the nurse pulled and wiped the sticky plastic with water to help to get it to release. Jack was screaming and writhing in pain—you would have thought we were operating without anesthesia on him. He was so worked up, he lost it—that point where he wasn't listening and wasn't thinking. The nurse finally removed the sticky and Jack was still screaming and bellowing in pain. She got the needle and the screams got louder. About this time, I'm wishing for earplugs. She pushes the needle in the port and the screams continue. Finally, we get the

MY NAME IS JACK JOHNSON...

crazed child to realize everything is over, the needle is in, the sticky is gone. Jack looks down at his chest and says "whew!" Then he looks up at me and says, "look, I have tears" while holding a few tears up for me to see. (If you have worked with Jack you know he can manufacture tears, squeeze them out into his hand from his eye, and hold them out for you to see to make his point!) Let's stop here for a moment—this child had brain surgery. The surgeon took part of his skull out, moved parts of his brain around, and cut a tumor out. Then he put it all back in place and carefully stitched the whole thing closed. My wonderful child never once complained but tell him we must take sticky plastic off your skin and he falls to pieces.

Tonight, was yet another car ride night. After dinner, Jack had to get his dad to take him on another ride. Tonight, Ben gave him the choice of cars to ride in—ours or WD's Cadillac (WD is BR's husband.) Jack chose the Caddy. Ben put in a jazz cassette, and they left. Ben said Jack looked over at him and said, "This is very relaxing!" I am so glad after his trip to the Cancer Center he got to do a little relaxing.

Heavenly Father, thank you for the ability to relax, the ability to laugh, the ability to love, the ability to heal. Amen.

Something has occurred to me after our many trips to the hospital. With Jack being a teenager, the doctors, nurses, and other personnel all introduce themselves to me and to Jack. I have not properly taught Jack about how to shake hands and what to say when others shake your hand and say, "Nice to meet you." So, yesterday Jack and I had a chat about what to say and do when someone sticks out their hand for you to shake. I told him the way to do it was when someone puts out their hand for you to shake, you put your hand in theirs, not too hard and not too soft, and you shake their hand, again not too hard and not too soft. We did a few rehearsals while we shook each other's hands. Then I told him when he shakes someone's hand and they say, "Nice to meet you", you say "Nice to meet you too." We practiced this too several times. Then Jack says he might say "Same here" when someone tells him "Nice to meet you." Then he starts coming up with several other things he can say to them when they shake their hand with his. Then I showed him what to do when someone introduces themselves to you and shakes your hand. I put my hand out to him and said, "Hi, I'm Jill Johnson." I told Jack he needed to say, "I'm Jack Johnson" and how he could then say "Nice to meet you." We practiced this over and over several times and yet again Jack starts making up different things to say. Some of his etiquette statements do not meet the stan-

...BUT I'M NOT THE SINGER

dards of any etiquette book ever written and some are silly. After coming up with all kinds of good and bad remarks, he finally says, "I know what I will say... I can say, 'My name is Jack Johnson, but I'm not the singer.'"

JULY 23, 2010—We went to the Cancer Center and Jack had his first radiation treatment yesterday. It didn't take as long as I thought it would. He has this entourage since he has an anesthesia doc, a nurse who takes vital signs, and several radiation techs that must move him into position each day after they put him to sleep. During his radiation treatment, he lies on his stomach with his head and face in a mask contraption that they use to put his head in the position it needs to be to aim the radiation in the right spot. The mask cradles his head and shoulders and is made from a honeycomb material that is imprinted on Jack's face once his treatment is finished. He did get his needle out today which made me happy. He is so marked with ink and stickers on his back he looks like someone played a trick on him and put blue stickers all over him. They are the markers they use to guide them during the treatments. If one falls off, I am supposed to mark the spot with a Sharpie. After yesterday's treatment, he started complaining about feeling sick. He even went to the bathroom thinking he was going to be sick but as he said, just spit instead. They had prescribed anti-nausea meds for him after the surgery, so after a call to the radiation nurse, I crushed and made him a pill cocktail. He slept the rest of the afternoon. Today he also complained about nausea and I gave him a pill. Yesterday he also had a headache, today his ears hurt. This treatment is supposed to affect his ears and his hearing because the radiation beams are shot into the back of the brain from ear to ear width. I think the radiation oncologist said 70% would have damage, 40 to 50% will require hearing aids. They are now better since I made another pill cocktail with ibuprofen. I am a little shocked that he is having these side effects so soon. The nurse said the nausea would start around the 3rd week of treatment. But she said some have it earlier than that. Lucky Jack to get his nausea early.

Today the drywall went up at the house. I almost cried when I saw it—it is the first significant sign of moving forward. I haven't seen walls in my house since May. Jack wanted to see them, so we carried him over there. He smiled at the walls, at his room, and at the cats. We love smiles.

Thanks, God, for happy smiles, medicines that make us feel better, people who make us feel better, and the promise of better days. Amen.

JULY 24, 2010—Today was hard. First thing when I got up, Jack wanted

MY NAME IS JACK JOHNSON...

breakfast, I got it ready, he sat down to eat, tells me he doesn't feel well, and he goes to the bathroom and vomits. He has had two radiation treatments, and he is already vomiting! The only thing he has had today to eat is a container of Jell-O because he is afraid everything will make him vomit. He has had two anti-nausea pills today. I don't know what to say or do. I sit here and beg and plead and try to get him to eat anything but he refuses. I feel so useless and helpless right now.

This afternoon Benny and I went to the house and moved furniture and cut and pulled up the carpet in his room. The drywall guys were there putting up the drywall mud, but we stayed in Benny's room and did a lot of sweating. There was also a lot of huffing and puffing and sounds of pain coming from Benny...ha! No, that was me.

God, thanks for hard times that make us appreciate the good, thanks for staying with us through both. Thanks for the foods we eat, for the minds you gave us, for helping us understand, and for loving us even when we fall short. Amen.

JULY 25, 2010—Today was a little bit better than yesterday but not by much. All Jack has had to eat is one container of Jell-O and four cheese sticks from Sonic. He did eat some chocolate pudding, but it all came back up. I wish I could remember which doctor or nurse told me when they irradiate his brain— since it is the same area as the tumor was and affects the same parts that control the vomiting reflex— he might be sick again. That person needs a gold star for being right on the money. Jack is just like he was those last few weeks before his tumor diagnosis. He tries to eat, then he vomits. I wish so badly I could make this all go away, but I can't. The only thing I can do is talk to the doctors tomorrow and see what the heck we are going to do. He cannot go like this for long. Today was a Pawpaw Sunday where my family gets together to eat Sunday dinner. Jack stayed at home with Ben while Benny and I went to Dad's. I brought Jack his favorite foods from Dad's: green beans, roast beef, and mac and cheese. He didn't want them.

Thank you, Lord, for Your Word, for the foods we eat, for all the things we so stupidly take for granted, for good health, for friends that hold us up, and time with family. Amen.

JULY 26, 2010—Needle day and all went well with it. Numbing cream is a wonderful invention. I do hope the inventor is filthy rich because he or she saves so many children and their parents a lot of heartaches.

...BUT I'M NOT THE SINGER

Radiation went without a hitch. We got home, Jack took off his shoes, went to the bathroom and vomited. I talked to the doctor today first thing and told him about the vomiting and the lack of food. He prescribed Jack with steroids, again, just when we thought we had started to get rid of the steroid acne that at one time covered his whole body including his bottom and stomach. The doctor said the radiation is causing the brain to swell where the beam is aimed—the same place where the tumor was located. Hopefully, the steroids will take effect soon and will also increase his appetite.

We have our cable hooked back up to the house. A step forward. The drywall guys were there today again with coat of mud number two. Sanding is next. Progress. Slow, but progress.

Dear Lord, thank you for the sunshine and the storms, thanks for the ability to think and feel emotions, thanks for progress of all kinds, and thanks for this day. In His name, Amen.

JULY 27, 2010—Another day, another vomiting episode, another 1/2 Jell-O container and a little chicken and diarrhea. I talked to the doctor again today. They will start taking his weight every day and, if needed, will go up on the steroids a little more, but only if needed to stimulate Jack's appetite. Tomorrow we also will start our weekly trip for a small dose of chemo. It is not the chemo regimen we will be taking in a few months, but a small dose to work with the radiation treatment. If the vomiting wasn't severe enough, let's go and add a little chemo!! Even without eating and with being sick, Jack has had a pretty good day. He felt good enough for a car ride out Columbia Highway and onto West Harpeth Road. I haven't ridden out that way in years myself. I was just glad he went for his ride.

Thank you, God, for patience, for our earthly bodies, for our earthly homes, for more patience, for land not developed, and for my children and all children because they are all beautiful. Amen.

JULY 28, 2010—Thanks to all the people from church who are bringing us food. I don't know what we would do if I had to plan, shop and cook right now. Thank you! We went today for radiation treatment number 5. We added chemo today, too. As soon as we arrived at the Cancer Center, Jack had to go to the bathroom to vomit and had diarrhea too. Ben went with us today because of the added chemo and oncology visit. I'm glad because I couldn't have done it without his help. He took Jack to the bathroom while I checked him in. He got his radiation. We got him awake (not an easy task!), we put him in

MY NAME IS JACK JOHNSON...

a wheelchair and made the trek to VCH. Once we got there, we talked to our case manager, the doctor, the nurse and the child life specialist. Jack has now lost another 11 pounds, not something we need right now. We are still hoping and praying the steroids kick in and boost his appetite. It was a hard day emotionally for me. All the talk about chemo, white blood counts, hemoglobin, platelets, and on and on are swimming in my brain.

Dear Lord, thank you for mothers, thank you for people who care for us that aren't related by blood, thanks for letting us be comfortable, thanks for miracles that we can see and ones we can't, and thanks for your beloved Son. Amen.

JULY 29, 2010—Another day, another treatment. Tomorrow's is #7 with 23 more to go. I know because they gave me a new schedule. I never dreamed I would receive a calendar schedule made by a cancer center. It still is like a dream gone wrong when I hear the word cancer. How could my son have cancer? I can only take bits and pieces of reality at a time. Too much and I fall apart, or I start to tune things out. A preservation mechanism. I found this the other day: God doesn't give us what we can handle; God helps us handle what we are given.

Jack's treatment went well. They were late taking us back to get started, and he wasn't happy about it. He told them so. He walked down the hall to the treatment room with that "I just told you" walk of his with that head held up high, arms swinging at his sides. I was kind of snickering watching him and thinking, "now that's my Jack." Not much of him left in those sagging clothes, but that is my Jack. Everything I read about this cancer and the treatments says there will be some cognitive side effects. So, seeing him walk down that hall in front of all those highly educated doctors and technicians who made him wait after he just told them about it, there is no cognitive shortage there. He makes me laugh. He also has eaten more today than yesterday. But of course, it wouldn't be another day without another vomit. If I never see or hear the word vomit again, I will not be upset.

Thank you, Lord, for understanding, for people who hold us up, for people who care for us, for people who have freely opened their doors to us, for eyes that see things others don't, and for all children, healthy ones and especially sick ones. Bless them all. Amen.

JULY 30, 2010—Jack has had a good day so far. Mommy finally got smart—it takes a while—and took Jack's toothbrush and toothpaste to the Center with

... BUT I'M NOT THE SINGER

us. Jack told me and Ben that the awful taste in his mouth from the anesthesia makes him sick. So, I have been trying to figure out what to do about this and if this is really what is causing him to vomit and not the treatments themselves. Today, I took the toothbrush and toothpaste and we stopped by the restroom to brush. I had explained to him in advance so he would be open and understand the idea. We stumbled our way to the bathroom, a giant feat since, as Jack says, he is drunk from the anesthesia. Here he stood with a big red plaid blanket wrapped around him in front of the sink while I tried to hold him steady while also putting toothpaste on his brush. His toothbrush is one of those battery-operated brushes that you push a button and the brush does the up and down motion for you. I turned the brush on after the paste was on and the paste went flying into the sink and down the drain. I tried again and turned on the brush and there went the paste again. Next time I squeezed the paste INTO the bristles and Jack got it in his mouth before the paste went flying again. I love the new sinks that the water comes on by itself when you wash your hands, but not for brushing teeth. That little eye that sees your hands doesn't see a toothbrush quite as well. So, every time I would help him put the toothbrush down to get water, it would not turn the water on. I would have to put my hands under the faucet to get it to turn on. After he was finished, there was blue toothpaste and water everywhere. But we made it and he hasn't vomited!

Jack received a compliment today if you can call it that. (I did) There are several smaller children in front of Jack getting their radiation treatments. So, while we are waiting, the younger ones are in recovery trying to wake up from the anesthesia. Some are very quiet. Some are combative. Some are very loud. Today was a loud day with the anesthesia doctors commenting on how bad things had been trying to get the little ones to wake up. After Jack's treatment, the anesthesia doctor said, "You know it has been a hard day when your teenage patient with autism has been your best patient all day"

Dear Heavenly Father, thanks for today, thanks for moments that we share with each other that mean nothing to others except us, thanks for friends that keep us in their thoughts and prayers, thanks for friends that bring us food to eat especially homemade sweet rolls, and thanks for keeping us safe in your arms for today. Amen.

CHAPTER 20

AUGUST 2, 2010—Today was needle day, the day they put the needle into Jack's port, leaving it until Friday when they take it out. The first nurse (that is not a good way to start the sentence) didn't get the needle into the port and had to take it out. The second nurse hit it the first time. Jack was his great self again. He looks a little goofy with his vomit bucket (his words, not mine) shoved underneath his mouth with one hand while the other hand is holding his nose because he doesn't like the smell of alcohol. The elbow of the hand holding his nose is pointed to the ceiling because the port is near his left breast and the nurse needs to get to it. I'm not sure if it is physically possible to vomit if you are holding your nose. I do know he is a goofy goober sometimes, but we love him all the same. We have had no vomiting today, some spitting up, but no vomiting. He hasn't had much appetite only eating Jell-O (he calls it gelatin) until late this afternoon, and he asked for Ritz Bits. Ben went to the grocery and got some for him. At dinner time, we asked Jack if he was hungry and he said no. While I was putting up the Ritz Bits I know why: he ate almost the whole box!! Hey, they are full of protein in the peanut butter, so I can't complain. I'm just glad he ate something, and it stayed down. Small victories!!

Thank you, God, for the food that we eat to help our bodies stay healthy, for people who care for us in many ways, for families and friends, and for the strength to face the bad days. In Jesus Name, Amen.

AUGUST 3, 2010—Jack and Ben went for another car ride today out to Leipers Fork, and past Boston where 840 is being built. The rides are a huge treat for Jack as he counts down the minutes until his dad comes and picks him up. He acts like a teenager waiting for a date. He says things like "Dad will be here soon" or "I can't do that... I'm waiting for Dad to pick me up." It's funny to me that it's something so small that thrills him. I think we are the luckiest family to be able to have a great time in a car, riding through the countryside, looking at electric poles......

... BUT I'M NOT THE SINGER

Thank you, God, for eyes that truly see, hearts that truly know love, skin that can feel another's hug, and for giving us the opportunity to see others through your Son's eyes. Amen.

AUGUST 4, 2010—It was a long day. Jack went to have his radiation treatment at 8 am. I think the recovery nurse didn't take the extra sleepy medicine out of Jack's port before she flushed it because he was extremely sleepy for quite a while afterward. We oozed him out of the Cancer Center into a wheelchair and got him over to the hospital for his weekly chemo treatment at the oncology center. He slept most of the time he was there. His new oncology doctor, Dr. E., said that Jack was holding his own and showing signs of weight gain (ounces!!). The doctors are talking about lowering the dosage of steroids and starting with an acne treatment. The doctor wants to try to get a lot of it healed before Jack starts chemo because acne, caused by bacteria, can cause an infection. An infection of any kind is to be avoided at all costs. After we talked to the doctor, Jack got his chemo. Jack did spit up some before we left but he brushed his teeth again (he had already brushed them before he left home and before he left the Cancer Center!!) and that seemed to help with the spitting up. He is going to have the cleanest teeth in town.

After we ate lunch, we went back to VCH and waited to see the assessor for Jack's cognitive assessment. Jack had completed an assessment before he had his surgery, so this was his 6-weeks follow-up assessment. They will assess him again in 6 months. She thinks it is amazing the way Jack can memorize things. On the assessment, she asked him to look at a list of words, memorize them, and repeat them back to her. She said he asked her if he could repeat them backward to her instead. He did, and she was amazed. After the assessment, we went to see the neurosurgeon, Dr. P. He showed us before and after MRI pictures of Jack's brain and tumor. He explained we no longer need his services and released us from his care.

Thanks, God, for easy days, for happy days, for hot days and cold days, for healthy days, for safe days, and for watching over us days. Amen.

AUGUST 5, 2010—Today was, as Jack calls it, a two-person easy trip to the basement. He and I went to the Cancer Center where he got his treatment. Uneventful trip getting there, going to the treatment room and being put to sleep. After he got to recovery, he was hard to wake up again, and he was Shrek, the name I give to him when he wakes up screaming and making ugly sounds. We had to stay longer to see Dr. T. which made Shrek even madder.

MY NAME IS JACK JOHNSON...

We got his teeth brushed, got to the car and before I could get out of the valet lot, he had grabbed the trash bag and was heaving. Several cars were waiting behind us, so I had to find a better place for him to get sick. We drove a little, I found a parking lot with lots of shade, tore up a towel we had in the car, wet it with my water and put it on the back of his neck. He felt a little better, so we drove home. Once there, he headed straight for the bathroom where he heaved and spit a little more. He never actually vomited, a good thing, but all that dry heaving is just as bad if you have ever done it. My heart breaks when you stand there with him while his thin body shakes and heaves. It is the most helpless and useless feeling in the world. Cancer sucks! What an amazing kid he is. I told him the other day he was my new hero. Anyone who could fight cancer like he has becomes a warrior hero in my book. I think he liked that.

Thanks, today, Lord, for the rain, for the thunder, for the lightning, for the storms. Without them, we would not know how to appreciate the sunshine. In His Name, Amen.

AUGUST 8, 2010—Ben and I worked on Benny's bedroom at the house yesterday painting it orange. Yes, ORANGE! It screams ORANGE! We worked last night until 11 pm, and I dreamed about orange things like giant citrus fruit and monster basketballs. I'm kidding about the dreams but not about the late night and the ORANGE!!

While we were at the house, Benny called and told us Jack said his hair was falling out. When we got back to our home away from home, Jack's hair was indeed falling out. He already had a big bald spot in the back that was in the same spot as the zipper scar and where the radiation beam is aimed during the treatments. The radiation oncologist had told me Jack would lose his hair in the back first where the radiation beam kills the hair cells. When I saw it for the first time, it made me cry. I was just whistling through the weekend and bam! it smacked me in the face. Seeing his hair coming out was a neon sign screaming at me—THIS IS REAL. I don't know what I was thinking, the doctors had told me and I have seen other children without hair. But I guess it was the fact of just giving up another sign of normalcy—there is nothing that screams cancer patient more than a bald head, especially on a child, no matter what age. I have cried several times. This morning, he has the look of a middle-aged man who is losing the top of his hair with the sides intact. If you run your fingers over the sides of his head, your fingers will be covered with hair. It won't be long before it is all gone. At this moment, Jack and Ben are traveling the countryside scouring the roads for electric poles. Ben found

... BUT I'M NOT THE SINGER

and borrowed a hat from WD and Jack has it on. This is the picture: Ben is driving WD's Cadillac, Jack is in the passenger seat with a big safari hat on, t-shirt, basketball shorts and house shoes, and black sunglasses. They are probably listening to jazz and there is not a word spoken. The Sunday afternoon drive....

Thank you, Lord, for strong, healthy bodies, for Sunday afternoons, for the gift of sight so we can see and enjoy all the colors of life, and for making us in Your image. Amen.

AUGUST 9, 2010—Monday was needle day and we lived through another one. Jack was very impatient with the doctors again but they lived through another one too. Jack is on so much medicine I finally broke down and bought a medicine reminder box thingy or whatever they are called. I couldn't keep up with all the meds and what time he was taking what. Guess that old age thing is coming on sooner than I thought. I meticulously go through each prescription dose and what time he should take each. I open each little time of day box, put all the pills that go in each, the doctors change everything around and I must do it all again. It happened again today—the radiation oncologist wanted us to give Jack his first anti-nausea medicine before we left home to get in his system before they put him to sleep. Jack had been getting his first morning dose in his IV port when we got to the Cancer Center. He OK'ed for Jack to drink a very small amount of liquid to mix the crushed pill in, it had to be clear juice. Today we tried apple juice and he didn't vomit. After his treatment in the recovery room before he even got off the bed, he started gagging and trying to vomit. Nurse K. and I got him into the bathroom and he vomited all the apple juice up. He was groggy from the anesthesia while trying to aim and vomit into the toilet. Nurse K. and I both agreed that Dr. T. was going to have to change Jack back to getting the meds in the port. I got Jack to the car and as soon as we got on the interstate, he started vomiting again. He vomited most of the way home. I never knew how hard it is to drive with a vomiting passenger in the car with you. Tomorrow three things will change (1.) Jack will get his first dose in the port per a call from Nurse K., (2.) Ben will have to start going with me and Jack to drive so I can take care of Jack, and (3.) I will have to redo the pill box yet again!

Thanks, God, for laughter, for people who work to care for us, for people who look out after us, for people who open their home to us, for people who have cooked for us, and for the people who pray for us daily. Amen.

MY NAME IS JACK JOHNSON...

August 10, 2010—I checked off my three things that I was going to do different today. First, Jack was not going to take an anti-nausea pill but take the medicine by IV port. Check! Second, I took all anti-nausea pills for morning out of the pill pack or whatever it's called. Check! And third, Ben drove me and Jack to the Cancer Center. Check! And I'm glad he did. Poor Jack had to have an extra X-ray so they had to give him more sleepy medicine. He vomited most of the way home. He sat in the front passenger seat, I sat behind him, and held the "puke bucket" as he calls it under his head when he needed it. When he wasn't sick, I sat forward and rubbed his arms. He didn't have much in him but bless his heart, he just gags and retches over and over. I'm getting to where I really hate this cancer thing. I will say this: I have never seen a child take something so horrible as this in stride like my Jack does. He never cries, through all the getting poked, prodded, putting to sleep, and getting soooo sick. He just does it. Now don't get me wrong, he doesn't smile or laugh or cut up like he used to. Some days he hardly even talks. I think, "what would I do if this was me," and I would be a boohoo, snot-faced, feeling-sorry-for-myself wimp. Not Jack. He is showing me yet again what a great kid he is. I am finding myself more and more looking up to him as an example of strength.

The house is still there. The tile guys are getting ready for the tile to come in and doing the preliminary work. The tile comes in tomorrow. My morale is at an all-time low. Between Jack being so sick and the house still not ready, I am feeling down. Even Jack said this weekend that he wishes he could be back in his bedroom. He hasn't said that in a while. If I just had a magic wand...

Lord, thank you for miracles, for healing the sick, for feeding the hungry, for forgiving us when we fall short, for the blessing of life. In Your Son's Name, Amen.

AUGUST 11, 2010—Today is the half way point for Jack's radiation treatments. We have been through 15 as of today and have 15 more to go. I pray the next 15 go very quickly.

Last night Ben convinced Jack to let him shave part of his head. Jack's hair is falling out all around his head but not on the top. Ben said he looked like a well-worn baby doll that some little girl had drug around for many years and most of its hair had been rubbed off. After the shave, Jack looked in the mirror and said he thought he looked like an old man. With Jack's hair gone, his zipper (what we call his scar) stands out.

... BUT I'M NOT THE SINGER

Heavenly Father, thanks for the kindness of strangers, for laughter, for medicines that heal, for the people who give us those medicines, and for another day of life. Amen.

AUGUST 14, 2010—Today was finishing up the orange and white bedroom. With the help of our generous friends from church, our downstairs now has paint as well. They also helped us move furniture around upstairs so we can get the kid's playroom ready for hardwood floors. Our new church friends are truly a gift to us from God.

God, thank you for old friends who know when we need a pick-me-up, for new friends who give their time to make your life better, for the many colors in our world and for the eyes to see them. Amen.

AUGUST 15, 2010—Jack has had a good day today even coming to the house and playing Game Cube in his bedroom. He laughed and screamed at the game, and it sounded like home again. Too bad I was pounding staples into the newly laid hardwood floors with my dad and sister. But I got to hear him, and it was music to my ears.

Dear Lord, thank you for sore muscles that we had forgotten were there thank you for the sound of children laughing, thank you for family and friends, thank you for strong bodies. In His Name, Amen.

AUGUST 16, 2010—All went well with Jack's needle today. Nurse K. had tried to insert the needle a few weeks back, and it didn't work. It freaked her out and freaked Jack out. She was afraid to try again and upset Jack, so she got another nurse to try it. Nurse L. got it on the first try. Jack remembered this and told Nurse K. first thing, "You better get this in the first time." Poor Nurse K. was frazzled as soon as he said that. The whole time she was getting the needle ready, he was verbally reminiscing about Nurse L. and "her beautiful, long, red hair which was lovely and how she got the needle to go in on the first try and it didn't hurt.... blah, blah." Nurse K., let me introduce you to my unfiltered son, Jack, who will say whatever his mind thinks.

God, thank you today for sneaky family helpers, for houses that turn into homes, for nurses who take very good care of us, for sleep that heals the body, and for children who love their mothers. Amen.

AUGUST 17, 2010—We made it through another day. I found out today we are in the middle of the brain boost, where they are treating the tumor bed in the

MY NAME IS JACK JOHNSON...

2010   Jack and Mia, the cat during his radiation treatments

brain with a higher dose of radiation. I always thought motherhood would be this wonderful ride—like a Hallmark Card commercial. Happy mother, happy children, happy family. No one ever thinks this will happen. Don't get me wrong—up to now, motherhood has been a joy, even with the autism. There were some very rough patches, but they were patches, not vast valleys of medical treatments, pills, pills and more pills, gagging and lack of appetite, and not knowing the outcome. Cancer is hell on earth for a child and their parents.

Lord, thanks for friends that help us when we need help, for a mother's love, for a child's happy smile, for healthy bodies. Amen.

AUGUST 18, 2010—Today was chemo day, and Jack has lost more weight—down to 122. He has completely lost his appetite. I don't know how to make him eat more than he feels like eating which right now is not much. While we were in the oncology department, we talked to a nutritionist. She talked about

...BUT I'M NOT THE SINGER

getting the doctors to give him an appetite enhancer. Like every other day he gagged, heaved, and spit several times today. Every time I talk to the doctor, I tell them how sick he has been and ask if there is anything else they can give him. Today the doctor said she wanted to try Benadryl to see if it would help. They put it in his IV port and soon after he felt better for a while. We haven't seen that in a while—Jack feeling well and not having his puke bucket close by (remember, puke bucket is his term, not ours!).

Lord, thank you for the soaking rain, for nurses with big hearts, for workers with incredible skills, for drugs that make us feel better. Lord, look out for and bless the families who struggle with diseases where they lose control of their normal lives. Please send them healing, understanding, and love. Wrap your arms around the children who hurt in so many ways. Amen.

AUGUST 19, 2010—Jack has not felt well most of the day. I am not surprised because he had chemo yesterday. I am noticing the longer we continue with treatments, the less well he feels. Today, he played Game Cube for about 15 minutes, sat up only to eat a small lunch and a smaller dinner, sat up several times to drink fluids and when we went to see the house tonight. Other than those times mentioned, he has been lying on the couch. Now he has no appetite, no energy, no hair, and no bedroom. My poor child…

Lord, thanks for patience, for supportive friends and families, for times when we feel good even if it is for a moment, thanks for hands to hold when we reach out to each other, and for hearts that feel love. Amen.

AUGUST 23, 2010—Saturday Ben and I had to buy the floor trim for the upstairs and rent the flooring gun for one more day!! After lunch, we all went to the house. Jack wanted to go, but we had to take his new TV, his Game Cube, and sheets to put on his bed so he could lay in his OWN bed and watch TV and play games. It was like old times. He had fun, something he doesn't seem to get much of these days. We worked on the floors, got all of them finished except for a closet and got back to our temporary home. Up again Sunday, Ben and I got the boys going, and left again for the house to start putting in the floor trim. We came back, got the boys ready, me and the boys went to Pawpaw dinner, ate and had a birthday celebration, went back to the house and worked again. This time Dad and Amy came back with Dad and Ben finishing the hardwood upstairs and me, Benny, and Amy cleaning the downstairs for the hardwood floor guy who was coming this morning to start finishing the downstairs floors. (Thanks, Dad and Amy for all your hard work.

MY NAME IS JACK JOHNSON...

Maybe one day we will all not hurt when we move.) The kitchen cabinets are in, and the bathroom tile is finished. We are starting to have a house again not just joists and studs. Jack was with us but stayed in his bedroom with Mia the cat. He loves Mia, and she loves him when she wants to.

This morning was needle morning. Jack woke up first thing sick and got sick again after his radiation treatment. When he got sick at the Center, you could hear the heaves coming from deep inside him. He must be sore from all of it, but in true Jack style, he has not complained. I was talking on the way to the Center this morning to Ben about the little things we need to buy for the house to get it complete like door knobs, ceiling fans, faucets, etc. Jack didn't say one word all the way there. A few minutes ago, after he had had a good nap and a very small lunch, he said he heard what I had said to Ben about shopping for things for the house, and maybe we could go shopping for him a new ceiling fan, something I told him he could get for his bedroom with the generous offer a friend of ours has said she wanted to do. Who knows? Maybe a shopping trip is in our future.

Thank you, Lord, for the ability to work hard, for the ability to laugh at ourselves, for the ability to be friends with others, for the ability to love with all our hearts. In His Name, Amen.

AUGUST 24, 2010—Tuesday has been a quiet day. We went to the Cancer Center, and nothing out of the ordinary happened. Of course, he got sick, but that happens almost every day now, so that is not out of the ordinary. He has lost more weight—down to 121 and a half. That is not ordinary. Jack makes us all laugh at the Center because he tells the nurses now what needs to be done and in what order (taking weight and vital signs, flushing his port, getting his anti-nausea medicine, etc.). They are very good natured about it all and think he is funny too. On the way to the Center, our gas tank was low on gas with the gas light coming on in the car. You would have thought he was watching a clock ticking down the time to the end of the world. He was fidgety and complained about the traffic because he was so nervous we were going to run out of gas. Ben finally just had to stop and go ahead and get gas just to make Jack happy. Made me happy too. I didn't need to walk an unhappy, semi-bald, apparent cancer patient with autism to a gas station to get gas for the car. Or sit in the car waiting with an unhappy, semi-bald, apparent cancer patient with autism fussing and crying because his dad didn't fill the car with gas. Don't know which scenario would be worse, but I am glad I didn't have to live through either one.

. . . BUT I'M NOT THE SINGER

I had written yesterday that Jack and I would be going shopping for a new ceiling fan for his bedroom. We did! He said he wanted to go look for a new fan and if he feels like doing things like that right now, by golly, we are going. After we arrived at the store, I repeated to him if he got tired, he just needed to say something and we would figure out what to do. He kept saying "Ok, Mooooommmm" in that disgusted voice that only teenagers have. I told him we could possibly get a wheelchair, which they provide for their store patrons (something I didn't know or ever paid attention to). We made our way to the ceiling fan department. I must inject here that I truly wonder what it feels like for Jack to go into the ceiling fan department knowing full well that he can buy any ceiling fan he wants, knowing also, how much he LOVES ceiling fans. What a rush for him to be standing there looking up at all the different fans with their different light kits, fan and light pull strings, different number of blades, color of blades, and the different brand names. We hadn't been in the fan department long until I saw him leaning and holding on to the shelves. I asked him if he was getting tired and this time he quietly said yes. I told him we could go see what they had in the way of wheelchairs and we back-tracked to the front of the store. They had four different wheelchairs: a plain wheelchair, a wheelchair with a basket in the front and two wheelchairs that looked more like scooters. I asked Jack if he would like to try the scooter wheelchair but he said no. Jack chose a regular wheelchair and we returned to the ceiling fan department. We had so much fun talking about ceiling fans, their cost, their overall width, and the different colors of the blades. He chose his favorite and after buying bulbs for it, we proceeded to checkout. What a sight we must have been (since the young checkout people were looking like they had seen something scary) with me pushing this young man in a wheelchair, with a ceiling fan in a box across the arms of the chair he was sitting in. We will install the new ceiling fan this weekend and make Jack's dream of a new ceiling fan come true. I am thinking seriously about talking to the doctors about a disabled parking pass and finding out about borrowing a wheelchair.

God, thank you for letting us know how to have fun whatever it is for each of us. Thanks for letting us share our lives with others. Thanks for the feeling of pure happiness. May our lives be full of pure happiness for many years to come. Amen.

AUGUST 25, 2010—Wednesday turned out to be a busy day. We went to the Cancer Center and to the oncology floor at VCH. Jack, of course, vomited first thing this morning and right after his radiation treatment but has not been

MY NAME IS JACK JOHNSON...

sick or complained of a stomach ache since. The radiation oncologist talked to us this morning about what happens after Jack finishes radiation treatments. Talking about the future without radiation was nice. After we left the Cancer Center, we wheeled over to the oncology center. Jack's blood work is still in the good range, his weight is still dropping, and therefore he is now on an appetite stimulant. He has been completely taken off all steroids. The oncology nurse also talked about our upcoming future of no radiation treatments. She has already scheduled Jack for an MRI Sept. 23 because they also need the MRI for future reference. Jack will also have a pre-chemo kidney function test and another hearing test. The chemo he will receive is really several different chemo drugs that when given together have successfully treated this type of cancer. Each chemo drug has its very own set of side effects two of which are hearing loss and kidney damage. These two body functions will be monitored carefully while he takes the chemo, so they need a baseline point to start measuring from. We also talked about the handicap parking pass which we now have. I talked to Dad, and he has a wheelchair that he saved for future use but who would have ever thought it would be for Jack.

The house is coming along with the hardwood floors downstairs getting their stain today. The first coat of finish goes on tomorrow. The countertops are supposed to be installed Friday. The plumber comes Monday if Ben and I get the plumbing supplies bought before then. We are starting the countdown with both the house and the radiation treatments.

Thank you, Lord, for answering prayers, for all the people that have prayed for us for so many days and weeks, for all the people who have helped us get to this point, for all the love we have received through this time. Please continue to send us support and love through Your angels here on earth. Amen.

AUGUST 27, 2010—Ben and I have been very busy getting everything wrapped up on our end of the house stuff so we can get it finished. The plumber comes on Monday to start putting in fixtures, so we have been shopping for all the fixtures. I thought I would be more excited about shopping for them, but it's just another day of making decisions. Makes my brain hurt. Ben and I had planned to go to one store, but after a visit from a member of Brentwood Baptist Church, our plans changed. BBC had helped in our neighborhood earlier in the flood aftermath and somehow had Ben's phone number. One of the members called asking to meet him at our house. So, before our shopping trip, Ben met a gentleman from this church who gave us a VERY generous amount of gift cards from Lowe's. What a pleasant surprise

... BUT I'M NOT THE SINGER

for us. God had a hand in this one, giving us a wonderful gift at the very time we needed it. The church representative had no idea about Jack and our new battle. We all agreed God was working through the BBC that day. Thanks, Brentwood Baptist Church for being one of God's angels for us and others in our neighborhood.

After we got to Lowe's, God stepped in again and helped us out. This time he sent another angel in the form of a Lowe's worker, MW. Let me stop here and say while at Lowe's, since we had no one to watch Jack, he had to tag along. Lowe's does not have plain wheelchairs but has scooter chairs I can say Jack is now an awesome scooter chair driver going both back and forward with ease. He even drove it with the attached basket full of plumbing fixtures. Mr. W. saw us with Jack and his scooter looking at fixtures and, of course, he started asking questions. We talked about everything that had happened over the last few months and Mr. W., being a Christian, felt he needed to do something. Mr. W. personally took care of finding everything we needed in all departments and checked us out giving us a discount. What a kind and thoughtful gesture! We are still always touched by the giving hearts we have encountered during all of this. There are angels in our lives. I guess sometimes we really must be in need for them to appear and we must have the ability to see them. Thank you, Mr. W., for your prayers, your generosity, and your thoughtfulness.

So, with a lot of help from a lot of angels, our house is getting ready for us to think about moving. I was recently reminded the other day that one of the football moms still had some of my good china at her house. She took some of it home to clean for us since we had no water, and has kept it stored for all these months. Another angel. One of my sisters and Ben's sister have some of our clothes that were wet and took them home to clean. Angels again. I must add all our food angels who have kept us well fed through these past months. And all our volunteers who have put our house back together. The angels who opened their doors for us to have a place to stay. I know I am leaving others out who have cleaned and stored some of our stuff for all these months. Just like angels have wings to help guide and support them during their journeys, our angels have been our wings with their selfless support of us. Please know we are incredibly grateful to each of you.

Dear Lord, thank you for angels you send to help us, thank you for the kindness of strangers and the constant love of family and friends. Amen

AUGUST 29, 2010—Jack had a good day yesterday with no vomiting, and his ceiling fan was installed in his room. Ben worked hard on getting it installed

MY NAME IS JACK JOHNSON...

with it taking two tries and help from Rivers and Andy to get it to work. (Thanks to both of you for the help!) But it is up, and Jack is proud. He told us he is happy, how good his fan looks and how quiet it runs. Ben said when they got home yesterday from the grand installation, Jack fell asleep. All that ceiling fan excitement wore him out.

Lord, thank you for blessing us with friends, with happiness, and with health. In His Name, Amen.

CHAPTER 21

AUGUST 30, 2010—Needle day but the last one for radiation!! Hooray!! I think the nurses are going to miss Jack and his quirky sense of humor. I'm sure it's not every day in a nurse's life that the patient tells them what to do step by step.

Jack hasn't had a very good day today. He woke up sick and got sick again right after radiation treatment. When we got home from treatment this morning, Jack and I napped, I woke up at the normal nap time but Jack slept on to 2 pm this afternoon. When I thought about it, he has slept more this weekend than he has before, so I am sure the radiation is getting the best of him. He told me yesterday that when he gets up and walks in the house, it makes him feel like he has been exercising. Everyone I have talked to about all these treatments has said fatigue is a huge problem, so I guess we are at that stage now. He hasn't eaten anything much all day: 3 bites of cantaloupe, a slice of cheese, a thin slice of turkey sandwich meat, three pieces of apple and a grilled cheese sandwich. That's not very much at all.

God, today, thanks for caring nurses who look at the people they treat as people and not just a job, thanks for old friends and new friends, thanks for the food we eat, thanks for the kindness of strangers, and thanks for the cooler weather. Amen

AUGUST 31, 2010—I feel like a kid the night before Christmas. Jack has his last day of radiation tomorrow. Yay! I'm not sure anything will be different but just knowing it's the last one is such a relief. He was gaggy and sickly first thing this morning and right after radiation, but that was all. He has lost yet another pound—down to 119 and a half!!—but he is not hungry. I have racked my brain trying to think of something he will eat that he loved to eat before the brain tumor, but he pooh-poohs everything I mention. I am happy to see him eat even if it is a bird size meal. Also, tomorrow is chemo day, and I am supposed to get my calendar of appointments from them. Now that's fun, going to the doctor and getting an itinerary for the next several months. I know most of you are jealous and wish you could be like us...right?

Lord, thanks for a mother's heart, for a doctor's knowledge, and for patience and understanding. Amen.

SEPTEMBER 1, 2010—This has been a hectic day. First, we had radiation OUR LAST!! Happy, happy, happy. The nurses had a mini celebration for Jack and A., a three-year-old princess that had been getting radiation too. There were balloons and a cake decorated with their names, but since it was vanilla cake and vanilla icing, someone we know wouldn't touch it. Mr. Chocolate did get a gift card to Ben & Jerry's so he could get his chocolate fix whenever he wants. A. always wore the cutest outfits to radiation and was so dainty. She also had lost all her hair and wore the cutest hats to match her outfits. Ben said it was like Shrek and Fiona—the big grouchy ogre who won't eat a vanilla cake and the tiny princess in her matching hat, outfit, and feathered Crocs. What a funny picture!! Our next stop in our Wednesday journey was the oncology department better known as "Clinic." Of course, we had an ogre-sized wheelchair and ran into every wall and door frame from one building to another. At Clinic, Jack got weighed, vital signs measured, had blood drawn, and got chemo. Mom and Dad got more prescriptions to fill, more instructions to go with those prescriptions, a urinal and a urine jug for a 24-hour urine collection party we will have on the 27th of Sept, a calendar of each month we will be having chemo treatments which to our surprise goes through Sept. 2011, and information on Jack's upcoming Make-A-Wish wish. Whew!! We were busy. Jack will start back with his cancer fight on Sept. 23 with an MRI, the 27th is urine collection day, 28th is office visit, urine drop-off, and hearing test, and the 29th is check-in day at VCH for his first round of chemo. We are going to try to enjoy the next three weeks without anything.

Heavenly Father, thank you for princesses and ogres, for doctors and nurses with big hearts, for rides in the country, and for roofs over our heads that protect us from the elements. Amen.

SEPTEMBER 2, 2010—First day post radiation. This morning after I got up and moving, Ben came and got me and said we have a problem. I hate when someone does that to me especially with the year we have had, your mind goes through pictures really fast of all the horrible things that could happen that so far haven't been on our list of horrible things that we are living through. (Sorry for that terrible running sentence!) After my mind stopped running through my book of horrible things, Ben said Jack was very upset. I walked into the room and found him crying, sporting puffy, red eyes, and a red nose that matched his eyes. Oh, how my heart just ached to see the tears, the red nose. So, I leaned real close to his face, while I ran my hand across what little hair is left and in my best mommy voice say, "What's the matter?" He sniffs, a few tears fall onto his pillow and in a small, low voice he says, "I miss the church exit signs." Oh, my goodness!! My child is crying because he misses seeing exit signs! I must really try not to laugh, not at him but at the comedy of the whole situation. Here is God working in my child, my life, my family's life, and my very sick child cries to check on God's house and make sure others are protected in case of emergency. You know that in case of a fire at the church, the lights of an exit sign brightly shine through the smoke to lead members to safety. That is what Jack should be to us all, a bright light for all that see or know him, to show us how God works in ways that we don't necessarily understand. Maybe Jack is leading us, through God, to a place God wants us all to be. I asked Jack if he was ready to go back to church on Sunday. He said he didn't want to be around all the people, he just wanted to see the exits. I told him easy-peasy, I could call the church, talk to the pastor, and see if we could walk through the church to look at the exit signs. Of course, our pastor, Dr. H., said yes and met us in the lobby. Thank you, Dr. H., for your help and for letting Jack have the run of the church. Jack and I strolled through the church, down stairs, up stairs, and through passageways I didn't know existed but he knew so well. I took my camera and took shots of all the exits, even taking some in the darker hallways without the flash so the lights of the sign would be illuminated. You could have wrapped an expensive toy for a gift, and it would not have meant anything to him, but let him look at exit signs and he is on cloud nine. What a great kiddo he truly is!

Dear Lord, thank you for days without struggles, for struggles that are easy to overcome, for letting us as parents have time with the little ones you gave us, for the gift of love, and for time to let our hearts heal. Amen.

SEPTEMBER 7, 2010—Ben and I have worked on the house both Sat. and Sun. nights until 10pm. I was so sore both nights when I would go to bed, I couldn't sleep because my muscles were so tight and wouldn't relax. Monday, we got up, bought a van to replace the one we lost in the flood, and returned to our house to work. Jack went with us some but not much because we still do not have water for the bathrooms. But when he did come to the house, he

MY NAME IS JACK JOHNSON...

stayed in his bedroom and played his Game Cube and laughed and laughed. Music to my ears. He feels so much better not being put to sleep every day, not having his brain fried with a daily dose of radiation, and not being sick or retching since we stopped radiation. We did go to the Cancer Center to get weighed and he still just weighs 120 pounds. There is still not much of an appetite and he seems to have lost his hunger for treats and pleasurable goodies, like milkshakes, cookies, ice cream, that he used to love to eat. We have a new prescription for appetite stimulants—10 pills a day. He has smiled several times and when he does it just lights up his face. The cable guy comes tomorrow to fix his TV in his bedroom so he will be willing to spend more time there at the house if he can watch Game Show Network. If I can get Jack to go to the house during the day, I can get more work done. It has really been a challenge for me knowing that there is so much I could be doing at the house but I can't leave Jack here by himself. So, with GSN on his TV, he will be willing to go and I can get some of those little things done.

For everyone who has cooked, sent gifts, and helped with the house, a very large—thank you! We are so thankful to have support from our family, friends, and from this community. I don't know what we would have done without each of you!

Dear Lord, thank you for giving us family and friends that love us in so many ways, thank you for able bodies that work hard even when we hurt, thank you for smiles and eyes to see them with, and thank you for hearts that ache with love when our eyes witness a sincere, innocent smile. In His Loving Name, Amen.

SEPTEMBER 8, 2010—Today it has been four months and eight days since we had to escape the rising waters of the Harpeth. 131 days, 3,144 hours. I am so sick of not living in my own home with my own stuff. Every day I must look in the face of my sick son and explain why we can't stay at the house. Today he tells me he misses my cooking at home. Bless his heart; he has never said that before. The cable guy came today and got all TV's upstairs running. Jack got to watch some of his game shows while I worked on getting some of the boxes unpacked. We have running water, electricity, and the stove and frig are in the kitchen. The floor guy comes tomorrow for the last coat of finish. After it dries, I am going to try to get us at least living upstairs until we can get the final inspections on the first floor.

God, thank you for our houses, large and small, thank you for giving us the ability to make them homes, thank you for the feeling of love, the ability to see it,

... BUT I'M NOT THE SINGER

hear it, and give it. Thank you for strong bodies and minds. Help us to use them in ways that serve you. In His Name, Amen.

SEPTEMBER 14, 2010—A quick note to update everyone—WE PASSED FINAL INSPECTION!! Hooray!! We will be taking our time moving back in because there is still a little touch-up paint, shoe trim, floor trim, etc. that needs to be done. But we are moving back in... I can't believe I am writing that. I have cried several times since the inspection man left. I told him he made my day.

God, thank you for the blessing of a home, the gift of family and friends, for Your listening to prayers, and for the young man who was so kind and wrote us the occupancy permit. Amen.

SEPTEMBER 19, 2010—Jack is eating like the Jack of old. He decided today after church (yes! We went back to church—the first time since around March when Jack got sick there!! Jack even received applause when one of the pastors publicly welcomed Jack back to church! The whole church clapped, and Jack waved while I cried.) that he wanted Olive Garden, so we made the trek to Spring Hill.

Dear Lord, thanks for leading us, through Jack, back to Your house: for the wonderful sound of music, for the message, the prayers, the hugs, the people. Thank you for showing us Your love through them. Amen.

SEPTEMBER 20, 2010—We are back up and running at the Johnson house. That is with the internet. Thank you, AT&T for getting here. Ben and I now have a bed to sleep in. We have been sleeping on the mattress on the floor but now we have an actual bed. Jack is feeling good. He had school today with his homebound teacher, Miss T., and asks almost every day for a ride in the country and almost every day his dad takes him on one. There is so little right now for Jack in the way of pleasure and it shows. Some days he doesn't seem to smile at all. Other days his smile can light up a room. I don't know what the difference is—I guess just good days and bad days. One day, last week, he and I had been somewhere and we were on our way home when I heard him sniff. There was Jack, all teary eyed, snotty nosed, and I immediately asked him what was wrong. He was so upset he couldn't even talk. Finally, he said he felt like he didn't have fun anymore. I asked him what he meant by that because I didn't understand. Fun for him and what I think of as being fun are two different things. He said we usually go to the lake and have fun, we hadn't been

MY NAME IS JACK JOHNSON...

this year at all, and with us talking about selling the boats we won't have fun at all without them. That was what I understood with all his sniffing and crying while he was saying all of that. I had to explain that if we sold the boats we could always buy more later when he felt better. But right now, our mission (our meaning me, Ben, Benny and Jack) was getting him well. There would always be boats to buy and he could even help decide what kind of boat we would buy next. Right now, our top priority as a family was getting him well. He seemed to understand it and gained control of himself. I think since he has gotten back in the house he has realized that summer is over, we missed it! For all of us, our lives have been in la la limbo for the last four-plus months and we missed summer fun. Jack has not been swimming at all or to the lake. Those are his two favorite summer activities and he missed getting to enjoy them. It finally hit him when he started to think about everything and how it is now September. Heck, I almost choked on my spit when I walked into Publix and saw PUMP-KINS!! Pumpkins! I can't believe it is so close to Halloween. Summer is over. We missed it. Hey Jack, buddy, I could cry too.

We had to buy a new washer and dryer because our previous ones floated around in the wash room per Ben. So, I bought some of the new front-loading ones. They make me want to slowly pull my clean, fresh laundry out and put it to my face and sniff it like they do on commercials. Too bad my shoes all were ruined in the flood. I could put on my old heels and take my clean, fresh laundry out making it float in the air before I sniffed it. My favorite thing about them is the finished beeper. My old dryer signaled when it was finished with a load with a real LOUD Bbbbbuuuuzzzzzz. You could hear it outside. My old washer didn't have a buzzer or beeper; it just got quiet letting you know the clothes were washed. The new, front loader washer and dryer have a little ting, ting, ting song they play when they get finished. It is such a happy little tune you just can't wait to see your friends, Mister Washer and Madame Dryer, in your heels, with your hair pinned up, pulling your floating, clean, fresh clothes out...

Dear Lord, thank you today for people who do what they say they will, for the soft feeling of clean sheets at night, for the sounds of happiness, for the ability to cry and smile, for the love of children, for looking into the eyes of your loved ones, for hands to wipe away tears, and for healthy imaginations. Amen.

SEPTEMBER 29, 2010—Just a quick update... Jack's MRI was clear! Dr. T. said there was no enhancement (which would mean leftover tumor or new growth.) Thank you, God. Jack has gained ten pounds which made Dr. T. very happy.

... BUT I'M NOT THE SINGER

God, thank you for good news. Amen.

SEPTEMBER 29, 2010—We are at Vanderbilt Children's Hospital. It has been a long day of waiting. We got here at noon, and they finally got us a room at 5 pm. This place is always full, and that means there are too many sick kids. We are on the sixth floor and have the worst view we have ever had in the times Jack has been here. Previously I have enjoyed some of the views of downtown and Hillsboro Village but not this time. We are looking at buildings here at Vanderbilt. Boo hoo!

Jack is now asleep. They had to put in a hand IV along with his port. So, he got two needles today—one in the port, and one in his hand. He hates the hand IV's. Then earlier tonight he had to swallow 3 chemo pills, something we have been working on for weeks. His gag reflex is so sensitive he has had a very difficult time learning to swallow meds. But tonight, after lots of tries and frustration and 18 ounces of fluid, he got them all down. Another prayer answered. We really needed God's help on that one. Thanks, God. Now he is in the process of getting the other chemo. One drug they give him by injection and he has already received it. The last one takes six hours by IV. It is the reason we must stay at the hospital. This drug damages the kidneys so they are required to give him fluids before, during and after they give it to him. He has already had two hours of fluids, then the six hours while they give him the drug, and then he needs to have eighteen hours more of fluids to flush the drug out of his system where it will not damage the kidneys. We will not have a restful night because they told us we will be going to the restroom all night to get rid of the fluids. And we are asked to measure his output. Right now, he is hooked up to four bags of different drugs and fluids. He also has a pump to give him a steady dose of anti-nausea drugs that he can push a button for more when he needs it. These are powerful drugs: we had to wear gloves to hold the chemo pills he swallowed earlier. We are supposed to wear gloves when we make our bathroom visits so we don't get chemo waste on us. Here we are trying to fight a monster you can't see with drugs we are not allowed to touch. Sometimes life is so very strange.

Dear Lord, thank you for the small blessings, the abundant blessings, and blessings in between. Thank you for caregivers, doctors, and nurses. Thanks for their caring hearts and healing hands. Help them to care for the sick and disabled. Bless them with Your love and grace. In His Name, Amen.

MY NAME IS JACK JOHNSON...

SEPTEMBER 30, 2010—Journal Warning: If you are sensitive to talk about urinating and the male anatomy, please do not read this entry. Thanks for not getting offended.

Have you ever had one of those times where you questioned God about why He made the human body the way He did? I had one of those times last night. Poor Jack is receiving fluids at a very fast rate so they can keep any chemo from staying in his kidneys for any length of time. They had warned us that he would be up and down all night going to expel the extra fluids. I understood this and knew it would be a long night. But Jack has the bladder of an elephant and can hold water for long periods of time—something I had not previously known or thought I would ever need to know. Until last night. The nurse made me wake him up the first time because they wanted him to go as close to every two hours. So, I woke him up and told him he needed to go try to urinate. I am a stickler for germs in hotels and hospitals in the places that you might overlook or not get disinfected completely. Beds, linens, towels, washcloths, and floors to name a few. So, I want Jack to always wear his house shoes when he gets out of bed. Also remember he is hooked up to an IV pole with IV tubes coming out of his chest port and his hand. I woke him up out of a deep sleep telling him he must get up and try to pee. He sits up, I unplug the IV machines, and while I am putting on his house shoes he sleepily says "Hurry." I grab him and the IV pole and we shuffle into the bathroom. I think my only job is to keep him steady and hold and guide the pole. Ha, how dumb I am. Jack gets to the toilet and says hurry again and I say OK, we are here. Let me add here that the nurse asked if we would both wear rubber gloves when Jack goes in the night because we really don't want to get the chemo waste on our hands. So, we put on gloves here. I can get both of my hands gloved. I forgot my child has an IV in his hand, really can't use it for much or get a glove on it, and now is in desperate need to get his pants pulled down. I have a grip on him, got his pants pulled down, he sits down on the toilet, but heck, I forgot the urinal. By now, he is saying "hurry, hurry, hurry!" and I am getting flustered, there are too many things I am required to do and not enough hands. I get the urinal in place and Jack starts to relieve himself. And he goes, and he goes, and he goes. But it is in spurts and not a single flow. Women's pipes are different and a woman is not naturally born to understand spurts. I asked Jack if he is finished and he says yes, he thinks so. Do not believe any male person who says to you while you are holding his urinal in a squatting position in front of him in a small bathroom in the middle of the night that he thinks he is through urinating. Naive, sleepy me takes the urinal

... BUT I'M NOT THE SINGER

away and Jack started going more. It went all over me, the floor, the trash can, the toilet paper, on his IV tube, and down his legs. So much for the protection of rubber gloves! I said to Jack, "I thought you didn't have more," and he says... get ready for this one... he says he thought so too. What? That doesn't make sense—you either have got to go or you don't. Which is it? I cleaned Jack, me, the floor, the IV tubing, to heck with the trash can and threw out the wet paper. I tried to get him up but all I did was get him semi-up and when he stood, he hit his head on the paper towels dispenser. Why would anyone put a paper towel dispenser on the wall directly across from the toilet in a little bathroom and at a level where you WILL hit yourself on the way up? Wow, this place can provide doctors who can open brains and take out tumors but watch that paper towel dispenser on the bathroom wall. I did get Jack back to bed after we rolled over his IV tubes several times and got the IV pole tangled in the many cords. I certainly dreaded the next trip to the bathroom with him during the night and I was correct in my dread. That's the way they all went. Jack with his elephant bladder, me—a woman who doesn't have the same parts and has no understanding of the workings of male parts, the urinal, the bathroom, the mess. The idea of the rubber gloves went the way of chemo waste: down the toilet. So, after one of these trips in the dark of night, I laid on my uncomfortable couch/bed and wondered why God made men the way He did. Could it be He made woman because He saw this flaw in man? Or maybe since He is all knowing, He knew at some time down the pike this would be a problem for the female caregiver.

Lord, thank you for the human body, no matter how flawed, disabled or ill. Please give us understanding, patience, and a sense of humor to get through difficult times. Amen.

SEPTEMBER 30, 2010—We are coming home tomorrow morning, first thing. Jack is finished with chemo and is now in the 18-hour fluid flush period. I can't wait to get back to my comfy bed. It has seemed like a cruel joke that after all those months of sleeping on different beds, couches, and air mattresses and finally getting to sleep in my own bed again, that I would have to come here with Jack and sleep on yet another uncomfortable couch. I would say this so-called bed would be comparable to a jail bed but since I have never slept on a jail bed (I don't want to give anyone the impression that I have) I can only imagine that a jail bed would be like this thing. Now Jack on the other hand has slept like a baby. No nausea, no vomiting, no pain. I was invited to join the doctors in rounds this morning when they talked about Jack. They

MY NAME IS JACK JOHNSON...

said as the treatments continued, the nausea and vomiting would get worse. They also said that this time the nausea and vomiting could be delayed for a couple of days and that Jack would be feeling bad after he got home. They are sending lots of meds home with us for this. It is strangely comical how they use drugs to treat this disease, those drugs cause side effects, so they prescribe more drugs to help with the side effects of the first drugs. And it goes on and on. Jack and I have been plagued with an IV machine that has had beeping sessions many times today. Since I don't know what the heck is going on when the warning beeps, I must call a nurse to take care of it. Sometimes the IV bag needs to be changed, sometimes the IV tube gets twisted, and the reasons are as many as the times it beeps. Later this afternoon, it went off again and before I could get the nurse, my son reaches over and turns the thing off. I said, "Jack, you can't do that!" His reply: "That's what the nurses do!" Needless to say, the nurse and I had to explain that is their job to decide what needs to be done to the IV machine. I'm glad we aren't staying longer—he might figure out how to do other things around here!

Lord, thank you for the technology that we all take for granted, thank you for the ability to use it. Thanks for the comforts we have in our daily lives. Thanks for the people who give us comfort too. Amen.

OCTOBER 3, 2010—We finally got home from the hospital on Friday before lunch. It takes forever to get admitted into and released from hospitals. Jack came home with lots of new pills. As the weekend has progressed, he is losing his appetite again. I told Ben today that Jack looks hollow-eyed—his eyes look like they are deeper set just because they have dark circles around them. He has slept most of the weekend. I guess his body needs to build itself back after being beaten up by the chemo. Hopefully, since this was Jack's first chemo treatment, he won't stay down long. Jack is not very steady on his feet. He has a condition that is caused by one of the chemo's he has been taking that causes his feet to hurt. So, he flounders along shuffling his feet. And he also has a slight balance problem too. Friday, we set up a twin bed for him in the master bedroom's sitting/dressing area. This way he can sleep downstairs, doesn't have to go up the stairs, is close to a bathroom, and close to us.

Dear God, thank you for truthful people, for sleep that helps the body and soul, for tears we shed when times are tough and when times are wonderful, for the ability to love each other like you have loved us. Amen.

...BUT I'M NOT THE SINGER

OCTOBER 5, 2010—We had a terrific Tuesday today. Jack felt better today, better than he has since before chemo. He had a great appetite and did not sleep all day today, something he has done every day since his chemo. If you could see me right now, you would see a happy mother.

God sent another angel to help us out. This one came in the form of a young man who works for a local utility business. We had not had a certain utility meter replaced since the flood. It must have been time for lots of utility meters on our street to be replaced because when Ben called the utility company, they had a person already on our street. The young man who came was the nicest guy. He was going to replace our meter but before he did, he made known how upset he was about our big trash pile. He couldn't believe the city was charging us flooded residents for trash pick-up. We talked about it for several minutes with him telling me about how our neighbors had told him about us. But what he didn't know was about Jack's brain tumor and cancer treatments. Mr. Nice Guy did not like our situation with the trash pick-up and said he would do something about it. This company was one of the companies in this area that helped a lot with flood clean up in our neighborhood. They even set up a table and brought food for us for several days so all of us who were working on our homes everyday would have a free meal. I personally was impressed with their generosity. Now there stands this guy who doesn't know me at all but feels the need to help us out. From what I understand he got in touch with his supervisor and got him to come to our house. Mr. Nice Guy showed his supervisor our trash pile, told him our story and somehow within the next hour or so, the trash hook truck was picking up our trash. We had sent the city mayor an email asking if he would dismiss the $100 fee our city is charging flood victims for construction trash but had not heard anything back from him. But this man shows up to turn on our utilities and somehow gets the city to pick up the trash. Thank you so much, Mr. Nice Guy, for getting the city to do what they told us they would do originally. You are truly an angel driving a utility truck.

Lord, thank you for sending us angels on earth who see a need and fill it, for cooler weather for riding in cars with the windows down to feel the autumn air, for blessing us with so much we want to share some of our blessings with others, for hunger, health, and happiness. Amen.

OCTOBER 6, 2010—Jack and I made our trip to the oncology department at VCH. He got his dose of chemo for this week and a flu shot. He did a lot of screaming with the flu shot. He thinks his port makes him immune to any other needles. He screamed at me and screamed for his dad, like pass-out-

MY NAME IS JACK JOHNSON...

at-a-needle Ben would help him. If Ben had been there, he would have been standing out in the hall. I took the bait and gave Jack my cell phone and told him to call his dad. He huffed and puffed and then screamed why was I being so mean to him. Oh brother, it was such a sad scene. He got his flu shot and everything was fine. The pain of worry is so much worse than the true pain. Otherwise Jack has had a pretty good day. He had lost 2.5 pounds but we will try to get it back. I did find out that all of us in this house will have to get the flu shot as well. When I informed the B's in this house, you could have heard a pin drop. I know their faces dropped. I saw them.

God, thank you for the kindness of strangers, the medicines we have that help us to stay healthy, for family and friends that continually amaze us with their love and support, and for Your only Son. In His Name, Amen.

OCTOBER 13, 2010—Jack and I are getting this down—this meaning the trips to VCH for weekly chemo. We got there on time (2:30), they took us back, weighed him, put his needle into his port (which Ben and I had put numbing cream and Press 'n Seal on before we left home), talked to one nurse, two doctors, answered lots of questions, took blood samples, got the chemo and we were back home at 4:15 so Jack could see his favorite game show, Catch 21, at 4:30. Let me write here, yes, I said Press 'n Seal that you buy from the grocery. It is easier to remove than regular bandages which leave big red marks on his chest that hurt on the same place that they put in the port needle. We are now big fans of Press 'n Seal plastic wrap. Jack had gained more weight to 132 pounds. That is four pounds since last week!

Many of our visits to the oncology clinic were after radiation and sedation, but since we are finished with radiation, Jack is wide awake and being his charming self to the pleasure of the nurses and doctors. It's nice to have a patient that responds when you ask and responds in ways that you don't expect. Jack has that gift to put a smile on your face when he is his true self. If you have had the pleasure to be around Jack for any length of time, you understand what I am saying. Let's say Jack is making his presence known and everyone is enjoying meeting him. Even though it was for chemo, we had a good time going to the oncology clinic.

Dear Lord, thank you for autumn days, for downpours of water and downpours of leaves, for quick wit and quick laughs, for people who rescue the needy, for giving and receiving love. Amen.

OCTOBER 14, 2010—Jack had school which meant homework and then listening for one hour and a half. When we worked on his homework yesterday, and again this morning, his handwriting was worse than usual. Jack has never had the best handwriting, but his cursive is near perfect. It was awful when he wrote during his homework. I hope it is not another side effect of any of this treatment. His most prominent side effect right now is the pain in his feet. I looked the name of this side effect up, and it's called peripheral neuropathy. It is a side effect of vincristine, one of the chemo drugs he is taking. It affects the nerve endings in patient's hands and feet. So far, Jack has only had trouble with his feet. The doctor has given him drugs to help with the foot pain—we have had to increase his dose because of the pain. He has had a problem with balance causing us to hold on to him because he is so unstable on his feet. Jack told me at the doctor's office yesterday that he hasn't been sleeping well at night, waking up with his feet hurting and not going back to sleep, giving the doc a reason to go up on his meds. I wonder if this will be the rest of my life: watching, looking, and worrying about every pain, ache, difference, or look that Jack has that I haven't seen before. Will I ever relax and enjoy life again?

Lord, thank you for bodies that work hard, for the sleep that helps them rest, for the light of day and the dark of night, for friends, family, and pets that love us for who we are. Amen.

OCTOBER 17, 2010—For all of you who remember the trash pile that grew in our yard for weeks and how I wrote the mayor an email asking the city trash department to pick it up and not make us pay the $100 fee for trash pick-up... And how a hero from a local utility company got our trash picked up for us charging us nothing in the way of a fee...I finally got an email back from the mayor, and he politely told me they would not dismiss the fee, that they gave us notice. So many people have done so much for us and for that we are truly grateful. You would think if someone personally asked you to help them cut in a situation like ours, they would be kind enough to want to help Guess not everyone is an angel sent from God.

Dear Lord, thank you for the sunshine and the warmth it provides, for the smell and colors of autumn, for the breeze that blows the colorful leaves, and for the ability to love each other. Amen.

CHAPTER 22

OCTOBER 20, 2010—Jack had Vanderbilt Home Health Care come today to take his blood. We should hear tomorrow about his results. The nurse, Nurse T., who came, had been praying for Jack through her Bible study class and just figured out that the Jack she had been praying for is the same Jack she was coming to see today. It is a small world. She was very kind to Jack explaining everything she was doing to him. He knew what she should have been doing because he had memorized what the other nurses at the Cancer Center had done when he was getting his port accessed every week. She told me after she was finished that he had made her nervous. But when your patient is telling you step-by-step what you should be doing, it would make you nervous. Maybe next week she will feel more at ease. Jack's feet are hurting. The doctor's office will be calling tomorrow with his blood results, so I am going to say something about his pain and how uncomfortable he is. I so wish I could help him with his pain, but there is not much I can do. Hopefully, the oncology doctor can.

God, thank you for family, friends, and strangers that have become our support group, for providing us with shelter and food, for eyes to see the face of a loved one, for letting us have this day to spend it the way we have. Amen.

OCTOBER 27, 2010—As I sit and type this Jack is taking a shower and screaming his head off. I don't know why. His dad is back there with him, so I can only hope he has it under control. Well, I had to go and see what all the ruckus was about. Jack was having a bad shower day: the water was too hot, the soap fell in the bottom of the shower, the floor was slick, his balance was bad, and he might fall, and the list went on. He is now talking with this high voice that we don't know where it is coming from. I asked him one day where did he get his new voice, and he said it was his tired voice. But he said it was his tired voice in his regular voice. I had to turn my head so he wouldn't see me laugh. While he was screaming during his shower, he was doing it with

... BUT I'M NOT THE SINGER

his new high voice, so it sounded like Ben was helping a girl take a shower. Sometimes I feel like we live in a different world than the rest of you...

Today was blood work day. Nurse T. came, and she missed the port! She had to take the needle out and put it back in. All the while, I am holding poor Jack's hand which he is gripping mine for dear life. She got it the second time, took his blood, took out the needle, packed her bag and left. I can see in my mind poor Nurse T. hightailing it out of our driveway and down the road while she sips something from a flask.

Benny's birthday is tomorrow. He was born at 8:30pm, so when I think back, I was in the hospital 16 years ago, waiting to go into labor. What a joyous time that was—the excitement, the waiting, the anticipation, the dreams, the hopes all coming at once. And he hasn't disappointed us yet—he is everything we dreamed of and more. Thanks, Benny, for being a great son. And Happy Birthday!

Heavenly Father, thank you for the vivid blue skies after the storms, for battles won and lost, for the wonderful gift of children and the joy they bring, for eyes that look to You for comfort, for hearts that come to You for rest, for family, friends, and strangers whose hearts You have opened to give us love and support, and for giving us Your only Son. Amen.

NOVEMBER 1, 2010—Jack had a great Sunday, and I mean great. He had gotten sick again Saturday, vomiting again for no apparent reason, but then Sunday, the sun was shining and the sky was blue and Jack was his old self if only for that day. He ate lots of food, asking for seconds and dessert. He cracked jokes, he laughed, he told his dad that he was going to take him for a car ride. It was great. Ben and I were smiling. Even Benny was smiling because Jack was being so funny. He is taking his medicine by swallowing the pills and we are not crushing any, at all!! You just don't know how big this is for us and for him. He can control when he takes them, and we are not crushing pills and mixing them with juice, making sure the consistency is just enough to get past his autistic sensory issues. Tonight, he even got up, went to the cabinet, and got his pill container out. He brought them over to the couch and just looked at the pill container. He rubbed his hands over the little daily boxes and said, "All these pills!" Then he took out the Monday night selection and proceeded to take them. Jack is like the statement people have always said about Tennessee weather: if you don't like the weather today, just wait and it will be different tomorrow. That is our Jack. One day he feels awful, looks terrible, makes me cry just to look at him. Next day he is the sunshine in the house. I truly love the sunshine days!!

MY NAME IS JACK JOHNSON...

Dear Lord, thank you for our pets and the happiness they bring us, for the joy a smile can deliver, for the sunshine that comes through the clouds, for memories we laugh at and memories we learn from, for the support You have sent us in time of need, and for the love You have shown us through Your angels on earth. In His Name, Amen.

NOVEMBER 4, 2010—Jack's blood work results came back today. I was a little shocked and so was the nurse who called me. She had told me last week that Jack's counts would not go down any further than they had but they had really dropped from last week. A little medical talk: a neutrophil is a type of white blood cell that fights infection. They measure how many neutrophils Jack has in his blood every time they take his blood to see if he could fight any infection he encounters since we fight off many infections we don't know we have even been exposed to. A regular neutrophil count should be 1,500 to 7,000 in the way that they measure it. Anything below 1,500 is mild neutropenia (the condition of having low neutrophil counts). Anything under 1,000 is classified as moderate and under 500 is classified as severe. Jack's count is 800 which puts him in the moderate category. My cancer bible has a list of things to not do when you have neutropenia. Some are just common sense like washing hands thoroughly, staying away from people with illnesses, etc. Then there are those things that I haven't really thought of like watching how you cut your fingernails, don't touch your acne, do not use floss, avoid stagnant water in flower vases, humidifiers, to name a few. Like I didn't have enough to worry about I now need to worry about Jack flossing his teeth (yeah, right!), that water in that vase of flowers Ben brought home (fat chance!), and Jack cutting his own fingernails (hahahahahahaha). Seriously, some of these things I will take seriously and change a few of my family's bad habits. The nurse thinks Jack's blood count will go up but they will check it on Monday. If it hasn't gone up, we might have to move out his next hospital stay for round two of chemo. She also said Jack will feel so much better and it would be noticeable. I thought he felt good now! Cancer is a sly, cunning enemy.

Dear Lord, thank you for placing people in our lives just when we need them, for healthy bodies and minds, for listening to us when we whine and cry, for hearing our prayers, for loving us no matter what, and for giving us Your Son. Amen.

NOVEMBER 7, 2010—BR came by and took Jack for an afternoon car ride. When he came back, I heard sniffing and when I looked at him, he was crying. I asked what was the matter and he blurted out that he had been on his last car ride because it was going to get cold and he wouldn't be able to go. I reassured him that he could still go car riding when it was cold as long as he stayed in the car. I asked him if he was like a dog and had to ride with his head out the window. When he said no, I said as long as he didn't act like a dog, he could car ride in the cold weather. He still cried. I asked him again what was wrong and he boohoo-ed that everyone loves him like Mia, the cat, and me, and BR. Our names were said through loud sobbing. I had to finally sit with him and rub his back to get him to stop. But it is funny—he was in such a good mood before Saturday. On Friday, I asked him in passing if he was OK. He said yes and Ben said to him how people sure worry about him a lot. Jack said, "Yeah. I've got too much love." A day later he cries because he is loved by us.

God, our Father, thank you for the many blessings of life, the ones we see every day and the ones we take for granted, for the sunshine that warms our face on cold days, for land that is still "the country", for the strength to hold others when they don't have any strength left, for the angels You send to us to love for as long as we can and for caring for the hearts that are broken here on earth. In His Name, Amen.

NOVEMBER 8, 2010—Jack and I made our trip to the clinic at Vanderbilt Children's Hospital today, collected urine sample in hand in a bag. The nurse in oncology took Jack's blood. We left the sixth floor and went to audiology. We had a different audiologist today but our regular one came in and cleaned out Jack's ears. Jack was in a great mood even though he knew we were going to VCH. But when we arrived, he changed. Dr. Jekyll/Mr. Hyde come to mind. We had to wait in the waiting room and there were a few babies in there doing what babies do best—cry. First, Jack says in a thunderous voice, "I don't like crying babies!!" As usual, I told him to be quiet. Then he says. "I wish I had some duct tape to put over their mouths to make them be quiet!!" Duct tape???? I tried to quietly tell him that the babies were sick and didn't feel well and crying was all they could do. He looked at me and said some gibberish that he says when he gets mad at us while making some awful face that no person should make in a dark room much less in the lobby of a doctor's office.

Lord, thank you for new friends and old friends, for peace to accept the things in this life we must accept, for giving us the ability to love and hope, for keeping us safe for another day, for the blessings of today and the blessings to come, and for time to enjoy everything life has to give. Amen.

MY NAME IS JACK JOHNSON...

NOVEMBER 10, 2010—We are in a room at Vanderbilt Children's Hospital better known as Monroe Carrell Children's Hospital. We arrived at the oncology clinic at 1 pm. There were more small children at the clinic today, and Jack said yet again how much he dislikes babies and loud little kids. He goes on to say he is never going to have a girlfriend or wife and he is never going to marry anyone. Then he says he is never going to date a pregnant girl either. I don't think Jack understands, do you??

We finally got a hospital room at 3pm. Our nurses came in and said the doctors had prescribed Jack some IV anti-nausea medicine that would mean another IV put in his hand. He didn't like that. So, we gave him a choice, did he want the IV and not vomit or did he want to skip the IV and take a chance that he could get sick? The nurses did great getting the IV in and were so complimentary of his bravery. Next the nurse told us Jack needed to pee so we did in a urinal provided. I wrote down the amount and promptly flushed it down the toilet. Oops, I was supposed to give the specimen to the nurses so they could send it to the labs for testing. The first nurses went home for the evening and the next crew came in. These nurses were not happy that mother threw away the urine. They proceeded to worry the heck out of Jack and me about his need to pee. We have heard "Jack you really need to pee" about twenty times. I guess this is where the saying "worrying the pee out of someone" comes from. The person who first said that must have stayed at Vanderbilt Children's Hospital/Monroe Carrell Children's Hospital on the sixth floor. Finally, yet another nurse came in (probably the other nurses had told on us for not making urine on command) and fussed and fussed until Jack said he would try. He did add, if he peed, would that mean they would leave him alone and let him sleep. So, he peed and now he is asleep and we are still waiting for the lab to test his urine.

Pray that I get at least a whole two hours of sleep tonight because Her Majesty the Nurse has been in here asking how we want to be woken up every two hours for Jack to pee. She will wake us, or we can use my phone alarm. I am so glad Jack said she could wake us up because Her Majesty doesn't know how electronically challenged I genuinely am. I'll hold the urinal, Jack can do his business and Her Majesty the Nurse can wake us up. What a team effort!! Her Majesty has already been in here waking Jack up to pee again. And it wasn't two hours!! Bless his heart... it's going to be a long night.

Heavenly Father, thank you for people who help us when we need it, for the love of family and friends, for the pets we have that help us feel better, for the medicines we use that keep our bodies healthy and strong, for the faith we hold on to in difficult times. Amen.

NOVEMBER 11, 2010—Thursday—same recliner, same room, same hospital, different day. Jack has had all his chemo. We are now in the hydration period. He will be finished with hydration at midnight, and we will be coming home tomorrow if his blood count is OK. It was a long night with the chemo not even starting until midnight because the first urine test did not test well and we had to wait for him to go again and then test that one. That test came back at midnight, so we were up taking the oral chemo, getting the intravenous chemo and the infusion chemo, all at once. He had to wear gloves again to take the oral ones, and after he took all his chemo, I had to flush the toilet twice when I flushed his urine. Never mind that we had accident issues again during the night, but I flushed twice anyway. Jack, of course, has been a trooper again taking all of this in stride. We had one extended period of sleep from midnight after the chemo until 3 am. Then we were up every hour from then on. Ben got to the hospital at 7:30 am, brought me some breakfast, and we had coffee until 8:45 am. Then we had visitors, nurses, doctors, and therapists until noon. We had a busy morning.

I noticed last week as I was giving Jack a glass of water, he took it from me with his hands curled. I asked him why he was holding his hands like that, thinking he might have had something on his hands or fingers. He told me his fingers were curling up for no reason. He showed me how when he laid his hand flat with his palms up, his fingers slowly curled into a fist. Jack said his fingers do it all by themselves. So, while we were at the clinic before we were admitted, I told the nurse about it. She looked at Jack's hands and said it was the same as the pain in his feet—a side effect of one of his chemo's. The chemo can make the feet and hands drop, curl, and hurt with this side effect. An occupational therapist came to see us this afternoon and brought us therapy putty and a squeeze ball, so Jack can begin exercising his hands before the muscles in his hands shrink and stiffen in a curled position. A call has been made to the school system to see if therapy can be added to Jack's routine. I had noticed weeks ago that his handwriting had become very messy, messier than usual. He complained that his hands got very tired when he tried to write for extended periods during homework. Little did I know it was all associated with this side effect.

Dear Lord, thank you for brightening our day with the smiling faces of visitors, for the support of family and friends, for the help of caregivers, for Your

MY NAME IS JACK JOHNSON...

help in giving caregivers hearts of gold, for the relationship of a parent with a child, for the cry of ones in need, for making sure their need is met, and for unconditional love. Amen.

NOVEMBER 12, 2010—What a long day. We waited today until 3 pm to be discharged from the hospital. We still didn't get all the occupational therapy equipment they had wanted to give us before we left. They are making hand splints for Jack to wear daily when he is just sitting around or when he is sleeping to keep his hands and fingers in a normal position instead of the curled position he is currently comfortable with. The therapist that we saw yesterday said if not corrected, Jack's hands could become so stiff that they could start to turn inward at the wrists. I am still so very amazed that the chemo that could save his life is the same chemical that is causing all these side effects. At least we are home!! It feels good. My bed will feel wonderful. Jack has finally showered and is nice and warm and clean in his own bed.

Lord, thank you for the kindness of caregivers, for the hearts of earthly angels, for the feeling of your child's hand in yours, for the feelings of love and joy, and for the people You have sent us that make each day wonderful. Amen.

NOVEMBER 14, 2010—This weekend, Jack has felt good. No vomiting, no stomach issues, a good appetite, sitting up on his own like the therapist at the hospital said he should. He has been in a good mood, happy, watching one of the cable music channels and not 24/7 Game Show Network. Benny had a football banquet and received an award for keeping a 3.5 GPA during football season. Very proud of him. The Family Mission Group from our church, Franklin First United Methodist Church, returned and cleaned up our pitiful yard. There were zillions of leaves, bushes that needed cutting back, and a half-built patio that needed attention. In six hours, the leaves were all gathered and put at the roadside so the city can come with their giant leaf vacuum and suck them up. The yard was given Weed & Feed and aerated. The patio pavers were put together like a puzzle and stabilized with sides, landscaping nails and lots of sand. Flowers and bulbs were put in the ground and in pots. They will bless our yard next spring. Mulch covers all our landscape. Our yard looks so beautiful with color. And now we have hope that next spring, life will come again after the cold of winter and bring a smile to our faces. Thank you, Family Mission Group, for all your raking, digging, planting, mulching, sweeping, and getting dirty. Thanks for giving your time, sweat, and support to us.

Lord, thank you for strength, in our bodies, souls and minds, for others who

... BUT I'M NOT THE SINGER

so gladly and lovingly give their time and love to us, for the beauty of a flower, for the smile of a child, for the love of a teenager, for the clean water that we use to quench our thirst, and for strange, wonderful, beautiful days. Amen.

NOVEMBER 17, 2010—It has been a long day. Jack and I were at VCH again this morning at 10am and left at noon. He told me he wanted to eat lunch out, chose Rafferty's, and proceeded to tell me which exit on I-65 to get off. It has been a joyful day with him. At the doctor's office, he was pretend-playing The Match Game, the game show that was on TV in the 1970's. He has been watching reruns of it on Game Show Network and has started to memorize the questions and some of the answers. He knows all the 1970's stars that were on the panel and has the host Gene Rayburn's voice and mannerisms memorized as well. So, I had to play The Match Game with Jack while we waited for his blood counts to come back. He became the entertainment for the nurses. His nurse practitioner could not believe how different he was than the person he had been previously, but he has always felt so bad before and today he felt good. While we were getting ready to go this morning, I was in the bathroom in my underwear when Jack had to come in to brush his teeth. His toiletries are in our bathroom where we don't have to get him up the steps to brush his teeth since he is not good at going up or coming down steps. He comes in the bathroom, sees me in my underwear and says, "Is today wear your bra to the doctor's office day?" Funny guy. He has been like that much of the day. I love it. He got his hand splints today and doesn't like wearing them. They are bigger than I thought they would be, and he can't do anything with them on. I worked with him this afternoon on some OT things and noticed his abilities in his hands have regressed. He complained that it hurt his hands. Tonight, while doing homework, I asked him to write some vocabulary words on index cards. He could hardly hold the pencil and when he tried to write, he didn't have enough strength in them to force the pencil down on the card. I am shocked that his hands are this bad. Jack's blood counts were good and he hasn't lost any more weight. He is still very unsure on his feet and we must hold onto to him all the time. I think he is walking funnier than he did but it could be my imagination. He cannot loop his jeans button or zip the zipper, but he can remember the questions from The Match Game and what each star's response was. My, what a strange and wonderful world we live in.

Lord, thank you for our amazing minds, the magic of a good memory, for the laughter of our children, for the gift of good health, for nurses who care for

MY NAME IS JACK JOHNSON...

us, for medicines that heal our illnesses, for the homes where we live, and for a blessed day like today. Amen.

NOVEMBER 18, 2010—Today, Jack had school, and the occupational therapist came by to assess Jack for therapy. She asked him lots of questions and squeezed his hands and feet to see how strong/weak they are. He has not drawn pictures in a long time because he doesn't have control or power in his hands. Sadly, this is a child who loves to draw. The therapist will be back next week for two sessions. She also mentioned that she felt he could use leg braces again for extra leg strength and control.

Dear Lord, thank you for strong bodies and minds, for the love we have for each other, for the ability to laugh and smile, for a strong arm to help us when we need it, for a loving family and good friends, and for another earthly day. Amen.

NOVEMBER 22, 2010—It's nap time here at the Johnson house. Jack takes an afternoon nap about this time every day now. He puts his hand braces on and gets in the bed. We have just finished his homework and a full session of Mommy and me OT. There were lots of screams and groans but we got through it. We are supposed to do them three times per day but I haven't had time to schedule all of them into my day. I have written several times about his lack of balance and how we walk everywhere with him now because of fear of falling. Well, it happened. At least it wasn't down the stairs and thankfully, he didn't get injured. Saturday, he got up from the couch and just fell in the floor. Ben was already up, Jack had just gotten up, and Benny and I were still in bed. I laid in the bed and listened to the mayhem between the fallen and the rescuer. Jack, with his strange noises, Ben with trying to be helpful to one who doesn't like a nurturing dad. Jack complained about some pain but couldn't describe where exactly it was hurting. Jack has been a bit more cautious since the fall. He stayed in his room upstairs all day long yesterday playing and laughing at his video games. He told Ben that playing video games was good for his hands. Now he is an occupational therapist! He hasn't been sick and has felt otherwise good. We went to my sister's house Saturday night for Thanksgiving with my family. I pray God blesses us with many years of holidays together.

Dear Lord, thank you for the blessings we have this time of year, for the blessing we have all the time, and for the blessings we take for granted. Let us this season open our eyes to each blessing we have and learn to be thankful every day, not just this time of year. Let us know how blessed we are to be togeth-

...BUT I'M NOT THE SINGER

er every day, to be surrounded by loved ones, for our good health, our food, our homes, our lives. Help us to share what we have with others so they may know Your love. Wrap Your mighty arms around the needy and sick and let them feel Your strength. We ask these things in Your name, Amen.

NOVEMBER 26, 2010—We hope everyone had a glorious Thanksgiving with family, friends, food and lots of laughter. We had our steak Thanksgiving here at home, and we all shared what we were thankful for this year. I was thankful we were home, quiet and together, Ben was thankful the rest of us were well, Benny was thankful we were back in the house, and Jack was thankful to have me, Ben, and Benny to help take care of him, a statement he shared without prompting or asking.

Tonight, we picked up Ben's mom, and we all went to eat Mexican. I had a margarita, and Jack asked what was in it. I told him it was an adult beverage because it had alcohol. He said, "Don't you know that's a drug, Mom? It has alcohol fluids, and they are drugs!!" I have never heard the term alcohol fluids, so, it's pretty accurate to say Jack has been full of himself. And I am so thankful for it!

Dear Lord, thank you for happy days, for out-of-the-mouth-of-babes times, for all the blessings we are thankful for, and for friends and family that check on us through this website every day. Please allow us to have many more Thanksgivings to spend with loved ones. Amen.

NOVEMBER 29, 2010—Jack has been in a great mood this weekend. It was the let's-take-advantage-of-Jack's-good-blood-counts weekend. When we went to Bunny River's house Saturday night, Jack ate well except for the green beans—he said they tasted like sweat socks. They didn't. The beans were just not as cooked as he is used to. And I can't recall him ever tasting sweat socks. Maybe that is what he does upstairs in his bedroom.

Saturday Jack announced that he wanted to go to church Sunday morning. Not just to Sunday School but to church too. We all got up, dressed and went. He got exhausted during the service, and he couldn't walk all his secret stairways to see the Exit signs, but he got to go and eyeball as many exit signs as he could. Thank you, Misses Luna, for helping with Jack and his Exit sign checkup. He is so pitiful, walking around now with his feet causing a funny walk while his thin and curled hands stick out to help with his balance. But his excitement was so worth the trip. His face lit up, a strange contrast to the rest of his body. I only hope and pray all these side effects are temporary and not permanent.

MY NAME IS JACK JOHNSON...

Dear Lord, thank you for the loved ones You have put in our lives, for the love we share with them, for happy times we will never forget, for the moments we will cherish forever and for another day shared with them. Amen.

DECEMBER 2, 2010—Tonight, Ben was working, and I was talking to my dad when Jack announced to me he was ready for his shower. I told him I would be there as soon as I got off the phone. Well, what do you know? When I got off the phone, I couldn't find the rascal. I looked in all the familiar Jack sulking places, and he wasn't there. I found him in the shower with the water running and washing himself. Someone has been sandbagging us again. All this time he couldn't turn the water on in the shower himself, or get his washcloth, or get in the shower, or take off his socks by himself. Well, well, Mr. Sandbag, you did it tonight. We won't be falling for that song and dance again. He was not happy about doing it himself, saying to me that he couldn't wait for me anymore. Very funny.

Last night, as we were talking small talk with Jack, he hit us with another one of his Jack-isms. We were talking about all the things we do for him, like getting certain foods when he wants them, waiting on him most of the time, helping him up and down the stairs, helping him with dressing and shower time and all the other things we have had to do for him since this started. Jack was saying how much he appreciated all of this and said I was the world's best mother. So, of course, Ben asks "What about me?" Jack says never missing a beat, "Well, you're almost the world's best dad."

Dear Lord, thank you for days that make us smile, for the blessing of children who brighten our winter days, for healthy bodies that work when we ask them to, and for the ability to think, feel, and love. Amen.

DECEMBER 5, 2010—I have a story to tell about a great opportunity we took advantage of this Saturday. In the newspaper, there was a tiny article about Nashville photographers who were participating in a world-wide event donating portraits to families who couldn't otherwise afford them. The Saturday event was called Help Portraits. At the end of the article was a website address that I sent an email to see if we would qualify for the event. A person emailed back, told me yes, we qualified, and they would be in Franklin as well. They told me where, when, and were excited to meet us. So, Saturday, I rounded up several unhappy fellows, and we had pictures made. The Help Portrait photographers had donated their time to give other families a lasting memory. Our photographer had volunteered next door at our neighbor's

... BUT I'M NOT THE SINGER

2010 Help Portrait picture of Jill and Jack expressing his displeasure

house in the flood aftermath, and he knew exactly where we lived. Both the photographer and his helper could not have been kinder to Jack, making sure they took plenty of pictures of him but not pushing too far to make him feel uncomfortable. We left with eighty-four photos on a DVD that we can reproduce any way we want, a group picture of us framed, and several photos they printed for us as gifts. When we left, we left amid hugs and smiles and promises to see us again next year after Jack has hopefully finished chemo and is on the road to recovery. God has blessed us with so many earth angels who give so much of themselves in so many ways. I never realized that amid so much hardship and sadness, angels come, pick us up, wipe our tears, and show us the goodness of man and the pure heart of God.

Jack fell again Saturday. He stood up from the couch to go to the car and just fell face first to the floor. Of course, Jack had to be Jack after he fell with one of his Jack statements. When we got him up and off the floor, he said, "It's all your fault. You should have raised me better." He also had a nose bleed Friday, and he never said a word about it. It occurred to me that his platelet

MY NAME IS JACK JOHNSON...

count was very low last week when Nurse T. took his blood, probably the cause of his nose bleeding.

Dear Lord, thank you for friends to share life with, for angels who know what we need even before we do, for family gathered around the table, for hands that hold up, pick up, and heal, and for unexpected special moments in life that we share with loved ones that will permanently be in our hearts and minds forever. Amen.

DECEMBER 7, 2010—Tuesday... school and therapy day. Jack was not a happy camper today. He had to think and move, two things he is not in the habit of doing or shall I say doing well. He was a little short with the teacher and very ugly to the therapist, but he was ugliest to me, with his angry faces, screams, huffing and puffing, and just being downright mean. His TV time went away because of his ugliness, so he soon became Mr. Apology. Mr. Tears soon replaced Mr. Apology. It was a sad day for Jack. Ben and I had to go to the grocery store tonight after dinner. We left Benny in charge of Jack. Benny was hooked up to his iPod while playing on the laptop so sneaky Jack turned on the TV and watched Charlie Brown's Christmas. He later looked me in the eyes and told me he did it. I hope he enjoyed it because the only thing he will see on TV tomorrow will be his reflection on the screen.

I talked with the OT today, and she believes a physical therapist will start seeing Jack around the 19th of this month. She also explained he has dropped feet, they are probably causing his falls. She shared with me that when he picks up his feet, his feet point downward causing the toe of his shoe to trip him which makes him fall. She showed me several exercises we can start doing to help with this. I don't know how I am supposed to do all the things people want me to do... OT—three times daily, homework, housework, cook, wash clothes, get food and drink for Jack on demand, write bills, unpack boxes, put unpacked stuff away, put up Christmas decorations, shop for Christmas... and it goes on and on. I'm going to do what I can, and the rest can wait. Maybe I should ask Santa for a clone.

Lord, thank you for the patience we have with our children, for the love that we have for one another, for being able to laugh at ourselves, and for this wonderful season of giving to others. Amen.

DECEMBER 9, 2010—Jack has had school today and therapy. After his teacher left, he had an hour before the therapist arrived, so he got in my bed to rest. I got in the bed with him, and we talked, laughed, and had fun.

...BUT I'M NOT THE SINGER

Thanks, God, for days like today, for times spent close to loved ones, for coats to keep us warm on these cold days, for our pets that love us unconditionally, and for days with no pain or sickness. Amen.

CHAPTER 23

DECEMBER 15, 2010—Wednesday means blood count day and a visit from Nurse T. Nurse T. came in all happy to see us especially her friend, Jack. I had all her supplies out for her, and we were ready and waiting. (You probably know where this is going…) Nurse T. got her gloves, the cleaner for Jack's port, the tubes that the blood goes into, puts the needle in, and you guessed it, missed the port. She said in her sweet Nurse T. voice, "Oh, Jack, Miss T. missed." Jack screamed, "Failure!!!" She took the needle out, and after trying again, she got it in. Nurse T. was so upset with herself, she forgot the blood sample, but I caught her before she left the driveway. I told Nurse T. not to take to heart what Jack said. Ben and I have been fired from being Jack's parents so many times I cannot count them all, and all the poor teachers Jack has fired over the years. Jack is not the easiest patient but still loves Nurse T.

God, thank you for the gift of good health, the gift of this day, the gift of children, the gift of kindness and love, and the gift of Your Son. Amen.

DECEMBER 16, 2010—Today, Jack had school and therapy back to back. His therapist, Miss E., has put in an order for yet another pair of braces for Jack's hands and wrist. I asked Miss E if she thought it would be a good thing for Jack to use a walker here around the house until we see the PT. I am very concerned about his balance which seems to get worse every day. She must be concerned too because she said a walker would be good for him right now. We have the one that belonged to Adele, Ben's grandmother, in the attic. I haven't told Jack yet about it because we haven't gotten it out of the attic. Who knows how he will react? Tomorrow per Miss E., Jack will have to get up every two hours and walk around the house. There will be screaming sometime during the day tomorrow. When Miss E. told him this, his response was "Oh, great." Long face, sad voice. Miss E. got him up and walked him around the dining room table, but he could only make three steps at a time before he had to rest. Today has been a hard day for Jack.

... BUT I'M NOT THE SINGER

When I received the call on Jack's blood counts, I found out our regular nurse is on maternity leave, so we have a substitute. Nurse A., our temporary replacement nurse, said that since Jack's red blood, hemoglobin, and white count were all low, he would be extra tired. Nurse A. was correct. Nurse A. also told me things to look for in Jack that could signify his blood counts were too low, like ashen complexion, white lips, and unusually tired. He explained to me what to look for when Jack's platelets were too low, like nosebleeds that take 5-10 minutes to stop, unusual bruising, and little red spots that look like a rash but aren't raised and the parts of the body they could show up on. Nurse A. was a fountain of information. I thanked him profusely. Now I feel more secure about my knowledge in what to look for in Jack where his blood counts are concerned.

Today when Miss E. had Jack up and walking, Mia, the cat, got Jack and Miss E.'s seat on the couch while they were walking. Mia was not going to move on her own, so I had to move her. She was not happy at all. She tried to bite me! Not like her at all. Jack told Miss E., "Mia really likes to be near me. I'm Mia's man."

Dear God, thank you for the angels that surround and support us here on earth, for our pets that make us smile, for the words that come out of the mouths of babes, for the ability of walk and talk, for the miracle of our own bodies, and for helpers who take the time to give of themselves. In His Name, Amen.

DECEMBER 20, 2010—Jack had a great weekend. He loves the walker!! He can go anywhere with it, and it has given him so much confidence. He asked tonight if he could go to the grocery with Ben and me. I wouldn't let him, but he truly wanted to go. I was and still am shocked that any male living in my house would want to go to the grocery. We went to church yesterday too. Jack took the camera and during Sunday School time he and his helper, Misses Luna, walked the church and Jack took pictures of Exit signs. Thank you, Misses Luna, for your patience and love where Jack is concerned. Jack was thrilled at the pictures and being able to walk with his walker through the halls and floors of the church.

Dear Lord, thank you for balancing the unbalanced, for the joy of the Christmas season, for the color of Christmas lights reflecting off the faces of children, for the sound of laughter, for the innocence of the young, and for the baby and His birth we celebrate. Amen.

MY NAME IS JACK JOHNSON...

DECEMBER 22, 2010—It has been a very long day. We got up at 6:15am, left the house at 7:30am, got to the hospital at 8am and got home tonight at 6:30pm. It was a long day. I got Jack and our cart, full of our things to do today, unloaded from the van and we wheeled—me with the cart and Jack with the walker—into the hospital and to the elevators. We got on the elevator on the first floor and rode to the second. There were other folks wanting to get on but when we stopped and before they could all get on, a loud deep voice said, "Get your own elevator!" Several people snickered as I told the guilty party with the big mouth to hush. Again, the elevator stops at the third floor and you guessed it, that same voice says, "Get your own elevator." After the next reprimand, he didn't say it again. We got to the oncology floor, Jack got weighed (has gained six pounds!!), checked out, and got his port accessed. They then took his blood and sent it to the lab for blood counts. Since his counts were good, we had to have pre-chemo fluids. This chemo is again one that will affect the kidneys in a negative way if not flushed through the system. Jack had fluids put in his IV and around noon, the chemo finally started. It took it an hour or so to finish, then we had to have six hours more of fluids. Did I say it has been a long day?? Once settled in our infusion room spot, Jack noticed his surroundings and shouted, "Ohhhhh nooooo, a baby!!" Are you sure I have said it was a long day? With each trip to the bathroom, Jack had to take his walker and I oversaw the IV pole. With all the intelligence it takes to come up with all the new technology we have today, why hasn't someone invented a better IV pole? The pole isn't so bad if all you must contend with is the pole but when you add in a walker, there will be a problem. Have you ever tried to maneuver a walker and an IV pole into a bathroom with a door that automatically closes? I could not for the life of me hold the door open for Jack and his walker, get him in the restroom, and get the pole in the restroom all at the same time. I know that sounds stupid but there is not enough IV line for him to get out of the doorway and into the bathroom, not enough space in the doorway for me, him and the walker, and not enough arm length on my body for me to be able to grab the pole while holding the bathroom door open and Jack to be inside the bathroom. I have discovered that my foot is no longer capable of holding a closing door while the rest of me is awkwardly stretched in the opposite directions. I have also realized that Jack is not capable of holding a closing door with either one of his hands, and his tolerance for pain when the IV line is pulled is very low. And lastly, I have found out things about my son's bathroom habits that I didn't know before like: (1) you only squirt one push of soap into his hands—not two, or you will be cleaning the bathroom floor, (2) when your hands don't work well you can't push or pull

...BUT I'M NOT THE SINGER

your own pants up and down in the bathroom, (3) automatic flushing toilets are scary, and (4) you must use four paper towels to dry your hands to get them completely dry...every time you wash your hands. Ah, the life of the patient with autism and the ones who love them.

God, thank you for healthy bodies, for young minds, for the knowledge you have given us to try to find cures for diseases, for caregivers everywhere, for nurses and doctors, for mothers and fathers, for children, and for the ability to love no matter the circumstance. In His Holy Name, Amen.

DECEMBER 23, 2010—I feel as if I have taken root in a straight back, no padding chair on the sixth floor of the doctor's tower at Vanderbilt. We got there at 8 am and left at 5 pm, a whole hour less than yesterday. They had said it wouldn't take as long as yesterday, so I was expecting like three instead of 5 pm. Jack feels quite awful. He got up this morning and vomited. He was up two times last night to pee. He feels so bad tonight he has decided to sleep in the twin bed in the master bedroom. And he hates that bed, but he hates feeling bad worse. I think he is scared he will be sick in the night and can't make it to the bathroom. With the twin bed downstairs, the bathroom is not too far away. But upstairs, the bathroom is farther away from his bedroom, and he passes by the staircase which scares me. He could easily lose his balance going past the stairs and fall. I am happy he is sleeping downstairs.

Dear Lord, thank you for the givers in our lives, the givers of care, the givers of hope, the givers of love, the givers of knowledge, the givers of their hearts. Please help us to receive in a way that is pleasing to You. Keep us all safe at this time of togetherness. May there be peace on Earth. Amen.

DECEMBER 26, 2010—We hope everyone had a great Christmas. We visited with family Christmas Eve morning and more family Christmas Eve night. We ate lots of delicious food, laughed, sometimes I teared up, but mostly we had fun. Jack has felt surprising good with tiredness his only problem. He has not been sick or feverish—a nice blessing. Physically, he has been fine. Mentally he was a little off. Christmas morning was difficult: he didn't like the idea of going anywhere in the snow. It took a bit of coaxing and answering a lot of his questions, but we got him up and to Christmas morning breakfast with family. Once he got there, he did a lot of complaining which in turn turned into tears. He boohooed and was so sad, and I couldn't get out of him what was wrong. Of course, when he cried, I tuned up myself. He got in the extra bed at his Aunt Amy's house and covered himself up and cried. He told me to just leave him

MY NAME IS JACK JOHNSON...

alone but I couldn't just leave him lying there crying and not knowing what he was upset about was killing me. Finally, after several minutes of checking up on him and talking to him, he finally told me he was sad because he hadn't gotten what he wanted for Christmas. Holy Moly! Why, oh, why, couldn't he just tell me that to begin with!! Jack had asked for more Garfield stuff because he loves Garfield, the big orange cartoon cat. He has several stuffed Garfield's now, several books about Garfield, a stuffed Odie, Garfield's best friend, but he wanted more. I know him so well, I knew who to tell to get him Garfield stuff and I knew Ben and I would be giving Jack more Garfield stuff as well. Since we had been to two family Christmas celebrations, he must have thought I had forgotten about his request. I explained to him that I remembered what he wanted for Christmas and that Christmas was far from being over for him. That got him out of the bed and, at least, in the same room with the rest of us. We had our big Christmas breakfast, cleaned the dishes, and passed out the presents. My sister, Jan, (I have three sisters) had gotten one of Jack's wishes as his gift. She was sitting next to me and I was sitting next to Jack. He opened a couple of presents, said his thank yous, and got to one of his wish gifts. I will never forget the look on his face when he opened his stuffed new Garfield, who is holding his favorite stuffed animal, Pookie. To say Jack's face lit up is an understatement. Jack's face glowed. He smiled from ear to ear, something he hadn't really done in days. He looked at Garfield with Pookie in his arms, and put Garfield to his chest hugging them both tenderly. I looked at Jan who had been watching Jack open the gift and she had tears in her eyes. Jack got the gift that at the time he needed to make his Christmas bright. Finally, a Merry Christmas for Jack.

    As for me, I have been a wreck. I have held up well in front of family but inside my stomach has been in knots. I am not sure if anyone has felt the same thing but the whole time this Christmas in the far reaches of my mother's brain, I have been thinking about how I hope this is not Jack's last Christmas. I know I shouldn't be thinking this way but I just can't help it. I guess that is why it hurt me so when Jack was upset because I wanted this Christmas to be very special for him, for him to be happy, to not be in pain or sick to his stomach. Every day I get out of bed afraid of the future. I try not to dwell on it and just keep living, but it's always there, lurking in the back of my old brain. It doesn't cripple me or keep me locked away. It's just too close to me now. It's not just a fleeting thought when you hear it happens to someone else. It walks and lives in the house with me. One day I hope and pray it leaves. I pray Jack will be healthy one day, and cancer will be gone from our lives for good. But until that glorious day, I will live in fear. Dang, this house is not big enough

...BUT I'M NOT THE SINGER

for all of us. There's Ben, me, Benny, Jack, three cats, one outside cat, one guinea pig, autism, and now fear. It sure is getting crowded in here..................

Dear Lord, thank you for glowing smiles, for loving hands, for the tenderness of a heartfelt hug, for family and friends, for the joy of celebrating together, for the gift of food, shelter, heat, for the sound of laughter, and for the wonderful gift of love. Please watch over and hold in Your heart all the ones who grieve for the loved ones no longer here with us but with You. And thank you most for the greatest gift of all, Your Son. In His Name, Amen.

DECEMBER 28, 2010—We have had lots of guests. Jack saw the physical therapist for the first time, delivery of his new wrist splints, and a replacement occupational therapist for our usual one who went to California for Christmas and came back with a cold. The new PT decided he didn't need PT as much as he needs braces to help with the tightness in his feet. I hadn't noticed how Jack's feet point east and west of the center point of where they should point. He has started to overcompensate for the fact that it is so hard to walk with dropped feet that he points them out further to keep himself from tripping and falling. So, the PT left with the paperwork and orders to start the process of getting foot braces for Jack. He also has new wrist splints to wear at night that will keep his wrist in the correct position instead of his hands curling in.

Dear God, thank you for humor that sustains us through difficult times, for helpers that make our lives easier, for our homes, for family and friends, for times that make us ponder, and for the love and support we get from each other. Amen.

DECEMBER 29, 2010—Today Jack and I went to Vanderbilt for his chemo treatment. We arrived on time for our 10 am appointment, valet parked the van, went to the hospital, and walked to the elevators. We were the only ones waiting for the elevator and the only people to get on. Jack walked into the elevator, pushed the sixth-floor button, and moved his walker in front of the elevator doors with force and purpose. He placed his walker right up against the doors hoping it would keep others from getting on the elevator! I had to talk with him again about how we aren't the only people who have to use the elevators, and we must share them, and he can't stop others from getting on... blah, blah, blah. He took it well. Luckily, we went to the sixth floor without stopping for other passengers.

As with every other trip to VCH, they must take Jack's blood before they can give him chemo to make sure he doesn't need a transfusion. He didn't need a transfusion, but his ANC (measurement of neutrophils that fight infection) was very low. Jack now has a condition called neutropenia, or they say he is neutropenic. This means that Jack's infection-fighting white blood cells are so low that he is not able to fight infections. While he is neutropenic, he cannot: leave the house, eat fruits with their outer skins, touch his acne, roughly brush his teeth so they will not bleed, and he must continuously wash his hands. In fact, all of us will have to wash our hands regularly, not go around people who are sick, take off or clean our shoes before we enter the house, the list goes on and on. Jack has been close to the magic neutropenia number, but now he is there. We have repeatedly been told that this would happen eventually, so it wasn't a huge surprise. I need to be extra, extra careful about making sure everyone washes their hands, we keep the bathrooms and kitchen extra clean, making sure that Jack is not touching his face, and making sure he isn't running a fever. The nurse today said it shouldn't last long, probably until next week's blood counts. Jack had to wear a mask when we walked out of the hospital. He wasn't very happy about it, but he tolerated it without any problems. We keep getting further and further into the land of side effects connected with treating this cancer. Jack still hasn't complained as much as I thought he would. He complains a lot when asked to do schoolwork or therapy but most of the time, he goes on like this is all normal. Just don't get on an elevator with him...

Dear Lord, thank you for healthy bodies, for clever minds, for all the things that keep us safe and protected, for patience and understanding, for giving us a sense of humor, for the ability to complain when we need to, for encouragement from friends and family, and for Your constant love for us even when we fall short of Your expectations. Amen.

DECEMBER 30, 2010—It is almost the end of 2010. Wow. It seems like we just started the year and now it is ending. For us, 2010 is the year that never was; it was just a blur. I remember things that happened at the beginning of 2010, but those things seem like a lifetime ago. So, we say good riddance to 2010 and OH NO to 2011. For us, nothing has changed. There are no resolutions to make and not keep. There is nothing really to look forward to. It's the same old stuff that we will end 2010 with: fighting cancer. Personally, I am looking forward to 2012. Surely, we will be finished with cancer treatments by then.

Dear Lord, thank you again for friends and family, for spending time with them, for laughter and moments of happiness, for the smile of a child, and for

... BUT I'M NOT THE SINGER

the joy of the season. Let hope guide us through rough times and love hold us in a tight grip. In His Holy Name, Amen.

JANUARY 4, 2011—Today, Jack was bright eyed and bushy tailed. He has been drawing again today. He told me he was working on the electric poles from Auburntown to Lascassas. I am so happy he is drawing poles again. Drawing is such a good OT exercise, and it also means his fingers are getting easier to use for him. I do love progress.

Lord, thank you for warm winter days, for walks around the block, for the shelter of a home, for the ability to remember the good and the bad, for friends that always think of us, for another birthday of a loved one, and for giving us your only son. In His Name, Amen.

JANUARY 5, 2011—Jack has been very busy again drawing a hundred pictures of electric poles that he has memorized from his last car ride. He has poles from Auburntown and Lascassas, and now he is getting close to Smithville. Each picture has a pole and whether the pole has a transformer, a light, the different numbers of wires, whether it is made of wood or metal, and the list goes on. I am not up on my pole knowledge. I know there will be a trip to buy more copier paper in my future. After you realize the remarkable memory that Jack has, remember this is a child who in June had brain surgery. That same child had thirty brain and spinal radiation treatments where he was put to sleep for each one and has had three-to-four different chemo drugs over a period of five months. What a testimony to God that he gave us such a magnificent organ as the brain. God gave Jack a brain so very different from ours that so many people have judged him as strange, different, and disabled, but he can memorize electric poles from a twenty-five-plus mile trip and still be able after surgery to draw each one he remembers. I wish all the nay-sayers who didn't think Jack would learn, be productive, or have a good life could see him now.

Dear Lord, thank you for everyday miracles, for doctors with steady hands and open hearts, for eyes that see all your many blessings, for the love we feel for one another, for uneventful days, and for another day shared with the ones we love. Amen.

JANUARY 6, 2011—I got the results from Jack's blood count, and all I can say is how low can they go??? His neutrophils are down to 250 and in the dangerous category. Jack will not be leaving the house anytime soon. And everyone else who lives here will be spraying their shoes with Oust and sanitizing their hands A LOT.

God, our heavenly Father, thank you for the ability to think, to feel, to speak, to listen, to plan. Thank you for time to work, to think, to be busy. Thank you for family and friends, for without their support and love, we would be lost and alone. In His Name, Amen.

JANUARY 11, 2011—Today E, the occupational therapist, called, to let us know our insurance has decided they are not going to pay for any more OT for Jack. Don't you love days like that when a phone call can mess up your whole day? I called Jack's case manager, Nurse L. at Blue Cross Blue Shield, something you get when you have a serious health condition, and she told me she was on it. Nurse L. said she was working hard on changing some minds there at BCBS. As she said, it would be much better and less expensive for Jack to receive OT to keep his hands from stiffness now than to wait and do surgery on them later down the road to correct them. I knew insurance would come into play somewhere down the road during this treatment. I didn't know when. If people thought with their God-given common sense, we wouldn't have problems with insurance and the medical community. So, we wait to hear if Jack's OT treatments will continue to get paid for or not. So much for that happy new year...

Dear Lord, thank you for the sunshine, for the smile of a child, for the bright red of the cardinal in the winter, for the hope of spring, the love we share with each other and the faith we have of eternal life with You. Amen.

JANUARY 12, 2011—Nurse T. came today and took a blood count draw from Jack. He did bleed a little more after she took the needle out, something he has not done before, but a dead giveaway that the platelets are low. They were low but not too bad, and the good news, Jack is no longer neutropenic. He feels so good right now it is scary. I hate the fact that he feels so good now and next week we start the whole cycle over again. He also woke up this morning with some new shedding as he calls it. His hair is beginning to fall out again. I doubt this time it will grow back.

At Jack's physical therapy session today, his therapist had him up and exercising. There was a lot of sighs, growls, and mean faces but he did everything she asked him to do. I was shocked he could do some of the things he did, like standing up for a whole minute without any support. Yay for progress!

Dear Lord, thank you for the time we have with our babies, for their hugs

... BUT I'M NOT THE SINGER

and kisses, for their smiles, for the happiness they bring us, and for the peace only You can give when they are gone. In His Name, Amen.

JANUARY 13, 2011—Last night, Ben said for just one moment, Jack was a typical teenage boy just like Benny. No autism, no brain tumor, no side effects, just a boy kidding around with his dad and his big brother. Jack has discovered YouTube videos, old TV shows and commercials—a Jack favorite. He recently had been on YouTube and found one of those "Messing with Sasquatch" commercials. If you have never seen one, it is a Bigfoot creature—a Sasquatch—and the people in the commercial play jokes on the Sasquatch and it retaliates in a way only a Sasquatch would do. Jack found a commercial where some young people were out in the woods and they encounter a Sasquatch bent over a body of water to get a drink. One of them take a towel and pops the bent over Sasquatch on his fanny. Sasquatch grabs the person and throws him across the body of water and the person's shorts come off and you see his bare bottom. Jack thought this was the funniest thing ever. He laughed harder than Ben had ever seen him laugh. Jack couldn't wait to show this to Ben and Benny. This is sooooo typical behavior from a 14-year old male. Ben was taken back by the feelings of normalcy—no disability, no tumor, just plain old silliness shared by one of his sons. Our eyes get so clouded by the fluff of the unique and strange, that we forget to look at the human being Jack is. I wish everyone could see the disabled this way. I know it was a treat for one proud dad.

Dear God, thank you for being with us in good times and bad, for loving us when sometimes we don't deserve it, for the feeling of hope when things are at their worst, for faith that You will always be with us, and for the support of family and friends who hold us up when our bodies and minds are weak. In His Name, Amen.

JANUARY 14, 2011—It has been a very long MRI day. We left the house at 1:15, stopped at the bank, got on the interstate and was at the hospital at 10 minutes until 2. We got checked in at the desk, got our matching wristbands, and I politely chained Jack to his walker with his wristband. He was sitting in a chair with his hands resting on the arms of his walker when I taped his wristband shut I had mistakenly taped his wrist and the top of the walker in the wristband together. He had the funniest look on his face and said "Hey, Mom!" and pulled his wrist away from the walker and you could plainly see my mistake. The ladies at the front desk thought it was a hoot but Jack was not as humored as they were. Our old friend and favorite radiology

MY NAME IS JACK JOHNSON...

nurse, J., came and got us. J. took us back, got Jack in bed, got him a gown, and accessed Jack's port. Jack was full of himself. He cracked jokes, he said funny things, he didn't seem to mind any of this at all. He watched J. get all the things together that it takes to access Jack's port. Of course, there is the needle, the tube that attaches to the needle, the saline that you flush the port with, all the medicines that kill germs, the gauze that goes under the needle because the needle doesn't go all the way into the skin (Jack calls it the pillow for the needle) and the bandage that covers the whole thing once it's in place. Jack knows each piece, when the nurse should do each thing and what should come next. J. did it just right and Jack didn't complain at all. When it came time to put the needle in Jack says, "And here comes the bride!" We have no idea where that came from but we all had a good laugh. Once the needle was in place, Jack was thrilled when the MRI technicians came for him. A short trip down the hall and Jack was in the MRI room. The nurses called us around 6:20 to come back to the recovery room. Once awake, Jack needed to use the bathroom so three of us and the wheelchair squeezed into the restroom. Jack did what he needed to do and started vomiting. One of the nurses went to the emergency room and found Jack two containers of grape juice. Jack drank both and he wasn't sick again. We got him dressed, in the van, and on the way home he told us what he wanted to eat. We got home about 7:30. Jack ate and soon was ready to go to his room and his bed. It has been a long day. I must say I have never seen a child as strong and stoic as Jack. I have said this before, and I am sure you are sick of hearing me say it, but I have never seen a child so unaffected by things like he is. I am amazed at his sense of trust with all the different people touching him, the roll with the punches attitude he has with all the different places we have had to go, and his overall outlook. He said out of the blue today that if this thing kills him then he will leave us all his pole drawings and we can look at them and always remember him. How could I ever forget this child! No way!

Lord, thank you for another day, for nurses who treat us with kindness and love, for strong bodies and minds, for each moment of every day we have with loved ones, for faith that You are with us, for hope that news will be good, and for peace that only You can give us. Amen.

JANUARY 17, 2011—Jack and I went to clinic and I received the MRI results. ALL CLEAR! Praise God for good news. Jack's blood counts were good too. He is not neutropenic; his white blood count and platelets are in the normal range. He also had a hearing test today and the results of it were good too.

... BUT I'M NOT THE SINGER

The audiologist said there was no change in his hearing even though Jack had complained to me several times about ringing in his ears. But for now, the news was good and we will take it and enjoy having good news. Since Jack will be going into the hospital Wednesday and having the next chemo treatment, Ben asked Jack if he could go and spend some time with him at the hospital and give Mommy a break. Jack got mad at his dad and said, "Mommy must be with me always!!" Good thing Ben doesn't wear his feelings on his sleeves. I must say, Jack and I have a very unusual relationship. I can most of the time finish his sentences for him or translate what he has trouble saying to others. I can get him to do almost anything (and that's a big almost) and I understand him when Ben sometimes doesn't. I explain things to Jack in the way he needs to hear them. I give him reasons for things that he doesn't understand. Case in point: today at the hospital there was a child that came through the waiting room at the audiology floor that had a serious medical condition. My uneducated guess would be the little girl was born with some condition that caused her not to have a full-size brain because her head and face had an irregular formation. I am not sure of the name of the condition, and, as I said, I am not educated on all the different conditions. Jack saw her, made a very ugly face right there for everyone to see, and asked really loud, "What was wrong with that kid?" We had to have a talk about what is the right and wrong thing to do when you see someone who has a physical disability. We talked more about it on the way home with Jack almost crying because the whole thing just made him sad. It did me too. Hopefully, he will be more understanding next time he sees someone with a physical condition he hasn't seen before. Jack knows that Mommy will answer his questions, understand his answers, and love him all the same. Not that Ben wouldn't do the same, but we all have different roles with our children and they depend on us for those roles. So, I will be at the hospital with Jack and Ben will be Benny's best pal. And everyone will be happy.

Dear Lord, thank you for healing hands, for news we need to hear, for the blessing of support from family and friends, for healthy children, for ears that hear, eyes that see, and minds that think. Thank you for your only Son who died for us. In His Name, Amen.

JANUARY 19, 2011—I only thought today, when we left the house, we were going to the hospital. But when we arrived, we arrived at a zoo. I am not sure what was going on here today but there was a swarm of people here. Jack and I got to the sixth floor and waited for our turn to go back. In the

MY NAME IS JACK JOHNSON...

lobby, there is a TV that is usually on. It is usually on the Disney Channel or some other show that Jack doesn't watch anymore. He calls them baby shows. Today it was on a baby show channel and he was not happy. It was one of those baby shows that was a lot like the old Teletubbies show which at the time was one of Jack's hidden pleasures. He loved the Teletubbies. Today, when we sat in the lobby and the new and improved Teletubbies look-alikes came on the TV, Jack was absolutely horrified. He started sticking his tongue out at the TV. You know, you just haven't lived without sitting beside someone who is sticking their tongue out at a TV while waiting in a crowded lobby. Some days I must decide if crawling under the furniture will be better than sitting there doing nothing. Jack is always an adventure. We were called back and Jack had his port accessed and blood drawn. The nurses found out it would be an hour or two before our hospital room would be open so we could go out for lunch. We decided to go down the street to The Sportsman's Grille and not to the food courtyard here at the hospital since that will be all we get to choose from for the next few days. Since it wasn't too cold outside at the time, we decided to walk. It is only about a block and a half to the restaurant from the hospital. The physical therapist said Jack should get up and walk as much as possible while he was here. So, we decided we would try to walk. First, we had to catch an elevator down to the first floor again. Every elevator that stopped to pick us up was semi-full, and there would not be enough room for all of us and Jack's walker. Five elevators stopped with no room for us and we waited forever between the elevators stopping. There was a lady waiting too that was pushing a cart of vending machine snacks. She was waiting along with us for an elevator with enough room for her and her cart. Finally, an elevator stopped going up instead of down but it didn't have many people on it. All of us, snack lady, cart and walker, piled into the near empty elevator. We had to take the scenic tour of all the floors of the Doctors Tower here at Vanderbilt Children's Hospital just to get back to the first floor, but we did get there and started the block and a half walk. We didn't take into consideration that Jack has only walked behind his walker on smooth surfaces, not on anything too rough. The sidewalks are well used here and have lots of drive entryways that slope from sidewalk height to street level, cracks, pits, divots, and seams. When you walk on those drive entryways you must walk on a slope. When Jack walked on the slope, his walker went with the slope and so did Jack. He was really getting mad at all the slopes and cracks the sidewalk had. There was lots of moaning, groaning, and he got close to screaming a

... BUT I'M NOT THE SINGER

few times. Soon he started to slow down because he was getting tired. Ben started to help and that made Jack mad too. Finally, I just sent Ben on into the restaurant while Jack and I took our time, or rather Jack took his time. We finally got there and had a nice lunch that wasn't Taco Bell, Pizza Hut, or Subway, which is the menu here at the food courtyard. We ate, we paid, we left. We had no sooner gotten out of the restaurant and around the corner when Jack got off the sidewalk and into the street. It was not really sidewalk height at that point but the road and the sidewalk had a huge wide, wet crack between the two. In the blink of an eye, the walker wheel hit the road crack, Jack lost control of the walker and himself, and his legs folded under him. He wasn't hurt, thank God, and surprisingly, he didn't get upset. Ben and I couldn't quite figure out what had happened to Jack; it was like he was our height and then he was gone. I hate to admit it but Ben and I got tickled and snickered at the sheer confusion of it all. All we wanted was to eat a little lunch but it turned into another adventure. Needless to say, Jack went to sleep early. He was tired. We finally got a hospital room this afternoon at 3:15. It is late now, and we still haven't started the big chemo. Jack has had the oral chemo and the injected chemo but not the six-hour chemo drip. After the chemo, we have eighteen hours more of fluids. We will get there sometime tonight, I hope. We did get a room with a view, at least, seeing parts of Hillsboro Village and Belmont from our window.

Dear Lord, thank you again for healthy bodies and minds, for times when a snicker is all we can do, for times when turning around is the right answer to a problem, and for the knowledge to know what to do when life makes us fall. Amen.

JANUARY 20, 2011—It has been a long day especially when you don't get to sleep at night. We were up all night with the nightly checks, the beeping machines, taking chemo, filling the urinal, finding a nurse to check the urine—it was a long night. I couldn't sleep not only with the constant parade of nurses but because the bed for parents to sleep on is not comfortable. So, at 3 am, I decided to try the recliner, the other piece of furniture for parents to sleep on. It was not much better, but I did finally fall to sleep but was woken up thirty minutes later. I am not whining. I'm just tired. Jack was up as well but did sleep in between interruptions. They are giving him medicines to keep nausea in check, and these meds make him sleep. He has slept most of the day. And the nurses have not been in as much since the chemo is finished and we are on flushing medicines.

MY NAME IS JACK JOHNSON...

Heavenly Father, thank you for long healing naps, for days with no pain and nausea, for nurses who work hard at taking care of their patients, for family and friends who support us every day, and for the hope that there will be a day without cancer. Amen.

JANUARY 22, 2011—We are back home. Jack is doing great. He is very weak in his legs and feet again so Ben and I rode to my dad's house and borrowed his bathroom bench/chair for people who can't stand in the shower/tub. Jack loved it because he didn't have to try to stand up and shower on his own. He sat in the shower so long that his cheeks were red when he got out.

Lord, thank you for those times in life when things change so we can appreciate our normal times, for caregivers, nurses and doctors, for quiet time spent with the ones we love, for the smile of a child no matter their age, for the softness of a bed, the warmth of a blanket, the joy of comfort, and for being blessed to have them. Amen.

JANUARY 24, 2011—Jack has not felt well today. His laptop stopped working a few minutes ago, and he said he was depressed because his computer is down. He doesn't get depressed over the things that depress me like chemo, side effects, cancer treatments, doctor's visits, general poking and prodding. He gets depressed over his things not doing what he wants them to do. I wish for just one day I could see the world through his eyes. I bet the view is so different and wonderful. People wouldn't need drugs and alcohol to make them feel happy. Happiness would come from car rides, electric poles, and YouTube videos. Wouldn't the world be a better place if our doctor said our sickness would get better with a good old car ride in the country?

Dear God, thank you for car rides in the country, for strong bodies and minds, for friends that support us with their prayers and love, for family that continue to love us daily, for the vision to see the wonderful differences we each have, and for showing us how to love and embrace each other despite those differences. Amen.

JANUARY 25, 2011—The only way to describe my youngest son right now is bad. He feels bad. You can tell by the way he looks, the way he sits and the way he is eating; Jack feels bad. He hasn't been sick or had any pain. He doesn't feel good at all. I haven't seen him smile today at all. His appetite has left too. And we go back to Vanderbilt for more chemo tomorrow. I feel guilty letting these people poison my child like this, but I don't have a choice. But it does make a parent feel bad when they see their child so down and out. He feels bad, and it makes me feel bad.

Dear Lord, thank you for the snow even when we have seen enough of it, for the hope that winter will soon be spring, for days when watching out the window at life is just fine, for the anticipation of a smile from someone we love, for the wonderful world of the teenage soul, for making us in Your image, and for giving us a heart like Yours to use to love our neighbors, friends, and family. Amen.

JANUARY 26, 2011—Jack went to the clinic today for an infusion of chemo. His blood counts were good, but he had lost 6 pounds. He seemed to feel a little better today, and after we got the good news on his blood counts, he wanted to eat out for lunch. He wanted to stop at Logan's Roadhouse. We had a nice lunch together, even though he is not much of a conversationalist.

I did see Jack smile today. He smiled at the hospital because the first elevator we got on went all the way to the sixth floor non-stop with only us two on it. That got a smile and a big "Yes!" He smiled again this afternoon after we got home because Mia, the cat, was rubbing on a lamp so hard because she was happy to see him that she almost knocked it over. That made him smile too.

Dear God, thank you for the joy of an empty elevator ride, for the wonderment of a smile, for days without pain, for the support of friends and family, and for the hope we have for a cure for cancer. Amen.

CHAPTER 24

JANUARY 27, 2011—Fighting cancer is a rollercoaster. One day, Jack feels completely awful, the next he is feeling better. He did sleep a lot this morning, but he woke up, ate a good lunch, had school with his homebound teacher, and now he is back upstairs drawing pictures. I am not sure of what he is drawing, probably electric poles. He announced sometime before he went to the hospital last week that he had finished his trip-to-Smithville poles. I cannot imagine how many poles that would be, but I bet he does.

I was reading the story of a child named D. who died from a brain tumor in 2009. His parents gave his tumor to researchers who have made the tumor cells continue to grow in the lab. Can you imagine losing your child and the only thing left of them is the cancer that killed them? Please continue to pray for all children fighting cancer and all the families that lose their children to this awful disease.

Dear Lord, thank you for the promise of spring with its burst of colors and warmth, for the hope of another day on earth, for the ability to learn and retain what we are taught, for healthy bodies and minds, for the ability to dream of better days, for the never-ending support of family and friends, for the humor of a teenager and the love of a pet, and for life everlasting with You where there is no pain and sorrow. In His Name, Amen.

FEBRUARY 2, 2011—Tuesday was slow; Wednesday made up for it. Jack and I had to be at clinic at 11am. We left here at 10:30ish and got to Vanderbilt at 11 on the nose. Of course, it does take a while to valet park and get Jack and his walker out of the van. Jack and I got to the sixth floor, where Jack found a chair in the corner where he could sit and not see the TV with the baby shows. No sticking his tongue out at the TV today. Jack was called back, was weighed, and other vitals were taken. He had lost four pounds since last week. We had Nurse MM. today, who is always such a sweet

... BUT I'M NOT THE SINGER

nurse. She really likes Jack and has told him before if she sees his name on the board she will put her name down as his nurse. Someone who chooses Jack—you must love her! Nurse MM. had to access Jack's port. She had a hard time because she said the port was a little tilted today and when she put the needle in, the tilt made the needle slide off the side of the port. She had to try again and Jack was not happy. Jack told Nurse MM., "You weren't a failure, the port was just messed up today." They put us in a room and we waited for his blood counts. On the way to Nashville, Jack and I were listening to the radio on a pop music station. There is an artist named Kesha who Jack used to like but for some reason he doesn't anymore. One of Kesha's songs came on the radio and he turned the volume down. Then he started in on the reasons he didn't like Kesha and her music. I told him some people like Kesha and her music and some didn't and that it was OK. After they put us in a room after his port was accessed, Jack went back to the Kesha conversation. He just went on and on about her. Then he started in on Katy Perry, another pop music artist. He says he thinks both are "sex artists" because they wear too much make-up. Don't ask me where that one came from because I have no clue. I told him maybe he felt they were being too sexy because they don't wear enough clothes. He told me no, it was because they wear too much make-up. Another nurse came in and we talked about Jack's next big overnight stay in the hospital. After he left, Jack started back on Kesha and Katy Perry. The nurse practitioner came in, we talked, she left, Jack started again on Kesha and Katy. He finally stopped and closed his eyes for a few minutes while we waited for the chemo. I looked up and saw this sad face on Jack so I asked if he was alright. He said, "Yah. I just think I like Lady Gaga better than Kesha or Katy Perry." Finally, before I pulled my hair out, Nurse MM. came in and gave Jack his chemo and we got to leave. And Jack left Kesha, Katy Perry, and Lady Gaga in room six on the sixth floor of Vanderbilt Children's Hospital. I hope someone washes all that make-up off their "sex artist's" faces.

Since Jack's neutrophil counts were still good, he wanted to eat lunch out again. This week he chose Applebee's. Jack was hungry, eating six mozzarella cheese sticks, five chicken strips, and fries, and then a big chocolate dessert with ice cream. I was glad to see him eat. We got home about 3 pm this afternoon. After Jack got home and we did homework, he went upstairs to draw electric poles. He is drawing the poles going out Lewisburg Pike. Ben told me later this afternoon that Jack called him upstairs and said that a lot of the poles on Lewisburg Pike were the same. So, Jack had drawn the differ-

MY NAME IS JACK JOHNSON...

ent poles and asked Ben if he would copy the different poles on the copier machine. Jack took each pole picture he had drawn and told Ben "I need five copies of this pole, three copies of this one, eleven copies of this one..." I love my little strange, unique, whacky Jack.

Dear Lord, thank you for the kindness of strangers, for the patience and mercy we receive from nurses, for the gift of getting to eat whatever we want... sometimes, for the wondrous gift of love, and for making us in Your image with no two of us the same. Amen.

FEBRUARY 7, 2011—Today, after lunch, Jack laid on the couch to wait for the PT. He fell asleep. Later in the day, the PT called to let me know if no one else had told me that our insurance is no longer going to pay for Jack's physical therapy. They had already let us know they were not going to pay for occupational therapy and now they are not paying for physical therapy. No one from the insurance company has called to tell me anything. I get to hear this wonderful news from Jack's therapist. And insurance companies wonder why we hate them as bad as we do?? Are you kidding me? My child cannot walk without his walker. Jack has no balance, no ability to lift his feet without his own feet tripping him. He can't stand unassisted for one minute without touching something to steady himself. I know this because this was one of the exercises the PT was working with Jack on. But nnn-nnnooooo, the insurance gods won't spend their money to help him. I bet they will all get their million-dollar bonuses for their good work for saving their insurance company money by taking away from children's services that they truly need. I am so disgusted by the whole thing. I can't wait to hear their excuse.... "well, your son has to have a foot injury before we can authorize more physical therapy...blah, blah, blah." We don't have the money to pay out of pocket for therapy. We already owe the hospital money for other expenses in Jack's treatment. If there is one thing I have learned in the past year, you faithfully pay your insurance premiums for years thinking it will be there for you when you need it. That is the line we have all been told, its why we all buy insurance. But when you need it to do what you have paid all those years for, they will use every trick in the book to try to get out of paying for anything they can. And it doesn't matter what type of insurance —flood insurance was the same way. So, I will regroup and put on my warrior mom clothes and start another battle over what's right and what's wrong. Jack needs to be the young man that he was before the brain tumor and treatment.

...BUT I'M NOT THE SINGER

Dear Lord, thank you for the gift of laughter, for the children You give us to protect and love, for people who genuinely care about others, and for making me see the good of today through all the bad. Amen.

FEBRUARY 9, 2011—My Dad was telling me the story about his doctor visit today. He was talking to his doctor about his inability to stay asleep during the night. His doctor asked if he had more than usual on his mind. Dad told his doc about how his grandson had had a brain tumor and was taking treatments. The doctor didn't say anything, but he thought they needed to pray. Dad and his doctor prayed to God for Jack, for us, and for our whole family including Dad. I am always so amazed at how a small drop of news can have the ripple effect to so many people. Please keep Jack and all the other children fighting pediatric cancer in your prayers. Let's all make a wave instead of a ripple.

Dear Lord, thank you for the promise of spring, warm weather, and time spent outdoors, for the gift of family and friends, for giving us the ability to heal all wounds in our bodies and our minds, for hope that tomorrow will come, and for the ability to love. Amen.

FEBRUARY 15, 2011—Jack has had a good day. We got up and went to Vanderbilt to see Dr. McGrew, Jack's autism pediatrician. Since she is retiring to explore the art world, today was her actual last day. We talked a lot about what she will do about another autism doctor, how well Jack was doing with treatments, and our insurance situation. Dr. McGrew praised Jack for his ability to endure all he has while living with autism. We also talked about the insurance company's stance that they don't have to cover any more therapies because they only cover trauma of the hands and feet. Dr McGrew believes, like us, that this is, in fact, trauma. She looked at his hands and said she could tell he has lost muscle in his hands. And of course, his feet are stiff and cannot move the way our feet do. Dr. McGrew asked me to talk to Jack's case manager nurse and find out the medical director's name and number so she could talk to him about Jack and his condition. I called as soon as we got home and our case manager nurse said she would set up the appointment for Dr. McGrew and the medical director to talk. Hopefully this will help. Jack was very sad that Dr. McGrew was not going to be his doctor anymore. She talked to him and told him she would continue to keep up with him through the CaringBridge site and if he needed her, he could email her anytime. That seemed to help him. When we left, he hugged her. I teared up, of course, because I could see his face and he had tears in his eyes and his bottom lip

MY NAME IS JACK JOHNSON...

was quivering. It is very hard to give up people who have made a huge impact on your life. We all have them. It could be a favorite school teacher, a special friend, a mentor you have leaned on in times of need. They have made our lives better even though they didn't set out to become that important to us. They were just doing their job, but for us—the ones who they touched—it is more than just an obligation. It made a difference in our lives, it changed the course of our sails. It sent us in a different direction from where we were headed. It truly made a difference. Thank you, Dr. McGrew, for changing the direction of our lives so many years ago. I don't know where Jack and all of us would be today if you hadn't shown us the way. Jack is the strong fighter he is today because of the guidance of people like you. Enjoy your family, your art, and your retirement. May God bless you and your family.

Lord, thank you for the people You send to help us make our lives the best they can be, for the warm sunshine and a few minutes to enjoy it, for times when we need to cry in sorrow and in happiness, for the love of family and friends, and for every day we share with our loved ones. Amen.

FEBRUARY 16, 2011—Today started with our weekly visit from Nurse T. She came in as usual smiling and started right into the job of getting a sample of blood from Jack. We had Jack all numbed up and ready for the dreaded needle. Nurse T. felt around Jack's port, aimed, pushed the needle in, and nothing. No blood. She took the needle out, redid the whole process with a new needle and fresh and clean Jack, and again nothing. Jack was very upset, Nurse T. held her cool, and I tried to keep Jack from getting any more upset. Again, we went through the whole process again with a new needle and with Jack cleaned and ready, and again nothing. The needle was going into the skin but not into the port. Nurse T. said she was not going to try again, that 3 times would be all for her to try. She would call her office and see what they wanted her to do and call me and let me know. By this time, Jack was in tears, he was scared, tired, and upset that things did not go as he had thought it would. This is the first time I can remember Jack crying over a botched access. Her boss called me later and told me we would have to go to clinic to have his port accessed. Since it was lunchtime, we ate lunch, and Jack and I readied for our new plan to get to the clinic. We left home, got there at 1:30 and were soon called back. The nurse took us back to the blood sample room and got Jack comfortable on the table. When she felt Jack's port, she said it felt like it was turned. She asked another nurse to come and feel and the new nurse also said the port felt turned. But they still had to have a blood count so Jack

...BUT I'M NOT THE SINGER

had to choose between a needle in the arm or the hand for his blood sample. Again, he was not happy, raising his voice in response to the two choices. Finally, with the help of the nurse and a little freezy spray, Jack finally gave the blood sample we had been trying for most of the day. Bless his heart, his chest where the port sits under the skin is now bruised with small holes where the needles were put in, like a pin cushion. We were asked to wait in the infusion room, the big room where kids get their chemo in lounge chairs with overhead TVs. Soon the nurse came and told us that Jack needed an X-ray to see exactly what was going on with the port. We left the clinic sixth floor and went to the hospital's first floor for an X-ray. Again, after waiting for a little while, we were called back and Jack had two X-rays of his port. We then went back up to the sixth floor and waited for the results to come up on the computer. But like the rest of the day, the X-rays situation was messed up too. The results would not come up on the computers. Our nurse practitioner came and talked to us and told us that more than likely the port has flipped in Jack's chest. It is not uncommon for this to happen and they really don't know why. I guess it's just the constant push and pull of the needle that finally makes it flip. The only thing they can really do is take it out and put a new one in its place. That means surgery, again. Yes, it is a minor surgery but it's still surgery. Jack got a little upset yet again on hearing the "S" word but after talking about it, he calmed down. We find out tomorrow if Jack will have surgery and when this surgery will happen.

What a day! And if it has been a bad day for me, you know it was twice as bad on Jack. All that sticking and sticking and sticking and pushing and pushing and pushing on the same bruised spot over and over just wore Jack out. By late this afternoon, when a nurse would come near him, he would say, "just don't touch my port!" We got home at 4:15 and still had homework to do. I think Jack was happy to have something to take his mind off the day because homework was a breeze.

Dear Lord, thank you for the blue skies and the warm weather, for the blessing of another day to spend with loved ones, for the ability to help others in their time of need, for the love of family and friends, and for the calm that a touch of another can bring in times of turmoil. Amen.

FEBRUARY 17, 2011—Hooray! We found out today... No surgery. The port was fine on the X-ray. Our nurse practitioner called and told us the good news and said that she wanted us to come in next week for Jack's weekly blood counts so the nurses there could be the ones to access his port. That way if something feels wrong to one of them, we will be right there at the hospital if needed. Jack's chest is still bruised and still has puncture holes. Looks bad and still hurts him. But in true Jack style, he hasn't let it bother him.

Dear Lord, thank you for family and friends that walk with us through our journey of life, for the tiny green of the bulbs pushing through the soil in promise of the beautiful flowers coming soon, for the smile of a child, for the shelter and food we are blessed with, and for time spent with loved ones. Amen.

February 20, 2011—We have had a busy weekend. Benny had a lacrosse tournament Saturday in Knoxville. Since the weather was going to be warm and since his blood counts were good, Jack got to go. While we were at the ball fields, Jack had to go to the bathroom. We drove to the facilities, got out his walker, and got him out of the van. The parking place was six to ten feet away from the bathroom and concession building but there was a slight incline up to the building. You would have thought we had asked Jack to scale a skyscraper with all the whining and loud noises he was making in that short climb. I know it must be hard to push the walker (which is not light) and make your feet walk (which don't cooperate on demand) but do you have to scream like we are taking you to the guillotine? Poor Ben was trying to help because Jack was pushing and walking and screaming all at the same time and his pushing was making the walker ease toward the edge of the sidewalk. Ben was trying to pull the walker back into the middle of the sidewalk and Jack started this long, loud, "NNNNNOOOOOO!!" in front of everybody. And people wonder how Ben's hair got so gray. We finally got to the bathroom and Ben eased Jack and the walker into the men's room. I stood outside the door feeling like some type of sicko, whacko, middle-aged, overweight lunatic while all these men came in and out of the bathroom. I watched while these two lacrosse players walked up the sidewalk, talking like teenage boys do, and one of them puts his hand on the men's room door handle, pulls the door, and from the bowels (no pun intended) of the men's room comes this animal-like, little girl, shrill scream. One of the teenagers looks at the other one with this strange look and says, "I think I'll wait." They walk off still talking. Out comes Jack, the walker and poor Ben and we head back to the van. The walk down to the van was easier than the walk up, but still there was a lot of loud cries and even louder wails of trouble and woe. The good news was that we made it, safe and sound!

Dear Lord, thank you for the wonderful land, water, trees, and mountains we have, for the time to enjoy them, for the amazing animals and wildlife You share with us, for giving us an incredible sense of humor we can use to help us get through our lives, for hugs we can give to those around us who are heart-broken or hurt, for our ability to love and be loved, and for faith, hope and love You gave to us to share every day. In His Name, Amen.

FEBRUARY 27, 2011—We have had another Knoxville weekend. Benny had lacrosse games this Saturday again in Knoxville and again me, Jack, and Ben made the trek as well. Jack enjoyed getting to see all the electric poles along the way. During our trek on the scenic route to Knoxville, the three of us (Benny rode with his team on a bus) stopped to have lunch in Crossville, Tennessee, at the local Cracker Barrel. We parked in the disabled parking space, got Jack and the walker out, and went into the restaurant. We ate, we talked, we left. While we were inside the restaurant, another car parked in the disabled parking spot next to our van, making it a smaller space for Jack to get his walker through. I was walking ahead of him so I could open the van door. Since he was watching the ground and his feet, he didn't see that there was not enough room for me and him and the walker. I opened the van door for him, turned around to get out of the way but he had come behind me, trapping me between the van and the car next to us. The open van door was behind me and Jack and his walker were in front of me. Not thinking I said, "Jack, you have to use your brain in situations like this. There is not enough room for all of us and you should have waited for me to get out." Without missing a beat, Jack says in a loud voice, "I DON'T USE MY BRAIN!!" Ben and I got tickled at Jack because of the things that come out of his mouth. You never know what he will say or do and when he does do something, you can't help but laugh at his whacky, wonderful, off the wall remarks. He keeps us in stitches all the time.

Thank you, Lord, for the sunshine on our face and in our hearts, for the promise of a place called heaven where there is no pain and sorrow, for the ability to know when to plan for changing weather, for the nurses and doctors that make us healthier, for the support and love of friends and family, and for Your never-ending love, forgiveness, and grace. Amen.

FEBRUARY 28, 2011—Jack and I went to the hospital today for pre-admit stuff. He had another hearing test, and we dropped off his urine collection. He asked the audiologist to make sure his ears were cleaned before she started the test. The little skunk LOVES to have her clean his ears because "it feels good and relaxes him." Jack was under her spell even though she said his ears were not very waxy. By the time she finished, he couldn't even hold his head up. I had to keep reminding him to sit up tall in his chair because he was relaxed and was leaning into the arms of his walker. He did pass his hearing test with no change at all in his hearing. I was a little surprised he hadn't slobbered on himself.

Dear Lord, thank you for loving us and giving us all the many blessings we have, for the friends and family we share our lives with, for the rains that will soon bring the flowers and trees back to life, for the ability to smile and laugh, for sending us people who make our lives better, and for Your Word, no matter who shares it with us. Amen.

MARCH 2, 2011—Surprise! We are not at Vanderbilt as we expected we would be. They were full; no available beds. The oncology floor is divided into 3 sections of rooms and all rooms were taken. When children who are on chemo come into the office sick with anything, they take the first rooms available. Then the children who are scheduled to take chemo inpatient are next. They didn't get to the chemo patients who were scheduled. The rooms were full. The hospital is supposed to call tomorrow as soon as a room comes available with Jack being top on the list. Jack and I did go to Vanderbilt and had his blood counts taken with them being in the good range. Even for the short time we were there, he was full of himself. First, he said very loudly from the elevator to a waiting mom with a giant stroller and lots of kids to "get her own elevator." Lovely, Jack. Then after we were finished and were leaving, he told me to hush talking so much to the nurse practitioner. I was talking to her about his feet and his walking. He opens the door to the waiting room by himself, uses himself and his walker to hold the door open and loudly says to me, "Stop with the yak yak yak yak yak yak!" The waiting room was full of people who now know Jack as the loud, nasty boy with the walker. We call him Mister Sunshine.

Thanks, Lord, for surprises, for the ability we have to accept surprises when they happen, for strong bodies and minds, for good health, for days filled with happiness and laughter, and for our daily blessings that we sometimes take for granted. Amen.

MARCH 3, 2011—Jack and I got the call from the hospital at 11:45 am about the same time I was getting lunch ready. I told them we could be there in an hour, but I keep forgetting it takes that long to get Jack and his walker in the van. We arrived at about 1:30. He has been full of himself all day. Earlier he said to me, "What does a guy have to do around here to get a table to draw on?" Oh, brother! The table was two feet away. All he had to do was ask. Tonight, after he gobbled his dinner down and before I got finished with mine, he commented, "I think it might be time to get the drawing table back." I replied, "What does a girl have to do around here to get to eat her dinner?" He didn't like that. I am happy Jack is in such a good mood, and that one of us is enjoying his time at Vanderbilt.

Lord, thank you for healing the sick, for the sound of laughter and how it makes the world look brighter, for nurses and their ability to make us feel better in body and spirit, for budding trees and the blooming buttercups, for the support of family and friends, and for the love we have for each other. Amen.

MARCH 7, 2011—While at the hospital, Jack and I were trying to nap Friday afternoon. I watched the clock and at 2:30 he fell asleep, and I got comfy in my chair/recliner. I started to count the number of times we were interrupted—five times—by nurses coming in and out of his room within an hour's time. Sleep does not happen at a hospital.

Today Jack has been very nauseated. He had the dry heaves which can be awful. He has complained several times about his stomach hurting. When he feels bad, he feels terrible until his anti-nausea meds kick in, then he feels good again. One minute he is close to tears from the stomach ache, give him a pill, and within another few minutes, he is playing and laughing.

His physical therapist came back today for the first time since the insurance company refused to pay. Dr. McGrew, Jack's autism pediatrician, talked to the insurance company's medical staff about Jack's inability to walk and his history with toe walking. (Thank you again, Dr. McGrew!!) The insurance representative told her that our insurance would pay for PT, it was the language the therapist had used that made them stop paying for it before. OH, PLEASE. I smell a game to try to get out of paying for services. Anyway, Jack will be getting PT again, and the insurance company will continue to pay for it. Occupational therapy is another story, but the school is checking into whether they can start seeing Jack for OT. I am still waiting to hear back from them. Jack's PT said today that Jack's feet are worse than what they were the last time she saw him. I could have told her that, but hey, I'm just the mom here.

Jack was his loveable self in the short hospital stay. He had lots to say to everyone who came in and a lot to say to me. We had our usual fumbling, bumbling, urinal use. It is difficult to hold him up to pull his pants up and down, get him up and down, and take care of business. The nurses wanted

MY NAME IS JACK JOHNSON...

Jack to drink lots of fluid even though they are giving him lots of IV fluids, which makes any patient not want to drink more fluids. Jack just refused to drink for me until a nurse came in and said to me (not to Jack which makes me mad. He understands what you say fine. Just tell him!) that his urine density was close to the dangerous level and Jack really needed to drink more fluids. So, I "interpreted" for the nurse and told Jack he needed to drink more fluids because his urine density was close to the dangerous level. Jack started drinking more and I kept pushing fluids. One of the nurses and a caregiver came in and loveable Jack hollers out how his mommy is trying to get him drunk! The nurse and caregiver stop and look at me. Oh brother—surely, they don't think I am giving my child liquor? I had to explain to them that Jack thinks that if you drink too much of any fluid you get drunk. To him, drunk is the full feeling you have when you drink a lot of fluids. Everyone laughed at this point—ha ha ha.

After we got home from the hospital Saturday, Jack wanted to go and play in his bed in the master bedroom. He was happily playing on his laptop having a big time when Ben walked back there to check on him. Ben asked Jack if he would like for him to stay with him for a while. Jack looked up at Ben and said, "Well, I never thought I would say this, but I do kind of enjoy your company." The next thing I knew, Ben and Jack are in the bedroom together but doing different things. Jack had missed his dad, and his dad had missed Jack too.

Dear Lord, thank you for nurses and caregivers, for words that make us smile, for fathers and sons, for friends and family, for the blessing of good health and feeling good, for the gift of children, and for the ability to love with our hearts. Amen.

MARCH 9, 2011—Today was a mixed bag day for Jack. We got up, got dressed and ready to go to Nashville. Jack had his blood counts taken, which were all good. His port is still tilted but the nurses there at the oncology clinic have no problem with getting it accessed. I talked today to the nurse practitioner about my concerns with Jack's feet and how bad I think they are getting. To explain this to you I will paint you a visual picture. When we lie down in the bed or the couch with our feet up, our feet rest with our toes pointing toward the ceiling. Try it and you will see this. When Jack is lying flat in that position, his feet point in the same line as his body. And that IS his resting position. He has dropped feet so bad he has overcompensated by walking with his feet pointing outward or as I call it east to west, instead of his feet

... BUT I'M NOT THE SINGER

pointing north and south (straight ahead). The physical therapist also said he is also turning his feet inward at the ankle. None of this is good. I asked today if Jack's chemo that he was scheduled to take could be reduced because it is the chemo that causes the neuropathy and dropped feet. I have been reading more and more about this particular chemo, the neuropathy it causes, and the chances of permanent damage. I told the nurse what I had read, what the PT saw, and voiced my concerns. The doctor came in and looked at Jack's feet and asked Jack several questions about his legs and feet. I explained to the doctor and the nurse how part of the problem with Jack is his lack of communication skills. With Jack you must understand you don't always get a true picture of what is going on with him. When the doctor started asking Jack specific questions about his feet and legs, he told us 1) that sometimes he has tingling in his legs and feet, 2) that his feet and legs sometimes "go to sleep", and 3) that this has been happening for quite some time. I told them both that I needed their help in knowing what to ask Jack about since he just doesn't volunteer his symptoms. Autism does make this harder with the lack of communication that begins with Jack but ends with the rest of us. With this new information, the doctor decided to skip today's chemo and next week start the chemo back but at a lower dose. As the doctor said, "We want to kill the cancer but not make him crippled." Comforting words. Pray we have caught it in time and permanent damage has not already happened.

Speaking of not making a big deal over things: since Jack's surgery, he will not wear his glasses. Flatly refuses to wear them. I still don't know why.

Bless his heart... Jack has also had another hard day with nausea and stomach aches. He hasn't eaten much today again. Once today I heard him whispering to himself "please stop hurting, please stop hurting" repeatedly. I wish so badly that I could make it stop for him. If I could whisper "please stop hurting" and it would stop, I would use my last breath saying it. I think about how I would be in his shoes, and I would be crying and whining to everyone and making everyone around me miserable. Not Jack, he quietly whispers to his stomach in a voice only his stomach would hear. No tears, no whining, no complaining. Just a whisper...

Dear Lord, thank you for the power of words and the blessing of communicating with each other, for the blessing of good health and the miracle of our bodies, for the caring hands of loving nurses, for the sound of a whispered plea for help, for the promise of a land with no pain and sorrow, and for the love and support of family and friends. Amen.

MY NAME IS JACK JOHNSON...

MARCH 14, 2011—I am glad last week is behind us. Jack felt so bad, didn't eat much at all, and complained of stomach pain a lot. He did get sick again on Friday, after stopping one toilet up with paper, he went to the other downstairs bathroom, had to go again and vomited in the trash can. Yuck. Saturday, he was a different guy. He felt good, ate better, and went to a family member's birthday party.

Today Jack had PT, which he didn't enjoy very much. He now thinks the PT is "giving him torture." He even told the PT he was ready to do his homework and that she could leave. That's a first...Jack wanting to do homework. We should have a little torture session every day before homework.

Dear Lord, thank you for the burst of colors from the blooming trees as they shout with pink, white, and purple "Spring is here," for the joy in a child's face, the sound of laughter, the ability to love and be loved, for the wonder of the brain and how it works, and for the gift of life, no matter how short or long the time we have together. Amen.

MARCH 16, 2011—It has been a long day but shorter than we thought it would be. Ben, Jack, and I were up and on our way to Vanderbilt at 8:30 am. We went to see the pediatric orthopedic doctor. Everyone there wanted to know all about Jack's story: the previous leg braces, the autism, the months of vomiting, the tumor, surgery, and treatment. I think we repeated the story three times. There were no X-rays taken. There was no need. The doctor said that Jack could not put his foot into a brace now because the heel cords are so tight his foot would not lay in the brace properly. The only thing the doctor said could be done was surgery to relieve the tightness. Oh goodie, there is that "S" word again. If we do the surgery Jack would be in casts—both legs—for a while and then should wear braces after the casts come off. Bless his heart... will this ever end?

Dear Lord, thank you for the opportunity to be blessed with the gift of children, for the short time we get to see them grow, for all their smiles, their laughter, their growing pains, for scraped knees and hurt feelings, for all their dirty diapers and nasty noses, for the feeling of love we feel when they make us proud, for fears, tears, and hugs, and for the memories we parents will hold on to forever. Amen.

MARCH 21, 2011—Sunday, Jack demanded we go to church because he hadn't checked the Exit signs in a few weeks. When Jack checks the Exit signs, he also likes to take pictures of them. We got to church, parked, and while walking with Jack into the building, he asked me if I brought the camera. I told him no, that it wasn't my job to remember the camera for him to take pictures. He screamed out, "God dang it!" After church, I told him how ugly that was, how we don't use bad words, even though he hears them, and how it is not right to say them. Without missing a beat, Jack says, "I guess I need to go to anger management classes!" Today, the physical therapist came for her weekly session. She was making Jack stretch out his legs while standing at the kitchen bar, not a favorite activity for Jack. By the way he was acting and the faces he was making, one would assume she was breaking his legs. Last week, he called her the torturer. As she was stretching his legs, I was explaining to him how to point his feet and move his weight to both legs. He looked up at me, made the ugliest face and called us both "monsters." The therapist told me later that she enjoys coming to see Jack because he makes her laugh with all his antics. I will say it again... he is one of a kind.

Dear Lord, thank you for the moon and the stars, for the light of day and the dark of night, for houses that become homes, for the laughter of children, for the joy of finding a lost item, for the ability to think and speak, for the words that come "from the mouths of babes," for the support and love of family and friends, and for the opportunity to worship You with song and praise every week. Amen.

MARCH 23, 2011—Jack, Benny and I went to Vanderbilt today for Jack's blood counts. Nurse MM. accessed Jack's port by herself and got it on the first try. Jack has decided he is changing Nurse MM.'s name to Shirleen. We don't know where that came from but MM. didn't mind. I love a good-hearted nurse.

Dear Lord, thank you for time spent with the ones we love, for being able to laugh with each other, for days with tears of sadness and tears of joy, for the caring hearts of caregivers, for much-needed sleep that calms the soul, and for days that teach us some of life's small lessons. Amen.

CHAPTER 25

MARCH 29, 2011—Jack and I went down memory lane today at his follow-up appointment with his radiation doctor. Jack's radiation doctor was glad to see he had grown and continues to gain weight. He is concerned about Jack's weakness in his hands and feet and wants us to get help for his weak hands since the PT is working on his feet. Jack has been very tired, very pale, and has dark circles around his eyes. The physical therapist came today after we got back from Nashville and I had to wake Jack up just to have therapy. The PT had Jack up and standing against the kitchen bar doing exercises for his feet and legs. She observed how Jack is not balancing equal weight on both legs but putting most of his body weight on his left foot. She was showing him how to balance and put weight on both legs at the same time. Jack started repeating word for word a commercial he has heard on TV for a product called Glucerna. The PT and I looked at each other because we don't understand. Then Jack repeated, "Helps you maintain balance." Glucerna is for diabetes and balancing your blood sugar levels. Jack heard balance and that is what came to his mind. Oh, how I love the autistic brain and the many roads it travels.

Dear Lord, thank you for walking with us through happy times and times of sadness, for the knowledge and trust we have that You will never forsake us, for the hug of old friends, for the smile on the face of a child who is feeling poorly, for healthy minds and bodies, for the miracle of the brain and how it works, for our pets who love us unconditionally, and for the never-ending always present love and support from family and friends. In His Name, Amen.

MARCH 30, 2011—Jack and I made our weekly trek into Nashville and VCH. It was a zoo today on the oncology floor. The infusion room was overflowing with people. The nurses were moving people around just to get kids into chairs to give them chemo. There were children sitting on the floor, in chairs, and in strollers. It is so very sad to think that many children are that sick. Today the port was too tilted for Nurse B. to get it accessed. She put the needle in but it missed the port. Jack is getting so much better at tolerating accesses to the port. I am proud of him for hanging tough, not firing his nurses, and watching the words that easily fly out of his mouth. I try to help him as much as I can, constantly reminding him that it is not the nurses' fault that the port is tilted. Nurse B. got another nurse to get Nurse MM. who has conquered the tilted port for the last few weeks. Jack was happy to see her. Nurse MM. showed Nurse B. how she finds the port with her fingers, holds the port in place with one hand, and puts the needle in with the other. She did it today on her first try. Jack was a trooper, not with a smile on his face, but still a trooper. When I think about how hard this is for any child, I am truly amazed and shocked that my child with autism handles all of this so well. Jack is a warrior!!

Jack's blood counts were still good—a surprise to me. He has slept 75% of today. His color is not right, his ankles are weaker than usual, and he has the darkest circles around his eyes. He did eat well today, and he hasn't been sick again. He is still taking an extra anti-nausea pill—that makes five each day. Hopefully the rest of the week, Jack will start to feel and look better.

Dear Lord, thank you for doctors and nurses who care for us and give so much of themselves, for blessing us with good health and watching over us when we are sick, for the rains that give the grass its green color, for the songs of the spring birds, for the colorful spring flowers, for the gift of sight to see the green grass, for the gift of hearing to hear the songs of the birds, for the gift of smell to smell the sweet aroma of flowers, and for the gift of life to enjoy all that You have given us. Amen.

APRIL 4, 2011—Today was physical therapy day and with all the stormy weather, Jack was very compliant. On one exercise, he was trying so hard and for so long that he broke a sweat and was physically shaking. When I work with him, it's like his feet and brain don't communicate anymore. He can't get his feet to do what his brain tells them to do. I got Ben to stretch out Jack's feet last night because it is too hard for me to push on them. Ben was so surprised at how stiff Jack's feet are. Ben is a strong guy, but even he couldn't get Jack's feet to move. It pains me so to see Jack struggle with his feet so much. His left foot is not the problem as much as the right foot. When he puts weight on his right foot, it bows out at the ankle. The physical therapist is seeing him start to extend his knee backwards to overcompensate for the weakness in his right foot. It makes me wonder how much worse can his feet get before

MY NAME IS JACK JOHNSON...

chemo is completed in July? I just hope we can continue to use the walker and not have to go back to using the wheelchair before the chemo ends. I think of Jack controlling a wheelchair; the unfiltered mind connected to the uncaring mouth sitting in an unstoppable chair with wheels. If that happens, I will just wear a sign that says, "I'm sorry" in big bold letters because that is all I will ever need to say in public.

Lord, thank you for showing us the power of nature, for the rain that grows the plants and trees, for the gift of the connection between the mind and body, for the pure joy of a car ride in the country, for the blessing of friends who share with us their knowledge and experience, for the humor of this life and sharing that humor with others, for the pleasure of a smile and how it can brighten a room, for the opportunity to be a parent to the individual children we have, and for the blessing to be able to share with others everything that life has given us. Amen.

APRIL 9, 2011—Fifteen years ago tonight, I was in St. Thomas Hospital in Nashville, awaiting the arrival of child number two, another boy. I would not change a thing that has happened to each of us since that day fifteen years ago. Not that I would wish autism or a brain tumor on my child, but if it hadn't been for the life with autism and that dang tumor, I would never have seen the wonderful, strong, funny, beautiful person that little baby has become. Who would have ever thought that baby would become a warrior, that he would teach his mother what courage and perseverance look like in the face of a hostile enemy, an enemy with no face or feelings, whose mission is to take, as much as it can, away? That faceless, heartless enemy has met its match in Jack. Happy Birthday, Jack. May we celebrate each year together, celebrating the day you came to this world and all the obstacles you have overcome. I love you more than I did the first time I saw you fifteen years ago!

Dear Lord, thank you for the love shared between a mother and her sons, for the memory of our children's first cry, for the strength that appears from You when we are met with enemies in this life, for time we have here and for the time to come with You in eternity, and for the unending support and love we have and continue to have from family and friends. Amen.

APRIL 15, 2011—All I can write is THANK YOU! Thank you to everyone who came out to our benefit in support of Jack and us, thank you for all the silent auction items, thank you to each of you who bought the auction items. Thank you to the songwriters who shared their wonderful music with all of us.

...BUT I'M NOT THE SINGER

Thank you to all the people who helped with working the children's area, the auction area, the selling of T-shirts, the photo booth. Thank you to Sodium for letting us use their awesome facility. Thank you to everyone at Poplar Grove School for all their hard work. And thank you to MJ and LD, for your hours of hard work to put all this together. If you were there and I missed getting to say hello, please forgive me. We were so very grateful to everyone!!

Dear Lord, thank you for putting so many wonderful people in our lives and knowing when we need them the most, for letting us witness the outpouring of love and support that we saw tonight, for letting us feel the hugs that were given, for letting us share the time we had with each other, and to know through it all You were there with us, in every giving heart tonight. Thank you for the blessing of friends and family. Amen.

APRIL 18, 2011—Tonight I feel as if I have been beaten with a big stick. Jack and I went back to the hospital today to find out if he could go ahead with chemo. His blood counts were back up which meant he could have chemo. We arrived this morning at 8:30 am and left tonight at 6:15 pm. It has been a long, long day. I have had to sit in a straight back chair all that time because that's all you get. The patient gets a recliner (thank you VCH, for comfy recliners) so Jack was comfortable. But to my old bones, the chair started to feel like an old wooden chair after a while. Today was also Jack's worse nightmare day: not just one but two crying babies sat beside us... for about eight of our ten-hour hospital stay. Please don't get me wrong... I truly feel sorry for the poor babies who are fighting cancer, and I feel sorry for the parents who must sit there all day trying to console a frightened, ill child. But that constant screaming all day long starts to get to you after the first few hours. Even the nurses commented on the fact we had crying babies all day. Once when Jack had to go to the bathroom, luckily for me, he waited until we were in there to say, "Both the baldies are annoying!" I was so happy we were in a place where I could talk to him and tell him how ugly it was to call the babies "baldies" because they had lost their hair just like he had. But I must admit, I secretly wanted them to go home, but they stayed as long as we did. Maybe tomorrow when we go back for round two of this chemo, we will not have crying babies around us.

Again, I need say to each of you, a big thank you for your support of the Jammin' For Jack benefit. We had an awesome turnout, and the amount of money raised blows our minds. We are so grateful to everyone and all the contributions made to the benefit.

MY NAME IS JACK JOHNSON...

Dear Lord, thank you for giving us a voice to let others know when we are in pain, frightened, or unhappy, for the care and love that only a nurse can give, for all the healthy children in our lives, for the hope that all children will one day be healthy, for the night—a time to relax, rejuvenate the body and mind, for all the love and support we have received from family and friends, and for Your love and grace that we may always know that You are with us always. Amen.

APRIL 19, 2011—Another "beaten with a stick" day. Another 8:30 am to 6 pm day. My shoulders hurt, my back hurts, and my bottom hurts. The oncology floor was full again today but not as many crying babies. As of right now, we have finished six of nine chemo treatments. Jack is tired, and so am I.

Dear God, thank you for the nurses who take such good care of us, for friends who come to visit when we need it most, for watching over everyone who daily drives in the fast lane, for the blooming flowers that remind me of the family that now live with You, and for the constant support and love of family and friends. Amen.

APRIL 21, 2011—Today was not a good day for Jack. He woke up this morning complaining about a stomach ache. He ate some breakfast, laid around for a while, ate very little for lunch and then spent a couple of hours on a stool in front of the toilet. He was so nauseated that he didn't want to leave the bathroom. He did have moments of heaving and gagging but never really vomited. I think he felt awful. My heart breaks all over again when I see him feel that bad. I hate that helpless feeling of not being able to do a darn thing to make him feel better. Isn't that what we are supposed to do as mothers, take all the boo-boos and ouchies away? I hate feeling helpless, I hate chemo, and I hate cancer.

Dear Lord, please bless all people living with a life-threatening disease. Please give them comfort and compassion as they go through treatments. Please give their families patience and understanding. Please help the researchers in their battle for cures. Thank you for every day we get to spend with our loved ones, for the colors of spring: the green trees and grass, the blue skies, the purple irises, for the beautiful sound of laughter, and for days without pain or sickness. Amen.

APRIL 25, 2011—Today Jack asked for his glasses. I have no idea where it came from or what changed, but out of nowhere he asked if I still had his glasses in my purse (yes) and could I get them for him (yes). He put them on

...BUT I'M NOT THE SINGER

and continued watching his video games and his computer. He still has them on right this minute. He has not worn his glasses since he had surgery back in June of last year. I had started to wonder if his eyesight trouble was a part of the growing tumor but now I don't think so. Could be he just figured out the ability to see would help him win his video games. Who knows? Earlier Ben and I asked Jack if he was sleeping downstairs in the big bedroom with Ben and me. Jack so calmly replies, "I'm yours." Ben and I laughed at what a true statement that was for Jack to say. He has been "ours" since the day he was born and continues to be "ours" every day and in every way. Out of the mouth of babes...our "babe" is fifteen years old and holds nothing back. We love that this child is ours!

Dear Lord, thank you for the technology we have today to help keep us safe in threatening weather, for sometimes being able to speak our minds, for the sound of laughter, for time spent with the ones we love, and for the support and love of family and friends. Please watch over and protect us from the impending weather. Amen.

MAY 4, 2011—Today was blood count day, and his neutrophil count is very low. He is classified as neutropenic again. He has been exhausted, not feeling well at all, and not eating much. He has complained several times about his stomach hurting, especially when you touch it. I had the doctors look at his stomach today, and they said the extra blood work they did showed nothing major was wrong but for us to be on alert for any change in urine output, bowel movements, and fevers.

Dear Lord, thank you for the wonderful sunshine, for the warmth the sunshine brings when it touches our skin, for the miracles of our living and breathing bodies, for the people who help us stay healthy, for the researchers who are always busy looking for the cures to our diseases, for helping hands when we need them most, for the gift of children, and for the support and love of family and friends. Amen.

MAY 9, 2011—I hope all mothers had a wonderful Mother's Day. Today I did something no mother should ever have to do: shave her child's head. A few days ago, out of the blue, Jack's hair started to fall out again. He lost most of it while he was getting radiation. The nurses have been warning us he could lose it again while taking chemo but he continued to have a head full of baby soft, off-colored hair. I guess after that last chemo treatment, the hair cells waved the little white flag and lost their grip to the scalp. Over the last few

MY NAME IS JACK JOHNSON...

days, it had progressively gotten worse becoming too much for Jack. The hair was getting in his bed, going down the neck of his shirt, and making him miserable. He asked earlier today if he could shave his head but Ben and I both thought that it wouldn't all fall out and talked Jack into a wait and see attitude. But I guess he just couldn't stand it anymore. I think I should rewrite my earlier statement—I didn't do all the shaving, Ben did most of it. I shaved some and I'm glad Ben took over for me because it was hard. I never thought it would be hard but it wasn't easy to watch Jack's hair fall to the floor in clumps. While the shaving was going on, there was not much anyone could say. All you could hear was the sound of the clippers/shaver and the sound of the vacuum we used to get the hair off the floor. I guess Jack will now be bald until he stops chemo in July. I hate cancer!

Dear Lord, thank you for giving us time to be ourselves, for the joy of laughing and spending time with friends, for the gift of children and wonderment of parenting, for helping us to see that beauty is not always in the outward appearance, but it is in the heart, for days without pain and sickness, for the quick moments of fun and happiness in the hardships of life, for the unfailing love and support of family and friends, and for Your never-ending love and grace. Amen.

MAY 11, 2011—Jack and I went to Nashville to the hospital for blood counts today and surprisingly, his counts were back up where they should be. It was a good trip except for the part where Jack told someone that the elevator was crowded and to get their own elevator. He was right—the elevator was crowded, and every squeezed-together person in the elevator with us heard him tell someone to get their own elevator. When I told him that wasn't a nice thing to say he told me it was true, the elevator was crowded, and those people needed to get on the next one. He is making it hard to argue points lately.

Dear Lord, thank you for days with good news, for days with lots of smiles, for all nurses and their caring spirits, for giving us a sense of humor so we can laugh as we go through life, for the amazing brain and its many capabilities, and for family, friends, and sometimes even strangers who support us in so many ways. Please be with those in pain from heartache, sickness, and grief. In His Name, Amen.

MAY 14, 2011—Just a quick weekend update... Jack's MRI went fine. We do not have the results yet but will know next week. I must say he was full of himself yesterday before the MRI. We first had to go to the oncology floor

...BUT I'M NOT THE SINGER

to get his port accessed and as we walked in the doors of the infusion room, Jack began hollering "Nurse R., Nurse R.!!" When we arrived at the radiology department and the nurse came to get us, he told her "I've got my Mom trained just like an animal!!" I don't know where that came from. They put us into a room with several beds divided by curtains. Jack, Ben, and I were in one area and the nurses brought in a little girl with her dad and put them in the area next to us with the curtain drawn between us. (But, of course, we could hear everything that went on next to us.) The doctor came in to talk to the little girl and Jack listened to every word. He started making faces at some of the comments we could hear. Ben and I were trying not to burst out laughing. The doctor asked the girl if she was a Twilight fan because she had on a Twilight T-shirt, which, of course, piqued Jack's interest in knowing about Twilight. So, he loudly asked us "What is Twilight?" Continuing to eavesdrop on the conversation next door, he glanced over to us and said, "I'm receiving information." At this point, Ben and I were trying not to laugh out loud, when Jack looked over at us and very straight-faced said, "I think I am becoming an entertainer, aren't I?" And finally, on our last elevator trip of the day, he was well behaved but a little over the top with his imitation of an elevator doorman. He stood in front of the floor buttons and asked the riders, "And which floor do you need? OK!" He was a hoot!!

Dear God, thank you for the miracle of our brains, for giving us a sense of humor, for laughter, for doctors and nurses, for technology that might one day cure more diseases, and for the sheer joy of love. Amen.

MAY 16, 2011—A good news/bad news kind of day for us. Since I really like good news, I will start with it first. Yesterday, we all rode motorcycles in the Rides for Kids, a fundraiser for the Pediatric Brain Tumor Foundation. We arrived at Jim Warren Park at the correct time and, of course, had to wait for the ride to start. Jack got to ride in a sidecar that had a top, so he was nice, warm, and dry. Benny rode behind a nice gentleman who had a big, shiny bike with matching jackets and helmets that were outfitted with a walkie-talkie system. Ben rode in the sidecar of another gentleman and sat behind a windshield, but he said he still got cold. I sat behind a gentleman whose bike also had a sidecar. One of the other cancer survivors' sibling rode in it. I didn't get too cold even though my helmet had no visor, my hands were exposed, and the temperature never got out of the fifties. Even though it was cold, we had a fun 90-minute ride through some of Jack's favorite car riding spots. We estimated that there were around three hun-

MY NAME IS JACK JOHNSON...

dred motorcycles at the event. The survivors and their families were the front riders and we had full police escort. Everyone was so nice and very glad we were there. After the ride, tents were set up in the football fields at the park prompting Jack to use the wheelchair instead of the walker. Under the tents, we were treated to a light lunch before the presentations and accolades to the biggest contributors started. There were three kiddos who had cancer: M., the youngest at eight years old is cancer free but deals with lots of side effects, J., sixteen years old, who has been cancer-free for years but recently found out she has new growth in her brain, and then there was Jack. All three, while on stage, shared their story. On the stage, Ben stood with Jack who was ready to go home. He was chosen to reach into a large bottle to pull out the winning ticket for a new motorcycle prize. He enjoyed pulling out the name and holding the giant check announcing the amount of money made and donated to the Pediatric Brain Tumor Foundation—a huge amount of one hundred seven thousand plus!! After all the prizes were given out and all the clapping had stopped, we were finally on our way to the gate when one of our hosts stopped us and asked if we would wait a little longer so the survivors could have their pictures made with the prize winners and the biggest fundraisers. Jack wasn't happy he couldn't leave. The photographer staged Jack and the girls as the center of the picture, surrounding them with each sponsor, winner, and highest fundraisers. Jack would smile for the picture but in between each picture, he was a terror saying things like "Get me out of here!" and "Watch it buster, I'm not even in your fan club" (this line comes from the Cars movie video game and is one of Jack's favorite lines!). The photographer was getting tickled at Jack and his antics. Unfortunately, not everyone understood Jack and his off the wall comments. It was fun, we will do it again next year, and will look forward to it. Now for the bad news...if you don't like bad news stop reading now. You have been warned... Jack's recent MRI results are questionable. Something is showing up in his spine. I talked to the oncologist today, and he doesn't know exactly what we are dealing with. He will talk with the pediatric radiologist and Jack's neurosurgeon to get their opinions and where we go from here. To say Ben and I are heartbroken is an understatement. We are a scared and confused wreck. We know there is not much we can do but wait and see. Sometimes the wait and see is pure agony. The doctor said it could be something as minor as a radiation artifact (a side effect of radiation) or something as significant as a recurrence. We don't know right now. We have chosen not to tell Jack because we really don't know enough to try to explain anything to him. We will let everyone know as soon as we hear something ourselves.

Dear Lord, thank you for the years, days, hours and minutes we are given to spend with our loved ones, for giving us caring hearts when we need them most, for the support and love of family and friends, for listening to our prayers and our needs, and for filling us with Your love and understanding. Amen.

MAY 17, 2011—This has been one of the longest days for us because we have been in wait mode all day. I don't think doctors have ever had to wait for information like what they are making us wait or they wouldn't do it to anyone again. I didn't want to get out of the bed this morning but I finally did. I wore my PJs around the house until 11am and didn't even feel like eating anything for breakfast. I really do hate limbo land—the land where parents are made to wait for any information about their sick child. Finally, about 4 this afternoon, Jack's doctor called. The news was we still don't know what this lesion/neoplasm/tumor is. The doctors still don't have enough information to give us a diagnosis. Jack will be going into the hospital for chemo as planned tomorrow but the doctor will be scheduling another MRI and a PET scan for some time in the next few days. A biopsy was mentioned as well. The pediatric oncologists, pediatric radiologists, and the neurosurgeons, better known as the Tumor Board, meet on Monday mornings to study cases together. Jack's case will be discussed at this meeting on Monday so his doctor would like to have all the tests completed by then. The radiologist does not think it is a radiation artifact (something that radiation causes—even after lots of research I still do not understand what exactly it is) nor do they think it is an infection. The mass is on the 7th cervical (neck) vertebrae in the bone marrow. It is not in the spinal column where a typical medulloblastoma recurrence would be. Worst case scenario it could be a medulloblastoma bone cancer whose prognosis is not good. But this is a very rare scenario. Until the doctors can get enough information to make a definite diagnosis, we will continue to wait. We had to tell Jack that something new is going on because of all the new tests scheduled. He took it well, no tears or too much shouting. He didn't like it and said so but we will let him vent as much as he needs to.

Dear Lord, thank you for letting us laugh while being surrounded by chaos, for technology we rely on for our health issues, for the gift of children and the joy of parenting, for more patience and strength when we have used up our patience and strength, for tears that we cry to relieve the stress we face, and for the support and love of our amazing family and friends. Amen.

MY NAME IS JACK JOHNSON...

MAY 18, 2011—Jack and I are here at Vanderbilt Children's Hospital tonight. He has already had one chemo in pill form but needs to have more fluid before the six-hour chemo starts. He will need eighteen hours of fluid after the chemo. Ben and I talked to the doctor today about Jack's new upcoming tests. He is already scheduled for an MRI on Friday, and they are trying to get a PET scan scheduled in the next few days. These tests should show the doctors what we are dealing with—something caused from all this chemo, something else minor or a rare recurrence. The doctor showed us the lesion on Jack's MRI and explained a little bit more about the where and what. But of course, we must wait for the critical information after the other tests are completed.

Dear Lord, thank you for giving some of us the heart and knowledge to become doctors, for making Jack just the way he is with all his quirks and antics that give us so much joy, for watching over us when we are walking down the hard roads of life, and for giving us such wonderful family and friends who hold us up today. Amen.

MAY 22, 2011—We got up early today to go to church. It was good to see everyone who loves Jack this morning. I almost cried several times during the music—right now I am walking around with a lump in my throat constantly, just waiting to burst into tears. I think it goes with living in limbo land, the land of not knowing what will happen tomorrow. Thanks, Misses Luna, for being Jack's special friend today. I think his autism has gotten a little worse recently—not sure if it is a physical reaction to all his many medicines or just his coping mechanism for everything he has and is now going through.

Some days in life we glide through, no problems. Then some are what I call bad hair days when we seem to do everything wrong, things are harder than usual, or it's difficult just to get through the day. And then there are the Twilight Zone days where you feel as if you have been put into a different world. That was Friday for us—a Twilight Zone day. (For those of you who don't remember or didn't watch, the Twilight Zone was a TV show back in the days before color TV where the actors were in situations where things were not the way they seemed or the story ended in a strange twist.) Ben says our whole trip to the hospital last week was that way with it building to a head Friday. It started when we got into Jack's hospital room, the commode seat was about to fall off the commode. I had to fix it before Jack needed to use it. That night Jack and I got no sleep. I slept for only about 30 minutes and during those 30 minutes, I dreamed one of my teeth fell out so it was not a pleasant sleep either. Thursday was a bit better with a surprise free lunch

...BUT I'M NOT THE SINGER

from Chick-fil-A at the Ronald McDonald House room at VCH. I was thrilled I didn't have to eat Taco Bell, Subway, or Pizza Hut—the only options I get while at the hospital with Jack. A big thanks to Chick-fil-A!! Late that afternoon things started to get real crazy. The hand that Jack's IV was in puffed up like a blown-up rubber glove. He didn't freak out about it but he wasn't happy about it either. Jack's doctor had worked his tail off trying to get Jack worked into the schedule for an MRI with sedation and a PET scan with sedation before we left the hospital and as luck would have it, he accomplished both The doctor had previously explained to us that the PET scan would highlight the glucose in Jack's system. Therefore the fluids they were giving Jack needed to be changed before the scan to a glucose-free fluid. When they do the PET and if the new lesion was a medulloblastoma, it would be highlighted on the scan. He said the changeover was in the schedule and the nurses knew their orders. He had all of Jack's "ducks in a row" so he could have all the scan results with him on Monday when he presented Jack's case to the Tumor Board that meets every Monday morning. The PET scan was scheduled for 11am and the MRI was scheduled for 5pm on Friday. We didn't really like the idea of Jack being put to sleep twice in one day but if it had to be done, it had to be done and we would live with it. Early Friday morning during doctor's rounds, the doctors discovered Jack's fluids had not been changed over to the glucose free. Oops! Since it took so many things falling into place (i.e.: PET scan schedule, anesthesiologist schedule, etc.) to get the PET scan scheduled and with it being the day of the scan, they didn't have the anesthesiologist to do the PET scan later in the day. We now had two choices: Jack could have the scan without anesthesia or we could reschedule the scan for the next week and wait yet another week to find out what the lesion is and to present Jack's case to the Tumor Board, since they only meet on Monday mornings. Jack started to lose it since the doctors were trying to talk him into doing the scan without being put to sleep. They tried to explain how other children do them all the time, how they don't hurt, how they are not loud, and on and on. I talked to one of the nurses who is on rounds with the doctors about what to expect in the PET room so I could try to explain things to Jack. She called down to the PET scan room with my many questions like; what is the room like, what is the machine like, how will Jack have to lay—on back or face down, does it have flashing lights, etc. Once I got the best picture I can, I tried to explain all of this to Jack but he has just shut down and will not listen. He still thinks he should be put to sleep and get his scan no matter what. Well, folks welcome to our world of autism. Once Jack gets his mind set a certain

MY NAME IS JACK JOHNSON...

way, it is very hard to change it. He really has a hard time picturing something verbal in his mind without seeing it. And he is so literal with his thinking that saying things like "the scan will be inside a tube," is, in his mind, whatever his idea of a tube is—like the IV tube or a tube of toothpaste. If he has never seen the tube, he thinks about the tubes he has seen and that is what he visualizes. What about the expression of "having to be completely still" while the scan is going on? In his mind, he is thinking he can't blink his eyes or breathe because to him both are movements he needs to make. Will he have to stop them also? (I hope that makes sense!) Not only are we fighting his definite hard head attitude but we are fighting his autistic mind. He shut down and said he would not, under any circumstance, do a scan without being put to sleep. He got sick from all the stress of this situation. I started to lose it. Why is my son being put in this terrible position because someone didn't do their job? Someone did not change over the fluids like they were supposed to. My child had his head in the vomit bucket because he was completely stressed. Can you tell I am furious? I must leave the room and go outside to cry and figure out what I need to do. Ben and I both feel that all the tests need to be done as soon as possible because we do not know what this lesion is growing in our son's body and that every day without knowing, could be another day of no treatment if it can be treated. Remember, this lesion was not in the January 2011 MRI but a mere three months later it is here, shining in the last MRI. We can't get rid of Jack's autism, we can't take him, kicking and screaming, to have the scan, and we can't punch out the nurse who failed in changing over the fluids. Helpless and hopeless, we let the doctors know that Jack cannot and will not do the scan and we will have to reschedule it out another week. And then my phone rang and it was my oldest sister, Amy, who dangled the ultimate carrot in the face of stubborn Jack: his own iPad! Something we just don't have the money to buy. But even the carrot iPad didn't work with Jack. He told my sister he wasn't having the scan no matter what she offered. End of story. We were sick with sorrow for being put in this situation and for having to reschedule this very important medical test another week. Sometimes life is so unfair with its many mishaps and goof-ups caused by something someone else does that affects us in so many ways. So, we sit and wait for the upcoming MRI, happy that we didn't have to depend on someone else to make it happen, when a little voice from the hospital bed says, "Mommy, there is a tiny voice in my head that says I can do this." I asked him, "Do what?" and the music to my ears that comes out of his mouth said, "Do the scan without being put to sleep." This child with autism, the one with the

... BUT I'M NOT THE SINGER

hard head and stubborn streak, decided that he would have the scan without being put to sleep. I asked him several times if he was sure and he said yes, something was telling him he could do it and I thanked God for putting that voice in his head. First, I cried from anger and disappointment, now I'm crying from happiness and pride. Jack called my sister to tell her that her purse will now be lighter. We let the nurses know and soon they are coming to take us all down to the adult hospital to get the PET scan. A very kind man came from the hospital transport department and took us through the turns, twists, and elevator of the children's hospital into the twists, turns and elevators of the adult hospital. We went to the PET department knowing that Ben and I could stay with Jack in the PET scan room, that Jack would get a slight sedative and dye for the scan, and that we had to wait an hour before the dye did its job. Jack got his sedative and dye and we waited. Ben and I went into the scan room to see the machine before we took Jack, giving us a chance to talk to him about it before he started humming loudly from the sedative. There was not another mother in the world on Friday, May 20th at that time that was as proud of her child as I was. For him to push all his fears, concerns, and his autism to a place only he knows about and let this scan take place is HUGE!! For any of you who work with children or adults with autism, you know how truly big this is for any of them. When it was time for Jack to get the scan, he got up on the table and kept as still as he could for a total of 13 minutes. Ben and I reassured him the whole time, telling him how great he was doing and to continue to keep still. I will never forget thankfully, Jack lying on the scan table with his stuffed Odie from the Garfield cartoons snuggled down in his shirt with its little face looking up so lovingly at Jack as the scan machine hummed away. Quicker than I thought, with no problems, it was over. The time now was 3-ish and we had to be at the first floor of the Children's Hospital by 4 to start the MRI preparations. The technician in the PET department called the transport department to get us back into the Children's Hospital. We wait for our escort and were at their mercy because there was no way Ben and I could remember the way we came. Our person with the photographic memory was having a hard time holding his head up and his speech was slurry from his slight sedation. So, we waited... and waited... and waited. Finally, Ben said he was going out into the hall to see if he could find out where we really were in the hospital and see if he can find a way to get back. Jack and I are left to sit, him in a wheelchair and me in a chair. Jack looked around and said, "This must be the dark side of Vandy" because where we found ourselves was not painted in fun colors nor had

MY NAME IS JACK JOHNSON...

dinosaur stickers on the walls. Ben came back and said he couldn't find anyone to ask a question to. Do-do-do-do... do-do-do-do... I can hear the Twilight Zone music playing. Where the heck did everyone go? Ben left again to search for a way out after we both checked and had no cell reception where we were. Jack and I were waiting for the transport person or for Ben to appear with news of an escape. Finally, Ben came back right before the PET tech reappeared! She said that transport was backed up (duh!) so Ben asked her how we could get back to the Children's Hospital since it was now 3:35 and our next appointment was at 4. We finally found our way out into the sunshine and to a familiar spot where we could get back into the hospital even though it wasn't the way we came! We never saw transport again. They must have gotten lost in the dark side of Vandy.

We got back to Jack's hospital room, the nurse called the radiology department and found out we didn't have to be downstairs until 4:30. So we waited. At 4:30, the radiology department came and took the three of us down to the first floor to a place we were very familiar with. Jack was wheeled into the same room where this whole journey started after his first MRI in June of last year when we found out about the tumor. We were greeted by the same nurse, J., we had that day in June. We are all familiar with each other now, calling each other by name. So again, we waited... and waited... and waited. J. walked to the MRI room to get a time for our wait since there was another child getting an MRI. He came back and told us it would be another 30 minutes. So, we waited and waited and waited some more. If you have ever been around someone with autism, you know they HATE to wait. Some of Jack's worse come-aparts were because of waiting. He just doesn't wait and gets very vocal when he is forced to wait. Jack started asking things like "when is the snot-nosed brat going to get finished" and I thought how proud I was earlier and how that feeling was disappearing. I was trying to explain and told him how we must continue to wait and how that child needs to have a good MRI so his family can know what exactly is wrong with him... blah, blah, blah, but nothing worked. Jack was more verbal with each passing minute. I started to pray that God would intervene and help the MRI go faster so we could get Jack away from other people and put to sleep before we needed to apologize for his verbal abuse. J. checked again on the time, comes back long-faced, and doesn't even want to say anything... but the new number ends with a zero and starts with a four. Forty more minutes of waiting with Jack!!! I am thinking, "Oh no!" when this loud, boisterous voice says, "Son of a bbb!!!" and just as my hand flew to cover his mouth, he finished "bbbbbiscuit eater!!!" Ben and

...BUT I'M NOT THE SINGER

I looked at each other and just fell over laughing. We both had no clue what that child was going to say and both of us were moving in slow motion trying to stop Jack from saying something bad, right there in front of everyone. Our MRI appointment was for 4pm but the MRI techs came for Jack at 7pm. We got an unhappy Jack delivered to the MRI room and, in a sick way, Ben and I were relieved for the much-needed break from Mr. Happy. While we grabbed some dinner, the radiology department called us to say they were closing and that Jack would be taken to the third-floor recovery after the MRI was finished around 8pm, where they would meet us and take us back to him when he woke up. Ben and I walked back to the Children's Hospital and got to the third floor waiting room, another place we are familiar with because we spent a long day there with family and friends in June of last year. But when we got off the elevator, the only people we saw are the janitorial service cleaning up the waiting area. They looked at us oddly and we mirrored that look. On the waiting room podium is a sign that said to please go to one of the office windows and sign in if no one was at the podium. Ben and I walked over to the first window—nothing. Second window—nothing and no one. Third window—a tablet with the cover sheet of "please sign list below." I lifted the sheet only to find the list below had the date of Monday, May 23rd written in bold letters at the top. Do-do-do-do... do-do-do-do... there was that tune again. So where was everyone? Where was my child? Ben and I decided to go to the sixth floor where Jack's hospital room was located. Thankfully, they had not put someone else in the room and it was the way we left it. Ben and I walked to the nurse's station and told a nurse our sob story. She called the radiology department and found out they wanted us to go to the third floor waiting room where they would meet us when Jack's MRI was finished. Again, we waited... and waited. Once they called, we headed back to the third floor, walking again through the janitorial workers still cleaning the waiting room, and finally were greeted by a friendly nurse who was glad to see us. She took us back into the main surgical recovery area, a place we haven't seen since Jack's big surgery, and to Jack's bedside. About thirty minutes later, Jack finally decided he was ready to wake up and we were told we must go back to the sixth floor so Jack's needle could be removed from his port, something they did not do in recovery. Do-do-do-do... do-do-do-do... Once into Jack's sixth-floor hospital room, the nurse cannot find his release papers. Good grief—will this day ever end? Another nurse asked me to step outside where she asked me if I signed the release papers earlier and asked what I did with my copy. Double good grief! I had signed the papers, was given a copy, and found their copy

MY NAME IS JACK JOHNSON...

of Jack's release papers in the file she was holding. Somewhere in my mind I heard the voice of Rod Serling saying, "The Johnson family came to have medical tests only to find they had stepped into the Twilight Zone." Finally, they removed Jack's port needle, we got him in the wheelchair, and we were out the front door to wait for the van. I was sssssssooooo glad to see home, I almost cried. Jack and I did nothing all day long Saturday but rest and take naps. It was a long, long hospital stay. Or were we really in the Vanderbilt Twilight Zone?

Dear Lord, thank you for letting us sometimes change our minds, for the pride only a parent can feel for their child, for letting us be together to worship You, and for the support and love of family and friends and their unselfish generosity when we need them most. Amen.

MAY 23, 2011—Right now I really don't know what to say. We heard from Jack's doctor today and the tests results were not what we had prayed for. The doctors feel Jack's cancer has spread to the bone marrow and Jack will have a biopsy to confirm this on Thursday. I don't know where we go from here. The doctor told me last week when he was explaining the MRI results that when medulloblastoma spreads to the bone marrow, the treatment plan is very limited and the prognosis is not good. Ben and I are in shock and this burden is very heavy. Jack is the wonderful son he always has been; drawing pictures, laughing, and being his funny self. It is so hard to think that something so evil is growing in him. It rips you from end to end. Right now, the fight has gone out of me and has been replaced with this overwhelming feeling of being crushed. I know I have got to let myself cry and get mad before I can put back on my mommy armor and fight like the crazy mad mom I know I can be. I know that I don't have to ask for each of you to pray, I know you will. I will ask that you continue to stand beside us and fight this battle with us until we get what we want. Jack deserves the best that life has but it is going to take a fight. So please tell your family, friends, and neighbors about Jack and his fight and get them to tell their family, friends, and neighbors and let's pray hard. I want God to hear Jack's name every day, every hour and every minute.

Dear Lord, thank you for the blessing of children, for how they forever touch our hearts, for the sound of their laughter, being able to see their smiles, for letting us watch them grow, and for every second we get with them here on earth. Amen.

...BUT I'M NOT THE SINGER

MAY 26, 2011—Today was another fun-filled day at Vandyland. I think we will start calling it that because it sometimes fills like we are on a ride at the fair. Today's ride was called the Biopsy Scrambler. We got to the Children's Hospital at 8am and tried to check in at the computer check-in but no appointment was listed. Not a good sign. Our favorite nurse, MM., came in the waiting room and told us to go back to the access room. Then she asked what we were there for. Uh? Aren't they supposed to know this? Bless her heart, she accessed Jack's port, took his blood, hunted down where we were supposed to be, and personally took us there. A big thank you, MM., for being our calm in today's storm. What MM. found out was that Jack was going to have the biopsy at the adult hospital in the radiology department close to where Jack had his PET scan. Did anyone tell us this? Nnnnooooo! We waited for a while in the waiting area and right before Jack started to get loud and unhappy about waiting, they came and took us to a small, separate room with thankfully lots of privacy. The best move of the day! Ben and I got Jack out of his clothes and into a gown, and Jack's nurse, a big burly guy named C., started asking the thousand questions you answer every time you see someone new at the hospital. I was a little unsure about C. because he was such a hulky guy made larger by lots of curly hair and had a very serious bedside manner. This was sometimes not the personality that meshed well with Jack's demanding attitude and literalness. While C. is asking questions, he excused himself and left the room. Shortly, he returned with another person in tow who introduced himself and politely apologized because an anesthesiologist to put Jack to sleep to perform the biopsy was not scheduled. And the Biopsy Scrambler was kicked into "on" mode. Can you believe that? They are going to put a needle into my child from the front of his neck and move it past all his vital organs into the bones of his spinal column and THEY DON'T HAVE AN ANESTHESIOLOGIST!!! Are you kidding? Mystery man informed us that we would have to reschedule the procedure until tomorrow. Could we come back tomorrow? He couldn't be sorrier, yadda, yadda, yadda. Jack started falling apart because heck, he was ready, willing, and able to go then and you know how hard change can be for kids with autism. Ben and I were furious, but of course, we were in the catacombs of the hospital and our cell phones do not get service that far underground on the basement floor of a tall concrete structure. Then Mystery Man said, "There is one person who is an anesthesiologist that I am waiting to hear back from that might be able to help us out but it's a long shot." Continuing, he said he should hear from this person in about 30

MY NAME IS JACK JOHNSON...

minutes if we wanted to wait. We waited and fumed. How do you schedule everything for this procedure and not schedule the most important person? Ben and I were amazed and mad that we had wasted all this time and energy. We were also mad that we would have to explain the situation to Jack while trying to get him to leave the hospital. Thankfully, about twenty minutes later, Mystery Man told us that he had found someone who would be Jack's anesthesiologist and that it was one of the head doctors of the pediatric anesthesiology department. Thank you, God, for bringing us the unique gift of Mr. Department Head. Jack was so happy to have his biopsy, he was almost giddy. With all that said, Jack's biopsy went well but of course, we won't know the results for a few days. Nurse C. turned out to be a very kind nurse, making sure Jack had everything he wanted. Jack did not complain about anything the rest of the day. No pain, no stomach hurting, no anesthesia side effects. He amazes me more and more each day. The Biopsy Scrambler ride ended about 3pm.

Dear Lord, thank you for Your interventions in our daily lives, for the technology we have today to improve our health, for the doctors and nurses who help us when we are most vulnerable, for our beautiful children who fill our lives with love and hope, and for the constant support and love of family and friends, their encouragement and their prayers. Amen.

MAY 31, 2011—We have had denial weekend. We had not heard anything about last week's biopsy, so we just decided to wrap ourselves in a denial blanket and not think about the hard things in life. It was nice.

I did talk to the doctor today about Jack's biopsy results. This will be strange, but they still don't know anything. The results came back inconclusive, meaning they didn't find the medulloblastoma they were looking for, but they did find something not right. It could be too early to get a good medulloblastoma biopsy, or it could be something completely different. So, the doctors will retake the biopsy results next Monday to the tumor board and present the new information and see what the neurosurgeons have to say. There is a possibility that we will have to wait for a while and see if the lesion grows which will show that it is more than likely medullo or there is a possibility that Jack could have surgery to remove the affected bone. They don't know until all the doctors have had a chance to review Jack's case. So again, we wait. We will continue with the chemo schedule we are on now until we know something different. Ben and I are going to start collecting all of Jack's records and start sending them to some of the leading doctors in pediatric brain tumor research and get lots of opinions before we make any decisions about any surgery. Maybe someone somewhere has seen something like this before and can give us some expert knowledge. But one thing stands out to me: there is a very tiny, but very bright ray of hope shining through all the muck and mess of all of this. It's like when you are in a completely dark room with blackness all around you, and there is that one tiny ray of light that seems to be brighter than it is but can light and make some of the blackness go away. Well, that's what I am holding on to right now. That one tiny ray that's coming through that tiny crack in all the darkness of this situation. Maybe it's just me, but I think the world would be a terrible and dark place without Jack and his light!

Dear Lord, thank you for sometimes letting us live with denial, for giving us children and letting us experience their life journey, for the much-needed sounds of children playing and laughing, for the tiniest ray of light in the darkest parts of life, and for the support, love, and prayers of family, friends, and strangers. Amen.

JUNE 1, 2011—Today was blood count Wednesday which meant a trip to the Children's Hospital. Jack's blood counts were good. Ben did get to talk directly to the doctor, and he got a chance to ask him all the questions he wanted. These are the things that we know today: 1) Jack's case will be presented to the tumor board on Monday morning, 2) Jack's doctor will call us and let us know what the recommendation was—whether to wait and see if the lesion grows or do a surgical procedure on the lesion to find out for sure what it is, 3) we are going to continue until otherwise decided to stay on the current chemo protocol except we are discontinuing the one chemo drug that causes Jack's neuropathy, and 4) we will go back for more blood counts next Wednesday. There is still a tiny ray of light to base our hope on so that is what we will do.

Hope is a funny thing—you must have it for so many things in life and you truly don't know you have it until it's taken away. Going through this journey makes you really think about life and its true meaning. It also makes you think about God, His grace and love, and the suffering in the world, and how they all go hand and hand together in this world. When I think about Jack, I see all the suffering he has gone through in the past with his autism and now with the cancer. If it wasn't for God's love and grace, Jack wouldn't be here with us, as Ben and I only had a six percent chance of having another child after Benny. And if Ben and I hadn't asked for a test to make sure I would be able to carry Jack in those first few months of his

MY NAME IS JACK JOHNSON...

pregnancy, I would have miscarried. Then I think about all the people who Jack has touched and how they are all praying and getting others to pray, and I think—wow, isn't that what God wants us to do? To not think of ourselves but to think about others? To love one another and do for others as you would want to be done for you? And isn't it funny that Jack has been the one to get people to pray. The kid who lacks every social grace known to man. The kid most likely not to be a college graduate, a rocket scientist, the president of the United States. He will probably have a very menial minimum wage job, will probably care less about his appearance, won't own an automobile or house. However, he touches people with something so completely different that you can't help but feel it and know that sometimes the things in life we all think are important, are stupid and superficial. Sometimes God does His work in the most unlikely places.

Dear Lord, thank you for days without tears, nights with sleep, for rays of hope and the blessing of Your grace, for making each of us different and wonderful, for doctors and nurses, for the ability to see the physical and see what's inside us all, and for the support and love of family, friends, and strangers. Amen.

JUNE 2, 2011—I didn't get a chance to tell the story of Jack and the elevator from Wednesday's trip to the hospital. I do not know why it is just now occurring to me but using an elevator is a very social event that we, the typical, take for granted. For the socially challenged like Jack, it is one big old social scene where so many challenges await. For instance, if there is a crowd of people waiting for the next available elevator and some were there waiting before you arrived on the scene, but the nearest elevator to you opens, do you wait for the people who have been waiting the longest to get on the elevator before you or do you get on the elevator and hold the door for everyone who wants to get on? What if one of the people waiting is disabled like Jack is right now—do you let them get on first? As you see, some of these questions we can answer, but for others, they might be a challenge. For poor socially challenged Jack, the elevators are always tricky. He is very prone to blurt out to others to "Get your own elevator" when the one he is on is full and has stopped at another floor for someone else. Wednesday, as we were leaving we walked out to the elevators and found a crowd waiting. Jack has a hard enough time right now with walking Standing while waiting is hard on his legs and feet as well. So, we are all standing around waiting, some waiting longer than others. And, of course, Jack started his usual unsocial behavior with his unfiltered mouth

... BUT I'M NOT THE SINGER

going off with unneeded comments about the slowness of the elevators. And, of course, I was talking to him about when the elevator stops for him to wait because others have been waiting longer than us. But, of course, the elevator door right in front of Jack opens and he thought it was his elevator because it stopped right in front of him. I got him to let two older ladies on the elevator first. For no reason, the elevator doors started to close and instead of hitting the open-door button, the ladies let it shut without anyone else getting on. At that second, I got the same feeling as any mother would when she has accidentally left the diaper bag home, is out in public with her sweet baby, and sees that pruned up, red face on her soon to be smelly child! I know a bomb is going to go off. Jack started with the "What the???" comments and started talking trash about the elevator. Now, we are the latest and easiest form of entertainment to everyone waiting for the elevators. Jack pushed his walker up to the elevator that-got-away doors and would not back up. He was so mad at the elevator that he said the next time the doors open, he would get on it. Behind me, I heard a sound and wondered if someone was making popcorn to eat while watching this scene. Ben walked up to Jack and quietly told him that no one could get off the elevator if the doors opened. Jack's response: a growl. I gave Ben one of my "please leave Jack alone" looks and he backed off. I am still talking to Jack and trying to get him to understand that it wasn't the elevator itself that closed the doors, but the fact that on other floors, there were lots of people just like us waiting who had pushed the elevator up and down buttons. The elevators were busy. Benny walked up and told Jack again that having the walker up against the elevator door was not a good idea. Jack's response: he hissed. Wow, this was really going well, don't you think? I could see Jack was struggling to stand, holding on to the walker. I lovingly suggested he pull the walker's seat out and sit for a minute. No way, that boy had that walker up against the elevator door and he was not moving it away. Some battles are worth the fight, others are not, especially in public places. An elevator dinged behind us and when the doors opened, it was full. So, we continued to wait in a lobby full of others waiting, but Jack was the only one who had a walker that looked as if it was held with a magnet to the elevator doors. Another elevator dinged, we all turned around and the doors opened. By this time, I didn't care about social graces and just wanted to get Jack on an elevator. I might have run over someone trying to get on but I don't remember. All I know is that Jack turned around from the elevator he had been attached to and proudly and loudly proclaimed, "Did you see I kicked that elevator before I turned around?" Needless to say, we went down on a not so crowded elevator because I think by this time, the waiting crowd had decided to forgo riding with us. Sometimes autism can be the best people repellent like bug spray repels bugs.

Dear Lord, thank you for the gift of life, for each day, hour and minute, for the ones we have around us to share our lives with, for love and its many different sides, for letting us see, hear, smell, and feel all the things around us, for the support and love of so many, and for Your Son who You sent us to save us from our sins. In His Name, Amen.

CHAPTER 26

JUNE 8, 2011—I must share how we went to the hospital today, spent quite a bit of time there, rode the elevator several times and did not have one episode of elevator abuse by Jack. He was on his best behavior or maybe the elevators were. It all depends on how you look at it.

Wednesday, Jack had his blood counts taken and is very neutropenic and his platelets are very low. He had to wear a mask when we left the hospital and we had to come home to eat lunch, not a good day for lunch at a restaurant. He feels fine and is in good spirits but he didn't like the fact he is neutropenic. Nurse MM. had to poke him twice today because she missed his port the first time but Jack only complained a little. We are now quarantined for a while. After blood counts, we went upstairs to see the neurosurgeon. He sat down with me and Ben while Jack was napping on the exam table and showed us pictures of Jack's scans and the mystery lesion. Dr. P. plans to go in through Jack's neck from the front, move things around in his neck that need to be out of the way, and get to the vertebrae. He will then try to get a good sample of the bone lesion with a needle biopsy while looking at the needle and the lesion. Then the sample will be sent to pathology right then and tested for exactly what it is. If it is a good sample and is medulloblastoma in the bone marrow, he will sew Jack up and we will go from there. If he doesn't get a good sample from the biopsy, he will drill a small hole into the bone and get a sample from the lesion. That sample will go to pathology and if it is medulloblastoma in the bone, nothing will be done from there. A non-medullo sample will be sent again to pathology and if it turns out to be something that really doesn't need to stay, Dr. P. will remove the bone with the lesion, replace it with another bone, and fuse it with the surrounding vertebrae. Jack will have to spend the night at the hospital the night after the surgery to make sure he doesn't get an infection of any kind because his system is so compromised by the chemo. The surgery could last two-to-four hours, depending on what they find. Dr. P. also said he had never seen anything like the lesion because it has not compromised the bone, is well

MY NAME IS JACK JOHNSON...

defined, and is only in one bone. He said all the radiologists who have looked at the scans say it is a relapse of the medulloblastoma to the bone marrow. He was not so sure, so this is the plan we know today. The powers that be are trying to schedule the surgery next week. Hopefully, by the time we get the surgery scheduled, Jack's counts will be on the upswing and he will not need an infusion of platelets. So, we—I bet you know what I am going to write—wait again. Wait, wait, and more wait. I am starting to hate that word. Because with waiting comes patience and I am running out of patience.

Dear Lord, thank you for the ability to learn, become doctors, and help others in need, for the patience and caring you give to nurses, for the sheer miracle of the human body and all its working parts, for the support and love of so many around us, and for Your grace and love for us even when we fall short. Amen

JUNE 17, 2011—Jack is out of surgery and has been for quite some time. We are in a holding pattern of waiting for an available room. We arrived at the designated time—a very early 6:30am. They took us back at 8am. Surgery was scheduled at 8:30am and they had to work hard to meet that deadline. Jack was his usual self, saying Jackisms and keeping the nurses on their toes with his ever-present instructions. The nurse who had the task of accessing Jack's port missed two times. He didn't fire her or tell her she was a failure but she wasn't going to try again and found another nurse who had more experience with port accessing. Nurse Number Two got it on the first try. Jack's response to the nurse: "I love you." Something he doesn't tell me very often. They took Jack back at exactly 8:30. His neurosurgeon was standing outside the pre-op room waiting for Jack. And, of course, Jack was the trooper he has been through this whole journey. Somewhere around noon, the neurosurgeon came into the waiting room to talk to us. The surgery went well. He tried to get a needle biopsy through the bone but decided to go into the bone and remove as much of the lesion as possible. The lesion material and medulloblastoma are almost identical in cell pattern under the microscope. So, pathology cannot say exactly what the lesion is. They now have enough material to run extensive tests and we will have the final verdict within the next week-to-week and a half. We really don't know anything and are in the wait and see land of parent hell yet again. The neurosurgeon said since he took out as much of the lesion as he could, there should not be much left. It didn't sound as if there was any new growth but hard to tell with just looking at the sample. We are relieved the surgery is over and are guarded on the final diagnosis.

... BUT I'M NOT THE SINGER

Dear Lord, thank you for the rain, for the smell of magnolias, for the sound of children's laughter, for the feel of a sleeping baby on our chest, for our homes that protect us from the rain, for our beloved pets and their unconditional love for us, and for the support and love of friends, family, and strangers. Amen.

JUNE 20, 2011—We still do not have any news about Jack's biopsy. Waiting again.

Happy Father's Day to all fathers. Ben's was uneventful. Benny and I went to my Dad's for Pawpaw Sunday dinner. Jack did not feel up to going, and Ben wanted to stay home and do whatever he wanted since it was his day. But when Jack decided to stay home, Ben's plans changed. Especially after Jack made the following comment to Ben: "Dad, I think we should do what all fathers want to do on Father's Day, and that's make their kids happy by taking them on a car ride." Guess what Ben did on his special Father's Day at home? Not only did it make Jack happy to get to go on the ride, but it also made Ben happy too. Jack even picked out the radio station for Ben to listen to while Jack listened to his iPod. Ben tried once to change the station, but Jack told him it was the station that Jack wanted him to listen to for Father's Day. So, poor Ben had to listen to rap and pop music and drive Jack around for his Father's Day gift. We don't think Jack truly understands the idea of gift giving, but sometimes just being with the ones you love, no matter the music or scenic route, is what is important. Ben had a pretty good Father's Day.

Jack has had some problems with pain from his surgery. He has a two-inch incision on his neck. First, it was his throat that was giving him the most pain, but now it's his backbone where the neurosurgeon took out most of the lesion. I am sure that it is very uncomfortable—the pain associated with removing most of the bone marrow in one of your neck vertebrae. This morning Jack woke up complaining of pain in his back and shoulders. I think the shoulder pain is coming from the fact that he is moving differently because his back hurts so much. I have been giving him ibuprofen since there were no pain pills prescribed for home. The ibuprofen has been helping. I know at the hospital Friday night after we finally got into a room (at 8:45pm!), Jack was hurting and groggy from the anesthesia. I turned out all the bright lights in his room, there was nothing on the TV, and he was not in the mood to talk. So, the two of us sat there together, Jack in the bed, me sitting in a rocker next to his bed, holding his hand, in a semi-dark room,

MY NAME IS JACK JOHNSON...

not a word spoken between us. We didn't even look at each other because Jack couldn't move his head toward me since turning his head hurt his throat. So, I sat and looked at him while he stared ahead at nothing. Funny how silent moments like that can take your breath away. There are not too many moments like that in life where you can feel so close to someone without speaking a word. And how just a touch of a hand can signal the heart to love even more. I must say there is a special bond between a child and his or her caregiver—the person who comforts them when that is what they need most. I'm not saying Ben is not a good father; his role has always been the playmate and big pal to the boys. When they are sick or need love and understanding, they come to me. When they need advice or a big buddy, they go to their dad. So, if Ben had his moment with Jack and his Father's Day gift, then I had my moment with Jack that night at the hospital.

Dear Lord, thank you for the gift of life, for the health we have and take for granted, for all children, healthy ones, sick ones, disabled ones, for loving us even when we least deserve it, for quiet moments for reflection and love, for the moments we experience that make us grow, and for the support and love of so many that hold us up in these times of fear and uncertainty. Amen.

JUNE 22, 2011—Jack's doctor called and it is NOT cancer!!!!! I have screamed, I have thanked God, I have cried, I have laughed. I haven't wet my pants but the day isn't over. I feel the weight of the world has come off my shoulders. Jack asked me what was the matter with me so I told him. In true Jack form, he said "good." The doctor said there was no malignancy at all. So not only is it not medulloblastoma in the bone, it is not another cancer either. I am so happy I could burst! I can't hardly believe it! This means that Jack has a chemo treatment next week and then we only have one more to go!!! I was sooooo afraid to even think that far but now I feel I can. Are we in the clear? Not really. This is still a type of cancer that has a high rate of relapse. Can we let our guard down? Not really because the radiation and chemo Jack has been receiving will leave parts of his body not working correctly for years. We still have a long road ahead. But it wasn't a relapse this time and for that we are absolutely delighted. Hard to believe but this is the first good news we feel we have heard for over a year. Your support, prayers, and love have kept us going through all this darkness we have lived through the past few weeks. Thank you so much, even though saying thank you seems so small a gesture to us. When you travel this horrible, senseless road, you cannot do it alone. But it is all we have to give at this time so thank you! thank you! thank you!

... BUT I'M NOT THE SINGER

Dear Lord, thank you for listening to prayers, for lessening our burdens, for the time we are given with our children here on earth, for the opportunity to love and guide them, to watch them grow, and if it is Your will, to be with them when they go to heaven, for the promise of everlasting life, and for sending us Your Son. In His Name, Amen.

JUNE 26, 2011—Our Church's Family Mission Team came to our house again this past Saturday. In just a few hours, they turned our dried up, weed-infested landscaping into a blooming, happy yard. We now have beautiful, colorful flowers that will brighten our summer; new, fresh mulch, several beds of weedless flowers, mulched and trimmed trees and shrubs, a mowed lawn, and a clean, unstained driveway. I am truly amazed at their giving spirits and their unfailing energy. The Family Mission Team from Franklin First United Methodist Church is indeed the perfect picture of the "good and faithful servant." We will never be able to give back what they have given to us. But we are so very, very thankful for them and all they have done for us. Thank you, Family Mission Team, from all the Johnsons. You have changed us forever with your example of giving to others. We are blessed to have you in our lives.

Dear Lord, thank you for time spent together with family, for people who give so much of themselves and never ask for anything in return, for days with happy news, for letting us look forward in life with hope and promise, for flowers that brighten our lives, and for the support of family, friends, and strangers. Amen.

JUNE 28, 2011—Jack has been a pill today. His physical therapist came by for a therapy session and he was full of himself. We didn't have therapy last week because of his surgery and when you get off the old beaten path for Jack, he is hard to get back on the road. He was very unhappy to see his therapist, to have therapy, to just move, or uncover his head with a blanket. Sometimes we parents have those proud moments with our kids. Jack's was today. First, he was defiant, then he was obnoxious with his "Pull my finger"—saying it over and over, then the constant burping and not saying "excuse me" but instead saying "Juicy!!" Oh yes. I was a very proud mother. He had one of his stuffed animals who he so nicely introduced to his therapist by saying "This is my therapist who torments me!" When the therapist asked Jack to stand up at his walker, he told his stuffed animal "Watch how they torture me!" Later, when the therapist had Jack standing at the bar, holding on to do his exercises, she

MY NAME IS JACK JOHNSON...

was scratched by one of our cats for no reason at all. Jack laughed and said, "Good job, Mia!" (Mia is the cat.) So proud, yes so proud. Luckily for us, Jack's therapist understands and loves Jack anyway, despite all his shortcomings. She has actually said that she looks forward to seeing Jack because he is never boring and always makes her laugh. Jack and boring do not go together. So, I must say I am a little apprehensive about going to the hospital tomorrow with Mr. Happy in tow.

Dear Lord, thank you for giving us the ability to dream, thank you for more time to hope for a life filled with love, for the gift of a sense of humor and the ability to laugh at ourselves, for getting to watch our children grow and mature, for the never-ending support and love of family, friends, and strangers, and for Your grace and love. Amen.

JUNE 29, 2011—Today has been another long day. We arrived at 10 am for our hearing test appointment, happy to say Jack passed the test with flying colors. So far, at least hearing loss is not a problem...yet. Jack's regular audiologist was at a doctor's appointment, and so another person stepped in. Jack was OK with it but also a little sad. Ben came with us today, and he likes Jack's audiologist too, not because she cleans Jack's ears, but because he likes to look at her. She is young, petite, and very attractive. Ben was sad, too, that she wasn't there. After Jack's test as we were waiting for an elevator, Jack's audiologist got off, so her and Jack got to see each other. Ben was happy to get to see her, too. I was just happy that Jack passed the hearing test. I am also glad Ben didn't drool.

Dear Lord, thank you for putting people in our lives who know us and help us any way they can, for being able to glance into the future, for giving some of Your people the urge to want to take care of others for a living, for the wonder and mystery of the body, for uninterrupted sleep, and for the love and support of so many friends, family, and strangers. Amen.

JULY 3, 2011—We did make it home Friday from the hospital at about lunchtime. Thursday night, Jack went to sleep around 9pm so I was very quiet and took a much-needed shower and got ready for bed. But of course, I couldn't sleep. I watched a little TV, played on Jack's computer, and read a book. Still at 11pm, I was wide-eyed and just couldn't get the old mind to stop. Somewhere between 11:30 and midnight I had at least gotten comfortable on my couch/bed, when the nurse came in to take Jack's vital signs. And, as usual, he woke up and immediately had to urinate. I always ask for two urinals just

... BUT I'M NOT THE SINGER

in case the nurse hasn't come in to collect the first one, then we have an extra to use. When Jack goes during the night, I leave the full one in the bathroom and the empty one is beside his bed. After he uses the empty, I swap the empty and full urinals, the full/not full dance of the urinals. So, Jack needed to go, I got in my position to do my part of the job and wait while Jack does his part. To my surprise and shock, he has been saving up and was about to fill the empty urinal to the top. Now I reiterate again, I am not an expert on the male plumbing and tell Jack to stop while I get the empty urinal out of the bathroom. It becomes very obvious we are going to have to make a urinal exchange. I grabbed the full one while holding the empty and somewhere in the exchange the full urinal overflows onto the bed, Jack's PJs and underwear, down his leg, down the bedrail, into his shoes, and splashes to the floor. Oh great! I haven't had much sleep at all, it's late, I'm tired, Jack was not happy, and I had this huge mess to clean up. Jack, besides not being happy and not feeling very well, decided that he would just sleep on wet sheets with wet pajamas because "They will dry overnight." Bless his heart—he just wanted to sleep. But no, we must change the pajamas, underwear, clean the floor, the bedrail, the shoes. After getting him in clean clothes, I moved him to the chair so I can get the sheets changed too. So here I am, wiping and cleaning, and moving wet clothes, and then I started to change the sheets. If you have never changed sheets on a hospital bed, they don't have mattresses. They have some-kind-of-plastic-wrapped-foam-inserted-thing they pass for a mattress that is attached to the bed itself. I know it is for safety purposes so the mattress won't slide off the bed frame itself, but in the middle of the night changing wet sheets, you do find some sense of humor in the fact that it is like fighting an alligator just to get a fitted sheet on a bed. Then add in the fact that Jack was saying things like "Oh no, it doesn't fit!" and "You are never going to get this right!" At that moment, I am wondering what other people's lives are like that don't live this way. I can only imagine how bored they must be. Finally, I got the sheets back on, got Jack back in the bed, got everything wiped and cleaned up and back to my couch/bed. You would think by this time there would be an AAAHHHH! coming from me but nnnnnnooooo. My mind was hashing over and over about the chemo left in Jack's urine and how much got on him and how much might have stayed on his skin and went into his pores. And what about the chemo urine that was on his leg. Oh no, I didn't use soap and water, I just wiped it off with a wet rag. Oh no, we will wake up in the morning and the chemo will have eaten holes in his skin and his clothes. Will the chemo eat through the big plastic mattress because I didn't use soap

MY NAME IS JACK JOHNSON...

to clean it either? Will the chemo eat the finish off the floor? At this point, I am about to wake my now sleeping son back up, put him in the shower, burn his pajamas with the sheets, ask for a new hospital room when I think to myself: stupid woman... they are making him put a chemo pill in his mouth and swallow it and he hasn't exploded. They are pumping chemo into his veins and through his bloodstream and he is still asleep. Funny how I thank God for the mystery and the miracle of the human brain and in my sleep-deprived stupor, I wonder where mine has gone. So, we lived through our last, hopefully forever, hospital stay and lived to tell about it.

JULY 5, 2011—We're back! Jack and I are back at the hospital. Jack was having vomiting issues and with the vomiting, he started having pains in his lower abdomen, wouldn't eat anything except Jell-O and pudding, and did not want to drink much of anything. Today, he started screaming about the pain and he cried—hard and lots. He was just not himself. Ben and I became concerned and I called the clinic. We decided to drive down and let the doctor look at Jack. He had lost five pounds since last week when he went into the hospital but his blood counts were good. They also did an X-ray of his abdomen and luckily there was nothing there except some constipation. But because there was a possibility of a fever and the doctor wanted to give Jack lots of fluids, they admitted us. Jack has not truly vomited since Sunday but he has had several episodes of heaving and spitting up. Being his mother and knowing this child better than anyone, Jack felt BAD. Really bad. He cried a lot at clinic just because he felt so dang awful. While I held his hand as he cried, I cried too because I knew he felt awful. He is now asleep, is on his second liter of fluids, ate another Jell-O for dinner, took his meds, and had a very small urination. So far, no fever. Hopefully tomorrow he will feel better and we can go back home. Hopefully he will want to eat something besides Jell-O and pudding and the vomiting and heaving will stop.

Dear Lord, thank you for the time You have given us to be with our children, for love shared between parents and their little ones, for Your promise of a place with You where there is no pain and suffering, and for the gift of going to You in prayer for others who are in need. In Jesus' Holy name, Amen.

JULY 6, 2011—Well, we are still here. Jack is getting more fluids, a little slower than before but he is still getting them. He feels better and is giving everyone grief for not letting him go home today. He wanted to fire the nurses, but when they explained that they had nothing to do with it, he wanted to fire

...BUT I'M NOT THE SINGER

his doctors! He almost pushed the nurse's emergency button to tell them he was ready to go home. He has wailed ("I miss my cats and my bed and my Wii and my TV and my ...") and fussed ("It is time for me to go NOW!") and gotten very mad ("I am going to talk to someone about this"). Doctors rounds should be quite delightful tomorrow morning. I must say Jack is making a legacy for himself here at the Children's Hospital. One nurse told me today that she had never had Jack as one of her patients, but she had heard about him. I bet she had. Wonder which Jack story she heard about—the "get your own elevator" or telling nurses "you have failed!"

Dear Lord, thank you for the patience and caring of all nurses everywhere, for the ability to laugh at some of life's most unfair situations, for patience when dealing with our children, for days with surprises, and for the love and support from family, friends, and strangers. Amen.

JULY 11, 2011—Jack is feeling better. All the fluids he received at the hospital helped. Saturday morning, we got up early to get to a 5K run/1 mile walk for a brain tumor foundation at Edwin Warner Park. The run/walk track was straight uphill which made it hard to get Jack up the hill in a wheelchair. Benny and I gave it a good try but only got up about one-quarter of the way and turned around. Then it was a struggle for us to hold on to Jack's wheelchair on the steep downhill incline. Jack weighs about 165 pounds and that old wheelchair of his weighs about 25 pounds. So, Benny and I (mostly poor Benny!) were pushing around 200 pounds of Jack and chair and then trying to hold on to about 200 pounds on the way down. Jack was so mad we had to turn around. The autistic mind doesn't like to "not finish" anything even an uphill climb. I finally told him to get out of his chair if he wanted to finish the race and push his chair himself. Here is Benny, huffing and puffing and sweating, then there was me, huffing and puffing and sweating and turning red in the face, and then there is Jack, all cool and comfy in his chair screaming at us to keep going. But when he thought he might have to push his own chair, he changed his tune. Of course, near the end of the after-the-run/walk program, Jack got bored and was ready to leave. First, he loudly says, "Hurry up! My time is valuable!" Then he grabbed the wheels on his wheelchair and made it move. Too bad he didn't realize you need to steer the wheelchair and he drove himself into the grass. My niece told me later that her five-year-old is now telling her to hurry up because his time is valuable. Jack is such a trendsetter!

Dear Lord, thank you for another day here on earth to do Your will, for the awesome opportunity to be parents and to know the love that comes with it, for

MY NAME IS JACK JOHNSON...

the smell of a baby, for the hug of a small child, for the memory of holding your child in your arms, for the continued support and love of so many people, and for the promise of a place with You where there will be no pain and sorrow. In Jesus' Name, Amen.

JULY 20, 2011—Jack and I had to go to the hospital today for blood counts. Jack has been sleeping more, not unusual for a chemo patient on steroids but a little more than Jack's usual. Today when we went in for blood counts when asked if I wanted Jack's needle removed, I told them not until his blood counts came back. And as luck would have it, his platelets were extremely low, making today the first day Jack has had to have a platelet transfusion. Someone was not happy about it. He said, "I can't believe it" and "hurry up because my time is valuable." It took a whole fifteen minutes to do the transfusion, it took forty-five minutes to wait for the platelets. And you know why Jack was so not happy? Because it was taking time away from getting to eat! Lately he has been eating like a pig. I worry about him eating too much but I also think about how sick he was just a few weeks ago after that last chemo so I try not to worry. I was very happy that my mother instinct kicked in and I didn't let the nurse remove Jack's access to his port. He really would have been mad. I did explain to Jack about what platelets are, how they are a part of our blood and that our body needs them to do lots of different jobs. Glad he didn't ask which jobs because I couldn't answer that one. So, to be prepared in case this happens again, I looked it up: platelets are blood cells that prevent us from bleeding through our cuts, scrapes, and through the walls of our capillaries. If they get around 20,000 or less, there is a risk of bleeding in the brain. Jack's were down to 22,000. So, to be on the safe side and in fear that they might go lower, he was given a transfusion. When you think of transfusion, you probably think of the big bag of red blood. Platelets are the color of butter with a creamy consistency. Since I like to explain as much as I can to Jack and what I think he can handle, I explained to him that his platelets were so low that he had to get more and the ones that he was receiving came from someone's blood. Jack said, "that is gross!" So, as he received his platelet gift from someone, Jack laid on the table while I sat and held his hand, per his request.

Dear God, thank you for the gift of prayer, for allowing us to pour our hearts and minds out to You in prayer, for the opportunity to be parents and to know the unconditional love that goes with it, for the blessing of living in this time of knowledge and technology, for the sense of touch and the feelings that come with it, for hope that there is a place with You where there is no pain and

... BUT I'M NOT THE SINGER

tears, and for the support and love of family, friends, and strangers that make the burdens of life easier for us. In His name, Amen.

JULY 21, 2011—Today was physical therapy day for Jack. He didn't want to cooperate but that is usually how he is with PT. He got mad at me because he didn't like how I was helping his PT. The funniest thing about it is the PT's name is Jill too so we kid Jack about having two Jills to deal with. He has already told us once that he dislikes Jills. Today he got out of control with his kidding me about fighting like they do on the Jerry Springer Show, something he found on TV at our last stay at the hospital. I complained before when they wouldn't show the Game Show Network because some of the shows are a little questionable but they will show the Jerry Springer Show. So, thanks to Vanderbilt Children's Hospital—my son with autism really likes to watch the Jerry Springer Show because the guests are always fighting. The show also bleeps out the bad words, another thing my son with autism loves. He thinks it is so funny to hear the bleeping. So today, while doing his hand weights with the PT, we were telling him how to pretend he was punching someone and he says, "like the Jerry Springer Show." We, the Jills, innocently and unfortunately agree and he proceeds to get a little out of control, taking a weak swing at me. It was weak but it did hit me. Well, punching is not allowed in our house and he knows this. Jack goes from Muhammad Ali to snotty and crying out of control. Geez...he went from one extreme to the other in five seconds flat. His PT was surprised to see how upset he got by the whole situation and I was surprised myself. We did get him to finish his PT session but as soon as Jill walked out the door, the tears started flowing again. Jack was very sorry for punching his mother which didn't hurt at all (as I said it was very weak) and wanted to be punished. We decided on the punishment, got all the tears dried and the nose blown, and not another word has been mentioned about it.

Dear Lord, thank you for the many people who spend time trying to help us become healthier, for giving us a sense of humor and the gift of laughter, for being able to say we are sorry when things go wrong, for days with buddies and friends, and for the love and support of family, friends, and strangers. Amen

JULY 27, 2011—Another Wednesday, another trip to the hospital for blood counts, and another day with a platelet transfusion. I sort of thought that there might be something going on with Jack's blood, but I figured it would be a neutropenic kind of day. Jack has still been a sleepy boy, a lot more

MY NAME IS JACK JOHNSON...

than usual, but it was low platelets again. After waiting for the blood counts to come back, we had to wait for the platelets to come up from the blood bank at the hospital. It took quite a while, but Jack did OK with the long wait. Near the end of the wait, he was starting to tell the nurse to "bring on the platelets" while making some strange hand motion with his statement. He asked me how I liked his hand movements and at that point, what do you say? It wasn't an obscene gesture or something he really shouldn't do so I told him it was OK. Bless his heart, he has done so well with all the waiting that seems to go with getting all these treatments, and I am so proud of how he has handled it. So, Jack, make your silly, nothing-a-typical-teen-your-age-would-do hand motion while you wait, yet again, for another day. Happily, the platelets arrived after the second nurse's call to action and accompanying hand motion for platelets that Jack did for anyone watching.

And, of course, we can't go to the hospital without an elevator experience. Today's "As the Elevator Climbs" installment starts with us waiting with another mother and her son who is in a wheelchair. Two construction workers were also waiting but let us have their spot on the elevator and waited for the next one. The elevator is full of both the big wheelchair and the walker so every time the elevator stopped at a floor for more riders when the door opened Jack would say, "There's no room for any more people." I didn't say anything because he was right and the boy in the wheelchair didn't look like he felt very well, and I was thinking about him getting sick on the ride up.

Dear Lord, thank you for days with surprises, for every day we get to spend it with our loved ones, for making us all different in so many ways, for the love between parents and their children, for spending time with the ones we love when they need us the most, for the wonder of the human brain, for the kindness of strangers, and the love and support of family and friends. In His Name, Amen.

AUGUST 1, 2011—We have had to make some parenting decisions this weekend. As I have written before, Jack discovered the Jerry Springer Show on one of our trips to the hospital and thoroughly enjoyed the fighting and the bleeping of bad words that is what the Jerry Springer Show is about. I really didn't want to let him watch it but as parents we sometimes make decisions on giving our children freedom to choose and taking freedoms away when those freedoms are abused. It is never an easy decision to let our children experience life with all its rights and wrongs but sometimes it is the only way they will learn. Jack loves to watch it, I don't like it but agreed to let him watch it—1) because he says that Jerry Springer is a TV show with a Y14 rating which means since he is fifteen he is old enough to watch it, and 2) he emphatically said he would not imitate or repeat anything he sees or hears from the show. I had written last week how Jack had taken a swipe at me while he was play fighting, imitating what he had seen on the Jerry Springer Show. This weekend he gets angry (it came from out of nowhere, somewhat of a surprise) and tells me I am "a donkey, you know like a jack ___!" He did not say the other word but his insinuation was undeniable. I was surprised there wasn't a bleep sound with the word "jack" because that would be exactly what they would do on that show. Later, he was angry at a pop singer that he totally doesn't like (Kesha) and said he was going to show her parts of his body that he had seen ladies do on the Jerry Springer Show. Ben and I sat Jack down yesterday and explained to him how when we agreed to let him watch Springer, he agreed he would not imitate or repeat things he heard from the show. But here he was imitating and repeating the awful things on the show which is not acceptable behavior. Jack's response was to tell us that he was fifteen years old and he could watch shows that were Y14. We had to further explain to him that just because you are old enough to watch a show doesn't mean you are mature enough to watch a show and that being mature means you know which things on the show are appropriate to repeat and which things are not. After further explaining how showing body parts in public is against the law and how repeating bad words is not good either, it was a unanimous decision that Jack stops watching the Jerry Springer Show. Jack was not happy but understood that when you watch bad behavior, it can rub off on you. You are probably thinking Jack will sneak and watch Jerry Springer when we are not around. That is typical behavior, what a typical child would do, but, when you have a child with autism, once you make a rule, they will stick by that rule. They are very rule-oriented children and adults. It's one reason why I love them so! Goodbye, Jerry Springer, goodbye!

Dear Lord, thank you for the food we eat, for the coolness of air conditioning in our homes, for the ability to laugh at ourselves and each other, for the gift of coming to You in prayer, and for the support and love of family and friends. Amen.

AUGUST 4, 2011—Yesterday when Jack and I were at the oncology clinic, I left feeling low. It wasn't because of Jack or anything anyone did; it was just so depressing to see these poor children in all stages of cancer treatment coming in to get more treatment. When Ben's grandmother was living in a nursing home, I thought that was the most depressing thing I had ever seen, all those poor seniors walking around looking lost and alone. Or the ones that would grab you and talk to you when you would walk by them because they were so lonely. Ben and I would leave and cry afterward. It was just awful to see how some of us spend our last days on earth alone, confused, and senile. But to see those poor children at the clinic and know that some of them don't know what it feels like to feel good, is worse to me than the elderly. At least the elderly had a life that was once filled with choices and promise. These sick children don't have a say; they spend their time fighting just to live another day, week, or month. They are swollen and bloated from the drugs they must take, some of them have feeding tubes because the drugs take away their appetites and they are too young and small to stop eating. Some of them sleep, some of them cry because they feel so bad, or some cry because they remember how the drugs make them feel. It makes me mad, very mad. Life is not fair, and this unfairness disheartens me.

Dear Lord, thank you for life—with all its up and downs, for our health and for reminding us how truly special good health can be, for the blessing of children, for the gift of love that we feel for each other, for giving some of Your children hearts of gold and showing them the road you put before them, for eyes and ears so we can see and hear You calling, and for the love and support we have had for so many months on this journey. In His Name, Amen.

AUGUST 8, 2011—Today was physical therapy day with therapist Jill coming to make Jack work out. And since it was a bit cooler, we decided to take Jack outside to walk. He was so unhappy, but we made him anyway. He walked from our house to the neighbor's house and back. He grumbled and mumbled the whole time, even screaming several times because the tiny twigs from the trees were too much for him to push his walker over. I am glad none of the neighbors were home because they might have called Child Services on us because of the ruckus Jack was making. He broke a sweat, one not caused by a fever or chemo, and, unfortunately, he hadn't put deodorant on and smelled awful. Poor therapist Jill told us today that she is changing jobs and will not be Jack's therapist after next week. Jack screamed, "Yay!" when she told us but since she has gotten to know him, she just laughed and told him how much she was going to miss him. Jack later told me he was happy Jill wasn't coming back because he was tired of therapy. Poor Jack "YAY'ed" Jill's leaving because he thought he wouldn't have to have therapy anymore. I had to explain to him that Jill was leaving but that didn't mean he was stopping therapy; it just meant a new thera-

... BUT I'M NOT THE SINGER

pist would be coming. I don't think that made Jack happy.

Dear God, thank you for the much-needed rain that has already made the grass grow, for giving us strength in times of need, for healthy bodies and minds, for the beauty of flowers, for times with laughter and smiles, for nurses and therapists who always give us so much, and for the love and support of family, friends, and strangers. Amen.

AUGUST 10, 2011—Jack and I got up early this morning, packed all our goodies for a long day of chemo, fixed our lunch so we wouldn't have to eat "hospital food," drove through lots of nerve-wracking traffic, and all for nothing—Jack's neutrophils were too low for chemo. Jack was furious that his last chemo has now been put off for another week. Me too but I didn't act quite as bad as he did. Jack was full of himself today at the clinic. He had the ever-popular burping that Jack does in all volumes of sound and duration. I told him once that I would only accept three responses after he burps: "Excuse me," "Pardon me," or "I am so sorry." But nooooco. Jack burps and his three responses to his burps are: "Spicy!" "Juicy!" or (my favorite) "Excellent Vintage!" So, with his case of the burps, Jack amused the nurses with his inappropriate responses. I was not impressed. When his nurse practitioner came in to tell us his counts were low, Jack starts saying, "I hate you. I hate you. I hate you." The nurse practitioner looked at me, and I could tell she was confused by his statement, but I knew he wasn't talking to her exactly. He was talking to himself. So, I asked him who he hated, and he said his neutrophils. His nurse practitioner laughed and said that was the first time she had heard anyone say they hated their neutrophils.

Before I could get out of the clinic, Jack was already getting on an elevator. And luckily for us, there was only one other person on there when we got on. Jack has now decided if he pushes the "close door" button on the elevator, he has the power to control the elevator. With his new-found power, he also believes if he constantly taps the "close door" button on the elevator, it keeps the elevator from stopping to let someone else on. So today when we got on the elevator with one other person, a male employee of the hospital, the poor man is riding on an elevator with a very-happy-about-the-elevator-not-being-crowded young man and his mother and having to listen to the elevator close door button clicking all the way down six stories. We will try again next week for the LAST CHEMO!

Dear Lord, thank you for our differences, for sometimes letting us see the world through another person's eyes, for the miracle of the human body and how well it works when it is healthy, for the body's ability to heal, for the

MY NAME IS JACK JOHNSON...

kindness and understanding of strangers, for the ability to laugh when life gives us cherry pits instead of cherries, and for the support and love of family and friends. Please watch over our children as they head back to school. Keep their minds and bodies strong and able to learn the lessons in life. Please give the teachers the power to reach deep in the minds of the children and share their knowledge. And please keep them all safe. In His Name, Amen.

AUGUST 15, 2011—Today was Jill, Jack's physical therapist, last day. I have had such a wonderful time with her as she worked with Jack and she has truly fallen in love with Jack. Jack called Jill and me the evil Jill twins today. Both of us Jills laughed at that one. I told him we were the Jill and Jack Oreo cookie—a Jack in the middle and two Jill's on the outside. At first, he didn't think it was funny, but after Jill left, Jack said the idea of the Jill/Jack Oreo was funny. Then he said it will be sad for Jill not to come anymore. We will miss her!

Dear God, thank you for the cooler weather, for the beauty of a full moon, for the sound of laughter and for too much-laughter pains, for helping us through our everyday struggles, for letting us see the inner soul of a person and not just their outward appearance or manners, for being able to love each other despite our flaws, and for the love and support of family and friends. Amen.

AUGUST 18, 2011—We are officially finished with chemo! In the past six months, I didn't know if we would ever get here but here we are, and it is a wonderful feeling!!

Dear Lord, thank you for the knowledge we have that one day may help us find cures for diseases, for hard-working nurses, for days without pain and sickness, for everyday miracles we overlook or take for granted, and for the love and support we have received from friends, family, and strangers. Amen.

CHAPTER 27

AUGUST 25, 2011—Yesterday, Jack and I got ready for an appointment with a dermatologist who will look at Jack's newly acquired and very plentiful stretch marks. The marks are on his legs, his upper arms, his sides, and cover his bottom. They are even showing up on the back of his knees. The oncologist had never seen quite so many, that quickly formed, and the strange lack of a stretch pattern. Once on the interstate, we got stuck in traffic at Cool Springs for a wreck that had happened at the Old Hickory exit. I somehow had remembered the new doctor's number at the hospital, called the number, spoke to the receptionist, explained the situation with the traffic, and was told if we were not there by 9:30 the doctor might not see us. Well gee, what can you do? I forgot to recharge my helicopter accessories on the van so that was out of the question. I did notice the longer we sat in traffic the more autistic Jack was acting. He was talking to himself, making clicking sounds, jerking in his seat—things I have not seen him do in years. Occasionally, he would say something about the traffic and how we needed to start moving. Finally, traffic started moving and of course, by now, everyone who was sitting in traffic either starts to drive erratically because they are now very late, or they are driving white-knuckled with one foot on their brakes. We left home for our appointment at 20 minutes after 8am and got to the hospital at 9:15. As usual, it takes us a while to get inside the hospital, wait for an elevator, and get checked in so we arrived at our appointment at 9:20am. Didn't need the helicopter accessories after all. We sat down and waited our turn to be called back. Jack was still jerking in his chair, clicking loudly and talking and laughing to whatever he was saying. I asked him several times to be quieter. He did, but slowly got louder again. I think I heard someone say Johnson but who could hear with all the laughing, talking, and clicking. Finally, a nurse walked nearer to us and said "Johnson, last name, Jack, first." Now me and "Clicky" were on the move. The nurse took us back to a room, Jack got up on the table, and laid down. While the nurse and I were talking, Clicky turned into Burpy,

MY NAME IS JACK JOHNSON...

not holding anything back. A couple of his burps rattled the walls. I quickly shared Jack's autism diagnosis. It is very hard in new situations like this when this young man who walks with a walker because his feet are visibly turned outward, surprises the unexpecting public with his lack of public manners. "Excellent vintage" is not a proper response to a long, bellowing burp! I politely said, "excuse you" while giving Jack my best beady-eyed stare and shoved his iPad at him. That kept him happy and the burps magically disappeared. Keeping with the protocol of today's medical community, we must first see the doctor's "fellow" which means they are in training to be a doctor. The female "fellow" came in and we went over all the nurse's notes of all the questions/answers. The "fellow" looked at Jack and took notes. She left to get the real doctor, a dermatologist, who came in shortly with 2 other interns in tow. We were all in an exam room that was not much bigger than a closet with Jack on the table, 3 room chairs, one stool, a computer on wheels, a sink, a very kind real doctor, one female "fellow," two interns and me. I was praying quietly to myself that Jack would not take this opportunity to show his new audience his skillful burping or some other equally skillful body function. To my amazement, he was quiet, listened and answered the doctor's questions, which were put in a question form for Jack's cognitive level. As Jack twisted and turned, the doctor/fellow/interns all leaned in to examine Jack's stretch marks. The real doctor started asking Jack questions that had nothing to do with skin—like do your knees sometimes hurt? Or do you have trouble running? I was wondering; "what does any of this have to do with stretch marks?" The doctor explained that Jack probably has a condition called Joint Hyper Mobility Syndrome which has the symptom of stretch marks in places on the body where stretch marks normally do not happen. This syndrome affects the collagen in the body, that in turn affects the joint ligaments and the collagen in skin which gives skin its elasticity. The syndrome makes the joints hurt but also makes big muscle groups like the muscles in your legs stiff which can make running difficult. Jack has never, never, ever been a good runner except when he was a toddler and the autism was at its peak. There is no test to confirm this Syndrome diagnosis and there is no cure. Doctors just treat it as it happens; prescribing ibuprofen and hot/cold compresses for the pain associated with it. I suspected his stretch marks were not normal and so did the oncologist. But as we who have had children know, there is not much that can be done for stretch marks except dousing them in lotion. Time will fade them. So, for now, Jack will have to continue to look like a road map of stretch marks. One doc visit down, one more to go.

... BUT I'M NOT THE SINGER

We left the eighth floor and took the elevator down to the sixth. I told the appointment computer we had arrived and saw we did not have an appointment in the computer, but know we are scheduled to be there. Jack found his favorite seat in the lobby and we waited. And we waited. And we waited. Nurse MM. came out and explained to Jack, after one of the other nurses told her she had an unhappy Jack in the waiting room, that she was very busy and would be with him in about five minutes. Jack responded with a loud, "Uh! Don't you know my time is valuable!!" Poor MM. I tried to nicely tell Jack that MM. had other patients that had been there a while that also needed her attention and that she would be with him as soon as she could. Jack's response: "Snot-nosed brats!" And now the clicking started along with some heavy breathing and ugly faces. My blood pressure was rising not because of the wait but because Jack had no understanding of waiting and we had already done so much waiting. We had been in small spaces with lots of new people, we had to sit in traffic with lots of people, and not one of these things is on the favorite-things-to-do list for people with autism. I also knew with all the talking, laughing, clicking, and burping, Jack's autism was "really big," the term we use when we feel the autism is taking over Jack. MM. came back to the lobby, explained she had one more thing she must do, and then she will be back to get Jack. I saw MM.'s face was red and I wondered if she was pushing herself to hurry up for my ungrateful child or if she was pooped from the morning she had had. One of the receptionists stopped by, said hi, and got a mouthful from Jack. She explained how she understood it had been a terrible day for everyone, especially on the sixth floor, because they had already seen ninety children that morning and it was only 11:30! (They open at 8am so that is about thirty children per hour!) Finally, MM. came and got us and the beast that Jack had become mumbled under his breath all the way past the nurse's station, where I saw them look and snicker, down to the blood specimen room. Of course, when we got there, it was full and Jack must sit to wait on his walker's chair. As we were waiting, Jack's nurse practitioner stepped into the hall from her office and saw Jack. She said hello and Jack said, "I'm having to wait again. Don't you people know my time is valuable!" I start to wonder if hair makes a sound when it turns gray and if it does, mine should be playing a symphony. I apologized for Jack, yet again. He got his port accessed by MM. and unfortunately for her, she forgot to do something but Jack corrected her. God bless her—she told Jack thank you for reminding her because she forgot. Jack and I found a seat in the infusion room and

MY NAME IS JACK JOHNSON...

waited for his blood counts to come back. Jack again started clicking and talking. A baby cried somewhere and Jack loudly said, "Oh no!" By this time, I had politely asked Jack to calm down, asked him to be quiet a few hundred times, and threatened to put his things in time out. But when he said, "Oh no!" I was close to my personal edge, that place where you have had about as much stuff that you can handle.

Jack was still causing a scene. Next to us, I noticed the patient in the chair was propped up in his recliner getting his chemo with a rolling table in front of him with his DVD player playing a Tom and Jerry movie and, at the same time, playing a very loud video game in his hand-held device. Jack also noticed this, looked at the boy's stuff, and started to jerk in his chair. He also began to talk to himself loudly again, and I realized the sound of the video game is making Jack's autism bigger. When I told Jack to be quieter, he growled at me and gave me his ever-popular "loser sign" where he sticks out his tongue, makes an "L" with his hand, puts the "L" to his forehead and sticks his other arm straight out. The funniest thing about his loser sign was, instead of the forehead finger making a letter "L" for loser, Jack's finger was backward and, instead of a loser sign, he was making a strange right-angle sign. Yes, we have told Jack several times that he was doing the "L" wrong, but he was too cantankerous to listen. Well, if people haven't noticed Jack by now, he made it a certainty. I was done, I had nothing left to say or do besides rendering some form of child abuse and was too tired even to do that. I tried to change the subject by telling Jack how we were going to Benny's football game Friday night and how much fun it was going to be to watch the Cougars play. He turned to me and said, "I'm not going! My Friday night TV show is new, and I'm not missing it!" I told him in my nicest voice that it was time for us as a family to support Benny and that the game Friday night was the first game that Benny played as a starter. Jack said a little louder, "I'm not going, and you can't make me!" I replied that we would talk about it later when it was just the two of us, and he replied, "I'm not going to no stupid football game!" Jack's blood counts came back as neutropenic, not the dangerous, quarantine type, but in the be-very-careful zone. After MM. took out Mr. Happy's needle and we stood to leave, she hugged me and told me I needed respite care for Jack and especially for myself. I told her I needed a nice quiet beach all by myself.

On the way home, the subject of the football game came up again, and again Jack said he was not going. We talked calmly about it for a while with me explaining how every family member who would be a babysitter

... BUT I'M NOT THE SINGER

for him would be at the game so he must go. He told me that I would just have to stay home with him to which I said that I would be at the game, that I have two sons not just him. He looked at me and said, "You want me to give up my show for a ball game. You never give up anything for me!" At those words, I reached my limit. I did not speak to Jack nor him to me for quite some time. We stopped at Logan's for lunch and as we were walking in, I stayed with him to help him get his walker over the wide cracks in the sidewalk. I had a grasp on the front of his walker in case he got to a big crack so we would get the walker over the crack. One last crack was coming up and I had my hand on his walker when it suddenly stopped. I looked at his walker and noticed he had the brakes on. He said through clenched teeth, "I don't need any help." We ate lunch in silence. I got us home and crashed. I cried and cried. I cried for all the children who are fighting this damnable disease. I cried for the kid at the clinic whose brain tumor has distorted his face to the point that one eye has now shut and his jaw is inches lower on one side than the other. I cried for myself and how some days I can only take so much. I cried for all parents watching their children fight an enemy that shows no mercy. And I especially cried for my son who will never understand in this life how much both of his parents and his older brother have given up for him. How much we have given to make his life as happy as possible. How much we have given up so he could have the best chance at a productive life. Oh, how I wish he truly understood!

Dear God, thank you for the gift of good health, for giving us more patience when we need it, for the feeling of love we feel for each other in good times and bad, for nurses who care for us and give so much of themselves, for the blessing of a healthy sense of humor, and for the love and support of family, friends, doctors, nurses, and complete strangers. In His Name, Amen.

AUGUST 27, 2011—Jack did go to the game. Since last night's game was the first game of the football season, the school had a tailgate party in the parking lot. Ben, Jack, and I went early to enjoy some of the food that was served at the tailgate party. We avoided the crowds and stayed at our van near the stadium. The three of us ate our dinner on the sidewalk outside of the stadium. The tailgate meal was a hamburger, chips, and a dessert. Each of our desserts were different—two chocolate chip cookies, two tiny brownies, and an oatmeal raisin cookie. Jack got to pick his first and unfortunately picked the oatmeal raisin cookie, took a big bite, and when I looked in his direction, he was gagging, spitting and picking the cookie out of his mouth. I really

MY NAME IS JACK JOHNSON...

thought our night was going to end right there in the parking lot. We got his mouth rinsed out but it was close. He recovered but refused to eat anything else. For those of you who don't understand, a chocolate chip cookie has a smooth texture with sweet chocolate chips. An oatmeal raisin cookie has the rough texture of the oatmeal through and through. It was that rough oatmeal that made Jack almost sick. Jack made an outstanding recovery! Next, we had to get him into the stadium. We had the experience of going to scrimmages to help us form a plan as to how to get Jack in the stadium without causing a scene, up the stairs without having to fight the crowds, and how we needed an aisle seat in case he did have to go to the restroom or we had to leave the game early for some unforeseen reason. The game started at 7pm and since we were already there for the tailgate party, Ben went into the stadium at 6:15, found us seats that fit the bill, left our stadium seats and blankets to reserve the seats and came back to get Jack. It took both of us to get Jack up all the ramps and stairs of the stadium, and to take care of the walker when we got him seated. Of course, we had to endure several of Jack's little girl screams getting him up the steps to our seats but we got him there unharmed. I was thrilled to see two of his old classmates from Poplar Grove come and speak to him during the game. They have no idea how much I appreciated that. So, if any parent reading this was told by their child who went to PGS that they saw and spoke to Jack at the football game, I am so thankful your child took the time to speak to Jack. He glowed when he talked to them.

I must say, Jack got into the ballgame. He called plays. He booed the refs. He did his backward loser sign and did quite a few thumbs down gestures. He called a referee a bad word, something I told him was inappropriate. Jack's response was, "I haven't been watching Jerry Springer if that is where you think I heard it!" At the end of the game, he told me, "You mean I gave up my TV show, and the Cougars lost? ARH!!!" Even with all his antics, we had a fun time.

Dear Lord, thank you for our days spent here with our loved ones, for giving us time to make memories that will last forever, for the gift of children, for Your awesome grace and understanding, and for the promise of a place with You where there is no pain and suffering. In His Name, Amen.

SEPTEMBER 1, 2011—Jack had school today. Jack's teacher and I have been talking about Jack's impending school reentry. Today's conversation was walker versus wheelchair because Jack tires so easily that the wheelchair would be the better choice for getting around the school but the walker makes

...BUT I'M NOT THE SINGER

him use his legs which in the long run will make his feet better. But if we use the walker to keep his feet active and moving, then by the time he got to class he would be too pooped to participate. And this problem is only the beginning of all the challenges he will be facing like being able to go to the bathroom, sit in class for specific amounts of time, physically write, and the list goes on and on and on. And that doesn't count the cognitive problems he might face.

I found this quote today that reminded me so much of Jack and how he touches so many with his unique and quirky take on life:

> "I am what I am because of other people, and they are what they are because of me being around."
> - Maasai Tribe proverb

Dear Lord, thank you for giving us the people we are surrounded by daily, for the opportunity to be parents to our children, for being able to protect them from harm and to hold and love them when we can't stop the monsters, for the true miracle of the human body with all its different but interacting parts and systems, for the love and support of so many wonderful, giving people, for the gift of prayer, and for the promise of a place with You where there is no pain, no sorrow, no disease. In Jesus' name, Amen.

SEPTEMBER 7, 2011—Today was our weekly trip to the clinic for blood counts. There was a mechanical problem with an elevator but we got to the sixth floor with no problems. The whole ride up, Jack kept a silly smile on his face. As we waited in the lobby, I noticed Jack was full of himself, making him loud. I asked him once to not be so loud and his reply was, "Like Gaga says, I was born this way!" Nurse MM. came and took us back to the specimen room to take Jack's blood. Jack gave MM. a gift which she was thrilled to get. MM. had tears in her eyes. She shared with me how it took her about three months before she "got" Jack with all his quirkiness and unusual behaviors. She leaned over and whispered something in Jack's ear that I couldn't hear. She got the needle ready to access Jack's port, counted to three, put the needle in, and missed the port. Jack told her to take it out and do it again and if she missed the next time, he would just have to take his gift back. I am glad MM. really likes Jack. In fact, I asked him later what MM. had whispered in his ear and he told me she said she loved him. MM, we love you too.

MY NAME IS JACK JOHNSON...

I must share a conversation Jack and I had during the ride to Nashville this morning. The radio was on, and one of the commentators said something about how close the holidays are. I said to Jack how we all need to start thinking about Christmas and what we really would like to get as gifts. I also asked him if he knew who the hardest person was for me to buy gifts. He said who and I told him it was him; he is the hardest person for whom to buy. He goes on to tell me that last year he didn't tell me what he wanted but thought it and Santa Claus heard his thoughts and brought the desired gift to him. So, this year, as Jack went on, he is not going to tell me what he wants—he is going to think it, and Santa will hear his thoughts. I explained to him how Santa is an old man and needs help with making sure he has the gifts all the children have asked for. I tried to explain how children have been working for years to help Santa by writing their wish lists and that is what we needed to do this year. All four of us need to sit down and make a list of things we want for Christmas so we can share it with grandparents, aunts, and uncles. Once we write it, Santa will know too. It worked, and Jack didn't say anything else, but that might only mean he thought I was crazy and he told that to Santa in his thoughts. Christmas will be interesting again this year.

Dear Lord, thank you for the promise of a place with no pain, sickness, and sorrow, for the promise we will be with our loved ones again in that place with You, for the gift of children whether healthy or sick, for the possibility of one day finding a cure for the many diseases here on Earth, for the amazing gift of love, and for the blessing of so many people who have held us up in our time of need. In His Name, Amen.

SEPTEMBER 11, 2011—We have had a strange and stressful weekend. It all started Friday, around lunchtime. Jack's physical therapist was scheduled to arrive for therapy anywhere from noon until one. I knew Jack wanted to eat lunch around that time so I offered to feed him at 11:30. He ate his lunch and was ready for the therapist when she arrived a little after noon. Soon after she arrived, Jack needed to go to the restroom. When Jack came back, he was complaining about his stomach hurting low in his abdomen. The therapist and I got Jack up and outside much to his displeasure. He walked for a little, not as much as usual, and we all came back inside. Jack sat down on the couch and started his leg exercises. Suddenly, he screamed "Oh no!!" and stood straight up off the couch. Then he hit the floor with a bang. I ran over to where he was and he started crying and screaming. First, he cried because he has fallen, then he cried because he had pooped his pants, and then he cried because he

... BUT I'M NOT THE SINGER

had hurt himself. And when I say he was crying, I don't mean a little boo hoo; I am talking about an all-out assault on the ears, blood-curdling screams that made the cats run and hide. While I stood over him, he started to get incoherent, jabbering away about how he had pooped on himself and he couldn't get up. I asked him several times in a quiet voice to calm down so we could take care of everything. We must do one thing at a time with the first step being calming down. I reached down to grab his hands to help him up, but he says he can't stand up on his own. I reached down and put my hands under his arms and pull, almost falling on top of him. He is no help at this point and has started to get upset again. I tried again and with all my might, pulled him up and aimed him for his walker. Once I got him up, he started screaming again, this time yelps of pain, and turned himself toward the couch and plopped down on it. He was crying and was not happy. The room was beginning to smell awful. The therapist and I got Jack back up and behind his walker, but he is in pain, letting us know with his screams. We got him to the bathroom, leaving a trail of destruction behind. The therapist who is young and doesn't have children, decided to leave for her next appointment. I let her out the door. My poor Jack was sitting on the toilet, smelling, crying, screaming and half naked where he has taken off and dropped his clothes from the waist down in a stinky pile on the bathroom floor. He tried to clean himself up and made a bigger mess than before. Poop was everywhere—the couch, the floor in the living room, the floor of the bathroom, on the discarded clothes, all over Jack, all over the toilet and now that he tried to clean himself up, it is all over the toilet paper roll and the wall around it. There is no way I can get him clean while on the toilet so we tried to talk about what to do next. Oh, and I forgot to mention, he was in come-apart mode, that place where kids with autism get when the world becomes too much. Too much for them to process, too much information coming to their brains and their brains not knowing the answers. He was hurt somewhere, he was confused because he had pooped his pants (something people just don't do in his mind; babies poop in their pants not teenagers!) He was embarrassed because the therapist was here when he pooped himself, and he was raving mad because he fell, something he had been very scared about doing. After several attempts at trying to get his attention and to stop his crying and screaming, I just screamed back at him. I know, it wasn't the best thing to do, I'm supposed to be the adult but if he can't hear what I am saying, how can I talk to him? My scream caused him to take a small breather and I got to talk to him calmly about what I thought we should do. I told him that we really needed to get him out of the bathroom and

MY NAME IS JACK JOHNSON...

into the shower to get him cleaned off. Through big tears and a very loud voice, he said he was afraid he would fall again and that he can't do it. Then a big wail comes out of his mouth and again he is falling apart. I tried to get him to listen again, but the wailing and boo-hooing are just too loud. I forgot to mention, Ben had left earlier in the day to run some errands for work and I had no clue when he would be returning. At this point, I realized that I was going to need help from someone and Ben would just have to come home now. I called and when Ben answered the phone, I asked him where he was and luckily, he was on our street right then. I told Ben before I hung up to come into the house immediately and hurry. Ben knew when I said something along those lines, there was a big problem. The wailing and crying was still going on while I explained the story to Ben. In true caveman form, he thought he could pick Jack up and carry him through the dining room, living room, and master bedroom to the master bathroom and into the walk-in shower. Good luck with that one! Jack was not moving and he told us so with a little wailing and screaming in between each word. He said it hurt too much to move and he could not move without hurting. I got Jack's attention and he stopped wailing long enough for me to ask him if he remembered how football players who are hurt get off the field? If they don't need a stretcher but they can't walk by themselves, the coaches get the hurt player to put his arms around their shoulders and they hold on to the player's arm and waist. The player holds his hurt foot up and walks on his one good foot. I have Jack's attention on this one. It doesn't last long. He was not fully understanding what he needed to do. I told him the weight of his body would be distributed between me and Ben, and we would keep him from falling again. We would help to get him off the toilet. That last one had me too because the bathroom where he was currently toilet-parked was just a half bath and there was not enough room for two people to be on either side of him. Again, Jack burst into another chorus of wails. Don't get me wrong—I love this child so much and I am not making fun of him, but sometimes, as any parent knows, a child can be their own worst enemy when it comes to their total lack of understanding and hard-headedness. Unfortunately, kids with autism are the first-place prize winners in the race for the hardest headedness, lack of understanding, and sheer unwillingness to be cooperative when the situation warrants. Ben and I discussed our options and scratched them off one by one all in earshot of the one who needed to hear. Calling an ambulance—scratched that off. Getting the wheelchair—scratched. Calling a neighbor for help—scratched. Leave Jack where he was—scratched, but it got his attention and he reluctantly

... BUT I'M NOT THE SINGER

agreed to try to become a hurt football player. We had to get him up and in position to get his arms around our necks. Ben leaned over Jack, Jack put his arms around Ben's neck, and tried to stand while Ben pulled Jack upwards. Well, it didn't work—and Ben had thought earlier about picking Jack up and carrying him to the master bath by himself. Maybe in an earlier life but not today. Second try got Jack up and off the toilet while Ben and I moved our arms up and around our heads while moving our bodies up and around Jack's body. It was mass confusion maneuvering a very, very stinky, screaming Jack! I got in position, under one arm of Jack's, Ben under the other, and we inched our way through the dining room and into the living room. From what I can make out through all the commotion of the last thirty to forty-five minutes, Jack had a hurt ankle and could not put any weight on it. We inched our way to the master bath while stopping every few feet for a break. Not only was this not easy for any of us but Jack was screaming, loud blood-curdling screams of pain in our ears. We got about five feet into the living room, stopped for a break, and Jack stopped screaming and said, "I'm breaking into a sweat!!" I replied through my sweat dripping bangs, "Me too!" Off we went, walking sideways, me under one of Jack's arms, which was around my shoulders, Ben on the other side, with a naked, screaming Jack between us. We finally got Jack to the master bedroom which luckily Ben had the foresight to get ready for Jack's arrival. Ben got him into the shower and sat him on his shower chair. Jack told us it was his left foot that hurt and showed us exactly where. He somehow hurt the back area of his ankle, not the side where you would normally sprain or break your ankle. We asked him on a scale of one to ten how bad was the pain. He told us a ten. So, while Ben was getting Jack clean in the shower, I called the doctor's office at the hospital to see what they wanted us to do. I described what happened to the nurse, what Jack told us and she said to come to the hospital for an X-ray. And we had to be there in an hour! Now, we had to get Jack ready, carry the wheelchair downstairs, get Jack in the wheelchair, and in the van and drive to the hospital all within an hour. Ben got Jack dressed and brought the wheelchair downstairs, I packed up our things and put them in the van. We got Jack in the wheelchair and Ben had to construct a makeshift ramp so we can wheel the wheelchair and Jack out to the van. Thank the Lord we had not gotten rid of the extra plywood that was left after the flood rebuild. We got to the hospital's oncology floor, checked Jack in, went down to the first floor and waited to get the x-ray. After the x-ray, we took Jack back upstairs to the oncology floor, they put us in a room, and we waited to see the doctor. Nurse MM. saw Jack and as soon as

MY NAME IS JACK JOHNSON...

he saw, she started talking sweet to him. He tuned up to cry again. The doctor came in and told us there were no broken bones (thank you, God) and no fractures. He looked at Jack's ankle, pushed and moved it around. Jack was in visible pain but his ankle was not swollen, blue or hot to the touch. The doctor told us to keep Jack off the ankle all weekend and to watch for redness and swelling. If it was not better in a week, we would need more tests. Jack has been in the wheelchair the rest of the weekend. I will have to say Jack cried more Friday than he cried through the whole brain surgery, radiation, and all the chemo combined. He cried because he pooped his pants and other pieces of clothing, he fell, was embarrassed he pooped his pants and fell, and because he was hurting. He cried because he had to go to the hospital and was sorry that he had fallen and gotten hurt. He cried because he wanted to go to the football game Friday night and might not get to go, and he cried because he wouldn't get to see the electric poles on the way to the football game. He cried in torrents, like how rain blows at angles during a storm. He cried in quiet, run-down-your-face tears when he thought about how he had screamed in our ears while we were walking him through the house. He cried with his bottom lip hung low the same way he did when he was a baby and he didn't get his way. When I tried to talk to him about ways we could do things better if we ever had a situation like that again, he apologized. He kept saying he was sorry for each and everything we said. He finally said, "I'm just Mister Sorry!" But the thing he wanted and cried for the most was to go to the football game and by gosh, we were going to take him no matter what!

Ben and I were both, by this time, spent. There wasn't much get up and go left in us but we were going to take Jack to the football game. I had not had lunch—can you guess why?—so after a bite to eat we went to the Antioch/Centennial football game at Antioch High School in Nashville. We couldn't find the handicapped parking so Ben decided to go to the ticket booth, get our tickets and find out where the handicapped parking was located. While asking, a Metro policeman heard Ben's question and told Ben to drive his car to the ticket booth and he would get us closer to the stadium. We drove up to the front of the stadium and the policeman asked to get in our car so he could show us the way. He told Ben where to turn and park the van close to a gate that is only used by the players and coaches. Mr. Policeman told the gatekeeper that he had given us permission to park there and that he, the gatekeeper, should allow us access to our van if we need it. The officer told Ben that we were his guests and the gatekeeper would see to it that we got in and out with no problems. Ben told him that he already paid for our way in and thanked

...BUT I'M NOT THE SINGER

him for everything. The policeman stopped me while Ben was pushing Jack in his wheelchair through the gate and asked if Jack had neck or head surgery. When I told him Jack had brain cancer, the officer said there was no way he would let us pay to get into the game. He went to the ticket booth, got our money back, came and found us on the visitor's side of the stadium and gave us our money back. Thank you, Antioch High School and Mr. Metro Policeman for your kindness. We will not forget how you treated us without even knowing what our day had been like. You made us glad we made the effort to go. Centennial beat Antioch 31-8. Everyone treated each other with respect. It doesn't matter the score on the field, what really matters is how you play the game in football...and in life.

Dear Lord, thank you for strong healthy bodies, for the ability to cry when life becomes too much for us, for days without pain and sorrow, for the giving hearts of strangers, for the opportunity to be a parent, for loving us when we sometimes don't deserve it, for days of happiness and contentment, and for the love and support of family and friends. Amen

SEPTEMBER 14, 2011—It has been another rough day in Jack land. Jack's digestive system has been off since the incident with diarrhea on Friday. Today, he went to the restroom twice and on the third trip vomited up all his breakfast. I am not sure if just being all messed up digestive wise caused the vomiting or not. It has been a very long time since the last chemo, and I really can't imagine the vomiting was a late effect of it. I am so very glad that his next MRI is Monday the 19th so we can have at least that fear removed. Even Jack said he was happy to have the MRI coming up so he would know that the thing is not growing back. These MRI's are the love/hate medical tests of the brain tumor world. They can be wonderful when they show the all clear or can be the point where new treatments start, but they are a necessity, and we have the next one Monday.

I want to send a big thank you to two of the Centennial High Cheerleaders who came over to Jack last Friday night just to say hello. They were classmates of his for many years, and they came by just to say hello to him and ask him how he was doing. Thank you, S. and C., for making a point to say hi to Jack. You made Jack feel important and brought tears to his mother's eyes.

Dear Lord, thank you for old friends and new friends, for the life we have in the time we are in and with the technology we enjoy, for the miracle of the human body and mind, for every day without pain and sorrow, for hugs on the days we need them most, for the wonderful gift of a smile that lights up our day,

MY NAME IS JACK JOHNSON...

and for the love and support of so many who have followed us on this journey. In His Name, Amen.

CHAPTER 28

SEPTEMBER 21, 2011—Finally Some Good News! Jack's MRI was clear. No evidence of disease! We are so happy we could pop. We talked with the doctor about starting the long process of weaning Jack off all the drugs he has been taking. We have already stopped a few that we feel he does not need now. He will still be taking quite a few pills daily, but at least it is a start.

Dear Lord, thank you for life, for making us in Your image, for healthy bodies and minds, for all the many blessings we take for granted each day but would have a hard time living without, for friends who walk with us, for family that holds on to us, and for strangers who pray for us. Thank you for the doctors and nurses who give so much to try to help us, for the upcoming autumn and the cooler weather, for faith in You, for hope for things to come, and for love—for You, from You, and to each other. Let us never forget where all things come from. In His Name, Amen.

SEPTEMBER 28, 2011—Jack saw his radiation oncologist yesterday. It was just a follow-up from being a year out of radiation treatments. Dr. T was pleased to see how well Jack was doing and so far, no serious side effects from radiation except for the mystery bone enhancement that the radiologists (back in June) thought was metastasized medulloblastoma to the bone.

While at the hospital, we went to the sixth floor to wait for a nurse to give Jack his flu shot. Nurse MM. was there and, of course, would be the one to give Jack his shot. She made over him as she usually does and he asked her in front of the other nurses, "MM., how many of these shots have you done?" Naturally, that question got lots of laughs from all the nurses (they probably give shots in their dreams!) and MM. went along with Jack telling him she would try to give him her best shot. Then out of the blue Jack becomes a comedian, cracking jokes about the nurses and asking them all questions like "are you the shortest nurse here?" and "how old are you if you have been nursing for thirty years?" He had all the nurses giggling and laughing, but when he started asking how much they weighed, I had to stop him. Nurse MM. gave him his shot; he asked if it was over, a good sign that he didn't feel the shot.

Dear Lord, thank you for the gift of children, for the opportunity to be loved and show love, for days with beautiful weather especially after life's storms, for the promise of a place with no pain and sorrow, for doctors and nurses who care for us when we are sick, for the feel of warm sunshine on our face, and for the love and support of family, friends, and strangers. Amen.

OCTOBER 2, 2011—Friday, Ben, Jack, and I went to see Benny play football at Centennial. After the game, the three of us hung out to let the crowd thin out so we could get Jack out with as little fanfare as possible. While sitting there, Ben decided to take our seats and blankets to the van while we were waiting. Ben returned explaining to us how the powers that be had locked the gate near the handicapped parking and we couldn't get out that way. Jack was not happy with this news, afraid he would have to walk twice as far to the van and through the remaining crowd that were talking and waiting to see their players. I asked Ben to find a policeman to ask him if he would open the gate for us. Ben went to find a policeman while Jack and I continued to wait in the bleachers. While we were sitting there, the CHS band was lining up to walk past the stadium seats on their way into the school. All the band parents were lined up at the front of the bleachers with cameras in hand waiting for their band member to march by. The band made its way past us and I heard Jack sobbing. I asked him what was wrong and he said, "I guess I will never be able to be in the band like I was planning to!!" I had no clue he even thought about things like that! He has never mentioned it before. First, it's the gate being locked and now it's the band that has put Jack over his emotional edge. Ben came back and told us he found a policeman who really didn't want to unlock the gate, even asking if Jack COULD go out the main gate. Ben responded by asking the officer if he would want to walk through the crowd behind a walker. The policeman unlocked the gate. Ben asked Jack to stand up, stood in front of him pulling him up to a standing position. Jack stood up face to face to Ben, they shuffled their way to the aisle toward the handrail so Jack could grab it. But somewhere in that space of a few inches, between their shuffling and the handrail, the two of them lost their balance and fell. Ben turned his body in a position so Jack would fall on him and took the brunt of the fall. Jack was fine having landed on Ben but in true Jack fashion, he let out a blood curling, little girl scream on his way down. I pulled Jack up while Ben pushed from below, got Jack to the handrail, helped

...BUT I'M NOT THE SINGER

Ben up, and the three of us made our way down the six or so steps to the waiting walker. Of course, we had drawn a crowd. The band parents that were left after getting their pictures, stood there in front of us, their mouths gaped open watching the scene that had just unfolded. After seeing their dumbfounded expression, I said loudly, "You can move along now, we have it under control!" That brought them back to life and one of them asked if we needed help. Uh, maybe a few minutes ago but we were on our way to the van now. Ben was not badly hurt, just a big scrape down his back where his back and the bleacher seat met. Just another Friday night with the Johnsons!

Jack decided he wanted to go to church as he felt so much better. We haven't pushed going back to church, just letting him be our guide. Finally, with the good week he had last week, and how well he feels, he was ready to go back. We planned to get up and go to church like we did before cancer. But NNNNNOOOOOOO! Jack woke us up about 3 am saying he didn't feel well and vomited again. Where in the world was this coming from? We are baffled and have no clue as to what brought it on. Jack had been eating so well last week. So, dance with me as we go back and forth with the medical two-step Two steps forward, two steps backward...

Dear God, thank you for times without pain and sorrow, for the opportunity to parent our children even in the worst of times, for giving us the gift of love which keeps us battling through life, for keeping our tongues quiet amid the chaos life can bring, for letting us dance our way through life, and for the support and love of family, friends, and strangers. Amen.

OCTOBER 4, 2011—For weeks now I have let down my guard and started at least thinking in terms of the future. Not too far but thoughts of Jack going back to school and church, thoughts of going on a vacation, and thoughts of us just living life again. I used the adage of the light at the end of the tunnel, in my mind's eye seeing the light, all bright and shiny, at the end of this journeys long and dark tunnel. It gave me something to look forward to... something to get up every day and strive for. Today's trip to the orthopedic doctor took away my light. Dr. B, who is not an orthopedic surgeon but an orthopedic doctor, said she agreed with Dr. L, the orthopedic surgeon, that Jack will indeed require surgery on both legs to help with his walking. Dr. B said Jack's Achilles tendon is so contracted that his feet will not lay flat on the floor. Also, his ankle is tending to the outside of his leg, keeping him unbalanced. After surgery Jack would be in leg casts for a length of time. Jack with his now 165 pounds and the weight of two casts could be too much for me and Ben to handle. There would be

MY NAME IS JACK JOHNSON...

rehab for Jack, an amount of time to be determined by the surgeon. Then Jack would have to wear leg braces and could have to wear them for three-to-four years. Years! Not months! Dr. B said she would also recommend a test for Jack called an EMG, which measures how and if all of Jack's nerves in his legs are still working correctly. The surgery would give Jack back his ability to balance his body but if there is nerve damage, it might not give him back his ability to walk unassisted. Interpretation: if there is nerve damage, Jack will never walk without a walker. We are shell-shocked, to say the least. We can forget about any plans for anything in the future because, yet again, we have no foreseeable future that doesn't involve surgeries, doctors, nurses, and therapies. I am just a tad bit angry. When Jack has surgery, he will be wheelchair bound until his legs heal. That means he will have to sleep downstairs for as long as his recovery takes and, as I said before, that could be years. We will have to have a better, lighter wheelchair and will have to install a wheelchair ramp. Life could change drastically for us, yet again. Ben was so upset by everything we heard today and by all the ensuing thoughts, that while backing out of our driveway, he backed into Jack's homebound teacher's car, putting a large dent into her expensive car. Like we needed anything else. As far as Jack is concerned, he hasn't asked any questions or made any comments. He has so much faith in me and Ben and knows that we only will do what is best for him. And, of course, we will. I just wish life would cut him some slack, give him a break. We just want him to be happy, without pain and suffering. As a parent watching this from the sidelines, you just want to make all the bad things go away. No more monsters, no more boo-boos, no more sadness. But life just keeps beating on him and we have no control. I hate this helpless feeling that comes with this journey. I am going to admit something here I have never said: I used to think Jack's autism was the worst thing ever. How dumb was that? I see all these parents of kids with autism and I think you have no clue how lucky you are to just have autism. Autism was so easy compared to this. If I just had my child with autism back I would be the happiest mother ever. No more tests and surgeries and doctors and pain. If only.

Dear Lord, this is a hard one. Thank you for all the blessings we have even when life gets in our way, and we can't see them. Thanks for being beside us when things don't go our way. Thanks for understanding us when we don't always understand life. Thanks for never leaving us. Amen.

OCTOBER 5, 2011—Jack took a bubble bath tonight, something he hasn't done in years. And, for goodness sake, he cried. And cried... and cried...

...BUT I'M NOT THE SINGER

because he missed bubble baths. Goodness gracious! I feel all of a sudden we have a teenage girl in the house. Bless his heart, we know he can't help it, but it sure is a different situation for us.

Last night Ben and I were watching TV and Jack was sitting with us playing on his iPad. Out of the blue comes the sound of piano playing. You guessed it! Jack had found an app that I had put on his iPad a while back that is a piano keyboard you can play. He started playing a song that I remembered he played when he played the piano. Jack stopped playing the piano after he became sick before the tumor diagnosis. I looked at Ben and he looked at me and, of course, tears rolled down my cheeks. When Jack finished playing, he looked at me and I asked him if the notes were with the keyboard. Jack says, "There are no notes. I just remember them." He looked at me with that big round face of his with a huge smile and says, "Hey, now I am going to play the song the washer makes when it gets finished' and proceeds to play the little tune our new washer plays. Ben and I were totally flabbergasted. Jack has heard the washer tune for the last few months and could sit there and not just hunt and peck for the right keys but could play the silly little washer tune by ear. All Ben and I could do was look at each other, me through my tears. Now you might think I am crazy or just a little off here but with all the bad news we got yesterday and all the bad feelings that were dredged up, we really needed something extra special to happen to bring us back, to show us things are going to be OK. Both Ben and I think that tiny, odd washer song was a sign, a sign from God, telling us that we would be OK, that we can handle anything, that Jack hasn't lost himself and neither have we lost him. Jack is still Jack no matter what physical shape he is in and we must believe that. Miracles can happen. Of course, they are not the Biblical miracles that Jesus performed but they are the moments in life for us where something takes our breath away and, in that moment, we feel the presence of God. And yes, we felt His presence in that moment when our child who has been through the proverbial wringer, who, at this time, is not cognitively equal to his peers, who cannot walk without a walker, who cannot even stand without the assistance of a wall, chair, or rail, who has been, for the past few days, wearing Depends diapers because he was so afraid of bowel accidents, who has a terrible crop of black hair growing in some places on his head and in other places still very bald, played the washing machine tune on his iPad keyboard from just hearing it. God does work in mysterious ways and we needed Him to teach us a lesson on hope, yet again.

MY NAME IS JACK JOHNSON...

Dear Lord, thank you for the gift of music, for being able to see the smile on the face of a loved one, thank you for autumn weather, for the smell of freshly cut grass, for how great a warm bubble bath can make us feel, for the opportunity to be parents of children, for our pets and their unconditional love, for promising us a place with no pain and sorrow, and for the love and support of family, friends, and strangers. We are forever grateful for all our blessings. Amen.

OCTOBER 12, 2011—Have I ever mentioned how emotionally strong my youngest son is? Have I ever written about how he just takes all that has been dealt him and never blinks? Well, I will say it again. My youngest child is amazing! I truly cannot say I would do as well as he has if it had been me instead of him. Today we arrived at the Vanderbilt Clinic, rode the elevator down to the basement and couldn't find the doctor's office where we had an appointment. Jack had to stop and go to the bathroom which takes a while even at home, but when you are lost in the basement of any part of Vanderbilt, it seemed like it took him forever. We found out we had to go back to the main floor and find another set of elevators. The trip got a little longer and we were a little late for our appointment. The nurse came and took us back to the EMG room and got us started. After Jack put on a gown, the nurse came back in and started the EMG. She attached wires to Jack's left leg a few inches above the ankle and while using a wand that reminded both me and Ben of a police officer's Taser, she shocked Jack's nerves in his legs and feet. She moved the wires around, measured the nerve reflexes at different places on his lower legs, watched the computer screen for the nerve responses, and ran copies of the response reports. Jack did excellent! He never complained about the shocks or cried in pain at all. He did make some funny faces and he told the nurse that she was electrocuting him but other than that he did wonderful. After the nurse finished, she said the doctor would be in to do the last part of the EMG. The doctor would be inserting a needle into a few of Jack's leg muscles and measuring whether the muscle was working properly. He inserted three needles in three different muscles and all muscles worked. I did have to hold Jack's hand while the needles were being inserted and I am not sure if I was holding his hand harder than he was holding mine. But he never cried, screamed, fussed, or refused to let the doctor insert the next needle. There were no numbing creams or freezy sprays that we could use to numb the pain. I did tell him to breathe each time the doctor inserted the needle and that helped him. Afterwards he said it really didn't hurt that bad but he had to move the muscle that the needle was in and that made me hurt to see it. But Jack didn't complain. Ben was sitting in a chair in the corner and when the needles came out, I did notice a little green tinge in his color. At least we didn't have to get the smelling salts for Ben. If he had passed out, Jack would never let him live that down especially since Jack was the patient. The doctor said that Jack has nerve damage from the middle top of both legs down to his toes. Some nerves did not even register on the EMG. Whether the damage is permanent is yet to be seen. Nerves will heal in some cases but at a very, very slow rate of about one inch per month. When you are talking about Jack's nerves and where they stop working in his legs, you are looking to at least two years of healing and it is not a given that they will. The doctor said Jack has the leg nerves of a sixty-year-old diabetic—Jack is only fifteen. Additionally, we still have the tendons that have contracted making it difficult for Jack to put his foot flat on the floor. The doctor also said Jack might wear braces for three-to-four years after the casts come off. I think she could tell how bad Jack's legs really are but didn't want to say anything definite without further tests. So, we are adjusting to the fact that we will have mobility issues for at least three-to-four years and maybe longer. Maybe forever.

Dear God, thank you for the strength to get through the hard moments of life, for the comfort that comes from the touch of another, for healthy bodies and minds, for days without pain and sorrow, for all the blessings we have that we take for granted, for the wonderful children you personally blessed me with, and for the love and support of family, friends, and strangers. Amen.

OCTOBER 13, 2011—Jack went to school today for a dress rehearsal, which meant he sat in on his class while class was in session. His assistant, Ms. N, stayed with him and I sat in the back of the class. Jack is a little behind in his math because he has been homebound all this time. He will get caught up to where the rest of the class is today. Jack got in the hallway during class change and said hi to kids he knows from Poplar Grove. We also saw Benny and his girlfriend walking down the hall and holding hands. Jack and I both laughed at that one, even though I wanted to cry. It was the first time I had witnessed my oldest holding some other female's hand that wasn't mine. I am getting hit from all sides right now by my two kids.

Dear Lord, thank you for making us all different in so many ways but also for making us in Your image, for loving teachers who give so much of them-

MY NAME IS JACK JOHNSON...

selves to help our children learn lessons for life, for days without pain and days with a healthy appetite, for teenagers even when they do things they shouldn't, for healthy bodies and strong minds, and for the love and support of so many people we have been blessed to have in our lives. Amen.

OCTOBER 16, 2011—We have been on the hunt for a new to us wheelchair. Jack has been using one that we borrowed from my dad that he had for my grandfather when he lived at Dad's house. The wheelchair is an older model made with lots of heavy metal. Again, thanks Dad for letting us use it all this time. But with the prospect of Jack having to use a chair every day at school, we felt a newer, lighter model would be easier for me to lift in and out of the van every day. I went on craigslist and found a chair for sale in Columbia. When I inquired about it, a lady replied that she still had it and wanted to get rid of it. The wheelchair had been her mother's who had recently passed away. I emailed her that the chair would be for our son but we were afraid it might be too heavy. She then replied that our son could easily pick up the chair. I replied that the chair was for our teenage son and that I would be the one who wanted it to be light in weight because I was the one who would be picking it up and down all the time. She wrote back a little perplexed that she thought I could lift it and she was sorry about my son needing a chair. Ben and I decided to go see the chair and let Jack sit in it. So, Saturday afternoon we all jumped in the van and headed to Columbia. We found the house, Ben knocked on the door, and a young pregnant woman answered. All this time I had in my mind that the woman who I had been emailing was older, around my and Ben's age. This woman was a lot younger. She got the chair out with Ben's help and the three of us talked about it and looked it over. She said again that it had been her mother's chair but that when she died, it was no longer needed. In her ad for the chair she was asking $85. Ben and I agreed we both liked the chair but, of course, the final decision rested with Jack. So, Ben took the wheelchair over to the van and Jack got out and in the chair. As the woman stood on her porch watching Jack, she got a very funny expression on her face. I have said before if you are not expecting Jack to look like he does, it can be a shock for people who have not been exposed to kids with cancer. I quietly told her that Jack had brain cancer, that he was now finished with treatments, and the chair was going to help him get back to school. She looked at me with big tears in her eyes and said that she was so sorry. I told her I was sorry that she had lost her mother. She then said her mother had had lung cancer and that it had spread to her brain before she died. I am standing there with a pregnant, teary-eyed woman who was watching my child with brain cancer sit in her mother's wheelchair who had died because her lung cancer had spread to her brain. I asked her when her baby was due and she said Nov. 8th. Ben asked the woman if she would take seventy-five dollars' cash for the chair and she says, "I don't want anything for the chair, just take it." Ben and I convinced her to take at least $50 and she agreed. We both told each other good luck with both of our changing lives and we left. On those days when I feel my lowest and so very alone in this fight, I find a person like her that ups my spirit. I bet her mother is somewhere looking down on this situation and smiling that her wheelchair is helping someone else who just needs to get around in life. Thank you, E. in Columbia, for helping us when we needed it.

Dear Lord, thank you for working through each of us in our own way, for the gift of children, parents, friends and strangers, for equipping us with hearts and minds that give and receive love, for the promise of a place with no pain and sorrow, for surprises of all kinds that bring a smile to our faces, and for the love and support of family, friends and strangers. Amen.

OCTOBER 19, 2011—Jack had his first day of school today. For him, this was a big step—the first time he has been in the classroom with other students since his last day of eighth grade. That seems like a lifetime ago for us. He will go with a new-to-him wheelchair, disinfecting wipes, masks, tissues, rubber gloves and lots of hand sanitizer. I have a bag attached to the wheelchair for all the germ-fighting items listed above. The bag also has a few Sharpies attached so Jack can ask whoever he wants to sign his bag like people would do if he had a cast somewhere on his body. It was only one class, but it was his start back to school. He had a great time as small a time as it was. His assistant was pleased with Jack and the work he did for her today.

Dear Lord, thank you for the cool weather, for the healing power of a good night's sleep, for days without pain and sorrow, for healthy bodies and strong minds, for love, faith, and hope, and for the support and love of so many. Amen.

CHAPTER 29

OCTOBER 25, 2011—Today was consultation day with the orthopedic surgeon. Our appointment was at 3:30, they called us back a few minutes to 5pm and the doctor talked to us for fifteen minutes. I have a theory about doctors who are late for their appointments by that much: they are either poor planners or they are thorough and meticulous with their patients. I always hope it is the latter of the two. Dr. M came in, looked at poor Jack's stiff feet, made him stand up and walk, had him lie down and he pushed and pulled on Jack's feet and legs to gauge the range of motion which isn't much in his feet. As with the other doctors, Dr. M thinks surgery will help by releasing the tendons in Jack's feet so they will lie flat on the floor. He also feels Jack will always have trouble with balance issues. Since Jack's big toes are uncontrollable because of the nerve damage, Jack's ability to walk properly will be hampered. He didn't say to what extreme, I guess we will have to see how the surgery goes and how Jack adjusts to wearing braces. The surgery will be out-patient with the chance of an overnight stay. There will be pain involved but once the pain gets better, Jack should be able to get around with his walker again for support. Both legs will be done at the same time with walking casts for six weeks so Jack can be mobile after the surgery. Bathing will be a challenge. After the six-week casts, Jack will be fitted for braces and he will wear them "for an extended time." (Opinion number two doctor said for three-to-four years.) Dr. M also said there is a small chance that he can clip the tendon in Jack's right ankle to help relieve it if he sees that it is necessary. The doctor made a point to tell us the incision would be small and hardly noticeable. Who cares about another scar now in our journey! Jack has so many now with all the operations, the steroid induced acne, and the body covering stretch marks. What are a few more scars at this point? Dr. M said he would get his scheduler to call us to set it up. We are hoping the surgery will be scheduled as soon as possible after Nov. 17th. We are going on Jack's Make-A-Wish trip Nov. 13 through

... BUT I'M NOT THE SINGER

17th and really don't want to have to deal with leg casts at that time. Jack is not thrilled about the whole thing, who would be, and he is especially not keen about being in pain. We talked about how nice it will be to go swimming next year and be able to walk and stand in a pool. We told him how the doctor will not let him hurt but will give him medicines for the pain. This poor child has been through so much in such a short time. We really hate this must happen, but it really needs to be done. We know this and we think deep inside Jack knows it as well.

Dear Lord, thank you for another beautiful autumn day, for healthy bodies and strong minds, for time spent with the ones we love, for the ability to learn, for the gift of children, for the blessing of friendship, and for the support and love of family, friends, and strangers. Amen.

OCTOBER 27, 2011—I talked to his special ed teacher about the new to Centennial Buddy program where they match a regular ed student with a special ed student. Jack has always enjoyed having people to talk to, and I think he misses it. He has never had what the rest of the world classifies as friends—someone who you do things with outside of school, like sleepovers, going to parties, and hanging out. Jack thinks if someone talks to him and they can laugh together, then they are his friend. He used to say, "Mom, I have lots of friends." He would be as loyal to a friend as a puppy. Just maybe, he will get that chance.

Dear Lord, thank you for the beautiful colors of autumn, for the sound of laughter, for the opportunity to be parents to awesome children, for the gift of good health, for days without pain and sickness, for the memory of the miracle of birth, for the promise of a place with You with no sorrow and suffering, and for the loyal lurkers and the guest book signers who have held our hand through this journey we have been on. Please bless them with Your grace and love. In Jesus' Name, Amen.

OCTOBER 31, 2011—Today was Jack's first day adding another class to his school day, and his special ed teacher said he did great. Hopefully his day tomorrow will be as good as today. We finally heard from Make-A-Wish today about our upcoming trip to the Bahamas on a Disney cruise ship. Make-A-Wish is coming to our house this Thursday to present Jack with all the information on the trip. It's starting to get exciting! We are going to all experience things on this trip we have never had the chance to do.

Dear God, thank you for giving us the opportunity to enjoy special occa-

MY NAME IS JACK JOHNSON...

sions in our lives, for the smile on a loved one face, for the gift of children, for the joy of time spent with friends, for the blessing of good health and strong minds, and for the support and love of so many people who continue to follow us on this journey. Amen.

NOVEMBER 2, 2011—The surgeon called, and Jack is scheduled for surgery on January 9th, 2012. We can at least make it through the holidays but, of course, it also means we must start with all the insurance co-pays and deductibles. Have I ever written how I despise the insurance companies? Jack and I went to the clinic today to get his port flushed, and I asked to see if they could schedule his port removal surgery at the same time. It is in the works as I type. That way Jack will only be put to sleep once for both surgeries. His next MRI is December 19th, and if that one is clear, he can have the port removed. One less thing to worry about and hopefully one less surgery and being put to sleep.

We had a tire that kept losing air and needed to get it looked at by professionals. Ben and I had to take it to Walker Chevy so they could figure out why it was constantly getting low. This is where my sister, Amy, works and Jack loves to go there and look at their Exit signs. So, of course, he had to go with us to pick the van up when they were finished with it and, of course, he had to go inside and inspect the Exit signs. Ben set Jack's walker by the car, Jack got out, and he was gone. He didn't wait for Ben or me and just politely walked in the showroom door like he owned the place. Amy has taken Jack there so many times that everyone there knows who Jack is and knows what he is looking for. One of the salesmen opened the door for Jack, and thankfully Amy was already on her way downstairs to the showroom. Amy and Jack did the Exit sign route through the building and came back downstairs. Thanks, Amy, for making his day with the Exit sign tour and thanks to everyone at Walker for putting up with Jack and his antics. After one of Jack's Exit sign trips to Walker, church, or now school, he comes home and draws each Exit sign he sees. He colors them the way they are with or without lights, cuts out each sign he makes and keeps them together. I will catch him now and then looking through his stacks of Exit signs. He can remember where each of his colored signs is located facility wise and where they are in each facility. The brain is a truly amazing creation.

Today Jack and I went to clinic for his port flush but before going to the Children's Hospital, we met Ben for lunch at Logan's in Cool Springs. I had just picked up Jack at school and he was full of himself. I can tell that

... BUT I'M NOT THE SINGER

school is agreeing with him by his excitement level when I pick him up. He was excited and talkative and just a pleasure to be around. I ask him every day about his day and who he saw at school and each day he tells me what happened. Today when I asked he said he was making friends in one of his classes because a new girl had talked to him. He told me her name and said that he didn't know her from Poplar Grove. Then he said that this girl gave him the "eye." Not knowing what he was really talking about, I asked him what kind of "eye." He told me the friendship "eye." While we were talking, I looked over and noticed that not only is hair returning on his head, but it has also returned to his upper lip! It is getting quite long, thick, and black. So, I said to him that we needed to shave his upper lip, that the hair is growing back now. He very firmly tells me "No," that he is in fact not shaving his mustache because it is sexy! I had to look away to keep from laughing. We arrived at the restaurant and met Ben who had us a table. We shared with Ben our conversation about the "eye" Jack received and how he is not going to shave his sexy mustache. Then Jack said, "I hope the girl who gave me the eye doesn't want to date me!" Ben said, "Jack, it's probably the sexy mustache that got to her and made her give you the "eye." Then he started licking his top lip and his mustache with his tongue. I asked him what he was doing and he said, "tasting my mustache and it tasted like hair!" We had a great lunch with a very lively conversation. Something must have happened on the way to Children's Hospital that I didn't notice because our friendly, talkative son became a beast somewhere on the trip. We arrived at the hospital, left the van with the valet, and got an elevator to the sixth floor, Nurse MM. came and got us and took us back to get the port flushed. Everything was fine or so I thought. We talked to MM., some of the other nurses, saw Dr. E, and talked to nurse practitioner, T. When it came time to leave, Jack was up and running out. He got to the door, of course, before me and when I got there, he was trying to bulldoze the door open with his walker. I told him to stop, that I was coming, and he screamed at me, "I'm not even in your fan club!" Being a little taken back, I asked him what was wrong and he said it was time to go. We were waiting in the elevator lobby and he was fussing the whole time. I don't even know what he was saying now. When the bell rang to announce the arrival of an elevator, Jack pushed his walker to the elevator door while I was telling him to wait for others who might be getting off. The door opens to the elevator and it was full. I told Jack to back up because the elevator was full and he blows! He screamed, "Dang it! I waited all this time and the elevator is full! " He was standing right in front of the full elevator,

MY NAME IS JACK JOHNSON...

screaming this to all the people in the elevator. I watched their expressions as this mad person with a weird hairstyle, holding on to a walker, screamed about how the elevator is full. Some of the people looked like they had seen the devil, others looked down at their feet. Happily, the elevator doors closed and the people on there were safe from the demon. I would have loved to have been a fly on the wall of that elevator as it went down. I bet someone said something along the lines of how very happy they were that they were on a full elevator and didn't have to travel with the screaming, walker demon. Demon boy and I stood with several other people and waited yet again for the next elevator which was not full and we all get on. I know that some of the people getting on with us felt like they were putting their own lives in jeopardy by riding with Jack. And, par for the course, he wasn't done yet. We got on the elevator on the sixth floor, the elevator stopped on the fifth floor, again on the fourth floor, and so on and so on. On about the third floor, Mr. Happy loudly said, "Is this thing going to stop on every floor?" You could almost feel the fear in the other riders as they considered whether they should just get off on the next floor or ride with wild man. And somewhere, I forget where, the elevator stopped again, some waiting people looked to see if there was enough room for them and Mr. Happy says, "Get your own elevator!" I gave him my meanest, dirtiest, boy-you-are-in-so-much-trouble look, he started to say something else, and I reached up and covered his mouth with my hand. At this point, all I saw was my hand over his mouth and his beady eyes staring at me when the demon sticks out his tongue and pushes it between my fingers. Well, at this point in the story, you might be saying the demon won, the poor mom lost. Oh, but the power and fear of germs had made the mommy hero use hand sanitizer at every sanitizer dispenser and now demon boy had a mouth full of hand sanitizer. I must say, hand sanitizer makes a demon spit and sputter like crazy. We walked out the front door of the hospital with him still spitting, sputtering and complaining about me and my hand sanitizer, while I verbally listed all the things that would be in time out when he got home. The gentleman who works the front door of the Children's Hospital asked me what was wrong with Jack and I shared the story with him and when I told him about the tongue getting a dose of sanitizer, he had to walk away he was laughing so hard. Demon boy and I still had to go to his physical therapy session at One Hundred Oaks. By this time, he was more subdued and was very tired. He had a hard time with all the therapy but we made it through without incident. Later tonight after the demon left, Jack apologized for his behavior. We will talk more about it tomorrow when he feels good again. I will leave with this parting thought—please, for me, hug your children tonight. They are truly a gift from God on their good days and their demon days.

Dear Lord, thank you for healthy bodies and minds, for days with sunshine and laughter, for our children on happy days and not so happy days, for letting us see the humor in our daily struggles, for giving us the ability to love, and for the support and love of family, friends, and strangers. Amen.

NOVEMBER 10, 2011—The countdown is on. We are counting the days until we leave on Jack's Make-A-Wish trip and we are down to two days. I think I am going to call this trip "The Johnsons' Great Adventure." As for Jack's day, I was out running errands, so Ben picked Jack up from school. Ben said the ladies in the office had been told a good Jack story and shared it with Ben. It seems the school is having a contest with students voting for other students who exemplify outstanding qualities and are the ultimate Centennial Cougar student. Today one of Jack's teachers was sharing it with the students in her class. She was explaining the contest and said that the prize was a chocolate cupcake. She went on to say that it was up to the students to find and vote for the person who they thought was the perfect example of a Centennial Cougar. I am not sure if he raised his hand or just said it out loud, but Jack says to the class and the teacher, "I'm going to vote for the guy in the wheelchair!" My son is just too funny!

Dear God, thank you for the change in the weather we had today, for tears of joy and tears of sadness, for the wonder of the human mind and how it works, for giving us hearts that feel love, for the gift of children, for the sound of laughter, and for the love and support we have been blessed with from so many on this journey we have been given. Amen.

SUNDAY MORNING, NOVEMBER 12TH. Make-A-Wish Day! We were up at 3:30am, trying to get dressed, last minute items packed, and ready for the limo who was due to arrive between 4:30 and 5am. We had so much luggage—including a wheelchair and a walker—that some of our stuff had to ride in the limo with us. Jack was grinning from ear to ear as we rode on the interstate, made our way into Nashville and to the airport. We checked in our luggage, and after a small problem with Jack not being able to walk through security, we waited for our flight. Jack and I have never flown on a commercial plane and this was a first for both of us. Jack was so happy just to be going that he wasn't nervous at all. He sat by the window and wanted me to sit with him.

MY NAME IS JACK JOHNSON...

Benny and Ben sat behind us with Benny having the window view. During takeoff, Jack and I held hands and laughed as the land below became smaller and smaller. We arrived in Orlando about two hours later and were met by thousands of other travelers going on some type of Disney excursion. We took turns pushing Jack, with his sweatpants and a hoodie with the hood on his head, in a wheelchair, aimlessly walking around, hauling all our carry-on bags, stopping to read every sign, annoying the heck out of all the people who are going somewhere and know where they are going. We couldn't have looked any more touristy! At least, we didn't have on Hawaiian shirts and cameras around our necks. No, we still had on our winter clothes with the temperature outside the airport in the warm seventies. We are directed to go to the buses, where Jack was lifted wheelchair and all into a Disney bus that would take us to Cape Canaveral, where we would meet our ship, the Disney Dream. After we got on the bus taking us to Cape Canaveral, Jack was mesmerized by lots of electric poles. We arrived at the dock and the huge ship was there in front of us. Its size was massive. Just seeing it builds your excitement for the trip.

We left the buses and stood in line with a few thousand of our closest friends. Once properly ID'd, we walked through a metal detector, received our "Key to the World" card, got in line to get on the ship with thousands of other people, and were stopped to have our pre-cruise picture made. Disney loves to take pictures of you whenever and wherever you visit them. Finally, we stepped from the dock to the ship and entered the main lobby. There we were asked our last name, and our arrival was announced to everyone in the lobby. "Welcome to the Johnson Family!" Funny, but most people in the lobby weren't listening; they were trying to find their way to somewhere on the ship. By this time, most of us who are on the ship are just hungry, looking for food. We were directed to the eleventh floor where there was a huge restaurant waiting for us to come and grab something to eat. With each restaurant we entered, a person was standing in front of the door handing out hand sanitizers to each person coming into the restaurant. Jack does not like the paper hand sanitizers and grudgingly cleaned his hands. Hunger was a wonderful motivator! We found a wheelchair friendly table, left Jack and started exploring the food. We enjoyed our lunch and the eleven stories high view out the nearby window. We were still docked, and people were still arriving with their names being announced in the lobby where no one is paying attention. We were also informed that our stateroom was not ready for us and would be ready at 1:30 pm.

We made our way to the eighth floor and found all the rooms roped off from us entering. We were alone waiting, Jack in his chair, the rest of us

... BUT I'M NOT THE SINGER

2011 Jack on his Make-A-Wish cruise to the Bahamas

randomly sitting on the stairs. It amazed us how people got off the elevators, looked at the four of us sitting there and proceeded to go to their room until they reached the rope blocking their entry. Why did they think we were sitting there? The elevators would open again, and more people would get off, look at us, and walk to the hallway only to find the rope of no entry. It happened again and again until the lobby was almost full, but still, people would get off the elevators, look around at all the waiting people and walk over to the hallway only to find the rope blocking their entry.

We were finally given the OK to go to our room. We found our stateroom, number 8616. The room had two separate bathrooms, one with a sink and shower/bathtub and one with a sink and the toilet, a very convenient and well thought out feature. There was a queen size bed, desk, couch that made into a single bed, closet with a personal safe for all our valuables (yeah, right!) and a small refrigerator. Benny's bed dropped down from the ceiling above

MY NAME IS JACK JOHNSON...

the couch bed, making a bunk bed. He was too long for the bed sometimes moving the curtain that divided the queen bed from the living room area during the night with his feet. The room ended with a veranda, a cool name for a small three-person-at-most balcony that was connected to all the other balconies but each separated by a dividing wall that was open at the top and bottom. I loved sitting out on the veranda until the Marlboro man who was two doors down lit up his smokes. First it was just cigarettes, then he ventured into the cigars. I really hate the smell of a bad, smelly cigar. There are some cigars that have a pleasant smell; some are just plain awful. Just plain awful was on this cruise. Jack didn't get to enjoy the veranda much because he hates cigarette smoke and I really didn't want him around it. But it was a beautiful view of the water during the day and at night. You could sit out there, see the stars and the moon, and the reflection of the moon on the water. Ben and I had some time out there just relaxing and enjoying the view. Marlboro Man liked it too, forcing us inside to escape the fumes. Our luggage was not due to arrive in our stateroom until later so we left our room and went exploring the fourteen floors of our ship.

Later that afternoon, we had to be present for the emergency drill where they showed you the proper use of the life jackets. They sounded the emergency alarm so we would be familiar with it just in case, and they showed us where to meet according to our room number. Instructions were given on the lifeboat plan. This was not a Jack favorite. He didn't like to hear talk about emergency plans and wore his noise reduction headphones during the emergency alarm which was an extremely loud blow of the ship's horn.

We headed back to the stateroom and had just enough time to change clothes and head to dinner. First, we were greeted with our pre-dinner hand sanitizer. For our first night, we were scheduled to have dinner at the Animator's Palate restaurant with the theme being the artwork from all the Disney films. There were pictures of art in all stages of completion on the walls of the dining room. We met our servers who followed us to each different restaurant for every dinner while we were on the ship. We met Edi, a young man from Thailand who would be our drink server, Felipe, a guy from Peru who was our head server, and Zita, our hostess for our section who was from Sweden. The restaurant's walls were covered with film art, pieces of memorabilia from each movie, and large TV/computer screens that showed different scenes from the movies. Once everyone was seated, the screens came to life with scenes from underwater and the characters from Finding Nemo, Jack's favorite movie. One character was talking to the tables in one section and then

... BUT I'M NOT THE SINGER

moved to another screen in another section. Our table was under one of these screens with Ben and Benny's backs facing the screen and Jack and I facing the screen. Jack was mesmerized by some of his favorite characters playing games and singing songs to the guests. On the screen behind Benny and Ben, one of the turtles from Finding Nemo came up. I grabbed my camera, put it up to take a picture, and the turtle on the screen said, "Hey, you, the dudette with the purple shell holding the black box. What's your name?" I was thinking, "who the heck is this turtle talking to?" I looked up at him, and he said, "Yeah, you." Ben and Benny were laughing hysterically while I had this very public conversation with an animated turtle. The turtle asked my name, where we were from, said he had never been to Tennessee, even held his flipper up to his ear to make sure he heard my answers to his questions. He asked if I wanted a picture and told everyone else who wanted his picture to get ready and he posed for pictures. The turtle turned into a ham, hamming it up with his many poses and expressions.

NOVEMBER 14, 2011—Hello from somewhere in the Atlantic Ocean, the beautiful blue water surrounding the Bahamas. I have never seen water this blue. This ship is flying through these waters! We are eating well and often and trying new foods that we have never eaten before, except for Jack, who tonight ordered from the kid's menu. Everyone has been extremely nice and kind to us. Tonight, we played shuffleboard on the deck while Jack watched, cheered, and booed our playing. He has had a few episodes of bad behavior and crying. I think he is having a really good time though. We are taking lots of pictures and making lots and lots of memories as we rock and roll across the blue sea. Lots more to tell and lots more to do on our end. Just a quick update to everyone we love and cherish.

Dear Lord, thank you for the blue of the deep ocean, for the kindness of strangers, for the smile on the faces of our children, for the beauty that surrounds us every day, and for family, friends, and strangers. Amen.

Monday morning, I woke to the sound of strange creaking and popping. The sun had barely come up, so I went to the veranda window to see what was happening. We were closing in on Nassau, heading for the Nassau port where several other cruise ships were already docked. The water was bluer than I have ever seen in my life. Ben woke up shortly after I did and we sat on the veranda and watched the docking process as it was happening. I am amazed at how they can dock those very large ships in such a small place.

We got dressed, ate breakfast at the Cabanas restaurant, and got ready for

MY NAME IS JACK JOHNSON...

our excursion into the city of Nassau. We had already made reservations to go to the Atlantis Resort and tour the aquarium per Jack's request. First, we had to find our way off the ship to depart, showing our identification again to get off the ship. Nassau was a busy place, and traffic was horrible. We were ushered to an area where the tour buses loaded and there we had to wait for a bus. Jack had to get out of his wheelchair, walk up the bus stairs, and the tour folks put the wheelchair on the bus after everyone else had been seated. Much to Jack's surprise, the steering wheel of the bus was on the left side of the bus, and we rode on the right side of the road, very fast, and very close to the other cars, trucks, and buses! I sucked air several times while we were making our way across town. Jack loved it, looking at all the electric poles. The roads were very crowded and very narrow, sometimes barely squeezing between the buildings of downtown. Atlantis Resort sits on its own island joined to downtown Nassau by a bridge. The Resort is huge with nine swimming pools, three condo towers, a casino, lots and lots of high-end shops, many restaurants, and the aquarium. The aquarium starts in the main area of the resort and winds its way underground and around the resort. Jack liked all the fish; it didn't matter what kind.

After the tour, we got back on a bus and rode through Nassau again with all its twists and turns and traffic. Once we were back at the ship, we headed upstairs for lunch. We ate, change into our bathing suits, and headed to the pool. Jack was beyond excited to get into the pool. We found four empty chairs and, with Ben on one side and Benny on the other, we hauled Jack to the pool. This was a huge ordeal because we had to take him up four stairs, down two stairs into the water with dozens and dozens of kids and adults around us. Of course, doing this caused a big scene and cleared out a spot in the pool. Parents pulled their children out of the way and took them to the other side of the pool. Little kids swam away, looking afraid that they might catch whatever Jack has. I must say it has been quite some time since I have looked closely at Jack's feet. They are a mess. His feet are so misshaped and contorted, it is hard to believe he can walk on them at all. They don't look quite as bad in shoes but without shoes is another story. Jack, Ben, and Benny found a clear spot in the pool and watched the movie above them on the big screen. I sat on the side of the pool and put my feet in the water while taking pictures of my boys. Jack later decided to try and get into the hot tub, another ordeal. First, we had to wait for an empty spot in the hot tub, and then we had to get him out of the wheelchair, up four more steps, and down a few more into the water. Once there, he loved it.

... BUT I'M NOT THE SINGER

Soon it was time to get ready for dinner. We all had to shower and get dressed. The second night, our dinner was in the Enchanted Garden restaurant. We were given our complimentary hand sanitizer before we entered the restaurant. I had forgotten or thought I had forgotten the dinner tickets that we must show the host/hostess at the door. Benny went back to our room to find them while the rest of us waited in the lobby. We had just received our hand sanitizers when Jack said that he is not going to use his. There were people waiting to get seated all around us and Jack started to get very ugly about the hand sanitizer. He said very loudly, "I am not using it and no one can make me!" Benny was still not back and Ben left me and Jack to work out the sanitizer issue to help Benny search for the dinner tickets in our room. I pulled Jack as far away from others as I could and explained to him we were given hand sanitizers because the crew of the boat doesn't want us to have any germs on our hands as we come into the restaurant and that it is easy to spread germs on a ship with lots of people especially little children and blah, blah, blah. I thought I was making headway with my explanation but as soon as I stopped to take a breath, Jack said, "Too bad! I am not using a hand sanitizer and that's final!" By this time, he had everyone's attention within a twenty-foot radius and all eyes were on him. I gave him a choice of paper hand sanitizer or the liquid sanitizer. He began to scream something else and I, without thinking, quickly put my hand over his closed mouth which still had the paper hand sanitizer in it. We locked eyes and I said calmly and firmly that he would use sanitizer or we would go back to our room. He looked at me and loudly said, "You touched my mouth with hand sanitizer!" Please understand—no sanitizer got into his mouth, just on the outside. Now he was talking to me through lips that he will not let touch each other and with his tongue poised midair in his mouth. Finally, he said something I could understand "You got sanitizer in my mouth" and closed his mouth to make a huge ball of spit so he could spit it out. There we were.... Jack with a massive ball of spit in his mouth, me standing there watching him "walk" his wheelchair to the only trash can in the lobby where everyone who had used their paper hand sanitizer properly disposed them. He got the wheelchair to the trash can but could not get his head close enough to the trashcan to spit his spitball into it because the footrest of the wheelchair kept the chair from getting closer. At this point, I did what any other person would have done in this spot: I opened my paper hand sanitizer and let the boy spit into it, right there in front of all those moms, dads, grandparents and kids dressed up in their Cinderella and pirate outfits. By this time, I am exasperated with the whole situation and reached in my purse for my liquid hand sanitizer, got my hands and Jack's

MY NAME IS JACK JOHNSON...

sanitized and, by some strange chance, touched the left pocket of my pants, felt something unfamiliar and found our dinner tickets that Ben and Benny were frantically searching our room for at that very moment. I really enjoyed "the drink of the day" that night at dinner.

Our servers Felipe and Edi were there at our table again, and both men signed Jack's germ bag. Zita, our hostess, also signed it. It was another good meal. We ended our second night, full of dinner, relaxed and happy.

Tuesdays on Disney's cruise ship, the Dream, is Castaway Cay day, Disney's private island in the Bahamas. We had traveled the sea Monday night and woke up Tuesday at the island. The island itself is three miles wide and two miles long. Disney has doctored the island with man-made barriers along the coast to keep control of the ocean. The water in the Cay is crystal clear. Once on the beach, Jack fell asleep, I sat near the water, and Ben and Benny went snorkeling. After Jack woke up and Ben and Benny got back, we tried to get Jack in the ocean. We had been given a sand wheelchair—a life saver—and we took Jack in his chair as close to the water as we could get him. Since we were a Make-A-Wish family, Disney had given us complimentary floats for the day. Jack wanted to sit in a donut style float. It took two of us to get him out of his wheelchair while the other person held the float. Much to our surprise, the water was cool, not too bad once you got used to it, but Jack didn't get used to it and soon wanted out of the water. So, we had to reverse our getting in the water with him to getting him out of the float and the water. It wasn't an easy task and, of course, we had the attention of everyone within the sound of a scream distance.

After the float fiasco, Jack got hungry, and we went in search of lunch. And with Disney, you don't have to go too far to find food. Lunch was a buffet of hamburgers, hot dogs, chicken, ribs, and all the fixings. Seating was at picnic tables.

We stayed a while longer on the beach and headed back to the ship. We all had a shower and dressed for dinner, but before dinner, we visited the eighteen and older side of the ship. We sat while listening to a guy playing island music on the steel drums. Jack liked the steel drums. Ben and I had a few adult beverages while we sat by the ceiling to floor windows, listening to the steel drums and watching the ship pull away from the Castaway Cay dock. That night on the ship was pirate night and all the servers dressed in pirate garb. The menu that night was all pirate-themed regular foods with pirate names. I had a Rusty Anchor for a before dinner drink. Rust should always taste that good.

... BUT I'M NOT THE SINGER

That night was our first night to eat at the Royal Palace. Of course, our servers, Felipe, Edi and Zita, were there to serve us. The evening before Zita had given Jack a challenge—to find something he really liked because he didn't like the menu choices and was ordering from the kid's menu. Zita was never told Jack had autism and would not stray from his regular Jack selection of foods. But he had let it slip that he liked Dory from the movie, Finding Nemo. Dory used to go everywhere with us. Dory went to church faithfully and even had her picture with Jack in one of our church's brochures. That night at the Royal Palace, we were led to our table which turned out to be very close to the door. But it was one step up from the floor which meant Jack would have to get out of his wheelchair, step up one step, and walk to a regular table chair. Felipe and Edi were close by to help. Jack, on the other hand, was not very happy about having to step up and change chairs. Loudly he said, "Hey, hey. We want another table!!" But there sitting on our table right in the middle of it, looking straight at us was a new, clean, stuffed Dory, smiling right at Jack. But in true Jack form, he was too busy complaining to even notice. Benny saw her first and said, "Hey, Jack, I think someone is waiting for you at our table." Jack was still mouthing about a new table when he looked and saw Dory's smile and her big, beautiful, fish eyes looking right at him. That's all it took. Jack was trying to get his wheelchair closer to the table and was grabbing the railing beside our table to help himself get to that table that two seconds ago he would not sit at. The smile on his face was worth it to us and to Zita as well. It turned out to be a very nice dinner. A big thanks to Zita, Felipe, and Edi for making Jack's night.

We woke up on our last day of the cruise, ate breakfast, and explored for a while. That night was our last night to eat dinner on the ship and our last night to see our servers and hostess, Felipe, Edi, and Zita. We ate our dinner in the Royal Palace again. When it got close to time to leave, Jack started crying. I had been walking around all day with this huge lump in my throat myself. My mind had been on the fact that this could be the last vacation the four of us would ever take together. I know some people will tell me how stupid that thought was and how I need to have faith. I do have faith, but my faith is that whatever the future holds for us, God will never leave us. And I know that all the prayers in the world cannot stop whatever our future holds, they might make it better or easier but bad things still happen even when we are very faithful, pray daily, and trust in God. So, when Jack started crying, I cried too. Zita came by while we were teary-eyed and our tears became her tears as well. Here we are in one of the happiest places on earth boohooing because we

MY NAME IS JACK JOHNSON...

don't want to leave this magical place. Jack was crying because he didn't want to leave, I was crying because I don't want him to leave either. Zita told Jack through her tears that she hoped in a few years that he would come back and see her again. The ship would still be there and so would she and that they could see each other again. Tears continued streaming down our faces. Jack enjoyed his taste of fun and magic. I had enjoyed being away from reality.

When we got back to our stateroom, Mickey was waiting on the bed for Jack, a stuffed Mickey Mouse that is. Jack got invited to a special party the morning of the Castaway Cay day. He got to meet the ship captain and Mickey Mouse and had his picture made with them. The new stuffed Mickey was also signed by Mickey himself. Jack cried over the new Mickey as well.

We woke up that last morning, got ready, and headed back to the Royal Palace where Felipe, Edi, and Zita were waiting for us again. And, of course, Jack started crying again when we left. We all hugged each other and were directed to the exits. We left the ship and boarded the bus that would take us back to Orlando. We got to the Orlando airport and had time to kill before our next flight out to Raleigh-Durham, NC, our connecting flight airport. We walked around and ate lunch. We waited a little longer for our flight and finally could board the plane.

We arrived in Nashville that night. It was a long day waiting in different airports. Our limo was waiting, and so was our luggage, just sitting there all by itself where it had been taken off the wheel of luggage.

All in all, we had a wonderful time. Disney did lots of extras for us because Jack was a Make-A-Wish kid. There was always a note card with a gift inside or a plate of treats for us to enjoy in our room. Our beds were always made and ready for us at night, complete with a towel or blanket shaped into an animal. We were treated so well by all the staff everywhere we went on the ship. We will treasure our Make-A-Wish trip forever. Hopefully, in the years to come, we can take another cruise together and enjoy it one more time! And while I'm hoping, I hope Jack is walking the whole way!

NOVEMBER 18, 2011—We are officially home. We got home last night, but we were all so tired that as soon as we ate dinner and unpacked the things we needed, we were all in bed.

After reminiscing about our trip, I must say that Jack was great on this trip. Now we did have a few episodes, but even his episodes were not that bad. I didn't have to apologize to anyone for his behavior even though I could have in some instances. He learned how to cover his loud and unexpected burps, he didn't make anyone mad, and he seemed to enjoy himself thoroughly. But hey, what is there not to like on a cruise. I think all of us would have stayed another few days if given the option. I must say a huge thank you to all the people who helped us on this trip. First, there was the limo company who picked us up bright and early Sunday morning at 5:15 am and met us last night at the airport and brought our tired, weary bodies home. Then there was the whole Make-A-Wish organization that made all of Jack's dreams come true. Next, a big thank you to all the people at Disney who went out of their way to help us in some capacity. We had wonderful people who served us all our dinners and personally made it special for Jack. And Disney also gave Jack all kinds of gifts to make his trip a little more special. For those of you who have wondered what Make-A-Wish is all about and would consider giving to a worthy case, MAW is truly a wonderful organization for children with life-threatening illnesses. They make wishes come true for kids who have or are fighting terrible diseases and need something positive and happy in their lives. Parents of these children don't have the extra cash it takes to make their child's wish come true. So please, if you are ever asked to give to Make-A-Wish, remember Jack and how much it meant to him to have a little fun.

Dear Lord, thank you for all the technology it takes for us to get from one place to another, for the look of joy on our children's faces, for the comforting feel of another's touch, for the opportunity to be parents to wonderful children, for healthy bodies and minds, and for the support and love of family, friends, and strangers. Amen.

CHAPTER 30

NOVEMBER 21, 2011—We had a good weekend back home from our Make-A-Wish trip. Ben, Jack, and I got up and went to church Sunday morning. After church was over, we went to the Fellowship Hall where Jack met up with his special friend. While waiting for Sunday school to start and enjoying the time between church and SS, drinking coffee, and talking with friends, one of Jack's peers came over and hugged him. Jack didn't reciprocate, keeping his posture very stiff, his hands in his lap and making one of his famous unhappy faces. This peer knows Jack and understands that she is probably not going to get a hug back, but she hugs him anyway. Later at lunch, I said to Jack how nice it was that Caroline had hugged him. He said, "I'm sexy, and she knows it!" (Lyrics to a song that he has recently heard!)

Dear Lord, thank you for the blue oceans, for the ability you gave us to build ships that cross the oceans, for eyes that see the beauty of the colors of water and sand, for the animals and sea life that exist only in water, for time to spend with our loved ones, for tears of sadness and tears of joy, for the comfort a touch can give and for the support and love of our family, friends and complete strangers. Amen.

NOVEMBER 28, 2011—Over Thanksgiving break, Ben painted a family picture for us. This was one of my wild ideas wanting something unique for a big old bare wall in our family room. I had looked at all the cool canvas art that is available for sale everywhere but why should I have to buy art when an artist lives right here under this roof? After figuring out what I wanted, Ben painted it for us. The artwork reflects our family. The art is a combination of all the things we love: the water, the sunset and how it reflects off the water and something that represents the four of us. Four trees represent us. Each of us painted on it. Of course, Ben did the majority of the painting but the three of us painted a few spots on the trees. I wanted something people would see as soon as they walked into the room and it is an eye-catcher. The Johnson family picture.

... BUT I'M NOT THE SINGER

Dear Lord, thank you for the loved ones we will celebrate the birth of Christ with this year, for the gift of love even when it hurts, for the time we are given with all our loved ones on earth, for Your promise of a place without pain and sorrow, for the health some of us enjoy daily, and for the love and support we have had from family, friends, and strangers. In Christ Name, Amen.

NOVEMBER 30, 2011—Every morning Jack gets up and walks from our bedroom to the family room where Ben is usually waiting for him, and Ben always says, "Here he comes to save the day!" This morning Jack walks into the family room, and before Ben can say it Jack said, "Here I come to save the day!" And he has been like that most of the day. I took Jack to school this morning, and when we turned onto the road the school is on, he was so thrilled to see that one lane of the road was blocked because of electric line work. You would have thought he was seeing his favorite movie star or hero. He said, "Oh, look. They are doing my favorite thing. They are working on the electric poles!!" I had to tell him they weren't working on the poles themselves but were stringing more electric lines of some kind onto the poles. The workers were in the bucket trucks, up in the bucket, and the bucket was close to the poles. That was all it took. And then when we were pulling into the school parking lot, a Lady Gaga song came on the radio. He heard the song 'Come On' and said, "And wow, there's my girl's song on the radio!" His girl...Lady Gaga.

Dear God, thank you for days with smiles and laughter, for the warmth of sunshine on a cool day, for good health and strong minds, for being able to find a ray of sunshine on a cloudy day, for the comfort of a friendly voice, for the opportunity to be parents to amazing children, and for the support and love of so many as we continue to travel through this part of our journey. Amen.

DECEMBER 12, 2011—Saturday we had our picture made courtesy of Help Portraits. Help Portraits is the one day out of the year where all professional photographers give their talents and experience to people in need. It is a worldwide day of giving for photographers as they take pictures of people who don't have the money to have a recent photo of their family, or for single mothers who cannot afford a professional family photo, or for people like us last year who had suffered through the flood or any natural disaster, or for people again like us who have a sick child and want a recent photo of the child and with their family. We had our picture made last year at Help Portraits. Jack had finished radiation and was starting chemo. He was so thin.

MY NAME IS JACK JOHNSON...

pale, and didn't have much hair. We went back this year for more photos with Jack being a one-year cancer survivor! We finally will have a recent family photo of Jack with his hair back. Thank you, Help Portraits, for the updated family picture with this year's healthy-looking Jack.

Dear God, thank you for time that heals, for good health and strong minds, for the crisp cold of winter, for warm coats and houses for shelter, for the spirit of giving to others, for the smile on the face of a child, for friends and family time spent together, and for the love and support of so many people who walk with us on this journey. Amen.

DECEMBER 21, 2011—Today was our trip to the State Capital and Jack's Make-A-Wish event—Cookies and Milk with Santa and Governor Haslam. We left home a few minutes before two to give ourselves plenty of time to find a parking place. Fortunately, when we arrived at the Capital, the guard at the gate of the driveway instructed us to a handicapped parking place right beside the Capital. Thank you, Mr. Guard! The wheelchair ramp into the Capital started right in front of our newly found handicapped parking place. We wheeled Jack inside and were directed to the elevators. We got to the first floor where we were to meet the MAW people and were directed with a few other families to another room. The camera crew started setting up. More and more families arrived until there were about ten families with their Make-A-Wish child and their other children. A lady came and asked for all the MAW children to follow her. Me and another parent had to go too because we had to help our children get to where they were going. We were led into the Governor's office where the Governor himself came out and spoke to each child. He shook hands with each one except for Jack who gave him the fist bump. The Governor asked the kids questions about Christmas but not very many were in a talkative mood. We then were led back to the original room where Ben and Benny and the other families were waiting. Santa had arrived while we were gone and was waiting for the kids. Santa introduced his elves, two young attractive ladies dressed in skimpy elf costumes, who helped the kids into Santa's lap and passed out gifts. Jack leaned over to me and said, "Wow. I didn't know Santa would bring real elves with him!" Bless my son's heart. On the other side of me, Ben and Benny were admiring the elves themselves but in a different grown-up way. All the children gathered around Santa and his elves and Santa read the "T'was the Night Before Christmas" story to the kids. And there sat our big, teenage Jack right in the middle of it all. I asked Jack later what his favorite

... BUT I'M NOT THE SINGER

thing about the trip was and he said when Santa read the story. Then each kid was given the opportunity to sit in Santa's lap, talk about what they wanted for Christmas, and have their picture taken. Oh, and were there pictures taken!! This was supposed to be about the kids not the Governor and I didn't like that the Governor's photographers were always in the way of the parents trying to take pictures of our kids with the Governor. There was this one guy who had on brown pants (I know this because those pants and his backside are in lots of my pictures) who was constantly walking in front of us parents so he could get the best shots of the Governor. One time when all the kids, the Governor, Santa and the elves were all posing, there was not a clear shot for any parent to get a shot without a photographer in it. All the photographers were in the way. Hopefully, Make-A-Wish will have some good pictures to share, and maybe Mr. Brown Pants won't be in them all. Jack had fun. Benny had fun too but he won't admit it. We got lots of pictures of Jack and some guy's brown pants. But it was another gift for me this Christmas.

Dear Lord, thank you for watching over us, for the gift of children, for the blessing of good health, for the innocence of children, for the ability to laugh at ourselves, for the love and support of family, friends, and strangers, and for the true meaning of the season, Your Son. Amen.

DECEMBER 27, 2011—For us, Christmas was hard. Harder than Christmas last year. We live each day in the shadow of cancer, and the shadow doesn't lift because it's a holiday. None of the pretty lights or magical carols playing over the airways make it take a break. So, if I sound like "Debbie Downer," let me say sorry, but it is the way we live.

Lately, Jack has suffered from croaky burps that once made him vomit. The closer Christmas got, the worse the burps, the more he kept us up at night, and the less he ate. We went to the Capital on Wednesday, and that was Jack's last good day. He went downhill from there. He didn't want to eat at all, he made trip after trip to the bathroom all day and all night, and he didn't feel good at all. But he had no fever, no diarrhea, no headaches, no other symptoms. Then on Thursday night, he vomited again. He kept saying he was hurting in his stomach area, a place he had pointed out to us many times before and he had pointed this same place out to all the doctors who he saw before his diagnosis. Jack was vomiting, not feeling well, not eating, hurting in his stomach area, going to the bathroom, and not sleeping because of going to the bathroom so often and having the croaky burps. And if you had lived through

MY NAME IS JACK JOHNSON...

the hell we have lived through in the last year and a half what would you be thinking? Well, so was I. I tried not to but with each skipped meal and seeing him lose a little more weight each day, I couldn't help it. I prayed every breath for God not to let this happen again. I pleaded with God; I started making deals with God. Please, God, don't let this be happening again. Ben is always the picture of optimism, and I'm the protective pessimist, thinking the worst to prepare myself just in case it happens, but every day seemed worse than the one before. We asked Jack several times what was going on and he said he was upset over Christmas, something we didn't understand. So, we kept asking and kept asking until finally on Friday he told us he was worried about what he was getting for Christmas. What? Was he this sick with worry over a Christmas gift? So, we asked what gift he was the most worried about, and he told us Nermal, a stuffed cat from the cartoon character Garfield series. I couldn't believe anyone could be this worried over a stuffed animal. A friend told me to give Jack the thing and get it over with. But I knew if I did, I would have to use the worry-making stuffed animal the right way for several reasons: 1) Jack still believes in Santa and just pulling the stuffed animal out of a closet would open a big can of worms that, if he really were sick with worry, would add to his stress, 2) I really needed to use the gift to get him motivated to rejoin the land of the living again and start to eat and sleep again, and 3) I didn't want him to go further into a funk if giving him the gift was all he wanted for Christmas and because he got it before the actual day of Christmas then why would he go anywhere else if that was all he truly wanted. I hope that makes sense. Don't forget—we are not just dealing with the side effects of cancer here; we still have good old autism in all its glory to contend with too. We must approach everything we do with that in mind as well. So, I devised a plan: Ben and I had to go out anyway to pick up a few things, and I would tell Jack that while we were out, we were going to stop in at the mall and talk to Santa about Jack and his whole situation. This seemed to help Jack who perked up just a little. I went to the hidden Christmas gifts in our special hiding place and got the Nermal stuffed animal, wrapped it in my jacket, and Ben and I left for our errands. When we got back, I had slipped the Nermal into a gift bag that I had that was a cross between a gift bag and a stocking and we went inside the house. I sat down beside Jack and told him that we had talked to Santa and Santa was not happy. With that, Jack said, "Oh, no!" I told him Santa was not happy that any child no matter its age would be that sick over a gift, and that Santa agreed to let Jack have the gift early if Jack would eat more than he had and stop worrying over gifts. Jack said to the air, "Oh

...BUT I'M NOT THE SINGER

Santa, I will do my best" and I gave him the stuffed animal. I was expecting fireworks and sparks to fly, but Jack just softly smiled and put Nermal on the couch beside him. At dinner time, Jack ate a little bit and said he hoped Santa would not be disappointed in him but he couldn't eat much. At least he tried to eat, more than he had done before. That night Jack slept longer than he had in a while but still had to get up and go to the bathroom and still had the burps. On Christmas Eve morning, we got up, and still, Jack didn't feel good. He went to the bathroom as soon as he woke up and vomited again. My heart sank. Even Ben lost hope. The arrival of the 'yearned for gift' hadn't made anything better at all. I cried the whole time I was showering. Ben said a few choice words under his breath. Jack felt so bad he really didn't want to go anywhere but after my cry, I decided that we were going to go anyway and make the best out of this Christmas as we could. Jack still didn't eat anything but yogurt for breakfast and he opened his gifts but you could tell he really didn't feel well at all. Ben and I smiled, tried to laugh and act normal, but it was too hard sometimes and tears came out anyway. We left one family gathering, went home long enough to load up again and went to another family gathering. And all the while we were smiling through the tears and hurt we were carrying around. Jack ate yogurt for breakfast and a few bites of food for supper and that was all he ate all day. Jack slept well Christmas Eve night. He didn't really care about getting up to see what Santa had left for him but he did. We all got dressed and ready for our Christmas morning last family gathering. We arrived at the gathering, Jack ate yogurt again for breakfast, and went and sat by himself. He said he didn't feel like opening gifts and would open them later. My sister tried to coax him but he wouldn't move. The rest of us opened our gifts and before the gifts were all opened, Jack decided he would join us. He opened his gifts, said his thank yous, and went back to where he had been before. He looked so sad, and didn't feel well, and the color of his skin was ashen. It was so hard to make it through all the festivities but we did. Finally, we were all back home. Jack sat down at his favorite seat on the couch and said, "I am glad that is over. Next year I am not going to ask Santa for any gifts because I worry too much about them!" And that was the declaration that changed his world. Since then, he has started eating, the burping has all but stopped, he is laughing and happy, no more stomach pains and his color has come back. He has slept quite a bit but when he is awake, he does all the things Jack has always liked to do like watch his favorite things on YouTube and his favorite shows on TV. He has even used some of his new iTunes cards to download some new music to his iPod. Ben and I are shocked

MY NAME IS JACK JOHNSON...

to say the least. How can a kid make himself so sick over a Christmas gift? For us, it was like a switch was turned off in Jack sometime last week and then it turned back on Christmas Day. What caused this, I cannot say. I have never seen anything like it. Was it a virus? I do not think it was because he never had a fever, no chills, no runny nose, or sore throat or diarrhea, or any other symptom you could name. As he said, he was worried he wouldn't get what he wanted for Christmas and that was the only explanation he could give us. Today, I am, for lack of a better term, shocked at the whole thing. I am not sure if this was caused by the stress of worrying over a gift or something we can't see or know about today. Ben and I are calmer than before but until we get this upcoming MRI over, we will not be completely back to normal ourselves. As Ben put it—he has a lot grayer hair now than he did before Christmas. Even if there is no evidence of cancer on the MRI, it will take us a while to get over the last few days. I, like Jack, am so happy Christmas is over. Now if we could just get this next MRI over.......

Dear Lord, thank you for the gift of Your Son whose birth we celebrate this time every year, for the many blessings we have that we sometimes take for granted, for spending time with family and friends, for the joy of giving, for the sound of the laughter of children, for the miracle of the human body, for the gift of good health and strong minds, for days without pain and sorrow, and for the love and support of so many who walk with us on this journey we have been given. In His Name, Amen.

DECEMBER 30, 2011—Jack had his much-awaited MRI yesterday. Of course, we do not know the results but have an appointment to go over the scans next Wednesday with Jack's oncologist. Jack did great yesterday. The MRI was not scheduled until 3:30 so it made for a long day of waiting. He woke up full of himself yesterday morning, saying as soon as he woke up, "The people there know me. They know I'm the man. And when I get there, I will say 'Here I am to save the day!!'" When he says things like that he truly is the man! We had to go to the oncology floor to get Jack's port accessed and to have blood drawn. Unfortunately, his favorite nurse, MM., was not there. The nurse we did have had a hard time getting the access needle into Jack's port. She attempted once, missed, and had to try it again. Jack was not happy but tolerated it well. He also had a few choice comments to the nurse like, "Who hired you?" and "I really think we need an expert now!" The nurse took it all in stride and laughed long and hard about the 'who hired you' comment. She told Jack that in her twenty-something years of nursing, she had never

... BUT I'M NOT THE SINGER

had a patient ask her that question. She has never been around our Jack. After the port was accessed, we went down to the radiology department where we waited. We were called back by our old friend and nurse, J. J. was happy to see us, or so he said, and Jack was happy to see J. Jack didn't give J. too much trouble but he was ready to have the MRI over. They took Jack back, and Ben and I waited until 6:30 pm when we were told by J. that they would have Jack upstairs on the surgical floor recovery and would call us back about 7 or 7:30. We waited with our nerves on edge until a nurse came and got us. When we got back there, Jack was awake and "drunk," his words, (like he knows what it feels like to be drunk) and had to go to the bathroom. Ben, the nurse, and I got Jack up and to the bathroom where we spent quite a few minutes. Jack finished, got back in the bed, and after another 30 minutes, he was ready to go home. When we got home, he had a touch of diarrhea and had a little touch of it this morning. He also told us this morning his throat hurt, and when I looked in his throat, he has matching red marks on either side of his throat. I presume these were caused by the breathing tube put in during the MRI. Next Monday we go back to the hospital for all of Jack's pre-op testing before his surgery scheduled for Jan. 9th.

Dear Lord, thank you for nurses and doctors who treat us when we don't feel well and are at our most vulnerable, for the winds of change bringing in the new year, for healthy bodies and strong minds, for the blessing of children and for the love and support of family, friends, and strangers. In His Name, Amen

CHAPTER 31

JANUARY 4, 2012—The sunshine of today brought good news...Jack's MRI was clear!! Ben and I are so relieved. I cannot describe the relief, just that we feel lighter. Thank you, God, for good news and clear scans! Thanks to each of you for your thoughts and prayers about this MRI. We could not go through this without each of you and your prayers and without our faith that God is with us daily.

Jack went to Walker Chevrolet where my sister works and watched the safety company come and repair Walker's Exit signs. To say the child was thrilled is an understatement. He had been looking forward to this since sister Amy mentioned it. Jack got to watch the Exit sign repairmen take Exit signs down and put new bulbs in the others. Jack told us the repair men's names were W. and B. He got to watch them do all their repairs and they also gave him some Exit sign fronts for him to keep. Jack got to sign the work form stating that the work was done correctly. He had a great time. Thanks, Amy, and all the people at Walker for letting Jack come and spend time doing something he thinks is so much fun!

Dear God, thank you for a day with sunshine especially after gloomy days, for doctors and nurses and the care they give us in our quest for good health, for the good health we enjoy and strong minds that learn something new every day, for the blessing of children, the gift of giving and receiving love, for the feel of a hug, the warmth of our homes, for time spent with loved ones, and for the support and love of family, friends, and strangers. Amen.

JANUARY 9, 2012—Leg surgery day. It has been another long day sitting around a hospital waiting room. Jack's surgery is now over, we are home, and so far, he is doing great. They got an earlier start on the surgery, starting at 2 pm instead of the planned 2:45. The leg surgery lasted a whole hour, and the port removal was a thirty-minute procedure. It took longer for Jack to completely wake up from the anesthesia than it took for the surgeries. Right now,

... BUT I'M NOT THE SINGER

as I am writing this, he is sitting in the recliner of the couch with both casted legs propped up on pillows, still a little silly from the pain meds, talking to himself about something.

We arrived at the hospital at about 12:30, went to the surgical floor and waited to be called back. The surgeon came to see us and again went over what exactly he would be doing, what to expect in the way of pain, how to manage the leg casts, and other details. During the surgery, the leg casts would be assembled after the incision was closed to keep the foot in the proper position while the tendon and the incision heals. The casts are light blue and start about two-to-three inches below the knee. They completely cover his leg all the way to the end of his foot, where there is an opening at the very end, and you can touch and see his toes. Standing and walking is optional right now because there is pain associated with this surgery and it could last up to two weeks. The doctor would love to see Jack walking after the pain has eased but until that time, he can use the wheelchair. Jack will wear these casts for six weeks; they will remove them, fit his foot for braces, reconstruct another cast to wear until the braces are completed, and then Jack will wear braces. There is no guarantee that this will make Jack walk better. This surgery today was the first step in trying to correct the problem by at least putting his feet back flat on the floor where normal feet usually are, but if the nerve damage is severe or there is damage somewhere in Jack's brain, the part that controls balance, he will still have issues. Hopefully, we will have a quiet night, but you never know when someone has had surgery.

Dear Lord, thank you for doctors and nurses, for their caring hearts and knowledge, for the advancements we have made in the care of our bodies, for the researchers that work hard every day to find cures for our many diseases, for the charities that sponsor the research for cures, for the many people who give to those charities, for the gift of a giving, unselfish soul, for days without pain and suffering, and for the support, love and prayers so many have done on our behalf. In His name, Amen.

JANUARY 10, 2012—It is very quiet in our house as I write this. Poor Jack is napping after having a couple of pain pills today. He had a good night, sleeping through most of it. I did not wake him during the night to take his pain medication so when he woke up this morning, he had been several hours without any. And he was feeling it. The doctor warned us that this was a painful recovery and could take two weeks to be pain-free especially when standing up completely. Jack has had some "burning pain" in his heels which

MY NAME IS JACK JOHNSON...

is exactly how the doctor said other patients had described their pain. Jack's legs are also prone to have leg spasms as the tendon heals back and from the stationary position his legs are in right now. We have a specific drug to give him once these spasms start but so far, he hasn't had them. He has not gotten out of his bed today, just deciding that watching TV from his bed was just fine. He has taken over that side of the master bedroom with all his signs, odd lights he likes, and his many stuffed animals. For Christmas, he got his very own Exit sign just like the ones put up in public buildings. I asked my dad if he could attach a regular electric cord to the sign and of course, my dad can do anything. (Thanks, Dad for the Exit sign cord.) Jack has his very own lit-up exit sign that he can take and plug into any electric outlet anywhere.

Part of his surgery yesterday was the removal of Jack's port-a-cath, the contraption that was put in his chest months ago so they could take blood and give him chemo and other drugs without sticking him in the arm each time. The surgeon who did the surgery took it out and gave it to us to keep. Jack and I laughed at the ugly port yesterday when I showed it to him. Thanks, God, for protecting Jack's body from infection while the port was in him.

Dear Lord, thank you for the gift of children, for the smile on the face of a child, for healthy bodies and strong minds, for the ability to come to you in prayer, and for the love and support of family, friends, and strangers who walk with us on this journey. Amen.

JANUARY 11, 2012—The second day after surgery and it has been a doozy. Jack woke up this morning needing to go to the bathroom. We must make sure Jack has his new cast shoes on his feet, the wheelchair must be put exactly at the right spot by the bed for person transfer, Ben bends over the bed, Jack wraps his arms around Ben's neck, Ben stands up and turns Jack's backside toward the wheelchair and easy as that, Jack is in his wheelchair. The wheelchair and Jack barely squeeze through the bathroom door and you need to back into the bathroom because there is not enough room to turn the wheelchair around in there. We pulled the wheelchair as close to the toilet as humanly possible and Ben repeats the whole thing over again except for putting the shoes on. When Ben has Jack in mid-air, between the wheelchair and the toilet, he must push or pull Jack's pants up or down, whichever way he is going at the time. It's no wonder Jack is having trouble going to the bathroom when it takes so much effort just to get there and seated. I don't know if I could do it by myself, all that lifting. Once Jack gets finished, Ben and Jack do it all over again and reverse the whole process to where Jack

... BUT I'M NOT THE SINGER

gets back into the bed. After a bathroom trip this morning, Jack was in a fair amount of pain. I say a fair amount by his actions, his body movements and his general attitude. This morning he was hurting. He cried, he couldn't get comfortable anywhere in his bed, and he just looked like he was hurting. He took a pain pill but between the painful trip to the bathroom, and then not getting any immediate relief from the pain pill, he just became a ball of nerves. He twisted and turned in the bed, we put his feet up with pillows, we put them back down. We talked about staying calm and how that helps with pain management. He cried and screamed. We talked him into moving to the couch and sitting in the recliner so his feet would be up without the pillows. But still the pain persisted. I wrote yesterday that the doctor had given Jack medicine for muscle spasms that go along with this type of surgery. The drug he gave him for the spasms was Valium. Ben and I made the executive decision to give Jack one of the Valium to see if he would calm down and let the pain medication take effect. Within thirty minutes, Jack was calm, pain-free, and humming a tune. He has been pain-free ever since. Oh, the magic of medicines!!

Jack will have something to look forward to when he returns to school. I have signed him up for a program they have at CHS called Best Buddies. Best Buddies is a nation-wide organization that matches special education students to typical students who want to be a buddy to them. I have seen a huge difference in Jack since he started going back to school for all four of his classes and lunch. He would be sad every time I picked him up. I asked him what was wrong and he would sadly say "nothing" but I could tell something wasn't right. I asked him several times about his new classes and if he knew anyone in them and he would tell me no. I asked about lunch each day (there have only been two days of lunch for him) and each day he told me he didn't want to talk about it. Not giving up, I kept at him until he told me that other students would sit with him but he didn't know them. So, for Jack, he has no one to socialize with at lunch. What do you do as a parent? I don't want to make Benny spend his lunchtime away from his friends so he can sit with Jack during lunch. I feel that is not fair to Benny nor to his friends. Benny has a life away from Jack/autism/cancer at school. I had heard about Best Buddies and had filled out the paperwork to get Jack started back at the first of the year but never followed up on it. Until now, when I found out Jack is virtually alone at lunch. I got back in touch with the person in charge of the Best Buddies program at CHS and he got in touch with the young lady who was chosen to be Jack's buddy. This young lady, K., has sent me an email and told me about herself. She sounds like a very mature girl to be only a freshman. She is excited to meet Jack. I so hope this will be the start to Jack making friends again. I look so forward to meeting K. and to watching my son have a friend again.

Dear Lord, thank you for pain-free days, for days of happiness and joy, for healthy bodies and strong minds, for the gift of friendship, for eyes and hearts that see the true soul of others, for parents who teach their children to be more like your Son, for the children who learn this lesson from their parents and the blessings they will receive from opening their eyes and hearts to others with differences, for the blessing of children and the joy of being a parent, and for the love and support of family, friends, and strangers who have given us so much. In His Name, Amen.

JANUARY 12, 2012—Today Jack woke up without pain. About two this afternoon, he spoke up and said it was time for a pill. He also said he wanted an "IB" and it took him a while to explain to me what an "IB" was—he was referring to ibuprofen. Last night when Jack got ready for bed, he was hurting especially his right leg, the leg that has always been affected the most. After Jack took his last pain pill before bed, his pain did not get better. We got him in the bed after he took the pill and one ibuprofen. We had been in bed for about thirty minutes when I hear this tiny, sad sounding, "Mommy" from Jack's bed. Funny how when Jack feels good, he calls me Jill. When he feels bad or sad, he calls me Mommy. I got up, went to his bedside, and he was still in pain. I gave him another ibuprofen, and within thirty minutes he was comfortable and asleep. What was ibuprofen last night turned into an "IB" today. Once Jack got comfortable around two this afternoon after his pain pill and "IB," he quietly slipped into an afternoon nap.

Dear Lord, thank you for the promise of spring with its warmth and new beginnings, for healthy bodies and strong minds, for the gift of children, for ears to hear our children say "Mommy," for the blessing of humor and the sound of laughter, for seasons in life when we need the presence of others and the seasons when they need our presence in their lives, and for the love and support of family, friends, and strangers who teach us so much about Your love and grace. In Jesus' Name, Amen.

JANUARY 17, 2012—This weekend was the first time Jack took a shower and not a bed-bath since his surgery. And it was so much fun... haha. At first, he told us "NO WAY" was he going to get up and move to the bathroom. Then it was

... BUT I'M NOT THE SINGER

"NO WAY" was he going to put rubber things on his casts. "NO WAY" was he going to stand up in his casts and get into the shower. (I write "NO WAY" in big letters because he was screaming it!) He also told me he was not going to stand up and walk on his casts to go to the bathroom for his shower. I think his words were, "I'M NOT STANDING UP AND YOU CAN'T MAKE ME." But I have learned if you just ignore him and let a little time pass, he will soon realize he is in no position to fight. Ben and I got his walker, helped him up and onto his feet, and after a few blood curdling screams, he stood on his own while holding on to the walker. We asked him to walk to the bathroom and you would have thought we had just asked him to walk across hot coals. He screamed, he made strange noises, he panted, he made faces, but he got to the bathroom without incident. Then we had to get him in the shower. Oh joy. Before we even got him to the bathroom, I had put up a shower curtain on the door frame of the walk-in shower. I didn't have shower curtain rings so I rigged up the curtain with shoe strings. Hey, don't laugh...it worked well. We got Jack in the bathroom, seated him on my bathroom stool. We then had to put the rubber covers on his casts. The rubber covers are a rubber bag with an opening in the top that has a stretchy elastic material that fits snug around the leg above the casts to keep the water from getting inside. You can't put them on before Jack takes off his clothes or the rubber material will make taking his pants off very hard. Here was poor Jack, naked, cold and shivering, waiting for me and Ben to get these wild looking rubber things on and over his casts. It took a while. We got the water warm before he got in the shower. Once the water is warm, Jack stood up while we held on to him, turned around so his backside is going into the shower first, and he slowly slid his legs backwards to the shower entrance. We had his shower seat in place facing outward into the bathroom, and we guided his bottom to the seat. Once Jack was seated, we closed the shower curtain pulling it down so I can see where to cut it so Jack's legs can be outside the shower and water will not get on the casts. We then propped his feet and casts up on my bathroom stool outside the shower curtain. Now you are thinking to yourself, if the casts are covered in watertight bags, why do you have to keep his legs outside the shower? Because Jack's autistic mind wants it that way. He was too afraid he would get his cast's wet and if it makes him a little more comfortable about taking a shower, who really cares. We don't. As of today, we have showered him twice. Each time there was screaming and lots of faces but at least he is clean and smelling fresh.

Dear Lord, thank you for the storms of change, for the technology that keeps us safe during the storms, for giving some people the ability to see others

MY NAME IS JACK JOHNSON...

as important and special when others cannot, for the ability to walk and run, to see and hear, to feel another person's touch, for the gift of children and the opportunity to watch them grow, for healthy bodies and strong minds, and for the love and support of family, friends, and strangers. Amen.

JANUARY 19, 2012—I have yet another story about Jack. We were watching the news the other night while I was cooking dinner. Jack was watching the news on the TV and his computer at the same time. A story came on about a wreck that had happened on a particular road. The newscast showed a picture of the road—a two-lane road with no houses in the picture, just farmland on both sides. Jack said, "Mom, is this the road Eli (his cousin) lives on?" I looked up and saw the road and told Jack that I didn't think so. He then told me he knows that road from somewhere. The newscast then said the road was Holly Tree Gap Road. About this time, Ben walked in and Jack told him that there was a wreck on a road that he remembered. I told Ben it was Holly Tree Gap Road and Ben said he and Jack had just ridden there on their last car ride together. Jack then brought up the picture of the road on his computer from the TV station's website. When Jack heard Ben say this, he said, "I knew I had seen that road because I recognized the poles!" Jack remembered the road not by the road itself, but by the electric poles!! I am amazed he can recognize a road by its electric poles but doesn't have any motivation to walk again. Living life with autism...such a strange world to me.

Dear Lord, thank you for the blessing of communication—how we can tell others our wants and needs, for ears to hear that same communication, for the gift of children even when they are not their easiest, for healthy bodies and strong minds, for the will to live the life we have been given, for the support and love of family, friends, and strangers, and for the promise of a place with You with no pain and suffering. In Jesus' Name, Amen.

JANUARY 20, 2012—I wrote an email to Jack's special ed teacher about his unhappiness regarding school. From what little feedback I had gotten from Jack, he is depressed over the cafeteria situation. I think eating alone was not what Jack had in his mind for his time at lunch. And who can blame him? Who wants to eat by themselves every day when you are used to having people around you 24/7 like Jack has for many years and especially in the last year and a half? She wrote me back and told me she would look into it. And in the mean-time, Jack got up, ate his breakfast yogurt, washed up, got dressed, and was ready to go to school with a whole different schedule than what he was used to. And remem-

... BUT I'M NOT THE SINGER

ber, Jack is only going to third, fourth, fifth, and sixth periods every day, not a regular schedule like every other student. Before we left the house, we got an email from the person in charge of the Best Buddies at CHS saying that the special ed teacher had gotten in touch with him and that he would have Jack's new Buddy come and meet Jack during his lunch break. Also, he shared with us an upcoming kickball game the Best Buddies are going to next Friday during school. (Of course, Jack cannot play kickball but he could go and cheer on the players.) On the way to school, I told Jack this, hoping it would give him something to look forward to. I silently said a prayer to God to watch over Jack and let things go well for him and his Buddy. Jack deserves it! Later, I went to pick him up, and when the assistant wheeled him into the room, Jack excitedly said, "I met my Buddy, and we had lunch together, and another student came and sat with us, and I liked my Buddy," and... and... and! I haven't seen him that excited in quite some time! He had a huge smile, lots to say and share, and was more animated and alive than what he has been. He had eaten all his lunch and felt good. We talked a lot about his new Buddy; what she was like, what she likes to do, what she looks like, and talked about the other student that sat with them too. Jack had so much to say and was so proud to share all their stories. It was hard for me not to cry. You have no clue how long it has been for him to share something cool with us that has happened to him. Something like what has happened while we weren't around or something he has done by himself. We have all been "together" since before his diagnosis, and I have wondered several times if he was going to be dependent on Ben and especially me since I was the one who took him back and forth to the hospital for all those months. But today I saw the old Jack, the one that I remember seeing walking down the halls talking to his friends from his social skills class. The one the teachers at PGS worried about when they suspected he had a crush on a girl because he was repeating the words to a song that he had heard titled, "Sexy Chick." I haven't seen him in so long—it was a huge treat for me. I got to see the child I worried we had lost and that was a tremendous and much-needed blessing.

Dear Lord, thank you for the blessing of children, for every day we have with them, for the opportunity to see them become the people they were meant to be, for healthy bodies and strong minds, for all the blessing we are given from You, for angels on earth and in heaven, for the support of family, friends, and strangers who help us get through the good times and the bad, and for the promise of that special place where there is no pain and suffering for any of Your children. In His Name, Amen.

MY NAME IS JACK JOHNSON...

JANUARY 25, 2012—Jack is loving having a friend to eat lunch with every day. When I pick him up from school, he is bubbly and full of things to say. Not the same kid I was picking up who would have his head hanging down and had nothing to say at all. He is walking better with his walker. Today I stopped him and asked him to let go of the walker and see how his balance was. After screaming at Ben and me, he did let go and held on to us, but he felt more stable with his balance than he has in some time. He is walking more and more with his feet pointing forward, not east and west, and with his feet flat on the ground. Just watching him walk makes me feel better. I talked to him this morning on the way to school about trying every day to stand on his own without the support of the walker or one of us. We need to see how well he can do without any support at all. He said he would try. He hasn't complained about his stomach hurting in a while and ate well for dinner last night. Showers are becoming old hat with him now knowing what to expect. His hair is growing back a little quicker now, and its texture is getting softer than it has since before his tumor surgery.

Dear Lord, thank you for the tiny flower buds peeking out from the ground, for the ability to hear thunder during the night, for the comfort of a big bed, for the need to be with the ones we love when we are afraid, for healthy, strong bodies, for friends to spend time with, and for the love and support of family, friends and strangers. Amen.

JANUARY 26, 2012—Today we had Jack fitted for a tux for next weekend's Best Buddies Prom. I think I am more excited than he is. Ben and I had wondered if tux pants would fit over Jack's casts and they do so he will be in full tux gear. I know I am going to cry when I see him all dressed up. Jack did better than I ever dreamed he would getting fitted for the tux. It even amazes me how far he has come in such a short time. Every day when I pick him up at school he has something new to tell me about his time with his Best Buddy and at school in general. He has been visiting other classes during his Health and Wellness Class period—aka PE class. The PE teacher, the special ed teacher and myself thought that letting Jack learn the ropes about getting himself around in his wheelchair during his PE/Health and Wellness class time would be good for him. It gives him the freedom to visit the other special education classrooms where he knows other kids. Therefore, he has had lots of stories to tell me about his adventures in wheelchair visiting. He also tells me stories about what he and his Best Buddy, K., have talked about at lunch. The other day he was sharing things they had talked about and it seemed to

...BUT I'M NOT THE SINGER

me by what he was saying that she was asking him lots of questions and he was answering but he wasn't asking her any in return. Ben and I talked to him about asking her questions to find out information about her likes and dislikes and to see what they had in common. We gave Jack several questions to ask her the next day at lunch. Surprisingly, he remembered the questions, asked, and found out some new things about her. Tomorrow Jack is going on his first field trip this year. The Best Buddy program is going to Ravenwood High School and play in a kickball game. Jack will leave school, get on a bus to Ravenwood, and play either Ravenwood's Best Buddies team or other teams from the school system. I'm not sure which one. He is excited about getting to go even though he won't be playing kickball, just watching. He was telling us that when he was at Poplar Grove and they would play kickball in PE, he would be the roller of the ball and that he had a mean roll. I don't know if that is true but he at least thinks he had a mean roll. I hope he has a great day watching kickball and being with his peers.

Dear God, thank you for days without sickness and pain, for watching our children grow and blossom into adults, for smiles of joy on the face of a loved one, for the flower buds telling us spring is near, for friends to spend time with, for the love and support of so many during the past two years, and for Your help and guidance as You walk with us daily in our lives. In Jesus' Name, Amen.

JANUARY 29, 2012—I received a text from Jack's previous special education teacher Friday: Jack was pitching for the Centennial Best Buddies team! He had told me he had a "mean roll" but sometimes Jack says things that turn out to be not true because of his view of the world around him. Now remember—Jack was sitting in a wheelchair while pitching... with casts on both feet... with a scar in the back of his head from brain surgery! I must confess I have been so scared that something will happen to Jack. I broke into a sweat thinking about all the germs that were on that kickball every time he touched it. But I must take a deep breath and relax and let Jack do what he wants to do (of course within limits) and let God do the rest. I'm not saying God will put up an invisible force field to protect Jack, I am saying that God wants me to see that Jack is a teenager first and foremost and that Jack needs to live his life the best he can. I can't live it for Jack or smother him to protect him from the world. He ought to be himself. So, there was Jack, sitting in his wheelchair, pitching a kickball with who knows what kind of germs on it, in the middle of a school gymnasium packed with the whole Ravenwood High School student body (around two thousand kids with all kinds of germs too) playing his little

MY NAME IS JACK JOHNSON...

heart out on a sports team! He has always told us that "sports are not my forte!" I was nowhere near him and he was having the time of his life! With every text I received, I cried a little bit more. I cried for the fact that the kid pitching for the Centennial team was my son who I have held when he felt so bad he couldn't hold his head up, who at one time we didn't really know how much time we still had with him, who has been through the toughest fight any child or adult faces when they face the cancer beast. I cried because that same child has stepped so far out of his comfort zone pitching a sports ball from his wheelchair in front of so many people who he doesn't know. I cried too because all those other students watching him have no clue that the Centennial Best Buddies kickball pitcher is not just a kid with special needs, he is the strongest person I have ever met with the soul of a true warrior. There are not many children who walk the journey of fighting cancer, much less one who already is challenged with special needs. And, of course, I cried out of pure joy and pride for the young man he was today. The first game was won by the Ravenwood Best Buddies but the second game was Centennial's. Two students on the team were awarded MVP awards and one of those was our own Jack Johnson. He even caught a ball while pitching and got an out as well. He is starting to become his own person and live his life the way he sees fit. And I'm slowly learning how to let go a little at a time, a little more each day.

Last Thursday night, I had cooked oven baked crispy chicken, one of my family's favorites. While I was cooking, Mia, Jack's favorite cat, decided she liked the smell of the chicken and got up on our kitchen bar to find some. This is a big no-no in my house; the cats are never allowed on the kitchen countertops. I told her to get down, and Ben sprayed her with water. Jack was so mad at us for getting on to Mia. He just went on and on about how mean we both were. So, in my most loving yet most sneaky 'parenting,' I devised a plan to show why we don't want cats on our kitchen countertops. I got Jack's plate of dinner ready, but just before I took it to him, I picked up one piece of chicken that I had already cut up for him and then took the tiniest bite out of that piece of chicken. I put it on the side of Jack's plate and took the plate to him. When I put it down on his eating table at the couch, I told him that the piece of chicken on the side of his plate with the bite out of it was the piece of chicken Mia had taken a bite out of since she had been on our countertops checking out our dinner. I told him since he was upset that Ben and I had stopped Mia from eating our dinner, then he wouldn't mind eating after Mia, but I didn't want to. The look on his face was priceless. He had no words, but you could almost see the wheels turning in his brain, connecting the dots of... if the cat gets up on our countertops... where our food is... and she gets our food... and we don't want to eat after the cats have eaten some of our food...! Needless to say, he didn't want to eat the chicken that the cat had eaten and made me take it away. I told him that was why we made the cat get off the countertop where our food was and that we will continue to keep all cats off our countertops. He agreed, and I ate the bite of "cat-eaten" chicken on my way back into the kitchen. Sometimes parenting is delicious!

Dear God, thank you for strong minds and healthy bodies, for giving us the courage and drive to step out of our box, for the gift of children, for time spent with the ones we love, for our pets and the unconditional love they share with us, for the buds of spring flowers, and for the love and support of family, friends, and strangers. In His Holy Name, Amen.

CHAPTER 32

FEBRUARY 1, 2012—Jack went to school on Monday, and his Best Buddy didn't come to school, so she wasn't there for lunch. Jack was brokenhearted. He told me he almost cried and he almost cried when he told me this. So, he had to eat lunch by himself. I understand these days are going to happen when the Best Buddy is not at school, but my son needs a backup plan. I told him if it happened again to pack up his lunch—he takes his lunch from home every day—and take it to the special education room and ask if he can eat lunch in there. If this doesn't work, I will call an IEP—an official meeting with Jack's teachers and the school administration—and we can formally have it put in writing what needs to be done to help Jack out when he has no one to eat lunch with him. My child deserves to be happy in school like any other kid, and if he is not happy and is stressed out, something needs to be done, and the situation needs correcting. The next day his Buddy was back at school, and everything was OK for him. I still think it's important that having another person there with Jack during lunch makes such a difference to him.

Dear Lord, thank you for the promise of eternal life, for the time we have with loved ones here on earth, for the blessing of children and the opportunity to watch them grow, for every day we live with healthy bodies and strong minds, for friends who ride through life with us, for the technology that lights our homes, for hope, faith and love, and for the support and love of family, friends, and strangers who continue to bless us by just being there when we need them most. In His Holy Name, Amen.

FEBRUARY 5, 2012—Jack was so handsome and mature looking in his tux for the Best Buddies Prom Friday night. He really did not like having his picture taken so many times by me. Jack thinks if you say you want to get a picture of him, you want one picture not the twenty or so I always take. We took him to school so he could ride the bus with the other students going to the prom. I think there were only five or six special needs kids who went and

...BUT I'M NOT THE SINGER

2012 Jack, with both feet in casts and with his walker, dressed to attend the Best Buddies Prom

the rest of the group were typical students who are in the Best Buddies program whose best buddy didn't go to the prom. But since it was a prom/party for the Best Buddies program, they went anyway, which was fine because Jack and the rest of the special kids got lots of buddy time. We arrived at the Vanderbilt Marriott, the bus unloaded, and we were directed to the prom. If I had to guess I would say there were around two hundred-plus kids there. There were kids of all shapes, ages, sizes, and abilities all there to have fun. They had food, music and dancing, and lots of smiles everywhere. I love these kids. They don't care what others think and they know how to have fun. You can't help but smile at their carefree attitudes. The girls were all dressed up and the boys had on suits or tuxes. When they arrived, they got to walk the red carpet and have their pictures made. K. pushed Jack down the red carpet. Ben and I went with the rest of the parents to the Parents VIP Lounge where the music wasn't so loud and we could have a conversation. We met up with some other parents whose child had had social skills class with Jack a few years back. We sat around enjoying talking about our children and sharing stories. I went to check on Jack at intervals. One of the chaperones came not too long after one of my checking trips and told me that Jack wanted to go home, not a surprise to us. We said our goodbyes and left the prom one hour before it was over. Not only did Jack wear a tux, we also bought him a corsage to give to K. because I wanted Jack to have the prom experience.

MY NAME IS JACK JOHNSON...

Dear Lord, thank you for the ability to enjoy life, for healthy bodies and strong minds, for parents who instill in their children a love for all no matter their abilities, for children who do not see the outside of a person but look inside of others, for the pleasure we feel as we watch our children grow up, for time spent with our loved ones, and for the love and support of family, friends, and strangers. Amen.

FEBRUARY 13, 2012—Jack is blossoming every day. His attitude has gotten so much better since he has found a friend. He has become more and more outgoing, the same way he was before cancer. Benny comes home sharing how kids on his football and lacrosse teams are now coming up to him and telling stories about Jack because they are in class with Jack. The last story was how Jack was teaching the class in geometry. Today I asked Jack if he taught the class again today and he said he did teach a problem for homework in class today. He went on to say that he gets on to the students who don't answer the question correctly. I am just glad that Jack feels so good and that he is enjoying his time in school.

Dear Lord, thank you for time with loved ones, for days filled with happiness and time spent making memories, for hearing our prayers of need and thanks, for healthy bodies and strong minds, for days without pain and sorrow, for the gift of children, for another birthday, and for the support and love of so many who walk beside us through this journey. Amen.

FEBRUARY 22, 2012—Yesterday was doctor day. We arrived at the Children's Hospital, valeted the van, and went to the fourth floor, Jack's orthopedic doctor's floor. The front desk lady says, "Dr. M. is a little behind because he had a surgery this morning that took longer than expected." The lobby was full of people waiting, the hallway was full of people waiting, and a nearby hospital waiting area held the overflow of waiting patients. After our two hours wait, we were finally called back to the cast room, the room where kids go to have casts put on and taken off. Jack had to have both. He got on the bed and the nurse immediately came after his casts with the saw. I explained what they were doing, step by step as she cut and removed them. This was the first time I had seen Jack's surgical wounds from the leg surgery. I was told that he would have a small one-to-three-inch scar on the back of his legs but he has three small incisions instead. They are much smaller than I had thought they would be. The doctor came in, looked at Jack's incisions, we talked briefly about the casts, the braces, and physical therapy. And then he was gone. The

... BUT I'M NOT THE SINGER

brace guy then started his part of the appointment. He marked, measured and fitted Jack for the leg braces. Once he had finished the nurse came back and washed Jack's poor dirty and stinky legs and feet with alcohol. She then started wrapping first with gauzy material, then with cast materials. Dr. M. wants to see Jack about a month after he has had the braces on so we are scheduled to see him on April 4th, the same day we see Jack's oncologist to get the results of our next MRI, which will be on April 3rd.

Jack asked Benny over the weekend to play with him, something I know is below Benny's maturity level. But he took the time and played with Jack for about five hours one day. It made Jack's day to get some one-on-one time with his big brother. I hope it made Benny's day as well. Life in the world of special needs doesn't just affect that person, it affects the family as a whole and individually. I am so very proud of both of my wonderful sons!

Dear Lord, thank you for the opportunity to be parents, to see our children grow and mature, to see them walk in their own lives, for the opportunity to share Your word with them, to watch them practice the things we have taught them, for every day, hour and minute we have with them, and for the life you gave them here with us and the life they will have with You one day. In His Name, Amen.

MARCH 7, 2012—Yeah! The casts are gone. Jack's poor legs and feet are a total mess. One leg and foot were swollen—I don't know from what. His feet and legs are just nasty looking from the lack of muscle mass and the dead skin that is yellow and ghastly. The braces themselves are white. Luckily, his old almost new shoes fit his new braces. Jack showed Ben and me how his big toes do not work anymore. He says he can feel them, but when he tells them to move, they don't. We will see what happens when we try standing him up on his bare feet with no casts or braces. We also talked to him about trying to walk some at school, but he does not like the idea of leaving the safety of his wheelchair. So, I guess Jack will continue to be in a wheelchair at school until his doctor or physical therapist helps him become more independent. Jack also told us on the way home that it was time to have a celebration dinner tonight and that he wanted pizza for his celebration dinner. So, we will be celebrating the demise of the big blue casts and the arrival of the white braces. A baby step in the right direction, we hope!!

Dear Lord, thank you for days to celebrate milestones in life, for the ability to stand, to walk, to see, to hear, and to feel, for healthy bodies and strong minds, for the many colors of spring, for the feel of sunshine on our skin, for the

MY NAME IS JACK JOHNSON...

love between a parent and their children, and for the support and love of family, friends, and strangers. In His Name, Amen.

March 13, 2012—Jack is getting settled into his new braces. Last night I had him walk barefoot behind his walker to the master bathroom. He complained loudly, but I could see his feet. He said it hurt a little in the back of his leg and on the bottom of his feet, but his feet were flat on the ground, and his right ankle did not bend outward. I was pleased even though he was screaming in my ear about how mean I was. The only reason he didn't fire me from being his mother was that he needed a shower and can't get in the shower by himself.

Dear Lord, thank you for the spring weather, for the colors of the blooming flowers, for the opening of the buds on the trees, for the gentle breeze that blows the smell of freshly cut grass, for healthy bodies and strong minds, for days without pain and sorrow, for the beauty of a full moon, for the blessing of children, for time in quiet solitude, and for the love and support of family, friends, and strangers. Amen.

MARCH 26, 2012—I will share that today was the first day in months and months that I saw my youngest son walk without support! He was at physical therapy, and the therapist was holding on to the back of his pants, but Jack was not holding on to anything—no wall, no walker, no one's hand—for support. It was strange to see his hands out in front of him wavering around in mid-air to help with his balance. I am not sure how he felt about the whole thing while it was happening, but later in the car, we talked about how many fun things he will be able to do when he can walk again without any help. I want to keep motivating him with all the fun things to try, so it will keep him actively wanting to get better and walk unassisted. The therapist said the surgery did give Jack more range of motion, but it still isn't in the normal zone.

Dear Lord, thank you for the ability to walk without help, for the power of the mind, for healthy bodies, for time spent with the ones we love, for the spring colors in full bloom, for taking time to think about others who have given us so much, and for family, friends, and strangers who have helped us in this journey. Amen

MARCH 27, 2012—What a strange day Sunday turned out to be. Sunday morning at church, his special friend, Misses Luna, came to our Sunday School classroom to talk to our group about a new program our church is offering and to enlist our help with the program. Jack came with her and sat nicely while

...BUT I'M NOT THE SINGER

Misses Luna spoke. Sometime during her talk, Jack started to jerk in his chair, something he sometimes does when he is in Jack's world and is thinking about something completely different than what is happening around him. He jerked around a little, jerked his head backwards and popped the back of his head into the brick-o-block walls of our class. He said he was OK and put his head down onto the seat of his walker and rested. I was a little concerned because he hit the area where his brain surgery scar is. After church, we checked Jack's head and there was no swelling or any red area where he popped it. He didn't have a headache and he felt great, playing and laughing the whole afternoon away. Since there was a snafu in thawing hamburger meat, we were left with a fast food dinner. Jack chose Arby's, one of his old favorites. After Ben got the food and we were all eating something strange happened. Ben, Benny, and I eat dinner at the kitchen bar and Jack eats at the couch with a hospital rolling dinner table, a yard sale find many years ago. While we were eating, Ben and I heard Jack sneeze. I said, "bless you" and Ben who was the closest to Jack said, "let me get you a tissue." Ben got up, walked the few steps to Jack, and discovered Jack had vomited all in his plate, on the couch, and on himself. Ben said, "Oh my God, he has vomited all over himself." At this point, Jack had not said a word, unlike other times when he has told us things like "I don't feel good" or "something is hurting" or "my tummy hurts." There had been no sign of him feeling bad at all. And even stranger to us, there was no sound of vomiting; no heaving sounds, no sounds of retching. Nothing. There is no reason to think anything other than Jack sneezed. Of course, we all went into action, getting washcloths, cleaning supplies, etc., as Jack continued to vomit—without a complaint, without any sound. Vomit came out of his mouth like lava out of a volcano. By that time, he had not said one word to any of us. Ben ran and got a "puke bucket" as we call them because Jack was still vomiting. Finally, he said "oh no" because it had gotten on his clothes. We got him cleaned up, the couch cleaned, the evidence discarded outside, and started to gather our thoughts. Where the heck did this come from? Why didn't Jack say anything? Why didn't we hear anything besides a sneeze? We asked Jack what happened and if he got sick right after he sneezed or did the sneeze cause him to be sick. Jack told us he never sneezed! Ben and I looked at each other like what the heck?? When we were far enough away from Jack, I asked Ben again (because I'm old and senile) if he heard Jack sneeze and he said the sneeze was why he got up to get Jack a tissue. Jack also said that he didn't feel any pain and didn't feel sick at all. He said it was like his body said that it didn't want that food and it pushed it out. He even said he had a bite in his mouth chewing when the rest of his food came up.

MY NAME IS JACK JOHNSON...

I know this is all gross but we are so confused by this. This has never happened before. Jack has been sick so many times here at home, out in public, at other people's houses, at the hospital and never, ever has he vomited like this. And the not remembering that he sneezed when the rest of us distinctly heard him sneeze. I don't know if the pop on his head at church had anything to do with this or if Jack had a slight seizure. We have no explanation for this from anything previously experienced over the last two years. We are so thankful that his next MRI is scheduled for next week so we can hopefully get some peace of mind. Since then and all of today, Jack has felt fine. No more stomach trouble, no vomiting, no complaints. This is the weirdest thing we have experienced by far through this whole journey. Hopefully we will get some answers next week from the doctor. And, in true Jack form, his response to the whole situation was, "I guess it's not really Good Mood Food!"

Dear Lord, thank you for giving us the blessing of children whether they are special needs or typical, for healthy bodies and strong minds, for the ability to feel something as deep and bonding as love for each other, for days without pain and sorrow, for times of gladness and times of tears, for giving others a strong foundation of goodness and joy, for giving us sight to see that goodness and overlook the bad in others, for the many blessings we all take for granted each day, and for the love and support of family, friends, and strangers who continue to walk with us on this journey of life. In Jesus' Name, Amen.

MARCH 28, 2012—I must share this one...

I picked up Jack today at school and on the way home, we talked about how he had seen his previous special ed teacher today at school. He was telling me about their conversation, and then I remembered that her children went to the Franklin Special School District schools. I said to Jack that I wonder what this teacher was doing with her children since FSSD was on spring break this week and the county school system is not, the system his previous special ed teacher now works for. Jack said he didn't know where her children were and I said back to him that her kids were in MAC, a school system-run Morning and Afternoon Care program for working parents. Jack then said, "You know... I used to think that MAC was when a tractor-trailer truck took you home from school." Think about it... I love this child!!

Dear Lord, thank you for the warm weather, for healthy bodies and strong minds, for the ability to laugh at ourselves, for getting the chance to look at life through someone else's eyes, and for the love and support of family, friends, and strangers. Amen.

... BUT I'M NOT THE SINGER

APRIL 4, 2012—No evidence of disease—the magic words of all cancer parents. We are thrilled. The past two days have been busy with the MRI and two doctor's appointments. I am dragging. Jack is living in autism world right now with the TV going and the computer showing his favorite videos. He has been full of himself for the last two days. Yesterday for MRI day, he was determined to take his favorite-for-now stuffed animal, Tails. Tails is a stuffed animal that comes from one of his video games/TV shows. Tails has recently gone to church with us and so I guess it was only the natural thing for her to want to go to the hospital as well. I type this as if Tails is a living, breathing animal and for Jack she is. You must understand in a strange way Tails is Jack's best friend. When you don't have friends that see life the same as you do, you will find some that do and to Jack that is Tails. Jack and Tails talk to each other: Jack in his regular every day Jack voice and Tails responds with her high-pitched girly voice provided by Jack. I have heard them carry on conversations before. It's like watching a ventriloquist except Jack's mouth moves. So yesterday in true Jack form, Jack and Tails provided the entertainment in the MRI prep and recovery room. All the nurses wanted to know about Tails and Jack was eager to answer all their questions. Wouldn't you be if it was your best friend? Jack had to change his clothes and put on his gown before the MRI, which also meant that he had to take off his shoes, socks, and, of course, his leg braces. Lucky for us, we had our handy dandy rolling box that we have learned from experience helps with keeping all of Jack's stuff out of the way and keeps us from having to tote all his stuff while he is having the procedure. After Jack was in his gown, the nurses came and told us the MRI techs would be coming shortly to get him. Then came the question of what to do with Tails—should she go with him or stay with us? Jack decided Tails would be safer with us. Since we had put all of Jack's clothing, shoes, and leg braces in the rolling box, I said to Jack that I would put Tails in one of his leg braces where she would be safe and comfortable. Tails said in Jack's best high-pitched girl voice, "I'm not getting in that leg brace!" Jack in his Jack voice asked Tails why not. (Jack was lying on the hospital bed while holding Tails who he turned to look at the leg brace and then back to him.) Tails said, "That leg brace smells like crap!" He said, "No it doesn't." She went on, "Sorry, Jack. I don't mean to hurt your feelings but you know it's true!" We could not hold back and the three of us (Benny was with us!) tried to stifle our giggles but couldn't. Jack and Tails seemed unfazed by our laughter. You never know what will come out of his mouth or out of Tails' mouth!

Today while waiting to get called back to see the oncologist, Jack was full of himself again. We had just eaten most of his lunch and ordered dessert. So

MY NAME IS JACK JOHNSON...

not only was his autism in full bloom but he was also sugared up from the Molten Chocolate Cake from his Chili's lunch. While waiting in the lobby, he starts laughing loudly at his iPad game and with his many repeated phrases. There was a baby in the lobby but it didn't cry at all and Jack was OK with it. When the baby was called back, it was laughing and when I said something to Jack about how happy the baby had been he said, "That baby looked like a vampire to me." He didn't say it mean or nasty; he said it in a matter of fact way. I said, "Jack, that baby didn't look like a vampire. It was happy and smiling." He said, "It still looked like a vampire to me." Glad the baby's daddy didn't hear. Jack went back to laughing loudly when I told him to be quiet. He looked at me and points his finger, made an ugly face, and told me to hush. I looked back at him and said, "Time out number one" which means he will be in trouble at home and something—one of his beloved things like the TV or computer—will be put in time out. He made another face and I said, "Time out number two." He then said, "Mmmmmoooooooommmmmm. I hate my parents. Stop bossing me." I told Jack Ben and I could leave and he could do this by himself if he wanted. Jack said, "No. I will only hate you for a little while." Other parents in the waiting room snickered at that statement. Once we were called back by Jack's favorite nurse, MM., he had to have his blood drawn. We had to wait outside the lab for a seat and while waiting Jack's nurse practitioner saw him and ran up to give him a hug. She hugged us too and turned her attention back to Jack. She told him how much she had missed seeing him and how he always makes her laugh. Jack said, "Yes. I AM an entertainer." It was nice to see everyone and good that it was a good news trip. Funny how people in the medical field become like family after you go through a long illness. And it is a sad and crazy thing but you do miss them too.

Dear Lord, thank you for each moment spent with our loved ones, for the blessing of children, for the gift of friendship whether the friends are real or pretend, for surrounding us with doctors and nurses who are blessed with giving hearts, for giving us a rare opportunity to see life through another's eyes, for the ability to love and be loved, and for the love and support of family, friends, and strangers who walk with us on this journey. In Jesus' Name, Amen.

CHAPTER 33

APRIL 9, 2012—Happy 16th Birthday tomorrow, Jack. We love you
   Dear Lord, thank you for every moment we spend with our loved ones, for the blessing of children, for healthy bodies and strong minds, for the ability to love and be loved, for time spent with family and friends, and for the support and love of so many who have continued to follow us on this journey. Amen.

APRIL 16, 2012—We are finally over the Twelve Days of Jack's Birthday. It was fun, he had fun, and we got to spend time with most of our families. He has been full of himself—I don't know if it was just the excitement of it being his birthday or if his autism was just way too big—but he has been a laugh a minute. His first remark was at Benny's lacrosse game. Jack put his head back into my lap (I was sitting one row up and behind him) and I could see that his little black chin hairs have grown back. I said to him, "Jack, we need to cut those chin hairs again" to which he replied, "Nope. Too sexy!" Yesterday, at my sister's house, he told my sister who had made her famous meatloaf recipe that her meatloaf was OK but he liked his mother's meatloaf better. On the way to my sister's house, I commented to Jack why he had left his church pants on to go to my sister's house and not put on something more comfortable. His remark: "Handsomeness!" and a little wave of the hand over his legs. I told him again today on the way to physical therapy that the chin hairs had to go and he protested loudly about how he wanted them to stay. I said that there were not enough of them to look nice and went on to explain that ten chin hairs do not count as a beard. He angrily said that he had more than ten chin hairs, pulled the visor mirror down, and counted them. There were twelve. I was off by two. Twelve chin hairs do not constitute a beard. The chin hairs were removed tonight after much protest. Also, today at physical therapy, he was spreading his own brand of Jack-ness. I can't remember everything and I asked several times where he was getting the things he was saying but he wouldn't tell me. One of his statements was

MY NAME IS JACK JOHNSON...

to his physical therapist; he told her "she smelled like a dead senior citizen's backside." And that was just one of the happy statements he repeated during therapy today. We had a very long and very detailed conversation on the way home about repeating things from TV and video games that do not make sense in certain situations and that are not socially appropriate. He was not happy and told me exactly where the new statements came from—a video game. Last week Benny came home and said that one of his teachers had told him some Jack stories from school that one of Jack's teachers had shared with her. Seems Jack went to school one day and his teacher had a new fresh hair color—red. Jack told her that he didn't like her color choice and that she looked like, "Girls gone wild." The teachers were laughing with each other about what kind of videos we watch here at home since "Girls Gone Wild" is a video of young females who let others film their escapades which consist of risqué poses and topless photos. It took me a while to figure it out but Ben has said before when the female cats in our house fight that they are "girls gone wild" since that is the term used to describe girls with bad behavior. Who would have thought using that term to describe our female fighting cats could have teachers wondering how Jack knows anything about "Girls Gone Wild."?

Dear Lord, thank you for the joy of parenting, for the awesomeness of a child's mind, for the gift of watching each day as a child grows, for healthy bodies and strong minds, for letting us see the humor in life, for the beauty of a sunset and a full moon on a dark night, for faith, love, and hope, and for the support and love of family, friends, and strangers who walk with us on our journey. In His Name, Amen.

MAY 6, 2012—We are so excited to announce that our Jack walked without the help of his walker. Now granted he didn't walk far, and he didn't want to and complained a lot, but he walked, and for that, we are very grateful. I wanted to see if he could, if he would, and it did take a little bribery. There were ugly words (from him, not me) and lots of ugly faces (again from him, not me) but he walked from his bed to our bed in our bedroom, a good twelve-to-fourteen foot. He walks like he did when he first learned how to walk years ago—with his arms and hands out in the air to the sides for balance. The first time across the floor and after he landed on our bed, he had the biggest smile on his face. Made my heart melt. He was proud of himself. To say Ben and I are overjoyed is an understatement, but we are still guarded. We are just starting this long road to recovery, and this is one of the biggest steps physically that Jack will have to make. So, we take baby steps and start walking across the bedroom and add steps wherever we can.

Dear God, thank you for healthy bodies and strong minds, for the ability to walk and run, for giving us loving parents who we miss once they have left us, for the blessing of children, for the joy of a smile, for days without pain and suffering, for every moment we have with the ones we love and cherish, for the opportunity to study Your word and to come to You in prayer, for the awesomeness of the warmth of the sun and the mystery of a full moon, and for the love and support of family, friends, and strangers who continue to walk with us on our journey of life. In His Name, Amen.

MAY 15, 2012—A milestone day for Jack. Today was the first day Jack did not use the wheelchair at school but instead used his walker. Everyone was surprised and very proud of Jack. One of his assistants said Jack was so proud of himself and enjoyed all the accolades. His classmates, teachers, and assistants were all so excited. Even students in the hallways said things to Jack. He was full of excitement with the way everyone reacted, and he was very excited to get to use a "real desk" since he had been using a lap desk all this time. I asked him if he wanted to take the wheelchair tomorrow just in case he got tired, and he told me "NO." The one assistant we talked directly to said Jack has a problem with turning corners and likes the idea of running into people turning the corner coming from the other way. Sometimes he can use his walker as a battering ram and will have to learn to make his way through crowds without my helpful guidance. But we reached a huge milestone, another step closer to becoming a cancer survivor and a step further away from cancer.

Dear Lord, thank you for the feeling of pride we feel when we have accomplished a hard-fought goal, for days without pain and tears, for healthy bodies and strong minds, for the blessed sunshine, for the unconditional gift of love, and for the support and love of so many who continue to follow Jack and our family on our journey. In His Name, Amen.

MAY 22, 2012—Jack and I recently rode motorcycles again in the annual Ride for Kids, the motorcycle ride that benefits the Pediatric Brain Tumor Foundation we participated in last year. The pediatric brain tumor survivors are called the Stars and receive all the attention. Jack and I rode with an older gentleman who had a very nice bike and sidecar. Jack rode in the sidecar, and I rode on the back. We met this gentleman's wife who was so sweet to

MY NAME IS JACK JOHNSON...

2012 Benny and Jack

give up her seat so we could ride together. I usually don't think of seventy-something folks as motorcycle riders, but they do and enjoy riding all the time. Funny—some retirees see the country in an RV while some see it from a motorcycle seat or sidecar. Our ride lasted an hour and a half, traveling through some of Williamson and Maury counties' beautiful countryside. After the ride was over, all the participants gathered under a tent for lunch, presentations, and door prizes, including new motorcycle giveaway. The Stars were brought up on stage and got the opportunity to share their stories. There were three Stars this year including Jack. I went up on stage with him because I never know what will happen and try to prepare for most any situation. He answered most of the questions that were asked of him. We had a wonderful day!

Dear Lord, thank you for days with smiles and happiness, for guidance in all the decisions we make in life, for love between a parent and child, for time we get with our loved ones, for the ability to hear laughter, for a goodbye hug, and for the love and support of family, friends, and strangers and for the opportunity to give a little something back to them. In His Name, Amen.

... BUT I'M NOT THE SINGER

MAY 30, 2012—Jack is walking WITHOUT his walker!! Jack and I went to Pawpaw Sunday dinner this past Sunday, and Jack used the furniture for stability and not the walker. So, when we got home I didn't bring the walker in the house and left it in the mudroom and told him since he didn't need the walker at Pawpaw's, then he didn't need it here. He has been walking on his own. He is still a little unsteady but gets around better than he has in months. Ben and I did not know if we would ever see this day, so it is such a joy for us to see Jack walking around the house! He does keep his hands up near his chest in an unnatural position, but we are working on that as well. With each step, he builds more and more confidence in himself, his legs, and his balance. He and I walked outside this morning for a little while, and he only grabbed for me once. He does say that if the floor/ground/road are not level, it makes him feel insecure. All of this will take time and effort. We will be working on this every day this summer.

Dear Lord, thank you for healthy bodies and strong minds, for the ability to love and be loved, for days full of memory making and days spent in solitude, for our pets and the unconditional love they give us, for the sunshine and the rain, and for the support and love of family, friends, and strangers and the lessons they have taught us. In Jesus' Name, Amen.

JUNE 5, 2012—Jack and I just got back from physical therapy. His therapist was surprised to see him without his walker. We also went to church where Jack got to walk into the church without his walker. Everyone has been so kind to say something to him. The comments boost his ego and make him try harder. He did well today in therapy, but his therapist and I noticed that he was off. She had to ask him several times to change positions after he finished one activity, something she usually says only once. She commented to me that he acted zoned out. I asked him on the way home why he didn't respond to her when she asked him, and he said he didn't always hear her. This was not a good sign, causing the therapist to mention seizures, something we have suspected he might be having for some time now. If he indeed has them, they are not happening all the time and are the kind of seizures that zone him out. I asked the therapist if what she witnessed concerned her and she said yes because she had never seen him like that before. She asked me how long will it be before he sees his doctor again. His next MRI and his first survivor's clinic appointment are at the end of July and the first of August. I will have to judge if I think that we need to see a doctor sooner.

Sunday after church we went to our favorite meat-and-three restaurant for

MY NAME IS JACK JOHNSON...

lunch. We got our food, everyone started to eat, and while eating Jack froze. He got that funny look on his face and said, "I don't feel so well." Ben got him up and quickly got him to the restroom (thank you, God, for the empty restroom!!), and Jack exploded. As soon as the vomiting stopped, he washed his hands, came back to the table, and started right back eating his lunch where he left off. I asked Jack a few questions about this latest episode today on our way to Nashville. My question: how did you feel before the vomiting occurred? He said he felt nothing different. He said while he was eating he burped and that started the vomiting. He has not felt bad since. In true Jack form, he calls refusing to eat anything after a vomiting episode his new diet.

Speaking of diets, Jack was watching TV the other night when a Nutri-System commercial came on. Whoever the spokesperson was, said, "This was me before Nutri-System, and this is me now." Jack said, "That was me in middle school. I ain't going back to that!!" Such a funny guy!!

Dear Lord, thank you for healthy bodies and strong minds, for the gift of being able to come to You in prayer, for each minute, hour, and day we spend with the ones we love and cherish, for days without pain and sickness, moments of laughter and smiles, and for the support and love of family, friends, and strangers who continue to walk with us on this journey. In Jesus' Name, Amen.

JUNE 12, 2012—I am starting out this entry the same as my last entry: Jack and I just got back from therapy. Except this time, Jack is sitting in time out while I type this. He ran his mouth a little too much, calling other children "snot-nosed brats" so now he has a few minutes to think about saying this statement aloud in public. He is not happy with me now (what's new!) and has had a lot to say before his punishment. He did a great job today in therapy, he just wasn't happy that there were other children around. He let it be known he didn't like them in true Jack form—just say what you think and to heck with anyone who hears it. (The punishment timer went off and I had to go turn it off and let him know he was out of time out. I also repeated my message: just because you think something, doesn't mean you must tell everyone!) Today when we first got to the therapy center, I grabbed with my left hand one of those on the wall hand sanitizers that squirts out foamy sanitizer. I pulled on the nozzle, it was near empty, and it squirted foamy sanitizer all over me, Jack, and the nearby couch, but not much in my hand. Jack had it in his hair, on his shirt, and saw that it was all over the couch beside him. He was not happy about the thing exploding foam all over us and talked quite a bit about it until he started in on the "snot-nosed brats." Who knew going to therapy would be so eventful. The therapist also commented on another episode of staring that Jack did during therapy. She is concerned about these episodes—the one today and the ones last trip—being seizures. I am too. I am also concerned because Jack has lost twelve pounds since his last MRI on April 4th. And I am concerned that he vomited again this past Sunday, making two Sundays in a row that he has vomited. I have been so concerned that I called the oncologist's office and Jack has an appointment tomorrow at 10:30am to see the oncologist and a nutritionist. I am so torn about talking about the seizures. On one side, my mother's intuition is screaming in my brain that these episodes are indeed seizures. Then there is the other side, the doubting side, that wants to wait and see what happens. But that could be the wrong thing to do. If these are in fact seizures, they could get worse and become more problematic. And if that happened, would he be in the shower, in a pool, with someone else, in school or at church when he had a big one? That thought gets my mother's intuition screaming even louder. I don't want him to have seizures at all and don't like the idea of even thinking about them. But I can't just ignore them. Sometimes I wonder about my sanity—do I know too much about the side effects that could affect him and am I just seeing something out of fear? I guess I don't want to be too cautious nor do I want to be not cautious enough when it comes to these episodes/possible seizures. The vomiting episode this past Sunday came on with shivering and dizziness. I don't know enough about seizures to know whether shivering, dizziness, and vomiting come with them or not. Trying to get Jack to tell me things is not the easiest either. He gets mad when I ask him too many questions. And you can't ask him vague questions because he can't answer them. I asked him if he felt funny before he got sick Sunday and he said no. Later, when I asked him about being dizzy before he went to the bathroom to get sick, he said first he got the shivers, then he felt sick and when he stood up to go to the bathroom, he felt dizzy. That was the first time he mentioned the shivers.

Dear Lord, thank you for healthy bodies and strong minds, for the gift of communication, for the time spent with the ones we love here on Earth and for the promise of seeing them again one day, for being able to love each other when things are tough, for the feeling of joy watching a child enjoy the pleasures of life, for the beautiful sound of a child's laughter, for the feel of their hand in ours, for the blessing of friendship, and for the support and love of family, friends, and strangers. Amen.

JUNE 14, 2012—We went to the oncologist office yesterday. Everyone was

MY NAME IS JACK JOHNSON...

so elated to see Jack walking without a walker or being in a wheelchair. And they liked the head full of hair and the mustache. He glowed more and more with each compliment. First, we saw the dietitian. We talked about Jack's lack of appetite, his autism, how autism affects Jack's eating habits, what he eats every day, the quantity of food he eats, and his weight loss. Jack did weigh two pounds more than he did last week but he had his shoes and braces on his legs and was fully clothed. She also would like to weigh him again in two weeks, and if he has lost more weight, we will put him back on appetite stimulants. Just when we thought we had gotten rid of all the medicines, we could have to start back on appetite stimulants. Have I ever told you how bad I HATE CANCER??

We also saw the oncologist. I told him about the vomiting and the seizure type episodes. The oncologist will get Jack an appointment to see his neurologist. He did say if the vomiting continued and Jack said he was dizzy along with the vomiting, he would move up the MRI to an earlier date. He said the word "recurrence" several times. Every time he said it, I wanted to act like a child, put my fingers in my ears and loudly said "Blah, blah, blah. I can't hear you!!" I hate that word. Jack will continue anti-nausea medicines until we have the next MRI. Now we wait to hear when our neurologist appointment will be scheduled. I received Jack's report card a few weeks ago. My heart broke when I saw he failed two of his exams. He would cry if he knew so I will not tell him. Even though he failed them, he still had good grades the rest of the year, so the failed exams dropped his grades only a little. The failed exams tell me several things—either he was not properly prepared for the exams or he is having trouble with memory problems—yet another side effect of all the treatments. One can be fixed; the other cannot. I am so bummed by this. This will come up in his next IEP, and it will be addressed either way. I can't remember a time when Jack failed a test this bad.

Dear God, thank you for patience, for the look of pride on a child's face, for the caring spirit of doctors and nurses, for time with the ones we love whether it is a short while or many years, for the gift of coming to You in prayer with our thoughts and needs, for healthy bodies and strong minds, for the blessing of humor so we can laugh at this world and ourselves, and for the support and love of family, friends, and strangers. Amen.

JUNE 22, 2012—Jack and I just got back from our second physical therapy session of the week. He has broken in yet another therapist this week. She had been watching him during some of his previous sessions with his other

... BUT I'M NOT THE SINGER

therapist and knew a little about him from her observations. This week he has been milder than usual and surprised her. He also surprised me today during therapy when he came to the bench I was sitting on to take a rest and get a drink of water: he smelled awful. When I asked him why he stunk, he said his deodorant was out, so he didn't put any on!! Oh, my goodness! Really? Like there's not three other people who live in this house that all use deodorant every day that would have shared theirs with him? His dad's deodorant was in the drawer right beside Jack's, but he didn't use any because he was out!?? And to not put deodorant on when you are going to physical therapy?

We also had our trip to the neurologist. She looked at Jack, poked, prodded, listened, and felt all the regular places. She tested his reflexes and noted that his right leg does not have much of a reflex. She performed all the neurological tests that he has had so many times in the last two years and that her associate had just done to Jack fifteen minutes before. I explained Jack's episodes that we had witnessed, told her about his two failed exams at school, and his ongoing vomiting issues. She didn't seem too worried (I have seen worried doctors before!!) about any of these but does want to do an EEG on him to check for seizures. The EEG is scheduled for July 16th, will be performed here in Franklin, and Jack will have to fall asleep for it. We will have to keep him awake the night before so he will be able to fall asleep once at the EEG center easily. She went on to explain that the EEG could show that Jack is having seizures but that sometimes they do not register if at the time of the EEG he doesn't have any at all. So, the EEG will tell us if he has abnormal brain activity at that time, but if he has one the next day, it will not register. Yet again another strange explanation from the medical world. Jack will have the EEG anyway, and we will see what, if anything, shows up and go from there.

Dear Lord, thank you for the blessings we have been given and the ability to see them, for each minute, hour and day we have with our loved ones, for the ability to laugh at life when things don't go our way, for nurses and doctors who care for us in time of need, for the feel of sand between our toes, for the sound of ocean waves, for memories made in good times and bad times, for healthy bodies and strong minds, and for family, friends, and strangers who continue to amaze us with their love and support. Amen.

JULY 2, 2012—We returned from a quick trip to the beach. It was nice to see the ocean. I love the ocean, listening to the waves, the smell of it, the wonderful color of it.

Yesterday, we went to church without Ben because he had to work. Jack

MY NAME IS JACK JOHNSON...

got to check his Exit signs. After church, we picked up a take-out lunch. During lunch, Jack said "Uh, oh" and when I looked he was puking his lunch up into his plate. Benny and I went into our vomit mode, finding a vomit bucket, wet rags, and clean up materials. Yet again, out of nowhere, Jack vomited. No reason, no warning, no upset stomach beforehand. I asked him how it happened, a question he hates to answer, and he said he felt funny in the head, then had lots of saliva in his mouth and his food came up. I asked about the funny in the head feeling, asking several different questions about what it felt like—dizzy, swimmy, funny eye movements—but he said he didn't have the words to describe the feeling he had in his head before he vomited. Helpless doesn't even come close to how this makes me feel. Jack had complained about a "hurting" stomach on Friday and after I gave him a Benadryl, he felt better. He regularly takes three anti-nausea pills a day and when you include the Benadryl, that was four anti-nausea pills for that day. I don't like this at all. I don't like the fact that he has vomited more in the last few weeks since April 4th than he has in a long time. I don't like the fact that he gets sick at all. I don't like the fact that I can't "fix" this. I am so proud of the fact that Jack is walking so much better than he was before. I like the fact that people notice and say things about it to him and to us. But just because you see him walking better doesn't mean we are on the road to recovery. I am not sure now if you truly ever recover from this.

Dear Lord, thank you for the ocean with its ever-changing waves and vivid blue color, for healthy bodies and strong minds, for people who find us in need and give us a helping hand, for time spent with the ones we love, for the gift of coming to You in prayer, and for the love and support of so many wonderful people that continue to walk with us in our journey. Amen.

JULY 17, 2012—Yesterday was Jack's EEG. I must say he was the best patient he has been in a long time. Our appointment was at 1pm, and we were home by 2:30 pm. Shocking. We are so proud of him for being, yet again, a big trooper letting people do what they need to do and not getting upset. As for the results, we don't know anything as of today. We should hear something sometime this week, but you know how that goes.

Dear Lord, thank you for the time we have with our loved ones here on earth, for the blessing of our children, for the opportunity to love and parent them whether they are healthy, disabled, or sick, for days without pain and sickness, for healthy bodies and strong minds, for the promise of a place with You where there will be no pain and sorrow, and for the love and support of family,

... BUT I'M NOT THE SINGER

friends, and strangers who follow us on this journey. Amen.

JULY 26, 2012—I heard back from the neurologist's office about the EEG results—Jack's was normal. Hallelujah! We are all so happy. We are scheduled to see the neurologist in August and will talk about the results in detail then, but for right now we are happy with normal. Jack had his first appointment for a much-needed tooth cleaning yesterday, and to our surprise and the dentist's, Jack's teeth are in remarkably great condition. Can I hear another Hallelujah!

Dear Lord, thank you for the gift of air conditioning on these very hot days of summer, for giving us the blessing of a sense of humor, for healthy bodies and strong minds, for giving us the blessing of children, for the wonder of the human brain, for doctors and nurses who take care of our bodies and minds, for the blessing of knowledge and the ability to use it for our own good, for faith, hope and love, and for sending Your only son so we might have everlasting life. In His Name, Amen.

CHAPTER 34

AUGUST 1, 2012—I don't know how to start.......

Jack's MRI results show a new tumor in his spine. This tumor is in his spinal cord area, is one centimeter in size, is inoperable, and cannot be biopsied. The radiologist who read the MRI believes it is a recurrence of medulloblastoma; Jack's neurosurgeon believes radiation could cause it. If you remember, we had something show up on a previous MRI that after two biopsies turned out to be something caused by radiation. This one is different. That first one was in one of Jack's bones in his spine. This one is in the spinal column; the place spinal recurrence would be. We are waiting for Jack to be scheduled for a spinal tap that will let us know if there are indeed cancer cells in his spinal fluid. Hopefully, this will be scheduled tomorrow or Friday so Jack's case can be presented to the hospital's Tumor Board on Monday morning. Ben and I are worried too about the tumor's location. If there are no cancer cells in the fluid, with this tumor being where it is, we are afraid it could be dangerous as well if it continues to grow.

How are we? Coping as best we can. I am the walking wounded, on the verge of tears. Ben wants to hit something. The nurse practitioner who gave us the news today told us with Jack in the room, and he almost freaked out. He loudly asked her if his wooly booger had come back. He was near tears. Bless his heart; I am not sure how much he truly understands. If he had cried, I am not sure I could have held back the dam of tears and sorrow I have put up myself. How ironic... we stopped by the school and picked up Jack's class schedule this morning. We were full of anticipation and trying to get Jack excited about a future at school. Can we say rug pulled out from under us? I have continued to keep up with the latest discoveries in the medical studies on medulloblastoma and know they are discovering new information every day to fight this type of cancer. It gives me hope.

Dear Lord, thank you for healthy bodies and strong minds, for the blessing of children, for bad days that make you appreciate the good days, for a small

... BUT I'M NOT THE SINGER

piece of hope that we can hold onto in times of need, for faith that You will always be with us, and for the support, love, and prayers of family, friends, and strangers who continue to follow our journey. In His Name, Amen.

AUGUST 4, 2012—Jack had his lumbar puncture (aka: spinal tap) yesterday. We arrived at VCH at 9 am, our appointed time to start the prep work. We went to the oncology clinic, and Jack got the pleasure of seeing his favorite nurse, MM. She had not been there last Monday before his MRI, so he was happy and relieved to see her. She was just as happy to see him and me and Ben too. And in true Jack form, he guided her through the placing of his IV letting her know where he wanted it in his arm and how much "freezy spray" she needed to apply. After the IV was taped and covered just the way Jack likes it and after our MM hugs—mine and Ben, not Jack's...only his lean in hug—we went to the third floor. We signed Jack in and received our matching hospital bracelets. We were called back and placed in a prep pod—my name for it, not the hospital's—which is a room with four-bed stations, each station having its own hospital room-like area and divided by curtains. Jack had his vital signs checked, was hooked up to monitors, and received his favorite thing—a warmed blanket to snuggle up in while we wait. And wait. And wait. Our pod was near the doorway, so we watched people as they walked past us, coming in and out of surgery and other pods. For us, it's a parade of familiar faces, faces we have seen many times in the last few years. Jack had his iPad and was enjoying his latest YouTube find: mad cats. Yes, real live cats who are mad, screaming, hissing, and clawing while their owners film them. If Jack is happy and he is not annoying the people around us, I am OK with it.

Finally, at 11am, the nurses and the nurse practitioner that specialize in lumbar punctures came and got us. They took us back to the room that is specified as the lumbar puncture room and started getting Jack ready. Of course, he was happy they started and he was not waiting anymore. As the nurse got the anesthesia ready, Jack asked for it. Yes, asked for it. And, of course, he memorized each step of getting put to sleep and knows it is time to get the "sleepy medicine." All the nurses in the room were becoming Jack fans, seeing how easy he can be and how compliant he is when it comes to medical procedures. I am sure they see a lot of screaming and tantrums and having a kiddo telling them what they should be doing and what needs to be done next is kind of refreshing. We were with him when the sleepy medicine did its job and were sent to a nearby waiting room where other families of children having minor procedures were waiting as well. The nurse

MY NAME IS JACK JOHNSON...

practitioner came in after 15 minutes to tell us the procedure was over, Jack was in recovery, and they would call us shortly. We waited for two hours and the whole procedure took fifteen minutes! Thirty minutes later we were taken back to recovery, another place we know too well. Our recovery nurse was someone who we have had in the past. She was quirky and funny and remembered Jack's name but said he looked so different than the last time she saw us. It took about fifteen minutes for Jack to be fully awake. We had apple juice nearby; the only thing Jack says helps with the bad taste in his mouth after waking up and the only thing that keeps him from getting sick. Soon he was up and ready to leave. The IV so skillfully inserted by Nurse MM. must come out before we could go home. Jack likes to take any sticky tape off himself, saying only he can control the pain of taking the sticky tape off his skin. He began the slow removal of the tape holding his IV in place with the guidance of Nurse K. First, he pulled on one side of the IV and then he pulled on the other side and before we know it, the tape was off with the IV still attached. Jack pulled his own IV out! He was speechless, his mouth and eyes were opened wide with surprise. We all laughed. He can be so silly. Now we wait for results.

Dear Lord, thank you for happy times spent with the ones we love and cherish, for healthy bodies and strong minds, for all our friends and family whose arms we feel holding us up when we face life's lows, for the blessing of children who You gave to us to love, and for faith and hope—the two things that sustain us through our hardest days. Amen.

AUGUST 8, 2012—Jack's doctor called today. The good news: the results were negative for medulloblastoma in the spinal fluid. HOORAY! We certainly love good news. I can feel the tension leave my body as I type those words. Of course, there is always a but... but we still have something growing in Jack's spinal column that is not supposed to be there. We have an appointment with the doctor tomorrow morning to talk about all of this. I will ask to see the MRI results to have a visual of what we will be talking about. The doctor's secretary—for lack of a better title—also said in our earlier, quick conversation today that we are not out of the woods since we don't know what this thing is and whether it will keep on growing which will not be good. There could be another MRI in a few weeks to check on the growth of the lesion. So, we have good news/not so good news today. Hopefully we will learn more tomorrow and at least have a plan or course of action. As usual, this waiting and wondering has consumed us. Limbo land is a horrible place

... BUT I'M NOT THE SINGER

to be and try to live like nothing is wrong. This journey is filled with gigantic ups and enormously low downs. I can almost feel myself aging with every day we live in this world. I need to admit on a few occasions while saying a prayer, I have prayed, "Dear God, Help!" because I know He already knows our problems and why bore him with all the crazy details when there are so many. Within the past week, Jack has vomited three times, has complained of a backache, and has had two headaches. These have all added to our tension and worry.

The boys and I went to Pawpaw's for Sunday dinner on Sunday. Of course, we adults were all talking about the new lesion, the spinal tap, and the what ifs. Jack was lying on the couch the whole time with his eyes shut, but he told me later that he never went to sleep. I was concerned that he might have overheard something we said that he wouldn't understand. On our way home, Jack told me he needed to talk to me. I told him he could talk to me with Benny there but he said he wanted to talk to me in private. I thought to myself that he had indeed overheard some of our earlier conversation and prepared myself mentally for the upcoming questions. We got home, Benny went upstairs, and I sat with Jack and asked him what was wrong. He said, with the longest face I have seen in a while, "You know my stuffed animal I love so much is really dirty and I think we need to order a new better one." I wanted to give him the biggest hug but thought better about it. We are talking about Jack. All this time, I was thinking he was going to ask me questions about his MRI results and he was worrying over a stuffed animal. I should have known better. I still think like a typical mother when I need to always think in Jack's world. The things that worry us don't always worry people who live in Jack's world and the things that they worry about seem so simple to the rest of us. Last night, I found out that part of the reason he has been so sick was that he has been worrying about the newly ordered holy grail of stuffed animals. Today after vomiting again he told me through tears that he was worried that it won't come. Bless his heart... he has no understanding of commerce. Guess that's my fault. I have tried to show him by taking him shopping with me and explaining the buying and selling of clothes and food. It could be the internet shopping that he is having a hard time with, who knows. But I do know he is making himself physically sick over this. Again, I feel like asking God for help. And school starts Friday. This is the first year for Jack to go full time to school This is also the first year Jack will go without the assistance of the wheelchair or walker. It is going to be a huge adjustment for him just waking up in the

MY NAME IS JACK JOHNSON...

mornings. He will also be riding to school with Benny each morning, something he says bothers him. He says Benny is not trustworthy in his driving. Jack has never ridden with Benny and has nothing to base his feeling on.

Dear Lord, help. In Jesus Name, Amen.

AUGUST 9, 2012—Today was doctor day. Jack's oncologist shared Jack's MRI with us. We saw the lesion/enhancement for ourselves. This thing is sitting right on the spinal cord and as the doctor explained, that is why it cannot be biopsied. From my meager, newly acquired knowledge, the spinal cord, sitting in spinal fluid in the spinal column, runs from the brain all the way down near your tailbone. It gradually gets smaller and ends at the curve of your spine near your tailbone. This new lesion is located at vertebrae T4/T5, thoracic vertebrae numbers four and five. Jack's previous questionable lesion in the vertebrae was at cervical vertebrae number C6. The spinal cord takes up more than half of the space in the spinal column. If the doctors were to try a needle biopsy, even the tiniest needle could damage the spinal cord, not something anyone wants. The doctor went on to say that everyone at the Tumor Board still thinks this could either be radiation effects, the very early stages of recurrence or the very early stages of a new cancer or growth. The only recourse is to wait for six weeks and do another MRI on the spine and look for change. If the lesion has changed or spread to other areas, then it is probably a recurrence. Medulloblastoma is a very fast growing malignant cancer and if it is there in an early stage, it will grow. If it doesn't grow at all it is probably radiation effects and will not do any damage. And if it grows in size and form but very slowly, it still could be another type of slow-growing cancer, a side effect of treatments from Medulloblastoma. The doctor did say that if it was recurrence that there are several chemo options available that are showing promise for recurrences. He also told us to watch out for any outward signs of tumor growth in Jack like pain in his legs or further balance issues. If Jack has any of these symptoms we need to let him know and he can get Jack scheduled for an MRI sooner. So, we wait. And pray its radiation effects. And wait some more.

Sometimes I feel like I'm in a strange tug of war. One day we celebrate good news, the next day we must put our guard back up and wait. I never knew cancer was so difficult. I always thought that the story went this way: you were diagnosed with cancer, you had treatments, you went into remission and you returned back to your life. Maybe this is just the uncertainty of pediatric cancer. Maybe I was naive or just ignorant of the world

...BUT I'M NOT THE SINGER

of cancer. Maybe I wasn't exposed to this or just didn't really see. But this is so hard. It pulls like a rope on your heart and your mind. You never know what is going to happen right around the next corner and there is always a next corner, waiting. One day the rope jerks you this way and the next day it jerks you the other. Jerk, jerk, jerk. I need to untie this rope and just live today. We all live our lives thinking about our plans for this weekend or what we will wear tomorrow or what is for supper tonight. We all live today thinking about the time ahead of us. We need to stop. We need to relish in now. Not five minutes from now, five days from now or five weeks from now. Right now. Today for us, Jack is symptom free, laughing at something on his computer, and will soon ask about his dinner because his tummy will be rumbling. Thank God for now.

Dear Lord, thank you for healthy bodies and strong minds, for time we have with our loved ones, for the sound of laughter and the cleansing of tears, for being able to come to You in prayer, asking for Your mercy and grace for those in need, for the blessing of a hug and the joy of a smile, for the support and love of family, friends, and strangers, and for the gift of today. Amen

AUGUST 13, 2012—I hope all the children had a great first day of the new school year. Jack on the other hand didn't even make it until the 11:07am early dismissal of the first day of school. He vomited at school and we had to pick him up. Bless his heart. He felt so bad when we picked him up that he came home and fell asleep. When he woke up later, I asked him about how school was for the time he was there. He tuned up to cry and said that he was left in class without a helper and he was left in the hallways by himself to find his classes without help. He was confused, got lost, had to ask for help and was scared to death that he was going to get into trouble if he was late to class. Is it any wonder he vomited? If someone from the school system had knocked on my front door after he told me this, I would have needed money to bail myself out of jail. I would not have been responsible for my actions. Are you kidding me? This is a child that has NEVER even "walked" the halls of this school without using a wheelchair or a walker! This is a child who has NEVER been without an adult assistant in his whole school career. Not to mention he has had cancer. He has autism. He is having problems with short-term memory loss. He is having vomiting issues again (Friday was the third time he vomited last week). He has mobility issues and DUH! he is wearing leg braces. And he has something new and not yet explained lurking, possibly growing, in his spinal column. What are they thinking? And yes, his IEP states he is to have adult supervision between

MY NAME IS JACK JOHNSON...

classes. I am so mad and thoroughly disgusted. I ask: what are they thinking? I just can't believe the school personnel would take that type of chance and put themselves in jeopardy for a lawsuit in case my child was injured. Even if he wasn't injured and just lost his balance by being in a crowded hallway with so many other students, neither Ben nor myself think Jack could even get up from the floor by himself. To say I am angry is an understatement. To say I do not trust them right now is also an understatement. To say I am hurt and disgusted is yet another understatement. For a kiddo who has fought as hard as my child (and the other warriors with cancer who fight every day!) to be treated with so little respect for his health and well-being is totally unacceptable. I was asked if there was another student who could "help" Jack get from class to class. Hey parents, is there any of you who would volunteer your high school student to be responsible for my child's safety, who could have physical symptoms at any time that the lesion on his spinal cord is growing? How often do you talk to your high school student about what to do if they are selected to be an escort for a child who might or might not have further issues with balance? Or who starts to have pain in his legs? Or who could lose the feelings in his legs? Don't you discuss this at dinner every night? Seems some people think you do. I personally think they owe my child an apology for the added stress to his already stressed mind. Sorry for the vent but this is absolutely ridiculous!!!!!

Jack's day was better today. His special education teacher is taking responsibility for Jack and his safety and is not leaving him alone in the hallways. He did stay the whole day and after school we stopped at the drugstore to pick up his new prescription. But before we could get home, he asked for the ever-present puke bucket and vomited yet again. While I sat watching my child retch and vomit in the parking lot of KMart, I told God how much I hate cancer. Between vomits, Jack told me he thinks the wooly booger is growing back in his head. How do you hold back the tears? I couldn't. I couldn't at church yesterday either. I have been known to tear up at certain oldie but goodie hymns that I grew up hearing in church. And I can never make it without shedding a few tears to the songs we so carefully picked out and sang at my mother's funeral. Yesterday was different. I am having such a hard time with the pressure of waiting to hear about Jack's newly discovered lesion. I get mad easily and am on edge most of the time. So yesterday in church when we started to sing "It Is Well with My Soul" the few tears I usually shed quickly became an unexpected downpour and I had to retreat to the bathroom. The tears just wouldn't stop. There are so many feelings I have that are "not well with my soul."

... BUT I'M NOT THE SINGER

Dear God, thank you for being able to see how a big smile can light up the face of a child, for the blessing of good health and strong minds, for days without pain and sorrow, for tears that cleanse the body of sadness and fear, for the gift of children—young and old, healthy and sick, able and disabled, for the awesome feeling of love and being loved, and for the support family, friends, and strangers give us when we need it most. In His Name, Amen.

AUGUST 15, 2012—Jack's first full day of school without vomiting and stress. He is completely worn out, but he made it and hasn't vomited. One small step to some, a giant one for us. He has complained of a headache, something he has been complaining about for several days now. I will have to watch this to see if this continues. My calendar, where I keep up with everyone's schedule, appointments, and comings and goings are now also filling up with Jack's daily vomits and headache. As I have said before, I am the ultimate "helicopter" mom. I think I have graduated now from that title to "blanket" mom. Call me whatever you want. If my child is happy, well cared for, and covered with love and understanding by those around him, I am happy too.

Speaking of happy, school has been trying hard to meet Jack's needs better than before. We have scheduled a meeting for Friday so everyone can "sing off the same song sheet." It's so obvious to me that as soon as Jack's needs are met, he stays longer at school and his stomach does not hurt as much. Yesterday I was called in to school because Jack was again in the clinic complaining of a stomachache. I rushed to the school, of course, with my now ever-present flowing tears from my eyes, and found him lying on the clinic bed. I asked him what was going on and he told me that he had a headache and his stomach hurt. I asked him if something had happened to upset him and he told me that in PE the other students were playing with balls. The balls were flying around and he was scared he was going to get hit with one of them. Thankfully, PE was over and so we talked about this. While we were talking, Jack's previous homebound teacher walked in. She asked Jack if she stayed with him and went to class with him, would he let her? Jack said yes and off they went. Just like that. Unbelievable. This child needs the security of having someone with him. The nurse took me to the assistant principal's office and we chatted (he talked and I talked through my tears) and he reassured me that they were working on getting Jack's needs taken care of and that things would be better. I appreciate his words but I am leery and not trusting. Just like Jack, I need to take it one day at a time and see if Jack is making progress. Thankfully today I saw a little progress and feel a little better. I am keeping an open mind but

MY NAME IS JACK JOHNSON...

every morning that I watch my two sons drive away from our house, I say an extra prayer that everyone, including my sons, will learn something that day. And that includes all teachers, school personnel, students, and even me.

I left school after Jack went to class with his homebound teacher and a little later was called back because Jack refused to eat lunch because he was afraid he would vomit yet again. I just brought him home early. He told me later that he was alone without any help in his last period class. Don't know if that was the problem but today he had someone in that class, and he stayed all day. I want to shout out and a big thanks to Miss T. for volunteering to help Jack. You were an angel sent from God for me. Another big thanks and shout out to the clinic nurses at school for keeping Jack calm and safe in your clinic. Also, a big thanks to Mrs. L., Mrs. J., and to anyone else who has gone out of their way to help Jack that I might not know about. You "get it" and for that, I am truly grateful. Hopefully, and with lots of prayers, there will be more people who "get it" after Friday's meeting.

Several of you have asked about the awaited stuffed animal I had written about a few entries back. Yes, the stuffed animal arrived. And yes, the smile on Jack's face was awesome. I check on him at night before he falls asleep to make sure he is OK. Every night he and his new stuffed animal are face-to-face, as he says, telling each other good night. Now, of course, he doesn't tell me goodnight, but if he is happy with his new buddy, I will be happy too.

Dear Lord, thank you for healthy bodies and strong minds, for using others for Your own good, for letting us see the goodness in others, for the blessing of children, for the open minds and open hearts of people who "get it," for hope and faith that help us when life lets us down, and for the love and support of so many who continue to walk with us on this journey. Bless them in ways only You can. In Jesus' Name, Amen.

AUGUST 21, 2012—Our meeting with the school was Friday, and it went well. Now everyone has personally received information from us on Jack and his many health issues today and what can happen. He is so much happier and at ease when I pick him up. He has someone with him all day and someone with him in the hallways. He is not going to PE class in case balls are flying around the gym.

I was amazed while doing my meeting research, the vast amount of procedures and surgeries my child has had over the last two-plus years. I was surprised to see the number of doctors who are now on Jack's medical team—fifteen different doctors and medical personnel now. I also found some

...BUT I'M NOT THE SINGER

not so pleasant statistics—kids with medulloblastoma have a survival rate of only 55.2 percent ten years out of diagnosis. That is a scary number for any parent. Jack is already two years out of diagnosis which makes it even scarier. It would be so easy to look away and put my head in the sand, but I think Ben and I both need to see those numbers. Even if Jack lives to be the ripe old age of one hundred, seeing those numbers pushes us to live each day as if it were our last. And that's what we are going to do!

Dear Lord, thank you for the blessing of children, for the life lessons we learn daily from them as their parents, for their smiles and laughter that brighten our days, for their innocence and resilience, for their hugs and kisses, for the memories of their lives. Thank you for the gift of life, time spent with the ones we love, and for the promise, we will see our loved ones again, whole and healthy with You. In His Name, Amen.

AUGUST 27, 2012—Friday night Centennial High School plays local rival Franklin High School. At the game, the schools will be selling Battle for Jack 2012 bracelets with the proceeds going to Jack's medical expenses. Benny will be playing in the game, something that makes us proud to know that he is playing on the Battle for Jack night. I also wanted to let everyone know tomorrow Culver's in Cool Springs is having a Battle for Jack day. If you eat at Culver's and mention Jack's name, 10 percent of their profit will be donated to Jack's medical expenses. What a wonderful gesture from the folks at Culver's. We are so fortunate to live in such a giving community

Dear Lord, thank you for the blessing of children, for healthy bodies and strong minds, for hearts that give so much to others, and for the love and support of family, friends, and strangers who bless us every day in this journey. Amen.

AUGUST 28, 2012—Last week Jack had a come-apart. For you who don't know Jack personally and have never seen a come-apart let me explain: a come-apart is a meltdown/temper tantrum that comes from nowhere and is set off by something minor or so it seems. There are lots of tears, thrashing of the body, sometimes self-inflicted injury, and all rational thought disappears. Come-aparts are something that some people with autism have when they have a hard time with the world around them. This one started because Jack hates homework and hasn't had homework since eighth grade. Remember kiddos with autism are creatures who thrive off routine and despise change. We have had to deal with lots of change this year. When it came time to do

MY NAME IS JACK JOHNSON...

homework, and with the fact that Jack's poor little mind is having lots and lots of difficulty with short-term memory loss, he was overly tired, frustrated with having to do homework, and upset that he couldn't remember things, and... and... and... KABOOM! He exploded. He cried and cried and cried until he lost all control over his emotions. He thrashed in his chair and beat his head with his hand. He screamed loud and fussed at every person in the world. I thought for a while he might make his throat sore from all the screaming. I tried to calmly talk to him but he would not listen. I had to just sit and watch him go through this. When he was younger and autism was at its peak—and before he could understand the world around him and communicate his wants and needs—he would have these come-aparts several times a day. To see Jack today, you would never believe he could be that out of control, but take it from me, he had them and often. As he has gotten older and his understanding grows, the come-aparts have become fewer and fewer. After an hour of coming apart, Jack told me he needed some time to himself and I told him that was good because I needed some time alone myself. I walked outside and cried. We have been through so much the last few years, and we have come so far since the beginning of autism land, that to see a full-blown come-apart again was so disheartening. Again, I had one of my "God—help" prayers. Jack did calm down and we did finish the homework but I am now worried that he will have a come-apart at school. This is not something the school and I have talked about. Of all the words I have written, please remember these: behavior is an outward response to something, whether it is bad behavior (ex: underage drinking in teens) or good behavior (ex: being well-behaved not because you want to but because you want to please others.) This holds true for people with autism; their behavior is a response to something they don't understand or don't have the capacity to verbalize. We haven't had any more explosions and I hope it will be years and years until he has another one.

Jack had his first real visit from a friend who is in his age group on Saturday. Ever. Jack's Best Buddy, K., came by Saturday and spent some one-on-one time with Jack. He was so happy to have an actual friend over. He cleaned up the couch and we didn't have to ask him to put on clothes, wash his face, or brush his teeth. They sat on the couch together—he on one end and she on the other—and talked about music, videos, and school. He wanted to share his world with her, all the things that mean something to him. She was shocked to see the stacks of Jack's electric pole pictures and to fully understand how awesome his abilities truly are when it comes to remembering each pole, where each pole is located, and how each pole is drawn in detail. I

... BUT I'M NOT THE SINGER

asked him when she looked at some of his pictures where the poles were and he so candidly said they were the poles from a trip to Center Hill Lake. Each pole drawn on a single sheet of paper are the poles going to the lake and every pole coming back from the lake, in chronological order as you travel the road to the lake and back. Pages and pages of electric poles, all different. After a while, Jack ran out of things to say and since I had stuck around to help if needed, I talked to K. about things in her life. She stayed for about an hour and a half. But for Jack, it was the greatest thing to have a friend his age come and visit HIM. He was so happy. A big hug and thank you to K. for taking time out of her day to visit with Jack. I cry when I think about it now.......

Dear God, thank you for continuing to show us Your love through so many people who surround us every day, for the blessing of children, for the gift of a true friend and the joy of friendship, for healthy bodies and strong minds, for eyes to see the wonders of this life, for faith, hope and love, and for the love and support of family, friends, and strangers who walk with us on this journey. In Jesus' Name, Amen.

SEPTEMBER 5, 2012—If you missed it, Centennial High School beat Franklin High School in Friday night's big matchup. It was the first win over Franklin High since Centennial High opened fifteen years ago. There were lots of people in attendance with lots of our family there to cheer on Benny and the Cougars. I am so happy for the whole Centennial football team, especially the seniors who will leave school at the end of this year with this win under their belts. I am especially happy for Benny who got to be on the winning team on the Battle for Jack night. He will remember it forever.

Jack sat and watched the whole game. He cheered, he clapped, he screamed at the referees. He gets so hyped up that I don't know what he will do or say next so of course, he surprised me Friday night. The refs made a penalty call that Jack did not like and he gave them the finger. Yes, you read that correctly—Jack gave the refs the finger. And it wasn't just the finger. Oh no, he had to put his hand up as far as his arm would go upward while giving the finger. I didn't even know he knew how to do the finger. And of course, I am at a loss to where he learned the finger. Take your pick: videos on the computer, school, TV, you name it. It is not something we do here at home. When I saw him, finger held high, I just turned and stared at him. He gave me that innocent face and said, "What?" Is that not the most typical teenage reaction to getting caught doing something you aren't supposed to do? I just continued to stare at him and he stared back. Not a stare-down kind of stare

MY NAME IS JACK JOHNSON...

but an "I am in big trouble" kind of stare. I finally said to him that the finger was inappropriate and he said he knew that. He then started with the "I'm sorrys" to which I just stared again. I told him that if I ever saw him do it again, he would be in big trouble and something would be put in time out for a lllllloooooonnnnngggg time. After we left the game, Ben and I talked with Jack about it again and told him to never do it again. We asked him if he understood the meaning behind the finger and he said no. I reminded him of our rule: you never repeat something when you don't know what it means. You ask your parents what it means. He said he would never do it again. I hope not. I could have crawled under the bleacher seat but I wouldn't fit. He also came home last week telling me how he told one of his teachers that if the referees called too many penalties on the Cougars that he was going to scream out the "F-bomb" at them. So, the incident of flying the famous familiar finger could have been worse. He could have added a few "F-bombs" so everyone could hear. Needless to say, we had another serious conversation last week about that word as well. Living with autism is so much fun!!

Dear Lord, thank you for giving us minds that can remember the things we enjoyed in the past with the ones we love, for the blessing of children, for each minute, hour, and day we have with our loved ones, for healthy bodies and strong minds, for tears of joy, tears of sorrow, for the sound of laughter, the feel of a hug, for the beauty of a creek, a lake, the ocean, for faith and hope of a day without pain and sorrow, and for the love and support of so many people who walk with us daily on this journey. In His Name, Amen.

SEPTEMBER 10, 2012—I want to thank everyone again for the outpouring of support we have received from so many people. To all the students at CHS and FHS, a big thank you for supporting us through the Battle for Jack bracelets. To everyone at Culver's and everyone who ate at Culver's, another big thanks. To the Quarterback Clubs of both Centennial and Franklin High Schools. To people at church who sold bracelets. To all the people who have sent us gifts. The list goes on and on. We are overwhelmed by the love we feel through each of you. It is unbelievable! I'm going to steal a line from my youngest son, who when we visited Culver's the day of the Battle for Jack and after I showed him the posters advertising the Battle for Jack, Jack said, "Wow, Mom. How do these restaurants know me?" So, I will steal from him and say, "How do all these people know us!" We are blessed beyond belief with how people have surrounded us with prayers, gifts, and support. Thanks again to each of you.

...BUT I'M NOT THE SINGER

Dear Lord, thank you for the coolness of fall, for healthy bodies and strong minds, for the blessing of children, for the gift of a hug from a friend, and for the love and support of family, friends, and strangers who bless us each day as we continue to travel on this journey. Amen.

SEPTEMBER 12, 2012—Yesterday, the radiology department was in rare form actually ahead of schedule for Jack's MRI. We were taken back by our favorite radiology tech/nurse, J., who didn't even call our name when he came to the lobby to get us. He just motioned. Not a good sign when the hospital personnel know you that well. J. was not happy to see us, considering our reason for being there. He also had to place Jack's IV which, of course, Jack coached him through. J. did have to find the Freezy Spray—spray that freezes the skin—but he was happy to do it. He said Jack was in too good of a mood. Another patient arrived in the recovery room next door to the prep room and started crying. Jack immediately started talking about "getting the duct tape" which made J. happy to know the old Jack was still with us. We also knew the anesthesia doctor who has put Jack to sleep many times during radiation treatments. He asked Jack several of the questions most people ask us: like his name, when he ate last, when he drank last, etc. Jack answered each one. He then asked me and Ben why we were having yet another MRI and we had to explain the new lesion. While we were explaining it, the anesthesia doctor made a face and said that they would take extra time since they were looking at a possible recurrence. I cringed at the "r" word. Ben told me later he did too. Jack got his IV, his gown, and was ready to go. When they came for him he was ready and pushed the button on the wall that opened the large metal doors while the doctor and a nurse from the MRI room pushed Jack's bed down the hallway. You can't help but laugh at the silly child especially when he tells the hospital personnel what to do. After two and a half hours, they called us back to recovery where we found a still half-asleep Jack. He did not want to wake up. After forty-five minutes and lots of prodding, he did open his eyes and put his clothes on. He did have a little extra dizziness but did fine with it. We left and were soon homeward bound. Jack was so thrilled have this MRI. He was so happy because he didn't have to go to school. Never mind the reason we had to have the MRI to begin with or the fact that he couldn't have anything to eat or drink. He was just so dang happy to not have to go to school. He is a funny creature.

Now, we wait for the results. We could call and ask for the results but sometimes living in total denial and la la land is not that bad. Some people might find that strange, but we are going to enjoy our ignorant bliss for one more week. That's us—ignorantly blissful...

Dear Lord, thank you for caring doctors and nurses, for working through them with healing the sick, for the ability to laugh at life's quirky moments, for time shared with our loved ones, for healthy bodies and strong minds, for days of ignorant bliss, and for family, friends, and strangers who amaze us each day with their love and support of us as we travel this road. Bless them all with Your glory and grace. In His Name, Amen.

SEPTEMBER 12, 2012—Do you remember as a child a person who made you do something that frightened you to your core? Like, force you into a pitch black, dark room? You could feel someone's hands pushing you into that room even though you didn't want to go. Anywhere but there. Maybe it was a haunted house or a dark, scary place. And you were being shoved into that place anyway...

Jack's doctor's office called shortly after I wrote about ignorant bliss and how I was liking ignorant bliss. Jack's regular oncologist is out of town and another doctor was filling in for him. He called and said he has the results from the MRI: Jack's mystery lesion has now doubled in size from the last MRI six weeks ago. (I really wanted to ask him if he had ever heard of ignorant bliss but didn't want him to think he was talking to a crazy person.) He had already talked to Jack's neurosurgeon who again said the lesion could not be biopsied without causing further neurological damage. The neurosurgeon said that trying to biopsy the lesion from the front of Jack's body (as he did before) would be risky as well because he would have to go through ribs and major blood vessels to access where the lesion sits. Since the lesion cannot be biopsied and has doubled in size in six weeks, the course of action is to treat it as a medulloblastoma recurrence and start a new regimen of chemo. Stand-in doctor said he would talk to Jack's regular doctor later that day or the next and let him know about the results. I asked if Jack's case will go before the Tumor Board on Monday morning and he said he would talk to Jack's doctor and see if he wanted to present it before the board. I asked if the lesion's growth was the common growth pattern for medulloblastoma recurrence and he said yes. Yet another rug pulled out from us again. We are again broken hearted, confused, and overwhelmed by this news. This is not what we wanted to hear or had hoped and prayed for. I have spent some time researching second opinion doctors just in case. I know there are children who have survived recurrences of medulloblastoma but the numbers are not good. I know

... BUT I'M NOT THE SINGER

we will not give up without a fight and we will try anything we can to stop this monster. I am holding onto my very small sliver of hope that there is still a chance this is radiation-induced and that it will stop growing.

Fight. Such a strong word. We think of wars, men in armor, swords, and guns. We never think in terms of needles and chemo and scans. Fight—to strive vigorously and resolutely. We are fighters. We are resolute. Until next Wednesday—our next doctor's appointment—we are going to continue to live life the best we can. We are going to do what we need and want to do. If you see us out, please don't tell us you are sorry or start to cry. I am already doing that enough for everyone. Just say hello, smile, and know we know you are there for us. I'm not going to ask for prayers because I know most of you will say them without my asking. Thanks to each of you for always being there.

Dear Lord, help. Amen.

SEPTEMBER 17, 2012—A tale of two feelings... Friday was a very frustrating day for Jack. First, he had a trying day at school. His memory is failing him. Things he could remember before he cannot remember now. He tried to take a quiz at school but couldn't remember how to do what was needed to get an answer for his Algebra problems. He had to be taken out of class and took the rest of the quiz later in the day. The teacher later told me Jack made a very good grade on the quiz. If you have ever known a person who has had a stroke, you have seen first-hand how frustrating it is to be unable to remember as you did before. It is aggravating and causes stress in the person's life. This is the way things are for Jack now. His brain is being affected by the side effects of his brain cancer and the treatments, whether it be by the radiation, chemo, removal of the tumor surgery, or by the tumor that grew in the brain. I have researched information about long-term side effects, and the loss of short-term memory is very common after treatments. Poor Jack also faces the everyday challenges of autism on top of the side effects he is experiencing today.

We went to church yesterday. The church is in the process of changing all the Exit signs that Jack has so carefully memorized and watched over the years. He was so thrilled last Sunday to see the new Exit signs I didn't know if he was going to be able to sit through church. He has sat for hours this past week drawing each new Exit sign at the church and carefully cutting each drawn sign out and then stacking each sign with the others like it. Now to go along with our eight-inch-high stack of electric pole drawings, we have piles and piles of carefully cut out and perfectly drawn Exit

MY NAME IS JACK JOHNSON...

signs... all in our family room. So yesterday was already going to be a good day for Jack since he was getting to see the new Exit signs again. Instead of going to Sunday School class in the Youth ministry where they talk about true teenage issues, Jack and his special friend for that week walked the hallways of the church and looked at each Exit sign. If the lights in the signs were out, Jack had a pad and pencil to write the janitors a note to let them know which sign was out and wherein the building the unlit sign hung. Since the old Exit signs have been replaced, he doesn't have to write notes, and he gets to enjoy looking at and touching each Exit sign. Yesterday he found an Exit sign that didn't sit well with him. A lesson in exit signs: each Exit sign has two punch outs, one arrow pointing left, the other pointing right. Once the arrow has been punched out, it lights up like the exit word and points to the direction of the nearest building exit. Jack found an arrow in a sign that had not been punched out, to point people in the right direction of the nearest exit. He decided he would punch out the correct arrow on the Exit sign to help guide people in case of emergency to the nearest building exit. He couldn't do it with his finger so he went to a nearby Sunday School class and asked the teacher for a pair of scissors. He punched out the arrow and kept the arrow for his prize. You have never seen a kid so happy and proud of himself as he was. He was giddy. He was so happy to show me and Ben what he had done. He even told us that since he punched out the arrow, people needing to get out of the building would not run into the wall if it was dark. They would see they needed to turn to the right to get out of the building. We all need to feel like we make a difference in our world. We all need to feel like we can accomplish something, whether big or small. You know the feeling, the feeling of pride that comes with success. This is especially true for people who have had difficulties in life that make them sad and inadequate as Jack had been feeling. Jack radiated pride. He was like a light bulb himself, lit from within. His face glowed and electricity ebbed through his body. I have never seen him like this before. I cried tears of joy for getting to see his excitement with himself. He told us several things on the way home. He said he saved people from trouble in case there was ever a fire and they had to get out. He said, "Now they won't run into the wall!" And the one that took my breath, he said, "Where would we be without me?" I pray I never find out.

Dear Lord, thank you for being able to feel feelings of self-worth, pride, joy, disappointment and sadness, for healthy bodies and strong minds, for days without pain and sorrow, for the days that we lose and days that we win, for

... BUT I'M NOT THE SINGER

the sheer blessing of children, for the rains that water the plants that will soon brighten our world with the colors of autumn, and for the continued love and support of so many people You use to show us Your love. Amen

SEPTEMBER 19, 2012—The day we have dreaded has now come and gone. Ignorant bliss and denial were our way of handling life but we have come back to reality. And reality really stinks. Jack's oncologist told us today that he and the Tumor Board are 95 percent certain that the lesion growing on Jack's spinal cord is indeed a recurrence of medulloblastoma. As of today, there is no cure for recurrent medulla. There are treatments that are "promising" but that is all there is. He gave us two options of treatment and of course, there is the option of not doing any treatment, but for us personally that is not an option for our Jack. Dr. E. is going to send out Jack's scans to other doctors around the country to get second opinions for us. Our two options of treatment are both chemo treatments—one with chemo and a stem cell transplant, the other just chemo. The chemo-only plan consists of three different chemo drugs, Jack would not have to stay in the hospital overnight for them, could continue to go to school (if things were OK physically), and the chemo would last for a year. The chemo/stem cell transplant would put Jack in the hospital for 3 weeks, isolated, while the chemo killed all cells in his body, before the stem cells were transplanted back into his system. Both treatments are clinical trials that we could or could not do; our decision. As I have said before, I do know of a few children who have been treated for recurrent medulla who are still living life to its fullest. Some have never had another recurrence while some have had a second recurrence. Either way, I think we all feel that any extra time that any treatment can give, is time the medical community could use to hopefully find a better treatment or, God willing, a cure. Until then, this is what we have. Our first step is for Jack to have another spinal tap to look yet again for cancer cells in the spinal fluid. That is not to say if there are no cancer cells that this is not a recurrence; it is a way to see if the fluid comes back positive for cancer cells then we know for sure it is recurrence. Dr. E. did say all neurosurgeons, pediatric and adult, on the Tumor Board said they could not operate to get a biopsy. After seeing for myself the MRI picture of the lesion from the top down, the lesion is growing around the spinal cord—not on one side of the cord nor in the spinal fluid surrounding the cord, I can see the neurosurgeon's point of view. They will try to schedule the spinal tap in the next few days. After we get the second opinions and if they are all in complete agreement, then we

MY NAME IS JACK JOHNSON...

schedule Jack for surgery to place another port-a-cath into his chest. Once Ben and I decide between our options, chemo will begin shortly after. Ben and I sent Jack out to the infusion room while we talked to the doctor. We told Jack on the way home that he would have to have chemo again because the "wooly booger" had grown back, this time on his spine. He said, "I always was scared it would grow back." He didn't like the idea of having to take chemo again but being Jack, he just took it in stride. I told him that I would be with him through it all just like we did before and he said, "I know." There is no way to describe the way we feel right now. If I could scream as loud and as long as I could, I would, but you can't do that in a neighborhood in the middle of town. Ben and I are numbed, but for me, I can feel the rumbling of anger deep in my soul that will need to come out eventually. We will not give up hope. We will always do what is best for Jack. I will say yet again: I hate, despise, detest cancer.

Dear Lord, thank you for the cool winds of change, for the blessing of children, for every minute, hour, and day we have with the ones we love, for the medical community that works every day to care for the sick and spend hours researching better ways to heal, for always holding our hand in our times of need, and for surrounding us with the love and support of so many as we continue our journey. Amen.

SEPTEMBER 27, 2012—Today Jack's oncologist called to let us know that the spinal fluid taken in Jack's latest spinal tap was negative for cancer cells. Ben and I are not sure how to feel about this. Let me try to explain: if the spinal fluid had come back positive for cancer cells, we would have known exactly what we are dealing with and would have a pretty good picture of what we must do in the way of treatment. A positive result would have opened the door to other possible clinical trials that must have a confirmation of recurrent medulloblastoma as a prerequisite to participate in those trials. Without a true confirmation that Jack's spinal lesion is definitely a recurrence, we are very limited on clinical trials. And without a concrete confirmation of a recurrence, we could have to be put in the position of giving Jack a year of chemo to treat something that looks and acts like a recurrence of medulloblastoma but has never been confirmed as a recurrence. I do understand where the doctors are coming from since the lesion is growing in Jack's spinal cord. I am a firm believer that we must do something to stop its growth but it would be so much easier to have that positive diagnosis of medulloblastoma recurrence. From my meager knowledge of diagnosing a

... BUT I'M NOT THE SINGER

tumor, the doctors look for size, shape, growth—the speed of growth and the pattern of growth, where in the body it is, whether it is a lesion growing after a diagnosis of previous cancer and the most important one—a cellular diagnosis of what type of cancer it is. The ONLY one of those factors that we don't have is the cellular diagnosis of the cancer itself. I am hoping that one of our second opinion doctors will know of someone who has seen this before or knows of a doctor who might operate to get a biopsy before we are forced to treat Jack for a recurrence. This is such a hard place to be in—not knowing what this truly is and knowing that we just can't sit back and wait since we know for sure the thing is growing. Knowing exactly what this lesion is made of would be a relief because then we could arm ourselves and plan our attack full well knowing exactly what our true enemy is. This is like fighting smoke and it brings doubt to the whole situation. Doubt really doesn't belong in a cancer fight especially when it's your child you are fighting for. I just pray the second opinions doctors have different ideas and this whole decision is not completely left up to me and Ben. Do you treat or do you not? A gamble with your child's life. A parent's worst nightmare. The doctor today told us that our second opinions should be back by the end of this week—tomorrow—or by the first of next week. So, we wait... tic, tic, tic, tic, tic...

Jack feels good. You would never know that there is anything wrong going on inside his body, except for his pale color. He doesn't have a healthy glow which is concerning for us. But he feels good and continues to be our Jack. Since our church replaced all their Exit signs, it has given him something to look forward to each Sunday. This past Saturday, one of Jack's special friends from church called and said she had a gift that she needed to drop by for Jack. When she and her son arrived, they had an Exit sign that had been removed from our church and had been replaced. The janitors had removed it, cleaned it up, (this Jack noticed saying how very clean and shiny it was) and had a plaque attached to it saying, "Jack Johnson, Thank you for all your help. Franklin FUMC 2012." The janitors had also attached an electric cord to the Exit sign so Jack can plug it in and the exit letters light up. There was not a happier child in Franklin that day. Publishers Clearing House could have brought him a million dollars, and he would not have been as happy as he was with that Exit sign. He sleeps with it each night even though he is sleeping in a twin bed. The sign is not small, being one of the exits with emergency lights attached to the left and right of it. Thanks to all the people at Franklin First United Methodist Church who had a hand in this. Thanks to

MY NAME IS JACK JOHNSON...

Nancy and Quinn for bringing it to Jack. He was the happiest kid around.

The other night he had an assignment for English where he had to write in his journal. He was given a topic and had to write a response. I have never looked in his journal before since it is something he does in class. I didn't know that the journal existed. The question was "Have you or someone you know ever been unable to make a person listen to you? How did it feel to be ignored? Did you finally succeed in being heard?" Jack said he didn't know what to write so I said to him, "Jack, you and I ignore each other all the time. We don't mean to but like when I'm busy and you ask me something sometimes I don't hear you and it seems like I might be ignoring you. And sometimes you do me the same way." So, he wrote, "My mother has ignored me when I ask her something. It makes me angry when I am ignored by her. I succeeded in being heard by yelling at her." No truer words were ever written. As I looked further into his journal, I also found this question, "What is your favorite book?" Jack's journal entry reply, "I really don't have a favorite book because I don't read. I actually think that it's for old people." Reading is for old people per Jack. So, for all of you reading this, Jack thinks you are old because you read. Ben and I have laughed about this so much this week. All I can say is... that's our Jack!

Dear Lord, thank you for patience, for the blessing of children, for healthy bodies and strong minds, for times of giving and times of receiving, for the gift of sight so we can see You in the people around us, for the ability to find humor in life, for the joy of a gift from the heart, and for the continued love and support of family, friends, and strangers who amaze us every day. Amen.

CHAPTER 35

OCTOBER 6, 2012—The last few days we have been celebrating Homecoming at CHS. I need to share that the Homecoming Parade Grand Marshall was none other than our Jack Johnson. He was technically co-Grand Marshall because another student was also a Grand Marshall. She is a cancer survivor as well. The theme of this year's homecoming was "We Believe" and some of the proceeds from the T-shirt sales, the Powder Puff football game, and the dance tonight go to Monroe Carroll Children's Hospital for cancer research in honor of Jack and the other Grand Marshall. Jack had a blast.

Dear Lord, thank you for letting us be young in age and young in spirit, for healthy bodies and strong minds, for memories of wonderful times that are etched in our minds, for the blessing of children, for each minute, hour and day we spend with our loved ones, and for the love and support of family, friends, and strangers who walk with us on this journey. Amen.

OCTOBER 11, 2012—We finally heard from Jack's oncologist today regarding one of the second opinions. St. Jude's Dr. G. called Jack's doctor and suggested one more MRI before starting any treatment. Dr. G. recommended that if the lesion has in fact grown even more than on the last MRI, then treatment is needed. If it hasn't grown more, then we could wait until the next regular follow-up MRI and continue to monitor the lesion. If it has grown, Dr. G. supported the three-chemo regimen that we have discussed with Jack's doctor previously. Dr. G. also said none of the surgeons at St. Jude's would risk a surgical biopsy either. Surgery is just too risky. A huge amount of growth would be a sign that the lesion is a medulloblastoma recurrence and treatment would be necessary. We are still waiting for Boston Children's Hospital's opinion which could come anytime. Dr. G. said he would schedule Jack's MRI six weeks from the last one, but Jack's oncologist would like to go ahead and schedule it for next week, at five weeks after the last one. Jack's MRI will be scheduled for some time next week, and we will go from there.

MY NAME IS JACK JOHNSON...

So again, we are now waiting for two things to happen: we are waiting to hear from Boston and get their opinion, and we are waiting to hear when the MRI will be performed. At least we are starting to move toward a plan of action. The waiting and waiting and waiting for others to get back to us, not knowing when or how long it will take is so disheartening.

Today was parent/teacher conference day at school. I didn't need to see any of Benny's teachers because he is doing well. For Jack, it is completely different. I talked with his four core subject teachers about how he is doing and what the future is for Jack medically. They all know what could be happening and plans are already in place in case we need them. Glad to have that in place, so we won't be faced with that if we need to hit the ground running with chemo. It was also good to hear Jack is doing well in school even though he does have some modifications. I so wish everyone could know how well this child does with all the complications he has had in his life. It amazes me, and I live with him daily. Most people think life is hard with an annoying paper cut! Just think what it must be like for a child with autism and brain damage from brain cancer who continues to learn what is asked of him as an eleventh grader in high school! I hear so many parents brag about the accomplishments of their children and I silently sit back and think to myself "Ha! They have it easy!! Let's see them do it with autism and brain damage. Then I will believe you!!" If only everyone could see...

Jack has taken his title of "Grand Marshall" of the homecoming parade a little too far. Last week he told me, "The Grand Marshall is hungry for dinner" with a big smile on his face. This week while at his foot doctor's office, he told me, "You cannot talk to this Grand Marshall that way!" when I told him to sit up the second time when the doctor wanted to examine him. I pray his majesty Grand Marshall starts to lose his uppity-ness soon.

Dear Lord, thank you for teachers who care, for healthy bodies and strong minds, for the gift of a sense of humor, for time spent with the ones we love, for days without pain and sorrow, for the joy of youth and the wisdom of age, and for the love and support of so many people who continue to bless us by walking with us on this journey. In His Name, Amen.

OCTOBER 20, 2012—The doctor called late yesterday afternoon. Ben talked with him and the MRI earlier in the day showed NO NEW GROWTH. The lesion in Jack's spinal cord has not grown since the last MRI five weeks ago. This is good news, but when you are dealing with cancer, it is still a guarded situation. Jack still has a lesion inside his spinal cord that has a history of rap-

... BUT I'M NOT THE SINGER

id growth. We are meeting with the doctor on Monday at 10 am to look at the MRI pictures and to discuss the situation. Ben said the doctor also told him that he heard back from Boston Children's, our second opinion on the lesion, and they suggested a treatment that Jack's doctor has never done before. Ben could not remember the name of this treatment, and he didn't write it down (argh!!), but we will find out Monday.

Dear Lord, thank you for all children—old and young, sick or healthy, here or with You, for the colors of autumn and the change of seasons, for the winds that blow the fallen leaves, for the glory of good news during our times of trouble, for the smile of a loved one, for being able to communicate our wants and needs no matter our age or ability, for prayers answered, for the patience to wait in life, and for the love, prayers, and support of family, friends, and strangers who bless us each and every day by continuing to walk with us on this journey. Amen.

OCTOBER 22, 2012—Ben, Jack, and I went to the hospital to talk with Jack's oncologist about the "stable" results of the latest MRI performed last Friday. I must share with you that I was very guarded about the results, knowing that if the results were as fantastic as they sounded, then why would the oncologist want to see us? Why didn't he just say "Hey, great news. We will see you at Jack's next regularly scheduled MRI in December?" Now we know. Jack's oncologist still believes the lesion in his spinal cord is in fact recurrent medulloblastoma. He still believes treatment is needed. We don't have a biopsy and no one from Vanderbilt, St. Jude's, or Boston Children's will perform a biopsy because of where the lesion is located. The lesion now has a measurable amount of growth in a measurable amount of time. The lesion is in an area where recurrence usually appears and the time factor—being in the first two years after the end of treatment—is the danger period for recurrence. Cancer does not have a set pattern of growth. Some cancers grow quickly and stop, some grow slowly and speed up, some grow at different times in different ways. There is no way to predict the growth of a certain cancer lesion. If Jack's lesion grows, it will most likely cause a physical issue, more than likely paralysis which could affect all organs and limbs from the location of the lesion down. In layman terms, the lesion is between Jack's shoulder blades as the general area. Paralysis is irreversible even if the tumor shrinks. We could gamble and wait to see if the lesion continues to grow, putting the chance of paralysis in our son's future. If that is not enough, the oncologist said waiting could also make treatment less effective if the tumor disseminates (meaning: scatters or diffuses) throughout the spinal fluid, spinal cord, and brain. With limited treatment options, we want the size of the lesion to be as small as possible. As of today, the lesion is still localized. From my research and the experience of other parents who have already walked this path, we had already decided, if needed, to choose chemo—a regimen of three different chemo drugs, two oral, one intravenous, given in twenty-eight-day cycles for a whole year, and watch to see if the tumor shrinks. If it doesn't shrink, it will not mean that the lesion was not cancer but could be that the chemo stopped growing. So, we will never fully know unless the tumor shrinks or disappears that we were giving Jack chemo for an actual recurrence. So... do we gamble and watch and wait to see if it grows, knowing full well the consequences of paralysis and possible hard to treat dissemination? Or do we gamble with the chemo, hoping Jack does OK with all the different side effects associated with taking not one, but three different chemo drugs? Do we go ahead and give him a difficult treatment for something we truly don't know for a fact is cancer? Ben and I decided to get second opinions from St. Jude's and Boston Children's since they have already looked at and given second opinions before this last MRI. Jack's doctor says he should hear something this week from both hospitals because, since the MRI was classified as stable, the second opinion doctors will not need to see the actual MRI scans to decide. A stable scan is self-explanatory. Ben and I are weary. We aren't just physically tired, we are emotionally drained and heavy with the burden of such an ominous decision. My head feels like it is being pressed in a vise.

Dear Lord, thank you for words and their meanings, for healthy bodies and strong minds, for the ability to think and make decisions, for the blessing of children, for eyes that see the beautiful colors of autumn, for the gift of friendship, the comfort of a hug, the joy of a smile, the gift of laughter, for giving us the gift of love, and for family, friends, and strangers who walk with us, love us, and hold us up through good times and bad times. You have blessed us in so many ways, and for these blessings, we are so very thankful. Amen

OCTOBER 26, 2012—Jack's doctor called and said he had heard from St. Jude's Dr. G. He recommended waiting another eight weeks and see if the lesion grows. He also said that the previous stable MRI made him just suspicious enough to want to wait and rescan again. Dr. G. has seen so many of these, and he is one of the leaders in research on pediatric brain tumors, so this news was music to our ears. Jack is scheduled to have this next MRI on Dec. 7th, not the eight weeks Dr. G. recommended but enough to see if any more

...BUT I'M NOT THE SINGER

growth has occurred. Ben and I feel the weight of the situation has lifted from us, only for a little while. We are so happy and eager to enjoy time with our boys. Benny turns eighteen this Sunday, and we are going to celebrate.

Thank you, Heavenly Father for the blessing of children, for hearts that give so much to others, for healthy bodies and strong minds, for each moment we have with the ones we love, for the joy of celebrating good news, for knowing what we need when we need it most, and for the love and support of so many people you have surrounded us with. Your love blesses us. Amen.

OCTOBER 31, 2012—We got up early Saturday morning, and as soon as Jack's feet hit the floor, he vomited. Sunday morning Jack did not vomit but did again first thing Monday morning. He went to the school clinic either later Monday or on Tuesday (I can't remember) but hasn't vomited since.

I am so glad Benny had a great eighteenth birthday. We have celebrated for days with too many desserts. I did not buy a card for Jack to give Benny for his birthday thinking I could coax Jack to make one since he loves to draw so much. So, I asked Jack to make his brother a birthday card to give him, and he did. This is what he wrote:

"From: Jack J. To: Benny J.
Yo Benny, it's ya birthday! You are now 18 and will soon be going to college. It will be all lonesome around the house without you. I am happy you are now 18 and want to wish you a happy birthday. I'll miss you while you're gone."

Several of us cried. What a wonderful expression of brotherly love. Happy Birthday, Benny. We are very proud of you and love you and your brother so much.

Dear Lord, thank you for always being with us during our greatest moments and our lowest lows of life, for healthy bodies and strong minds, for hearts that give so much to others in need, for the blessing of children, for being able to feel love and receive love, for the opening doors of change at different times in our lives, for the love and support of so many in the last few years, and for sharing Your only son with us so we always have an example of how You want us to live. In Jesus' Name, Amen.

NOVEMBER 7, 2012—Last Saturday, our church's Family Mission Team were here at our house cleaning up our yard. They called last week to let us

MY NAME IS JACK JOHNSON...

know they were coming. What would have taken us weeks and weeks to do (if it ever got done at all!) took them a few hours. They brought bulbs, flowers, and mulch. They planted, potted, and spread. They had blowers and rakes and cleaned every leaf from the ground and put them by the road where the city could vacuum them up. They amaze me with their commitment to helping others, their get in and get it done attitude, and their giving spirit. We are so honored to have the opportunity to get to know this exceptional group of people. So, a big thank you to the FUMC Family Mission Team for taking time to help us out yet again. And when they left, they said they would see us in the spring. What a wonderful picture of God's love!

Dear Lord, thank you for the promise of a home with You, for the gift of friendship with friends old and new, for the strength and bravery to trust in ourselves, for the blessing of a healthy body and the gift of a strong mind, for the joy of children, for time spent with the ones we love, and for the love and support of family, friends and strangers who continue to walk with us on this journey. In His Name, Amen.

NOVEMBER 14, 2012—Jack came home sick today. I say sick but he never really vomited. He gagged and "spit up some spit," as he says, but he never vomited. He was nauseated, and his stomach hurt. The school nurse called at 9:15 and said Jack had been in the clinic since 8 am. He didn't want to come home, thinking his stomach would get better. Ben picked him up 9:30. Jack finally woke up a few minutes ago, having fallen to sleep as soon as he got home. He says his stomach feels better. Again, I guess this will be our new normal—Jack having random stomach troubles. He has been completely off all anti-nausea pills for quite some time now, so we are a little surprised by this episode. He is not complaining of a headache, he has no fever, nor does he feel dizzy. It is just the same old stomach pains/nausea. Thanks so much, cancer and your treatments for continuing to wreak havoc on poor Jack's body.

Jack shared with me the other night after his shower that he is losing body hair again. For no reason, his body hair is just falling out in clumps again. So, let me sarcastically say again, thanks cancer!

Jack and I had a conversation last week about Jolly Old Saint Nicholas. If you recall, Jack has always believed in St. Nick and has a hard time each year with worrying over whether he will get the things he wants from Santa. He has worried himself into a frenzy, making himself physically sick. This year we have already had the chance to start the conversation. I told Jack that he needs to be thinking about some things that he might want for Christmas

... BUT I'M NOT THE SINGER

this year so we could start a list. He told me that this year he wasn't going to get upset over stuff like he has before. I told him that I needed to talk to him about Santa. I told him that Santa had a cut off age where he didn't bring gifts to kids over a certain age. I told him that age was 16. Luckily, Jack was very receptive to this. I went on to explain that Santa only makes toys for small children and since bigger kids want things like high tech games and gadgets, Santa had to let factories make those. Santa just doesn't have enough room to make new kinds of fun things. After the age of sixteen, Santa turns the gift buying over to the parents. Jack listened intently and said he would let me know the things he decides he wants even if it is something on the computer (aka: online shopping). I hope this ends the worrying and being sick over Christmas. Some of you might wonder why I just didn't tell him the truth about Santa. Let me explain: if I told Jack the truth, with his dislike for small children, he would find it a pleasure to share the truth with them. With his lack of social skills and understanding, he might tell every child he sees that there is no Santa. I am trying to avoid a heartbreaking scene for all children and to keep Jack out of deep trouble. So what if he still believes! Who does it hurt if he still believes in the magic of Christmas? Who doesn't want to believe that someone could magically come during the night and give you all things you wish for? I wish there was that person who could come and take away all the hurt and pain my son and others like him have to endure. I wish that there was no such thing as cancer and that no one got sick and died from it. If someone could take it away, think of all the children who would still be here to enjoy the magic of the season.

I need to share a story about a conversation Jack and I had last week on our way home from picking him up at school. Jack had had a pretty trying day at school and was not in a good mood when I picked him up. In fact, the conversation started with how much he hates school. He said, "I hate school so bad that I think I won't go back." I said, "You know that is against the law for you not to go to school. Kids that don't go to school go to juvey (our word for juvenile jail) to live."

Jack: "Well then, I'll just run away from home."

Me: "Run away from home? Who will feed you and wash your clothes?"

Jack: "I will just steal food."

Me: "From where?"

Jack: "From restaurants."

Me: "How will you steal food from restaurants? And remember stealing is also against the law."

MY NAME IS JACK JOHNSON...

Jack: "I will get someone who works at the restaurant to steal it for me."

Me: "Do you know someone who works at a restaurant who would do the stealing?"

Jack: "No, but I will find someone."

Me: "If you are running away from home, that will mean you will have to sleep outside in the cold, on the ground, in the dark at night. What will you do then?"

Jack: "I will pack me a suitcase and put my blankets in it."

Me: "What about a pillow? Will you take enough blankets to use for a pillow?"

Jack: "I will take a pillow in a suitcase too."

Me: "It will have to be a big suitcase. What about clean clothes? Sleeping and living in the woods outside will make your blankets and clothes dirty."

Jack: "I will just take another suitcase for clean clothes."

Me: "Wow Jack. That's a lot of suitcases to be carrying around while you are running from the police who will be looking for you since you ran away from home. Don't you think you will get tired carrying two suitcases while running in leg braces through the tall grass and trees in the woods?" Pause...

Jack: "Argh! I guess I have to go to school even though I hate it!"

Me: "I think you have to go too."

I love this kid!!!

Dear Lord, thank you for time we have with the ones we love, for the ability to make memories that will last forever, for healthy bodies and strong minds, for the gift of laughter, for the ability to run, to see, to hear, to speak, for endings and new beginnings, for patience and understanding, for the blessing of children, and for the love and support of so many who continue to walk with us on this journey. Amen.

NOVEMBER 28, 2012—We hope everyone had a wonderful Thanksgiving with friends and family. We left town on Friday and spent the weekend in the Smoky Mountains. We had talked about this for a while and planned it at the beginning of November. With Jack's next MRI looming on Dec. 7th and knowing that Benny will be in college this time next year, we decided it was a good time to go. We visited Gatlinburg, the mountains, and Pigeon Forge. We rode the ski lift in Gatlinburg, took pictures of the beautiful mountain streams and waterfalls, played putt-putt golf and rode go-carts. I think the trip did wonders for Jack because he has been in a good mood ever since. Benny has too. That makes it all worthwhile to me.

... BUT I'M NOT THE SINGER

Dear Lord, thank you for the blessing of children, for time spent with our loved ones, for the gift of laughter, for the beauty of places we have never seen, for patience, for hope, for faith, for love, for healthy bodies and strong minds, and for the love You gave to us through Your Son. In Jesus' Name, Amen.

DECEMBER 12, 2012—In this journey, one of the hardest things for me personally is to share our bad news. Jack's most recent MRI shows a definite recurrence of medulloblastoma. The cancer has now spread to several other areas of his spine, from his neck to his tailbone. The original new tumor has also grown. Jack's oncologist said the Tumor Board on Monday were all in complete agreement on this being a recurrence. No one present doubted. We again are crushed, pinned to the floor with grief. Nothing can prepare you for news like this. Luckily the cancer has not spread back into his brain but if not treated, it will. It's just a matter to time. The doctor is in the process of scheduling surgery to implant another port-a-cath into Jack's chest and to schedule a baseline kidney function test. One of the chemotherapy drugs Jack will be taking can have a negative effect on his kidneys, just like a previous chemo drug he had before. Again, we will have to watch this closely. I had already researched, in advance, the options available for recurrent medulloblastoma and had talked to Ben about what I found. We already agreed on which option we felt would be best. Jack's doctor is going to send the new scans to St. Jude's, just in case there is the slightest chance of a disagreeing second opinion. Neither one of us thinks the second opinion is going to be different. Jack's doctor wants to start chemo as soon as possible before the new lesions in his spine start to grow bigger and cause further health problems. Luckily, he has not had any problems yet.

My mind is a jumbled mess of thoughts and ideas. Funny how when you need your brain the most, it just can't focus. We have lived on hope for so long and pushed reality to the side but now reality is pushing back. Not to say that hope is gone—that will never happen here. We just know the reality of the situation and the consequence of this news. We need to be realistic and rethink our priorities, pushing the less important things aside for the truly important. We must think and talk about school, Benny and college, household bills versus medical bills, insurance, and all the other things in life that might need to be rearranged in our personal importance scale. In the spirit of the season, we might need to make lists—not the naughty and nice variety—but the what-is-truly-the-best-thing-to-do-now lists. I know God is still with us. He knows Jack better than anyone, even me. He also knows cancer better

MY NAME IS JACK JOHNSON...

than the doctors. So, I give this to Him, the One who knows. Take my son and his cancer and whatever happens is His will. Parents—our job is to love our children through the good times in their lives and through the lowest lows of their lives. God only lets us borrow His children. They have always been His. He lets us have them to love, hold, and cherish. But they are His. For me, that's the hardest reality of all.

Dear Lord, thank you for healthy bodies and strong minds, for hope, for faith, for love, for each precious moment we have with the ones we love, and for continuing to surround us with support and love from so many people. Amen.

DECEMBER 14, 2012—Jack is scheduled for surgery to implant his new port at 7:30 am Monday morning. We must be at the hospital at 6 am. Ouch. Tuesday, he has a kidney test from 8 am until 12—a four-hour test. He has had kidney tests before but this one will let the doctor know if his kidneys are still working properly and if they are, it will give them a baseline to have for future kidney tests since one of the chemo drugs can damage kidneys. On Wednesday, we start chemo. I am not sure if the chemo is one of the oral kind he will be taking or if it is the one he needs to take through his veins. I guess we will find out then. The oncologist said that we will need to test Jack's blood counts closely the first few months to make sure things are on track and the chemo is not affecting his counts. Jack will also have another MRI six-to-eight weeks after starting chemo to see whether the cancer has stopped growing or has at least slowed in its growth. Jack is OK with all of this. He is very happy to be out of school especially because next week is exam week. I hate to tell him, but he will have to take them anyway sometime in the future. He is not happy about taking chemo again, but he knows he needs to. I reminded him what a good team we made when he had chemo before. He said he remembered and he knew we could do it again. What a trooper.

It's been a long few days. I am tired, worried, edgy, and working hard at finding my strength. I must be strong for him. I know this because we have done this before. But I haven't found my legs yet—for lack of a better term—to be able to stand without falling apart. I did a little Christmas shopping today, and the sad Christmas music playing through every store's PA system has sent me crying to the car twice. This is so hard, much harder than I thought it could ever be. But I know it's in me... I have to keep digging deeper and deeper somewhere inside of me to find that extra mommy strength. I need to pick up and put my mommy armor back on and get ready for the next battle in this war. I must get past the crying and the heartache and fight again.

...BUT I'M NOT THE SINGER

Maybe this weekend, I can spend time gathering my thoughts. Building my emotional strength will help. Jack is so strong; I need to follow his lead. Lord help me, I love this child!!

Dear Lord, thank you for time—time we have with our loved ones, time we have to heal from emotional burdens and physical scars, time we use thinking and praying for others in need, and time we spend worshiping You. Please be with the families who lives changed forever today. Hold them close, give them the things they need, and surround them with love and caring. In His Name, Amen.

DECEMBER 18, 2012—Jack's port implanting surgery went well, no complications. He was as usual full of himself ready and willing to tell his nurse and doctor how to do everything. We were at the hospital at 6am. They took Jack to surgery at 7:30, and the doctor came to talk with us when he was finished at 8:45. We loaded a wobbly Jack in the van at 10:15 and were home around 11. A very busy morning for us all. We were back at the hospital this morning at 7:30 am for the kidney test and left at 12:45. We are now back home. Tomorrow we will be back at the hospital at 10:50 to start chemo.

Dear Lord, thank you for healthy bodies and strong minds, for the blessing of sleep when the body and mind are tired, for the touch of the hand of a loved one when they need it, for the gift of a happy smile, for hope that keeps us charging forward when we are not sure of what's ahead, for the blessing of children, for the opportunity to watch our children grow, for love between a parent and a child, and for the love and support of so many people who hold us up in time of need. Amen.

DECEMBER 20, 2012—I was looking forward to a little peace and quiet after our three days at the hospital but today has been a hard day as well. Yesterday was chemo day for Jack. Since his appointment was mid-morning, I had planned on him going to school for a few hours and picking him up on the way to the hospital. But he woke up with an itchy rash all over his neck, chest, and arms so I kept him home. I thought I would let the doctor look at it before we did anything. As I have said nothing in the medical world gets done in a fast manner. There is a lot of waiting involved whether you are waiting to get called back to see the doctor, waiting to have a test run, or waiting to get the results of a test, and so on and so on. Of course, yesterday was a hurry up and wait kind of day. Jack and I arrived before the appointment time and waited in the waiting room which was filled to capacity. We were last to be called back.

MY NAME IS JACK JOHNSON...

On Monday, the surgeon who implanted Jack's new port told us that the port was implanted where the old one was but the tubing was inserted into another artery that runs horizontal in Jack's upper chest near his shoulder and the tubing ends in one of the chambers of his heart. It was for me a too-much-information moment. Jack had to have his port accessed—the beginning stage of getting his first dose of chemo. Our nurse took her Jack instructions—"find the port, get the needle, count to three before putting the needle in"—and followed them. But something was wrong and the needle would not work. She had to take it out and try again. Let me add that she is working with a newly placed port, which was implanted under the new incision which has just barely healed since the surgery to put it in was just two days earlier. It hurt me just to look at it much less touch it with your hands and especially not a sharp object like a needle. She tried again and again it didn't work. She asked Jack to lie down so she could try again with him on the table and not in a chair. We got Jack up and moved to the bed and she tried again, but it wasn't going where it needed to go. This time when she took the needle out, blood ran down Jack's chest coming from the needle hole. Seeing the blood freaked Jack out and he started to tune up to cry. I stopped him, got him to look me in the eyes, and asked him if I was upset about the blood. (He and I have a pact of sorts that says when Mommy looks worried and upset, then Jack can be worried and upset!) I reassured him that it was just a little blood and it was nothing to worry about. She tried twice more and on the second time, the needle was finally where it needed to be. Jack was hurting and upset over the blood. I am sure it had to hurt even with the numbing cream we had applied before we left home. The area was still healing from the surgery and then having to endure repeated needle pokes, his whole chest had to be tender. Jack did an excellent job of keeping it all together! The oncology floor does not order chemo from the hospital pharmacy until the patient arrives, gets checked in, and has any tests done to make sure they can get the chemo that day. While we waited for the chemo to come up from the pharmacy, Jack was given an anti-nausea drug and Benadryl for the rash. He rested and soon felt better. After a little lunch, he quietly fell to sleep thanks to the Benadryl. The doctor came in with all the papers for me to sign and sat with me and explained all the side effects of these three new chemo drugs. Listening to the what-ifs is very scary. The chemo finally arrived around 2pm and the infusion started. The first of two chemo drugs took ninety minutes to infuse; the second one took an hour. The doctor had written a prescription for Jack's oral chemo drug which was sent to the hospital pharmacy for me to pick up before we left.

...BUT I'M NOT THE SINGER

When I saw the last chemo getting near the end, I left Jack in the hands of the nurses and headed downstairs to the pharmacy. I have a troubled past with the hospital pharmacy. I was told once at the beginning of this journey years ago that the doctor had sent a prescription and I needed to pick it up. Naively, I went to the pharmacy, waited my turn nicely, and asked so politely for Jack's prescription. The person who waited on me went into this verbal tirade about how doctors think they can just send in a prescription and it should be ready in just a few minutes when the pharmacy has other orders ahead of that one doctor from other doctors who think the same way... blah... blah... blah. It went on and on, like I caused it. I was just doing what the doctor told me to do but I was getting called out for it. I did tell Jack's doctor how bad I was treated and asked that he never send any prescription there again. But he said he had to send chemo drugs to that pharmacy since they keep them on hand for oncology patients. So, I went downstairs finding only one person ahead of me in line, a nice surprise. I asked politely again for Jack's prescription and the salesperson went to find it. She couldn't find it. She went to the pharmacist in the back and the two of them began whispering. Then the pharmacist walked over to the counter and said, "Mrs. Johnson, did anyone talk to you about the price of this drug?" I told her no and prepared to hear "a couple of hundred dollars." She said, "This drug will cost 3,000 dollars and your insurance is refusing to pay." I am totally at a loss for words. Three thousand dollars!!! Insurance refusing to pay. My mind cannot wrap around those words. I gave her our secondary insurance but the pharmacy does not accept the insurance. We talked strategy, she gave me the pharmacy business card and I walked away without Jack's chemo drugs. Oh, and I forgot to add, the 3,000 dollars is for five pills! Not a typo—five pills. Ben and I are still working with the doctor, our insurance companies, and pharmacies in our area trying to get this price down through our insurance companies. As of today, Jack has not had his third chemo drug. Now I'm going to vent so if you don't want to hear it, then skip this part. How does anyone think anybody can afford 3,000-dollar drugs? To say we are stunned is an understatement. We have just geared up to try to do anything in our power to save the life of our son from some stinking cancer that has no known cause and did not leave his body the first treatment go-round. And then you get the news that one of the drugs that shows promise in killing this monster is going to cost 3,000 dollars for five pills. Five pills he will have to take each month for twelve months. That's a total of $36,000 for twelve months. No wonder people find themselves in financial ruin from medical expenses. So, while we are down, facing a year of chemo that shows

MY NAME IS JACK JOHNSON...

promise in treating Jack's cancer but is not a cure, we get kicked by the price of one of the drugs that could save his life if it works the way it has for others facing this same demon. Life just isn't fair sometimes and this is one of those times. Ben and I are determined to keep working with everyone involved to find a solution to our 3,000-dollar dilemma. It was a long and hard day.

Dear Lord, thank you for moments without pain and sorrow, for healthy bodies and strong minds, for the gift of children, for the blessing of friends who are there when you need them most, for parents and family, for the abundance of food we enjoy, for the beauty of the lights at night during this season, for the love and support of so many people who walk with us on this journey, and for this time of year when we celebrate the birth of Your Son. In His Name, Amen.

DECEMBER 22, 2012—A Christmas Miracle... Yesterday was like riding on a ride at an amusement park. The only difference was there was nothing amusing about it. When I wrote my last entry, we were in the process of trying to get our hands-on Jack's third chemo—five pills that we found out were going to cost us 3,000 dollars and our insurance was refusing to pay for them. When taking chemo, the doses of the different chemo drugs used are given at certain times in the treatment process, ensuring the optimal amount of each drug used is doing its specific job at just the right time in conjunction with the jobs of the other chemo drugs. Since Jack had already received the other two chemo drugs on Wednesday, we had just a small window of opportunity to get that third chemo in him so all three chemo drugs could do their specific jobs in unison per his treatment plan. Thursday night I went into Walgreens and talked with a pharmacist, my second conversation with her that day, (thanks C., for all your help and advice!) and found out that they did not accept either of our insurances, which if they did, could help with the cost of the drug. I also asked why any drug would cost this much. She explained that the cost has to do with the research involved with a drug and since this drug was new, it had quite a bit of research behind it making it cost higher than most. After talking to her and knowing that Walgreens would not accept either of our insurances, Ben and I decided to get up Friday morning, call the oncologist office, have the Walgreens order cancelled, and try other pharmacies in hopes to find one that would accept both insurances. No sooner than my feet hit the floor, I called the doctor's office and left a long message for the doctor's administrative assistant, K. After I left the message, Ben and I got ready to go Christmas shopping—something we have put off for so long, waiting to hear the results of the MRI, then dealing with the results, and hav-

...BUT I'M NOT THE SINGER

ing to adjust to live in chemo land again. Before we left the house, K. called and I told her that we were trying to find a pharmacy that would use both insurances. She told me to call her if we found a pharmacy and she would talk to the pharmacist and send them the prescription. She also told me that I could have her paged when we found a pharmacy. Ben and I started our hunt for the elusive pharmacy that would take both of our insurances and cover some of the cost of Jack's chemo drug. We stopped first at the Kroger close to our house, walked to the pharmacy, asked for the pharmacist, and found out they did indeed accept both of our insurances. Jackpot! I made the call to K., had her paged, but she didn't answer. While I was on hold waiting for K. to answer her page, the pharmacist looked up the chemo drug in his computer, told us that the drug is no longer manufactured in a 250-milligram dose, and that the price for the five pills would now be $4,000 instead of $3,000. Holy Moly! We were worried about trying to come up with $3000 and now that price is up to $4,000 in the blink of an eye. We took the pharmacy's phone number and left to try to Christmas shop. While shopping, Ben and I were coming up with plan after plan to make this chemo situation less expensive and wondered how the heck we are going to pay for a whole year of this drug. K. called and told me that the Kroger pharmacy will have to order the drug and because of the holiday will not be able to get the chemo drug until next Friday. We can't wait that long so K. said she was going to try something else and would call me back. We continued shopping while thinking about the black cloud shadowing our lives. K. called again and told us she was talking to the pharmacy at the Children's Hospital in hopes that someone there could help us. Shopping was hard with all the chaos of the crowds, the horrific drivers who seemed to lose all sense of etiquette, and the fighting and haggling over prices between the customers and checkout personnel over sale prices. Around 4pm, I got a call from K. She had been working closely with the hospital pharmacist and asked if we could get to Nashville by 5:30pm. She explained that the hospital pharmacist had sent the prescription to the main hospital at Vanderbilt, not the Children's Hospital and we needed to pick it up by 5:30. K. also asked if I wanted to hear some good news (of course I did) and told me the prescription would be FREE! FREE, yes, totally FREE! The drug that was going to cost us at least $3,000 we are getting for FREE! (Sorry for the capital letters but I love typing that word!!) I don't understand how K. did this or if it was the pharmacist at the Children's Hospital or a pharmacist at Vanderbilt Hospital but my poor tired, feeble mind can only comprehend the word FREE. I thanked my new best friend, K., told her I wanted to meet

MY NAME IS JACK JOHNSON...

her next week at Jack's next appointment, and she agreed to meet and talk next Wednesday. Ben and I left, trying our best to get to Vanderbilt Hospital's Clinic Pharmacy by 5:30. I have heard and experienced so many times in my life where things have been presented to me as free and in reality, were not, that I was a little skeptical about getting a $3,000 drug for free... totally free. I found the pharmacy while Ben waited in the car, stood in line, and waited my turn, and gave the pharmacy tech Jack's name. She found the drug. I talked to the pharmacist and got specific instructions, and finally, in my little hot hands, I got to hold the most expensive drug I have ever heard of and there, written in little numbers on the receipt, underneath the true price are lots of zeroes. It is truly FREE. As I walked through the halls of Vanderbilt back to the waiting car, two things happened: I gave thanks to God and I physically skipped in the hallway while tears of joy fell down my cheeks! I got a few looks from others in the hallway but I did not care. Now will the drugs be free from now on out? No, but we have one dose down, eleven more to go. Did this solve the problem of cost and insurance? No, but we will worry about that next week. Will we still be faced with uncertainty about how much the drug will cost? Yes, but next week when Jack goes in for blood work and we get to meet K., we will also meet with the hospital social worker and try to come up with a plan of action. But for now, Ben and I are FREE from a huge financial burden here at Christmas time. For poor Jack, he has started yet another chemo drug that could eventually make him nauseated and sick. That's the worst part of the whole picture.

Dear Lord, thank you for surrounding us with others who give from their hearts, for the ability to love, for every moment we share with the ones we love, for the gift of a smile, for the blessing of children, for showing us Your love through the actions of others, for the love and support we receive from family, friends, and strangers, and for the miracle of Christmas—the birth of Your Son. In His Name, Amen.

DECEMBER 29, 2012—We hope everyone had a great Christmas, visiting with family and friends. We had a busy Christmas, going here and there to visit with family. We did have one special gift for Jack this year. One of my sisters with the help of my dad put a sign on the nearest electric pole to our house that has a transformer attached. The sign says, "This electric pole belongs to Jack." He loved it. He talked about how it would now be his job to make sure the light on the pole was working at all times. If it goes out, he can call the electric company and have them come and change the bulb. When I

...BUT I'M NOT THE SINGER

asked my sister if she had the electric company's OK for this, she said no, but maybe they won't care. So, if anyone reading this works for the electric company, there is an electric pole on our street that now belongs to Jack. We hope that is OK. If not, please let us know before anyone takes down the sign or someone will have his feelings hurt. And it won't be pretty... someone could get fired!!

All in all, it was a good Christmas. Jack even commented last night about how nice it was for him not to be upset with worry over Santa and what Santa was bringing him for Christmas. I must confess it was bittersweet for me from beginning to end. In my mind, I constantly wondered if this would be our last Christmas together and that made me cry several times. Each Jack ornament I put on the tree, each gift I wrapped for him, each present he opened, I thought that same thought. I pray that it won't be and I pray this chemo will work wonders. But reality is not on our side, and I know this. I so wish Santa had brought Jack a gift, a small box with the word "Cure" on the side. But as of today, Santa has not brought that box. For Ben and me it has been a hard Christmas.

Reality hit home on the day after Christmas. After Jack woke up and ate his yogurt, he suddenly jumped up and ran to the bathroom and vomited his breakfast up. Luckily, he hadn't taken his "the most expensive pill ever" chemo pill. Hate for him to vomit up his 700 dollar-plus chemo!! Update on the chemo drugs is that we have an army of people working to find a solution to this expensive chemo. We have so many different routes to take and each one is being carefully examined. Hopefully, we will have a plan in place in the next few weeks. In the meantime, Jack has another hospital visit for chemo on Wednesday, Jan. 2nd. What a way to start a new year!

Dear Lord, thank you for the gift of friendship, for the love of family, for the blessing of children, for the time we have with our loved ones, for healthy bodies and strong minds, for the sound of laughter and the sight of a smile, for faith and hope, for the abundance of food we are blessed with, and for the continued love and support of family, friends, and strangers walking each day with us on this difficult journey. In Jesus' Name, Amen.

DECEMBER 31, 2012—Reflections...

An idle mind, a quiet house, no New Year's Eve party, and a brain full of reflections over 2012. What's a girl to do? Write them down.

Reflecting over the last year was easy for me. I remember so much: Jack's leg surgery, getting his port taken out, a year without chemo, several no evidence of disease MRI's and then the game changer in July. "There is another

MY NAME IS JACK JOHNSON...

lesion." I am a big believer in not dwelling on the past, and I don't necessarily think reflecting is dwelling. Reflecting is the act of looking back and looking for the good and bad in a year, but not looking backward to point fingers, blame others or yourself, or causing feelings of guilt.

With my thoughts reflective, I will write notes to others...

To all of Jack's loyal followers,

What would we do without you? No one can fully understand how terribly lonely this journey truly is until you walk it yourself. People sometimes avoid us—whether in person or by not calling/coming around us anymore—because it is very hard for us to live in this cancer land, much less come to visit on a regular basis. There is no light-hearted-spontaneous-let's-go-do-something-fun attitude in our home. We are slaves to cancer in what we can and can't do and where and when we can or can't go. Our wallets are empty with the cost of medical expenses and most fun activities in this world cost money. And, hey, cancer is not fun. It is not fun or enjoyable to watch another human being become sick and frail through no fault of their own. Cancer brings up feelings of fright: "Could I be next?" Or feelings of grief: "I remember Aunt Agnes and how she suffered." And who wants to be reminded of past grief or thoughts of their own mortality? So, for all of you who so diligently follow Jack's journey, leave messages of hope, send cards of encouragement, continue to want to be with us in some way, we are truly thankful. I have said it so many times that sometimes it might sound trite and small but I mean it with all my heart. It is always fun to have companionship with others when life is at its fullest, with fun and happiness. It is not always fun to be a spectator of the other side. You are a blessing to us by just continuing to support us through this long and difficult journey. I will forever be grateful for each of you.

To our Heavenly Father,

I must say You have surprised me. Not only is it a surprise no parent wants to get—a diagnosis of his or her child's cancer—but for You to turn cancer into a surprise view of a different side of life is another. You have made me see for the first time. You have made me see the things I have read about so many years in Your book. I have witnessed the good in people that only You can move them to do at just the right time. People do not move for any reason; You make them move. People do not love for any reason; they love because You opened their hearts to love. On the darkest days when my

... BUT I'M NOT THE SINGER

heart hurts, You move someone into action. When we have had an unexpected need, You have moved someone to fill it. We have never had to ask for anything; our meager needs have been fulfilled through You. You didn't cause this cancer to happen; man has done this to himself. You can't take it all away because then there would be no catalyst to move others to do Your work. Why my son from all the sons in this world—I hope one day I will understand. He has taught me so much about life, myself, and this world and for that, I am truly grateful to You. During some moments in this journey, I think I have seen the face of Jesus, not in the flesh, but in the faces of others. Thank you for loving me enough to show me this part of life that most people do not see.

To my wonderful son, Benny,

I am in awe of you. You show me things I never thought you would. You were such a funny, free-spirited, imaginative, hard-headed, little dark-haired boy. Wasn't that just yesterday? I often wondered what hellish behavior you would share with us that would embarrass and humiliate us—your parents. But life has had other plans for our family and you have had to become a person of character, feelings, and compassion. A life most children never live. You have to be a big brother to a brother who, through no fault of his own, is sometimes very, very difficult. You have had to learn to understand that the broken toys and hurt feelings were not caused from meanness but from an invisible member of our family who came to live in our house uninvited and unwelcomed. Sometimes you have been referred to not by your name but by who you are related to. Sometimes you have had to do things that you didn't plan to do or go places you didn't plan to go because our lives dictated that we had to do or go to those places to keep peace in our family. You have seen behaviors of others—good and bad—that have shaped you into the young man you are today. I always thought you were afraid to have friends over who would see what life was like in our house. But now I understand it was a defensive strategy—why show them the truth when they aren't mature enough to understand the situation. Now at this age and maturity level, you chose to surround yourself with people who do understand and support you with their friendship because they care for you. You could let all of this become a burden and bring hate into your heart, but you chose to wear it like a piece of clothing—something you wear without too much thought or care. Please continue to see others for who they are. Do not judge them by what they have or who they know but live your life for yourself. Do not waste time on the unnecessary wants of life but by the needs of yourself and others. Give your

MY NAME IS JACK JOHNSON...

time, your love, your gifts whenever you can. Be proud of where you have been and where you are going. You are remarkable. You are loved.

To warrior Jack,

You are a teacher and you have no idea that you are. You are teaching me so much about life and about myself. Life would be so boring and mundane if not for you and your uniqueness. I find myself sometimes feeling sorry for other parents who don't have a child like you in their lives. How boring life must be for them; so normal, so typical. Most parents have children and lives that are the primary colors: green, red, blue, and yellow. Because of you, our family has the whole color wheel in life—the greenest greens, the darkest reds, the brightest yellows, and the most vivid hues of blue. Life has never been boring since you were born. Then life gave us our first bump in the road. I had to watch as some hidden force took over your mind and you became someone different. It was hard to watch you fall further and further away from us. Autism makes you do things out of the ordinary. I have watched as people walk farther and farther away from you. It has been so hard to witness. But it also brought a whole new set of people into our lives that most people do not know. I discovered the world of special needs—a community of families who live each day in a way so different and so meaningful—most people don't realize exists. It is almost a secret society where people give to others who are different in many ways. Some are therapists, some are teachers, others are families, and then there are others who just get IT—the IT being the realization that we are not made the same as others and that is a wonderful thing. It was like going to the World of OZ, where the colors of the world were brighter, the people were more understanding, and the whole world revolved around love, not hate and discrimination. You know nothing about this world as your mind is being bombarded by the world around you—a world your brain is not ready to see, feel, hear, or touch. At the beginning of your new strange world, you needed a guide—someone who would guide you through the maze of this world. I stepped into that role willingly. Your Dad took the reins of our everyday world and I became your world tour guide, guiding you through the world of learning to live in a world you didn't understand. Hand-in-hand, we have stumbled and fallen, picked ourselves up and plowed ahead. I have never truly understood your world but have tried to learn everything I can so I can help you navigate my world. I am your advocate, helper, teacher, therapist, investigator, translator, guide, activist, counselor, doctor, nurse, mother, and friend. I have researched this disorder until

... BUT I'M NOT THE SINGER

my head hurts. It hasn't been easy—learning your world and trying to teach you to live in ours. The road has been long and bumpy but we are persevering. Our family sacrifices so much so life will be easier for you and Benny in the future when Ben and I are no longer here. My relationship with you is not one of just a mother and son. It is much deeper than that. I have seen others look at me for direction when they didn't know what to do or say around you. I have seen you look at me for direction when you have been put into a situation you don't understand. I understand you more than any other person on this earth because that is my job. My job from the beginning is to help you get through this life and you are. You exceeded so far past my help and have relied on yourself and the knowledge you have learned. You use the skills you have learned to be the person you want to be. You have succeeded beyond my wildest dreams! Life took another unexpected swing at you and I became your guide and interpreter again. This new chapter brought new challenges and changes. In moments when the pain for you was great and your body wretched from the strong medicines, I so wished I could carry your burden I wished it was me and not you. I prayed every day that your burden and pain would be eased. I thought the prayer had been answered. But it wasn't. And yet again we face the beast once again. Hand-in-hand we will fight together! As I have told you several times, you and I can do anything together. I will not give up. I will fight with you if I must. I will sacrifice to save you. Wars are fought by warriors, strong and brave. You are a warrior. You have faced the foe with strength and bravery. I am proud of you and I will gladly wear my armor to face another battle for you. You are my hero.

And for you... Cancer,

I despise you. I hate you with a burning hate that any mother who has fought this battle for their child feels. You are a coward, stealing from the innocence of the young. You have robbed my child, my family, and our lives of so much. You have taken our monetary assets, our future, and our sorrow and tears. You have scarred my child and left him unable to walk unassisted. You have brought pain and sickness to him. You have taken from him the ability to remember things that once were so easy to remember. You have aged us and turned mine and Ben's hair white. I so wish you didn't exist. But there are things you cannot take from us. You cannot take our happiness because we will continue to look for the joy in this life's battle. You cannot take our faith in God who will always be with us. You cannot take our hope because we have an endless supply. You cannot take the support and love of others who hold us up

MY NAME IS JACK JOHNSON...

during your visit. You will not take my son without the biggest fight of your life. You will not win. Together we will kick your cancerous butt!!

These are my reflections of 2012. I make no apologies. I will make no resolutions that I wouldn't keep anyway. 2012 has been another roller coaster ride with its ups and downs, its twists and turns. I am not sure what 2013 will bring, but I know I will still be thankful to each of you who stay with us during this battle. I will still be thankful to God for all our blessings. And I will continue to fight, not only for my child but for every child who fights this battle.

Happy New Year. Be safe. Have fun. Enjoy.

Love to all!!

CHAPTER 36

JANUARY 6, 2013—It's so very quiet in my house. Bless his heart; poor Jack is on nap number two for today. He has not had a good day, or for that matter, a good weekend when it comes to his health. He woke up yesterday morning and vomited, but the rest of the day he felt good. Today he woke up and vomited but has never really gotten to where he has felt good. I have taken his temperature twice, but there is no fever. He just doesn't feel good.

Jack did feel well enough to attend a party in his honor last night. There are three wonderful ladies who each Sunday spend their Sunday School class time with Jack. They walk the church building with him as he checks each Exit sign. One week one of the ladies jokingly called their unusual class "The Walking with Jack Sunday School Class"—a take on the "Walking with Jesus" Bible study—and the name stuck. The ladies of the Walking with Jack SSC decided he deserved a party with all his favorite activities and foods. At the party, we had apple slices, pepperoni and sausage pizza from Papa John's, and red velvet cupcakes... all of Jack's favorites. There were also "Jack" rules we had to follow: no smoking or underage drinking, no crying babies, and no music except his iPod. Ben got in trouble with Jack because he was caught with a beer, but he didn't have to leave the party. Miss D's birthday is today (Benny's girlfriend), so Jack rapped a birthday song for her in front of everyone at the party. Took everyone completely by surprise because none of us knew he would rap in front of so many people nor did we know he knew a rap song enough to repeat it. Thankfully, it was a clean rap song too.

Jack had another chemo treatment this past Wednesday. It was one of those days that wasn't a "good" day at clinic. Jack's nurse accessed his port with a needle to take blood and to give him his chemo but for some reason he complained once the needle was in place that it hurt. Just saying something hurts is so general so I had to get Jack to give us a more descriptive explanation to what and where it was hurting. He said the port hurt in his chest and that on the pain scale the pain was about an eight. Jack is not a complainer

MY NAME IS JACK JOHNSON...

unless something is extremely wrong so I knew he really must be hurting. I asked him if we needed to get the nurse to take the needle out and try putting it back in but he said he would tough it out and wait and see if the pain got better. While we waited for the blood work to come back, I asked Jack several times if he was still hurting and he told me he was but not as bad... a four or five on the pain scale. Then he rolled over on the examining table and accidentally touched the needle and he cried out in pain. I knew then we had to change the needle. I found his nurse and she immediately took the needle out and placed another one in his port. At first, Jack complained that it hurt as well but eventually the pain subsided. This was a first for us. Jack has never, ever had pain with getting his port accessed. There have been occasions where the act of getting the needle into the port had hurt especially if the needle had to be put in the port and taken out several times because it missed the port in his chest. But this was not the same. I hope this is the last time this happens. Once the needle was safely in place and not hurting, the blood work came back with flying colors, and the drugs were started. First, he was given his anti-nausea drug and some Benadryl, which also helps with nausea. The Benadryl also puts Jack to sleep and soon he was out. While he was out, a small child in the big infusion room (Jack's nurse had put us in a room usually reserved for sick children) started to cry. In the beginning, it was soft cry, then it became louder, and then the child, between loud sobs, starting screaming, "Stop. You are hurting me!" This poor child cried and screamed about how someone or something was hurting them for thirty minutes. Between seeing Jack in so much pain with the accessed needle and then hearing this other poor child suffer, it was too much for me. It is bad enough hearing any child crying in the infusion room because we know how horrible this truly is on them. But for this child to cry and be in pain for so long... it is in a strange way a form of torture for these children. Not too long ago, a young child was waiting in the infusion room while we were waiting to be called back into a room. His nurse came to take him back to the room where they are set up to access the children's ports—I couldn't tell the age of the child five, six, or seven-ish if I had to guess—but he wasn't stupid and knew where he was being led. When it dawned on him, he started to resist and was physically taken away by two nurses to the access room. It was horrible to watch. I sat and wondered what goes through their minds as they are being led to where ever they are going. If every person had to watch these things happen to children every day like I have, I feel in my heart that there would be a cure for childhood cancer tomorrow.

... BUT I'M NOT THE SINGER

Thankfully Jack slept through the crying child at last Wednesday's appointment. He did ask about the little boy who didn't want to get his port accessed. He even said to me that day that he understands that getting his port accessed is not that bad and doesn't take long. He still amazes me, and I am so glad he understands as much as he does.

Dear Lord, thank you for days without pain and sorrow, for caring nurses and doctors, for healthy bodies and strong minds, for the comfort of a hug, the sound of "I love you," for the touch of a gentle kiss, for the blessing of children, for the joy of friendship, and for the support and love of family, friends, and strangers who continue to hold us up during this journey. Amen.

JANUARY 13, 2013—Jack is doing OK. He feels good, hasn't had any vomiting, but, boy, is he in a bad mood. He fussed at me Friday, yesterday, and again today. He was bad in church, but things were different for him... someone was in our back-row seat, and some of his "Walking with Jack Sunday School" ladies were not there. There was also a crying baby two rows behind us that screamed out several times which made Jack cover his ears (I'm OK with that), turn around to look at the baby (I'm not OK with that), and hiss like a cat at the baby. (I'm definitely not OK with that!) I understand that he has trouble with the sound of loud crying. Who knows what his cancer treatments have done to his thanks-to-autism sensitivity to loud sounds? But the turning around in your seat and hissing in the general direction of the baby is not acceptable. In between the hands flying to the ears, the looks and hissing, he is burping, very loudly. To make matters worse, sitting in church on the other side of me is Ben, mister-I-can't-sit-very-long-without-falling asleep who is in a perpetual state of nodding in and out of consciousness and finally gives in to the feeling, giving himself away with the sound of a snore right in the middle of the sermon. Here I sit between the sound of snoring and the face and sound of a hissing man-cat. What a great day of worship for me! I might have enjoyed the sermon, but I don't even remember what it was about.

Jack also had an adventure on Friday. The special education class at CHS has an outing day once a month. On this day, the special ed students who want to go are taken out with teacher participation into the community and are given a chance to learn first-hand how to act in a public environment. On these days, they are taken to a restaurant, learn how to order their meal themselves, how to pay for their own meals and how to figure and leave an appropriate tip to the waitress/waiter. After lunch, they usually go to a store and can buy an item they might need or want. This exercise teaches them how

MY NAME IS JACK JOHNSON...

to make choices, how to pay for the item, and how to act in a public place. Some of these Jack can do already on his own and some not. The special ed teacher had asked me several times if Jack would like to join them, but he had never really wanted to or had something else happening that day. On Friday, he wanted to go. He had fun being away from school with some of his special ed friends (including the teachers) and learned a little too. He told me about ordering his own food and leaving a tip for his waiter. I had mixed feelings previously about him being away from his classes and missing the lessons for that day in those classes. But after seeing him Friday afternoon and how happy he was when he got home, I am not so sure I made the right choice by not letting him go sooner. Thank you, Ms. L., for asking Jack and for letting him participate.

Dear Lord, thank you for a sense of humor when things in life are not funny, for the joy we see in our everyday life, for the blessing of children, for healthy bodies and strong minds, for being able to feel love, receive love and give love to others, for being patterned in Your likeness, and for the continued love and support of so many people who bless us each day with their presence. In His Name, Amen.

JANUARY 20, 2013—Last Wednesday was chemo day for Jack. Jack and I arrived on time and prepared to stay for the day if necessary. You never know how long you will be at the clinic on chemo days. Jack's favorite nurse MM. was there. MM. had been out for a while and we had not seen her in months. It was nice to see her. She was also Jack's nurse for the day which started his day off well. First for Jack is always getting his blood counts, and for those counts, his port needs to be accessed. MM. accessed his port, first try and without much pain, and Jack was very happy. Once the needle was in the port, the blood was taken, the urine they had to test as well was collected, and we waited to see the doctor. Jack knew we would have to stay and was very excited to find just the right spot in the infusion room where we would spend our afternoon. Jack always gravitates to the corner chairs so there would only be other people on one side of us. Unfortunately for him, all the other families think the same way and most of the time the corner chairs are the first to go. Fortunately for us, the clinic was not crowded, and Jack got a coveted corner chair.

Jack's blood counts and urine came back fine, and we were sent to the infusion room where our corner chair awaited us. There were a few other children with their families getting their treatments but no crying babies... always a good sign. After Jack was given anti-nausea medicine and Benadryl, it

...BUT I'M NOT THE SINGER

wasn't very long until I was sitting with a sleeping patient who only woke now and then when a small child would cry out somewhere in the rooms. I left the Children's Hospital, leaving Jack in the good hands of Nurse MM., and walked over to the Vanderbilt Clinic Pharmacy where Jack's next dose of the-most-expensive-chemo-drug-ever was waiting for me to pick up. Just like last time, I was charged nothing. I must add here that I do think that God heard all our prayers because my-new-best-friend, K., Jack's doctor's secretary, told me that one of our health insurances said they are going to pay for the drugs and so far, they have.

Jack surprised me last week with a telephone call from school. He called because he wasn't having a very good day at school, he had been ugly to his special ed teacher over taking notes in class. He called me to talk to me about it. I don't know why. It's not like I can make the teacher do anything nor can I make Jack do anything different. But he needed to hear my voice, and he needed some reassurance that things would be OK. I picked up the phone, said hello, and Jack said, "Mom." "Yes, Jack." "I am having just the greatest day... can you tell I'm being sarcastic?" He has heard me say that and repeated one of my lines. I love this funny kid.

Dear Lord, thank you for unexpected surprises, for the blessing of children, for every day we have with our loved ones, for the comfort and security of a friendly voice, for inquisitive minds, for healthy bodies, for days without pain and sorrow, and for family, friends, and strangers who continue to love and support us through this journey. In His Name, Amen.

JANUARY 23, 2013—What a week and its only Wednesday. Did I write before that Jack vomited first thing Sunday morning? We didn't go to church, not knowing if the vomiting was a one-time thing or something else. He was fine the rest of the day. Monday, he was fine. No vomiting, no feeling sick, but he was a little tired, more than usual. Tuesday the school nurse called at 10:30ish. Jack had been in the clinic since 8:30, refusing to call home, thinking he would feel better if his headache went away. Once he got home after Ben picked him up, I gave him one of his prescription pills for headaches. Jack is not supposed to take ibuprofen or Tylenol because one of his chemo drugs can cause extra bleeding especially in the brain and taking over the counter remedies for headaches impacts the blood.

Today he woke up, ate breakfast, was washing his face/brushing his teeth/brushing his hair and from nowhere, he vomited. Not just one vomit but several. He was so mad. His morning pills, his breakfast, and his drink all came

MY NAME IS JACK JOHNSON...

up. Between vomiting episodes, he screamed out about how he hates chemo. "I hate you, chemo!!" Vomit. "Why, chemo, why." Vomit. "This is not fair!" Not only do you, the parent, know how hard this is for your child's body—the cancer, the chemo, the vomiting—but then to hear them shout out to the one thing that is at this moment keeping him here with us, it's just unfair. It was a "take your heart out and stomp it" moment. As I have said so many times before, the hardest thing is watching and knowing your child is suffering and there is not a darn thing you can do. I hate cancer with every fiber of my being. I wish all children came into this world with a care package. And in this package, a parent could find an instruction manual, a roll of duct tape to tape our hearts back together after our children break them, ear plugs for the screaming baby and teenage years, and a magic wand, so we have the power to make things better for them in times like these. If only...

Dear Lord, thank you for healthy bodies and strong minds, for times to live life to its fullest and times to reflect, for the blessing of children, for each day, hour and minute we have with the ones we love, for the promise of a beautiful place filled with love where there is no pain or sorrow, and for the love and support of so many who walk with us on this journey. Amen.

JANUARY 29, 2013—This entry comes with a disclaimer. Some might call this entry a pity party. It is not intended to solicit pity. It is a true picture of our lives as we live them out today. Maybe, just maybe, someone reading this will see how very minor their problems are today and give extra love and hugs to the important people in their lives. Every day is a gift. Don't take any of them for granted.

In one word: school. I don't know where to start. I try so hard not to badmouth the school but it is very hard when my child's needs and welfare are not taken seriously. Some of you may remember how Jack's school year started. His first day this year was also his first day at high school as a full-time student. His freshman year was spent at home being a homebound student while he took treatments and his sophomore year was his first year in a high school building but only for four hours each day with an assistant at his side the whole time. So, his first day this year was his actual first day of high school as a full time junior student. But someone in the special education department did not read his IEP and he was left alone, without an assistant, lost in a school he does not know, in crowded hallways. He called me in tears. You do everything in your power as a parent of a special needs student to make sure all the necessities are listed on the IEP, all the people are in place, all

... BUT I'M NOT THE SINGER

the documents signed. And then someone drops the ball and it all falls apart. After Christmas break and the first of the year, if students are taking half courses, they will have a schedule change, changing to the next half course they are signed up for. I told Jack he would have a new schedule at the first of the year and he understood. A week later Benny's girlfriend, Miss D., asked me why Jack was not in class, a class she was in too. She said the teacher had been asking about Jack and asked if anyone knew what was going on. Miss D. waited after class and told the teacher who Jack is since most everyone at school knows something about the boy with cancer. Yet again someone had dropped the ball and Jack missed the first whole week of class because no one looked at this schedule, no one told Jack about the change, and no one got him to the right class. Where was Jack, you might ask? He was still going to his class that was supposed to be PE but since he can't do PE, he was in a quiet room resting. Jack is put in his new class, already a week behind, and per my request is given an assistant. Again Miss D. tells me what is happening in class. Seems the assistant is not assisting with Jack but is sitting in the back of the class and not with Jack. One day, Jack asked the assistant for help and she loudly said, "You mean you asked me over here for that?"—loud enough that other students heard it too. Jack was asking her for the time because he gets to leave his classes early so he is not in the hallways when they are full of students trying to get to their classes—a stress factor for Jack. I got in touch with Jack's special ed teacher who assured me things would be taken care of. The assistant moved this time to the front of the room, still not within helping distance of Jack. When asked why, the assistant said the classroom is not spacious enough for her to have a chair next to Jack. Then what the heck is she there for? I find out that since Jack has been out so much and he started this class already behind, that he was supposed to take a makeup test with others who needed to take it while the others in class took another test. These make-up test-takers are sent to the hall to take their tests. Jack's so-called assistant opened the door for Jack and the others and shut the door behind them, staying in the classroom and not with Jack who she is in the room to be with. Jack went out in the hall and sat in the floor of the hallway while the others took their tests—with no supervision at all. In Jack's other classes, he is to wipe his desk daily with sanitizing wipes before he sits down, making sure he is not exposed to any extra germs—per his IEP. He is now sitting down on the floor of the hallways where every germ known to man is lurking.

Oh, and there is more... this weekend while talking with Jack, I asked him about his school day yet again. I asked this time if he now has an

MY NAME IS JACK JOHNSON...

assistant in every class. He said yes, all except for band. So, I asked, "What happens in band? Are you playing music on your xylophone?"—which we pay for every month on a rental plan. Jack said, "No. I'm not playing much." "What do you do then?" "Oooohhh, I mainly sit and watch the others play." "You sit in the room and watch the others play their instruments?" "No, I'm in a room off by myself and I watch them through the window." "What kind of a room is this?" "It's one of the practice rooms." "Do you ever practice in there?" "Yea, I did some but not much anymore." "Does the teacher give you music to practice with?" "He brought me some but not some every day." "Does the teacher come in the room and say anything to you?" "He sometimes says hi but not all the time." "So, let me get this straight, Jack. You are in a room by yourself, you have your xylophone in there, but you don't get music to practice with, the teacher does not come in there and tell you what you need to do, he only says hi every now and then and you spend class time watching the other students play music through a window?" Innocently and with pride he said "Yes. I watch them and know when it's time to leave the class when they start to pack their instruments up!" I am close to tears. He has goals in band on his IEP. I let the special ed teacher know, she contacted the band leader who asked who is supposed to help him—referring to Jack—and is told: YOU. Today, we got a call from school that Jack is not having a good day and needs to come home. He is not sick, does not have a headache, nor is he upset. We picked him up and asked him what happened. Per Jack, after second period, he was too tired to work anymore. He went to Coach somebody's class to rest on the classroom's bean bag chairs. Seems our little buddy fell into a long nap, missing his next three classes. And since one of those classes is the class with the evil assistant, no one looked for him. He woke up and went to his regular lunch classroom where his special ed teacher finally found him. She talked with him about letting someone know where you are and how you are not supposed to miss class. He went back into the lunch classroom where there was an Uno card game played every day. He was pulled out by the special ed teacher in the middle of the game and when he got back to the game, a player gave him a "pick 4" card. And Jack fell apart. It is so easy with all the chemo and the blood counts and the talk of cancer that we all lose sight of the fact that Jack still has autism. It hasn't disappeared nor was it replaced by cancer. It is still there, alive and well waiting to come out. Ben and I noticed when we picked Jack up from school, he had dark black circles under his eyes. And the list of errors goes on and on. I am going to talk with Jack's doctor tomorrow about homebound requirements

...BUT I'M NOT THE SINGER

since a doctor must ask for a patient to be homebound. We are scheduled for a meeting at school this Thursday morning.

At our last MRI, we were asked a question we have never been asked before. We are asked by the anesthesia doctor if Jack has a DNR. A DNR? After thinking about it, it makes me sick to think this is where we are, talking about getting a "Do Not Resuscitate" order. I am shocked by the thought of it. Then recently I was asked to pray for another child who was fighting brain cancer. He was only five years old, had already had surgery and treatment, had relapsed, and had taken more treatment. But the cancer grew back quickly, so quickly there wasn't anything else the doctors could do, taking his parents by surprise. It happened without warning. One day they were fighting still filled with hope, the next their rug was pulled out from beneath them. This precious child died. Fear is something that goes along with this battle. Once you have had your rug pulled out from under you by the words "Your child has cancer" you have crossed into a world where fear of losing your child is your constant companion. I work hard to push fear away but it rears its ugly head like a "Whack-a-Mole" game. It comes up and you beat it down. It comes back up and you beat it down again. It's a constant struggle. When reading about these other children it dawns on me how close we are to the edge, the edge of the unknown. We have no clue if this new chemo treatment will or will not stop this monster. If it doesn't, we have options but with each failure we have fewer options. It is a scary place to be. Then you read a story so close to your own and it gets harder. Jack has suffered with several headaches. He also complained about his back hurting. He woke up this morning and had to go to the bathroom—at 5am—something he never does. Today, he had yet another bad day at school and we had to pick him up early. He is falling more and more behind on his school work because he is either out with chemo, he is sick from the chemo, or he just cannot handle the pressure of being at school. My world is spinning out of control. I feel like I'm in a vortex, surrounded by IEPs, and rude assistants, and chemo drugs and... and... and I can't seem to stop the constant spinning. Nothing stops the vortex as it moves along. I don't know where to go, how to get out of this situation. If I could just leave and take my family away from this confusion, and worry, and fear. If we could outrun it all...

Dear Lord, thank you for healthy bodies and strong minds, for the time we are given with the ones we love, for letting us find humor in the darkest times, for the blessing of children, for happiness and serenity, and for the continued support and love of so many who walk with us on this journey. Amen

MY NAME IS JACK JOHNSON...

FEBRUARY 1, 2013—Jack had chemo again on Wednesday. We arrived at our appointed time, waited for a few minutes, and after getting weighed and his vitals taken, we were put in an examination room. Jack has lost four pounds in two weeks. His favorite nurse, MM., found us and took Jack back to the lab to get his port accessed to take blood for counts. MM. knows Jack so well now that she knows his favorite things and the way he likes things done. She follows how Jack has coached her to a T, which he loves. She has accessed his port the first time each time she has been his nurse since we have been back on our every two-weeks chemo schedule. It is such a blessing for me to be a witness to someone who cares for your child and his welfare while under her care as Nurse MM. does. I know she would not hurt him unnecessarily. I know she will not get mad at him for reminding her of his personal needs. She has been a blessing to him and me. After his port was accessed, we went back to our examining room and soon the nurse practitioner came in. We discussed how Jack is doing with me relaying his issues with vomiting after chemo, his issues at school, and the added stress it has been for him, and the side effects that the new chemo drugs have caused. She gave him a new prescription for another drug to add to his current anti-nausea medication that will help with the vomiting.

We talked further about school, how Jack is feeling pressured by the workload and how he is falling further and further behind in his present work because of his many absenteeism's. As I suspected she would, she told me she doesn't want Jack to be stressed out and would prefer he be homebound schooled than be so stressed. We agreed. She explained how one of the drugs could cause a brain bleed or bleeding in other parts of his body. She told me what to look for and what to do if I see any of the signs that Jack could be having unusual bleeding. Jack's blood counts were fine, and his urine sample was normal, so we went to the large infusion room. There are only a few chairs left. The first choice was between a woman and her six children and a woman holding a baby. The second choice is between a baby on one side and small child on the other. Jack's first choice was the six children/one baby, but when five of the six children started moving around in the small space each patient is allowed, some of them got too close to Jack. He decided to move to choice number two. One of the patients in the corner finished their chemo and Jack upgraded to the coveted corner chair... with his own TV.

We have experienced the infusion rooms so many times that we come prepared with noise-reducing headphones for Jack. It didn't take long before one baby starts to wail and Jack put the headphones on. MM. saw what

... BUT I'M NOT THE SINGER

was happening and jumped into action. She got Jack's first two medicines prepared and ready to go since one of the medicines would put Jack to sleep. Soon he was hooked up and asleep. While he was asleep, I went downstairs in the hospital and got a sandwich for my lunch. When I got back, the room was a little more crowded than when I left. A couple of ladies had joined the family of six, holding in their hands musical instruments. I thought to myself surely, they are going to take the children who are not receiving chemo out to another room to play music. But NOOOOOO. There are several drums, a xylophone, some shaking things, and a guitar. Soon the room is full of offbeat drumming and shaker noises, lots of guitar strumming, and notes played on a xylophone that are nowhere near the rhythm of the guitar strumming. Jack sleeps soundly through the whole thing! Nurse M.M. came over to us with a horrified look but I assured her Jack was happily sleeping. Thank you, Benadryl, for the gift of sleep you give. Me, on the other hand? I got a headache. I called Ben so he could hear what I was hearing. Now I don't mean to sound insensitive to the needs of others and know that it must be terrible to have to bring your whole brood with you so one of your children can get their much-needed chemo drug. But what about the rest of us? What about all the children who don't feel like listening to your musical party? Is there not another room in that whole hospital that could be used for this? Hey, what about the lobby? That would be good for the other children waiting their turn to see their doctors. Maybe a little music to soothe their nerves. But NOOOOO, I am treated to a concert of drumming, strumming, and beating of musical instruments. I ate my lunch and got indigestion. Finally, the concert was over and the instruments and music ladies left. Silence is golden and I love it.

We had a meeting yesterday with school personnel. I had made of list of complaints and read from the list. Ben and I got the feeling there were several people in attendance who were not happy besides us. We did not get finished with the business at hand and will meet this Tuesday morning again. With everything that has happened and taking Jack's safety and happiness into consideration, we decided to keep Jack in school for the immediate future. We have changed his day and dropped two of his classes. We have lessened his workload in hopes of relieving his stress. If Jack is still stressed after the changes have been made, we will look at homebound schooling again. The homebound paperwork will be completed, and homebound schooling will be on standby for lack of a better term. In case Jack's health changes or his side effects worsen, we will educate him in our home

MY NAME IS JACK JOHNSON...

with homebound services. But by having the paperwork completed and in place, homebound services can begin quickly in case things change.

Ben and I agonized over what we wanted for Jack. This past summer without anything to do, both of us felt like Jack was becoming very depressed. Near the end of summer, he was lifeless and didn't want to do anything. Once he got into school after the horrible beginning, he did have some good days. He enjoys spending time with some of his friends and being in the company of peers. He has always enjoyed learning when it is presented in a format geared toward his learning style. We had planned for all of this and things were listed on his IEP for his benefit, but since the IEP was not being followed and things were not being done to help Jack, he became stressed. Ben and I were promised things would change by the administrator who attended our meeting. I lost it and cried in the meeting, something I hate to do. I had not slept well for several nights with just too dang much stuff on my mind. I don't think some people at school realized how very serious all of Jack's issues are and how not realizing this could put him and their own wellbeing at risk. I pray they get the full picture now. And I pray Jack has fun while he continues to learn beside his peers.

After the meeting, Ben and I had to run and pick up some items for Jack's lunch and take it back to school for him. I ran it into his lunch classroom barely five seconds before he did. I talked to the classroom teacher for a while and got the opportunity to see Jack interact with his friends, both special needs, and typical friends. He was sitting at a table surrounded by friends, first eating and talking, then playing Uno cards. He was glowing. His smile was from ear to ear. He joked with them, and he laughed with them. He was having fun. I teared up just watching him and his school buddies. After agonizing over Jack's school day, and sitting for hours in that meeting, and crying tears because I have lost trust in the people who are supposed to care and keep my child safe, I saw that big smile and heard the laughter and saw the interaction of a kid who needs to be with others. It certainly helped me know we made the right decision for today.

Dear God, thank you for the blessing of children, for healthy bodies and strong minds, for tears of joy and tears of sorrow, for the time we have been given with the ones we love, for the sound of laughter and the gift of a smile, for eyes that see the beauty of a snowflake, and for the continued love, support, and surprises from family, friends, and strangers. In His Name, Amen

... BUT I'M NOT THE SINGER

FEBRUARY 5, 2013—The week we thought we would have has turned into the week we didn't know was coming. Sunday morning, we all woke up with plans to attend church. Everyone was clean, almost ready except for Jack. Before we could get him ready, he walked into the bathroom and exploded. Bless his heart... he vomited so much. It wore him out. He slept for the next three hours. Monday morning Jack got up expecting to go to school but instead vomited again. And again, after being sick, he slept three hours. Today he again woke up expecting to go to school but again vomited. He slept until 10am. Needless to say I really don't think the new anti-nausea medicine is working. If he vomits again tomorrow I will call the doctor's office for another med. You never fully understand how completely different we all are until you see so many people, whether children or adults, who take the same drug but suffer so many different side effects. It is very eye-opening for me. This morning Jack also complained about not having any balance. This could be a side effect from the anti-nausea drug, or from the cancer itself, or from just being so out of sorts. Who knows. All of this is just a guessing game— whether this drug will do this or that, whether the tumors will grow or shrink, whether the vomiting will quit altogether tomorrow... who knows? We live in a world of information, usually very concrete information. We ask a question and we get answers or we know where to find them usually with a click of a few buttons. But our family seems to live in world of vagueness; a place where factual answers to questions do not exist. Funny how we Christians when in this situation ask God for guidance and wisdom. But in those moments when you watch your child puking his guts out from a trial chemo that may or may not stop a cancer that has grown from a mysterious cause, you don't pray for guidance and wisdom. You pray your child gets relief from the sickness and you pray for someone else to receive the guidance and wisdom so your child and hundreds like him can live their lives happy and healthy and get to see adulthood. Faith is your constant companion: faith that you are making the best decisions you can for your child from the information you are given, faith in the doctors who are giving you that information, and faith that God is giving all of us the things we need whether it's a day without sickness or finding the needle in the haystack that will one day be a cure. We hope that these things will happen, with faith we believe they will and with love, we clean up the mess left behind a sick child and give them a hug. An abnormal view of faith, hope, and love.

Later this afternoon Jack became bored and sad, missing school and not seeing his friends. I had so much to do, but my heart just dropped seeing his sadness. So, we played a few card games of rummy. I had so much fun watching his face light up as we played. He made all kinds of noises, good ones and bad ones for the times when he had a good play or when I had a good play. I so wish I had a recorder in my mind of times like that, when taking out a camcorder would ruin the moment. To see him go from a moody teen to a happy little boy again was priceless. It made my day.

Dear Lord, thank you for the time we have with our loved ones, for faith, hope and love, for healthy bodies and strong minds, for days without pain and sorrow, for moments with smiles and laughter, for the blessing of children, for the memories we make every day, and for the love and support of so many people who continue to walk with us on this journey. Amen.

FEBRUARY 14, 2013—Jack's MRI was Monday. It was an uneventful MRI. We left for the hospital at 10 am and pulled in our driveway at 6 pm. Wednesday, we were back at the hospital at 8:40 am. Nurse MM. was there and accessed Jack port on the first try. Jack was a happy boy. Dr. E. came in with the MRI results. Good news: the tumors in Jack's spine are either less enhanced on the MRI or have shrunk in size. The chemo Jack is taking is working!! This is wonderful news, and we are very happy.

Since the chemo is working and Wednesday was a regularly scheduled chemo day, we made our way to the infusion room to find a chair to spend our next several hours in. Nurse MM. hooked Jack up to the IV pole with his anti-nausea medication before she started the chemo. Twenty-five minutes after the anti-nausea medicine started, Jack fell asleep. He woke up after about an hour's nap and had to go to the restroom. I unplugged the IV machine, got Jack up, grabbed the pole with one hand and held on to Jack with the other. He went to the bathroom, an uneventful trip, and soon we were back sitting in our corner chair in our curtained off spot in the infusion room. Jack nodded in and out of sleep. He said he was not hungry or thirsty and just wanted to nap. MM. came and went, checking on the chemo and changing the different IV bags as they emptied. Jack suddenly gave me a funny look and said he needed to go to the bathroom again. MM. was re-calculating the IV machine because we were near the end of one of the chemo bags. She told us to go on to the bathroom, warned me that the IV machine would probably "beep" while we are in there, and showed me where to turn off the beeping noise while we are in the bathroom. Again, we made the trek to the restroom, I got Jack inside, and he did his business. He looked up and told me again he was not feeling good and said, "My mouth is feeling swimmy" which is what he says happens

...BUT I'M NOT THE SINGER

before he gets sick. I had to get him up out of one position, get him over the potty making sure his IV tubing was not in the line of fire, and he started heaving. Bless his heart, he had the heaves. And he heaved and heaved. He did not have anything in him because he had not eaten much for breakfast and he had not eaten lunch. The chemo was still making him sick. After a couple of heaves, the dang IV machine started beeping and I turned it off. I was trying to make sure Jack stayed in the correct position for vomiting (Jack tends to not bend over the commode when getting sick and gets it everywhere) as I was going back and forth to the sink to get him cold paper towels for his face and neck when someone knocked on the door. I said, "Just a minute" and went back to Jack. He was still heaving, the IV machine beeped again, and yet again someone knocked on the door. Argh!! Of all times for someone to need the bathroom and for the IV machine to keep beeping. I made sure he was OK and had himself steadied, opened the door, and asked the closest nurse to find MM. for us in hopes I could get her to ask Jack's doctor for some more anti-nausea medicine that hopefully will stop the heaving. When I opened the door, there stood a lady holding a baby who I assumed was the person who had been knocking on the door. I told her that my son was sick in the bathroom, that he would be a while, and that there was another bathroom down the hall. She told me she really needed the bathroom we are in because it has a baby changing table. Oh goodness. I didn't think about us being in the bathroom with a changing table but there are other bathrooms that have changing tables but not in the oncology department. There was one in the lobby but I guess she didn't know or had forgotten. I wished I could have helped her out but until Jack was finished vomiting, we were not going anywhere. Poor Jack continued to vomit for a while. Nurse MM. did get the message to the doctor and he did prescribe Jack another anti-nausea medication (the 3rd one of the day!) which was given to Jack in his IV. It took effect quickly and Jack did not get sick again.

Dear Lord, thank you for the blessing of children, for the act of giving to others, for the gift of a smile, for nurses and doctors, for days without pain and sickness, for healthy bodies and strong minds, and for the love and support of family, friends, and strangers who continue to amaze us by walking with us on this journey. In Jesus' name, Amen.

FEBRUARY 19, 2013—Sunday was the Best Buddies Prom at the Bridgestone Arena in Nashville. Jack's Best Buddy, K., had sent me a text asking if Jack was coming to the prom. I had RSVP'd that he was coming just on the off chance he would feel good enough to go. I figured if he wanted to go he would just wear a nice pair of slacks, a dress shirt, and tie, all of which we have here at home so we would not need to rent a tux. When I asked him if he wanted to go he didn't know until the last minute, then he decided he did want to go. Ben and I hit the ground running knowing that we didn't have long to get him and ourselves ready. Ben ran upstairs and found an old suit of Benny's that miraculously fit Jack. What a wonderful surprise! I ironed the pants and a shirt and before we knew it, Jack was transformed into a prince for his prom. We stopped at school where the Best Buddies were gathered for pizza and pictures and to ride a bus together to the Arena. Ben and I followed in our van and watched the prom from the Inclusive Zone in the Arena, the place where parents can watch the festivities below. Jack walked in the arena prom area, found a comfy chair and there he spent his prom time. He did get up once for picture taking but spent the time he was there in the most comfortable chair he could find. He stayed longer than he did last year, but he didn't dance or sing karaoke like some of the other participants did. But he did have his picture taken with his best buddy and few other girls from school. I hope he had a little fun, at least he said he did. He wore noise reduction headphones during the whole prom. For Jack, they are a prom attire accessory.

Dear Lord, thank you for the blessing of children, for ears that hear the sounds around us and for eyes that see the beauty that surrounds us, for days without pain and sickness, for letting us see a person's heart not just their outward appearance, for the joy of a smile and the gift of laughter, and for the love and support of so many who continue to walk with us on this journey. Amen.

CHAPTER 37

MARCH 15, 2013—Some days our house feels like a pressure cooker with all the stress associated with living with a family member with cancer. Jack had some homework he needed to do, nothing long and drawn out, just a few questions to answer and the writing to answer them. But he threw a fit about it. I didn't give in to his fit, gave him time to cool down, and finally sat with him to help get the homework finished. He wasn't happy and let me know how he felt very loudly and as often as he could... he still had to breathe. I took it as long as I could and finally mentioned something about punishment for bad behavior. We had a verbal meeting of the minds even after he finished the homework. He just kept on and on and eventually said something about how he was going to kick my butt, not the term he used. There is nothing about being a caregiver that is fun. You are there for that ill person day and night every day. It is a very hard job.

Still mad at me, Jack got his dad to help him in the bathroom when he needed help later that night. While in the bathroom together, Jack started telling Ben how he was going to run away from home, a story he has told me before after another disagreement. Ben did exactly what I did before; he asked Jack questions about the how, the where, and the what of his living on his own. (The conversation below is through lots of tears and wailing...)

Jack: "Dad, I am going to run away from home. That will get Mommy.' Wailing....

Ben: "Jack, where will you go?"

Jack: "I don't know. Somewhere away from HER!" More wailing ….

Ben: "What will you do for food?"

Jack: a pause for a huge wail..."I guess I will have to eat innocent animals." More wailing "I don't even know what bird or squirrel taste like!" Another huge wailing.

Ben was proud of himself because he didn't laugh out loud to that last statement.

MY NAME IS JACK JOHNSON...

The next day Jack slept too long at school during his nap, and the teachers became concerned and called me. I talked to Jack on the phone to make sure he sounded alright. He said he was upset over our fight. We talked about it that afternoon, and things are back to normal. I wish I could take away all his anxiety and heartache but I cannot. I wish I could make life easier for him but again I cannot. I wish life weren't so hard for him, but this is what we have, whether we like it or not. I hope he never has to taste bird or squirrel.

Dear Lord, thank you for the sunshine, for the peeks of spring colors in the flowers and trees, for healthy bodies and strong minds, for the blessing of children, for days without pain and sorrow, for the comfort of a hug, the sound of the words "I love you," for hope and faith, and for the continued support and love of so many who walk with us on this journey. In Jesus' Name, Amen.

March 22, 2013—Jack's Best Buddy, K., wanted to come by and visit Jack. We talked, planned a certain day and time, and I told Jack about her upcoming visit. A couple of days later but before K.'s visit, Jack told me he was drawing a surprise to give to K. He was hunched over his rolling hospital table working on his drawing. Finally, he told me he was finished and asked me if I would like to see it. He handed it to me, and I saw he had drawn a whole comic strip with the characters of K., Justin Bieber, and Jack. Each drawing of the characters was pretty accurate with Jack wearing his glasses and sporting a mustache and goatee. The comic began with K. and Justin Bieber "hanging out." The next picture depicted a mad Jack opening the door to the room where the other two are hanging out. Comic strip Jack said to Justin Bieber, "Stop right there! Get away from her!" Jack and Justin exchange ugly words, Jack gets madder and wiggly lines of heat come out of his head. Jack then proceeded to "Beat the crap out of Justin Bieber." He leaves Justin on the ground in pain and then leaves with K. It was a very artistic comic, and each character's likeness was accurate, but the funniest thing was Jack had, in his first draft, included several bad words that I made him remove. K. loved it! We did too!

Last week the Best Buddies organization had their yearly kickball game at Ravenwood High School. Jack participated last year being the kickball roller from his wheelchair. This year he kicked the ball and ran the bases, completely taking us by surprise! I never know what he is going to do or say but for many years he has told us when we asked, that sports are not his "forté"—one of his many Jackisms. Fast forward to this past Tuesday and there he was with his leg braces with hairy Velcro, his low blood counts from chemo, a port-

...BUT I'M NOT THE SINGER

a-cath in his chest, and he was kicking a dang ball and running bases where someone could easily throw a ball at him to get him out and hit him in the head or chest. The thought of it makes my stomach hurt. Even an administrator at school called me and reiterated that there would not be a nurse with Jack at the kickball game. I had to tell her that I fully understood and would not hold them accountable if something was to happen to Jack during the game. Jack was adamant that he was going. And like last year, Jack was declared the MVP from Centennial High School. Last year he shared the title, this year he was the CHS MVP. He was so proud of himself. He wore his MVP ribbon home under his coat and flashed me with his ribbon. He talked about how the announcer had said his name as the MVP from CHS over the loudspeaker and how all the students cheered. There was not a prouder student around. He grinned from ear to ear and glowed from the inside. He couldn't wait to show Benny and Ben and constantly talked about what he was going to say. I was proud too, for more reasons. Jack had put himself out there. He had forgotten about his port in his chest. He felt good enough to do physical activity. He forgot about his leg braces and kicked with all he had. He was just another kickball player, not the kid with cancer. He got up and moved even though there are very few muscles left in his body, something I blame on cancer. He didn't worry about getting hit with a ball or that someone would laugh at him or that he couldn't do it. He just got up and did it. Something that is not his "forté" became his reason to feel pride. There are so many things Jack cannot do and will probably never do like drive a car, have a girlfriend, go off alone with kids his own age without adults around... all the things typical kids his age are doing. But for one day for two hours, he was not just a cancer warrior; he was a kickball champion. He is my hero. I took a picture of happy Jack holding his MVP ribbon. I didn't even have to ask him to "say cheese." He was still grinning from ear to ear. Wednesday morning Jack got up, walked into the family room, sat in his chair, and vomited. Ben and I think the previous day's activities wore his body down. Chemo reared its ugly head and reminded us where we are in life. Jack slept until 11 am. He was exhausted. His smile was gone. But he hasn't lost his pride and still has his MVP ribbon nearby.

Dear Lord, thank you for the blessing of children, for eyes that see a happy smile on the face of a loved one, for healthy bodies and strong minds, for days when we feel like running through life, for the courage to walk outside our comfort zone, for days without pain and sickness, and for the love and support of family, friends, and strangers who walk with us on this journey. Amen.

MY NAME IS JACK JOHNSON...

APRIL 5, 2013—Wednesday was chemo day. Nurse MM. was there which made Jack's day. Gnash, the Nashville Predators mascot stopped by the oncology department to say hello to all the cancer patients. Jack and Gnash had their picture taken together. Chemo went as well as chemo can. Thursday Jack had his leg braces worked on with the old Velcro removed and replaced. The technician who did the work laughed when he saw the Velcro. The tech was shocked the braces were staying on Jack's legs because the Velcro was so hairy looking, having lost its ability to stick together. The Velcro was replaced, and now Jack doesn't click when he walks. I laughed with him about how he can now sneak up on people, but he would never do it.

As of Monday, Jack's school day will be different. We are going to go to homebound school for the classes Jack has in the morning, and Jack will go to the actual school at 11:30 each day. Because of his many absenteeism's, Jack has fallen further and further behind in one of his early morning classes and had gotten into the habit of not paying attention. And as the year continues along with chemo, he becomes more and more unable to keep up in some classes because of his lack of stamina. Parenting a child with Jack's unique needs has become a very big challenge for me. I am constantly trying to figure out what is best for him, for his health, for his education, and trying to juggle these is hard. I don't want him not to learn—I want him mentally stimulated but how much does he really need? And how much is too much? And how do you tell? And where do you draw the line? And? And? And? There is the fear that I will make the wrong decision and it might affect Jack's health or push him over the autism edge. I wish these decisions would be easier.

Dear Lord, thank you for the warmth of spring, for the blessing of children, for the gift of a smile, for hope, love and faith, for each day we share with our loved ones, for healthy bodies and strong minds, and for the love and support of family, friends, and strangers who continue to walk with us on this journey. In Jesus' Name, Amen.

APRIL 10, 2013—Happy Birthday, Jack. Seventeen years old today. How can that be? We have spent the day with our friends on the sixth floor at the Children's Hospital. Cancer doesn't take a birthday so instead of cake and ice cream Jack received chemo. The nurses gave him a special gift, wrote special wishes, and signed his card. His friends from school that he eats lunch with and plays Uno with sent him a video of themselves wishing him a happy birthday. We will have a little just-the-four-of-us party tonight, nothing fancy or loud. Just a little celebration in honor of Jack. All in all, he has had a good

...BUT I'M NOT THE SINGER

day. He is sitting and drawing pictures as I type this—his normal typical Jack afternoon. Happy Birthday to my unique and wonderful son. May God bless you with many more.

Dear Lord, thank you for the blessing of children, for the spirit of giving, for healthy bodies and strong minds, for days without sickness and pain, for the gift of a smile when things are troubling, and for the love and support of so many people who love our Jack. Amen.

APRIL 16, 2013—We had a small birthday celebration on Wednesday night of last week—just the four of us—with Jack opening his gifts from us and getting to choose where he wanted his birthday dinner to be. His choice of dinner was here at home with take-out Steak and Shake: a cheeseburger, fries, and a chocolate shake.

Saturday, we had a pizza party here at the house for family and a few close friends. Before everyone arrived, Jack made a list of his party rules. The written rules at Jack's birthday party per him:

"House Party Rules"
"1. No saying bad words
2. No smoking
3. No going into other people's bedrooms
4. No peting Mia, which is my cat. (his spelling of the word petting.)
(Note: She is the gray tanish cat. She also hates guests at the house.)
(Tanish – again his spelling.)
5. No fighting
6. No crying kids
Violators will be asked to leave my house party."

Everyone followed the rules as close as possible, and no one was asked to leave. Jack had a blast, smiling most of the night. It was a fun day celebrating our Jack.

Dear Lord, thank you for the blessing of children, for the colors of spring flowers and blooming trees, for the gift of loving another human being, ourselves, and You, for friends who bless us with love and laughter, for times of solitude and times of fellowship with others, for days without pain and sickness, for healthy bodies and strong minds, and for the love and support of so many who continue to walk with us on Jack's Journey. In His name, Amen.

MY NAME IS JACK JOHNSON...

APRIL 25, 2013—Jack had chemo yesterday. It was an uneventful hospital trip. Later, Jack got a haircut, looked in the mirror and pronounced to everyone, "Man, I'm sexy!" I haven't decided if that was autism or the male ego speaking there.

Now for a little cleansing of my tired soul. As you read the words below, please understand this situation does not have to happen but happens every day at some school, somewhere in our country. Teachers, if you see yourself in my description, please retire or find another career. Sorry if my words are offensive to anyone but actions like these need to stop.

Dear anonymous teacher,

I want to publicly thank you for your total lack of concern for my child and his education. He has been in your classroom for the last ten months if you didn't notice. He has struggled in your classroom and struggled with cancer treatments. He has been absent many times for medical reasons and sometimes, when he has physically been in the classroom, his mind couldn't attend to what you were saying. You saw his struggles... you shared it with Ben and me. Your words at the Parent/Teacher conference were:

Us: "We are Jack's parents. How is he doing in your class?"

You: "He does fine. The special ed teacher is with him."

Us: "Are there any problems with Jack that we need to know about that you have seen?" You: "No. He has given his special ed teacher some trouble, but she handles it."

Us: "Is there anything you would like to know from us about Jack, his medical issues, his side effects issues?"

You: "No."

Us: "If there is anything we can do, please let us know."

You: "OK. Thanks for stopping by."

I knew as soon as I walked out in the hall. I have seen your kind before. My first remark to Ben was: "That was a waste of time." You showed no concern for your student, our son. As the year went along, Jack got further and further behind in your class. You did not let us know. Jack was absent for chemo and began to feel terrible at times and couldn't come to school. You said nothing. We had several meetings but you never came. You never got in touch with us with your concerns. I am not in your classroom and must have a blind trust in your knowledge and ability as a teacher, an educator, that my child sitting in your class has needs that are or are not being met. You might say that is my responsibility as a parent to be aware of my child's grades. I was fully aware of my child's grades from his progress reports and report cards. But I

...BUT I'M NOT THE SINGER

have no way of knowing how far behind he is in your class unless you, the person responsible for educating him, lets me know. Then you finally called, 6 weeks before the end of school. You let me know that Jack is indeed behind and that you are sending a contract for me to sign to promise that I will get Jack caught up before the end of the year on all his missed or needed assignments. Forty-five pages of work that needs to be completed by Jack so he can pass your class... in a month; four weeks. I must ask... is this contract for Jack's sake or for your sake since YOU are graded on his passing grade? I wonder where your concern is for the children we as parents entrust to you every day? If one of your students is struggling, is it not your job to help them with their education, being that you have a degree in education? I, with all my heart, understand that your job is hard. I would not want to teach high school students the information you need to teach them. But isn't this YOUR job? Do I not pay for your salary with my taxes? Do you, as a teacher, not have an obligation to all parents, students, and taxpayers to do the job you have been asked to do? Maybe for you it is just a job. Maybe you are too tired or have been at this too long. Maybe you are riding the "tenure train" to retirement. I don't know. What I do know is that I sent my child to your classroom every day, on days when he didn't feel good; on days when he had just received chemo to fight cancer. On days when I truly hated to send him. And to think that you didn't take the time to notice that he was there, that he was trying, and that he was struggling. We opened the door for you to come to us at the Parent/Teacher conference but you told us basically that he was the special education teacher's responsibility. Where is your accountability to a student who you have had in your classroom for the whole school year who has a contract with you and the school system for his educational needs, a contract you were given? Did you read it or was it filed and not opened? So, thank you. Thank you for your service to my child. Thank you for adding stress to my life and that of my sick child. Thank you for making me appreciate the amazing efforts of Jack's other teachers who so graciously stepped up to the plate and helped him through the material they gave him. They read, followed Jack's contract, and showed a level of concern for his welfare and educational needs in their classrooms. They fully understood their role as Jack's teacher and fellow human being. If they did it, why didn't you? I also love the fact that they have grown to care for my child as he continues to fight cancer. It hurts me to think that you missed a wonderful opportunity to get to know one of the most amazing students you will ever get the chance to teach. He has the strength and resiliency of a warrior. It's a pity you never noticed

    From the parents of one of your students.

MY NAME IS JACK JOHNSON...

Please let me also publicly again say thank you to Jack's other teachers from this year. They have come to meetings, voiced their concerns, and showed him and us a huge amount of respect, and in some cases have gone out of their way. From the bottom of my heart, thank you, teachers, for the care, concern, understanding, and educational help you have given Jack this year. It has not gone unnoticed and is greatly appreciated by me, Ben, and Benny. Thanks for "getting it" and for caring for your students, including mine.

Dear Lord, thank you for healthy bodies and strong minds, for being able to show others kindness and love, for the blessing of children and the responsibility of parenthood, for nurses who give of themselves in the care of others, for teachers who have a love to teach the young minds in their care, for giving us the ability to see not only the outward appearance but the goodness in others, and for the love and support of so many who walk with us on Jack's journey. Amen.

MAY 6, 2013—Last Friday, Jack was going shopping and out to eat with the Transition class at CHS. Jack is not in the Transition class but goes out with them for social time when they go out into the community on Friday of each week. Last Friday, the Transition class of Independence High School was to join our class on this social outing, meeting up for lunch at a local downtown restaurant. Jack's past best friend, JT, goes to Independence High School. I asked the Transition teacher at our school if she knew if JT was coming. She did not know but said she would ask the IHS Transition teacher. A little replay background on Jack and JT's friendship: Jack and JT were both in the Waves Developmental Preschool when they were toddlers. They both started preschool together at Franklin Elementary and moved to Poplar Grove Elementary School together as well. They were in class together until they graduated from Poplar Grove in 2010 right before our world turned upside down. JT is not as verbal as Jack but that has never stopped their friendship. I have seen them together, no verbal communication between them but quietly sitting together and laughing with each other about nothing. They taught me that being together means so much more when words are not needed. They also taught me that fun and laughter come from within and not necessarily from some outside source. I have so many Jack and JT stories. I badly wanted them to have a chance to have lunch together. I am always so afraid and wonder whether something we do will be a "last time" to do it. Cancer brings on that fear. Thanks to the Transition teacher from both schools, JT and Jack were to have lunch together. I couldn't resist going and taking a few pictures and was

...BUT I'M NOT THE SINGER

there when the two of them saw each other. JT was already seated at a table waiting for the others to arrive. Jack was to come with the other students from CHS on the bus. The bus parked, the students got off, and I saw them, Jack in front, walking down the sidewalk. Jack looked up and saw JT first and his face lit up while he mouthed JT's name. As he got closer, JT saw and recognized Jack and quietly said Jack's name. There were no hugs, no high fives, no "good to see yous." But there was something, an invisible beam of love between old friends. Jack was all smiles and so was JT. They sat together at the table and I overheard Jack ask JT what he was having for lunch. When JT answered, "a cheeseburger" they both smiled at each other, the same way they did for so many years. I didn't stay and have lunch but wanted Jack to have time with his friends. I started to cry before I got to the van and bochooed all the way home. How a simple smile of happiness can say so much between friends who have never carried on a true one on one conversation. Never forget the power of true friendship.

Dear Lord, thank you for the blessing of children, for days without pain and sickness, for the gift of friendship, for tears of joy and for tears of sorrow, for healthy bodies and strong minds, for the act of remembering the past, the ability to live in the present and the promise of tomorrow, and for the love and support of so many who walk with us on this journey. In His name, Amen.

MAY 10, 2013—Jack had his chemo Wednesday. It was a strange trip. We arrived on time, he was weighed in (he has gained another pound; hooray!) and we were put into an examination room. It was chilly even for me in the room so I got Jack a blanket, nothing unusual there. He laid down on the examining table, curled up into a Jack ball, and covered himself (including his head) up with the blanket. Nurse MM. told us she would be in as soon as possible to access Jack's port. In the meantime, the nurse practitioner came in to see Jack. She and I talked about any changes in the last two weeks with Jack and his health, still nothing unusual as we have this talk every two weeks. We talked about school, Jack's headaches, body aches, overall day to day activities like we always do. She asked, "Jack, where are you going to the beach?" No reply. I said, "Jack, answer Ms. T's question—where are we going to the beach?" No reply. The NP uncovered Jack's face and asked him if he heard her question. Jack said, "Yes, I heard your question and I am not going to college." The NP chuckled and said, "Jack, we weren't talking about college. We were talking about the beach." Jack said, "I am not living in a dorm either when I go to college." With that, I am up and out of my chair and with the NP's help, we

MY NAME IS JACK JOHNSON...

got Jack sitting up. He had a hard time sitting up and wobbled a little as he sat upright. We told him we weren't talking about college; we again told him we were talking about the beach. My heart was about to stop. What was going on with him? The NP made Jack look at her and started doing her examination for brain activity she does every two weeks. Both of us were scared that something had happened to Jack as he was still a little fuzzy about what was said. Ben thinks that Jack had fallen asleep and had dreamed he heard people talking about college, since here at our house we do a lot of talking about college right now with Benny. But Jack knows he is not going to college and will not be living in a dorm. I think he must have fallen asleep bringing on the talk about college instead of answering the questions about the beach. That is the only answer I can come up with. It is so scary though to hear your child incoherent like that. Knowing what I do about Jack's condition and the previous and current treatments, it was a jolt for me to hear him babbling about something so far out of touch with him. The NP reassured me that his examination was fine and that made me feel better. But then today Jack told me he took a shower last night when I know he did not. I told him no that he did not take a shower last night, that he was watching "Swamp People" (one of Jack's new favorite TV shows on Thursday night) but he was still sure he had. Finally, I convinced him and he realized he had taken his shower yesterday morning and not at night. Still I feel something was just not right with him. I took him to school anyway today and haven't heard anything from him. Still a mother has certain "mommy intuitions" and I hope and pray my feelings are off base. Thankfully Jack has an MRI next Tuesday which will we hope relieves some of these fears.

Dear Lord, thank you for all mothers, for their love and understanding, for their cheers of joy and support, for their sacrifice and giving spirits, for all the lessons they shared with their children. Thank you for my children who have blessed me in so many ways, for their love to me, for the opportunity to be a parent to them, for the memories I will cherish forever. Thank you for every day we spend with our loved ones, for healthy bodies and strong minds and for the love and support from so many who follow us on Jack's journey. In Jesus' Name, Amen.

MAY 17, 2013—Jack did have his MRI Wednesday. The MRI was long, longer than usual lasting five excruciating hours. Jack had just been brought back to recovery when they called us back, so it took another hour for him to wake up. His throat was terribly sore from the breathing tube, and the roof of

...BUT I'M NOT THE SINGER

his mouth has been sore as well. He has had a deep, raspy voice ever since but in true form, he has gone on to school to finish up his tests. What a trooper he is!! We had not heard from the doctor on the MRI results so, not wanting to wait the whole weekend wondering, I called. One lesion has not changed, but there are new suspicious places in his spine and this time in his brain. This is not what we wanted to hear. I know enough to think it is not good since Jack is still taking chemo to stop any new growth, and I know enough again to say there could be a greater chance for us to have to change our plan of attack against this beast. I also know enough to say I was happier—if I can use that word in this context—when the growth was contained to the spine. But now there could be growth in the brain... not good. I know too that there are more options, more treatments, and clinical trials still available, so all is not lost.

Dear Lord, thank you for the blessing of children, for watching them grow from an infant to a young adult, for days without pain and sickness, for hope when all seems lost, for being able to come to You in prayer with our pleas and concerns, for strength when our knees are weak, for guidance when we feel confused, and for the love and support of so many who hold us up when we need help on this difficult journey. Amen

MAY 23, 2013—Sunday was the Ride for Kids motorcycle ride to benefit the Pediatric Brain Tumor Foundation. This was our third ride, a family favorite, and this year didn't disappoint. The motorcyclist's numbers were down this year but still a lot of money was collected for pediatric brain tumor research. Jack rode again in a sidecar, but this year he got to ride in a 1958 antique sidecar. Of course, he didn't know how special his sidecar was, but the rest of us did. Ben, Benny, and I rode shotgun—if that is the correct word to use—with motorcyclists willing to let us ride. Benny rode with a guy named Bobby from Indiana. Bobby was a big man with a beard. He gathered our family together and told us a story. Bobby plays Santa Claus at Christmas for children in his area. He makes and gives each of them a handmade bell. He tells each child that when they ring the bell it signifies that God loves them. Bobby presented each of us with one of his handmade bells. We will cherish them forever. Everyone at the ride was extra sweet to us, to Jack of course, and to Benny as well. He received so many well wishes for his high school graduation. I am so amazed by the spirit of motorcycle riders. Most of us only see the leather jackets, facial hair, and tattoos but on the inside, they ride with hearts of gold. So, a special thank-you to everyone who had a hand in making our day special. You enrich our lives with memo-

MY NAME IS JACK JOHNSON...

ries we can keep forever.

For us, the rest of the week has been tough. We heard from the doctor on Monday and went into the hospital yesterday. As I had shared, the recent MRI showed new growth in areas where we had not seen growth. We decided to go ahead with giving Jack his regularly scheduled chemo which he received yesterday. We got to see the MRI results ourselves and talk in detail to Jack's oncologist. The original recurrent tumor in the spinal column has shrunk, hardly even showing up on the MRI. There is a new growth in the spine that wasn't there before. There is also new growth in the brain, something we haven't seen. But what makes this new growth especially ominous is that instead of being a solid mass it is diffused. On the MRI, it looks like someone threw sand into Jack's brain. Some in the medical profession call it sugar coating, or the technical term: leptomeningeal metastasizing. No matter what it is called, it is not a good thing to see in cancer treatment. It cannot be removed since it is very tiny, very spread out tumor growths. It cannot be radiated, something I had read up on, since it is so diffused. Most disappointing, it has grown while Jack was being treated with chemo, a chemo regimen that has shown promise for a possible cure. This is not good. If Jack was not taking chemo now, he would only have a small amount of time with us. There are other things we can do. Dr. E was going to find where Jack's tumor sample is in getting tested for subtype. If it is going to be a while, he will call St. Jude in Memphis to see if Jack could qualify for a clinical trial for subtype treatment. If so, St. Jude could perform a newly found blood test for sub-typing that Dr. E just found out about. Vanderbilt is not able to do any of this testing at their facility. There are a few other clinical trials available but none today are curative. Dr. E said we would have to go to another facility but that he would help us if we decide to go that route. We can continue to give Jack his present chemo but since the cancer is continuing to grow, it will eventually be futile. Dr. E went on to say that we could start palliative care if we decide that Jack's treatments are just too much—a quality of life decision. If you haven't understood where this is going, we are running out of treatments and time. Ben and I are brokenhearted to say the least. We told Benny but have decided not to tell Jack. What difference will it make if he knows? Are we giving up? No way, we will continue to fight as long as we can. But we might be faced with decisions no parent should have to make about their child's life—something we have thought about but have never really faced before to this degree. I hate cancer with a passion that is so great.

So, the plan today is: Dr. E is getting Jack's scans together to send to St.

...BUT I'M NOT THE SINGER

2013 Jill, Benny, Ben and an unhappy Jack having his picture made before Benny's Senior Prom

Jude's for a second opinion. He is tracking down the tumor sample to see how much longer it will take to subtype. He is going to talk with people at VCH about opening a proposed clinical trial there: how close they are to opening it and when that will be. If that will take too long for Jack's benefit, he will talk to St. Jude's to see if Jack can qualify for their clinical trial. So, we wait to hear from him.

Ben and I will have to become good actors. We will have to face all of this with smiles where Jack is concerned. We will have to smile through Benny's high school graduation and celebration. There is so much to celebrate. He has made us so proud. He has lived in autism and now cancer's shadow for so long and now this on one of his life's biggest days. I had no clue how life could be so hard, not an on-my-the-car-broke-down hard but a life-fighting hard against an enemy so strong and devious that it can grow in a chemically hostile environment. One day I want to ask God why? Why is there a thing like cancer that can take our loved ones away? Why?

Dear Lord, thank you for the blessing of children, for nurses, doctors, and medical researchers, for each hour and day we have with our loved ones, for giving us the gift of love, for hope and faith, and for the love and support we receive from so many as we continue to walk with Jack on this journey. Amen.

JUNE 2, 2013—We made it through Benny's graduation. Last weekend was a whirlwind of celebrating Benny. It was his moment in the spotlight. Benny, we are so proud of you and can't wait to see where you go in life!!

MY NAME IS JACK JOHNSON...

I did talk to Jack's oncologist last week. We are still waiting to hear back from St. Jude on a second opinion and waiting to hear back from the tumor sample that was sent weeks ago for sub-typing. The results could completely change our course of action with treatments but as Jack's doctor said yet again, "Anything from now on will only give us time, not a cure." I know he needs to keep reminding me of that, but I wish he would stop. I get the message too clearly and get sick of hearing it over and over. Doctors need to understand parents don't give up that easily when it comes to their children.

Jack has felt alright, not the best nor the worst. He has been sleeping a lot lately. He vomited half his lunch up today at O'Charley's, just out of the blue. He came back from the restroom, angrily sat back down and proceeded to eat the rest of his lunch. Bless his heart. He keeps going and never gives up. He is such a trooper! As for Ben and me, what can I say? I cry at the drop of a hat when something unexpected happens—a song on the radio, a memory, the thought of school in the fall. I have changed my prayers, asking God now for mercy for my son. Then we go to church and sing a song, and the word mercy appears several times. And I cry. People don't know what to say to us, so they say hi and pat us on the back. Or hug us. Or bring us food. Just between Ben and me, we talk about things that are a parent's worst nightmare, something no parent ever expects to have to talk about. But you know, by the grace of God we get by. We continue to live because we must. We have no choice. We laugh, we cry, we live...

Dear God, our Father, thank you for the blessing of children, for healthy bodies and strong minds, for days without sickness and pain, for every day we have with the ones we love, for getting to celebrate the milestones of this life, for Your abiding love, and for the love and support of so many who walk with us on this journey. Amen

JUNE 7, 2013—Thinking back to my childhood we always went to the State Fair in Nashville. Back in my elementary years, schools let out so kids could attend the fair. My grandmother used to take us, and my dad and grandfather would stop on their way home to join us. Now whether I remember that correctly—I don't know. My mind is not what it should be, and my memories can become jumbled. I do remember as clearly as if it happened yesterday one State Fair "ride" that I hated. It was the mirror fun house. I hated it because you could never find your way out. You would think you were headed in the right direction, but when you reached out your hand, you would touch yet another mirror. It only took one time for me to go inside the "fun house" to

...BUT I'M NOT THE SINGER

know I never wanted to do it again. When I look at our lives now, I feel like I am back in that mirrored maze, trying desperately to find my way out. This week we ran into another mirror...

Jack's oncologist called this week to give us the results of the tumor sub-typing that we had been waiting for weeks to have. Jack's tumor does not fall into the category of the subtype that they currently have treatment options for. Today there are four subtypes: Shh, Wnt, Group 3 and Group 4. The researchers know enough about subtypes Shh and Wnt that they have drugs that target the cancer's cell division pathways to try to stop its growth. They do not have enough information on Group 3 and Group 4, unfortunately. Those are the two that Jack's tumor subtype falls under. They do not know which of those his tumor falls under only that his tumor does not have the Shh nor the Wnt pathways. Not what we wanted to hear. Another treatment option is gone.

Since the beginning of this journey, I have been a member of several parent support groups of parents on this same journey. I am so ignorant of the technicalities of all this scientific information, I don't add my two cents because I don't have two cents. But recently another parent in the same place in their battle as we are presently mentioned that their child's doctor had suggested two different chemo drugs I had not seen mentioned before. So, I wrote them down and asked Jack's oncologist about them. He did not know much about them only that they are both chemo drugs used to treat other cancers and that both are FDA approved. (Anything new like clinical trials or new treatments I read or hear about I will take to Jack's oncologist.)

After the news about the subtype, our only hope was the second opinion from St. Jude. St. Jude's tumor board meets on Wednesday afternoons and Jack's doctor said as soon as he heard something he would call. He called yesterday and all the doctors in the St. Jude's tumor board agree that the results of Jack's last MRI show a medulloblastoma leptomeningeal disease or, in layman's terms, new diffused growth. Diffused growth cannot be removed by surgery nor can it be radiated again, Jack's doctor relays. But St. Jude tells him that there is a new two-chemo regimen that they are doing for kids like Jack who have relinquished all the standard treatments. St. Jude is doing an experimental trial on two chemo drugs, the ones that were mentioned on the parent support group that I had just asked Jack's oncologist about. St. Jude would like for us to try these drugs on Jack and see what happens. Is it a cure? No, but at this point we have very limited options. Could it work? They don't know. That's why they are experimenting with these drugs. These drugs have

MY NAME IS JACK JOHNSON...

shown "promise" in shrinking tumors in mice. Both drugs have had clinical trials and have shown promise for treatment, but they were individual trials—each drug tried by itself. Both trials showed promise shrinking tumors in many cases. So, they want to see what giving both drugs together will do. Jack's oncologist gave me the name of the doctor at St. Jude to call and we did. He, of course, had to call us back but at least it was in a very small time frame. He is the leading doctor on this trial and he took the time to explain the drugs, the previous trials and results, and what they are doing at St. Jude. He told me twice to remember these drugs are experimental and today are not classified as a cure. They could give us more time by shrinking the tumors, making the tumors completely go away, or do nothing at all. This type of cancer is a highly malignant beast whose first attack of treatment is the best line of defense. If it returns, there are no proven curative treatments today. But at least maybe something could give us the extra time.

On June 17th, we are headed to St. Jude's to start the process of getting more time with Jack. We will get our living arrangements, process our new lives, and move forward. Jack will see the doctor first thing on June 18th, and we will begin the task of getting all new labs, new MRIs, and a spinal tap. If all is well, we will start chemo on June 24th in Memphis. I do not know how long we will be in Memphis. That first week of testing we will stay in Memphis until the tests are completed. If Jack tolerates the chemo well, we could come back home. If there is a glitch, we will stay. St. Jude has a hotel where they house patients in active treatment, and we will stay there for free. If insurance refuses to pay, St. Jude will pick up the tab. Jack knows most of what is going on. I told him he and I were going to have another great adventure, this time in Memphis. He knows he is going for chemo that Vanderbilt does not have. Again, why tell him anything that might make him worry and miserable in the time we do have left?

Dear Lord, thank you for the blessing of children, for days without pain and sickness, for healthy bodies and strong minds, for each day, hour, minute we have with the ones we love here on earth, for the promise of a place without sorrow, and for the love and support of so many who walk this journey with us. Amen.

CHAPTER 38

JUNE 13, 2013—Writing this from the beautiful shores of St. George's Island in the state of Florida. We asked Jack what he wanted to do this summer and he told us he wanted to go to St. George's Island where we could have a house and pool all to ourselves. We are having a wonderful time in the sun, the sand, the rental house, and the private pool. Thanks to Sue and Tom (Ben's mom and her boyfriend) who have joined us here for we could not have done this without their help. Our beach house is good—not the fanciest or the most up to date. Jack has been inside most of the time doing Jack things like drawing poles and playing on his computer. He has been swimming a few times only going in the afternoon when the sun is behind the beach house, putting the pool in the shade. Yesterday, he and Benny played Star Wars in the pool with pool noodles, something they used to play over the years at the lake. Benny was so good to play with Jack again. Ben was touched by the whole scene, the two boys playing like they have for so many years. It upset him, he told me later, seeing them together playing. Funny how something so familiar is so heartbreaking to watch now. Benny and Ben bought Jack a T-shirt which put a huge smile on Jack's face. We love smiles. Jack has not been to the beach, not wanting to get hot or in the sun too much. He did tell me a few minutes ago that he wanted to go to the beach on Saturday, our last day, so we could all have our picture made together on the beach. How did he know I wanted one? He has almost fallen once when he was walking to the pool because, as he told Ben who was with him, his toe (the one he doesn't feel) tripped him up. But Ben was nearby to help him. He loves getting in the pool water because he doesn't have to balance or use his feet as his anchor to get around or maneuver his body. He loves to float and wears goggles so he can look at the bottom of the pool. I love to watch him play, or draw, or anything he wants to do. I cannot get enough of him.

While here, I have heard from St. Jude several times. We are scheduled to get there on Monday and stay until they say we can leave. I talked to our St.

MY NAME IS JACK JOHNSON...

Jude scheduler just a while ago, and there is a chance we could be there until July 6th; it all depends on what happens once we get there and how Jack's body reacts to the chemo he will receive after all the tests are completed. The tests are scheduled for the first week, some each day, and as we get the results, we can make plans from there.

Dear Lord, thank you for blessings that make our lives better, for the beauty of the oceans, the smell of the salt water, the sand between our toes, for time spent with the ones we love, for the blessing of children, and for the love and support of so many who walk with us on this journey. In His name, Amen.

JUNE 20, 2013—We are here in Memphis at St. Jude. We are having a free afternoon, the first since Tuesday.

Jack and I headed to Memphis at 12:30pm in the van while Ben followed in his car so he could drive back home the next day. We arrived in Memphis at 4 and found our way to St. Jude. It is a huge campus surrounded by a massive fence with entry gates in several locations. We were sent to the Memphis Grizzlies House, a hotel-like building with 100 rooms for families to stay overnight. Our room is spacious for a hotel room, consisting of a bathroom, a kitchen area, a living space, and a separate bedroom with two double beds. We are given meal tickets which also double as our room keys. We are allotted a certain amount of money for breakfast, lunch, and dinner each day we are here. If we go over that amount we pay out of pocket. The meal tickets are for the patient and one parent and are for the hospital cafeteria only. There have been two nights where local businesses have donated food to the guests at the Grizzlies House (GH) and we do not have to pay for that. There is a continental breakfast downstairs each morning supplied by the hotel that is also free. We get around the campus by way of a free shuttle service. You can walk too if you like, something we have done quite a bit of in the last few days. The hospital cafeteria is massive in size and has an array of different foods and several food stations. There is a pizza station, a deli sandwich station, a grill station with hamburgers and hot dogs, a meat-and-three station, a salad bar, a Greek salad bar, an ice cream station, a dessert station, a Chinese station, a huge area with all types of health foods, a pasta station/Mexican dish station, and an area with drinks and pick up foods and snacks like yogurt, chips and crackers. Jack is still limited with what he will eat, but at least we have choices. At lunchtime, the cafeteria is a mass of people and cafeteria trays. There are long lines and lots of waiting. But the food is always delicious, well worth the waiting and the crowds. Seating is sometimes a problem since most

...BUT I'M NOT THE SINGER

people who work here eat here for lunch. That says a lot if the people working here will stay and eat the food. Dinner time is not as good as lunch time. Most of the stations close and there are very limited choices for dinner, not a good thing for a picky eater like Jack. So far, we have found something he will eat. Our days are planned with appointments, and we have a schedule to follow each day. Our day starts with getting to the hospital either by walking or by shuttle, then registering each day where Jack gets a new hospital wristband each morning. Next, we follow the schedule we have been given with the help of a map to find our way to each appointment. We have walked several miles this week, back and forth, up and down hallways and floors. We are mostly on the first floor of the hospital where all outpatient appointments occur. Our appointments start each day at around 8 am and last well into the afternoon. Today has been our shortest day with our last appointment ending at 2:30. Tomorrow we start our appointments at 7:30. Jack has been measured, weighed, poked, prodded, photographed, twisted, turned, X-rayed, and monitored. He has been asked to walk, talk, look that way and the other way, push, pull, follow my finger, stand up, lie down, roll over, and sit up.

Ben spent the night with us Monday night and stayed with us most of Tuesday. He didn't want to leave us without knowing that we had what we needed and that we knew our way around. We are a few blocks away from the actual downtown Memphis area, being able to see the Memphis Pyramid out our room window. We can also see one of the bridges that crosses the Mississippi River.

Ben left Tuesday afternoon for home, leaving me and Jack here on our Big Memphis Adventure, as we call it. Yesterday was our roughest day yet. We arrived at the hospital at 8am, getting registered first. From there, we went to Jack's doctor's office to be cleared for his MRI. We left and went to the diagnostic department for a line nurse (a nurse who specializes in IVs and ports) to check Jack's port and the access he had received the day before for lab work. We went to the diagnostic department, checked in, and waited. Our appointment was a 10am with us arriving at 9:30 since another appointment was cancelled. Our prep nurse, J., took us back to the changing room where Jack changed into a gown and pants and had to walk through a metal detector and then the prep room. It was a larger room than what Jack is used to at Vandy, with different beds and lots of other equipment he had not seen before. New people, new surroundings, new ways of doing things—again, an autistic person's nightmare. Jack did well with me talking him through it. Nurse J. was nice and treated us both well, taking notes, temperature, and vitals, and started the fluids into Jack's accessed port. It didn't work, freaking out our patient. J. did not know what to do. He tried flushing it with saline and Jack cried out in pain. He could not get a return (medical term for trying to get fluids out of an access). The port, it seemed, was the problem. Different people, different equipment, different sights, long wait, and now port problems. Poor Jack. By this time, he was in pain on top of everything else. Nurse J. called in a line nurse to see what she could do with the port, thinking it could have a clot in it. She flushed and flushed, and each time Jack wailed in pain. Tears were flowing down his face and under his breath he was cursing, something he politely told me he was doing between his tears and screams. A couple of times he screamed so loud I had to cover his mouth, fearing his screams would frighten the younger children around us. Finally, the line nurse decided to take the access needle out and put it back in so she could try to clear the port of whatever was causing it not to work, something yet again Jack got upset about. But like the trooper we all love and know, he took it. The line nurse removed the first access but since Jack was going immediately into the MRI machine once he was asleep, they could not numb his access area because the fresh numbing med would interfere with the contrast given during the MRI. So, the line nurse removed the access and put a new access needle back in. I was completely shocked with the quickness as she got the needle into the port and Jack, prepared for the pain once again, was shocked as well since he hardly even felt it. Once he witnessed the working access, Jack was calm. Once they put him to sleep and I watched him drift off, I could breathe myself. I had asked the personnel if I could be called back as soon as they were finished with Jack's MRI of his spine and brain and the scheduled lumbar puncture, and happily they said they would. And true to their word, they called me back as soon as he was delivered to recovery. I sat with him and his nurse for the next hour, both of us trying to rouse our sleeping beauty. Finally sleeping beauty decided to wake up after we started rubbing a wet washcloth on his face and he responded by punching us. After I had just told the nurse how funny and wonderful Jack is, he wakes up throwing punches. (Do our children ever stop embarrassing us parents?) Even though he was awake, he was still groggy and not steady on his feet so we were given a wheelchair to get him back to our hotel room. But first he was hungry, not getting to eat all day and we made a quick run to the cafeteria to get some take-out dinner. The selection was very limited and Jack decided on a cheeseburger and fries. A lady in front of us in line lets us go before her, seeing that Jack was in a wheelchair, still wrapped up in blankets. I told the cafeteria worker Jack wanted a cheeseburger and

... BUT I'M NOT THE SINGER

fries and in return he asked if I wanted wheat or white BREAD. Oops, they have run out of buns and are using bread instead. This is not something Jack has ever seen before and he, yet again, freaks out, screaming things about eating a burger on bread and how nobody ever does that, blah, blah, blah. About this time, I realized how very exhausted I am physically and mentally and wished I was still at the beach, my feet in the sand. The nice lady who let us go before she turned her back to us and started ordering. I pulled Jack completely out of earshot of those around us so we could chat. He was starting to fall apart again, this time over white bread. He fussed and fumed and turned red. I finally convinced him to eat the three pieces of leftover pizza we had ordered (another freebie, a gift certificate for a free delivered pizza) and got him interested in a very nice slice of red velvet cake. Magic!! I got a salad and a piece of chocolate cake for me and we left the cafeteria, me pushing Jack in the wheelchair, him wrapped like a wiener in a blanket, having to hold our big bag of Jack's daytime toys (laptop, iPad, iPod) and my Nook and notes, and our bag containing our dinner both sitting in his lap. We found the nearest door to the outside and we left. Well, you know I can't end the story there. We went out a door that is on the back side of the hospital and we had to go all the way around to the other side, me pushing Jack, our gear, our dinner up and down curbs and sidewalks. Once the sidewalk ended and we walked up the street as cars coming from a parking lot drove by us. It took forever, or so it seemed, to find our way back to our home away from home. We did make it finally and all was well. It was a very long day.

Today I signed the papers consenting to Jack's participation in the experimental chemo regimen. I got to see his MRI results from yesterday which showed the tumors had not grown much at all. The lumbar puncture came back positive for medullo cells in his spinal fluid, a first for him. His spinal fluid has never had medullo cells, even in the beginning. Jack's doctor said it was not a surprise and was a sign that the cancer had indeed spread throughout his brain and spine, which was what we had seen on the scans. Doctor R., Jack's neuro-oncologist here, said it was good in a way for the fluid to be positive because it will give us a gauge as to whether the chemo is working. If the chemo is working the spinal fluid will become negative for cancer cells. If it remains positive, the chemo is not working. This way we don't have to solely depend on the visual scans and measuring the size of the tumors you can see on the scans.

Dear Lord, thank you for the blessing of children, for the gift of healthy bodies and strong minds, for the kindness of strangers, for doctors, nurses, and

MY NAME IS JACK JOHNSON...

researchers, for the sound of laughter and the sight of a smile, for the feeling of a hug, the reassurance from someone we love, and the continued love and support of so many who walk with us on Jack's amazing, Adventure journey. In His name, Amen.

JUNE 22, 2013—Saturday morning in Memphis, waiting for Ben's arrival from home. He is coming to spend the day with us and will go back home tomorrow. We are free for the day, already been to the hospital and back. Jack had blood taken this morning and had his port access taken out. It was a happy time for him to be rid of it for a while and a happy day for me as well because he cannot take a shower while it is in and must take a bath while I hold a cloth over the access. We struggle with holding the cloth over the access and trying to wash as many body parts as he can while arms—mine and his—go up and over and around and through each other's arms. It's a mess for both of us. It is hard for him to get up and down out of the tub and hard for me to hold on to his slippery wet body while he gets up and down. He dislikes the hair washing too because he holds the cloth while I use a cup to wet, wash, and rinse his hair. He sounds like a balloon letting air out while he tries to breathe, make sure the cloth is not getting wet, and just freaks and worries over whether the access is getting wet as I pour water over his head repeatedly during the washing. Tonight will be so much easier with Ben here to help and Jack getting to take a shower.

We are now officially scheduled to leave on July 1st. Jack will have the second dose of chemo on Friday, we will stay the weekend for observation, and if all goes well, we will be homebound on that Monday. We will see Dr. R. again on Tuesday for an examination. We also see his fellow doctor, Dr. T., a sweet Asian doctor with an Asian accent who talks without sometimes finishing her sentences or finishes them with "no?" She is sweet and treats both of us respectfully, as does Dr. R. We work with Dr. R.'s nurse, H., as well.

Jack had chemo yesterday. The infusion room here is called the medicine room. There are small individual rooms with glass doors all facing a huge nurse's station. The doors open and shut automatically with a whooshing sound. The rooms have a bed, a TV, some chairs, a desk, and all the other things you would find in a hospital room. Jack was happy to have a room and not just a chair like they have at Vandy. He was happy to have a TV but didn't even turn it on. The internet reception is not good at the hotel but is great in the hospital. He can't watch his YouTube videos at the hotel since the service is not good; it slows his computer down and it takes forever to watch

...BUT I'M NOT THE SINGER

a video, something that is driving him bananas. He has said a few times he wishes they would move us to the Ronald McDonald House so he could "get out of here" because he is upset the reception is not good. So, all day yesterday, he quietly laid in the hospital bed while receiving his chemo, laptop in his lap, headphones firmly attached to both ears, with a huge grin on his face. The chemo itself did not take long at all, maybe an hour. He also received a vitamin B12 shot prior to getting the chemo, something he will continue to get while on this chemo. I told the nurses about Jack's autism and told them I would need to help him understand what they needed to do. The B12 shot goes in a muscle so it had to be given in the top of his leg or his thigh. Given the choice, Jack chose his thigh. I was all prepared for his reaction but the nurse popped that needle in and popped it back out. Jack said, "That was so easy. I didn't even feel it!!" making us all sigh in relief. He is also getting three days of steroids around the time of receiving chemo and will have lots of blood tests to see how his bone marrow reacts to the drugs. We left the hospital yesterday at 3. We still had to pick up today's schedule, and while there picked up dinner at the cafeteria so we would not have to come back. We had hot dogs for dinner (yum, yum, not) something I knew he would eat since they had hot dog buns left and something I knew we could heat up in the room microwave. We spent a quiet Friday evening, me watching TV and Jack sitting up in his bed playing on his computer.

Dear God, thank you for healthy bodies and strong minds, for the blessing of children, for the ability to see not only the outside of each other but to see what's on the inside of us, for the generosity of so many who have made St. Jude a wonderful place for sick children, for the miracle of the human body and mind, and for the love and support of so many who continue to walk with us on Jack's Adventure journey. In Jesus' name, Amen.

JUNE 24, 2013—Today was scheduled to be an easy day, with only one hospital appointment and a lot of free time. But it didn't turn out that way. Our one and only appointment was with Patient Services, the part of the hospital that reauthorized our meal cards and reimbursed us for mileage. When we got to the PS office, we were told we had to move into the Ronald McDonald House since we have already stayed for a week and that we are scheduled to continue to stay until July 3rd. So much for leaving next Monday... looks like it is going to be Wednesday instead. Surprise to us! So, Jack and I are sent back to the Grizzlies House to pack and move ourselves to the Ronald McDonald House. The RMH is not on the hospital campus like the GH but is not too far away.

MY NAME IS JACK JOHNSON...

From now on, we will either drive to the hospital or ride the shuttle. We packed up (or should I say I packed us up while Jack watched TV) and loaded the van and we went to the RMH. The house is more like a two-story hotel with a high fence and a gated entrance. There are family rooms down hallways, with each room having two queen beds, a bathroom, a hotel style frig, a desk, one comfy chair, a walk-in closet, and lots of storage. We are not allowed to eat in our rooms but are assigned pantry space which we can lock, a part of a freezer and part of a frig for our groceries which we can buy with a gift card given to us by the RMH. There are lots of sitting areas throughout the house where people can mingle and watch TV. We must keep our rooms and our kitchen spaces, which are assigned to us as well, clean at all times. The kitchens are fully equipped with dishes, pots and pans, a stove, sink, toaster, microwave, and dishwasher. The house provides the cleaning supplies but asks us parents to keep things cleaned and washed. All dirty dishes must be cleaned in the dishwasher to make sure they are sanitized. We also must wash our own towels and sheets when needed. The kitchens are connected to a huge dining room where we can eat our cooked meals. The whole building is a joyful place with lots of artwork made by children who have lived here, colorful walls and furniture, lots of stuffed animals, and lots of places for families to have special time together. It is very quiet; I haven't heard any cries or running children in the hallways. We will not have our meal cards anymore. If we are at the hospital during lunch or dinner time, we will have to pay out of pocket. Jack is happy to get the chance to eat some of his favorite foods from home. After we were officially declared checked in and allowed into our room, I had to unload the van of all our luggage. Oh, did I write that it is very hot here, made hotter by lugging luggage in the heat. It took five trips back and forth to get it while Jack was in the room. I had to unload our frig stuff but waited until later to unpack clothes. After we got semi-settled, we drove back to the hospital for lunch because our meal cards were still good for that day. We planned to eat lunch, go back to Patient Services to pick up our Kroger gift card, and go to Kroger for our groceries. Jack ate a great lunch of fried chicken and mac and cheese, two of his favorites. He then had a piece of chocolate cake for dessert. After eating and getting our gift card, we left to go "Krogering." This past weekend while Ben was here, we found a Kroger store in a safe-feeling neighborhood and that is where Jack and I headed. Once we arrived just like we had this past weekend, we parked, walked in and Jack got an electric wheelchair buggy. I redirected him to keep him out of the way of others or out of the walkways. He usually does fine with one of them. He and I walked/drove into the produce

... BUT I'M NOT THE SINGER

department of the store, and I showed him where to stay while I walked around getting the fruits we wanted. Once I had them, I told him to back up and then turn through two produce aisles that would put him on the main walkway aisle through the store. But something happened. I don't know if he hit the gas too fast or the buggy lurched but Jack quickly turned the electric buggy into a beer display that was on the floor beside a produce aisle. It happened for me like one of those slow-motion movie segments, something I could see happening but couldn't stop. Jack took out two six packs of glass bottle beers. You could hear the glass breaking and I saw other bottles rolling across the floor. Beer was everywhere in the floor and even on Jack's buggy. He was upset and embarrassed by the whole thing. A clean-up guy gave us "the look" as I apologized the best I could. It was a difficult situation. I was shocked about what happened, concerned about Jack but needing to remind him about being careful, hoping he wasn't going to have a come-apart right there on an electric wheelchair in the produce department among strangers in a strange city, wondering what the store was going to do, if anything, about the cost of the beer, hoping no one fell into the mess Jack made, and trying to just get my shopping finished and get the heck out of there. Another Kroger employee came up to Jack and asked if he was alright which I so appreciated. It took me half of the store to get Jack to some level of normal after such a big jolt. First, he didn't want to continue to ride the wheelchair and thought he was "unworthy" to get to ride it anymore. He was ashamed of what he did and cried, while continuing very slowly through the rest of the store. I told him I would direct him the best I could to places where he would be out of the way and I would walk up and down the aisles so he could just stay in one place while I shopped a few aisles at a time. But he was still upset, his face was red with a look of sheer terror. After we paid, I helped him get the wheelchair back in its electric plug parking space and he took off across the parking lot, holding up his hands to stop the traffic for him to cross. On the way back to the RMH, I talked to him about how everyone at one time or another has made a mess in a grocery store. I told him how I once picked up a jar of pasta sauce off a grocery shelf and it just slid right out of my hand, breaking and exploding red pasta sauce all over the place. It happens to everyone. I will add that during our shopping, after the incident, I wished I had a few of those beers to calm my nerves. We are now settled in to our new digs with Jack sleeping the rest of the afternoon after his exciting trip to the grocery.

    I have done a little research on St. Jude Hospital and thought I would share what I have found out. St. Jude was founded by actor Danny Thomas. Mr. Thomas was a young actor trying to break into the acting business with a pregnant wife. Since he didn't know where the money was going to come from to pay for his wife's upcoming medical bills and a new baby, he prayed to St. Jude, the patron saint of hopeless causes. St. Jude, also known as Thaddeus, was one of the twelve apostles. It is believed Jude was a cousin of Jesus. After praying to St. Jude, Mr. Thomas' career took off. He promised St. Jude that he would build a shrine to him once he made it big. The St. Jude Children's Research Hospital is the shrine Danny Thomas built in honor of the patron saint of hopeless causes. Danny Thomas and his wife are buried here on the hospital grounds. There are statues of Mr. Thomas and St. Jude on the grounds as well.

Dear Lord, thank you for days without sickness and pain, for healthy bodies and strong minds, for the blessing of children, for faith and hope, for letting us see the kindness of others, for doctors, nurses, and researchers, for forgiveness when we do something wrong, and for the continued love and support of family, friends, and strangers who walk with us on Jack's Adventure journey. Amen.

JUNE 26, 2013—Jack had blood counts taken yesterday, and his platelet numbers have fallen drastically. Jack has not been sick, he doesn't have mouth sores, and he is still eating like a pig. But since he took that first dose of chemo, he has slept more and today has had two small nose bleeds; both are side effects of low platelets. Dr. R. said Friday morning before Jack's next dose of chemo that they will take more blood to see where his platelet count is and if they are too low, Jack will get a transfusion before his next chemo.

Dear Lord, thank you for the blessing of children, for healthy bodies and strong minds, for the gift of friendship and the joy that comes with having friends, for days without pain and sickness, for partners who walk beside us through our lives through good times and bad, and for the continued love and support of so many people who walk with us on Jack's journey. Amen.

JUNE 29, 2013—Yesterday was supposed to be chemo day but Jack's blood counts fell even further than they already had and his liver function numbers rose drastically. So, he did not get chemo. He is now classified as having neutropenia, which to remind you, means he is in danger of becoming sick when exposed to germs of any kind, even the common germs our bodies are exposed to every day and we fight off each time we are exposed to them. A healthy immune system protects us from these germs; an unhealthy immune system cannot. He must wear a mask over his nose and mouth when he is in

...BUT I'M NOT THE SINGER

the presence of others or in a public place. He is also limited on what he can eat—no fruit with a peel like grapes, one of his favorite fruits. That makes him mad too. Hopefully this will not last too long and his system will bounce back. Jack will have another blood count in the morning and if his numbers have improved, he will get the second dose of chemo Monday. If his numbers are still low, we will plan to have chemo on Friday of next week. Dr. T. and Dr. R. said some kids on this protocol need that extra few days to let their bodies recover from the first dose of chemo and Jack might be one of them. If his counts don't recover in that amount of time, we will have to reevaluate the situation. If Jack does have chemo Monday, we will get to come home Tuesday. If we wait until Friday, we will come back then and spend the weekend here just to be sure. Dr. R. is going to get in touch with Jack's doctor at Vanderbilt so they can take his blood counts there instead of us continuing to stay here. So, we are on hold until we see what tomorrow brings regarding Jack's blood counts.

We did have a productive trip to the hospital yesterday because we got Jack's leg braces fixed. Jack had told us before we went to the beach that his leg braces were rubbing the side of his foot on both legs. Every time his feet grow, it makes his braces hurt his feet or legs. We must have them readjusted which at home means a trip to downtown Nashville and a charge for the adjustment. I didn't know if someone here would or could adjust them. He has been having a hard time with them being uncomfortable since we do an extremely large amount of walking here. So, I asked his physical therapist here and she said yes, they have an orthotist who could adjust them. Yeah! We even got to move up our scheduled appointment with her after Jack's chemo was cancelled. Jack now has adjusted and comfortable leg braces again. Something that went as planned... love it.

Another thing we have done is met with a teacher rep who works here at the St. Jude hospital school, a school for children who are here for long amounts of time. Hopefully, Jack will not need the school at the hospital, but we still need to meet with the school personnel. The teacher we met with understands Jack's situation with our school at home and our medical plan. She also knows the problems these children have when it comes to learning. Therefore she is adamant about helping schools understand the issues that come with educating a child who has had treatment, the long-term and short-term side effects, the issues that face a child in active treatment, and how to effectively teach these kids who face or have been faced with cancer. She told me she would help in any way I needed to make the school understand these

MY NAME IS JACK JOHNSON...

unique needs and what they need to do to educate them. To have someone to bounce ideas off who completely understands the medical side, the educational side, and the disability laws is a dream come true for any parent in this situation. I pray I will not have to use her expertise but know now I do have someone there if I need her.

Dear Lord, thanks for the kindness of others, for the blessing of children, for healthy bodies and strong minds, for days without pain and sickness, for doctors, nurses, and researchers, for being able to worship you with others, for the technology that keeps us connected to our family and friends, and for the love and support of so many who continue to walk with us on Jack's Adventure journey. In His name, Amen.

JULY 2, 2013—WE ARE COMING HOME TOMORROW! We will have to stay here long enough for Jack to get a shot that will boost his immune system twenty-four hours after chemo. But then we are headed home. Both of us are so excited. Jack has been listening to music on his computer while dancing in his bed. I have caught him several times just smiling at whatever is going through that awesome Jack brain. I have already packed as much as I can and will continue to pack as we take showers tonight. There is lots of excitement in the air. Today was another long day. We had four appointments scheduled: having blood taken for counts, getting chemo, seeing a research nurse, and seeing Jack's doctors for the last time. Blood counts went fine, no problems. We went and had lunch because we had extra time between appointment number one and appointment number two. Lunch was good too.

I am going to stop here in the story to tell another story. Today, after lunch, we went to the "medicine room," the place where chemo is given at the hospital. I was told on one of our many tours that we didn't have to let people know we were waiting when we got to a department at the hospital. Instead, they would call for us when they were ready for us, something it has taken me a while to get used to. So, we arrived at the medicine room waiting area, found a seat and waited. Dr. T. found us and said we were going ahead with the chemo because Jack's blood counts were good. She said she had ordered the chemo and they would be calling us back soon to administer the chemo. After an hour of waiting Jack became angry with waiting so I went into the medicine room, explained Jack's situation and asked if she could give me an idea of how much longer we might have to wait so I could tell Jack. The lady at the desk said it would be around forty-five minutes more because it takes about an hour to an hour-and-a-half for the

... BUT I'M NOT THE SINGER

chemo to get to them. I thanked her and went back to the waiting room to an unhappy Jack who just became angrier when I relayed the information on our waiting time. Forty-five minutes came and went. Others came and were called back but not us. Jack became more and more angry with waiting and started telling me what he was going to do if they didn't call us soon. First, he said he was going to get up and go see someone about why he wasn't getting to go to a room. Then he said he was going to get on the shuttle and go back to the RMH without me, that he was sick and tired of all this waiting. I tried my hardest to talk to him but he was not listening to me anymore. He jumped up and said he was going for a walk and walked out the door. I was as tired of him as he was tired of me and waiting so I just sat there and let him leave. It wasn't long until I questioned my sanity. I had let a mad, unstable Jack loose on an unsuspecting hospital full of people, not knowing where he was going or if he was coming back. Then I thought about going after him but too much time had already passed and I had no idea which way he went. And if I left, he could come back and he would freak out if I wasn't there. So, hating myself for it, I had to sit and wait to see if he would indeed come back. Sitting there trying to be cool around the other patients and their parents in the lobby, I pretended to read my Nook. The clock kept ticking and still no Jack. My mind was racing, trying to figure out if someone would bring him back or if he got on the shuttle would the driver ask about his mom since we have ridden it together all week. Or would he be brave enough to just walk out the front door? Or would he go to his doctor's office and fuss to them? My mind then thought about how long should I sit and wait for him before I took off looking for him? What should I do? Mommy regret was making my stomach hurt when Jack walked through the door, still carrying his stuffed animals in his Jack bag and his blanket from home still hanging around his shoulders. I could have jumped up and hugged and kissed him but he would have really caused a scene then. He proudly told me that his walk had helped him calm down and that he felt better. I told him I was happy he felt better but unknown to him, I now felt terrible. After watching the next family walk in and get called back, I had had enough and went back in the medicine room to see the lady at the desk. She put us in a room this time, three hours late for our initial appointment. We missed the other appointments planned for that day but Jack's doctors found us and we got our instructions, our medicines for our next trip, and copies of our records to give to Jack's doctor at Vandy and copies for me to keep. The other appointment we just didn't get to. Did I say what a day?

MY NAME IS JACK JOHNSON...

Dear Lord, thank you for the blessing of children, for the giving spirits of others, for healthy bodies and strong minds, for days without pain and sickness, for nurses, doctors and researchers, for faith and hope, for the comfort of home, and for the love and support of so many who follow us on this journey we travel daily. In Jesus' name, Amen.

JULY 4, 2013—We are home. I finally slept in my own bed, took a shower in my own shower, typing this in my own office. I sound like a selfish kid with the mine, mine, mines. But it is nice to be home.

Dear Lord, thank you for the blessing of children, for days without pain and sickness, for the sound of an easy rain shower, for the gift of friendship, for healthy bodies and strong minds, and for the support and love of so many who continue to walk with us on Jack's journey. Amen.

JULY 16, 2013—I have to share this.

Brenda, my Dad's wife, got in touch with the Robertson family of the cable TV show Duck Dynasty. She told them about Jack, his story, and continued cancer treatments. They in turn sent him a box of Duck Dynasty goodies: autographed T-shirts and pictures, a bobblehead of Si, a member of the Robinson family, a replica of Si's tea glass that he carries with him in the show, a duck call, and his favorite: a Duck Dynasty cap with attached beard. As we all know, Jack has a love of facial hair. He now sports a wee-tiny, very thin mustache and sparse goatee which he thinks is wonderful and makes "the ladies think he is sexy." (His words, not ours!) Both of his patches of facial hair are from promises made by parents who don't always think with their heads and think from their hearts. At this point, we don't care as long as he is happy. So, for him to receive this cap with a beard attached was wonderful for him. He loved putting it on and wearing it to surprise Benny. We took pictures of him which he didn't mind either because he was showing off his new look. He also told us he wished we still had the houseboat so he could try his duck call and get the ducks to come to him. What a wonderful gift from people we don't know and who don't know us! Thanks, Brenda, for being bold and putting Jack's story out there to the Robertsons. Thanks to the Robertson family for making Jack's day and for letting us see him have fun, clowning around with me, Ben, and Benny, with a silly cap with attached hair. Blessings come in all fashions...

Dear Lord, thank you for the generosity of friends, family, and strangers, for the blessing of children, for the opportunity to celebrate the little things in

... BUT I'M NOT THE SINGER

life, for healthy bodies and strong minds, for the beauty of a smile and the gift of laughter, and for the love and support of so many who walk with us on this journey. Amen.

JULY 25, 2013—We have been to Memphis. We left Monday and returned yesterday afternoon. And in true Johnson family form, it did not go without a hiccup...Monday morning, Jack and I had to be at Vandy at 9:10 for his blood counts so we could get a read on where his liver enzyme levels were so he could receive the next dose of chemo. That morning it was raining, really raining. I don't like to drive in the rain even to the grocery store but much less on the interstate Once we got on the interstate, it was horrible. I had my wipers on the highest speed but still couldn't see the cars in front of me. The rain was coming down in buckets, and the spray from the other cars' tires gave the illusion of driving in a fog. There was water standing in places on the interstate as well. To make matters worse, some cars did not have their lights on. I looked in my rear-view mirror and did not see any cars but looked again and there was one without lights. Traffic was bad too with all lanes crowded with drivers, some like me who couldn't see how to drive. Not very long after we got on the interstate, with the white spray, the heavy rain coming down and pooling on the roadway, trying to keep up with where "no lights" were, and the constant beating of the high-speed wipers, a light flashed on my dash warning me of a "battery system problem." If you don't know Jack very well, I will fill you in on one of his "things": he doesn't like warnings. He doesn't like tornado warnings nor fire drills. He freaks whenever the low gas light comes on even after we have told him over and over that it means to get gas soon, not immediately. Ben and I have bought gas to make the light go off so Jack would stop worrying and complaining.

When the "battery system problem" light came on so did Jack. "Oh NNNNOOOOO! What is going on? What does that mean? OHHHHHH NNNNOOOOO!" Ha! I had no clue myself. The thing I did know was that the van was still running, that when I pushed the gas pedal it was still moving, and that the air conditioning, radio, and wipers were still working. I had my phone, but there was no way I could drive in the rain, the spray, with the "no lights" and the traffic and call Ben all at the same time, so I got Jack to make the call. Unfortunately, Jack doesn't have a cell phone and doesn't know how to use one. I cannot take my eyes off the road, and there is no way to get easily off and then back on the interstate in all the traffic, so I kept driving,

MY NAME IS JACK JOHNSON...

eyes straight ahead while giving Jack instructions on how to use a cell phone. Jack got Ben on the phone and told him about the warning light. I talked to Ben through Jack, and he told us to keep driving to Vandy and let him know when we got there. After we hung up, I got Jack to find the owner's manual in the glove box and told him how to look up the warning light definitions in the manual. After several tries, he found the correct information and read aloud what it said: turn off the radio and air conditioning, drive to a dealer and have the problem checked. So, now we are traveling through the rain, the spray, the traffic, the "no lights," the standing water, with the red warning light shining with no air conditioning! Boy, that was so fun!!

We made it to Vandy without any further troubles with the van. Being that it was Monday and we usually don't go to Vandy on Mondays, Jack had to have his blood taken by someone other than Nurse MM. and had to see another doctor besides Dr. E. After the trip there, he was open to all the changes. But, of course, Vandy was having trouble with their computer system and we had to wait for Jack's liver enzyme counts. His numbers were down enough for chemo which meant we were Memphis-bound that afternoon. But we have a small problem called "battery system problem." Benny had to have a car at home with him to go to work and Ben's car is a big old SUV that would cost us a fortune in gas to drive to Memphis. Ben called our mechanic who, luckily for us, could work on the van as soon as we could get it there. A very lucky break for us. We had planned on what time to leave for Memphis but that was before our "problem." We took the van to the mechanic, packed our bags and waited. Ben went to work and Jack and I waited here at home. For some reason, I walked over to the kitchen sink, looked out the window above the sink, and there on the inside of the window was a big black wasp. If you know me at all, you know I hate bugs. Any bug. Big bugs, little bugs, stinging bugs, harmless bugs, black, brown, green, spotted bugs, bugs with six legs, eight legs, a million legs, or with wings—it doesn't matter. I hate them all. And here right in front of me was one of their kind. Thoughts started running through my mind at a very fast pace. "Ben is not home... who will kill the wasp? Not ME!! I couldn't kill it because it is on the window between the over the sink lights and the wand on the window shade that turns the shade's blinds. But if I leave it alone it could fly and maybe sting me or, heaven forbid, Jack. And if it stung Jack what would happen? Could that make him sick? Were insect stings in any of the information the doctors have given me on cancer and outside dangers? Oh, Oh, Oh!" My mind went into overdrive. I did the only

...BUT I'M NOT THE SINGER

thing I could think of at the time: I covered the wasp with a plastic container. Yes, a plastic container that you put your leftovers in. Oh yes, I did. Just picked one up and covered that wasp up with it. He didn't like it either and started buzzing and flying around in his new smaller space. I felt his body beating on the sides of the plastic. Gross! Then it dawned on me... I haven't really thought this thing through... now what? I was standing in the kitchen holding a plastic food container against the window keeping captive a now very angry wasp when I thought to myself: how long will I have to stand here? I can't stand here all day. But I can't let this crazy mad wasp out in the room to terrorize me and Jack. So, I did what any other bug hating woman would do: I asked Jack to get the scotch tape off my desk and I taped the plastic container to the window. It wasn't pretty but it kept the container against the window and the wasp inside the container. Jack was happy, I was happy, the wasp was angrier. Ben came home so we could pick up the now fixed van and I asked him to deal with the wasp. He asked me where the wasp was and I told him it was at the sink. In true man form, he looked and looked around the sink but couldn't find it. I told him to look up and that was when the laughing started. "Ha, ha, ha. You taped the wasp to the window in a plastic container. Ha, ha, ha. I have never seen this one before. Ha, ha, ha... silly woman." I knew it was coming and really didn't care since the wasp was still captured and Jack and I were safe. So, macho Ben looked closely into the plastic container and in his manly voice declared the wasp dead, suffocated from lack of oxygen while taped to the window in a plastic container. I HAD killed the wasp! Yeah me!! Ben, still with an air of superiority, pulled the container from the window, the sound of tape ripping away from the glass window reminding me of my silly bug hating "woman" ways, followed by a "oh heck!" The wasp had been playing possum and was still alive. Superior macho man grabbed the dishtowel by the sink and proceeded to try to beat the wasp to death. I could hear the mad wasp buzzing between the sounds of the dishtowel hitting the sink. I looked up to watch the carnage happening in the kitchen, and I saw Ben, flowery dishtowel in hand, his whole body jerking with each movement of his hand going down, beating at the wasp who was trying its best to get out of the sink. Finally, after about 10 whacks of the flowery dishtowel, Ben finished the deadly deed. I almost wet my pants laughing at how Ben used his whole body and a very colorful flowery dishtowel to beat to a pulp an angry wasp. There is never a dull moment in our house.

    We arrived in Memphis later than expected. We checked in at the Griz-

MY NAME IS JACK JOHNSON...

zlies House and went to bed. Tuesday, we were up and downstairs waiting for the shuttle to pick us up to take us to the hospital. Jack received his chemo, and before we knew it, we were back in our room at the Grizzlies House. Jack complained that his head was hurting shortly after we got back to our room. Both of Jack's oncologists have now told me to give Jack a whole pain pill instead of a half of one that hasn't seemed to help the last few times he has had a headache. We gave Jack a whole pain pill. Ben and I had to snicker later when Jack started dancing in his bed and laughing at his computer while watching his TV. He didn't have a headache anymore, and everyone knew it!!

Wednesday was to be short day with just a blood count test, pick up a prescription, a dental visit, and head east to home. We expected to leave before lunch. But best laid plans never seem to materialize especially at a hospital. The quick dental visit took a little longer than scheduled. The prescription was held up for some reason. A nurse practitioner came to us and explained that three of the drugs Jack is taking can lead to heart damage when taken together for a long period of time. She was going to get Jack a scheduled EKG to check his heart and if it was alright, to have a baseline EKG on file for future reference. She told us she would call Vandy and get it scheduled on our next visit. We thanked her but as soon as she disappeared, she appeared again. Just on a chance, she called the pulmonary department to see how busy they were and they had an opening right then. We were off to the see the technician in the pulmonary department for an immediate EKG. It took about three minutes, less time than it took to get from Jack's brain tumor department to the pulmonary department in the hospital. Jack's EKG was fine and now they have a baseline for future reference. We waited again for the prescriptions and decided to eat lunch there at the hospital cafeteria. We were on the road by 1pm, two hours later than planned. We were home at 3:45.

School called to talk about what to do about Jack's upcoming school year. I am so confused about what I want to do. For the first time in Jack's school time, I have asked for a meeting with the school on what THEY feel is appropriate for Jack this year. Since we are back and forth to two hospitals, one four hours away, and on call when it comes to blood counts and chemo treatments, how do you schedule the time to learn? I can't believe I am saying this after spending years and years pushing and prodding Jack and the schools for his educational needs; I don't know how important an education is now. I want him well, free of cancer, enjoying life like he

... BUT I'M NOT THE SINGER

should be at this time in his life.

Dear Lord, thank you for the blessing of children, for days without pain and sickness, for good health and strong minds, for the caring hearts of nurses and doctors, for your guidance when our lives need direction, and for the continued love and support of so many who walk with us on this journey. Amen.

CHAPTER 39

JULY 30, 2013—A new week and another trip to St. Jude. Jack and I arrived here yesterday about 6ish. He had blood counts taken at Vandy yesterday morning which, I might add, took forever. Our visit yesterday took three-and-a-half hours for blood counts! It was painful for both of us... all the waiting.

Today, we were up early getting ready for Jack's chemo. He had his port accessed, blood taken again, all brain activity tests administered, and chemo. He has also been a pill. Yesterday was a trying day for him and for me. I knew we were on borrowed time with each minute we had to wait. I also know in a case like yesterday we were just one of the many who had to wait. Jack did fuss and so did I but I used a few colorful language words under my breath which Jack heard. It gave him an outlet to take his frustrations out on. So, last night he fussed and fussed about my using bad words. He even drew a graph to keep up with my bad language and with each level of bad language used, he listed the appropriate (to him) punishment for me. So, all day long today I have been under the watchful eyes and super ears of the cursing graph holder who was eagerly waiting for bad words to fly out of my mouth. And, no, I have no checks on his graph! It has never dawned on graph guy that some of my bad words could be instigated by him. No sooner than we got in our room last night he started with the instructions "can you find an electric plug for my computer?" and "where's my bag with my stuff?" and "can you...will you..." the whole time while I was trying to get our bags up from the van and taken off the luggage cart and returning the luggage cart. A little patience from him would have been nice but he doesn't see it that way. No, I should not use bad language but a little help from him in the way of understanding wouldn't hurt either.

Today, he has been in a better mood, spreading his Jack joy around. When it was time to access his port, about the time the nurse was readying to pull the trigger of the J-Tip (a needle-like syringe filled with a numbing agent that shoots the agent into the skin, making a "pull the top off a soda can sound"), Jack loudly said, "Fire in the hole!" I have no clue where that came from. Then at lunch, he had two pieces of sausage pizza which to his surprise were spicier than usual, and he said there were "devil sausages on his pizza." He continued with how he didn't know the devil could cook especially pizza but that the devil's sausages were hot. It is never boring with Jack around.

Dear Lord, thank you for the blessing of children, for days without pain and sickness, for the gift of humor and the joy of laughter, for healthy bodies and minds, for holding our hands on good days and bad, and for the support and love of so many who walk with us on this journey. Amen.

JULY 31, 2013—We are home. After I wrote the last entry yesterday, Jack and I went to the hospital cafeteria to see what was for dinner. He didn't feel well, had a slight headache, and was a bit more unstable on his feet as we strolled to the hospital. He wasn't sure what he wanted so I ordered a couple of sandwiches that I thought would be good for either one of us and would let him choose. Back at the room, I put the food on the table and told Jack to choose what he wanted and I would eat what he didn't. He sat in the chair but immediately jumped up, ran to the bathroom and vomited. I hate to see him get sick like that. Finally, the vomiting stopped but the headache became worse. He would not eat anything and was crying and holding his head in pain. I could not give him another pain pill and wondered if the vomiting and heaving had made the pain worse. I also knew that being a ball of emotions and stress could not help a hurting head so I calmly talked to Jack about relaxing and laying back in his bed. Talking to him in a slow and quiet voice, I told him how crying could make his head hurt more and how relaxing could help. After a few minutes, he stopped crying, was calm and relaxed, propped up with pillows in his bed. His head was still hurting some but not as bad. I gave him a few more minutes and calmly got him to agree to eat something to keep his head from hurting more. I bought him some plain potato chips and found some popsicles in the eating area of the hotel in the free to guest's freezer. He ate all the chips and messed around with the popsicle but at least he had something on his stomach. While we watched TV, his head got better, and soon he was ready for bed. He fell asleep quickly. Bless his heart. I really hate to see him that sick and in pain.

Dear Lord, thank you for safe travels, for the blessing of children, for healthy bodies and minds, for days without pain and sickness, for the awesome responsibility of being a parent, for nurses, doctors, and researchers, for the

MY NAME IS JACK JOHNSON...

gift of love, and for the support and love of so many who continue to walk with us on this journey, Jack's journey. Amen.

AUGUST 4, 2013—I had a meeting with school personnel on Thursday about what we are going to do about Jack's last year of high school. It was decided Jack will attend school for only two periods: lunch and a living skills class. Both periods are laid back times where Jack can have fun with peers. No pencils, no paper, no hard thinking, no tests. Jack will have no stress at school, just fun, fun, and more fun. If it is not fun for him, he won't go. Jack will be supervised by only a handful of people who will attend the next meeting when all paperwork is completed. Everyone will know what to do, when, and how, even me. He will have someone with him at all times, even when he goes to the restroom. I would rather we all be too cautious than not cautious enough, and something happens to Jack while in their care.

Friday, Jack and I went to Vandy for blood counts. Jack's counts were fine except his platelets. They dropped again and are very close to him needing a platelet transfusion. We will travel back to Vandy tomorrow morning and have blood counts taken again. If they are lower, he will receive a transfusion. We could tell his platelets were low because he has been having unexplained nosebleeds, something that goes with low platelets and the blood not clotting as it should. The little stinker has tried to hide it several times, but he doesn't cover the evidence very well in the bathroom trashcan. I don't understand why he doesn't want me to know and tries to hide it, but he does. Other times, he cannot hide it when his nose bleeds freely, wherever and whenever. We couldn't leave the hospital Friday because his nose started bleeding and I would not leave until it stopped. He had another one this morning before church and one yesterday. We do not have to go to St. Jude again until August 21. Jack will have his MRI on the 22nd, and we will get the results on the 23rd.

Dear Lord, thank you for each day we have with our loved ones, for the blessing of children, for days without pain and sickness, for the caring hearts of nurses and doctors, for making us resilient to changes in our lives, for the ability to worship You on this day and every day, and for the love and support of family, friends, and strangers who continue to walk with us on this journey. Amen.

AUGUST 6, 2013—Jack and I made the trip to Vanderbilt yesterday, and indeed his platelet count had dropped way below where it should be for a brain cancer patient. He had a platelet transfusion. I am so amazed by platelets. You

... BUT I'M NOT THE SINGER

would think since they are in our blood that they would be red, but they are the color of butterscotch. They are a little thicker than blood. I am reminded of glue for two reasons: platelets cause our blood to clot or glue together, and just the color and consistency reminds me of glue. I would love to see how they separate the platelets from the blood.

The transfusion didn't take long—a little under an hour—but still, we arrived at the hospital at 10 am and left a little before 2.

Hope is a word I never fully understood before. You hope it doesn't rain while you are at the beach. You hope you win the lottery. You hope your car doesn't run out of gas before you can get to the gas station. We hope for something in some form every day of our lives. But in the context of life and death, hope becomes so much more. Ben and I will never give up hope. As long as we have hope, we will do and make decisions about Jack and his health with the hope that he will live to be an old man. Hope means everything to us.

Dear Lord, thank you for healthy bodies and minds, for days without pain and sickness, for the blessing of children, for the mystery of the human body, for the gift of hope, for the sound of a loved one's laughter, and for the support and love of so many who walk with us on this journey of hope. In His name, Amen.

AUGUST 8, 2013—Jack and I went to Vanderbilt Children's Hospital yesterday for blood counts again even though he had counts taken Monday. He also received a platelet transfusion Monday because his platelets were so low. After checking them yesterday, the transfusion from Monday had only raised his platelets a little and not enough for him to be safe. So, he had another platelet transfusion yesterday.

Dear Lord, thank you for the blessing of children, for days without pain and sickness, for healthy bodies and minds, for the opportunity to be parents, for nurses, doctors, and researchers, for memories—good and bad, and for the love and support of so many who walk with us on this journey. Amen.

AUGUST 18, 2013—We just left our oldest at college. How could Benny be that old? It has been a hard weekend leaving him there. I miss him and cried again after we got home. I think I hear him coming in the door, but it's the cats doing something in the mudroom. I see the foods he likes to eat in the frig and the pantry, and I miss him. I walked to his bedroom upstairs, and it is all him, and I missed him again. I will learn to live with him not here, but like every other mother who has walked this road before me, it will take some time.

MY NAME IS JACK JOHNSON...

When Ben, Jack, and I got in the van to come home after hugging and saying goodbye to college boy, Jack said, "Now begins my life as an only child!" Leave it to Jack to ease our pain.

Dear God, thank you for the blessing of children, for healthy bodies and minds, for time we spend with our loved ones, for the privilege to be parents and watch our children grow into adults, for tears of joy and tears of sadness, for days without pain and sickness, and for the love and support of so many who walk with us on this journey. Amen.

AUGUST 23, 2013—We are back from St. Jude. It has been a long two days and two nights. Jack has been his wonderful self. More on that later.

The MRI results were not good. The cancer has continued to grow despite all the chemo we have been giving it. There is more growth of seeding (technical term: leptomeningeal disease) and two new areas of enhancement in the frontal lobes. We are crushed like a bug under someone's shoe. Dr. R. and Dr. T. were sad as well. Neither one knows of any treatment that would be successful at this time. Jack has now had full brain, and spine radiation and nine different chemo drugs and still nothing has stopped it. If the cancer was in a solid tumor form, Jack could have it removed but since it is leptomeningeal disease, they cannot. We could do radiation again, but they would only radiate again if they had a specific target, not just radiate the whole spine and brain. The two doctors talked to us about doing a high dose chemo to see if it would work; chances are it would not. Quality of life becomes an issue too. If there is nothing to stop this, do we want to keep throwing things at it, knowing full well there is no cure? High-dose chemo would require hospitalization for a long period. Is that what we want to do to Jack? Make him further sick, his hair falls back out, bloated by steroids? And it probably would not stop it? No parent should be faced with these kinds of decisions but hey, lucky us...

Our doctor at Vanderbilt had told us all the same things before we decided to try this experimental chemo. Two different hospitals, three different doctors—all with the same words. Dr. R. said the "room spinning" episodes Jack has recently complained about, the feeling of the unleveled floor, and the headaches Jack has had are all symptoms of what he saw on the scans. With the rate of growth from the last scan, Dr. R. estimates we have Jack for only a few more months. We are going back to Vandy now to talk with Jack's doctor about comfort care, aka palliative care, a step above hospice care. We will also get his opinion on the new scans. I feel he will agree with the St. Jude doctors.

... BUT I'M NOT THE SINGER

Have we thrown in the towel? NO! I am going to put out feelers on my parent support groups to see if there is anything anywhere that is showing any promise. Even though the doctors would be the first ones to know if there was, sometimes the parents get the scoop on new things coming up the pipeline at their children's hospital, things even the doctors haven't revealed to another doctor. At this point, we will search for anything and decide on it versus Jack's quality of life. Ben is just stunned. I have cried buckets of tears and screamed at the top of my lungs today driving home from Memphis since Jack was with Ben. I am mad and angry; at who, I have no idea. I am just mad. This is so senseless. Cancer is so mean. My poor child who has fought so dang hard through all the autism and for something like cancer to take all of that away makes me sick. I don't think God made us to comprehend something as evil as cancer. I know this hurts...

So tonight, I will ask you to say a prayer. Thank God for the blessings you have. Those blessings are not endless; they are fleeting. What you have today, you might not have tomorrow. Like the song says: count your blessings, name them one by one, and you will see what God has done.

AUGUST 26, 2013—Sunday, Jack didn't feel like church, so we didn't go. He did want and had already asked Ben if we could ride to the lake and look at electric poles. There was no way we could not give him what he wanted. He also requested that he would be able to sit in the front passenger seat so he could get a better look at the poles. The three us of got in the van, Ben driving, Jack in the passenger seat, and me behind him, and we rode to the lake like we used to for years and years. It brought back a flood of memories for us. Ben asked Jack if he remembered this and that of things we used to do when we had the houseboat. Jack told us his favorite things from that time were riding to and from the lake because of the poles, riding in the boat on the water, and watching Ben ski because he liked it when Ben wiped out. Only Jack would like those things! It was a bittersweet trip wondering if we would all be together the next time we traveled those familiar roads.

Jack has been busy drawing poles since we got back. We even had to stop and get him more paper to draw poles on because he had so many to draw. I love looking at life through his eyes and it is a treat to be with him when he is excited about the things he likes the best. While on our drive, he loudly announced that they had put up new poles since we had been there. He would say, "Look! That pole has a transformer on it now!" Once he looked straight ahead and said, "Look guys!" Ben said, "look at what?" Jack said, "Up

MY NAME IS JACK JOHNSON...

ahead!" I looked up thinking there was a new house or a construction site or something of interest. Jack said, "Look at those new poles. What a surprise. I wasn't expecting that!" He was so excited and engrossed with the electric poles and in his mind, he thinks we all love poles as much as he does. I love that innocent way of thinking and the sheer happiness he gets from little things in life. He could care less about the fact that he is not a typical seventeen-year-old guy. He doesn't worry or fret about his looks or what others think of him. He is so not like typical seventeen-year-olds with their needing acceptance from others to feel good about themselves, and it is wonderful. He is unique, funny, fun to be around, and happy being himself. There are not too many of us who are like him. He is such a wonderful joy to be with!

Until you go to the hospital with him. Last week's trip was a doozy. Jack and I left Wednesday afternoon, stopping for dinner before heading to St. Jude. We arrived around 7pm with our first appointment the next morning at 10:30. We walked to the hospital the next morning. Jack was checked in and tagged with his patient bracelet. His port had to be accessed and blood counts taken before his upcoming afternoon MRI. As soon as we walked in the front door, we heard screams of crying babies. They were everywhere. Cries were to the left of us, to the right of us, in stereo. Jack walked in and his demeanor and body language went from a happy Jack to evil Jack, who hates loud noises, especially crying babies. So, with scowl-faced, slumped over Jack, we walk into the check-in area. Jack slinks off to a chair where he proudly takes out his finger gun (he puts his hand horizontal, holds his thumb up like a trigger, and puts his index and middle fingers out like a gun barrel) and starts to take aim, while I look on in horror, shaking my head "no" and giving him my best "you better not" look. Thankfully we were called back to the room for port access. Our nurse was one we have had before. Jack and I were now in a heated argument over appropriate behavior when around crying babies: a conversation we have had over and over. The nurse snickered at the conversation she was overhearing. I asked her to excuse Jack's behavior at the moment because he has autism and has this thing about crying babies. He continued to have his finger gun out and cocked ready to shoot crying babies. The nurse tried to help by talking with Jack about how unhappy the babies are when she must stick them with needles and how it hurts their little bodies which makes them cry. He proudly told the nurse that if he put his gun away, he would just get the duct tape to tape their screaming mouths shut. The nurse chuckled about the duct tape. She helped us go out the back door so we would avoid any more babies. Jack was scheduled for an OT follow-up and there was a

... BUT I'M NOT THE SINGER

reduction of strength in his right hand. The OT gave Jack a new exercise band and pages and pages of exercises she wanted him to do daily. I love therapists. Most of them are young and eager and so optimistic. There is no way they could have children, giving page after page of OT homework. I know for a fact there is no way they could have autistic children! You could only be young and eager and totally optimistic to think a kid with autism is just going to drop everything they love to exercise with therapy putty and a giant rubber band. I do love their optimism.

We left the therapy department with our pages of daily exercises and a shiny, new, green therapy band and walked to the MRI department. The last MRI Jack had, we had to wait two hours before we were called back. On this trip, they called us back as soon as we got comfortable in our waiting room chairs. On most of Jack MRI's, we can be with him until they are ready to start the machine. We have been by his side when he fell asleep after he received his anesthesia. This time the nurse and anesthesiologist helped Jack walk to the MRI and helped him on the MRI bed. He was fully awake. I was not allowed to go in the MRI room since I still had some metal on my clothes. So, I watched from the doorway as Jack laid on the table. He asked for a pillow for his head, they attached an oxygen mask to his face, they moved around the room in preparation for the scan while poor Jack laid there on that hard table all alone. I felt so sorry for him. I so wanted to run to his side and hold his hand like he likes for me to do. But he never asked for me, nor did it seem to bother him that I was out of reach. If the nurses asked him a question he answered, no fear in his voice at all. I did talk to him from the doorway telling him how well he was doing and how well he was listening and following directions. I could have cried right there but I didn't. Soon they gave him the anesthesia and Jack fell asleep while I told him sweet dreams. He is such a strong kid and is my hero.

After several hours, I was called to recovery and Jack's bedside. He was still happily asleep after his MRI of his brain and spine and a lumbar puncture. The recovery nurses, both male, have been trying to wake Jack without much luck. After an hour of trying to wake sleeping beauty, he finally woke up but still will not open his eyes. And, boy, was he grouchy. He started saying over and over "But I don't want to wake up"—something he has heard from a video game or TV program. Jack is the last patient of the day, and the nurses are ready to go home, but all we got was "BUT I DON'T WANT TO WAKE UP" over and over and over. I finally got him to a place where he was talking with his eyes shut and would drink apple juice. I started the task of

MY NAME IS JACK JOHNSON...

taking off his gown and putting on his clothes. It was a task because Jack was a floppy ragdoll... with a very loud mouth.

With gown off, shirt on, shorts on, leg braces and shoes, we were finally ready to leave. I worked up a sweat tangling with a good size, angry young man who told everyone he was still "drunk!" The nurses had a wheelchair waiting, and once I had Jack loaded into the chair, I discovered another small problem that I hadn't thought through: how was I going to push Jack in the wheelchair while also pulling a cart? The pull cart has our waiting paraphernalia, like his computer, his iPad, my books, and my purse, Jack's blanket from home, and anything else I thought we might need to last us for the day. I tried to pull the cart and push the chair, but without two steady hands pushing both sides of the wheelchair, it wouldn't go forward in a straight line. I tried to wrap my arm in the handle of the cart, but that didn't work either. In desperation, I asked Jack if he could roll the wheels of the wheelchair like he used to do when he used a chair daily. Again, what was I thinking? I won't share his answer. Finally, I grabbed the pull cart handle and one of the wheelchair handles and pushed. It worked but was a handful of handles. We couldn't roll fast, or I lost my grip. My body had to push from an off-center position behind the wheelchair because the cart took up the room on one side of the back of the wheelchair. I walked with an uncomfortable stoop so I could keep a grip on the chair and the cart. The time was 6:20 pm. Jack was still "drunk," we had no food for dinner at the hotel, and the cafeteria closed at 7. We headed to the cafeteria with only minutes to spare. So do a lot of other people, all at the same time. The only food station open late was the grill. Here they cook hamburgers, hot dogs, fries, tater tots, chicken fingers, and other grill type foods. I pushed/pulled us into the line and continued to move us up while asking Jack what he wanted to eat. I couldn't leave him somewhere out of line for fear of what he might say or do. He announced while in line he wanted a cheeseburger with a bun. Sounds reasonable, right? Jack will not eat a cheeseburger without a bun. Period. We had had this problem before at this food station when they, in fact, ran out of buns. It got ugly. I was trying to avoid another scene, not thinking about the scene we were making just walking around while I, sweating and red-faced, was pulling/pushing an angry "drunk" kid in a wheelchair who was covered up completely by a blanket except for his unhappy face and constantly complaining mouth. I tried talking to him, pleading with him, so maybe he would not blow up as I imagined the poor guy behind the counter unknowingly telling us he didn't have a bun and Jack exploding. I could already see it in my mind, hear the screams of misery over a bun. I

...BUT I'M NOT THE SINGER

could feel the eyes of the other people around us boring down on me like I could change any explosion that happened.

As we got closer to our turn, in a last plea I told Jack he could just eat the cheeseburger meat without the bread to which he said through tightly gritted teeth, "NO!" Then he said, "They have buns because I saw them." But this is coming from a blanketed "drunk" kid with his eyes still rolled back in his head. Finally, the counter worker looked at me and asked if he could help me. (If he only knew how loaded his question was) I opened my mouth and said, "Two cheeseburgers please. One on bread and the other on a bun." And then he asked what kind of cheese and the world was lifted from my shoulders. Who knew a hamburger bun could bring such joy and relief. But it did. I pushed/pulled Jack, the chair, and the cart out of the way while I put covers on our plates of hot cheeseburgers. Jack turned around and said "pickles" which meant he was asking for pickles. I saw the condiments ahead of us and there was no one there. With the covers on our plates, I put the plates in Jack's lap and looked up to push/pull the chair/cart and saw two ladies who had gotten in line ahead of us at the condiment station. They were talking to each other when I heard one of them stop and say, "There aren't any pickles left, dang it!" By the time she left, she had stirred almost every pickle out of the pickle juice and put them on her plate. I was surprised Jack didn't say anything to her but he might have drifted off to sleep again, since he was "drunk." I managed to fish out four measly looking pickles and a few bits and pieces of pickles past. With pickles on Jack's plate, we pushed/pulled/rode through the rest of the cafeteria, picking up a couple of pieces of cake, two of Jack's favorites, so he could choose the one he wanted. We got to the drinks. Jack told me water and as I was getting the cup, then he changed his mind and wanted Hi-C punch instead. I reluctantly watched the pink fluid fill the cup, thinking about how big of a mess it would make if Jack dropped it. Jack wanted chips too but told me he only wanted Lays. I had to leave him and search for them but finally found one of three bags left. I pushed/pulled us through the cashier line with Jack holding all our plates of food. Once through the cashier line, Jack decided he wanted to eat in the cafeteria rather than take the food back to the hotel. I got us to the first table I found and started the process of moving all the food from Jack to the table. I moved the wheelchair and a table chair into position to move Jack from one to another as Jack exclaimed one more very loud "CAN'T YOU SEE I'M STILL DRUNK!" while getting lots of stares from those around us. I then got his condiments for his burger and napkins for his mouth. Finally, I sat down and we ate dinner in silence. I was tired, smelly

MY NAME IS JACK JOHNSON...

from sweating, and hurting in my back from all the stooping over pushing/pulling the chair/cart/Jack. I ate my burger while keeping an eye on Jack as he eagerly ate his bunned and pickled burger. He had not eaten all day. I was afraid he could choke. We finished. I threw away the garbage, cleaned up our area, and started the process of getting us to our room with all our gear. Jack made the transition from table chair to wheelchair without incident or screaming until we started to move the chair. He screamed one more time because his blanket had gotten caught in the spokes of the wheelchair. I got it loose but not before it got a new black mark on one side that probably will never wash out. It took a while, but we pulled/pushed/rode back to the hotel where I got Jack in bed, took a shower, collapsed, and did nothing for the rest of the night.

The next day wasn't a whole lot different. Ben was coming to Memphis, leaving early from home to meet us at the hotel so he could help load the van for us. He overslept and didn't make it to help me load up. Since we were only scheduled for appointments until early afternoon, we had to have our things out by noon, which meant I had to get us ready, get breakfast, pack us up, and load the van by myself. It wasn't an easy task. Once loaded, we drove the van to the hospital instead of walking since we would be leaving the hospital in the afternoon.

Dear Lord, thank you for another day with the ones we love, for the blessing of children, for days without pain and sickness, for healthy bodies and minds, for nurses, doctors, and researchers, for love, faith and hope, and for the love and support of so many friends, family and strangers who give so much of themselves and continue to walk with us on this journey. Bless them all, Lord. In His name, Amen.

AUGUST 28, 2013—Ben, Jack, and I went to Vanderbilt today to talk with Jack's oncologist about palliative care. Ben and I had the words of Jack's doctors at St. Jude repeating in our brains. The doctors there painted us a picture of three-to-four months life expectancy, no curative treatment available, and their feelings on what Jack could handle and what he could not. Jack now has two new lesions in the frontal lobe area of the brain and per the doctors, because of their location, they could start to cause seizures. The spread of cancer in the back of his brain has grown and can cause further balance issues. Any treatment forward would be considered palliative care because Jack's cancer seems to be a very aggressive type. They went on into a description of what this type of cancer's end of life looks like and what we should expect. The St. Jude doctors said we could try some very

...BUT I'M NOT THE SINGER

aggressive chemo that would be horrible on Jack, would make him very sick, and probably would not make any difference in the outcome. They left us with the feeling that we had no hope whatsoever. But they don't know I live for hope. Hope is what has been keeping me going through this whole journey. It makes me strong for my son and gives me strength to be his mother, his advocate, his friend, and his support. For the last few days, I have had a very hard time dealing with a life without hope. I have cried buckets of tears. I have truly felt like Job in the Bible, who ripped his clothes off in grief. How can a parent be open to the possibility of the death of their child? NOT me. I will do whatever it takes to fight for my child. I have fought for him for years and will not stop now because all hope is gone. So, I got on the computer and researched everything I could find about clinical trials associated with Jack's type of cancer and recurrence. So much of this my meager mind cannot understand but I don't mind finding someone who can help or asking the doctors. First trial I found, I wrote the doctors at St. Jude about and have already received a reply. I agreed with them once it was explained to me, that trial would be too hard on Jack now. Back on the computer researching, I found more trials.

Today at our appointment with Jack's Vanderbilt oncologist to talk about palliative care, we didn't get too far into our conversation before I pulled out my papers of clinical trials. Dr. E is going to consider some of them to see if Jack qualifies for them. If he does, we will have to look closer at the treatment side effects to decide if we want to put Jack through the treatment. Dr. E said all the same things as the St. Jude doctors: we have a limited time with Jack, there is no cure, Jack's cancer is considered very aggressive, and any treatment given to Jack now would be considered palliative care. But treatment could buy us time, not much but enough time for some new treatment to come along and help. Ahhhh, my glimmer of hope. Now mind you it is small, a very tiny sliver of hope, but it is there. If we can add a few months to Jack's life and some new research shows promise in treating this horrible monster, then we can try it. If no new treatments are found, then we have had a few more months with our awesome son. We have done all we could as his parents. These are despicable decisions no parent should ever have to make for their child. I never dreamed we would be where we are but nightmares do happen. How do you measure the life of your child? What is it worth to you? How far would you go to save your child? How far would you push his/her body? How sick is too sick to push your child? When is enough too much? Not unless you have worn these shoes would

MY NAME IS JACK JOHNSON...

you fully understand how hard this is. I know it is hard for the doctors to tell parents this because they are human and parents too. I thought the doctors at St. Jude were going to cry with me and Ben during our difficult MRI results discussion. The situation is made harder for them because they cannot give their personal opinions in fear they will be liable for what they say. They have spent countless hours in education, in practice and in research, and still there are cases that they just can't do a dang thing about. But for parents it is agony. The old proverbial "watching a train wreck and not being able to stop it" feeling. The images that plague me in my dreams wake me up nightly. I haven't figured out where Ben's head is in all of this. Men keep so much inside. He told me today it was so surreal for him right now. I envy his emotional control that has seemed to have left me now. I do have faith—faith that God will not leave us alone and faith that Jack will be safe and cancer and autism free one day. So, I will continue to fight with the hope that something will come along, perhaps buying a few more months, with faith that God loves us no matter what, and with the love and support we receive from our friends and family. We will continue to love our sons, both of them, and fight whatever battle we face.

Please know... I am not Superwoman or Super Mom. Every mother I know would do the same in my shoes. Each of you is privy to what is happening in our lives by my sharing our story. I am not stronger than you, or a better mother than any of you. I am just opening my heart and baring my soul in one of life's hardest situations. And if this kind of situation comes to your family, you won't think about being super or strong. You do what must be done. I was not given a choice; it was thrust upon me. We are not alone. We are just one family facing this situation.

Dear Lord, thank you for hope—the light in the dark—that gives us the will to go on, for the blessing of children, for days without pain and sickness, for healthy bodies and minds, for faith as small as a mustard seed, for nurses, doctors, and researchers, for the strength given all mothers, and for the support and love of family, friends, and strangers who walk with us on this journey of hope. Amen.

SEPTEMBER 6, 2013—This past weekend we were invited to Center Hill Lake by some friends of ours so Jack could take a boat ride. Our friend, T., invited us and we met her husband, A. They have a lovely boat at the other end of the lake from where we had our boat, but since Ben and I have had many boats over the years, we had at one time a boat docked on that part of the lake

...BUT I'M NOT THE SINGER

too. For us, it was another trip down memory lane, seeing places we haven't seen in years. Jack sat in the back of the boat enjoying the feel of the wind on his face and the wind blowing his hair backward. I caught him a few times talking to himself which made me want to know what he was saying or what was going through his mind. Jack doesn't share. It was fun to see him enjoying himself. A. and T. also took us to their cabin home while a storm passed by. Jack made himself at home, falling asleep on the couch. What a beautiful house in the woods to enjoy with friends and family. Thanks to A. and T. for sharing their boat and house with us.

During the time before the rain started, we docked the boat and left the dock for their house. Jack had to walk along the dock walkway, something that scared me. With two of us on either side holding his arms, we got him to the shore. He then had to walk up a very steep sidewalk to get to A. and T.'s SUV—not an easy task for a guy with leg braces that do not bend at the ankle. Ever so slowly Jack walked up the steep incline, his feet pointing outward and taking the tiniest baby steps, with two of us holding his arms. He cracked us up when he started yodeling a song he has heard from a game on The Price Is Right. Even the people walking slowly behind us laughed. What a guy. He can't walk like the rest of us because his feet are contained in leg braces. He was trying his hardest to get to a dry place away from an approaching storm. His inability to walk up the hill made the climb slower and very hard. We were all infringing on the people who were trying to leave behind us because we can't move fast enough out of their way, and Jack started singing a yodel from a game show! That's our Jack!

We had an appointment Wednesday with Jack's oncologist at Vanderbilt. We talked with him about our options to slow the progression of Jack's cancer. We also talked about some of the clinical trials I had given the doctor the week before. We have decided to review some information on one clinical trial's results before we make our final decision. This trial is a chemo-only trial but with four different chemo drugs Jack has not had. The trial's results have shown the drugs will slow the progression of the cancer but will not rid his body of cancer. It will buy us time. It could buy months and in some cases a year plus. I must have faith that some new treatment will come along in that time that will cure or at least stop the growth of this cancer. On the parent support group, I have found another clinical trial that has shown promise in cancers like Jack's. I have sent another email to the doctors at St. Jude on that one. I also listened to a seminar given by two doctors from MD Anderson who are involved with this promising trial and who have more trials coming in the months to come. There is hope... we just must find it. We are now waiting to hear back from the doctors at VCH and at St. Jude before we make any final decision or start any chemo.

Jack did feel well enough to make an appearance at school yesterday. He has not been to school at all this year, so this was a first. Lots of people were happy to see him. He got to work a puzzle and spend time with friends. Tonight, he is going to a Best Buddies party before the football game at school. Ben and I will have to stay nearby, but hopefully, Jack will have some more time with friends. From what I understand, Jack and all the Buddies will be presented as a group tonight before the game. After that Jack goes with a friend of ours and Ben and I will stay to watch the game. Date night... woo hoo.

Next week Jack will become an honorary member of the football team at UT Chattanooga. Years ago, I signed Jack up with a foundation (Friends of Jaclyn Foundation) that brings together sports teams with children with life-threatening diseases. The children become "members" of the team, spending time with them whenever they can. Jack has his first visit with the team next Friday night. This should be interesting. Our visit there also gives us time to visit with Benny too. I will share how it goes.

Dear Lord, thank you for the blessing of children, for healthy bodies and minds, for time spent with our loved ones, for the gift of laughter and a sense of humor, for days without pain and sickness, for words that encourage us to go on, and for the love and support of so many who continue to walk with us on this journey with Jack. Amen

SEPTEMBER 8, 2013—Jack attended the Best Buddies party Friday night before the Centennial/Brentwood football game. In case you don't know, Centennial beat Brentwood for the first time in the history of Centennial High School. (Congrats to the CHS football team!) Jack's Best Buddy, K., asked if Jack would like to bring his iPod and DJ the party. He saw lots of previous teachers and spent time with them, but his favorite thing was getting to share his music with the party attendees. He was grinning from ear to ear. Some of the other party attendees were up and dancing which made DJ Jack even happier. I cried while standing out in the hall, watching him smile and laugh—something we don't always get to see. If I could bottle that smile, that body language, the way he lit up from inside, I would. I so wish every parent enjoys their children as much as we enjoy ours. Happiness is not just a word. It's a facial expression. It's a place in time. It's fleeting. It's a gift and a blessing. I so wish every day was blessed with such happiness!

...BUT I'M NOT THE SINGER

2013 Jack's senior portrait

Please pray for Jack, of course, but also pray for Ben and me. We are making decisions for our son and his future that no parent should have to make. We continue to investigate clinical trials and have several that are interesting, with promising results. We need guidance and direction in which trial will be the right one for Jack. These are very hard and difficult decisions that make parents question themselves. The burden of this situation is so much heavier than we ever dreamed. With God's help, we believe we will make the right decision for Jack and our family.

Dear Lord, thank you for another day with our loved ones, for the blessing of children, for days without pain and sickness, for tears of joy and tears of sorrow, for faith that we will spend eternity with You, and for the love and support of so many who walk with us on this journey. Amen

SEPTEMBER 12, 2013—Jack had an appointment yesterday to start another regimen of chemo. This chemo will hopefully buy us time, and we can use some of this time to research more about the new things happening that show promise, or time for some new treatment to become a clinical trial. We also feel the pressure, like a clock ticking because Jack's last chemo treatment was July 29th which means his cancer has been left untreated for six weeks—not

MY NAME IS JACK JOHNSON...

something we feel comfortable about, knowing how malignant this cancer is. We agreed to and signed the papers to start the new chemo drugs as soon as possible. Of course, there is that little thing about insurance and how they don't want to pay for the drugs even though our policy covers them. ARGH! As I type this, we still haven't received the drugs! K. at Vanderbilt is doing everything in her power to find a way to get the insurance company to pay ASAP for the drugs so Jack can start the chemo. Thank you, K., for all your hard work and patience. You have lightened our load! And, as the doctors say over and over like little broken records, this is not curative. I am beginning to hate those words.

After our hospital trip which took forever, we had to rush back home and get Jack ready for his senior portrait appointment. He has already had his casual senior portraits made (again thanks to M. and J. and Milo!) with these portraits being the formal tux portraits. Ben and I worked frantically with hair and facial hair trying to get Jack to look his best. We quickly made the trip to the studio with Ben leaving me and Jack for the actual portraits. Another mother and daughter were ahead of us, so we waited. While waiting, the young lady working the studio asked me in front of everyone there why we didn't have an appointment for our casual portraits since they have a contract with Jack's high school to do all senior portraits. I told her, again in front of everyone, that Jack had already had his casual portraits done. She responded by asking me if I had OK'ed it through the yearbook person in charge at school... blah, blah, blah. I had enough with the public questions and politely got up, walked to her, bent down to her ear, and said, "Jack is dying from brain cancer," stood up and nicely as I could, said "I don't think they will mind." The young lady nodded and didn't say another word. She walked the mother/daughter to the studio and took her portraits. Ben arrived after picking us up some lunch and when the young lady called our name, we slowly walked Jack into the studio. There is no way to express how it felt for me to watch Jack get his senior picture made, full well knowing that there is a chance he might not be with us when yearbooks are released in the spring. It was a challenge for him to sit up straight for all the pictures. It was also a challenge for him to stand and put on the tux jacket and the graduation cap and gown that he had to put on next. It was a group effort. Tears rolled down my face when I looked at him, sitting there smiling that silly Jack smile of his. Every day is a chance to make a new memory and I will remember this forever. When we were finished, I stopped the young lady and apologized in case I had hurt her feelings. She tuned up to cry and said she didn't know me

... BUT I'M NOT THE SINGER

but felt she needed to hug me. We did, two strangers brought together by Jack, something that seems to happen more and more lately. We got home, ate our late lunch, Ben went to work, and I started to clean up our lunch mess. While in the kitchen, I heard Jack say, "uh oh" and before I could move, he was on his way to the bathroom where he vomited all his lunch up. Poor Jack. I felt so sorry for him. Then it dawned on me: the headaches, the unsteadiness, the feeling bad, the vomiting—all signs of swelling in the brain. We had talked to the doctor that morning about Jack's headaches, and the deteriorating unsteadiness so he prescribed Jack a steroid in case the brain had started to swell from the cancer and the lack of treatments. Ben ran to the pharmacy and picked up the steroids and Jack has been taking them and has not had any more vomiting or headaches. He is still unsteady but it is not getting worse. I just hope and pray that we have not left this cancer unattended too long and it's gotten worse. I hate cancer!

Dear Lord, thank you for the blessing of children, for days without sickness and pain, for the angels you send to help us make it through another day, for every minute, hour, and day we have with our loved ones, for healthy bodies and minds, for nurses, doctors, and researchers, and for the love and support of friends, family, and strangers who walk with us on Jack's journey. In Jesus' name, Amen.

SEPTEMBER 17, 2013—"But Sports are not my Forté!"

I usually don't title my entries but decided this one deserved a title. It all started Friday...

Friday morning, we woke up to a day of still not having Jack's chemo drugs from the hospital. If you have never dealt with a serious illness with a loved one, you have missed out on the games that are played between doctors, insurance companies, and money, over what the patient needs, what the doctor prescribes, what the insurance will or will not pay for, and the time it takes for the whole soap opera to play out. The chemo drugs were prescribed by Jack's doctor on Wednesday and we were supposed to start taking the drugs that day. When Ben walked downstairs at the hospital to have the drug prescription filled, we were told we would have to pay $3,500 for the drugs even though we have insurance and the drugs are covered under our insurance plan. The insurance company wanted us to pay for the drugs up front and then they would reimburse us our money later. We are now living into our fourth year of this battle with cancer. We are paying lots of out-of-pocket expenses, deductibles, and co-pays. We just helped get our other son settled into college.

MY NAME IS JACK JOHNSON...

Does anyone really think we have that kind of money sitting around with nowhere to go to cover another medical or college bill? Oh, my goodness. The wonderful lady who works for Jack's oncologist was appalled to think that any insurance company would think that would be an amount of money any cancer patient or their family would just have sitting around gathering dust, just waiting for someone to ask for it. So, our guardian angel, K., started working hard, talking to our insurance company, our drug insurance company and the pharmacy at the hospital. She found the right hospital pharmacist who talked to the right person at the insurance company who both agreed to help us out and after two and half days of wrangling and haggling, a deal was made between the two of them and Jack's chemo drugs were covered at no cost to us. A huge thanks and hugs to K. at Dr. E's office and to V. at the Specialty Pharmacy at Vanderbilt Hospital. We so appreciate your help!

But all that wrangling and haggling took time and we didn't receive the drugs until midday Friday. I had written before how Jack was going to become an official member of the University of Tennessee Chattanooga football team which was happening this past Friday afternoon. Waiting for the chemo drugs pushed our planned schedule out of sync but we were determined to get to Chattanooga in time for Jack's big football signing ceremony. Ben mashed the gas pedal and we sped southeast. I am sorry to all the people we sped by or fussed at on the way. His driving and our speed made me a nervous wreck. Jack slept most of the way which was a good thing because his daddy's driving might have upset him. We arrived in Chattanooga at the basketball arena a mere five minutes before the ceremony. Coach H, UTC's head football coach, was waiting in the parking lot for us. Benny, Miss D., and two of their new friends met us there, and we all walked into a room at the arena. Ben and I walked Jack into the room with almost one hundred pairs of eyes watching us. The coaching staff was there, along with the media, the representative from the Friends of Jaclyn Foundation, and the whole football team. Sitting in front of the room was a table with several chairs behind it. The table was covered with a blue cloth, a football helmet sat on one side and a football on the other, a couple of blue and gold shakers were on either side of them, and several copies of the team's programs were on the other side. Ben and I made our way to the table helping Jack along. We sat, Ben on one side and me on the other with Jack in the middle. Coach H introduced us to the players and explained how Jack came to them through the Friends of Jaclyn Foundation. He then asked me or Ben to share a little something about Jack. I told the team how Jack is my hero. I went on to explain how Jack had been diagnosed

... BUT I'M NOT THE SINGER

with autism and how afraid I had been when he was diagnosed with brain cancer. I shared with them what a strong kid Jack has been through all his many treatments, how he didn't cry for the longest time while going through grueling treatments, and how he continues to amaze me with his ability to just take whatever comes. Ben spoke a little, too, thanking the team and coaches for having Jack on their team. Coach H. then gave Jack his National Letter of Intent and Jack signed his name. He surprised me by not signing his name in a wiggly print "Jack J." like he usually does. No, Mr. Team Member took the time to slowly sign his name in cursive—something I haven't seen him do in a very long time. Coach then presented Jack with a team cap and his jersey, a navy blue football jersey, number 14, with the name Johnson across the back. Once Jack put them both on, Coach introduced to the players their newest team member, Jack Johnson. And with that the room erupted with eighty-seven young men giving Jack a huge standing ovation. Mr. Team Member sitting beside me became Mr. Ham Sandwich, putting his hands up and out over his head, taking in all the applause. What a ham! (Don't ask... yes, I did cry!)

2013 Jack's first day as a Chattanooga Moc with Mom in the stadium box seats

MY NAME IS JACK JOHNSON...

2013 Jack on the sidelines at a Chattanooga Mocs football game

Dennis Murphy, founder of Friends of Jaclyn and Jaclyn's father, spoke to the team and coaches about what life is like living in the shadow of brain cancer. Jaclyn was nine years old when she was diagnosed with the same type of cancer as Jack's. She has had a better outcome than Jack and is now a sophomore in college. Living in the cancer world prompted the Murphys to give back through their foundation which pairs children with brain tumors with sports teams throughout the country. Not only does the relationship between the brain tumor patient and the sports team lift the spirits of the patient and their family, it also changes the lives of the members of the teams. Mr. Murphy said the foundation has received many letters from team members who had completely changed their life path after their relationship with a child with a life-threatening illness. Some of those team members had gone on to become researchers and doctors. Once the ceremony ended, the team had to practice. Before they left the room, all eighty-seven team players walked past Jack giving him fist pumps, Jack's preferred handshake, or high fives. A newspaper reporter was present from the *Chattanooga Times Free Press*. Mr. W. and I had spoken about Jack earlier in the week. He was also on-hand for

... BUT I'M NOT THE SINGER

the signing and afterwards asked more questions, some directed to Jack. Mr. W. wrote a wonderful article about Jack and his signing in the *Chattanooga Times Free Press*.

That afternoon, the football team arrived at the stadium and walked through their fans tailgating under a pavilion across the street from the stadium. Jack, tired from his signing, sat in a chair, while the team walked past him and fist pumped him again. After the team was in their locker room, Coach H. helped us get into the stadium. We were given sideline passes, game tickets, and skybox passes for us and other family members and friends who had come along to be with Jack on this day. Before the game, Jack was allowed in the locker room while the team was getting ready. Jack got bored and asked for his iPad so he could play it while he was in the locker room. Some of the players watched Jack play and commented on his choice of iPad games. Ben joked that Jack was the only team member with an iPad and not shoulder pads.

Since Jack was also a team captain for the game, it was planned for him to be on the field during the coin toss. Jack was allowed to toss the coin after one of the referees gave him a quick lesson in coin tossing. The captains walked onto the field, including Jack who was escorted by Ben for physical support. Jack did a good job tossing the coin. Mr. T., one of the referees, presented Jack with the game coin after the toss. As Jack walked off the field, the stadium crowd clapped and cheered. Jack gave them several waves and salutes. (I would never tell him but the crowd was cheering because the team had run onto the field from the locker room behind us.) We stayed on the field for a while and then were given a cart ride to the entrance of the skyboxes. We were taken to the skybox, walking past the media, the radio booths, and the coaches boxes.

Coach H. had told Ben that Jack could be in the locker room after the game to celebrate with the team. When the clock ticked into the fourth quarter, we made our way down to the field. Once on the field, Ben and Jack went into the locker room to wait for the victorious Mocs, who won the game 42–10. After shaking hands with the opposing team, the team made their way to the locker room. The chair Jack had been sitting in earlier before the game happened to be in the area where the coach talks to the team. So once the team and the coach came into the locker room, there sat Jack front and center behind the coach. Since I wasn't inside the locker room, I will relay what happened per Ben who was inside with Jack. Coach H. stood in front of his players and told them, "Your performance on the field was what it was

MY NAME IS JACK JOHNSON...

2013   Jack with his sexy mustache

...BUT I'M NOT THE SINGER

supposed to look like. We have a good football team and that's how you are supposed to play the game." Then he adds, "And Jack is 1 and 0." Ben said what happened next, he will never forget. Neither will I from my chair outside the locker room. The whole team started chanting "JACK, JACK, JACK, over and over and over. Ben said most of them were jumping up and down while chanting. Me? I could hear it from my chair and covered my face so no one would see me cry. Jack? He was being a ham sandwich again, lifting his hands into the air, taking in all the chants of his name. In life, there are presents we love receiving. Kids love toys, some men love guy toys like cars and golf clubs. Women like jewelry and clothes. Parents of children with cancer, we want our child recognized for their bravery and strength through their battles that bring many adults to their knees. We received that gift. For that small period of time while the team chanted our child's name, he was not just the kiddo with cancer, he was a part of a team. He was alive and proud of himself. He glowed. He smiled. He laughed. He joked with us. It was a gift better than anything money could ever buy.

We want to thank Coach H. for agreeing to let Jack become part of the team. Thanks for treating us to a day we will never forget. Thanks to Mr. W. for being patient with Jack and writing about us and Jack's journey. Thanks to the Friends of Jaclyn Foundation for connecting Jack with the Chattanooga Mocs football team and for the bag of goodies we were given. Last but not least, thanks to the Mocs football team for making one young man the happiest guy in Chattanooga that night. Thanks for taking a child beaten down by a horrible disease and lifting him in body and spirit. We will always remember the sound of Jack's name echoing through the locker room.

There were plenty of Jack-isms over the weekend as well:

• At the signing ceremony, Jack told Coach H that sometimes when his team is losing, he has been known to use bad language. Coach said, "Me too."

• Again, at the signing ceremony, Jack told the team, "I just hope we don't lose. I have a nasty temper when it comes to losing."

• Jack told Ben he would be a part of the Mocs football team only if they didn't want him to play in the game.

• When Jack found out he was getting his own jersey, he asked if he would have to wear a helmet too.

• In the skybox after the coin toss, Jack told me about Mr. T. the referee who gave Jack the coin tossing lesson and the coin after the toss, "Mr. T. won't be my friend if he calls the team for a bad call."

• After finding out that the Mocs next game is an away game, Jack asked if

MY NAME IS JACK JOHNSON...

we thought the team would give him an away jersey to wear.
- While Ben went to get the van after the game, Jack and I were standing at the corner of two roads when a car came by and someone in the car told Jack goodbye out the car window. Jack said, "Bye. Drinks are on me!" I asked him why he said that and he told me, "that is what people say when they are celebrating." I think he watches too much TV.
- On the way back to the hotel after the game, Jack said he needed to get back to the hotel so he could get his beauty sleep.

There were more, but Ben and I can't remember them all. He was firing them off one-by-one all night. What a great weekend for all of us, especially Jack.

Dear Lord, thank you for the blessing of children, for days without pain and sickness, for healthy bodies and minds, for the gift of spending time with the ones we love, for seeing the smile of a loved one, for putting others in our lives when we are at our lowest, for the feeling of a hug, for giving us joy and hope in our lives, and for the support and love of family, friends, and strangers who walk with us on Jack's journey. In His name, Amen.

CHAPTER 40

SEPTEMBER 25, 2013—Jack and I just got home from our weekly trip to VCH for blood counts. Jack's platelets are starting to drop and will have to be monitored closely. Other than the platelets, Jack has felt great. His energy level has been very good, and his appetite has been massive. He has gained six pounds since last Wednesday. I think the steroids are doing their job. We are weaning him off slowly.

Jack went to school last Thursday and stayed for an hour or more. I stayed with him and tried to stay out of the way as much as possible. We got up Thursday, started our day, and I asked Jack if he was going to try to go to school. He replied, "Nah. I can say goodbye to CHS now because I am on a college football team." I had to deflate his little bubble and his big ego and explain reality to him, and he decided to go to school. He had fun, visiting with friends, working a puzzle, and just being out of the house. Thanks to everyone at CHS for making Jack feel so special when he is there.

Dear Lord, thank you for the blessing of children, for days without pain and sickness, for healthy bodies and minds, for each day we are given with our loved ones, for the gift of a hug, for mending broken hearts, and for surrounding us with family, friends, and complete strangers who support us and love us on this long journey. We give thanks in Jesus' name, Amen.

OCTOBER 2, 2013—It's blood count day. Jack's platelets dropped a little further down but not to the point of needing a platelet transfusion. We knew his platelets were down because he had a minor nosebleed this weekend, always a sign that his platelets are low. He had lost two pounds, a surprise, but it wasn't from a lack of eating. He is still eating us out of house and home; not a complaint, just an observation. He finished taking steroids yesterday, so we will see what happens with his appetite now.

The sixth-floor oncology department was a complete zoo today. Our appointment was at 10:30, we were called back at 11:30. Nurse MM. was there

MY NAME IS JACK JOHNSON...

today, and she even took Jack's vital signs because the nurse who usually does the vitals was so busy. There were no chairs in the infusion room nor the lobby. I overheard one mother whose son had not been there in a year say she had never seen it that way in all the time her son was a patient. She went on to say how sad it was this way because that meant so many children were that sick. I agree.

Jack received a call last Friday from the coach of the UTC football team. He asked Jack if he had any words of wisdom for the team before their game on Saturday. Jack told them, "Play hard and never give up."

Dear Lord, thank you for the blessing of children, for the opportunity to teach them and prepare them for life, for days without pain and sickness, for healthy bodies and minds, for the sound of laughter and a sense of humor, for the upcoming change in the seasons, for tears of sadness and tears of happiness, and for continuing to surround us with friends, family, and strangers who support us and love us each day on this journey with Jack. Let us continue to "Play hard and never give up!" Amen.

OCTOBER 10, 2013—Wednesday night after blood counts...

That night was the beginning of seeing a change in Jack. He was more lethargic, started to lose his appetite, and just plain felt bad. He had moments of feeling good and being hungry but things just seemed to change for him. Thursday, he woke up not feeling well and with more balance issues. In the last few weeks, Jack has held on to my arm for support when he is walking, and it has become, slowly but surely, more and more as he grips on for longer periods of time and with a much stronger grip than before. He didn't want to go to school on Thursday but we talked about it and he decided to go. I decided this time to sit out in the hallway to give him some peer time without his mother there. My agreement with the school is that I am present at all times with Jack when he is there in case he has a medical issue so the school is not responsible—something at this time I am in full agreement with. So, I found a chair and sat outside the classroom while Jack sat and palled around with his peers. I was hoping with me out of sight, he could have some Jack time—time to be himself without a parent in sight. With Nook in hand and in the middle of a good book, I sat and read while Jack worked a puzzle. After he finished he was ready to go home. He grabbed my arm especially tight and we went to the van. I asked him if he was alright and he said yes. But his attitude and body language told me something was off. We got home and he said he had a headache. He ate some lunch and took a nap. When he woke up, he still had a slight headache and was "bored." I finally had to give him a pain pill later when his

... BUT I'M NOT THE SINGER

head really started to hurt, something I do as a last resort. He had a minor nosebleed that night along with all his many acne blemishes itching, peeling, and bleeding as well. Friday, Jack didn't want to get up and complained, yet again, of a headache. Friday was homecoming at CHS and Jack had been invited to ride in the homecoming parade and be one of the two grand marshals of the parade, something he also did last year. Jack and another young lady from CHS who has also fought a battle with cancer were last year's grand marshals and were both asked to do it again this year. Jack was very excited to get to ride in the parade despite the headache he had. I gave him half of a pain pill and he seemed to feel better. He rode in the parade, waving a royal wave to everyone watching on the side of the roadway. Ben and I laughed because not only was Jack doing the royal wave but he was also nodding his head when he waved. We followed the convertible Jack rode in to the parking lot after the parade so we could get him home. Once in the parking lot, Jack had pictures made with some of his friends before we left. He scared me when during one picture taking, I noticed one side of his smile was higher than the other side. When Jack sees the doctor, he or she puts him through a series of tests to see if both sides of his brain are working the same. Jack is asked to blow out his cheeks, smile real big, stick out his tongue and wiggle it, and many other short physical tests to make sure he shows no signs of brain trouble. So, when I saw his crooked smile it scared me. I asked him to smile for me which he did and wiggle his tongue at me which was also fine. But when he smiled for a picture, his smile was crooked with one side of his mouth higher than the other. I knew I had never seen Jack have a crooked smile.

We left the school and came home. Jack napped, felt better, and ate a regular Jack dinner with his grandmother who came to sit with him while Ben and I went to the homecoming football game. Saturday, we had planned to go southeast again to Chattanooga to watch the UTC football team play another home game. Jack was looking forward to the ride so he could look at electric poles and he was excited to be with the football team again. Some friends of ours had heard we were going to come home after the football game so they decided to treat us to a hotel room for the night so we could spend the night in Chattanooga and spend some time with Benny. Once in Chattanooga, we picked up Benny and Miss D. and rode to the hotel to get checked in. We were greeted in the lobby by a big sign welcoming Jack to the hotel. What a great surprise for him and all of us! When we unloaded the van and went to our room, it was also decorated with UTC T-shirts, caps, shakers, and many other UTC paraphernalia, again another wonderful surprise for all of us. Thanks

MY NAME IS JACK JOHNSON...

to our anonymous friends and to the UTC Alumni Office for the room and all the surprises. All Jack could say was "wow" over and over. After a late lunch, we went to the stadium. Jack got to go to the locker room again and fist-bump all the players and coaches. We sat on the sidelines during the game where finally I saw Jack smile, something he had not done all day. During the game, he had a nose bleed, not something you want to happen in the middle of a game on the sidelines. UTC won the game and Jack was happy. He fist-bumped all the players again in the locker room after the game and was ready to leave. By this time, it took me and Ben walking beside Jack to keep him from falling. Once back at the hotel, Jack crashed. Sunday morning, Jack did not want to get up at all. He said he felt horrible. Finally, he got up very slowly. We got him to eat some yogurt for breakfast and started the arduous task of getting him out of his pajamas and into his clothes. His pajama shirt had blood on the front from a tiny nose bleed and spots of blood on the back where his acne was bleeding during the night. The three of us were sitting on the beds in the room while Jack was slowly putting on his clothes, his socks, his leg braces and shoes, when he looked up and said, "I'm scared." Ben replied, "Jack, what are you scared of?" I was frozen in fear... all this time I have wondered when Jack was going to ask the elephant-in-the-room question about his health prognosis. I had one of those moments where thoughts are racing through my mind like comets across a night sky: what will I say when he asks? Do I tell him the truth and upset him or just wing it? Oh God, please put words in my mouth now. Jack looked down and said, "I am scared about her". He was pointing to me. Scared about me??? Then Jack said, "I am scared Mommy will leave me. You know you guys are older and I am scared Mommy will die and leave me and no one will be here to take care of me." Ben and I looked at each other in shock. Where did this come from? Is Jack feeling so bad that he worries about who will take care of him in the future? Does he see how needy he is getting and worries about it? My heart broke. I looked at him through the tears I was holding back and reassured him that I am not going anywhere and that I do not plan to die anytime soon. Ben eased the tension a little by asking Jack if he could take care of him if anything was to happen to Mommy. Jack's reply, "I want Mommy to take care of me."

We drove back home, Jack had another nose bleed, and later that night said his mouth was hurting. When I asked him where, he said there was this thing in his mouth that was hurting. I got a flashlight and there on the side of the inside of his cheek was a large, gaping mouth ulcer. Bleeding, itching, peeling acne, unannounced nosebleeds, hair falling out, balance issues, (out

...BUT I'M NOT THE SINGER

of fear of falling we have now brought the walker out of the attic for Jack to use) and now a giant, nasty, painful mouth ulcer. I explained to Jack what a mouth ulcer is since he has never had one before even through all the many different chemo drugs he has had before. I have read about a rinse called Magic Mouthwash that is prescribed to cancer patients and knew that we had an appointment to see the doctor on Wednesday. I asked Jack if he could wait until Wednesday and he said yes. By Tuesday, the ulcer was starting to hurt worse, and he couldn't talk without it hurting. He didn't want to eat because it hurt so much. When I looked again at the ulcer, it had grown and there was another one beside the first one—both taking up most of the room on that side of Jack's cheek. I got Jack to the van—not an easy task for one person now—and went to Walgreen's where I asked the pharmacist about a temporary mouthwash we could use until our appointment the next day. Through all of this—the surgery, the treatments, the pain, the sicknesses—Jack has amazed me. Having autism with all its quirks is hard enough but to have to go through so much more with his autism has truly been a miracle to me. I don't know how he has done it as well as he has. And now, here we have to use a very pungent mouthwash, something he has never used before. He still uses kid toothpaste because the taste is milder than an adult's toothpaste! Once home I explained to him what we were going to do: I would pour some mouthwash in a cup and some water in another cup, he would sip some mouthwash in his mouth and keep it in his mouth. No swallowing. He would let it sit in his mouth on the side of his mouth with the ulcers and when he couldn't stand it anymore he would spit out the mouthwash in the sink and rinse his mouth out with the water. And he did it, no complaints, no gagging, no vomiting. I was so proud of him and told him so. He just looked at me and nodded his head because it hurt him so much to speak.

 Wednesday morning Ben stayed home to help us get ready for Jack's doctor appointment and I was so glad he did. Jack felt horrible when he tried to get up. He didn't want to eat and could barely hold his head up. He had decided earlier in the week that he would sleep downstairs in our bedroom so we know he slept through the night. He just felt bad. I tried to get ready while prompting Jack to eat some yogurt and start to get himself ready so we wouldn't be late. He refused. I stopped and sat down on his walker—it has a retractable seat—and asked him quietly what I could do to help him. He just shook his head at me. I asked him if he wanted me to feed him his yogurt and he nodded. Bless his heart—he felt so bad that he wanted his mommy to hand feed him even though he is seventeen years old. I knew he really felt

MY NAME IS JACK JOHNSON...

bad now. It took a while but he ate all of the yogurt and got up to get dressed. Ben washed his face, fixed his hair, and helped Jack finish getting ready. Jack looked bad. The acne was bad enough but now he had a face full of stubble because we could not shave his face in fear of cutting the acne and making it bleed worse than it already does. His color was very ashen. He talked without moving his mouth so it wouldn't hurt the mouth ulcers. He walked with the walker, his head hanging low. It broke my heart yet again. On the way to the hospital, it finally dawned on me what could be happening with Jack: his platelets could be extremely low. They were low the week before but they could have gone down further and he could desperately need a transfusion. By the time we got to the hospital, I was convinced that this was Jack's problem. We were taken back where Jack was weighed—lost six pounds from the week before. All of the nurses saw how much Jack had changed in that short amount of time. His regular doctor was out of town but we saw another one. Jack's blood counts came back and his platelets are low, not as low as the week before but still low enough to cause all the bleeding. His neutrophils had dropped from 229,000 to 79,000!! This drop is the reason for the new balance issues, headaches, feeling miserable and even the mouth ulcers. Remember neutrophils are the blood cells that fight off infections in our bodies. They keep us protected from everyday germs that could cause us to be sick. The neutrophils were a mere 25,000 away from us having to stop taking the chemo so Jack's blood could recover. The doctor warned me to keep a close eye on Jack for signs of a fever. Anything over 101, we are to come to the emergency room and be admitted into the hospital. He also prescribed the Magic Mouthwash, some appetite stimulants in case Jack continues to lose weight and some more pain pills for the headaches. We pray that Jack's system will start to recover on its own while he continues taking chemo. Have you ever heard me say how much I hate cancer?

OCTOBER 16, 2013—The weather outside is the way I feel inside: drippy, cloudy, dreary. Jack has had a horrible few days. He has vomited both Monday and Tuesday mornings. He has been constipated, going four days without a bowel movement. He has had headaches, screaming out in pain. He has been dizzy saying the floor was moving while he was sitting still. He has been weaker than he was last week, back to using the walker full time. I noticed one night just sitting on the couch his body was swaying slightly, a sign of further balance issues. He couldn't play Wii one night because his hands were shaking so bad he couldn't control the game controllers. Since he has vomited, he has refused to eat so eating anything has been an issue. We did get the mouth ulcers healed, a bit of happy amid all the "crap", as he calls it. I haven't been able to get him involved in anything. He sleeps a lot, saying he is bored. With his neutrophils so low, we haven't been able to go anywhere where he would have to get out of the van, which means I haven't been anywhere. Ben did stay with Jack while I walked a mile the other night. Otherwise we have been here. Don't get me wrong, I am not complaining. Right now, I would not want to be anywhere else than with Jack.

It's blood count day. Jack's neutrophil count is lower than last week, and he is officially neutropenic meaning he is very susceptible to all germs large and small. He has also lost twelve pounds since September. With all of Jack's new problems, the doctor decided to move Jack's MRI up from its original date—next Friday—to tomorrow. The doctor is also very concerned that Jack's new issues are a progression of his tumors, something I had been afraid he would say. The doctor talked about getting the DNR paperwork completed and signed and started talking about end of life issues. I heard part of it and then my internal volume control muted. I know the doctor has seen more of this than I have but I will not go there until we know for sure after the MRI. One step at a time.

I did find my ray of hope in all of this: Jack's symptoms started about the same time we changed one of his chemo drugs and I hope and pray that this drug change also caused his "crap." The doctor said that the chemo could be the reason. The MRI will let us know. As I type this, Jack is sitting in his place on the couch drawing electric poles. Such a normal thing for him to do despite all the other things going on. The human spirit is a wondrous thing. We will not know the MRI results until Friday.

Dear Lord, thank you for the blessing of children, for days without pain and sickness, for healthy bodies and minds, for strength on the days we need it and for peace on days we need it too, for the gift of normalcy in life, and for the love and support of so many who walk with us on Jack's journey. Amen.

OCTOBER 19, 2013—I know so many of you already know, but for those that do not, I will let you know where we are, what has happened, and what will happen in the future...

After getting Jack in his bed downstairs and Ben and I in ours, we fell asleep. Around 5am, Jack burped loudly several times. He has been doing this quite often so it didn't surprise me, but it woke me up. This time "woke me up" doesn't mean fully awake but a very groggy state where I could hear

MY NAME IS JACK JOHNSON...

things and ask questions but my eyes were shut. I asked Jack if he was alright, thinking he might be feeling sick, and his verbal response was incoherent. In my foggy haze, I'm thinking something wasn't right so I asked him again if he was alright and again I hear words that aren't really words but a garbled sentence I don't understand. The fog lifted this time and I nudged Ben awake and he asked Jack the same question and got an even shorter still incoherent response. Both of us hit the floor and got to Jack's bed, turned on a light, and found Jack unable to form words or even get his mouth to work properly. I have been in too many doctor appointments and have seen too many tests for brain activity, or lack thereof, and asked Jack to smile. One side responded, the other did not. I asked him to stick out his tongue, and it came out to one side. I asked him to puff out his cheeks but only one cheek puffed out because his lips would not hold together. Ben and I threw on some clothes, dressed Jack, found his wheelchair, and got in the van to get him to the hospital emergency room. We were so afraid Jack had had a stroke. Who knew at 6:30am there would be so much traffic but Ben floored it and we arrived quickly. The emergency room was empty and Jack was immediately taken back. By this time, his symptoms had gotten so much better and he showed no signs from before except for a little slurring of words. A CT scan was taken of his head and we were put in a critical care emergency room. Before we knew it, it was after 8am. Jack's oncologist got to the office and found out we were downstairs. He came in the room and told us that Jack's MRI from the day before showed more progression of growth of all the tumors and more tumors that were not there before. Again, chemo has not worked. Jack has not had a stroke but has hydrocephalus, meaning the spinal fluid in his brain and spine has been blocked by the tumors. The swelling of the brain is in response to the tumor growth. This fluid buildup has been the culprit of Jack's new symptoms that prompted moving up the MRI. A neurosurgeon was called but he was in a scheduled surgery. A nurse practitioner from the neurology department stopped in and told us she was going to consult with the neurosurgeon while he was in surgery and would let us know as soon as possible. Jack's oncologist informed us that Jack would more than likely need a shunt placed to keep the pressure from getting worse. He said that without the shunt, Jack would only have a few more days with us, with the shunt he could possibly live another couple of months. The tumors are growing at such a rapid speed and there are now so many that the outcome is not what we have hoped and prayed for. At this stage, putting a shunt in is classified as palliative care, giving comfort to the patient so they can continue living with some dignity and

... BUT I'M NOT THE SINGER

quality of life. Without a shunt, it is a matter of time before the fluid builds to a very uncomfortable point and comfort may not happen. Thinking about this is hard enough much less thinking about your child suffering. We will do whatever it takes to avoid as much suffering as we can for our much-loved son. Please don't be judgmental in our decisions. Unless you have walked in our shoes, you do not know what you would do. You might think you would but until you have lived it each day, breathed it, have it become such a part of your life, you have no clue how you would react. So tonight, I type this from our lovely ICU room from Vanderbilt. Tomorrow, hopefully, we will be moved into a regular room. Jack is to stay over the weekend, getting steroids every six hours to help with the brain swelling. Monday, he will have surgery to put in the shunt. The neurosurgeon agrees with the oncologist on placing the shunt for palliative care reasons. We do not have a definite time for the surgery only knowing it will happen Monday. It is not a complicated surgery nor is it an uncommon surgery. It will take about an hour. Jack will get to come home Tuesday if all goes well. He now feels great having had several doses of steroids. He has had us laughing at his antics. Earlier he was playing music on his computer and wondered if his female nurse would enjoy coming in the room to listen with him. He went on to say he wondered if she would dance if he put on a certain song. I am not sure what she thought of it all but he was certainly enjoying himself.

Ben and I are the walking wounded. I have cried my face into a red puffy mess. I don't know how to do this and never, ever thought this would be the journey's end. I so wish with every inch of my soul that I could make this go away but I am at a loss since nothing seems to work. I still have faith that God is with us and will not leave our side. He will be with Jack every day. He will help us and guide us through whatever is in front of us. It is going to be the hardest thing we have ever faced. We are afraid, confused, angered, and brokenhearted all at the same time. Benny is home for fall break giving me and Ben a much-needed feeling of family wholeness for a little while. No matter how hard this day has been, we have been blessed by doctors, friends, and family who have come to us with hearts as heavy as ours. Jack's oncologist almost cried while talking to us. Our pastor came to be with us after leaving a meeting with international members who all stopped and said a prayer for Jack. Friends magically appeared or jumped when I called. Family members have sent us messages of love all day. And, most of all to our amazement, our son has made us laugh, made us smile, and made us love him even more. What a wonderful unexpected blessing!

MY NAME IS JACK JOHNSON...

Dear God, we thank you for the blessing of children, for each day, hour, minute we are given with our loved ones, for days without pain and sickness, for doctors and nurses, for the gift of laughter, for hearts that feel love, and for the love and support given to us by so many. In His name, Amen.

OCTOBER 20, 2013—Finally a little quiet after a very busy day. We were finally moved into a room after our initial overnight stay in the ICU late yesterday afternoon. We still do not have a surgery time, only knowing we are not scheduled for the first surgery of the day at 7:30 am. From what I can gather, the neurosurgeon is new, having recently replaced Jack's original neurosurgeon who left and went to Orlando a short while ago. The new surgeon was in surgery Friday all day—from 7:30 am to dinner time. The steroids Jack is taking again to keep the brain swelling down haven't jump-started the fierce appetite we have had before but have started the grouchy inner old-man attitude that comes out when he takes them. He woke this morning mad at the world and didn't think twice about letting everyone know he was a grouch.

Dear Lord, thank you for the blessing of children, for days without pain and sickness, for healthy bodies and strong minds, for faith, love, and hope, and for the love and support of family, friends, and strangers who walk with us on this journey. Amen.

OCTOBER 21, 2013—Starting this with an "ARGGH!"

Six-thirty this morning while sleeping on my pull out, four-inch-thick padded bed, I feel a little shake on my arm and hear a whispered "Mrs. Johnson." After three people had told me Jack would not be the first surgery of the day, there in the dark, Jack's nurse is trying to wake me because Jack is scheduled for the first surgery of the day. Argh again!! The surgical team, the nurse continues to whisper, will be in Jack's room in thirty minutes to take him down to the surgical floor. Have you ever seen a mommy fire drill? Where some type of emergency makes a mom move at the speed of sound? I have had two mommy fire drills in the last four days. I am feeling it, feeling much older than my 35 years (haha, you didn't think I would say the correct age, did you?) and from my aching bones that have had to sleep on four inches of very used foam the last few days. Ben was luckily walking out our house door to get in his car to come to the hospital when the mommy fire drill started. In fifteen minutes, I had on make-up and clothes and they were all buttoned, smeared on, and zipped correctly. A quick curling iron in a few well-placed spots of my hair and I looked good enough to be seen in public

...BUT I'M NOT THE SINGER

without scaring small children. I don't like mommy fire drills. The surgery team was in shortly after the drill was over so Jack was awake, and ready to go. He didn't have time for fresh deodorant or a quick brush of his teeth but we were doing the best we could do. Jack had to take his stuffed animals, Sonic the Hedgehog and his friend Tails, along for the ride in his bed and to keep him company during surgery. One of the transport guys asked Jack about his stuffed animal friends and Jack introduced Sonic and Tails and then told the man, "I have raised them." We all got a snicker out of that one.

Downstairs in the surgical department, the world is abuzz with children being wheeled in and out of rooms, down hallways, and into their holding areas. Nurses and doctors are everywhere as well, going to and from the operating rooms. Funny how you can pick out the seasoned parents—the ones who have done this before—from the newbies just by the expression of worry on their faces. We met Jack's new neurosurgeon, who must be twelve years old—when did we get so old and everyone else didn't? He was dressed in dress clothes, looking dapper for the operating room. I bet he has a hard time finding clothes like that in the boy's department. Seriously, he was very nice, very young, very well- mannered and dressed, and did I say very young? We were asked the same five questions by everyone who walked past us. When was the last time Jack ate? Is he allergic to anything? Any previous trouble with anesthesia? Any heart trouble or kidney trouble? Any recent colds or a runny nose? Before we knew it, Jack was being wheeled away, and the last picture I saw of him was the bed being rolled down the hallway toward the operating room, Jack's head laying between two yellow ears on one side and two blue ears on the other, Sonic and Tails.

While waiting, I noticed the windows were being washed outside, something you see quite a bit. But today, the windows were being washed by superheroes: Batman, Spiderman, and the Green Hornet. What a great surprise for all the parents and the children still waiting to be called back to surgery when the superheroes moved down into view as they made their way down while washing the outside windows. Hopefully, Batman, Spiderman, and the Green Hornet washed away not only the dirt from the windows but a little bit of fear from the hearts of the children and their parents as they waited to be called back.

Jack's surgery was an hour-and-a-half long. We were called back for the consult with the neurosurgeon who walked in our consultation room still dressed in his snazzy business attire. I wondered if he took off those clothes or just covered them up with surgical attire during surgery? The doctor let us

MY NAME IS JACK JOHNSON...

know the surgery went fine. Jack has three small incisions, two on his head and one on his abdomen. Since they had to shave his head in two places for the surgery and his hair is falling out now from the latest chemo drugs he isn't taking now, Jack decided that while they were shaving his head in the operating room, they could shave his whole head so his head would all be the same. Jack now is very bald with several bandages. I told him later this afternoon that with his facial hair and bald head, he looks like a rough motorcycle rider. I tried to get a smile, but it didn't work.

Jack woke up after surgery and had to have X-rays taken of the implanted shunt to make sure it was placed properly and in working order. After the set of X-rays, we were brought back to his room on the sixth floor. After needing a urinal break, when Jack tried to get back in a laying position, his shoulder, where the shunt tubing runs down toward his abdomen, was in a lot of pain. He started screaming, stiffening his whole body in the process. And, boy, could he scream. I was trying to keep him calm, not doing a very good job of it while the nurse was hurriedly getting Jack some morphine for pain. I got him calmed down and got him to relax his whole body while the nurse slowly gave Jack the pain meds through his IV. Within thirty minutes, he was very comfortable and very asleep. While he was sleeping, our palliative care representative came to talk to Ben and me. Jack's oncologist joined us as well. We talked options, further treatments, and hospice care. We will meet a member of our hospice team sometime this week so we all can be familiar with them, especially Jack. We talked about paperwork and end of life issues, the way Ben and I want things to be for Jack; things you never think you will ever talk about in the same sentence with your child's name. We are still in some surreal state of shock about this because we are parents who desperately love and want to protect our child forever—a job we thought long and hard about before we ever became parents. I so wish I would wake from this nightmare that our lives have become. Ben and I must decide so many things that are still unsettled, things that might seem insignificant but need to be discussed in detail in the weeks to come.

Jack has been medicated most of the rest of the day. He hasn't eaten much, a few potato chips and Jell-O, but is resting easy. Benny has been by to spend time with him before he needs to go back to UTC. I hate this for Benny in so many ways but especially because, yet again, Benny's life—his upcoming 19th birthday—is being overshadowed by his brother's health. Benny doesn't seem to mind. He is just as awesome as his brother. Their interactions make me weak in the knees to watch now.

... BUT I'M NOT THE SINGER

Dear Lord, thank you for the blessing of children, for days without pain and sickness, for each minute, hour, and day with our loved ones, for the promise of an eternal home with You, for the gift of holding a loved one's hand during difficult times, and for the love and support of so many who continue to walk with us on Jack's journey. Amen.

OCTOBER 24, 2013—We are home. Of course, leaving the hospital took all day. It is so strange that the doctors will wake you up first thing on their morning rounds to tell you that the patient can go home that day, but then it takes all day to make it happen. Jack decided he was fine with leaving after the nurses told him he would be going home with pain pills. We got home safely and Jack went straight to his reclining sofa spot. He is such a creature of habit. Mia, the cat, was so excited and, as soon as he was in the chair, she was on the armrest comfortably close to Jack. He hunched over his computer for the rest of the night, which made his shoulder hurt before he went to bed.

2013 Jack at home under hospice care

MY NAME IS JACK JOHNSON...

It took us several tries to get him, his abdomen, and his shoulder comfortable, with the help of extra pillows, so he could relax and sleep. Once we found the right spot, Jack slept all night. I did too, for the first time since Thursday night last week. In fact, I didn't want to wake up and could have stayed in the bed all day. The phone rang, making the decision easier for me. I got up, answered the phone, and politely lied to our pastor when he asked if he woke me up. Why do we do that when someone calls? Why do we tell them no when they can tell that in fact their call got us up out of the bed? Sorry, Pastor H., for not telling the truth. I am sure he could tell and knowing him, would forgive me for lying. It was hard to cover my lie when my words were slurry and I called him by a different name. I don't seem to be good at anything anymore!

The hospice representative did indeed drop in and talked to us about Jack and their services. We have not signed any papers yet because we are just not there yet. Jack is still coherent, mobile, and feeling well except for the occasional pain from the surgery. She gave us some information to read about their services. She talked to us about grief counseling before the end of life counseling and after counseling. This is all just a little too much for Ben and me right now. I hear what the doctors are all saying, I have seen the MRI scans, I understand what they say. But my heart still beats with hope. From where it comes, I do not know. My mind is a jumbled mess of thoughts that bounce around in my brain constantly. I cry at the drop of a hat and then try to hide it from Jack. I cannot think about bills, household chores; even making a grocery list is arduous. It is a struggle to breathe, to move, to think. I am living in a land of quicksand where making the slightest motion is work. And we are being asked to sign our son's care over to hospice. Too much too soon for us.

Jack still feels well enough to be his funny self. At the hospital, we had to measure his urine output after his surgery so each time he went, he had to go in a urinal. We would write how much each trip was so the nurses could record it in Jack's medical chart. Once when Ben was there, Jack had to go. After Jack's surgery, we taught him how to go in the bed with the help of the urinal, not off the side of the bed, but in the bed. At first, he was afraid—something so different, like using the bathroom in the bed—but, after the first time, he liked not having to move or get up. Once, Jack had waited a little too long before letting us know he had to go and proceeded to rush his daddy to get the urinal and get it in the right place. Ben asked Jack, "Why do you wait until the last minute to go when you know it takes us a while? You need to not wait like this." Jack replied, "If you don't leave me alone, I am going to pour my urine sample on you!" Typical Jack.

... BUT I'M NOT THE SINGER

Dear Lord, thank you for the blessing of children, for days without pain and sickness, for healthy bodies and minds, for moving others to do your work, for every day we have with the ones we love, for helping us see You in our daily lives, and for the continued love and support of so many people for whom we are so grateful. In His name, Amen.

NOVEMBER 3, 2013—Tuesday I had a meeting to finalize Jack's educational contract with the school finally. It was a formality meeting so all the paperwork is in some order and all signatures are included. Jack has no instructional time at school, only fun time. There is no set number of days, just when he feels like it. Since the paperwork must say he participates, we must make sure it does and is signed by all parties. I have been in so many IEP meetings over the years, and I have always tried my hardest not to cry. Crying can be a sign of weakness, an expression of deep frustration, or an outward release of pure anger when you are in a fight with a school system over the educational needs of your child. Last Tuesday, from out of nowhere, I sat in that meeting and could not stop the sudden and very unexpected tears that blurred my vision when the teacher read the IEP to the other meeting participants and me. In the IEP contract, there is a place for parent's concerns. We are not concerned about his school day anymore; we hope he lives long enough to have more time at school. And the goals... where we had for so many years listed goals for Jack's educational needs, for him to learn and be taught in a regular classroom with his friends and peers, for a future full of time spent toward a regular education diploma, his goals are almost non-existent. It was all too much for my feeble, little mommy mind already damaged by the reality of Jack's medical situation and dismal prognosis. There I sat, embarrassed, tears streaming down my face, surprised by their presence, having to listen to the few things now listed on my son's IEP, taken aback by the realization of life, all in front of a whole group of people who were sitting there watching me fall apart thinking how thankful they were that their own children were healthy and happy and not in this situation.

On Wednesday, Jack had another appointment with his oncologist. This trip was a consultation on whether Ben and I wanted Jack to have another round of chemo. Surprising as it is, yes, there are chemo drugs we haven't tried. I spent Tuesday afternoon at the computer researching the new chemo the doctor had talked to us about previously that attacks the DNA of the cells, stopping them from growing; a drug Jack has not had before. Ben and I agreed to try the new chemo drug for this reason and because the side effects are slight. Jack starts taking the drugs tomorrow.

MY NAME IS JACK JOHNSON...

Thursday Jack went to school. It was hard for him because he is back in a wheelchair, his head is shaved with a prominent scar and a few lumpy places where the shunt is obvious. It was raining that day, and he had put up his hood on his jacket so his head wouldn't get wet. Once inside, he refused to put the hood down. I left him in the special ed classroom with his peers and sat out in the hall so he could have some Jack time. The teacher kept coming out in the hall to give me updates. Jack was quiet and didn't participate in any activities, but he was watching what the others were doing. Near the end of his visit, he did take his hood off. Jack was finally comfortable enough to let others see him. No one said anything about his new hairstyle, new scars, or his new mode of transportation.

Somewhere during last week, Jack had a meltdown of emotions. I can't remember what day it was because it continued for several days and now I am still on alert each day for the emotions to return. It started with a puzzle, a kitty puzzle we were working on together. I was in my office doing something—can't remember that either—and Jack was behind me sitting at the dining room table, working on the kitty puzzle. From out of the blue, I heard sniffles and the muffled sounds of crying. I turned around and found Jack boohooing at the dining room table. I jumped up and asked him what was wrong. He looked up at me, his face covered in tears and red from trying to hold back his emotions and he said, "These kittens are so beautiful they make me cry. They are too lovely. WAAAAAA" and the tears flowed in buckets. Well, the kitties are cute but they aren't THAT cute. I sat with him and we talked about the real reason for the emotional outburst. Seems Jack was bored. He had nothing to do that interested him. We had a heart-to-heart about what he wanted to do versus what he can do versus what he doesn't want to do. I listed lots of fun things we could do and he agreed to some and others he didn't. It is hard for me to know what is going on in that mind of his since he is so different from other kids because he doesn't just come out and say things the same way other kids do. I asked him to look straight in my eyes. I asked him if they looked different to him, like they were X-ray eyes that could read his mind. He told me no. I told him he must tell me when he wants to do something: go outside, for a car ride, to school more than once a week, to get a treat somewhere, and the list went on and on. After our talk, I got him outside in the sunshine, sitting in the swing in our front yard away from his reclining couch and the TV. While swinging he said, "You know Mom, I think I would like to go for a walk around the block." I have never been happier to go and get his wheelchair. We walked once around the block

... BUT I'M NOT THE SINGER

and then decided to do it again. We looked at the colorful trees and watched the many neighborhood squirrels. We talked about the birds and the flowers I shared with Jack how much the walk meant to me because it got me outside and pushing him in the wheelchair which was good exercise for me. He has been in a better mood since and I have been making a concerted effort to make sure he is entertained by something. Add to my list of titles: mom, nurse, maid, cook, companion, caregiver, hand-holder, clothes-washer, friend, and now entertainment planner.

Dear God, thank you for the blessing of children, for days without pain and sickness, for allowing us to be parents, nurses, maids, caregivers and entertainment directors, for healthy bodies and minds, for tears of joy and tears of sadness, for eyes that see inside a person and not the outside, for your protection in times of storms, and for the love and support of so many who walk with us on this journey. Amen.

NOVEMBER 13, 2013—Last Saturday, Ben, Jack, and I rode to Chattanooga. To see Benny of course, and to see the Chattanooga Mocs football team play their last regular season home game. I had promised Jack we could get up and stop at IHOP for breakfast if he wanted to and he did. He ate a huge breakfast of eggs, sausage, and pancakes with ketchup. (That always makes me make a face.) We arrived late into Chattanooga but still got there in time to see the game kickoff. The players and coaches were all happy to see Jack, again making him feel like a football king even though he was in his wheelchair throne. We sat on the sidelines and watched the game from there even though the day had a slight chill in the air. Jack was bundled up with lots of layers of clothes and blankets, so he was warm. After winning the game, in the locker room, the team cheered again for "Jack, Jack, Jack!" because every game that Jack has been to this year has been a winning game for the team. One of the coaches called Jack their good luck charm. Jack was thrilled and certainly enjoyed himself and being the center of attention. The five of us—Ben, Benny, Miss D., Jack, and I—left the game in search of dinner before three of us made the trip home.

I have written here before that we have not told Jack the seriousness of his cancer and what the prognosis is. Ben and I have always thought it would add to Jack's stress. This morning I was talking to Ben while all three of us were in the bathroom getting ready about how winded Jack was from walking from the family room to the bathroom. I said to Ben that the pharmacist had told me that one side effect of Jack's chemo was shortness of breath because

MY NAME IS JACK JOHNSON...

the drug could cause heart trouble. Jack heard that and said, "OH NO! Am I going to die?" His reaction verified for me that Ben and I are making the right decision in not telling Jack the whole story. I did answer his question. I told Jack "Yes, you are going to die, but I am going to die too, and so is Daddy." I went on to explain: "We are all going to die one day. Everyone we know will eventually die one day." I ended the conversation by reiterating that the answer to his first question was "yes, but not today." That explanation satisfied his curious brain.

Last week, Ben was out of town for his work, so I had asked Jack if he wanted to sleep in the big bed with me. He replied, "I just might do that." We snuggled together under the covers, and when I woke up each morning, I would stay there and watch him sleep. Those are moments that tear out my heart when I let the real world in.

Today, we went to VCH for blood counts. Jack's platelet count went from 135,000 to a mere 26,000 in one week. So today he received another platelet transfusion. He has had nose bleeds that were getting more and more frequent by the amount of blood in tissues he tried to hide in the bathroom waste can. Jack has, in the last week, complained of pain in his arms and legs, telling us that it "hurt in the bone in them." He also has bumps on his scalp that itch quite a bit. And he has been having trouble catching his breath when he walks from the family room to the bathroom and back. Our house is not that large where a small walk to the bathroom would cause shortness of breath. Today we talked about all of this with the doctor. The pain in the arms and legs, the itchy scalp, and the shortness of breath could all be caused by the steroids Jack is taking. We are dropping the dose amount to see if they get better.

Dear God, thank you for this day we have with our loved ones, for the blessing of children, for days without sickness and pain, for healthy bodies and minds, for laughter and smiles, for strength to meet another day, and for the love and support of so many people who walk with us every day on this journey with Jack. Amen.

NOVEMBER 16, 2013—Today was the final Chattanooga Mocs football game for the season and it was played at Samford in Birmingham, Alabama. Ben and I asked Jack if he felt like going that far for a game and he said he did even though he was very tired and not his normal self. He has been a little more quiet and lifeless since his platelet transfusion during the last trip to the hospital. We got up early that morning and went south to Birmingham. Samford's stadium sits in a bowl with hills around the field. The stadium

... BUT I'M NOT THE SINGER

seats are against the sides of the bowl shape, making entering and leaving the stadium a chore for pushing and pulling a wheelchair. We didn't know where the locker room was for the Mocs but then found out it was in a building that was up several flights of stairs. There was no way we could get Jack to the locker room at halftime so he could be with the team. We did push him in his wheelchair where he could be sitting in the area where the team would be entering and leaving the field to and from the locker room. Jack fist-bumped the team players and the coaches as they went past. He saw the game up close, where he could hear the tackles and what the refs were saying. He liked that part. Once I noticed he fell asleep, his head tilting slightly to one side of his body. He didn't like the fact that the game went into overtime and the Mocs lost the game. We knew Jack was not happy about the game but there was something else, something Ben and I couldn't really put our finger on. He wasn't our Jack.

CHAPTER 41

The next day, Ben and I discussed whether we needed to get hospice involved since we had put them off until the need was there. It was becoming obvious that something was different with Jack; whether it was his attitude or his health situation, something changed. Jack had a hard time getting up, so we didn't go to church. He also complained of a headache. I gave him a pain pill, but it didn't seem to help, and he got upset because he was hurting. I sat with him and calmly talked to him trying to get his mind off the pain and give the medicine time to work. It eventually did, but it was a struggle for him to be calm. That afternoon Jack's Best Buddy, K., came by for a visit and made Jack feel better. That night, Ben and I decided to call hospice the next day, a Monday morning.

Before I go on, I want to try to explain something. When you are going through a terrible, horrific situation, something different happens in your mind. Some call it surreal while others call it an out of body experience. I will explain it this way: when something really bad happens, which has happened to us several times during this journey, your mind cannot accept the horrors around it. Life continues to move around you, but instead of you being a part of it, it seems like you are watching it happen to someone else. You are there, breathing, moving, and participating, but it doesn't seem like you are there. There have been TV shows I have watched where a person is behind a video camera recording what they see, sometimes their own hands and feet coming into the video they are recording. That is what you feel like when you experience some of life's worst moments. You feel as if you are watching it happen in front of you, but it's not really happening to you. I know this sounds so crazy, but it is part of experiencing the shock in a situation that your mind cannot comprehend at the time. I am saying this because at this point in this story life becomes different, with me feeling like I am viewing what is happening through the lens of a camera.

...BUT I'M NOT THE SINGER

NOVEMBER 18, 2013—We are asking for prayers. Jack woke up this morning and had a massive seizure. This morning started like any other morning: getting Jack up, dressed, and fed his breakfast. Because of his new weakness and tremors in his hands, I fed him his morning yogurt. After he finished, he started talking incoherently again. Luckily for us, Ben was home at the time. I was with Jack when the seizure started, but since he had never had one before, I really didn't know what to do. I held him as he started to drool, his arms locked, and his breathing became raspy and inhuman. Ben called 911 while I wiped Jack's face with a wet washcloth and reassured him that "Mommy is here." The EMTs arrived, put my baby on the stretcher, and took him to the ambulance while I ran to put on clothes so I could ride to VCH with them. When I ran to the ambulance, Jack was awake but incoherent and fighting the EMTs' attempts at putting an IV in his arm. With four EMTs holding Jack, they finally got the IV inserted and Jack calmed down. The ambulance took us into Nashville to VCH, lights flashing and sirens blaring. Once in the emergency room and after answering a million questions about the seizure, Jack was taken for a CT scan. The scan's results let the doctors know the shunt is working properly and there is no fluid buildup. But unfortunately, the cancer has grown, causing the brain to seizure. Jack was admitted and once in the hospital room, he ate a little, slept, talked to us, and still was very confused. While Ben and I met with hospice, my sister Amy and my dad visited with Jack. He had another seizure. A nurse came and got us under the pretense that the doctor examining Jack wanted to see us. But when we opened the room door, Jack was having another seizure. I quickly asked for a wet washcloth and whispered in Jack's ear, "Mommy's here." As soon as I spoke those words, the seizure's grip lessened. He has not been coherent since the afternoon seizure. Please pray that Jack will not have any pain and will be comfortable. We are heartbroken but are surrounded by friends and family who love Jack. We love each of you who have made a place in your heart for him too.

NOVEMBER 19, 2013—A very quick update... Jack had a long night with lots of pain meds and Benadryl for itching from those same pain meds. He and I had several quiet Mommy/son moments that warmed my heart. There is not a stronger person I know today or who I have ever met who has the strength of this child. He has not had any more seizures but is plagued by vision problems. He is a little more coherent but still doesn't understand what all has happened, even telling the nurse and me that "I didn't have no seizure!" My

MY NAME IS JACK JOHNSON...

heart is breaking because I feel when we are released to go home, this will more than likely be the last time Jack will visit this hospital.

Thanks to everyone for all the kind words and prayers being said for Jack. We are forever grateful for each of you. With much love, the Johnsons.

MORNING OF NOVEMBER 20, 2013—Another short update... from what we understand, we are going to be released today into the care of hospice. Hospice is delivering a hospital bed, a potty chair, and a smaller wheelchair as I write this. Our wonderful friend Janie has set up a meal rotation for anyone who feels the need to help feed us, and she has planned for anyone dropping by with goodies, so please see her guestbook posting on how to get this information. Thank you, Janie, for being so organized and for getting this set up for us. So many of you over the last few months have asked what we need or what you can do, and I have said nothing at the time you asked, but also told you that there would come a time when we would need your extra help and support. We are at that place now.

Jack felt as good as he could yesterday, surprising most of us with his strength and resilience yet again. He has been put on anti-seizure medication to see if we can control the seizures but, of course, the doctor said, "it's a we'll-see thing." He has been quite talkative at times and sat up last night and played Candy Crush on his iPad even though his vision is not good and he weaves where his balance and trunk strength is not good. He hasn't been up on his feet so we don't know if he can. Physical therapy has been called in to assess his physical condition.

Ben and I talked to Jack about how things will be different when we get home; how he will have a hospital bed to sleep in now and that he will have to stay in our bedroom instead of going to the family room, but we will get his TV for his new area. We told him that he would have a special potty chair near his bed for potty time and he could use a urinal for quickies. He was thrilled about that. Who knew using a urinal would make his day!

He continues to be confused, not remembering things, confused with what has happened, even things that happened only hours earlier, and sometimes his speech is slurry and incoherent. He is fascinated by the time for some reason. I am guessing his internal clock has been damaged, which sometimes becomes a topic of conversation for him. His mouth took the brunt of the second seizure with his tongue left swollen and chewed on both sides. We are rinsing with Magic Mouthwash again to help heal the wounds quicker. So, as you can see through all of this, he continues to amaze us with his fighter spirit.

... BUT I'M NOT THE SINGER

NIGHT OF NOVEMBER 20, 2013—Jack was deemed too unstable to ride upright in our van and was brought home in an ambulance. He was happy to get here and into his new bed. Mia the cat got over the new furniture and newly configured bedroom. She hasn't left his side except for potty breaks and snack time. Benny said Mia has been sleeping outside Jack's bedroom door; we guess she thought that since he wasn't in his usual place on the couch that he had to be in his upstairs bedroom. Jack is either very tired or the seizures caused some mental damage, or the cancer is affecting his brain more because he is talking about things that have not happened or is mentally confused. He has a hard time remembering where he is. After being home for several hours, he looked around the room and said, "Hey, I am home." Or telling us how much better he feels after he used the potty after using his walker to get to the bathroom. The walker is upstairs, his new bed has bed rails, and he is physically incapable of standing up on his own two feet much less walk into the bathroom, sit on the potty, stand up from the potty, and get himself back into bed without us hearing any of it on the baby monitor. But he thought he did. I hope this is a temporary setback, but we will deal with this too if it isn't.

Thanks again for all the prayers and continued support. I will update some time tomorrow. With much love, the Johnsons

NOVEMBER 27, 2013—I have tried several times to write this past week, but we have been extremely busy keeping Jack comfortable and happy along with taking care of all the visitors he has had. I have been surprised at how many people have come by to see him. He loves their visits. Thanks to everyone who has been by and spent time with Jack. The visitors have been a blessing for us as well as it keeps us busy and not thinking about how close we are to the end of this journey.

Jack is set up in our bedroom in a hospital bed next to the windows where he can look outside during the day. He has watched the birds and the snow that came down earlier this week. He is mostly bedridden, getting up only to take a shower with the help of Ben and his wheelchair and getting up to transfer from the bed to the potty chair. He is taking quite a few pain pills to control the pain, with hospice having to change his previous pain pill to a stronger one last night. Today he has been very out of it, going in and out of sleep, one of the side effects of the new drugs. Our hospice nurse said it was a temporary side effect that will lessen once the drug gets into his system. Today was also the first day he has not eaten much, but it is hard to eat when you

MY NAME IS JACK JOHNSON...

are asleep. Since the seizures, he has had trouble controlling both his arms and hands, something that gets a little worse every day. He cannot pick up his pills to take them; I must transfer each pill one-by-one to his wiggling hands so he can take them one at a time. His vision is still giving him fits with his eyes not able to focus, the eyes themselves twitching either side to side or up and down. But even though his health is slowly changing, his wit and personality are still there, making us laugh each day.

He has also lost some cognitive abilities as well. He woke up Monday morning and vomited for no reason and did not remember it. He cannot keep up with what day it is, so Benny made him a flip chart that tells him what day it is each day. He doesn't remember having the seizures, such a blessing, and doesn't remember riding in an ambulance. I fell one day this week (I am alright, just hurt my pride) which made a huge noise and Jack didn't remember that either. He still will find humor in something and has even smiled and laughed a few times. I will repeat myself: there is not a stronger person around who could go through everything this kid has gone through and still find a reason to smile or laugh! Jack the Lionhearted!

As I said, his hands are very shaky which means we feed him quite a few of his meals. We will not leave him alone for a long period of time, so one of us sits with him most of the day. I do not want Jack to feel lonely. We truly hate being in this situation but are making the most of every minute we have with him.

Mia the cat has not left his side except for eating and potty trips for herself. She is like a nurse, watching over him every minute of every day. We were blessed by a visit from the chaplain from hospice. She visited with me and Jack, asking him questions about himself that he really didn't want to answer, but he did. Mia was sleeping at the foot of Jack's bed while the chaplain was here. As her visit came to a close, she asked Jack if she could say a prayer. If you know my son, you know he isn't a praying kind of guy. When the boys were young, we said a nightly prayer but as they grew up, we didn't pray as much at home. Once at a family gathering, someone said, "Let's give thanks" and Jack loudly said, "But it's not Thanksgiving!" Also, Jack has never understood the act of bowing our heads during prayers. He has always told me that if we are talking to God when we pray, then we should look up so God can hear us in heaven. This became one of those things for me that wasn't a big deal; to bow your head or not. When the chaplain asked us to bow our heads in prayer, I bowed mine. Knowing Jack like I do, I snuck a peek and he was sitting with his head up but was quiet and still. I also noticed in front of me,

...BUT I'M NOT THE SINGER

Mia had her paws in praying position and had her head resting on her paws. Mia was praying for her buddy as well.

To say this is difficult is so trite. This is a gut-wrenching situation. No parent should ever be in our shoes. Our visitors make it a little more bearable along with the meals being delivered to our door each day. The cards (I now call them "paper hugs") and gifts we receive help as well as we still feel the presence of so many people who we know pray for us daily. Even the hospice people have commented on the amount of love we have in our world. And that is what we will continue to do: love each other. Make each other laugh. Spend time with each other even if it is just sitting quietly together. Play games together. Watch TV together. There will be time for tears and heartbreak, but now is not the time.

Dear Lord, we thank you for all the blessing you have bestowed upon us. With thankful hearts, Amen.

NOVEMBER 28, 2013—We are in the hospice facility in Nashville. Jack took a turn for the worse and had to be brought here. He has lost the ability to swallow, meaning he cannot swallow his pain medication. He is now receiving pain medication via IV. We had so wished he could be at home, but Ben and I did not want our son to suffer from unnecessary pain. He also lost his ability to urinate, causing him to believe he needed to go all the time. He has told me he doesn't know what is wrong with his eyes and hands not working right. I told him I didn't understand either because I don't understand this whole despicable situation. The doctor had told us "things" would change near the end. Guess we are there.

Ben and I are worn out. We were up, fraught with worry, the whole night. Who could sleep in this situation? Our minds and hearts are heavy. I cannot leave my son's bed. I find myself wanting to touch him, love on him, kiss him, and have this motherly longing to get in bed with him and hold him. He is my baby and will always be my baby. He occasionally squeezes our hands in response to our voices and touch. Those squeezes are a gift to us.

The personnel here are wonderful at what they do. We are accustomed to the healing aspect of the medical community. There is no healing here. This place is for transitioning. A nurse came by and didn't like Jack's rapid breathing. She talked with a doctor, and another medicine was added to Jack's pain management. Before she left the room, she explained that if Jack moaned or his breathing became faster, they were signs he was in pain and needed more medicine to be comfortable. Comfort has replaced healing.

MY NAME IS JACK JOHNSON...

NOVEMBER 29, 2013—Holding my baby's hand. At this moment, he is getting a breathing treatment along with oxygen. It has been an extremely long day with four episodes where Jack stopped breathing and, after sixty seconds or so, started breathing on his own again. With each episode, we shed tears, told him goodbye, and gave him kisses. He would take a big breath and would return to a normal breathing pattern. Our nurse said it was not unusual for breathing to change at this time. These episodes have left us drained mentally and physically.

Oh, how we wish we could help him understand that it is alright to stop fighting, but a true warrior fights to the bitter end. If you didn't fully realize it before, I hope you see how strong our fighter is. My love for this child cannot be measured! Thanks for all your words of encouragement, support, and love. Love to all, the Johnsons.

NOVEMBER 30, 2013—Today Jack is resting. He was put on a pain management pump which gives him a continuous flow of pain meds. It has helped, and he seems to be more comfortable than yesterday. He was partially coherent yesterday, getting out his finger gun as Ben said to let us know he was still in pain. He squeezed my hand several times and shook his head in response to a few of our questions. He knows his Mommy, Daddy, and Benny no matter how many pain meds he is receiving. He has not responded since.

Ben and Benny went to our house to get clean clothes for me. While they were gone, I had alone time with Jack. As I held his hand, I told him he didn't have to fight anymore. I explained that there would be a time soon when Jesus would reach out his hand to him, and he needed to take it. I told him when that happened, he would be able to fly so he could spread his wings and leave here. I reassured him that we would be alright. I held his hand and talked about his long fingers and his piano playing. I sang his favorite song, *The Lazy Song* by Bruno Mars. While I sang, his hand moved in mine. I don't know if he made it move because he liked my singing or he hated it. I didn't stop, changing to singing Christmas carols. I will always remember this special time together.

I know so many of you are praying and thinking of us and especially our Jack. Please remember that yesterday seven children died from this same monster and today seven more will die. How many will have to die before all of us understand that this should not be happening? Love to all, the Johnsons.

... BUT I'M NOT THE SINGER

DECEMBER 1, 2013—Ramblings of a grief-stricken, sleep deprived mother...

As I sit here beside Jack's bed watching the ever so slightly changing ebb and flow of air making his chest rise and fall, the sound of the oxygen machine annoyingly getting louder every second, my mind is a jumble of thoughts, memories, and utter confusion. In some strange way, my mind feels it is preparing my son for an upcoming trip. He doesn't have to have luggage or toiletries nor a ticket or passport. We are waiting at the station for the mode of transportation to arrive, not knowing what exactly it will be. I am holding his hand, and every time I look down to check on him, he changes from this young man in this bed to a small boy in overalls and a T-shirt. He looks at me from time to time and his expression is one of complete and utter trust in me as his mother. I have talked to him about his destination not from a place of experience or memory but from the words of a good book written by historians and scholars. I am so scared for him, for myself because I am relying on something called faith, an invisible force I believe controls our lives. I have shared with him the things I think he will see: a landscape of color and light that he has never seen before, people who will greet him—most will be strangers—who have loved him forever. I warned him the way most mothers have about strangers but that these strangers are not dangerous like the ones in this world. They are filled with love and will fill him with that love as well. The places in his body now filled with an evil disease will be filled with peace and happiness, more than he has ever felt before. And inside my chest is a crushing pain held back by the warmth of his hand in mine, a pain I know will weigh my body down until I cannot bear it. But this is what I was called to do that day long ago when I was given this gift of life, that sweet baby whose tiny fingers wrapped around my one finger. Who knew that small hand on the day of his arrival would also be the same grown hand I hold today as we wait together for his departure.

God, thank you for this gift and for the time I have had with him. Thank you for your promise that when I open my hand, your hand will be waiting to take his. Amen

DECEMBER 2, 2013—Jack still amazes us with his mighty strength and his fighter spirit. He is in no pain, not cognitive, but is comfortable. Between our periods of rest, Ben and I loved on, talked to, and rubbed and touched Jack throughout the day and night. We feel it's important that he feels us with him always.

MY NAME IS JACK JOHNSON...

Yesterday the hospice chaplain came to visit us. After introducing herself, she asked if she could talk to us. I will never forget the first words she spoke: "We are sitting here on sacred ground. This is a place where people come to leave this world and pass to the next. It isn't just a place for people to die, it is the place where the body gives birth to the soul. Some people have pain as their soul leaves their body because, just like a woman gives birth to a child, our earthly bodies birth our souls." She told us what we could expect, to not be surprised if Jack looked like he was in pain or reached out just before he transitioned. She also said around the time of Jack's passing, he will shed a tear, one single tear, called the death tear. He would take one deep breath and he will be gone. She shared with us how she could feel the love we have for each other and for Jack by just talking to us. Then she asked if she could say a prayer and anoint Jack with oil. After her prayer, she opened her bottle of holy oil she received on her last trip to the Holy Land. The very small bottle was attached to a bookmark in her Bible. She opened the top, put oil on her finger, and touched Jack's forehead. When she put the top back on the bottle, the bottle had leaked extra oil which she rubbed on Jack's arms. I leaned down to kiss Jack after the chaplain left. He smelled oily, but he was touched by oil blessed by priests in the Holy Land.

I finally slept for a little while last night but woke up terrified. It dawned on me that Jack is not getting any fluids at all. I panicked when I thought about my son suffering because he was not getting fluids. Ben asked a nurse, and she explained how they don't give fluids to patients that are in the process of transitioning because the body doesn't need nourishment or fluids. Giving fluids could cause more pain and discomfort. For example, if the kidneys shut down and you are giving the patient fluids, that extra fluid could back up into the lungs, causing a feeling of drowning. I know in my brain this is correct (I looked it up on Google), but after years of seeking treatments for a cure, my heart agonizes from the realization of Jack's condition.

Thanks for all your words of love and encouragement which keep us strong for sweet Jack. I don't believe he ever fully understood how many people he has touched and how many people love him. Thanks too for the memories some of you continue to share. Those memories break up some of the pressure we feel now, giving us a little time of remembering those more carefree and easier times with him. Love to all, the Johnsons.

MORNING OF DECEMBER 3, 2013—Jack is still resting this morning. We are surprised at his stamina and continued strength. He had another

... BUT I'M NOT THE SINGER

bath (he had one Saturday) in his bed yesterday and looked so much better. The nurses are now turning him from side to side. He has never woken up during all this moving around or even moved on his own to readjust himself. For Ben and me, this is the worst-case scenario. Cancer has blocked off certain areas of Jack's brain but not all, so the process it takes to transition to the next step is prolonged.

Jack now has his favorite stuffed animals with him. I placed Tails and Sonic under each of his arms just like he would hold them if he were awake. A new-to-us nurse came in this afternoon. She shared with us how her mother had just passed away three weeks ago. She was very kind and loving to us. As she examined Jack, she quietly talked to him. Before she left his bedside, she leaned over his ear and sang him a song. She sang so quietly we couldn't hear the song she sang. We didn't ask her, thinking that song was a special moment between her and our son.

Unfortunately, this is the face of pediatric brain cancer. It is not a pretty picture. There was another pediatric cancer patient across the hall from us who lost his battle yesterday. It was a terrible scene right outside our door. My heart broke into a few more pieces for them. Now that empty room is a constant reminder for me of the emptiness parents feel in the aftermath of this disease. I am so sorry to share this part of our journey with you. But to follow this journey, you must travel the entire road we are made to walk. This path is ours. I pray some of you will develop a better understanding of this horrible disease on these innocent children and will be moved to help us find better treatments and God willing, a cure.

Love to all, the Johnsons.

DECEMBER 3, 2013—We are taking turns at Jack's bedside with relatives who come to visit. This afternoon Bunny Rivers came by, and I gave up my bedside chair for her to have time with our son. Jack took a breath and didn't take another one. Bunny Rivers looked at me, I jumped up, held Jack's hand and told him he could be free. My other hand was on his chest when another breath left his body, but his chest didn't move. At 6:43 Jack reached out and took the hand of Jesus. He is now pain-free, autism free, and cancer free. We love you Jack... forever.

Jack's passing caught us by surprise in a strange way since we had expected his condition to change. He didn't raise his arms to heaven, he didn't open his eyes, and he didn't have a pained expression. He took a big breath, and he was gone. But just like the chaplain said, there was one single tear

MY NAME IS JACK JOHNSON...

that left Jack's eye. It was sitting there on his sweet cheek, his death tear. Our baby, our son, our cancer warrior, our hero was gone. His fight on this earth was over.

Nothing prepares you for this. There are books, and I had read several. I had talked to other parents who had traveled this path. I had read other cancer warrior's stories who had left this earth way too soon. But there is nothing to prepare you for the pain, the sting, the sheer heartbreak a parent feels. Through this journey, I have thought so much about Mary, Jesus' mother. She so boldly did what God asked her to do. She bore a child while unwed. She almost lost her fiancée. She birthed him in an animal stable in unsanitary conditions, not like our germ-free environments today. She raised him to be what God had wanted. But she was not saved from watching him suffer and die. She knew the end was coming. She watched as he carried his cross. She watched as he was tortured. She cried as he died. For a mother, there is no worse feeling than to feel the sense of utter helplessness and despair than watching your child die. How many other mothers in my shoes thought about Mary too?

The nurses came and removed the medical equipment from Jack. When I walked back in his room, he was free: free of pain, free of suffering in this life, and free of the tubes and needles that had been his constant companions for many years. The nurses had moved his stuffed animal buddies, but I got them and put them back where they had been, in the arms of their buddy. We said our final goodbyes, touched him, kissed him, and loved on him. We will forever be thankful for the kindness and support we received at Hospice.

Four days later, on a cold and windy Saturday, our son was remembered in a special ceremony honoring the extraordinary and remarkable person he was. Jack Johnson, our unique, quirky, and funny son and brother, sporting a very sexy mustache and a slight beard, a hint of a small smile on his face, dressed in his number 14 Chattanooga Mocs football jersey while holding his favorite friends, Sonic and Tails, was laid to rest within sight of a nearby electric pole. We will forever miss Jack's light in our world.

AFTERWORD

Today, Jack has been absent from our present life for four years, nine months, and ten days. We have never been the same, nor do we expect to be who we were before. There is not a day that passes that we don't think of him in some way. We have concluded he will always be a part of our lives in a way so very different from what we had hoped and dreamed. Jack will never be forgotten by the people he influenced in his short life or by us.

You might wonder why I wrote this book. There are several reasons. My first reason is to tell the story of my awesome son who, despite his disability, touched so many people with his uniqueness, his sense of humor, and his view of our world. Every person has worth. It doesn't matter if you are wealthy or poor, beautiful or unexceptional, uneducated or intelligent, untalented or gifted. Sometimes we must dig deep inside of others to see their inner beauty, but it is there. We might come in different outside packaging, with different abilities, and from different places, but we all have something inside of us that is worth sharing. It is up to us to bring this inside treasure to the outside for everyone to see. Gems are just stones made to shine and catch our eye once they are refined and polished. Man gives them their worth. Yet we are all gems waiting for someone to see our shimmer and sparkle. It doesn't matter if we move in a chair, talk with a computer, or hear with a machine. We have something to give to others. We can give a piece of ourselves if we just have people who truly want to receive it. I hope Jack's example will open the eyes of someone, even if it's only one person, to the worthiness of all of us. If you are a parent of a special needs child, that child has a gem inside just like a typical child. You must see it, refine it, and share it with the world.

My second reason for this book is to share a story about a child with autism. Since Jack's diagnosis in 1998, the number of cases of autism has grown from 1 in 1000 children diagnosed with this condition to a whopping 1 in 45 children diagnosed. (Taken from an article from November 2015 at https://

MY NAME IS JACK JOHNSON...

www.autismspeaks.org) Children with autism are said to have Autism Spectrum Disorder (ASD) because no two children exhibit the same behaviors or characteristics. These characteristics can range from low functioning to high functioning along a spectrum with individual characteristics of each person with autism ranging from low to high functioning as well. I have heard it said, "If you have seen one person with autism, you have seen one person with autism." No two are alike but can be similar in behaviors and characteristics. Other facts from Autism Speaks:
- Autism prevalence figures are growing
- Autism is one of the fastest-growing developmental disorders in the U.S.
- Autism costs a family $60,000 a year on average
- Boys are nearly five times more likely than girls to have autism.
- There is no medical detection or cure for autism.

(For more information, visit https://www.autismspeaks.org)

Last, but not least, I want to shine a light on the devastating diagnosis of childhood cancer. Thankfully, so much money has been given to breast cancer research in the past that treatments are specialized by the different forms and stages of breast cancer. How do I know this? I was diagnosed with Stage 3 breast cancer eight months after Jack passed away. The difference in treatments and support for patients is astounding. Instead of the one-size-fits-all mentality of childhood cancer, breast cancer patients will have a specific treatment plan formulated for their type of breast cancer. Not all patients suffer through radiation and chemo. Some will have surgery based on their breast cancer. I was offered support in so many ways from support groups to free monthly housekeeping services to a personal assistant called a breast health navigator who walked me through several procedures and was available at any time for any question I might have during treatment. And those are just a few of the services I was offered.

When Jack was diagnosed, we felt alone. There was no one available at any time to answer questions. There was no support group to help us deal with the emotional, financial, and personal hell we were going through. In most cases of childhood cancer, if both parents have jobs outside the home, one will have to quit their job to be with their child during treatment. No one told us our options for treatment; we had no clue where to go or whom to ask. Having been in both positions of being a mother of a cancer patient to being a cancer patient myself, the difference between a childhood cancer diagnosis and a breast cancer diagnosis was staggering.

... BUT I'M NOT THE SINGER

Please do not take my observations as a negative judgment against breast cancer and its treatment in any way. I am pleased to personally experience how far research has gotten in the treatment of this disease. Many women are alive today because of the research and up-to-date treatment options available, including myself. I hope and pray we will one day have the same individualized treatments available to all other adult cancers and childhood cancers as well.

Just a few statistics on childhood cancer:

- The incidence of childhood cancer is on the increase, averaging 0.6 percent increase per year since the mid-1970s, resulting in an overall increase of 24 percent over the last forty years.
- Before they turn twenty, one in every 285 children in the U.S. will have cancer.
- Forty-three children per day, or 15,780 children per year, were expected to be diagnosed in 2014 with cancer (10,450 ages 0-14, and 5,330 ages 15-19).
- The average age at diagnosis is six years old, while adults' average age for cancer diagnosis is sixty-six.
- Childhood cancer is not one disease; there are sixteen major types of pediatric cancers and over one hundred subtypes.
- The average five-year survival rate for childhood cancers when considered as a whole is 83 percent.
- Survival rates can range from almost 0 percent for cancers such as DIPG, a type of brain cancer, to as high as 90 percent for the most common type of childhood cancer known as Acute Lymphoma Leukemia (ALL).
- In 2010, there were 379,112 childhood cancer survivors in the U.S.
- More than 95 percent of childhood cancer survivors will have a significant health-related issue by the time they are forty-five years old; these health-related issues are side effects of either cancer or, more commonly, the result of its treatment.
- Cancer is the number one cause of death by disease among children.
- Since 1980, fewer than ten drugs have been developed for use in children with cancer, including those specifically for children and those for both children and adults, compared with hundreds of drugs that have been developed specifically for adults. Equally important, for many of the childhood cancers, the same treatment that existed in the 1970s continue without change as of 2014.
- The average cost of a stay in a hospital for a child with cancer is $40,000 per stay.

MY NAME IS JACK JOHNSON...

- For 2014, the National Cancer Institute (NCI) budget is $4.9 billion. It is anticipated that childhood cancer will receive 4 percent of that sum or $195 million.

All statistics from The Truth 365 (www.thetruth365.org/cancer-facts/)

What can you do? You can give to organizations that support childhood cancer research or support families going through childhood cancer. I have included a few below. If you want to give to another organization involved with cancer research or support, please make sure the organization helps specifically childhood cancer or supports childhood cancer families. Unfortunately, not all cancer organizations support families or research of childhood cancer.

- St. Jude Research Hospital (www.stjude.org/Donate)
- St. Baldrick's (http://stbaldricks.org)
- Alex's Lemonade Stand Foundation (www.alexslemonade.org)
- Pediatric Brain Tumor Foundation (www.curethekids.org)

These are just a few of the many organizations, foundations, and charities that we pray one day will find a cure for this horrible disease and killer of children around the world. Please let Jack's story move you, so another family will never find themselves traveling the road of childhood cancer.

You can also give to individual families after any diagnosis. From my experiences, here are a few suggestions:

- Gift cards from local restaurants, grocery stores, gas for traveling, general Visa or MasterCard
- Give cash (no one knows the needs of a person more than the person in need!)
- Bring snacks for hospital stays, surgeries, or procedures
- Offer to watch siblings or have siblings over for play dates
- Give toys for all the long hours of waiting. Don't forget batteries!
- If you are told there are no needs at that time, take that as truth. Sometimes it is more work for the family in need if you are giving food to someone who has an overflowing refrigerator or who doesn't want a stranger to clean their house.
- Ask "How can I help" and listen to the answer. Never assume you know the needs of another.
- Send a card with a personal message. To know you are not alone in your situation is a comfort. I call greeting cards "paper hugs" because that card came from someone who thought of me while writing the message after they

... BUT I'M NOT THE SINGER

had personally picked that individual greeting card. Sometimes paper hugs are all it takes to know you are loved.
- Lastly, please do not repeat trite platitudes, overused phrases, or seemingly well-intended remarks to make someone feel better. Most do not. Give meaningful, heartfelt hugs, pray for them, and tell them about your prayers. Tell them you love them. So simple but so powerful.

My goal for this book is not a book on religion, but a book about my son and how God has played a role in our lives.

For believers like us, where is God in a family who struggles with autistic behaviors daily? Where is God in the death of a child? I wondered and searched for the answers to questions like these for many years after Jack was diagnosed with autism. On those occasions when the nightly news would share with us the pictures of victims of horrendous crimes, earthquakes, floods, tornadoes, and horrible accidents, where was God? I think this is a question we ask at every traumatic life event and we never seem to have an answer.

For my sanity, I came up with my own reason from my meager knowledge of the Bible. God is always with us through every storm in our life whether it is autism, death, or any other life event. He doesn't stop these life events because Adam and Eve opened the world to good and evil when the forbidden fruit was eaten. All the destruction of man was released. In other words, God doesn't cause the bad things to happen. He walks us through the bad things.

If you look in the Bible at the stories that pertain to disabilities and death, most are used to make a point or tell a story. Jesus healed Lazarus from the dead (John 11), gave sight to the blind man in Bethsaida (Mark 8:22-25), raised a widow's son from the dead (Luke 7:11-17), healed a leper (Mark 1:40-42), healed the withered hand of a man (Matthew 12:9-13), and healed a boy with a demon (epilepsy) (Matthew 17:14-18). These are a few examples although there are more in the Bible. With all the healing and miracles performed by Jesus and his disciples, there is a reason for the healing: Jesus was attempting to show the power he had given to him by God. His reason was to give a visual to the people for them to believe he was indeed the Son of the Almighty.

But if you look closer, several people in the Bible were not healed. Paul, in the New Testament, said "a thorn was given me in the flesh" that never was healed. He struggled with not being healed and was "tormented" by the pain.

MY NAME IS JACK JOHNSON...

"Three times I pleaded with the Lord to take it away from me. But he said to me, "My grace is sufficient for you, for my power is made perfect in weakness." (2 Corinthians 12: 7-9 New International Version)

My favorite example of Biblical people not being healed is found in the story of a thirty-eight-year-old, lame man being healed by Jesus at the Pool of Bethesda. (John 5:1-16) Picture in your mind a temple pool, surrounded by colonnades, the pool covered by some other material, perhaps draped cloth. The name of the pool, Bethesda, means "House of Mercy." Sitting around the pool in the shade are "a great number of disabled people who used to lie there—the blind, the lame, the paralyzed." Legend had it that an angel would come and "stir up the water" of the pool. The first person into the pool after the stirring of the water "was made well from whatever disease with which he/she was afflicted." The water was probably connected to an underground spring that would occasionally burst forth making the waters seem to stir. No historical account of the water healing anyone was ever found, but that small glimmer of hope in healing brought the "great number of disabled people" to the pool every day. Please remember, there were very few medical treatments in this time in history. I am sure most people were desperate to find relief from pain and suffering. The disabled usually could not work in fields or have a trade. Most were left to beg and most lived with family so they would have a caregiver to help with self-care needs. They also would need to have someone who could get them to the pool every day so they could wait another day by the water's edge for the healing that would never come. The hopelessness is obvious to us, but not to them in that period of time.

One day, Jesus walks in the area, knows which person has been coming the longest, for thirty-eight years, and asks the lame man if he wants to be healed. The man replied, "I have no one to help me into the pool when the water is stirred. While I am trying to get in, someone else goes down ahead of me." The man was frustrated with not being the first in the water to be healed, and he did not fully understand the question from this stranger. Jesus told the man, "Get up! Pick up your mat and walk." At those words, "he picked up his mat and walked." After thirty-eight years, the man was cured! Can you imagine the shock; a man who had been lame for thirty-eight years stood up and walked just because a stranger told him to? Can you imagine his joy? The scene around him probably became chaotic; the eyes of all the other disabled people amazed at the miracle they witnessed. They saw Jesus heal one of his flock. I wonder how many became believers the day they

... BUT I'M NOT THE SINGER

witnessed this miracle?

The story continues with the man being questioned by the religious leaders of that day and how, in his excitement, he told these questioners that Jesus had healed him, prompting the Jewish leaders to accuse Jesus of breaking the rules in their quest to prosecute the Son of God.

But what about the crowd of people who continued to wait by the pool for their miracle? They were not healed as the lame man was on that special day. As the now healed man walked away from the pool, the others continued their daily ritual of waiting for the waters to stir. Jesus did not heal them. Their lives stayed the same.

Just like the crowd around the pool left behind, not everyone gets their miracle. Some of us are disabled for our whole lives. Some develop an illness or have an accident later in life that require special needs to live our daily lives. We pray for God to help, to take away the pain or for complete healing. Does God not hear our prayers? Does He look the other way? Does He ignore our pleas for help? I do not think so. God's goal for us is to live our lives by the example He gave to us in the form of His Son. Even though God knows we will fall short, He expects us to live our lives by giving of ourselves to the poor, the needy, the disabled, the grieving, the hurting, and the hungry. God wants us to see, to step forward, to help in any way we can. God can do anything because He is all powerful. He could raise His hands and the lame could walk, the hungry be fed forever. But He doesn't... He wants US to do His work. If God took away all the needs of His people, how would we practice our faith? How would we give to the poor if there were no poor people anymore? How would we feed the hungry if God gave them all they could eat? If there were no trials and hardships in life, God would become a fairy godmother whose sole purpose was to meet our every need. God wants us to have faith, to believe He is the Almighty Creator, to work on His behalf. Faith is believing in something we cannot actually see and acting as if what we cannot see actually exists. If we love and believe, we will do as He has asked us to do. We are to show our faith in making sure all of God's people are treated with respect and dignity while we are here on earth. The hungry, the disabled, the poor and needy, the hurt and grieving all have a special place on earth as they have in God's eyes. Just as the crowd around the Pool of Bethesda were not healed on that day, the people in need in our world are there for us to love and help in any way we can. Our faith in God is supposed to stir us into action when we see and understand a need. I am reminded of the Biblical story of the healing of a blind man in John 9. Jesus is with his disciples spreading the word. "As he went along, he saw a man blind from birth. His disciples asked him, "Rabbi, who sinned, this man or his parents, that he was born blind?" "Neither this man nor his parents sinned, but this happened so that the work of God might be displayed in him." God wanted the blind man to be the catalyst that moves us to be giving, understanding, and selfless in this world.

In the case of death, our bodies were made to have an expiration date. Someone once said we are born to die. Our bodies are the shell that houses our soul and spirit. The body ages, gets diseases, and breaks down. This is not an "if" but a "when" situation; our bodies will eventually die. We are to protect our body, soul, and spirit by taking care of our earthly body, having a clean soul, and feeding our spirit with the word of God. Our soul and spirit will live on long after our body has stopped working. If we believe in God, our soul and spirit will live on with Him in heaven. And remember too, all the people who Jesus raised from the dead, eventually died when their time on earth was over. His miraculous intervention was not timeless.

Death is another situation where we are called on by God to fill the needs of others. In some cases, we will become sick, and because of this sickness, we will perish. Sometimes there is an accident of some kind that will cause death. Sometimes our bodies grow so old and weary, the parts that help sustain life stop working. In all these situations, we are called on by God to be in service to others by our prayers and actions. We visit the bereaved after a death. We support the sick or hospitalized by sending flowers or bringing them meals. These are situations where again we are asked by God to be his "hands and feet" to those in need around us.

The unanswered question to me is the "why" question. Why do children die? Why are they to suffer? Why my child and not someone else's child? Why do babies die? Why questions will never have answers. The Bible tells us we will know the things we did not understand in this world when we get to heaven. In the Bible, 1 Corinthians 14:12 says: "Now we see but a poor reflection as in a mirror; then we shall see face to face. Now I know in part; then I shall know fully, even as I am fully known." The hardest aspect of grief is living each day without the answers to our "why" questions.

I have seen so many parents question God after the death of their child. Once believers, living their lives as God would want, they have seen their own child suffer and die. They prayed fervently for a miracle, believing with everything in them that their child would beat the odds. But it did not happen. And since it did not happen, in their minds, there could not have

... BUT I'M NOT THE SINGER

been a God on the other end of their desperate prayers. They turn away from God, their faith broken at their feet, as they feel God turned a deaf ear to them. My heart breaks for these parents. God never promised us a life without hardships and agony. He did not say He would constantly protect us from evil and death. "I have told you these things, so that in me you may have peace. In this world you will have trouble. But take heart! I have overcome the world." (John 16:33) He did promise He would never leave us. "The Lord himself goes before you and will be with you; he will never leave you nor forsake you. Do not be afraid; do not be discouraged." (Deuteronomy 31:8) He cries when we cry; He mourns when we mourn. In my mind, I think if I believed God didn't hear our prays for Jack and I turned away from Him because I felt this way, I would always question my decision. If God did hear my prayer, but it wasn't meant to be, would I completely turn away from Him and take the chance that in my unbelieving, I could be missing a chance to be with my beloved child in eternity forever? Not just for today, but for eternity? In Isaiah 57:1-2, the Bible says, "The righteous perish, and no one takes it to heart; the devout are taken away, and no one understands that the righteous are taken away to be spared from evil. Those who walk uprightly enter into peace; they find rest as they lie in death." Today, I believe Jack was not blessed with an anticipated miracle but instead, he was spared from something far worse than being in heaven with God.

I have been asked about why I ended my journal entries with prayers of thankfulness. My prayers of thanks were given in response to the horrors of watching my child and other children live through the misery of pediatric cancer treatments. Some days finding the beauty of life was difficult. Some days I had to shut off the memory of some atrocity I had witnessed to find one thing to be thankful for. I had not known the brutality of cancer treatments on children until it was my child and those around him who accepted the constant barrage of stranger's hands, hurtful needle pricks, seemingly endless sickness, and the courageous strength to endure receiving chemotherapy over and over again for months and sometimes years. When the world you see and live becomes hell on earth, you give thanks for the blessings in life you have mistakenly taken for granted. Colossians 4:2 says, "Devote yourselves to prayer, being watchful and thankful."

As I said before, these are my beliefs, my meager attempt to make sense of the senseless. I do not have an education in religion. My words are only meant to be read, and if someone finds some sense of peace in any of this, it will be a true act of God.

May God bless each and every one of you as you journey through life.

ACKNOWLEDGEMENTS

I must include a word of thanks to the many people who walked with us during this journey. Thanks to all the doctors, nurses, therapists, teachers, paraprofessionals, our family, friends, our church family, and total strangers who helped us along the way. Each one of you played an important role in Jack's life and we will always be truly grateful.

Thanks to the many people who sent us gifts, cards, food, and prayed for us during our most difficult times. We were astounded by the spirit of giving we have witnessed. God spoke to so many of you and you acted. We will never forget your support!

A few personal thanks to those who helped make Jack's story into a book. Thanks to Gayle for your support and editing this book in its raw form. I know reading this was difficult in so many ways but you persevered. I will forever be indebted to you. A special thanks to our Dallas, TX angel, Mr. B., who has gifted us with his generosity. You have been an example of a "good and faithful servant." We are amazed by you!

A big thanks to James and Paula at Two Peas Publishing! Each of you have worked to make Jack's story a reality for me. I appreciate both of you, your talents, and your support. Thank you!

Lastly, I must thank God for the gift of Jack. What a gift he was! Thank you for watching over us and somehow providing us with love and support from your saints on earth. We felt your presence so many times. Thank you, God, for never leaving us alone. Thanks for giving me the ability to take Jack's story and put it into words. I hope and pray I have served you well and that something I wrote will touch another's heart in a special way.

ABOUT THE AUTHOR

Jill Johnson lives in Franklin, Tennessee with her husband Ben. She doesn't consider herself an author but describes herself as a storyteller writing stories from life experiences. *The Little Toad and the Big Flood* (at Amazon.com or Google Play) is an imaginative children's story she wrote about an actual toad living in their yard during the flood of 2010. For more insight into her background and beliefs, go to her blog at aviewfromtheslowroadoflife.wordpress.com. You can email her at slowroad1987@gmail.com

www.ingramcontent.com/pod-product-compliance
Lightning Source LLC
Chambersburg PA
CBHW032027150426
43194CB00006B/182